INSTRUCTIONAL TECHNOLOGY: FOUNDATIONS

I. Kirsch

INSTRUCTIONAL TECHNOLOGY: FOUNDATIONS

edited by

Robert M. Gagné
Florida State University

IEA LAWRENCE ERLBAUM ASSOCIATES, PUBLISHERS
1987   Hillsdale, New Jersey   London

Lawrence Erlbaum Associates, Inc., Publishers
365 Broadway
Hillsdale, New Jersey 07642

Library of Congress Cataloging-in-Publication Data
Instructional technology.

Bibliography: p.
Includes index.
1. Educational technology.   2. Instructional systems.
I. Gagné, Robert Mills, 1916-   .
LB1028.3.I565   1986   371.3′07′8   86-6328
ISBN 0-89859-626-2
ISBN 0-89859-8 78-8 (pbk.)

Printed in the United States of America
10 9 8 7 6 5 4

Contents

INSTRUCTIONAL TECHNOLOGY: FOUNDATIONS

1 Introduction

Robert M. Gagné
Florida State University

Several kinds of events must contribute to the confluence that defines a field of scholarly interest and effort. When such a field is not old enough to be counted as a traditional discipline, the influence of certain trends can be identified and observed as they converge, while other influences remain indirect and less clearly perceivable. Instructional technology is a field of this nontraditional sort. Broadly speaking, two sets of events have contributed to its development. One set comprises the continuing and remarkable growth of new things, processes, and ideas that constitute what we mean by technology. A second and equally essential factor has been the influence of a growing number of people of sound intellect with an analytical cast of mind, a dedication to the promise of human learning, and a vision of how to promote the spread of human knowledge. Clearly, this vision is one of bringing to bear on human beings the most sophisticated set of procedures and machines that can be designed for making learning readily available to all people, and in assuring its effectiveness in developing the capabilities that are learning's results.

The people who acquired this vision and led others to it in this century were often initially intrigued by the potentialities of hardware devices such as the stereopticon, the slide projector, the motion-picture camera and projector. Since learning always involves stimulation of the learner, it was apparent that these devices made possible stimulation for learning that was both *deliberately designed* and *replicable*. Consideration of these features raised questions for the intellectually curious. Could the stimulation required for particular learning objectives be designed and recorded on film, so as to be

1

presented many times to many different learners? Could such recorded presentations be employed to circumvent the unfortunate but often unavoidable variability in instruction quality that marked poor teaching? Could certain identifiable portions of presentations for learning, well established in their content and objectives, be made available for teacher use as standard segments of instruction, replicable from class to class? Could some kinds of stimulation for learning be presented by film-related devices that would be difficult or impossible to present in other ways? And as a possibility, could presentations be devised that in some respects captured the most ingenious techniques of superior teaching?

With the addition of synchronized sound to the visual display, the same kinds of questions were raised in the minds of people who now were able to characterize this field of interest as *audio-visual*. Sound, after all, added another sensory channel to the spectrum of stimulation available for instructional design. By so doing, it raised a host of possibilities about the potential synergy between the two sensory channels. Interestingly, many of these questions have not yet received satisfactory answers, and the investigation of visual presentations in relation to sound presentations continues today as a promising area of research.

As for the people who were attracted to this field of scholarship and professional activity, they evidenced a variety of preferences and interests. Some came to view the audiovisual field as made up primarily of the technical knowledge required to operate machines—cameras, projectors, recorders, and tape players, as well as the materials involved in their operation, such as film and tape. Others concentrated their attention on questions of accessibility of devices and materials of an audiovisual nature to the variety of users that might be present within an institution or a training organization. And still others focused their curiosity on the challenging and difficult questions of what good were these things for education? What characteristics made them of particular value for the promotion of learning? It was this third set of people, not large in numbers, but strong in their beliefs and their dedication, who collectively possessed the vision that foresaw the promise of instructional technology.

The central questions that came to dominate the audiovisual field defined areas of research. And research was accordingly carried out, by investigators in the field itself, as well as by those in psychology and in the communications field. Whenever research is done, it must have a reason, a theoretical or pretheoretical basis for investigation. And so it was with research on the nature and uses of audiovisual devices. The theoretical biases were various—they came from communications theory, from visual perception theory, from operant reinforcement theory, from learning theory of the associationist sort, and from several other sources.

A fair amount of systematic knowledge was gained from these lines of research. Some of it was "negative" (in the sense of the finding that color did not improve the learning effectiveness of instruction in movies). Others were positive, although limited in their applicability (such as the conclusion that concepts involving motion could best be learned from displays showing that motion). Notably, however, the various investigations that were done, on various theoretical grounds, did not pose the questions that lead to crucial experiments. That is to say, while several different theories may have been guiding different studies, the research did not arrive at the point of finding ways to decide which was best among these theories, or among the hypotheses to which they led. This state of affairs should not be viewed as surprising. Instead, it indicates that research in the field of instructional technology was, after all, a very new and youthful discipline, as it still is today.

The continuation of research efforts in this field did, however, contribute critically to another development: the definition and central focus of the field of instructional technology. The common core of research investigations, however based in theory, came to be recognized as studies of the *conditions for effective learning.* Some of these conditions were, to be sure, the capacities and qualities of the *individual human learner,* including such things as visual and auditory abilities, speech and print comprehension abilities, and so on. Other conditions, in fact the other large set, were *media-based* conditions, pertaining to the kind of presentation made to the learner, and to its timing, sequence, and organization. As research continued in this field, these latter ideas became increasingly prominent.

As a result of the continuing efforts of professional leaders to define the field, and of the influences exerted on it by the pretheoretical notions of various research disciplines, a comprehensive view of instructional technology emerged, and became the view that prevails today. First of all, this view accepts the definition of technology as *systematic knowledge derived from scientific research.* Proceeding from this vantage point, the next question to be addressed is, systematic knowledge of what? Obviously the answer is not the machines or the materials used for instructional presentation—the projectors, the films, the display screens, the computer programs. All of these have their own technologies, their own systematic knowledge of how they are designed and built; but that is not technology of instruction. The technology of interest for the latter purpose must focus upon the human learner, and particularly upon the capabilities and dispositions that are acquired by learning. The systematic knowledge of this field must consist of that set of techniques and procedures derived from scientific research, which tells us how to bring about the changes in human performance that we identify as resulting from learning.

KNOWLEDGE SOURCES

Knowledge about conditions that are effective for human learning comes from a variety of sources. One tends to think, first, of the developments in material systems—the message-carrying and message-recording devices such as satellites and laser optics and computer memories. Often it is these developments that open up brand new possibilities in the delivery of instruction. It is these innovations that give us better pictures, greater variety and flexibility of messages, and greater volume of information—all of which can scarcely escape being used in the improvement of instruction, irrespective of the original purpose of their design. A second source, of considerable prominence today, is the field called artificial intelligence. As a field of scholarship, this discipline is concerned with investigation of the nature of intricate and complex problems possible for computers to solve. It addresses the question of how intelligent a computer can be made to be. Technology in this field is increasingly oriented toward using computers to help solve difficult problems: medical diagnosis, the monitoring of equipment functions, and financial forecasting. Spinoffs from artificial intelligence help to illuminate the process of learning, and particularly the learning of strategies that learners use to control their own cognitive processes.

Notable advances have been made in the understanding of human learning by those psychologists who have used an information-processing model as a framework for the investigation of learning processes. The adoption of this model by learning psychologists represents a paradigm shift away from an earlier theoretical position based on stimulus–response associations. The modern view of cognitive processing makes it possible to consider learning as a multistage process involving feature perception, short-term storage, rehearsal, semantic encoding, long-term storage, and retrieval, as primary kinds of cognitive operations. In consequence, this view conceives instruction as comprising events external to the learner that are designed, each in its own way, to support internal learning processes.

The field of investigation of audiovisual communication continues to contribute to the body of knowledge called instructional technology. There were, to be sure, disappointments with the results of studies conducted during the 1960s, which sought to compare the effectiveness of media-based instruction with teacher-based instruction. The legacy of these findings, however, represents an advance in knowledge in itself, since it has convinced investigators that this is not the proper question for research to ask. Meanwhile, important research conclusions are being drawn, in various settings, from studies that seek to assess the effectiveness of particular characteristics of audiovisual media. These findings may be expected also to throw light upon the effective instructional uses of those most modern media combinations, computers and video-discs.

OTHER RESOURCES

Instructional technology as a field draws its strength from several sets of dedicated people, whose interests are diverse, but who share a belief that technology can be employed to improve the design and delivery of instruction. It is a field that is able to draw upon a rich background of scientifically based knowledge—in hardware innovation, in communication research, in artificial intelligence and computer science, and in cognitive psychology. It would seem likely, then, that there would be a common set of beliefs and ideals that characterize the field.

Conceptual Resources

An influential resource for the field of instructional technology is the set of continuing ideas that are the comprehensive generalizations arising from the work of practitioners and researchers. These have been expressed by other writers in various forms, for a number of years. What are the continuing beliefs that characterize the field?

1. Inventions in communications hardware and associated use procedures (often collectively termed *media*), while they may be primarily designed for other applications, often make possible new opportunities for means of delivering instruction. Instructional technology seeks to investigate, develop, evaluate, and promote the application of such techniques.

2. Since the purpose of instruction is learning, the central focus for rational derivation of instructional techniques is the *human learner*. Development of rationally sound instructional procedures must take into account learner characteristics such as innate capacities, experiential maturity, and current knowledge states. Such factors become parameters of the design of any particular program of instruction.

3. *Procedures* for the promotion of learning may include techniques that are independent of hardware media (such as the provision of review, the use of feedback), as well as those that are closely tied to hardware features (such as large-screen displays, motion displays, rapid access in changing presentations). Instructional technology includes the systematic discovery and formulation of techniques that are media-independent as well as those that are media-based.

4. *Research* has the purpose of revealing: (a) ways in which existing media can be most effectively employed in promoting effective human learning; (b) the conditions of optimal learning, including the properties and characteristics of media that can be used to establish such conditions; and (c) novel techniques of designing and delivering instruction that can be shown to improve its effectiveness.

5. On a rational basis, the media selected for instruction should be those whose characteristics best fulfill the requirements for providing the conditions of most effective learning. It is recognized, however, that practical considerations such as availability and cost sometimes dictate media choices. In such instances, the question to be asked changes to the following: Given these media, how can they best be used in delivering a specified module of instructional content?

6. *Evaluation studies* of the use of media have frequently failed to show an advantage for media-based versus non-media-based instruction. It is believed that these studies may have been inadequately formulated. Remaining as questions of high promise for research are those which investigate innovative ways of utilizing particular features of media (e.g., audio and visual coordination, pacing of learner responses, variations in feedback, flexibility or practice examples, elaboration of factual knowledge) to enhance the effectiveness of learning conditions. Such studies may lead to innovative procedures for using existing media, as well as to novel modifications of equipment.

7. A goal of research and development in instructional technology continues to be the ideal of being able to specify the characteristics of a system of media that would make possible a set of conditions for optimally effective learning that would exceed the capabilities of instructor-mediated instruction. Such a system would be aimed at many (but not necessarily all) learning goals. Properties of modern communications and computer equipment, as well as discoveries in human cognition, provide many prospects for the development of a media system for optimal instruction of this sort.

WHAT IS INSTRUCTIONAL TECHNOLOGY?

It is hoped that the preceding discussion has managed to disclose and explicate the forces, issues, and prevailing views that characterize instructional technology. I have pointed out that the field may be viewed, first, as a set of professional people concerned with the development and use of instructional techniques having the purpose of promoting effective human learning. The learning with which these people are concerned may occur in the school, in the industrial classroom, in the specialized learning center, or in the home. Learning is often initiated and brought about by communications to the learner, and these communications are frequently delivered by equipment and its associated procedures, commonly referred to as media. Currently, these media include such "high-tech" items as television and computer systems in their various forms.

The technical knowledge that constitutes instructional technology includes practical procedures for using existing media to deliver instruction, and also to deliver portions of instruction that supplement the communications of an instructor. Instructional technology includes practical techniques of instructional delivery that systematically aim for effective learning, whether or not they involve the use of media. It is a basic purpose of the field of instructional technology to promote and aid the application of these known and validated procedures in the design and delivery of instruction.

While instructional technology has its own set of concerns and accepted techniques of application to instruction, the field also draws upon systematic knowledge investigated and developed in other scholarly disciplines. Of course, one source of background knowledge comes from the technology of hardware systems themselves, and from the new inventions and modifications that continue to appear. Another source of fundamental systematic knowledge derives from the research of cognitive psychologists who apply the methods of science to the investigation of human learning and the conditions of instruction. The findings of research on human learning provide a basis for the formulation of techniques of instruction that focus on learners and their characteristics. Computer science, and in particular that branch of research called artificial intelligence, contributes fundamental knowledge of human cognition and problem solving. And research in the field of communication continues to provide a basis for the development and evaluation of instructional techniques.

The dedicated professionals who ally themselves with instructional technology appear to share a set of general beliefs, agreed to with individual degrees of fervor and misgivings. In general, these ideas incorporate attitudes regarding the promise of new developments in equipment technology coupled with understanding of processes of learning in bringing about improvements in ways of delivering instruction. In line with this view, research efforts in instructional technology seek to investigate and verify the features of communications to human learners that optimize learning, and to discover how these features may best be planned and executed with the use of the various communication media and their combinations.

CONTENTS OF THIS BOOK

All of these dimensions of instructional technology are intended to be represented in this volume. Our major purpose has been to collect between a single set of covers the knowledge that we now have of this field, including some indications of where it is going. It is only this general purpose that has guided the many authors of individual chapters and each has been encouraged to report the state of knowledge from an individual viewpoint. The task of writing chapters for a book of this sort, beginning with scarcely more guidance than a chapter title in each case, was undertaken with goodwill and immediate understanding. This fact itself reveals something about the field—that despite its disparate origins, there is a consensus in conceptualization of instructional technology as a field of research, development, and application.

From these various considerations, it will be evident that this book is *not a how-to-do-it manual*. Instead, its principal quality is the linking of systematic scientific knowledge with future prospects of instructional technology. The trends that are presaged by these writings include instructional research, design, development, application, and utilization of organized knowledge. For this reason, we view the book as a whole as describing *foundations of the field of instructional technology*.

The varied background of the authors assures not only broad coverage, but also reflects different viewpoints about how to describe both current knowledge and likely future trends. Some authors take a fairly conservative view in the sense that they attempt to state what is known even though familiar. Others, while acknowledging the current state of the art, emphasize the new and developing views in trends pointing to the future. Some chapters begin with new developments in equipment, and then proceed to instructional implications. Other authors prefer to start with a description of current knowledge about instructional principles, and then to interpret these principles in relation to media and their uses. Such differences, it appears, do not represent fundamentally conflicting views. Surely, though, they invite readers to make their own individual integrations.

Early chapters of the book are intended to provide background information to aid in the comprehension and appreciation of subsequently presented topics. A historical summary by Reiser brings together the several trends in thought and effort that contribute to instructional technology. The foundational knowledge of human learning that serves as a basis for instructional design is described in a chapter by Gagné and Glaser. A current conception of the design of instructional systems, based upon models employed during years of varied experience, is described by Banathy, accompanied by views of future trends.

Proceeding to chapters accounting for substantive procedures of instructional technology, the analysis of requirements for instruction is described by Kaufman and Thiagarajan, followed by a chapter on performance and task analysis by Paul Merrill. The ways in which instruction is influenced by learning situations, and the models that take account of these effects, are expounded by Reigeluth and Curtis. Characteristics of the learner as they relate to instructional design and delivery are discussed by Tobias, who suggests some directions for research and for the application of the findings.

A time-tested way of treating the problems of instructional technology is by dealing with the variables in displays and in the communication process. A summary of what is known about these variables is given by Fleming.

Next, the kinds of innovations in telecommunications equipment and media systems to be taken into account now and in the near future are outlined by Nugent, with discussions of their implications for instruction. An account of developments in computer-based instruction is provided by Bunderson, along with indications of future trends. The ideas of intelligent, computer-aided instruction (ICAI) is given an analytical account by Tennyson and Park, who include a review of alternative models of such systems.

The four following chapters deal with the processes of design and development of instructional systems, as seen by experts who have played key roles in the development and tryout of these procedures. Baker and O'Neil describe current formulations of techniques for assessing the outcomes of instruction, and for evaluating system effectiveness. Morgan draws upon his extensive experience in domestic and international settings to describe how planning for instructional systems is done. The procedures of developing instruction for programs and for total systems are given an exposition by Branson and Grow. Reflecting equally extensive experience with problems of instructional development, a final chapter by Burkman gives an account of the factors affecting utilization of the results and products of instructional development.

It is hoped that these chapters will be effective in conveying an impression of the state of the art in instructional technology. The individual chapters may provide the substantive framework for the various techniques that make up the field of instructional technology, the problems yet to be solved by research and development, and an indication of the remarkable potentialities for the improvement of instruction.

AUTHOR NOTES

Robert M. Gagné is a Professor in the Department of Educational Research, Development, and Foundations, Florida State University.

2 Instructional Technology: A History

Robert A. Reiser
Florida State University

What is instructional technology? Over the years, many definitions have been offered, but no single definition has been universally accepted. The term instructional technology has meant and will continue to mean different things to different people. Yet most definitions of instructional technology can be classified as one of two types. One type of definition equates instructional technology with a particular set of instructional media, often referred to as *audiovisual devices*. The other type of definition describes instructional technology as a process, often labeled the *systems approach process.*

Perhaps the best example of these two types of definitions is contained in a statement issued by the Commission on Instructional Technology (1970):

> Instructional technology can be defined in two ways. In its more familiar sense, it means *the media born of the commmunications revolution which can be used for instructional purposes alongside the teacher, textbook, and blackboard* [italics added]. . . . The pieces that make up instructional technology [include]: television, films, overhead projectors, computers, and other items of "hardware" and "software" (to use the convenient jargon that distinguishes machines from programs). . . .
>
> The second and less familiar definition of instructional technology goes beyond any particular medium or device. In this sense, instructional technology is more than the sum of its parts. It is *a systematic way of designing, carrying out, and evaluating the total process of learning and teaching* [italics added] in terms of specific objectives, based on research in human learning and communication, and employing a combination of human and nonhuman resources to bring about more effective instruction. (p. 21)

Today, many professionals in the field think of instructional technology as a systems approach process, "a systematic way of designing, carrying out, and evaluating the total process of learning and teaching." However, it is important to realize that most of those outside the field, as well as some of those who consider themselves to be part of it, still think of instructional technology as audiovisual devices. Thus, the two types of definitions still persist; instructional technology is thought of both in terms of the systems approach and audiovisual devices.

A third major concept associated with the field of instructional technology is the notion of individualized instruction. As the Definition and Terminology Committee of the Association for Educational Communications and Technology (1972) has indicated:

> The educational technology approach has been directed toward expanding the range of resources used for learning, *emphasizing the individual learner and his unique needs* [italics added], and using a systematic approach to the development of learning resources. (p. 36)

Audiovisual devices, individualized instruction, and the systems approach have helped shape the field of instructional technology. In examining the roots of the field, it is important to describe the history of each of these concepts, as will be attempted in the remainder of this chapter. The next three sections will focus on the history of audiovisual devices, the systems approach, and individualized instruction. For the most part, these concepts have developed independently of one another; accordingly, the history of each will be separately described. Throughout the chapter, the primary emphasis will be upon developments that have taken place in the United States.

AUDIOVISUAL DEVICES

Before beginning to describe the history of the use of audiovisual devices in education, a definition is in order. Audiovisual device means any piece of equipment, with associated materials, that controls through mechanical or electronic means, the presentation of visual or auditory communication for instruction. Thus, overhead projectors, television monitors, and computers would be a few of the many examples of audiovisual devices. The instructor and the printed text are media that would not be considered under the rubric "audiovisual."

Early Forerunners

The beginnings of the audiovisual movement have been traced as far back as the 1600s, to the work of Johann Comenius, who proposed that we initially learn about things through our senses and therefore real objects and illustrations should be used to supplement oral and written instruction. In the 1650s Comenius wrote one of the first illustrated textbooks, *Orbis Sensualium Pictus* (The Visible World in Pictures). Although Comenius' textbook was very popular, his ideas had little influence on instructional practice. In the early 1800s, however, the field of education was greatly influenced by another educator who advocated learning via the senses, Johann Pestalozzi.

Pestalozzi posited that words have meaning in relation to concrete objects, and therefore learning should proceed from the concrete to the abstract. He advocated an instructional approach known as object teaching, which became popular in Europe, particularly in Germany, in the early 1800s; in the United States, the method reached the height of its popularity during the 1860s.

The Birth of the Audiovisual Movement

While the work and ideas of Comenius, Pestalozzi, and others may have foreshadowed the beginnings of the audiovisual instruction movement, it may be more accurate to place the birth of the movement somewhere in the early twentieth century. It was at this time that school museums came into existence. As Saettler (1968) indicates, these museums "served as the central administrative unit[s] for visual instruction by [their] distribution of portable museum exhibits, stereographs, slides, films, study prints, charts, and other instructional materials" (p. 89). The first school museum was opened in St. Louis in 1905, and shortly thereafter school museums were opened in Reading, Pennsylvania and Cleveland, Ohio. Although few such museums have been established since the early 1900s, the district-wide media center may be considered a modern-day equivalent.

In the early 1900s, prior to the advent of sound films and other media incorporating sound, the movement that was eventually to be called "audiovisual instruction" was labeled "visual instruction," or "visual education." The latter term was used at least as far back as 1908, when the Keystone View Company published *Visual Education,* a teacher's guide to lantern slides and stereographs (Saettler, 1968).

Besides stereoscopes and stereopticons ("magic lanterns"), which were used in some schools during the second half of the nineteenth century (C. Anderson, 1962), the motion picture projector was one of the early audiovisual devices used in schools. In the United States, the first catalog of instructional films was published in 1910. Later that year, the public school system of Rochester, New York became the first to adopt films for regular instructional use. In 1913, Thomas Edison proclaimed: "Books will soon be obsolete in the schools . . . . It is possible to teach every branch of human knowledge with the motion picture. Our school system will be completely changed in the next ten years" (cited in Saettler, 1968, p. 98).

Ten years after Edison made his forecast, the changes he had predicted had not come about. However, during this decade (1914–1923), the visual instruction movement did grow. Five national professional organizations for visual instruction were established; more than 20 teacher-training institutions began offering courses in visual instruction; at least a dozen large-city school systems developed bureaus of visual education; and five journals devoted exclusively to visual instruction began publication (Saettler, 1968).

During the remainder of the 1920s and through much of the 1930s, the visual instruction movement continued to grow. Technological advances in film and slide quality, radio broadcasting, sound recording, and motion pictures with sound helped foster this growth and served to expand the focus of the movement from visual instruction to audiovisual instruction (Finn, 1972; McCluskey, 1981). However, McCluskey (1981), who was one of the leaders in the field during this period, indicates that, while the field continued to grow, the educational community at large was not greatly affected by that growth. He states that by 1930, commercial interests in the visual instruction movement had invested and lost more than $50 million, and that the Great Depression did not help.

In spite of the adverse effects of the depression, the movement continued to evolve. According to Saettler (1968), one of the most significant events in this evolution was the merging, in 1932, of the three existing national professional organizations for visual instruction. As a result of this merger, leadership in the movement was consolidated within one organization, the Department of Visual Instruction (DVI) of the National Education Association. Over the years, this organization, which was created in 1923, and which is now called the Association for Educational Communications and Technology (AECT), has maintained a leadership role in the field of instructional technology.

During the 1920s and 1930s, a number of textbooks on the topic of visual instruction were written. Perhaps the most important of these textbooks was *Visualizing the Curriculum,* written by Charles F. Hoban, Sr., Charles F. Hoban, Jr., and Stanley B. Zissman (1937). In this book, the authors stated that the value of audiovisual material was a function of their degree of realism. The authors also presented a hierarchy of media, ranging from those that could only present concepts in an abstract fashion to those that allowed for very concrete representations (Heinich et al., 1982). Some of these ideas had been previously discussed by others, but had not been dealt with as thoroughly. In 1946, Edgar Dale further elaborated upon these ideas when he developed his famous "Cone of Experience." Throughout the history of the audiovisual instruction movement, even in spite of recent questions about the validity of the notion (Dwyer, 1978; Heinich et al., 1982; Salomon, 1981), many have indicated that part of the value of audiovisual materials lies in their ability to present concepts in a concrete manner.

World War II

With the onset of World War II, the growth of the audiovisual instruction movement in the schools slowed; however, audiovisual devices were used extensively in the military services and in industry. During the war years, the United States government, through its Division of Visual Aids for War Training, produced 457 industrial training films (Saettler, 1968). The government purchased 55,000 film projectors for the military and spent $1 billion on training films (Olsen & Bass, 1982). This money was apparently well spent; in 1945, after the German surrender, the German Chief of General Staff said: "We had everything calculated perfectly except the speed with which America was able to train its people. Our major miscalculation was in underestimating their quick and complete mastery of film education" (cited in Olsen & Bass, 1982, p. 33).

In addition to films and film projectors, a wide variety of other audiovisual materials and equipment were employed in the military forces and in industry during World War II. Those devices that were used extensively included overhead projectors, which were first produced during the war; slide projectors, which were used in teaching aircraft and ship recognition; audio equipment, which was used in teaching foreign languages; and simulators and training devices, which were employed in flight training (Olsen & Bass, 1982; Saettler, 1968).

Post-World War II Developments

The audiovisual devices used during World War II were generally perceived as successful in helping the United States solve a major training problem, namely, how to train effectively and efficiently large numbers of individuals with diverse backgrounds. As a result of this apparent success, after the war there was a renewed interest in using audiovisual devices in the schools (Finn, 1972; Heinich et al., 1982; Olsen & Bass, 1982).

In the decade following the war, several intensive programs of audiovisual research were undertaken (e.g., Carpenter & Greenhill, 1956; Lumsdaine, 1961; May & Lumsdaine, 1958). The research studies that were conducted as part of these programs were designed to identify how various features, or attributes, of audiovisual materials affected learning; the goal being to identify those attributes that would facilitate learning in given situations. For example, one research program, conducted under the direction of Arthur A. Lumsdaine, focused on identifying how learning was affected by various techniques for eliciting overt student response during the viewing of instructional films (Lumsdaine, 1963).

The post-World War II audiovisual research programs were among the first concentrated efforts to identify principles of learning that could be used in the design of audiovisual materials. However, educational practices were not greatly affected by these research programs in that many practitioners either ignored, or were not made aware of, many of the research findings (Lumsdaine, 1963, 1964). A thorough description of the history of audiovisual research is beyond the scope of this chapter. Accounts of various aspects of that history can be found in such works as those of Allen (1971), Clark (1983), Saettler (1968), Torkelson (1977), and Wilkinson (1980).

During the early 1950s, many leaders in the audiovisual instruction movement became interested in various theories or models of communication, such as the model put forth by Shannon and Weaver (1949). These models focused on the communication process, a process involving a sender and a receiver of a message, and a channel, or medium, through which that message is sent. The authors of these models indicated that during planning for communication it was necessary to consider all the elements of the communication process, and not just focus on the medium, as many in the audiovisual field tended to do. As Berlo (1963) stated: "As a communication man I must argue strongly that it is the process that is central and that the media, though important, are secondary" (p. 378). Several leaders in the audiovisual movement, such as Dale (1953) and Finn (1954), also emphasized the importance of the communication process. Although at first, audiovisual practitioners were not greatly influenced by this notion (Lumsdaine, 1964; Meierhenry, 1980), the expression of this point of view eventually helped expand the focus of the audiovisual movement (Ely, 1970; Silber, 1981).

National Defense Education Act: Title VII

In 1958, the audiovisual instruction movement in the United States was given a big boost when Congress, in response to the Soviet Union's launching of Sputnik, passed the National Defense Education Act. Under Title VII of the Act, the federal government provided extensive funding for media research and for the dissemination of media research findings. During the ten-year period that Title VII was in effect, more than $40 million was spent on approximately 600 projects. Filep and Schramm (1970) summarize the effects of this legislation:

> Title VII had a substantial impact on educational scholarship and brought numerous new researchers into the field of educational media and technology. It also helped upgrade the quality of the research effort and contributed to the growth of many departments of instructional technology and related institutions. It was instrumental in several developments toward quality educational television and helped in the establishment of educational information-disseminating institutions such as the ERIC Clearinghouses.
>
> In general, funding from Title VII did contribute to the application of the systems approach to education, to providing more individualized instruction, and to securing greater teacher acceptance of the new media. (p. i)

Instructional Television

Perhaps the most important factor to affect the audiovisual movement in the 1950s was the increased interest in television as a medium for delivering instruction. Prior to the 1950s, there had been a number of instances in which television had been used for instructional purposes (Gumpert, 1967; Taylor, 1967). During the 1950s, however, there was a tremendous growth in the use of instructional television. This growth was stimulated by at least two major factors.

One factor that spurred the growth of instructional television was the 1952 decision by the Federal Communications Commission to set aside 242 television channels for educational purposes. This decision led to the rapid development of a large number of public (then called "educational") television stations. By 1955, there were 17 such stations in the United States, and by 1960 that number had increased to more than 50 (Blakely, 1979). One of the primary missions of these stations was the presentation of instructional programs. As Hezel (1980) indicates: "The teaching role has been ascribed to public broadcasting since its origins. Especially prior to the 1960s, educational broadcasting was seen as a quick, efficient, inexpensive means of satisfying the nation's instructional needs" (p. 173).

The growth of instructional television during the 1950s was also stimulated by funding provided by the Ford Foundation. It has been estimated that during the 1950s and 1960s the foundation and its agencies spent more than $170 million on educational television (Gordon, 1970). Those projects sponsored by the foundation included a closed-circuit television system that was used to deliver instruction in all major subject areas at all grade levels throughout the school system in Washington County (Hagerstown), Maryland; a junior-college curriculum which was presented via public television in Chicago; a large scale experimental research program designed to assess the effectiveness of a series of college courses taught via closed circuit television at Pennsylvania State University; and the Midwest Program on Airborne Television Instruction, a program designed to transmit televised lessons from airplanes to schools in six states.

By the mid-1960s, much of the interest in using television for instructional purposes had abated. Many of the instructional television projects developed during this period had short lives. This problem was due in part to the mediocre instructional quality of some of the programs that were produced; many of them did little more than present a teacher delivering a lecture. In 1963, the Ford Foundation decided to focus its support on public television in general, rather than on in-school applications of instructional television (Blakely, 1979). In many cases, school districts discontinued instructional television demonstration projects when the external funding for those projects was halted (Tyler, 1975b). Instructional programming was still an important part of the mission of public television, but that mission was now wider, encompassing other types of programming, such as cultural and informational presentations (Hezel, 1980). In light of these and other developments, in 1967 the Carnegie Commission on Educational Television concluded:

> The role played in formal education by instructional television has been on the whole a small one . . . nothing which approached the true potential of instructional television has been realized in practice. . . . With minor exceptions, the total disappearance of instructional television would leave the educational system fundamentally unchanged. (pp. 80–81)

Many reasons have been given as to why instructional television was not adopted to a greater extent. These include teacher resistance to the use of television in their classrooms, the expense of installing and maintaining television systems in schools, and the inability of television alone to present adequately the various conditions necessary for student learning (Gordon, 1970; Tyler, 1975b).

Although the problems and shortcomings associated with instructional television have prevented it from changing the educational system in the way that many of its proponents originally envisioned, the medium continues to be used in many school systems (Riccobono, 1985). In addition, some large-scale projects, such as the *Sesame Street* television series and the instructional television programs developed for Great Britain's Open University, while not unqualifiedly successful, have received much favorable publicity (Cook & Conner, 1976; Hezel, 1980; Liebert, 1976; Schramm, 1977; Seibert & Ullmer, 1982).

Toward a New View of the Field

By the early 1960s, many of the leaders in the audiovisual instruction movement had come to the conclusion that the field was broader than the term implied. In 1961, James Finn, who was then president of the Department of Audiovisual Instruction, established a Commission on Definition and Terminology, whose goal was to define the field and the terminology associated with it (Ely, 1983). To this end, the commission prepared a monograph, in which the chairman of the commission stated:

> The increasing use of the audiovisual label over the last thirty years has created a term with varied meanings. Some have defined the audiovisual field by listing machines, by listing sensory experiences, or by indicating what audiovisual is *not*, i.e., whatever is verbal. As newer developments in technology have been applied to the problems of education, the audiovisual label has become less useful to describe the field with accuracy. A call for unity and direction has come from many sources within and without the audiovisual field. This monograph attempts to define the broader field of instructional technology

which incorporates certain aspects of the established audiovisual field. (Ely, 1963, p. 3)

The commission indicated that those in the field should be primarily concerned with "the design and use of messages which control the learning process" (Ely, 1963, p. 18), rather than with the audiovisual devices that traditionally had been the focus of the field. This opinion, published by the professional organization most closely affiliated with the audiovisual instruction movement, marked an important step in the shift toward a new view of the field.

In spite of the exhortations of the leaders in the field, however, many practitioners still focused their attention on audiovisual devices. In 1964, Lumsdaine made this point when he indicated that instructional technology could be thought of in two ways. He indicated that in one sense, instructional technology referred to "the use of equipment for presenting instructional materials" (p. 372). In a second sense, he stated, instructional technology could be thought of as the application of scientific principles, particularly theories of learning, in order to improve instruction. Lumsdaine went on to indicate that most of the work done by those in the audiovisual instruction movement could not be categorized under the second definition of instructional technology; in other words, efforts in the field had not been greatly influenced by theories of learning or by models of communication. Four years later, Saettler (1968) expressed a similar viewpoint. And in 1970, the Commission on Instructional Technology indicated that instructional technology "in its more familiar sense . . . means the media born of the communications revolution" (p. 21). With regard to the view of instructional technology as a "systematic way of designing, carrying out, and evaluating the total process of learning and teaching," the commission indicated that "the widespread acceptance and application of this broad definition belongs to the future" (p. 21).

In the 1970s, there was increased movement away from equating instructional technology with audiovisual devices. The changes in nomenclature within the field during this decade are an indication of this shift. For example, in 1970, the membership of the Department of Audiovisual Instruction voted to change the name of that organization to the Association for Educational Communications and Technology (AECT). Two years later, the Definition and Terminology Committee of AECT (1972) presented a new definition of the field:

Educational technology is a field involved in the facilitation of human learning through the systematic identification, development, organization, and utilization of a full range of learning resources, and through the management of these processes. It includes, but is not limited to, the development of instructional systems, the identification of existing resources, the delivery of resources to learners, and the management of these processes and the people who perform them. . . .

The approach that is characteristic of educational technology is perhaps best revealed by three successive patterns of interest that have shaped the development of the field during the past 50 years: the use of a broad range of resources for learning, the emphasis on individualized and personalized learning, and the use of the systems approach.

It is these three concepts, when synthesized into total approach to facilitate learning, that create the uniqueness of, and thus the rationale for, the field of educational technology. (pp. 36–37)

By emphasizing the systems approach and individualized instruction, as well as audiovisual devices ("learning resources"), the committee was clearly attempting to expand the view of the field. In 1977, the committee attempted to expand that view further by presenting an even broader definition statement, consisting of 16 parts. The first sentence of the statement provides a clear indication of its breadth:

Educational technology is a complex, integrated process involving people, procedures, ideas, devices, and organization, for analyzing problems and devising, implementing, evaluating, and managing solutions to those problems, involved in all aspects of human learning. (Assocation for Educational Communications and Technology, 1977, p. 1)

As stated at the outset of this chapter, there are many definitions of instructional technology. Each of the definitions previously cited has its adherents. The view of instructional technology as audiovisual devices has been reinforced as new devices such as the microcomputer (to be discussed later in this chapter) have entered the educational scene. Among people in the field, however, the trend has been away from viewing instructional technology as audiovisual devices and toward viewing it as a systems approach for designing instruction, "a systematic way of designing, carrying out, and evaluating the total process of learning and teaching" (Commission on Instructional Technology, 1970, p. 21). The next section focuses on the history of the systems approach for designing instruction.

THE SYSTEMS APPROACH

What is the systems approach for designing instruction? Banathy (1968) describes it as:

a self-correcting, logical process for the planning, development, and implementation of [instruction]. It provides a procedural framework within which the purpose of the system is first specified and then analyzed in order to find the best way to achieve it. On the basis of this analysis, the components that are most suitable to the successful performance of the system can be selected. . . . Finally, continuous evaluation of the system . . . provides a basis for planned change in improving economy and performance. (pp. 15–16)

While Banathy's statement provides a good general definition of the systems approach for designing instruction, it should be noted that, as Dick and Carey (1985) have indicated, there is no single systems-approach model. There are many models for the design of instruction that could be properly characterized as systems-approach models. Many of these models have been reviewed by Andrews and Goodson (1980).

Where did the notion of a systems approach to the design of instruction originate? What are its roots? How did it develop? The answers to these questions will be discussed in this section.

Early Forerunners

In order to examine the roots of the systems approach in education, it is important to recognize that it is basically an empirical approach to the design and improvement of instruction. This reliance on empirical evidence can be traced to the 1600s, and to Comenius, who proposed that inductive methods should be used to analyze and improve the instructional process (Saettler, 1968).

In the mid-1800s, Johann Herbart, a German educator, proposed that scientific research should be used to guide instructional practice (Travers, 1962). The empirical orientation in education is often attributed to the followers of Herbart, including Joseph Mayer Rice, an American who conducted several studies of school systems in the 1890s (Baker, 1973).

While Rice's work was not widely noticed, efforts of another believer in the empirical method, Edward L. Thorndike, had a major impact on educational practice. Thorndike joined the faculty at Teachers College, Columbia University, in 1899 and taught there for 40 years. During that time, his work in such areas as learning theory, mental testing, and individual differences greatly influenced the educational community (Baker, 1973; Saettler, 1968). Saettler indicates that Thorndike "established empirical investigation as the basis for a science of instruction . . . [he] was the exemplar of what might be done by empirical theorizing and investigation" (p. 48).

During the 1920s, there was increased interest in the use of empirical methods to help solve educational problems (Baker, 1973; Finn, 1972). Among the primary advocates of this approach were W. W. Charters and Franklin Bobbitt, both of whom were pioneers in such areas as activity analysis (job–task analysis) and objective specification (Dale, 1967; Ely, 1970; Popham, 1969; Walbesser & Eisenberg, 1972).

The Great Depression and World War II

Interest in empirical approaches to the design of instruction faded during the 1930s. The Great Depression, as well as the growth of the progressive movement in education, both served to hinder progress (Baker, 1973; Finn, 1972). With the entry of the United States into World War II, however, there was renewed interest in the use of empirical methods to help solve educational problems.

During the war, a large number of psychologists and educators who had training and experience in conducting experimental research were called upon to conduct research and develop training materials for the military services. These individuals, who exerted considerable influence on the characteristics of the training materials that were developed, based much of their work upon instructional principles derived from research and theory on instruction, learning, and human behavior (Baker, 1973; Saettler, 1968). Today, recent principles derived from the same sources serve as the basis for many of the concepts associated with the systems approach.

Programmed Instruction

After World War II, the birth of the programmed instruction movement in the mid-1950s proved to be the next major factor in the development of the systems approach concept. The process Skinner (1958) and others (cf. Lumsdaine & Glaser, 1960) described for developing programmed instruction exemplified an empirical approach to solving educational problems: data regarding the effectiveness of the materials were collected, instructional weaknesses were identified, and the materials were revised accordingly. In addition to this trial and revision procedure, which today would be called formative evaluation, the process for developing programmed materials involved many of the steps found in current systems-approach models. As Heinich (1970) indicates:

> Programmed instruction has been credited by some with introducing the systems approach to education. By analyzing and breaking down content into specific behavioral objectives, devising the necessary steps to achieve the objectives, setting up procedures to try out and revise the steps, and by validating the program against attainment of the objectives, programmed instruction succeeded in creating a small but effective self-instructional system—a technology of instruction. (p. 123)

Task Analysis

The refinement of task analysis procedures during the 1950's was another major factor in the development of the systems approach concept. Task analysis is the process of identifying the tasks and subtasks that must be successfully performed in order to execute properly some function or job. Early work in this area had been undertaken by Frank and Lillian Gilbreth, as well as by Bobbitt and Charters. It was in the 1950s, however, that the process was refined, primarily through the efforts of Robert B. Miller, who developed a detailed task analysis methodology while working on projects for the military services (Miller, 1953, 1962).

In the early 1960s, Gagné (1962a) expanded on the notion of task analysis. He indicated that the tasks and subtasks identified through the task analysis process often will have a hierarchical relationship to each other, so that in order to learn readily to perform a superordinate task, one would first have to master the tasks subordinate to it. This leads to the important notion that instruction should be designed so as to ensure that learners acquire subordinate skills before they attempt to acquire superordinate ones (Gagné, 1985).

Behavioral Objectives

The methodologies associated with task analysis and with the programmed instruction movement both placed an emphasis on the identification and specification of observable behaviors to be performed by the learner. Thus, the behavioral objectives movement can in part be attributed to the developments in these areas (Gagné, 1965a). However, objectives were discussed and used by educators at least as far back at the early 1900s. Among those early advocates of the use of clearly stated objectives were such people as Bobbitt, Charters, and Frederic Burk.

After World War I, the testing movement in education focused educators' attention on identifying what students were expected to learn. Tyler (1975a) points out, however, that the objectives that resulted from this movement usually identified the content that would be covered on a test, but did not specify the behaviors students were expected to exhibit in relation to that content.

Tyler himself is sometimes considered the father of the behavioral objectives movement. In 1934, he wrote, "Each objective must be defined in terms which clarify the kind of behavior which the course should help to develop" (cited in Walbesser & Eisenberg, 1972). During the famous Eight-Year Study which Tyler directed, it was found that in those instances in which schools did specify objectives, those objectives were usually quite vague. By the end of the project, however, it was demonstrated that objectives could be clarified by stating them in behavioral terms, and those objectives could serve as the basis for evaluating the effectiveness of instruction (Borich, 1980; Tyler, 1975a). Specifying objectives in terms of observable behaviors is now standard practice among advocates of the systems approach.

In the 1950s, behavioral objectives were given another boost when Benjamin Bloom and his colleagues published the *Taxonomy of Educational Objectives* (1956). The authors of this work indicated that within the cognitive domain there were various types of learning outcomes, that objectives could be classified according to the type of learner behavior described therein, and that there was a hierarchical relationship among the various types of outcomes. These notions, as we shall see, had important implications for the design of instruction.

In spite of the work of people such as Tyler and Bloom, the behavioral objectives movement did not flourish until the early 1960s. As stated earlier, work in the areas of task analysis and programmed instruction spurred the movement on. But perhaps the biggest spur was the publication of Robert Mager's book, *Preparing Objectives for Programmed Instruction* (1962), a small, humorously written programmed text designed to teach trainers and educators how to write objectives. This book is now in its second edition, and has sold more than 1.5 million copies.

While Mager helped popularize objectives, Robert Gagné helped to identify the instructional implications of defining and classifying objectives. Gagné (1962b, 1965a, 1965b; Gagné & Bolles, 1959), like Bloom and his colleagues, indicated that objectives could be classified according to the types of learner behavior they described. The categories of outcomes identified by Gagné, however, were somewhat different than those that had previously been described. More importantly, Gagné indicated that the instructional conditions necessary for learners to acquire these outcomes varied across categories, and he identified the conditions he considered would facilitate acquisition of each type of outcome. Gagné's theories regarding the conditions of learning are frequently relied upon by those who design instructional materials (Sachs & Braden, 1984).

Criterion-referenced Testing

In the early 1960s, another important factor in the development of the systems approach concept was the emergence of criterion-referenced testing. Popham (1975) states that criterion-referenced tests are "used to ascertain an individual's status with respect to a well-defined behavioral domain" (p. 93). As early as 1932, Tyler had indicated that tests could be used for such purposes (Dale, 1967). And later, Flanagan (1951) and Ebel (1962) discussed the differences between such tests and the more familiar norm-referenced measures. Glaser (1963; Glaser & Klaus, 1962) was the first, however, to use the term "criterion-referenced measures." In discussing such measures, Glaser (1963) indicated that they could be used to assess student entry-level behavior and to determine the extent to which students had acquired the behaviors an instructional program was designed to teach. The use of criterion-referenced tests for these two purposes is a central feature of systems approach procedures.

Early Systems-Approach Models

In the early 1960s, the concepts that were being developed in such areas as task analysis, objective specification, and criterion-referenced testing were brought together and discussed in articles written by authors such as Gagné (1962c), Glaser (1962, 1965), and Silvern (1964). These individuals were among the first to use terms such as "system development," "systematic instruction," and "instructional system" to describe systems approach procedures similar to those employed today.

At about this time, the terms "systems approach" and "systems development" began to be employed to describe the instructional development processes used during some instructional projects. Montemerlo and Tennyson (1976) point out that the first attempts to apply the systems approach to the design of training were undertaken by the Rand Corporation and the Human Resources Organization (HumRRO). They indicate that the systems approach model used by HumRRO has served as a prototype for most of the models that have followed it. Another early systems approach model was employed during the "Instructional Systems Development Project," which was conducted at Michigan State University from 1961 to 1965 (Barson, 1967; Gustafson, 1981).

Support by the United States Government

United States government support of, and interest in, instructional development efforts can be traced back to the 1950s. The event often considered as having sparked that interest took place in 1957, when the Soviet Union launched Sputnik. In response to this event, Congress passed the National Defense Education Act, which provided significant amounts of money for curriculum development (primarily in the areas of science and mathematics), as well as for media-related research. In contrast to earlier curriculum-development efforts, which often relied on individual authors, the activities supported by this new legislation often involved teams of subject-matter experts and educators working together to develop new instructional materials.

Borich (1980) points out that since the materials these teams developed often were quite innovative, pilot testing and field testing of some of the materials took place. Materials were then revised on the basis of this testing. Thus, some of the curriculum-development efforts of this period involved a process we today would call formative evaluation. According to Baker (1973), the testing of curriculum materials that occurred during this period was erratic, and often took place after it was too late to revise the materials. Regardless of the degree to which evaluation and revision became part of the development process, new attention was focused on the need to develop effective instruction.

The curriculum-development work that began with the passage of the National Defense Education Act in 1958 was expanded in the early 1960s when the federal government, under the Cooperative Research Act, provided funds for curriculum development in English, language arts, and social studies. Also in the early 1960s, the government provided support for the creation of university-based research and development centers. Each of these centers was intended to provide research leadership and develop educational products related to a specific area of education, such as educational administration or evaluation (Chase & Walter, 1982; Salmon-Cox, 1984).

It was in the context of these earlier legislative actions that, in 1965, the Elementary and Secondary Education Act was passed. This legislation led to the creation of 20 federally-supported laboratories, whose primary purpose was to assess and help meet the educational R&D needs of the region they served. Often, instructional products were developed in order to meet those needs. At some of the laboratories, these products were developed according to systems approach processes. And, as the need for individuals trained to employ these processes increased, graduate programs were instituted (Baker, 1973; Popham, 1980).

Through the establishment of regional laboratories and research and development centers, the use and dissemination of systems approach concepts was fostered. However, for a variety of reasons, including cutbacks in federal funding, the laboratories and centers themselves did not all flourish. Of the 32 laboratories and centers established in the 1960s, in 1984 only 18 remained (Salmon-Cox, 1984).

The Elementary and Secondary Education Act not only led to the creation of regional laboratories, it also set forth the requirement that those who received funds under ESEA to develop educational programs or products, were to evaluate the impact of their efforts. Although not all ESEA-funded programs fell under this provision, it was significant that it was the first attempt by the federal government to require educators to collect evaluation data (Borich, 1980).

Formative Evaluation

The evaluation of instructional products is an important part of the systems approach process. Two types of evaluation are typically employed. Formative evaluation is used to improve an instructional product while it is still in the development stage. Summative evaluation is used to assess the effectiveness of the final version of the product. While some systems approach models do not include summative evaluation as a part of the process, formative evaluation is generally considered an essential element.

The terms "formative evaluation" and "summative evaluation" were coined not many years ago by Scriven (1967), who employed the terms to elaborate upon a distinction first made by Cronbach (1963). Yet, while the term "formative evaluation" is relatively new, the concept has a much longer history. Cambre (1981) traces its origins to the early 1920s, when research-ers used a variety of techniques to assess the effectiveness of an instructional film. However, this effort, and other early efforts to assess instructional effectiveness, involved the evaluation of products that were in their final form; hence, in a strict sense, these efforts cannot be placed under the rubric "formative evaluation."

During the 1940s and the 1950s, a number of educators, such as Arthur Lumsdaine, Mark May, and C. R. Carpenter, described procedures for evaluating instructional materials that were still in their formative stages (Cambre, 1981). One of the first individuals to describe the formative role of evaluation activities was Ralph Tyler (1942), who wrote:

> The process of evaluation is . . . a recurring process . . . The results of evaluation . . . will suggest desirable modifications in teaching and in the edu-cational program itself. (pp. 500–501)

In spite of the writings of educators such as Tyler, very few of the instructional products developed in the 1940s and 1950s went through any sort of formative evaluation process. This situation changed somewhat in the 1960s, as many of the programmed instructional materials developed during that period were tested while they were being developed. However, authors such as Susan Markle (1967) decried a lack of vigor in testing processes. In light of this problem, Markle prescribed detailed procedures for evaluating materials both during and after the development process. These procedures are much like the formative and summative evaluation techniques generally prescribed today.

The Late 1960s and Early 1970s

During the late 1960s and early 1970s, many individuals and groups gave increased attention to systems approach concepts. The systems approach literature grew rapidly as models for the design of instruction (e.g., Banathy, 1968; Briggs, 1970) were developed and numerous journal articles focusing upon various aspects of the systems process were published.

The names of several professional associations were changed so as to reflect an interest in systems thinking. Gone were names like the Department of Audiovisual Instruction and the National Society for Programmed Instruc-tion, replaced by the Association for Educational Communications and Tech-nology and the National Society for Performance and Instruction.

In academia, graduate programs in instructional design were initiated and on-campus instructional development centers were established (Gaff, 1975). Some organziations in private industry and most of the branches of the mili-tary also became involved in the systems approach movement by adopting systems models and hiring individuals trained in the systems approach process.

Recent Developments

The systems movement continued to grow through the late 1970s and into the 1980s. The number of graduate programs continued to increase, as did the number of organizations hiring people trained in such programs. The number of systems approach models also continued to grow so that by 1980, Andrews and Goodson were able to report on the characteristics of 40 such models. The literature expanded in other ways, too, as a large number of new books were written (Sachs & Braden, 1984) and the *Journal of Instructional Development* was established.

Perhaps the most important development was the increased attention in the systems approach literature to notions emanating from the field of cognitive psychology. As Gagné (1980) indicated:

> It can surely be said that the acceptance of cognitive processing as an idea that must be dealt with in theorizing about human learning is a welcome change. . . . In developing programs of instruction, one must solve the problems of lesson design and media selection by reference to mental states and mental processes, rather than simply in terms of behavioral outcomes. (p. 7)

Resnick (1984) suggests that cognitive research is likely to result in principles that will provide a firm foundation for major changes in educational theory and practice. To what extent will those who design instruction according to a systems approach adopt the learning principles that are derived from cognitive psychology? At this time the answer is unclear, but whatever the answer may be, it is likely to have a major impact on the future of the systems approach process.

INDIVIDUALIZED INSTRUCTION

The systems approach can be used to design instruction that will be delivered to students on an individual basis, or it can be used to design instruction that will be delivered simultaneously to a group of learners. Nonetheless, few of those who employ the systems approach would argue with Dunn's (1984) statement that "one of the primary tenets of the systems approach to education is that of gearing instruction to the individual student" (p. 75).

Instruction that is geared to meet the needs of the individual student may be labeled individualized instruction. In order to meet the needs of the student, one or more special instructional techniques may be employed. These techniques include allowing learners to set their own individual pace as they proceed through an instructional sequence. They permit the choosing of instructional methods, media, and materials for each learner in light of individual characteristics, and allowing the selection of the objectives each learner wants to pursue.

Early Forms of Instruction

Until the mid-1800s, individualized instruction was the common method of education. In the Greek and Roman eras, pupils were taught individually by tutors. This system persisted for hundreds of years. In the United States, it evolved into a system in which children of different ages met with one teacher in a one-room schoolhouse, with each child being called to the teacher's desk to recite from materials the child was studying individually (Grittner, 1975; Kulik, 1982).

In the early 1800s, the system of instruction employed in many schools in the United States changed with the adoption of the monitorial system of instruction, developed by Joseph Lancaster and Andrew Bell. This system involved having one teacher present instruction to a large number of student "monitors" who, in turn, presented that instruction to as many as 10 younger students. By the middle of the century, the popularity of the monitorial system was waning. At about the same time, however, the advent of the graded school resulted in group instruction becoming an even more dominant feature in the American educational system (Grittner, 1975; Kulik, 1982).

Grouping Plans of the 1890s

Graded schools led to what some believed was an unnecessary degree of instructional rigidity, with all the students in a grade or class receiving the same instruction at the same time. In the 1890s, in reaction to what was sometimes perceived as an inflexible instructional system, several school districts introduced plans to individualize instruction. These plans were built around the concept of homogeneous ability grouping, or differentiation. Under these plans, students in the same class or grade were placed in different groups based upon their academic ability. These groups either received different instructional programs or proceeded through the same program at different rates (R. H. Anderson, 1962; Butts & Cremin, 1953; Grittner, 1975; Kulik, 1982). Grouping plans like these are still used today.

Although the grouping plans of the 1890s provided for some degree of individualization, they usually did not account for differences among pupils in the same group. In the early 1900s, however, a number of individualized instructional approaches were designed to accommodate the needs of each learner.

Burk's Individual System

Perhaps the first truly individualized instructional system was the Individual System, which was developed in 1912–1913 by Frederic Burk, for use in the elementary school at San Francisco State Normal School, a teacher training institution. Burk, president at San Francisco State, became interested in the self-instructional materials that one of his faculty members, Mary Ward, was having her students develop. Burk and his faculty developed similar self-instructional materials for most of the curriculum from kindergarten through eighth grade. Each child enrolled in the school was allowed to proceed through these materials at his or her own rate (Grittner, 1975; Kulik, 1982; Mickelson, 1972; Saettler, 1968).

Dalton and Winnetka Plans

Two of the best-known plans for individualized instruction were developed by members of Burk's staff. The Winnetka Plan was developed by Carleton Washburne in 1919, when he became superintendent of the public schools in Winnetka, Illinois. In the same year, Helen Parkhurst developed the Dalton Plan, which was first implemented in a school for disabled children in Dalton, Massachusetts. During the 1920s, each of these plans was adopted by many schools in the United States. They are described in detail by Grittner (1975), Saettler (1968), and Tyler (1975a).

During the 1930s, with the Great Depression and the increasing influence of the progressive movement in education, interest waned in individualized approaches such as the Dalton and Winnetka plans. Nonetheless, these individualized approaches significantly influenced educational thought and practice in a variety of ways. Among the notions fostered was the idea that learners would be required to demonstrate mastery of one set of skills before being allowed to proceed to a more advanced set. Also fostered was the notion that all learners do not have to proceed through instruction in a lockstep fashion; instead, instruction can be organized so that each learner can proceed through it at his or her own rate (Saettler, 1968; Tyler, 1975a).

Programmed Instruction

After a period of relative dormancy, interest in individualized instruction increased dramatically in the 1950s with the advent of the programmed instruction movement. This movement is often said to have begun in 1954, with the publication of B. F. Skinner's article, "The Science of Learning and the Art of Teaching." Skinner pointed to the deficiencies of traditional instructional techniques and indicated that by using teaching machines many of those problems could be overcome.

Skinner's plan rested on several interrelated principles. He proposed that instructional materials should consist of a series of small steps, or "frames," each of which should require an active response from the learner, who would receive immediate feedback regarding the correctness of his or her response. Skinner also believed that learners should be allowed to proceed at their own individual pace. A teaching machine described by Skinner was designed to present instruction in a manner that incorporated these principles.

Although Skinner's work provided much of the impetus for the programmed instruction movement, the roots of the movement have been located in much earlier periods. Some authors have traced the origins back to ancient Greece and Rome where, they indicate, some of the principles were first postulated and employed (Dale, 1967; Gilman, 1972; Lawson, 1969; Saettler, 1968). Other authors have attempted to identify early examples of "teaching machines" and other programmed instructional materials. They have cited such items as those developed by Quintillian at the beginning of the Common Era (Lawson, 1969); Halcyon Skinner in 1860 (Kulik, 1982; Stolurow & Davis, 1965), Maria Montessori at the start of the twentieth century (Saettler, 1968), and various educators during World War II (Stolurow & Davis, 1965; Tyler, 1975a). However, those individuals most frequently identified as precursors of the programmed instruction movement are E. L. Thorndike and Sidney L. Pressey.

Thorndike is often cited as having foreseen the development of programmed instructional materials (Baker, 1973; Dale, 1967; Lawson, 1969; Saettler, 1968; Stolurow & Davis, 1965). In 1912, he wrote:

> If, by a miracle of modern ingenuity, a book could be so arranged that only to him who had done what was directed on page one would page two become visible, and so on, much that now requires personal instruction could be managed by print. (p. 165)

In 1925, at the annual meeting of the American Psychological Association, Pressey demonstrated a teaching machine he had developed (Pressey, 1964). Although the device was designed primarily as a tool to automate student testing, it incorporated many of the features that Skinner later described as essential: it allowed for self-pacing by the learner, required active learner participation, and provided immediate feedback (Lumsdaine, 1964). Pressey and his students developed several automated teaching devices during the 1920s and early 1930s; however, in 1932, because of his belief that the field of education was not ready for his innovations, Pressey discontinued his work in this area (Pressey, 1964).

In the late 1950s and early 1960s, with the publication of Skinner's work (1954, 1958), many in the educational community became interested in teaching machines and programmed instruction. Large numbers of programs were developed for use in schools, the military, and business and industry. Many private companies were formed to develop these materials. A journal devoted exclusively to the topic of programmed instruction was originated, numerous books and articles on the subject were written, various programming techniques were devised, and professional organizations such as the

National Society for Programmed Instruction and the Association for Programmed Learning were created (Corey, 1967; Hawkridge, 1978; Merrill, Kowallis, & Wilson, 1981; Morgan, 1978; Olsen & Bass, 1982; Tyler, 1975b).

By the late 1960s, the programmed instruction movement was coming to an end. Interest had waned for a variety of reasons. Research had shown that the instructional effectiveness of programmed materials often was no greater than the effectiveness of conventional instructional materials (Kulik, 1982; Tyler, 1975b). Furthermore, students often indicated that the programmed materials were uninteresting (Baker, 1973; Morgan, 1978; Tyler, 1975b). In addition, school administrators and teachers had difficulty adjusting to the new roles thrust upon them by the use of self-instructional materials in their classrooms (Glaser & Cooley, 1973; Tyler, 1975b). These were a few of the many factors that contributed to the decline of the programmed instruction movement.

Although interest in programmed instruction did not last long, the movement had many lasting effects on the educational community. Among other things, it pointed to the importance of evaluating instruction on the basis of the outcomes that are obtained, rather than the instructional techniques that are employed; it focused attention on the procedures used in the development of instructional materials; and it sparked a renewed interest in individualized instructional approaches (Armsey & Dahl, 1973; Baker, 1973; Kulik, 1982; Merrill et al., 1981; Morgan, 1978).

In the late 1960s, as interest in programmed instruction was waning, some educators began to turn their attention to other forms of individualized instruction. It was during, and just prior to, this period that a number of such systems were developed. These systems included the Personalized System of Instruction, Learning for Mastery, the Audio-Tutorial Approach, Individually Prescribed Instruction (IPI), Program for Learning in Accordance with Needs (PLAN), and Individually Guided Education (IGE).

Personalized System of Instruction

The Personalized System of Instruction (the Keller Plan) is a mastery-oriented instructional method that allows each student to proceed through an instructional sequence at his or her own rate. This method was developed in 1963 by four psychologists: Fred S. Keller and J. Gilmour Sherman, who were faculty members at Columbia University, and Rodolfo Azzi and Carolina Martuscelli Bori, at the University of Sao Paulo, Brazil. The Keller Plan was first employed in a short-term laboratory course at Columbia University in 1963. Since then it has been used in thousands of college and university courses throughout the world (Chance, 1984; Johnson & Ruskin, 1977).

Under the Keller Plan, a course is divided into a series of units, the number of units often being approximately equal to the number of weeks in a semester. The instruction in each unit consists of written material, usually a textbook and a study guide; lectures are not an integral part of instruction under this approach. Units are placed in a definite sequence and students are required to demonstrate mastery of one unit before they are allowed to proceed to the next one. Quizzes are used to assess student mastery of each unit. Students can take these quizzes whenever they consider themselves ready to do so. After taking a quiz, a student receives immediate feedback regarding his or her performance. This feedback is provided by a student proctor, or tutor, who has previously done well in the same course. The student who fails to pass a unit quiz is not penalized for doing so. Instead, the student is given the opportunity to review the materials for that unit and take alternative versions of the unit quiz until these are passed. This process continues until the semester ends or the student has demonstrated mastery of (i.e., passed the quizzes for) each unit. The grade for a course often depends on the number of units the student masters, as well as the scores on one or more cumulative examinations.

Keller (1968, 1974) has identified five features of his approach which he feels distinguish it from conventional instructional methods. These features are : (1) the unit mastery requirement, (2) the use of student self-pacing, (3) the use of student proctors, (4) the reliance on written instruction, and (5) the de-emphasis of lectures. Many of those who have implemented the Keller Plan in their courses have modified one or more of these features, but they remain as the principal attributes of the system.

Learning for Mastery

The Learning For Mastery approach was developed by Benjamin Bloom and his students at the University of Chicago. Bloom based this approach on the model of school learning developed by John B. Carroll (1963). Carroll had stated that "the learner will succeed in learning a given task to the extent that he spends the amount of time that he *needs* to learn the task" (p. 725). Carroll further indicated that the time the learner would need would be dependent, in large part, on the quality of the instruction he or she received. Building upon these notions, Bloom (1968) proposed an instructional system that allowed instructional time and materials to vary so as to allow practically all students to master each learning task.

Although the Learning for Mastery approach, like the Keller Plan, emphasizes unit mastery, it allows for teacher-paced instruction. Under this approach, instruction for each unit is initially presented by the teacher using conventional group-based teaching methods. Students are then given a "formative" test to determine whether they have mastered the unit. Corrective activities are prescribed for those students who fail to do so. These activities include small-group study, peer tutoring, and individual review of alternative instructional materials such as textbooks, workbooks, and non-print materials. Students are either given time during class to engage in these activities or are required to do so on their own time, preferably before group-based instruction on the next unit begins. Before that instruction does proceed, a parallel version of the formative test may be given to those students who have not demonstrated mastery on the first test. At the end of the semester, or sometimes more frequently, a "summative" (i.e., cumulative) examination is administered to all students to determine the degree to which they have mastered each of the units covered (Block, 1980; Block & Burns, 1976; Bloom, 1984).

The Learning for Mastery approach has been used in thousands of schools in the United States, primarily at the elementary school level. In some cases, entire school districts have adopted the system. In addition, the system has been employed on a large-scale basis in several foreign countries (Block, 1979, 1980; Brandt, 1979).

Audio-Tutorial Approach

The Audio-Tutorial approach was developed in 1961 by Samuel N. Postlethwait at Purdue University. The remedial package he put together included printed materials, slides, movies, experimental equipment, specimens, models, and an audiotape which presented "the conversation one would expect to use with a single student while tutoring the student through a sequence of learning activities" (Postlethwait, 1982, p. 4).

Under the Audio-Tutorial system, a course is divided into units, each of which lasts a week. During that week, students can proceed at their own pace through most of the learning activities for the unit. Many of the activities are presented via audiotape and other media. At the end of the week, students are placed in small groups and are given oral and written quizzes covering the content of the units (Postlethwait, 1981; Postlethwait, Novak, & Murray 1972).

Since its inception in 1961, many instructors have employed the Audio-Tutorial approach, or slight variations of it. Although it has been used primarily in science courses at the college and university level, it has also been applied in other types of courses and at other levels of the educational system (Fisher & MacWhinney, 1976; Kulik, Kulik & Cohen, 1979b; Postlethwait, 1982).

IPI, PLAN, and IGE

During the early and mid-1970s, the three most popular systems of individualized instruction employed in public schools in the United States were Individually Prescribed Instruction (IPI), Program for Learning in Accordance with Needs (PLAN), and Individually Guided Education (IGE). These three systems had much in common. All three were primarily developed during the mid- or late-1960s, all three included several of the same features, and all three reached the height of their popularity during the mid-1970's. However, in spite of their commonalities, each system possessed some unique features.

Individually prescribed instruction. IPI was developed in 1964 by the Learning Research and Development Center of the University of Pittsburgh. The IPI system consisted of instructional materials and procedures designed to allow children to proceed at their own rate through various elementary-school curriculum areas such as mathematics and reading.

Instructional procedures under the IPI system involved assigning a student to particular instructional units based upon the student's performance on a placement test administered at the beginning of the school year. The student would then take a unit pretest so as to identify the unit objectives already mastered. Based on the results of the pretest, a prescription was given, listing the materials the student should study. After these materials had been studied, the student was posttested. If the posttest revealed mastery of the objectives, the student was allowed to proceed to the next unit. Otherwise, the student was given further work and was retested until mastery could be demonstrated. In some instances, records of student progress were kept by a computer (Glaser & Rosner, 1975; Lindvall & Bolvin, 1967).

The IPI system was implemented for the first time in September 1964 at the Oakleaf Elementary School in a suburb of Pittsburgh. IPI materials and procedures were employed in grades K–6 at Oakleaf for reading, mathematics, and science. Within five years, with support from the U.S. Office of Education, the IPI system was being tried in approximately 100 schools. By the mid-1970s, the IPI system had been used in thousands of classrooms in the United States and abroad.

In the late 1970s, government funding for IPI was discontinued, and Research for Better Schools, the regional laboratory that had been responsible for field testing and disseminating the system, ceased activity in this area. Since that time, use of the system has waned. One of the directors of the IPI project attributes this decline in part to teacher resistance to the employment of a system that did not readily fit in with typical classroom procedures (L. M. Maguire, personal communication, Nov. 2, 1984).

Program for learning in accordance with needs. PLAN was an individualized instructional system that covered language arts, mathematics, science, and social studies in grades 1–12. In 1967, The American Institutes for Research (AIR), Westinghouse Learning Corporation, and 14 school districts from various regions reached an agreement to develop PLAN. John C. Flanagan of AIR headed the developmental effort.

PLAN was arranged so that each school that used the system could select, from among the approximately 6,000 instructional objectives that were part of the system, those objectives that were to be included in its curriculum. The objectives that a particular student attempted to attain were determined by student and teacher. They based this decision upon such factors as the student's previous educational history and performance on a placement test.

After the objectives a student would be working on were selected, the student was given learning guides that identified learning materials and activities that would help in the attainment of each objective. These learning materials had not been developed under the PLAN project; during the development of PLAN, it was decided that rather than developing new instructional materials, the project staff would identify existing materials that would enable students to attain each objective.

As with many of the other individualized instructional systems, when individual students considered themselves ready, they were given a test assessing attainment of a set of objectives. If mastery of the objectives was demonstrated, the student moved on to another unit. If not all of the objectives were mastered, the student was directed to some remedial activities and then retested. A record of each student's progress was kept by a computer (Flanagan et al, 1975).

By the 1973–74 academic year, approximately 65,000 elementary and secondary students in more than 100 schools in 19 states were participating in PLAN. However, as new instructional materials became available, PLAN was not updated to reflect how those materials could be used as part of the system. As a consequence, the system eventually became outdated and its use was discontinued.

Individually guided education.   IGE was an individualized system of instruction with many components. Key features were a method of instructional programming that allowed for the progression of students on an individual basis, and a model of classroom organization and school administration that facilitated individualization and improvement of instruction (Klausmeier, 1975, 1977).

The IGE instructional programming method was similar to that used in other individualized approaches to instruction. In schools that used IGE, a committee of the principal and several teachers identified the objectives to be attained by students. Teams of teachers and instructional assistants then worked together to assess the entry skills of each student, identify the objectives the student would initially attempt to attain, and plan an instructional program designed to enable the attainment of those objectives. The instructional program was either prepackaged or designed for a particular student. Programs were also likely to vary in terms of such factors as the amount of group and individual activities included and the types of instructional media employed. After instruction, students were assessed and—depending on whether they had demonstrated mastery—either received additional instruction on the same set of objectives or advanced to the next set.

The origins of the IGE have been traced to 1965, when a project designed to create a new organizational structure in schools was undertaken by the Wisconsin Research and Development Center. Herbert Klausmeier served as principal investigator for the project. As a result of this project, in the second semester of the 1965–66 school year, the age-graded classes in elementary schools in four school districts in Wisconsin were replaced by 13 instructional and research units. The next school year, seven elementary schools completely reorganized into instructional and research units. Reorganization of the administrative structure of these schools also took place that year. In 1971, the U.S. Office of Education provided funds for a large-scale implementation of the IGE system. During the next two years, more than 500 elementary schools in nine states adopted the system, and by 1976 there were approximately 3,000 elementary and middle schools using some form of IGE (Klausmeier, 1975, 1976; Kulik, 1982; Saily & Rossmiller, 1976). In the late 1970s, however, government funding for the dissemination of IGE ceased. Since that time, the number of schools using IGE has decreased.

Waning Trends in Individualized Instruction

In 1976, the Wisconsin Center began an evaluation of the effects of IGE. Results indicated that most of the schools had not implemented the system properly. Nearly 60% of the approximately 900 schools surveyed could at best be characterized as having only nominally adopted the system. In many of these schools, the "implementation" did not result in any real changes in instructional practices; often the IGE label was used to legitimize the maintenance of ongoing practices. Only about 20% of the schools could be classified as true implementors of IGE (Popkewitz, 1979; Popkewitz, Tabachnick, & Wehlage, 1982; Romberg, 1985).

Similar patterns were found in the schools that adopted the IPI system. According to one of the directors of the IPI project, the degree to which the system was properly employed varied greatly. In many schools, the system was not operated as it was intended to be, and in some cases it was implemented in name only (L. M. Maguire, personal communication, Nov. 2, 1984).

These findings indicate the difficulty of instituting change in schools. It has been suggested that those who would like to see change occur must consider the social, political, and educational context in which schooling occurs. The beliefs and interests of school members, as well as the community at large, must be considered, and the active involvement and support of school staff must be sought. Without that support, true innovation is unlikely to come about (Popkewitz, 1979; Popkewitz, Tabachnick & Wehlage, 1982; Romberg, 1985).

Although IPI, PLAN, and IGE are no longer prominent forms of individualized instruction, the development and dissemination of these systems was a significant phase in the growth of instructional technology. The innovations fostered by the use of these systems included sequencing instruction based upon a hierarchy of objectives, using criterion-referenced tests for diagnostic purposes, changing the role of the teacher from a purveyor of information to an instructional planner, manager, and tutor, de-emphasizing the grade-level organization of schools, and using the computer to assist in the management of instruction (Glaser & Rosner, 1975; Klausmeier, 1984; Kulik, 1982).

Computer-assisted Instruction

In the late 1970s, as interest in individualized instructional systems such as IPI, PLAN, and IGE faded, developments in computer technology, particularly in the area of microcomputers, led to increased interest in the notion of individualizing instruction by presenting it via the computer.

Due to its interactive capabilities, the computer can be programmed to adapt instruction to the needs of the individual learner. Examples of simple adaptations include those programs that allow learners to select only the pace at which they proceed, as well as those programs that select the next instructional step that will be presented to each learner on the basis of the response to the previous step. On the other hand, complex adaptations (cf. Park & Tennyson, 1983; Ross, 1984; Tennyson, Christensen, & Park, 1984) involve adjusting several instructional variables (e.g., the amount, type, and sequence of information, practice, and feedback) in accordance with several learner variables (e.g., previous knowledge, current performance, and expressed interest). Currently, as before, most computer programs incorporate fairly simple systems of adaptation (Kearsley, 1977; Ross, 1984). This fact should be kept in mind as some events in the history of computer-assisted instruction (CAI) are briefly traced.

Computers were first used in education and training in the 1950s. Much of the early work in CAI was done by researchers at IBM, who developed the first CAI author language and designed one of the first CAI programs used in the public schools (Baker, 1978; Blaisdell, 1976–1977; Pagliaro, 1983; Suppes & Macken, 1978). Another pioneer in the field was Gordon Pask, whose adaptive teaching machines made use of computer technology to teach such skills as card punching and object tracking (Lewis & Pask, 1965; Pask, 1960; Saettler, 1968; Stolurow & Davis, 1965).

During the 1960s, several universities, often in cooperation with private industry, took the lead in conducting research and development in CAI. One of the first major efforts in this area was undertaken by Richard Atkinson and Patrick Suppes, of Stanford University's Institute for Mathematical Studies in the Social Sciences. Collaboration between the institute and IBM led to some of the earliest applications of CAI at both the elementary-school and university level (Atkinson & Hansen, 1966; Suppes & Morningstar, 1969). Another collaborative effort, among the University of Illinois, the Control Data Corporation, and the National Science Foundation, led to the development of PLATO (Programmed Logic for Automatic Teaching Operations), a CAI system that is currently used in a large number of universities, public schools, and training centers. Other universities that took leading roles in the CAI movement in the 1960s included the University of Texas and Florida State University (Morgan, 1978; Suppes & Macken, 1978). In spite of the work that was done during this period, CAI had little impact on education during the 1960s (Pagliaro, 1983).

In the 1970s, the CAI movement continued to grow. A major event during this period occurred in 1972, when a group from Brigham Young University and the MITRE Corporation began work on the TICCIT (Time-shared, Interactive, Computer-Controlled Information Television) System. This CAI system, which is widely used today, was perhaps the first to be designed expressly so as to present instruction in accordance with an instructional theory (Pagliaro, 1983).

A second major event affecting the CAI movement during the 1970s was the development of microcomputers. Many educators were attracted to microcomputers because these devices were relatively inexpensive, were fairly compact, and could perform many of the instructional functions of large computers. Even with this increased interest in computers, however, by the end of the decade these devices were still a very small part of the educational picture (Pagliaro, 1983).

In the 1980s, there has been a tremendous growth in the use of microcomputers in the schools. In June 1980, approximately 5% of the elementary schools and 20% of the secondary schools in the United States had microcomputers which were being used for instructional purposes. By January 1983, however, computers were being used for instruction in more than 40% of the elementary schools and in more than 75% of the secondary schools (Center for Social Organization of Schools, 1983a).

Although many schools now use microcomputers for instructional purposes, it should not be assumed that individualized instruction now is a dominant feature in the schools. A recent survey indicates that, in schools that have microcomputers, on the average, less than 15% of the students in those schools use a microcomputer during any given week. Furthermore, the average amount of time those students spend using the microcomputer is less than one hour per week, and more than half of that time is typically devoted to learning about computers. Thus, in spite of their increased use, it appears that computers continue to play a small role in helping students acquire the skills that are traditionally taught in schools (Center for Social Organization of Schools, 1983b).

CONCLUSION

This chapter has reviewed the history of three concepts closely associated with the field of instructional technology. It is interesting to note that in each of these areas, scholarly interest has displayed shifts of one sort or another over comparable periods of time. In the audiovisual area, as each new device (such as television and the computer) has entered the educational scene, interest in that device has increased. In the systems area, the emphasis seems to be shifting from a strictly empirical orientation to an approach which also takes into account the theories of learning emanating from the field of cognitive psychology. And in the area of individualized instruction, interest has alternated between individualized *systems* of instruction, such as the Dalton Plan and the Personalized System of Instruction, and individualized instructional *materials,* such as those presented via teaching machines and computers. In addition, there appears to be a growing interest in truly adaptive approaches to individualized instruction, approaches that allow for complex instructional adaptations in accordance with a wide variety of learner variables (cf. Park & Tennyson, 1983; Ross, 1984; Tennyson, Christensen, & Park, 1984).

These changes in interest may be a healthy sign, indicative of a field flexible enough to change as new ideas or devices enter the scene. Or they may indicate that the foundation on which the field is based is weak or ill defined. Rather than attempting to judge the strength of the field in light of these shifts in interest, it may be best to do so by examining the extent to which the concepts associated with instructional technology have influenced education and training.

Over the last 25 years, there has been a growing use of audiovisual devices in education (Heinich et al., 1982). This growth has become particularly apparent during the 1980s as more and more schools employ microcomputers for instructional purposes (Center for the Social Organization of Schools, 1983a). However, in spite of the increased use of audiovisual devices, many questions about the instructional effectiveness of these devices remain to be answered (Clark, 1983; Petkovich & Tennyson, 1984, 1985).

The systems approach has been applied successfully in a variety of instructional settings (e.g., Mager, 1977; Markle, 1977; Shoemaker, 1976; Witherell et al., 1981), and seems to be gaining broader acceptance, particularly in training organizations (e.g., Miles, 1983). Nevertheless, in the United States it is difficult to find descriptions of situations in which the systems approach has been successfully employed to solve the problems of public education.

Individualized instruction, in such forms as computer-assisted instruction, the Personalized System of Instruction, and the Learning for Mastery approach, is being used in many instructional settings. Often, research results have indicated that these individualized approaches are more effective than traditional instructional methods (Bloom, 1984; Kulik, Kulik, & Cohen, 1979a). Nonetheless, many of the individualized systems of instruction developed during the 1960s have faded from view, and group-based instruction remains the predominant instructional approach.

Accordingly, it appears that instructional technology, whether defined as audiovisual devices, the systems approach, individualized instruction, or some combination of these concepts, has had some impact on the fields of education and training; yet many of those affiliated with the field would indicate that the impact can and should be far greater than what it has been.

In 1972, the Definition and Terminology Committee of AECT indicated that the field of educational technology is unique in that it combines the three concepts discussed in this chapter "into a total approach to facilitate learning" (p. 37). The committee went on to state:

> The combination of these concepts in the broader context of education and society yields synergistic outcomes—behaviors which are not predictable based on the parts alone—but outcomes with extra energy which is created by the unique interrelation of the parts. (p. 38)

In practice, however, this combination rarely occurs. As the field of instructional technology evolves, perhaps there will be more attempts to synthesize the three concepts discussed in this chapter. If that is the case, it is likely that the accomplishments of instructional technology in education and training will be substantially greater than those achieved so far.

REFERENCES

Allen, W. H. (1971). Instructional media research: Past, present, & future. *AV Communication Review, 19*, 5–18.

Anderson, C. (1962). *Technology in American education: 1650–1900* (Report No. OE–34018). Washington, DC: Office of Education, U.S. Department of Health, Education, and Welfare.

Anderson, R. H. (1962). Organizing groups for instruction. In N. B. Henry (Ed.), *Individualizing Instruction: The sixty-first yearbook of the National Society for the Study of Education, Part 1.* Chicago: University of Chicago Press.

Andrews, D. H., & Goodson, L. A. (1980). A comparative analysis of models of instructional design. *Journal of Instructional Development, 3*, 2–16.

Armsey, J. W., & Dahl, N. C. (1973). *An inquiry into the uses of instructional technology.* New York: Ford Foundation.

Association for Educational Communications and Technology (1977). *Educational technology: Definition and glossary of terms.* Washington, DC: Association for Educational Communication and Technology.

Atkinson, R. C., & Hansen, D. N. (1966). Computer-assisted instruction in initial reading: The Stanford project. *Reading Research Quarterly, 2,* 5–25.

Baker, E. L. (1973). The technology of instructional development. In R. M. W. Travers (Ed.), *Second handbook of research on teaching,* Chicago: Rand McNally.

Baker, J. C. (1978). Corporate involvement in CAI. *Educational Technology, 18(4),* 12–16.

Banathy, B. H. (1968). *Instructional systems.* Belmont, CA: Fearon.

Barson, J. (1967). *Instructional systems development. A demonstration and evaluation project: Final report.* East Lansing, MI: Michigan State University. (ERIC Document Reproduction Service No. ED 020 673)

Berlo, D. K. (1963). "You are in the people business." *Audiovisual instruction, 8,* 372–381.

Blaisdell, F. J. (1976–77). Historical development of computer assisted instruction. *Journal of Educational Technology Systems, 5,* 155–170.

Blakely, R. J. (1979). *To serve the public interest: Educational broadcasting in the United States.* Syracuse, NY: Syracuse University Press.

Block, J. H. (1979). Mastery learning: The current state of the craft. *Educational Leadership, 37,* 114–117.

Block, J. H. (1980). Promoting excellence through mastery learning. *Theory into practice, 19(1),* 66–74.

Block, J. H., & Burns, R. B. (1976). Mastery learning. In L. S. Shulman (Ed.), *Review of Research in Education* (Vol. 4). Itasca, IL: F. E. Peacock.

Bloom. B. S. (1968). Learning for Mastery. *Evaluation Comment, 1(2).*

Bloom, B. S. (1984). The 2 sigma problem: The search for methods of group instruction as effective as one-to-one tutoring. *Educational Researcher, 13(6),* 4–16.

Bloom, B. S., Engelhart, M. D., Furst, E. J., Hill, W. H., & Krathwohl, D. R. (1956). *Taxonomy of educational objectives: The classification of educational goals. Handbook I: Cognitive Domain.* New York: David McKay.

Borich, G. D. (1980). *A state of the art assessment of educational evaluation.* Austin, TX: University of Texas. (ERIC Document Reproduction Service No. ED 187 717)

Brandt, R. (1979). A conversation with Benjamin Bloom. *Educational Leadership, 37,* 157–161.

Briggs, L. J. (1970). *Handbook of procedures for the design of instruction* (Monograph No. 4). Pittsburgh: American Institutes for Research.

Butts, R. F., & Cremin, L. A. (1953). A history of education in American culture. New York: Holt, Rinehart and Winston.

Cambre, M. A. (1981). Historical overview of formative evaluation of instructional media products. *Educational Communication and Technology Journal, 29,* 3–25.

Carnegie Commission on Educational Television (1967). *Public television: A program for action.* New York: Harper & Row.

Carpenter, C. R., & Greenhill, L. P. (1956). *Instructional film research reports: Vol. 2* (Technical Report No. 269-7-61). Port Washington, NY: U.S. Navy Special Devices Center.

Carroll, J. B. (1963). A model of school learning. *Teachers College Record, 64,* 723–733.

Center for Social Organization of Schools (1983a). School uses of microcomputers: Reports from a national survey (Issue No. 1). Baltimore, MD: Johns Hopkins University, Center for Social Organization of Schools.

Center for Social Organization of Schools (1983b). School uses of microcomputers: Reports from a national survey (Issue No. 2). Baltimore, MD: Johns Hopkins University, Center for Social Organization of Schools.

Chance, P. (1984). The revolutionary gentleman [Interview with F. S. Keller]. *Psychology Today, 18(9),* 42–48.

Chase, F. S., & Walter, J. E. (1982). Research laboratories and centers. In H. E. Mitzel (Ed.), *Encyclopedia of Educational Research* (5th ed., pp. 1618–1627). New York: Macmillan.

Clark. R. E. (1983). Reconsidering research on learning from media. *Review of Educational Research, 53,* 445–459.

Commission on Instructional Technology (1970). *To improve learning: An evaluation of instructional technology* (Vol. 1). New York: Bowker.

Cook, T. D., & Conner, R. F. (1976). Sesame Street around the world: The educational impact. *Journal of Communication, 26*(2), 155–164.

Corey, S. M. (1967). The nature of instruction. In P. C. Lange (Ed.), *Programmed instruction: The sixty-sixth yearbook of the National Society for the Study of Education, Part II.* Chicago: University of Chicago Press.

Cronbach, L. J. (1963). Course improvement through evaluation. *Teachers' College Record, 64,* 672–683.

Dale, E. (1946). *Audio-visual methods in teaching* (1st ed.). New York: Holt, Rinehart and Winston.

Dale, E. (1953). What does it mean to communicate? *AV Communication Review, 1,* 3–5.

Dale, E. (1967). Historical setting of programmed instruction. In P. C. Lange (Ed.), *Programmed Instruction: The sixty-sixth yearbook of the National Society for the Study of Education, Part II.* Chicago: University of Chicago Press.

Definition and Terminology Committee of the Association for Educational Communications and Technology (1972). The field of educational technology: A statement of definition. *Audiovisual Instruction, 17*(8), 36–43.

Dick, W., & Carey, L. (1985). *The systematic design of instruction* (2nd ed.). Glenview, IL: Scott, Foresman.

Dunn, T. G. (1984). Learning hierarchies and cognitive psychology: An important link for instructional psychology. *Educational Psychologist, 19,* 75–93.

Dwyer, F. M. (1978). *Strategies for improving visual learning: A handbook for the effective selection, design, and use of visualized materials.* State College, PA: Learning Services.

Ebel, R. L. (1962). Content standard test scores. *Educational and Psychological Measurement, 22,* 15–25.

Ely, D. P. (Ed.). (1963). The changing role of the audiovisual process in education: A definition and a glossary of related terms. *AV Communication Review, 11*(1).

Ely, D. P. (1970). Toward a philosophy of instructional technology. *British Journal of Educational Technology, 1*(2), 81–94.

Ely, D. P. (1983). The definition of educational technology: An emerging stability. *Educational Considerations, 10*(2), 2–4.

Filep, R., & Schramm, W. (1970). *A study of the impact of research on utilization of media for educational purposes sponsored by NDEA Title VII 1958-1968. Final Report: Overview.* El Segundo, CA: Institute for Educational Development.

Finn, J. D. (1954). Direction in AV communication research. *AV Communication Review, 2,* 83–102.

Finn, J. D. (1972). The emerging technology of education. In R. J. McBeath (Ed.), *Extending education through technology: Selected writings by James D. Finn.* Washington, DC: Association for Educational Commnications and Technology.

Fisher, K. M., & MacWhinney, B. (1976). AV autotutorial instruction: A review of evaluative research. *AV Communication Review, 24,* 229–261.

Flanagan, J. C. (1951). Units, scores, and norms. In E. T. Lindquist (Ed.), *Educational Measurement.* Washington, DC: American Council on Education.

Flanagan, J. C., Shanner, W. M., Brudner, H. J., & Marker, R. W. (1975). An individualized instructional system: PLAN. In H. Talmage (Ed.), *Systems of individualized education.* Berkeley, CA: McCutchan.

Gaff, J. G. (1975). *Toward faculty renewal: Advances in faculty, instructional, and organizational development.* San Francisco: Jossey-Bass.

Gagné, R. M. (1962a). The acquisition of knowledge. *Psychological Review, 69, 355–365.*

Gagné, R. M. (1962b). Human functions in systems. In R. M. Gagné (Ed.), *Psychological principles in system development.* New York: Holt, Rinehart and Winston.

Gagné, R. M. (1962c). Introduction. In R. M. Gagné (Ed.), *Psychological principles in system development.* New York: Holt, Rinehart and Winston.

Gagné, R. M. (1965a). The analysis of instructional objectives for the design of instruction. In R. Glaser (Ed.), *Teaching machines and programmed learning, II: Data and directions.* Washington, DC: National Education Association.

Gagné, R. M. (1965b). *The conditions of learning* (1st ed.). New York: Holt, Rinehart and Winston.

Gagné, R. M. (1980). Is educational technology in phase? *Educational Technology, 20*(2), 7–14.

Gagné, R. M. (1985). *The conditions of learning* (4th ed.). New York: Holt, Rinehart and Winston.

Gagné, R. M., & Bolles, R. C. (1959). Factors in learning efficiency. In E. Galanter (Ed.), *Automatic teaching: The state of the art.* New York: Wiley.

Gilman, D. A. (1972). The origins and development of intrinsic and adaptive programming. *AV Communication Review, 20,* 64–76.

Glaser, R. (1962). Psychology and instructional technology. In R. Glaser (Ed.), *Training research and education.* Pittsburgh: University of Pittsburgh Press.

Glaser, R. (1963). Instructional technology and the measurement of learning outcomes: Some questions. *American Psychologist, 18,* 519–521.

Glaser, R. (1965). Toward a behavioral science base for instructional design. In R. Glaser (Ed.), *Teaching machines and programmed learning, II: Data and directions.* Washington, DC: National Education Association.

Glaser, R., & Cooley, W. W. (1973). Instrumentation for teaching and instructional management. In R. M. W. Travers (Ed.), *Second handbook of research on teaching.* Chicago: Rand McNally.

Glaser, R., & Klaus, D. J. (1962). Proficiency measurement: Assessing human performance. In R. M. Gagné (Ed.), *Psychological prinicples in system development.* New York: Holt, Rinehart and Winston.

Glaser, R. & Rosner, J. (1975). Adaptive environments for learning: Curriculum aspects. In H. Talmage (Ed.), *Systems of individualized education.* Berkeley, CA: McCutchan.

Gordon, G. N. (1970). *Classroom television: New frontiers in ITV.* New York: Hastings House.

Grittner, F. M. (1975). Individualized instruction: An historical perspective. *Modern Language Journal, 59,* 323–333.

Gumpert, G. (1967). Closed-circuit television in training and education. In A. E. Koenig & R. B. Hill (Eds.), *The farther vision: Educational television today.* Madison, WI: University of Wisconsin Press.

Gustafson, K. L. (1981). *Survey of instructional development models.* Syracuse, NY: ERIC Clearinghouse on Information Resources, Syracuse Unversity. (ERIC Document Reproduction Service No. ED 211 097)

Hawkridge, D. (1978). Epilogue: Next year, Jerusalem! The rise of educational technology. In J. Hartley & I. K. Davies (Eds.), *Contributions to an educational technology* (Vol. 2). London: Kogan Page.

Heinich, R. (1970). *Technology and the management of instruction* (Association for Educational Communication and Technology Monograph No. 4). Washington, DC: Association for Educational Communications and Technology.

Heinich, R., Molenda, M., & Russell, J. D. (1982). *Instructional media and the new technologies of instruction.* New York: Wiley.

Hezel, R. T. (1980). Public broadcasting: Can it teach? *Journal of Communication, 30,* 173–178.

Hoban, C. F., Sr., Hoban, C. F., Jr., & Zissman, S. B. (1937). *Visualizing the curriculum.* New York: Dryden.

Johnson, K. R., & Ruskin, R. S. (1977). *Behavioral instruction: An evaluative review.* Washington, DC: American Psychological Association.

Kearsley, G. P. (1977). Some conceptual issues in computer-assisted instruction. *Journal of Computer-Based Instruction, 4,* 8–16.

Keller, F. S. (1968). "Goodbye Teacher . . ." *Jounal of Applied Behavior Analysis, 1,* 79–89.

Keller, F. S. (1974). Ten years of personalized instruction. *Teaching of Psychology, 1,* 4–9.

Klausmeier, H. J. (1975). IGE: An alternative form of schooling. In H. Talmage (Ed.), *Systems of individualized education.* Berkeley, CA: McCutchan.

Klausmeier, H. J. (1976). Individually guided education: 1966-1980. *Journal of Teacher Education, 27,* 199–205.

Klausmeier, H. J. (1977). Origin and overview of IGE. In H. J. Klausmeier, R. A. Rossmiller, & M. Saily (Eds.), *Individually guided elementary education: Concepts and practices.* New York: Academic Press.

Klausmeier, H. J. (1984). *Executive summary of accomplishments of Herbert J. Klausmeier, 1949-1984.* Unpublished manuscript, University of Wisconsin, Department of Educational Psychology, Madison, WI.

Kulik, J. A. (1982). Individualized systems of instruction. In H. E. Mitzel (Ed.), *Encyclopedia of educational research* (5th ed., pp. 851–858). New York: Macmillan.

Kulik, J. A., Kulik, C.-L.C., & Cohen, P. A. (1979a). A meta-analysis of outcome studies of Keller's Personalized System of Instruction. *American Psychologist, 34,* 307-318.

Kulik, J. A., Kulik, C.-L. C., & Cohen, P. A. (1979b). Research on audio-tutorial instruction: A meta-analysis of comparative studies. *Research in Higher Education, 11,* 321–341.

Lawson, D. R. (1969). Who thought of it first: A review of historical references to programmed instruction. *Educational Technology, 9*(10), 93–96.

Lewis, B. N., & Pask, G. (1965). The theory and practice of adaptive teaching systems. In R. Glaser (Ed.), *Teaching machines and programmed learning II: Data and directions.* Washington, DC: National Education Association.

Liebert, R. M. (1976). Sesame Street around the world: Evaluating the evaluators. *Journal of Communication, 26*(2), 165–171.

Lindvall, C. M., & Bolvin, J. O. (1967). In P. C. Lange (Ed.), *Programmed instruction: The sixty-sixth yearbook of the National Society for the Study of Education, Part II,* Chicago: University of Chicago Press.

Lumsdaine, A. A. (Ed.). (1961). *Student response in programmed instruction.* Washington, DC: National Academy of Science—National Research Council.

Lumsdaine, A. A. (1963). Instruments and media of instruction. In N. L. Gage (Ed.), *Handbook of research on teaching.* Chicago: Rand McNally.

Lumsdaine, A. A. (1964). Educational technology, programmed learning, and instructional science. In E. R. Hilgard (Ed.), *Theories of learning and instruction: The sixty-third yearbook of the National Society for the Study of Education, Part I.* Chicago: University of Chicago Press.

Lumsdaine, A. A., & Glaser, R. (Eds.). (1960). *Teaching machines and programmed learning: A source book.* Washington, DC: National Education Association.

Mager, R. F. (1962). *Preparing objectives for programmed instruction.* Belmont, CA: Fearon.

Mager, R. F. (1977). The "winds of change." *Training and Development Journal, 31*(10), 12–20.

Markle, D. G. (1977). First aid training. In L. J. Briggs (Ed.), *Instructional Design: Principles and applications.* Englewood Cliffs, NJ: Educational Technology.

Markle, S. M. (1967). Empirical testing of programs. In P. C. Lange (Ed.), *Programmed instruction: The sixty-sixth yearbook of the National Society for the Study of Education, Part II.* Chicago: University of Chicago Press.

May, M. A., & Lumsdaine, A. A. (1958). *Learning from films.* New Haven, CT: Yale University Press.

McCluskey, F. D. (1981). DVI, DAVI, AECT: A long view. In J. W. Brown & S. N. Brown (Eds.), *Educational media yearbook: 1981.* Littleton, CO: Libraries Unlimited.

Meierhenry, W. C. (1980). Instructional theory: From behaviorism to humanism to synergism. *Instructional Innovator, 25*(1), 16–18.

Merrill, M. D., Kowallis, T., & Wilson, B. G. (1981). Instructional design in transition. In F. H. Farley & N. J. Gordon (Eds.), *Psychology and education: The state of the union.* Berkeley, CA: McCutchan.

Mickelson, J. M. (1972). Personalized instruction: How new is it? *Education Digest, 38*(3), 38–40.

Miles, G. D. (1983). Evaluating four years of ID experience. *Journal of Instructional Development, 6*(2), 9–14.

Miller, R. B. (1953). A method for man-machine task analysis (Tech. Rep. No. 53-137). Wright-Patterson Air Force Base, Ohio: Wright Air Development Center.

Miller, R. B. (1962). Analysis and specification of behavior for training. In R. Glaser (Ed.), *Training research and education.* Pittsburgh: University of Pittsburgh Press.

Montemerlo, M. D., & Tennyson, M. E. (1976). *Instructional systems development: Conceptual analysis and comprehensive bibliography.* Orlando, FL: Naval Training Equipment Center. (ERIC Document Reproduction Service No. ED 121 356)

Morgan, R. M. (1978). Educational technology - adolescence to adulthood. *Educational Communication and Technology Journal, 26,* 142–152.

Olsen, J. R., & Bass, V. B. (1982). The application of performance technology in the military: 1960-1980. *Performance and Instruction, 21*(6), 32–36.

Pagliaro, L. A. (1983). The history and development of CAI: 1926-1981, an overview. *Alberta Journal of Educational Research, 29*(1), 75–84.

Park, O., & Tennyson, R. D. (1983). Computer-based instructional systems for adaptive education: A review. *Contemporary Education Review, 2*(2), 121–135.

Pask, G. (1960). Electronic keyboard teaching machines. In A. A. Lumsdaine & R. Glaser (Eds.), *Teaching machines and programmed learning: A source book.* Washington, DC: National Education Association.

Petkovich, M. D., & Tennyson, R. D. (1984). Clark's "Learning from media": A critique. *Educational Communication and Technology Journal, 32,* 233–241.

Petkovich, M. D., & Tennyson, R. D. (1985). A few more thoughts on Clark's "Learning from media." *Educational Communication and Technology Journal, 33,* 146.

Popham, W. J. (1969). Objectives and instruction. In *Instructional objectives* (American Educational Research Association Monograph Series on Curriculum Evaluation, No. 3). Chicago: Rand McNally.

Popham, W. J. (1975). *Criterion-referenced measurement.* Englewood Cliffs, NJ: Prentice-Hall.

Popham, W. J. (1980). Two decades of educational technology: Personal observations. *Educational Technology, 20*(1), 19–21.

Popkewitz, T. S. (1979). Educational reform and the problem of institutional life. *Educational Researcher, 8*(3), 3–8.

Popkewitz, T. S., Tabachnik, B. R., & Wehlage, G. (1982). *The myth of educational reform: A study of school responses to a program of change.* Madison, WI: University of Wisconsin Press.

Postlethwait, S. N. (1981). A basis for instructional alternatives. *Journal of College Science Teaching, 21,* 44–46.

Postlethwait, S. N. (1982). Audio-tutorial instruction: History of the AT system. *International Society for Individualized Instruction Newsletter, 82*(1), 4.

Postlethwait, S. N., Novak, J., & Murray, H. T., Jr. (1972). *The audio-tutorial approach to learning* (3rd ed.). Minneapolis: Burgess.

Pressey, S. L. (1964). Autoinstruction: Perspectives, problems, potentials. In E. R. Hilgard (Ed.), *Theories of learning and instruction; the sixty-third yearbook of the National Society for the Study of Education, Part I.* Chicago: University of Chicago Press.

Resnick, L. B. (1984). Cognitive sciences as educational research: Why we need it now. In *Improving education: Perspectives on educational research.* Pittsburgh: National Academy of Education, University of Pittsburgh.

Riccobono, J. A. (1985). *School utilization study: Availability, use, and support of instructional media.* Washington, DC: Corporation for Public Broadcasting.

Romberg, T. (Ed.), (1985). *Toward effective schooling: The IGE experience.* Lanham, MD: University Press of America.

Ross, S. M. (1984). Matching the lesson to the student: Alternative adaptive designs for individualized learning systems. *Journal of Computer-Based Instruction, 11,* 42–48.

Sachs, S. G., & Braden, R. A. (1984). Instructional development in the real world: Book recommendations from academia and industry. *Performance & Instruction Journal, 23*(5), 5–7.

Saettler, P. (1968). *A history of instructional technology.* New York: McGraw-Hill.

Saily, M., & Rossmiller, R. A. (1976). The I/D/E/A change program for IGE: A response from the Wisconsin R & D Center. *Journal of Teacher Education, 27,* 217–219.

Salmon-Cox, L. (1984). *Institutionalized knowledge production for education* (Learning Research and Development Center Publication 1984/1). Pittsburgh: Learning Research and Development Center, University of Pittsburgh.

Salomon, G. (1981). *Communication and education: Social and psychological interactions.* Beverly Hills, CA: Sage.

Schramm, W. (1977). *Big media, little media.* Beverly Hills, CA: Sage.

Scriven, M. (1967). The methodolgy of evaluation. In *Perspectives of curriculum evaluation* (American Educational Research Association Monograph Series on Curriculum Evaluation, No. 1). Chicago: Rand McNally.

Seibert, W. F., & Ullmer, E. J. (1982). Media use in education. In H. E. Mitzel (Ed.), *Encylopedia of Educational Research* (5th ed., pp. 1190–1202). New York: Macmillan.

Shannon, C. E., & Weaver, W. (1949). *The mathematical theory of communication.* Urbana, IL: University of Illinois Press.

Shoemaker, H. A. (1976). The pay-off of instructional technology. *Improving Human Performance Quarterly, 5*(2), 47–61.

Silber, K. H. (1981). Some implications of the history of educational technology: We're all in this together. In J. W. Brown & S. N. Brown (Eds.), *Educational media yearbook: 1981.* Littleton, CO: Libraries Unlimited.

Silvern, L. C. (1964). *Designing instructional systems.* Los Angeles: Education and Training Consultants.

Skinner, B. F. (1954). The science of learning and the art of teaching. *Harvard Educational Review, 24,* 86–97.

Skinner, B. F. (1958). Teaching machines. *Science, 128, 969–977.*

Stolurow, L. M., & Davis, D. (1965). *Teaching machines and computer-based systems. In R. Glaser (Ed.), Teaching machines and programed learning, II: Data and directions.* Washington, DC: National Education Association.

Suppes, P., & Macken, E. (1978). The historical path from research and development to operational use of CAI. *Educational Technology, 18*(4), 9–12.

Suppes, P. & Morningstar, M. (1969). Computer-assisted instruction. *Science, 166,* 343–350.

Taylor, B. J. (1967). The development of instructional television. In A. E. Koenig & R. B. Hill (Eds.), *The farther vision: Educational television today.* Madison, WI: University of Wisconsin Press.

Tennyson, R. D., Christensen, D. L., & Park, S. I. (1984). The Minnesota Adaptive Instructional System: An intelligent CBI system. *Journal of Computer-Based Instruction, 11,* 2–13.

Thorndike, E. L. (1912). *Education.* New York: Macmillan.

Torkelson, G. M. (1977). AVCR—One quarter century: Evaluation of theory and research. *AV Communication Review, 25,* 317–358.

Travers, R. M. W. (1962). A study of the relationship of psychological research to educational practice. In R. Glaser (Ed.), *Training research and education.* Pittsburgh: University of Pittsburgh Press.

Tyler, R. W. (1942). General statement on evaluation. *Journal of Educational Research, 35,* 492–501.

Tyler, R. W. (1975a). Educational benchmarks in retrospect: Educational change since 1915. *Viewpoints, 51*(2), 11–31.

Tyler, R. W. (1975b). Have educational reforms since 1950 created quality education? *Viewpoints, 51*(2), 35–57.

Walbesser, H. H., & Eisenberg, T. A. (1972). *A review of the research on behavioral objectives and learning hierarchies.* Columbus, OH: Ohio State University, Center for Science and Mathematics Education. (ERIC Document Reproduction Service No. ED 059 900)

Wilkinson, G. L. (1980). *Media in instruction: 60 years of research.* Washington, DC: Association for Educational Communications and Technology.

Witherell, R. A., Morgan, R. M., Yoon, H.-W., Kim, S.-V. & Lee, C.-J. (1981). *Korea elementary-middle school pilot project: Project impact evaluation.* Washington, DC: Agency for International Development.

AUTHOR NOTES

Robert A. Reiser is a Professor in the Department of Educational Research, Development, and Foundations, Florida State University.

3 Foundations in Learning Research

Robert M. Gagné
Florida State University

Robert Glaser
University of Pittsburgh

The technology of instruction is based upon a number of different pursuits, including such practical activities as determining training requirements, designing training, selecting media, and others described in the chapters of this book. The "how-to-do-it" knowledge involved in these efforts has been rationally and empirically derived from a body of scientific knowledge that has accumulated over many years. This source comprises facts, general principles, and theories about human learning, including its associated processes of remembering, problem solving, and reflective thinking.

LEARNING RESEARCH

The systematic study of the phenomena of human learning, along with the accompanying theory development, has had a somewhat schizophrenic history. Since the time of Binet's work (Binet & Simon, 1916) in assessing the intelligence of school pupils, a succession of investigators has carried out analyses and experiments on the learning of school subjects such as arithmetic, reading, and spelling. Notable among psychologists who oriented many of their investigations in this direction are Thorndike (1913) and Skinner (1968). At the same time, learning psychology has continued to lean strongly in what may be seen as an opposite direction—a trend toward task simplification that views school-derived tasks as too complex for precise scientific investigation. The employment of nonsense syllables as learning tasks by Ebbinghaus (1913) is the classic example of this trend in learning psychology. Simplified tasks in the study of human learning have included conditioned responses of various sorts, serial lists of syllables and words, paired-associate syllables presented sequentially on a memory drum, and a variety of symbol-identifying and figure-naming tasks.

Some Basic Learning Principles

For many years, the dominant conceptual unit in learning theory was the *association* (Anderson & Bower, 1973; Bower & Hilgard, 1981). A number of basic theoretical ideas, verified by empirical studies, emerged from this period of scientific study, and are of continuing value for an understanding of human learning. Some aspects of learning appear to be universal in their occurrence. These are principles that can be observed when associations are learned, typically in the classical or operant conditioning of animals or human beings.

Contiguity. Certain events have to be experienced contiguously by the learner in order for learning to occur. The principle of contiguity stated by William James (1890) was that "objects once experienced together tend to become associated in the imagination, so that when any one of them is thought of, the others are likely to be thought of also" (p. 561). Pavlov's (1927) account of the conditioned response established the necessity for contiguity (or near-simultaneity) of the conditioned and unconditioned stimuli. Similar requirements for contiguity of stimuli have been shown to obtain in operant conditioning.

The occurrence of contiguity, and the effects of its absence, can readily be observed in many natural learning situations. The burnt child does shun the flame. The pupil who is learning to return a book to its shelf must have a stimulus (such as the closing of the book) contiguous with the stimulus (which may be internal) that initiates the action. A student who is learning a synonymous meaning for a new word must have one or more synonyms contiguous with that word. Actually, the condition of contiguity usually seems an obvious necessity for learning. Although the contiguity principle can be violated in designs for learning, one expects that to happen only rarely.

The Law of Effect. The learning of an association in which a response follows the presentation of a stimulus depends on the occurrence of certain consequences of the response (that is, its "effects"). This principle of learning, as stated by E. L. Thorndike (1913), was that when a connection between a situation and a response is made and is accompanied or followed by a satisfying state of affairs, that connection's strength is increased. This fundamental principle is generally considered to embody the same idea as Skinner's (1938) statement of the law of conditioning for an operant response. Skinner stated that if the occurrence of an operant is followed by presentation of a reinforcing stimulus, the strength is increased. The idea of strength in both Thorndike's and Skinner's formulations is generally thought to be evidenced by a change in the frequency, rapidity, or probability of occurrence of the response.

Similarly to the case of contiguity, it is truly difficult to find practical learning situations that do not include feedback, or knowledge of results. It is very natural for a teacher or instructional designer to make the attempt to follow an action to be learned with a set of events that provide feedback to the learner. But some kinds of feedback are more effective than others, and discovering or estimating their effectiveness is a challenging question that continues to be pursued in research. As a pervasive learning principle, however, reinforcement appears to have a dependable persistence.

Practice. The repeating of events in an association was originally considered a condition that would increase "associative strength." But the effect of the factor of practice on learning and on the retention of learning is not a simple one. Thorndike's studies of the Law of Exercise led him to the realization that sheer repetition of an act does not strengthen learning. Practice has its effect only when each repetition of the learned association is carried out with due provision for systematic contiguity and reinforcement. When these conditions are accompanying, practice has a substantial influence on learning.

When *multiple associations* are being learned by practice, the attempt to recall one may be made more difficult by competition from the others. This important phenomenon is *interference* (Postman, 1961; Underwood, 1964), which exhibits itself in many kinds of learning tasks. Interference is more likely to occur the greater the similarities among the different associations being recalled. Thus, the effects of practice on the learning of a word list (such as vocabulary words in a foreign language) may reasonably be viewed as overcoming the interference among the items of the list. If a strikingly dissimilar item is introduced for learning among a set of similar items, the interference with this item becomes drastically reduced (Wickens, 1972).

The effects of practice are perhaps most readily observed when a motor skill is being learned. James' (1890) discussion of habit employs frequent references to the gradual improvement of motor acts by learning. Typically, it is a motor skill that provides the classical picture of the *learning curve* that exhibits improvement rapidly at first, and with decreasing acceleration approaches an asymptote. As Fitts and Posner (1967) point out, measurable increments of improvement with practice may continue for very long periods of time.

The effect of practice on the establishment of procedural knowledge presents a contrast to the gradually increasing strength of a motor skill. If a rule about simplifiying fractions has been initially acquired, practice takes the form of making repeated application of the rule to a number of *different* previously unencountered examples. But such repetition appears to contrast markedly with the repeated attempts at execution of the same sequence of muscular movements, as is done in motor skill practice. It is often difficult to show gains in the "strength" of a learned rule resulting from increases in the number of practice examples from 3 to 20. When the practice is spaced, however, as in *spaced reviews,* the retrievability of procedural knowledge is increased, presumably owing to the recruitment of additional cues during each review session. Variety of examples also has the effect of improving the retention of learned rules.

Beyond the stage at which a rule or procedure has been initially acquired, additional changes can occur with continued practice. These are described by Neves and Anderson (1981) as: (a) composition, which includes the combining of rule parts into a larger production, and speeding up of the performance; and (b) the attainment of automaticity, involving a reduction in demands on attention (Shiffrin & Schneider, 1977). The notion of automaticity, in particular, has important implications for both theory and practice, as James (1890) realized. This kind of practice outcome may have an incidental influence in improving retrievability of the rule. Its main effect, however, is to reduce the interference offered by the automatic task to another task concurrently performed (Shiffrin & Dumais, 1981).

Importance of the basic principles. It would appear from this review that three principles considered basic to the phenomenon of human learning are still viable: contiguity, reinforcement, and practice. They are not entirely simple principles, though, because their actions are interrelated. The experiences to be put together by contiguity do not get associated without reinforcement, and in many cases also, not without practice. The learning events to be associated by the arrangement of reinforcement contingencies require either contiguity or the internal representation of contiguity; practice is also a condition whose effect cannot be ignored. Practice normally takes place under conditions that include both contiguity and reinforcement; when both are absent, repetition accomplishes very little.

Accordingly, after years of learning research on these principles, they remain with us as statements of influencing factors that continue to be valid. But what do we gain when we know and accept these principles? With reference to the design of instruction, or to instructional technology more specifically, the answer is, not enough. Once the operation of these principles has been assured for any given instructional unit (as of course it should be), the factors of contiguity, reinforcement, and practice provide no further guidance as to how to plan or to conduct instruction. Is a lesson on riding a bicycle to be conducted the same way as a lesson on adding fractions, even allowing for differences in content? Is a lesson designed to teach American history to have the same format of instruction as a lesson in geometry, or a lesson on avoiding drug abuse? All of these kinds of instruction can readily be planned to conform with the principles of contiguity, reinforcement, and practice. Yet it strains credulity to suppose that the techniques of instruction for each can be the same, or even closely analogous.

More must be known about human learning than is encompassed by these basic principles. Knowledge of ways to achieve a more highly analytic conception of human learning has come from studies of learning in the tradition of *cognitive science*. As a category, this phrase includes the cognitive psychology of learning, information–processing theory, and research on cognition and intellectual processes. Contributors to this field are psychologists, linguists, computer scientists, and researchers of artificial intelligence.

LEARNING AS COGNITION

Modern theoretical conceptions view learning as a set of processes having the function of information processing. Once the stimulation from external energy sources reaches the human receptors, it is transformed by them into patterns that can best be understood as conveying *information* (Attneave, 1959; Garner, 1962; Shannon & Weaver, 1949). Since the subject of information gets us into the realm of communication engineering, many of the useful concepts of that discipline have accompanied this point of view (Lachman, Lachman, & Butterfield, 1979). Information is conceived as traveling in channels, and as being limited by channel capacities. Coding of information may be employed as a means of overcoming limitations in channel capacity. Processing of information is often done in a serial fashion, but may also be accomplished in parallel.

These and other ideas about information processing have been successfully applied to the investigation of human intellectual functioning. The most prominent linking has been provided by computer scientists who conceive of the computer as a symbol-manipulating system, and draw the analogy with the operations of human cognition. Over a period of some years, a great deal of research has been devoted to the problem of intelligent action on the part of computers, and many advances are still being made in the field usually called *artificial intelligence* (see Bower & Hilgard, 1981, pp. 353–415). It was an obvious logical step for some researchers to begin to use computer programs as a means for simulating human intellectual processes, and to verify possibilities of actual human behavior by demonstrating that such programs were capable of solving intellectual problems (Schank & Colby, 1973; Simon & Feigenbaum, 1964). Perhaps the most influential work in this field has been Newell and Simon's *Human Problem Solving* (1972). Other major works that have made substantial contributions are Anderson and Bower (1973), Anderson (1976), and Norman & Rumelhart (1975). But many others have contributed theoretical ideas and empirical research findings in journal articles and book chapters.

The Structure of Memory

One set of theoretical ideas that are fundamental to modern views of learning pertains to the structure in which information processing takes place. Several black boxes, representing phases of processing, must be hypothesized to intervene between the input of stimulation to the senses, and the output of human performances. In particular, just as inputs to the computer are stored in a component called a memory, inputs that enter the human cognitive apparatus must also be stored in memory. Investigation of these human storage functions has led to the distinction of several kinds of memory, or more precisely several kinds of memory storage.

Short-term memory. One of the important distinctions in the realm of human memory is the short-term memory (STM). This is the kind of memory that stores limited amounts of information for a fairly short time interval. Perhaps the simplest common example is storage of a telephone number which one looks up in a directory and uses within a few seconds in dialing. Short-term memory is also exemplified by the well-known test of immediate memory span, measured by the number of digits or letters a learner can repeat after hearing them once. Single items stored in short-term memory, when further processing is prevented, die away in about 20 seconds (Peterson & Peterson, 1959). Following Miller (1956), most investigators consider the limits of capacity of this memory store as seven plus or minus two. However, some would set the limit lower, at four or five. Although an item in short-term memory was originally thought of as a single letter or digit, the phenomenon of *chunking* makes possible the storing of words or familiar letter combinations (such as ERA, NSF, IRS), and meaningful patterns, such as the groupings of pieces on a chessboard. These may be stored as unitary items, up to the capacity of the memory store.

A dominant mode of storage in short-term memory is auditory. That is, in retrieving a sequence of items from short-term memory, it is as though the learner were hearing them. When errors are made in recalling items that have been presented visually, they arise mainly from acoustic confusions, rather than from similarities of the items' appearance (Conrad, 1964). Although acoustic coding is a highly prominent mode of storage in the short-term memory, it is not the only mode. Under some conditions, coding may take a visual form (Brooks, 1968) and also a semantic one (Shulman, 1972).

The working memory. The short-term memory receives information coming to the learner through the senses. When serving this function, the short-term memory may be viewed as *primary memory,* where the information is stored in a transitory fashion. However, other processes that take place in the short-term memory lead to the conception of its function as a *working memory.* One of these functions is the comparison of incoming information with previously stored information (in the long-term memory), retrieved to the working memory so that the item is "matched" and recognized. A second kind of work done by this memory is the combining, or *integration,* of new material to be learned with an organized set of knowledge (sometimes called a *schema*) retrieved from long-term memory (LTM). And a third function of the working memory, most familiar of all, is *rehearsal.* This internal process, the implicit repetition ("saying over to oneself") of the material received in the short-term memory, permits the initially encoded items to be maintained over periods longer than the 20 seconds in which they would otherwise be lost.

Rehearsal in its basic form of repetition is considered to be the process by means of which material entering the cognitive system is renewed, so that the information can be encoded for storage in the long-term memory. Perhaps a more significant part of the process, however, is sometimes called *elaborative rehearsal.* Rather than simply being maintained, the rehearsal of stored materials is considered to invest it with additional semantic meaning. This process puts it in a form for storage in the long-term memory.

Fig. 3.1 depicts the flow of information from the sensory registers to the short-term memory and between short-term and long-term memories. The short-term memory is shown with its function of primary memory storage, and also the various kinds of work performed by the working memory. Information of some sorts (for example, shapes or patterns) may flow directly from the primary memory to the long-term memory. However, the main route, shown with heavier lines, is for the information to undergo rehearsal in the working memory, and thence proceed to the long-term memory in semantic form. Three kinds of material may follow routes for *retrieval* from long-term to working memory: (1) events employed in elaborative rehearsal, (2) items to be matched with incoming material (with

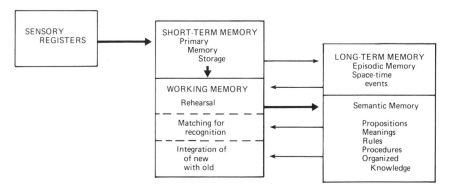

FIGURE 3.1.   Information flow in the short- and long-term memory systems.

resulting recognition of the latter), and (3) material previously stored in LTM with which the newly received items will be integrated.

Still another distinction is shown in Fig. 3.1. This is the two kinds of memorial material, conceived as residing in the *episodic memory,* on the one hand, and in *semantic memory,* on the other. Episodes, according to Tulving (1972), are personally experienced events occurring in particular places and at particular times. When a reader of a detective story recalls that, a few pages back, he noted a singular incident of bad manners on the part of one of the characters, this is an example of episodic memory. The episodic information has entered the short-term memory, perhaps has been briefly rehearsed, and has been stored as a spatio-temporal event in long-term memory. Upon being retrieved to working memory, the episode may be integrated with other information, perhaps newly received, that may take on semantic characteristics. For example, the reader may use the episode of the character's bad manners to become part of a line of thought that leads to his speculation about "who done it." Such meaningful sequential thought is stored as semantic memory, and may later be retrieved in that form.

THE IMPORTANCE OF SHORT-TERM MEMORY

One can think of the short-term memory as, first, a phase in the information-processing sequence in which newly received and to-be-learned material is maximally accessible to the attention of the learner, and is prepared by grouping, rehearsal, and elaboration for storage in the long-term memory. Second, the short-term memory, in its working-memory role, receives material retrieved from long-term memory, which is matched with new items so that the latter are recognized, or which may be combined with newly received material to form new entities for learning. These new entities may be different organizations of knowledge, procedural skills, problem-solving strategies, and the like.

Limitations of STM Capacities

The fact that the short-term memory is limited in both the amount of *time* items can be stored and the *number* of items which can be dealt with has some definite implications for learning. So far as is known, it is not possible to alter the limit of storage duration (20 seconds) by any learning intervention. It is, however, a limit that can be overcome by skillful use of rehearsal. A short-order cook, for example, may be observed to carry in his head orders that extend backwards several minutes, while at the same time receiving new orders in a continual stream. The time limit remains unaltered, as can easily be shown by introducing a momentary distraction to the cook, upon which the process of storage has to begin anew.

As for the limit on number of items, it has been found many times that individuals may increase their immediate memory span by practice. Older studies tended to show an increase of span from 7 to around 12 items. However, recent research has shown the possibility of large increases in the number of items that can be "held in mind" (Ericsson & Chase, 1982). By practice over a period of 20 months, one student was able to repeat back sequences of as many as 80 digits. The investigators reached the conclusion that he was doing this by methods that related digit sequences to meaningful knowledge in long-term memory, together with rapid retrieval. It did not appear to be the case that the limitations of short-term memory were being overcome by rehearsal.

The capacity limit of short-term memory is of particular importance to the design of tasks to be learned. Directions intended to tell the learner what to do ("first, look at the figure at the top of the page"), for example, must avoid describing more than three or four steps at a time, or indicating more than three or four stimuli to be attended to simultaneously. Otherwise, the capacity of the learner's short-term memory may be exceeded. When that happens, the learner may either: (1) be required to hear or see the instructions over again, or (2) perform the desired actions inadequately because too large a share of attention is being devoted to elaborative rehearsal of the directions.

When engaged in problem solving of any type, the learner's limited STM capacity for working with several processing tasks at once often constrains performance. In tasks of reading, for example, STM limitations appear to be involved in word decoding (Resnick & Beck, 1976) and in the comprehension of grammatically complex sentences (Richek, 1976). The limits of short-term memory also become readily apparent in mathematical problem solving, as in children's solving of word problems (e.g., Riley, Greeno, & Heller, 1983) and adults' solving complex mathematical puzzles (e.g., Wickelgren, 1974). Several of the strategies applicable to the latter types of problems, such as *hill climbing, establishing subgoals,* and *working backward* clearly have the effect of reducing the demands on short-term memory storage.

Accordingly, when the communication for learning consists of directions, rule statements, or passages of organized text, design for effective instruction needs to take into account the very definite limitations of STM capacity. And this requirement extends also to the kind of learning material that uses the presentation of a problem to be solved as a vehicle for learning. The learner will not likely be able to work with more in STM than four or five items, or steps, or operations. When more than this number are required, the learner must resort to rehearsal and chunking. Although these are effective processes, they also make demands on attention; consequently, using efficient strategies of storage and retrieval in LTM is very often the preferred route for memory processing. In sum, the instructional designer aims to avoid excessive demands on the working memory.

Long-term Memory

Stored in long-term memory (LTM) are concepts and associations between concepts (Bower, 1975). Concepts may be perceived objects or object features (for example, edge, round), relations (such as underneath, behind), or higher-order concepts like city and family (cf. Gagné, 1985, pp. 111–118). By most theorists, the concepts of LTM are assumed to be arranged in the semantic form of propositions, as depicted in Fig. 3.2 (Anderson, 1980; Rumelhart & Norman, 1975). Propositions are sentence-like entities, each possessing a subject and a predicate. Propositions are associated with each other through commonly shared concepts. Thus, the proposition of Fig. 3.2 may be expected to be linked through the concept *book* to other propositions about types of books, uses of books, sizes of books, and so on; and to be linked through the concept *Oscar* with propositions containing further information about Oscar. The typical contents of LTM, then, are *networks of propositions*.

Naturally enough, new propositions are continually being added to existing networks. Furthermore, new conceptual configurations are formed when new concepts or sets of concepts are acquired. Some theorists (Collins & Quillian, 1969) have proposed that propositional networks are arranged hierarchically in categories, so that *canary* is related to the superordinate category *bird*, which in turn relates to *animal* and to *living thing*. Another suggested organization for propositional networks is the *semantic feature model* (Rips, Shoben, & Smith, 1973), which proposes concepts to be defined, and differentiated from other concepts, by a collection of features. Thus the concept *cat* has the features of *fur, four legs, domestic pet,* and so on.

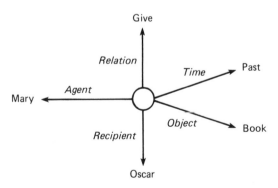

FIGURE 3.2. Representation in long-term memory of the proposition "Mary gave Oscar a book."

However they may be organized, the propositions of LTM appear to possess widespread relations with each other (Anderson, 1980; Klatzky, 1980). When a concept is newly presented to a learner, it produces a *spread of activation* to all other concepts in the network with which it is associated. Thus it is expected that a concept like *book* in Fig. 3.2, when activated by a newly presented stimulus, will occasion a spread of activation to such concepts as *pamphlet, university, and library,* among others. The notion of spreading activation has two main implications for understanding the nature of long-term memory. First, it underlies the prediction that speed of recall of a proposition will depend upon the number of concepts to which the activation must spread; similarly, for speed of recall of associated propositions. Second, it suggests a mechanism for the phenomenon of *interference.* The greater the number of different links with a concept are activated, the slower is the time taken to retrieve the proposition in which the concept occurs. The slowing of reaction time is taken as an indication of interference among the links of the concept within a network.

Propositional networks can also be used to account for many classes of things known to be present in long-term memory, though perhaps not all. Bower (1975) lists the following as LTM structures:

1. Spatial models of the world around us, including representations corresponding to images of objects and places.
2. Concepts of objects and their properties, and rules relating them.
3. Beliefs about people and about ourselves, and skills of social interaction.
4. Attitudes and values toward social events and goals.
5. Motor skills such as swimming, automobile driving, and others.
6. Skills for problem solving.
7. Skills (rules) for understanding language, painting, music.

Some Distinctions Among LTM Structures

It is apparent that elementary concepts and their associative links become organized into elaborate semantic networks in the long-term memory. These networks need to be further categorized into various *forms of knowledge,* if we are to deal with them in terms of the large questions of human learning and human performance. While the categories of Bower's list may serve a number of purposes of communication, there remain four kinds of conceptualization of LTM content that seem to require special mention. These are, first, the question of how images are represented; second, the distinction between "knowing that" and "knowing how"; third, the organized structures called *schemata;* and fourth, the idea that structures stored in memory constitute *human capabilities.*

Images.   Little doubt exists that an important variety of memorial content is the image. Almost everyone reports having internal images of perceived objects and events, although their types and intensities differ greatly among individuals, as Galton (1883) found. Although visual imagery is perhaps the most common variety, and usually prominent for most people, there are auditory images, tactile images, articulatory images, and other kinds as well. Research controversy has centered primarily on two questions: (1) whether storing material to be learned as images enhances the retention of material stored as verbal propositions (Kieras, 1978; Paivio, 1971); and (2) what is the nature of the representation of an image.

Current evidence indicates that adding images to the verbal propositions stored in LTM sometimes helps in recall of this material. Such enhancement of recall has been found, for example, in recall of stories by children (Lesgold et al., 1975) and in the recall of lists of words, such as foreign-word equivalents to English (Pressley, 1977). Other evidence suggests that images may be of particular help to retention in those individuals who score low in verbal ability (Cronbach & Snow, 1977; Salomon, 1979). However, it is not clear that adding images to material that is otherwise semantically well organized is always of benefit to retention; the results on this question are not yet all in (Allen, 1975).

Regarding the matter of how images are stored, it is clear that an image does not have to be a "mental picture." One might suppose, for example, that the geometrical plane figure, the square, would be represented by some spatially identifiable region containing points, lines, and right angles. However, Larkin et al. (1980) have shown that a square can be adequately represented by a *node-link structure* indicating relations among corners, edges, angles, and a surface, as shown in Fig. 3.3. Each link connecting parts of the square is a proposition, and the entire set of such propositions constitutes a representation of square. It is a representation no less real than the two-dimensional mental picture, since it omits no relevant property.

Declarative and procedural knowledge.   Distinguishing of declarative knowledge ("verbal knowledge," "knowing that") from procedural knowledge ("intellectual skill," "knowing how"), and the persistence of this distinction in modern cognitive theory, has led to significant advances in psychological research. While the origin of this distinction regarding what is learned extends back a substantial number of years, modern insistence on the differences in these two varieties of knowledge is to be found in the work of Newell and Simon (1972) and Anderson (1976). The former team of investigators of human problem solving posited a cognitive entity called a *production,* which entered into more complex *production systems,* assemblies of symbolic processing systems. Each production is described as being composed of a *condition* and an *action.* In other words, a production is a rule, an

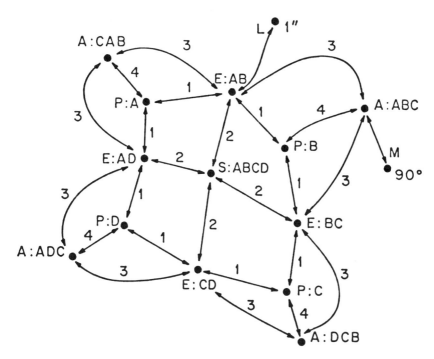

FIGURE 3.3. The representation of a square, described as follows: "Node-Link Representation of the Square, ABCD. Nodes represent corners (P), edges (E), angles (A), and the surfaces (S). Links connect corners with edges (1), edges with the surface (2), angles with edges (3), and angles with corners (4). Descriptors can be linked to nodes, as shown for the length (L) of Edge AB, and the magnitude (M) of Angle ABC." From Larkin et al., 1980. Copyright 1980 by American Association for the Advancement of Science, and reproduced by permission.

item of *procedural knowledge*. An example might be the rule for making plurals of certain words:

> IF the goal is to make a plural of a
>   word of Latin origin ending in *us*
> THEN replace the *us* with *i*

Of course, human beings learn a great many rules (Gagné, 1984, 1985). They are capabilities that make possible symbolic operations of many sorts: in using language, doing mathematics, composing and performing music, interacting with people. Knowing rules, in the sense of being able to apply rules to newly encountered instances, is not at all the same as *stating* a rule verbally. The latter performance falls in the class of *declarative knowledge*. Verbal knowledge in this category includes names and isolated facts as well as highly organized complexes of interrelated ideas.

While it is true that production-system and declarative-knowledge items can both be conceived as propositions (Anderson, 1980; Rumelhart & Norman, 1975), the difference between them is nevertheless one that deserves emphasis. Knowing rules implies human performance that is highly precise and predictable. Possessing declarative knowledge, in contrast, means being able to *state the gist* of some set of ideas, and to *construct* many of the details without great accuracy (Bartlett, 1932; Bransford & Franks, 1971). These differences have obvious implications for the question of how to assess the outcomes of learning. A rule is either successfully applied to a new instance or it is not. An idea of declarative knowledge may, however, represent the idea that was originally communicated very well, moderately well, or poorly, depending on the quality of the construction resulting from retrieval from LTM. Differences in the two varieties of knowledge also imply different requirements for instruction (Gagné, 1984). For instance, the prior knowledge relevant to the learning of a new rule is a specific set of prerequisite rules and concepts; the prior knowledge most useful in the learning of a new set of facts is a more abstract and comprehensive body of knowledge that cannot be considered specifically prerequisite. The two kinds of knowledge, however represented, possess different characteristics for learning, storage, recall, and transfer.

Schema organization.   Knowledge in LTM is often conceived of as forming itself into an organization called a *schema.* This is a set of knowledge organized so that the various concepts and propositions of which it is composed can be retrieved in terms of a more inclusive concept. A familiar schema is the *restaurant script,* a stereotyped description of going to a restaurant described by Schank and Abelson (1977). In an investigation by Bower, Black, and Turner (1979), considerable agreement was found among people who were asked to list events in going to a restaurant, with respect to such actions as sitting down, looking at the menu, ordering the meal, eating, paying the bill, and leaving. Schemata affect the encoding of newly acquired information, and also the nature of recalled events (memory *construction*).

The notion of a schema as a prototype organization for LTM storage has broad applicability. Rumelhart (1975) has suggested that people have a general kind of organization for simple stories, called a *story grammar.* The particular kind of storage and recall taken by the contents of a prose passage may be strongly determined by a *perspective* communicated prior to the reading of the passage (Anderson & Pichert, 1978; Sulin & Dooling, 1974). A picture may convey such a perspective (Bransford & Johnson, 1972), and thus activate a schema for recall. Other suggestions regarding schemata are as organizers of *patterns* (Posner & Keele, 1970) and of *scenes* conveyed by pictures (Mandler & Ritchey, 1977). When conceived as organized production systems incorporating intellectual skills, schemata play an important role in problem solving, about which more will be said later on.

Human capabilities. Modern conceptions of the information-processing route to learning and memory make reasonable the assumption that the answer to the question "What do humans learn?" is *capabilities.* That is to say, human beings do not learn responses, but the capabilities of making responses, and more particularly classes of responses. They do not acquire performances, but the capabilities of exhibiting certain classes of performance. Nor do human beings learn simply basic habits, or habit tendencies, because these provide too narrow a conception of the range and generalizability of human performances that we see about us. However they may be represented, it is *capabilities* that are stored in and retrieved from long-term memory.

A classification of human capabilities, the outcomes of learning, has been provided by Gagné (1984). Besides the declarative knowledge (verbal information) and procedural knowledge (intellectual skills) already mentioned, Gagné's taxonomy of capabilities includes cognitive strategies, attitudes, and motor skills. Of course there is no intention to innovate these categories; attitudes and motor skills have been recognized as different things to be learned for many years. As for cognitive strategies, these too are not novel, although their nomenclature has become broadly known only in recent times. They are capabilities that make possible the internal control of other processes involved in learning, remembering, and thinking, including the *control processes* suggested by Atkinson and Shiffrin (1968) in their original model of memory. Cognitive strategies also include the self-regulatory capabilities discussed later in this chapter.

Instructional Implications of Long-term Memory

Once a piece of information has entered LTM for storage, that information has been *learned.* For most varieties of things to be acquired by learning, this means that the processes of sensory registration, feature perception, short-term memory storage, and semantic encoding have operated upon the material entering LTM. Whether this last processing step means that every piece of stored information is in propositional form, or whether there may be a different form for images, is still a matter for further investigation. Whatever detailed form the learned material may take in LTM, the functional classes are five categories of capability: *declarative knowledge, procedural knowledge (intellectual skills), cognitive strategies, motor skills,* and *attitudes.*

While initial LTM storage is a defensible definition of learning, other changes may take place with further processing. These can be conceived of as advanced stages of learning. Neves and Anderson (1981) write of knowledge compilation beyond the stage at which a procedure is stored, as *composition,* meaning that productions initially learned in sequence are combined into single productions. Further practice of the productions (rules) may lead to *speedup* and ultimately to *automaticity.* These are stages of learning beyond the initial encoding of intellectual skills.

Other changes reflecting advanced stages of learning have been described for declarative knowledge. Presumably, following the encoding of items of declarative knowledge, added practice contributes added "strength," which results at least in part from the increasing size of the *fan* of associated propositions (Anderson, 1976; E. Gagné, 1978). Other kinds of advanced changes in material initially learned pertain to the organization of stored knowledge. Rumelhart and Norman (1978) distinguish three kinds of change brought about by learning. *Accretion* is simply the acquisition of a new set of facts; *tuning* occurs when the categories for interpreting new information (sche-

TABLE 3.1
Effective Learning Conditions
for Categories of Learned Capabilities

Type of Capability	Learning Conditions
Intellectual Skill	Retrieval of subordinate (component) skills Guidance by verbal or other means Demonstration of application by student; precise feedback Spaced reviews
Verbal Information	Retrieval of context of meaningful information Performance of reconstructing new knowledge; feedback
Cognitive Strategy (problem solving)	Retrieval of relevant rules and concepts Successive presentation (usually over an extended time) of novel problem situations Demonstration of solution by student
Attitude	Retrieval of information and intellectual skills relevant to targeted personal actions Establishment or recall of respect for human model Reinforcement for personal action either by successful direct experience or vicariously by observation of respected person
Motor Skill	Retrieval of component motor chains Establishment or recall of executive subroutines Practice of total skill; precise feedback

mata) are modified by learning; *restructuring* occurs when new cognitive structures are devised, allowing for new ways of learning, often after much time and effort.

These ideas about learning imply that instruction must be designed for initial encoding and LTM storage, as well as for other kinds of changes that extend beyond this initial stage. Conditions must often be provided for procedural knowledge to be practiced so that rules are combined, sped up, and automatized. When automaticity of productions is achieved, attention is freed for other activities that may be required for further learning and problem solving. Instruction must also provide for attainment of changes in organized knowledge, including the tuning of existing schemata and the formation of new and related ones.

The five different kinds of capability stored in LTM require different instructional treatments for most effective learning. After all, one does not expect the instructional arrangements designed for encoding of motor skills to resemble in detail the arrangements for encoding attitudes. Likewise, the design of instruction needs to support encoding differently for verbal information and for procedural knowledge (intellectual skills). Description of these differential requirements comprises the major content of *The Conditions of Learning* (Gagné, 1985). An abbreviated summary of some of the principal differential instructional requirements is given in Table 3.1. These conditions apply mainly to the stage of learning in which LTM encoding is initially accomplished. The attainment of automaticity of skills, or of restructuring of schemata, requires additional instructional arrangements.

LEARNING COMPLEX PERFORMANCES

Up to now, our account of learning and learning processes has been focused primarily on the learning of ordinary information that serves many of the purposes of life: the facts, the skills, the attitudes that provide people with the means of functioning in their everyday lives and occupations. But one can also view human learning as providing the way for unusual achievements—for solving unanticipated problems, inventing new devices and procedures, creating esthetically pleasing works of art or literature. What do we know about learning with such goals as these? Can a knowledge of learning processes be applied to the task of making people better able to solve problems, to think clearly and profoundly, to create novel original things and ideas?

In considering the learning that may underlie and facilitate various performances usually classified as complex behavior, it appears desirable to include descriptions of several phenomena that have been recently investigated under several labels. First, there is the concept of *control processes* proposed in the model of information processing by Shiffrin and Atkinson (1969). These processes, it may be supposed, operate through the media of *cognitive strategies,* that is, strategies of activation, use, and modification of the internal processes stored in LTM. Second, some account needs to be taken of the complexes of knowledge, including productions and strategies, that form the *mental models* that govern complex performances. Another source of significant ideas along these lines comprises studies of *problem solving,* including the contrasts in processing indicated by experts and novices. A fourth set of ideas, serving to integrate some of those previously mentioned, relates to the problem of improving intelligent behavior through learning. Presumably, this question pertains to the training of *self-regulation processes* that influence learning and thinking.

Cognitive Strategies

A prominent feature of modern thought and research on learning is the idea that among the processes available to the learner are processes of *control* that can manage other processes of attending, learning, remembering, and thinking. These control processes are engaged by acquired procedures called *cognitive strategies.*

The notion of cognitive strategy was given prominence by an investigation of concept formation (Bruner, Goodnow, & Austin, 1956). Over a period of some years, cognitive strategies have been found to affect a variety of information-processing activities. As processes of control, they can be seen to influence any or all of the processes of learning. When learners acquire new cognitive strategies of this sort, they can reasonably be said to be engaged in editing and regulating their performance and in *learning to learn.* To the extent that such strategies become and remain as capabilities in LTM, they may contribute substantially to the learner's intelligent performance (Detterman & Sternberg, 1982).

Strategies for learning. Cognitive strategies can be successfully employed by learners to control or modify incoming information. For example, strategies of *attending* to particular portions of material in printed text can be suggested to the learner by means of interspersed questions (Rothkopf, 1971) and also by including statements of objectives (Kaplan & Rothkopf, 1974). Readers can also be taught to summarize, question their understanding, and anticipate future events in order to guide their comprehension (Palincsar & Brown, 1984). When the features of material to be learned are emphasized or highlighted, as in using heavily outlined figures, these may suggest to the learner a strategy for *pattern recognition.*

Strategies for *encoding* information to be learned can be suggested to the learner either by verbal instruction ("make a diagram") or by some kind of organization that is actually imposed on the material to be learned. Variations in typography of a prose passage may be employed to organize learning material (Glynn & DiVesta, 1979), as may also semantically organized structures (Gardner & Schumacher, 1977; Glynn & DiVesta, 1977) or an author's use of text summaries to improve the reader's retention of a text (Reder, 1985). Another way that encoding can be influenced is by encouraging learners to use strategies of *elaboration*. Examples are suggesting to learners of paired associates that they connect the paired words by means of a sentence (as in "the BOY rides the COW"; Rohwer, 1975) or use mnemonic aids to learn a foreign language vocabulary (Raugh & Atkinson, 1975). Anderson (1980) interprets the idea of *depth of processing* (Craik & Lockhart, 1972) to mean that additional depth in the encoding of a fact to be learned is provided by linking with additional related propositions. Thus, a fact such as "the doctor hated the lawyer" may be encoded along with other propositions such as "the lawyer sued the doctor for malpractice," and "I (the learner) first heard this sentence on this morning's radio program." This kind of *redundant elaboration* is considered to provide more paths for retrieving and more opportunities for reconstructing the information when remembering is called for.

Strategies for remembering. It is difficult to separate clearly the cognitive strategies that may be employed for encoding of materials to be learned from strategies designed for retrieval via constructive memory. One prominent reason is the existence of the phenomenon called *encoding specificity.* The experimental finding is that recall of words is strongly influenced by the context in which they have been learned (Tulving & Thomson, 1973; Watkins & Tulving, 1975). Thus, when a word such as *black* is one of the words to be recalled, and it has been originally learned when presented together with another word (*train*), the probability of its recall is increased when the latter word is presented as a cue. Strategies for remembering overlap with strategies for encoding, particularly when the latter are conceived as providing specific cues for retrieval. A review of evidence regarding the use of cues in instruction has been provided by Wright (1977). A variety of cognitive strategies can be brought to bear by the learner on the task of remembering declarative knowledge (Brown, 1978), and still other varieties affect the recall of procedural knowledge (Rigney, 1978; Tennyson, Tennyson, & Rothen, 1980).

Strategies in problem solving. Problem-solving activities of human beings can be analyzed to reveal the presence and the use of cognitive strategies. In science problems, mathematics problems, or problems of a social nature, people use cognitive strategies, in which the content is more or less specific to the problem at hand (Gagné, 1985). Useful strategies can be learned and used by children in performing arithmetic operations, such as mapping written subtraction moves onto blocks (Resnick, 1981). Strategies employed by students in constructing geometrical proofs have also been identified and described (Greeno, 1978). Children solving arithmetic problems acquire strategies that aid them in transforming word problems into mathematical form. Specific *task strategies* are applicable to many different kinds of problems. Are there more general strategies that are broadly applicable to any and all problems that human beings try to solve? This question is discussed in a following section.

KNOWLEDGE ORGANIZATION FOR PROBLEM SOLVING

Information-processing studies of problem solving in the 1960s and 1970s accepted the tradition of early experimental psychology in concentrating primarily on the study of "knowledge-lean" tasks in which competence can usually be acquired over short periods of learning and experience. Studies of these tasks illuminated the basic information-processing capabilities people employ when they behave more and less intelligently in situations where they lack any specialized knowledge and skill. The pioneering work of Newell and Simon (1972) and others described general heuristic processes (such as *means–end analysis, generate and test,* and *subgoal decomposition*), but provided limited insight about the learning and thinking that require a rich structure of domain-specific knowledge.

In more recent years, investigators have examined knowledge-rich tasks that require hundreds and thousands of hours of learning and experience in an area of study. Studies of expertise have attempted to sharpen this focus by describing contrasts between the performance of novices and experts. The results force us to think about high levels of competence in terms of the interplay between *knowledge structure* and *processing abilities.* The data illuminate a critical difference between individuals who display more and less ability in particular domains of knowledge and skill, namely, skilled individual's possession of rapid access to and efficient utilization of an organized body of conceptual and procedural knowledge. The work on problem solving in adult experts and novices has shown fairly consistent findings in quite a variety of domains—chess play, physics problem solving, the performance of architects and electronic technicians, and skilled radiologists interpreting X-rays. This work has shown that relations between the structure of a knowledge base and problem-solving processes are mediated through the quality of representation of the problem. This *problem representation* is constructed by the solver on the basis of domain-related knowledge and the organization of this knowledge. The nature of this organization determines the quality, completeness, and coherence of the internal representation, which in turn determines the efficiency of further thinking. The representation of a problem consists essentially of the solver's interpretation or understanding of it, and greatly determines how easy it is to solve.

Knowledge and the Perceptions of Experts

Demonstrations of the influence of knowledge on problem-solving processes were provided by de Groot (1966) and by Chase and Simon (1973a, 1973b) when these researchers explored what makes master chess players different from less expert ones. de Groot obtained protocols from former world champions and from some fairly skillful club players as they tried to find the best move in a given situation. Surprisingly, he found no strategy differences. All looked ahead about the same number of moves as they tried to evaluate each move, and used the same strategy to guide this search. However, experts simply recognized the best move and gave it first consideration, evaluating the other moves only as a way of double-checking themselves.

The implication of this research is that when experts look at an apparently complicated situation, they are able to represent it in terms of a small number of patterns or chunks. This ability to perceive the problem in a way that restricts the problem space has since been shown to occur in other areas as well. For instance, in medical-diagnosis research, both experts and novices are found to use the same kind of generate-and-test heuristic. The experts, however, start with a more accurate hypothesis (Elstein, Shulman, & Sprafka, 1978). In electronics, Egan and Schwartz (1979) found that skilled technicians reconstructing symbolic drawings of circuit diagrams did so according to the functional nature of the such elements in the circuit as amplifiers, rectifiers, and filters. Novice technicians, however, produced chunks based more upon the spatial proximity of the elements. When Akin (1980) asked architects to reconstruct building plans from memory, several levels of patterns were produced. First, local patterns consisting of wall segments and doors were recalled, then rooms and other areas, then clusters of rooms or areas. In other words, they exhibited a hierarchical pattern of chunks within chunks.

How Structured Knowledge Facilitates Problem Solving

How does this structured knowledge facilitate problem solving? Remember that the initial representation of a problem is very important in determining how easy the problem is to solve. Just as a chess player's knowledge allows a representation of a given situation to be formed, a problem solver's knowledge determines the problem representation. Then the proper problem-solving procedures, if they are known, must be retrieved from memory and applied. It is the problem solver's representation that guides retrieval of appropriate solution procedures.

In order to consider this point in more detail, it is helpful to use the concept of a *schema*. As previously noted, a schema is a modifiable information structure that represents generic concepts stored in memory. Schemata represent knowledge that we experience—interrelationships between objects, situations, events, and sequences of events that normally occur. In this sense, schemata contain prototypical information about frequently experienced situations, and they are used to interpret new situations and observations (Rumelhart, 1981). In many situations, information that is essential to an interpretation is absent; understanding the situation requires filling it in by means of prior knowledge. Estes (National Academy of Sciences, 1981) explains this point by describing the following vignette: "At the security gate, the airline passenger presented his briefcase. It contained metallic objects. His departure was delayed." In order to understand this common-place incident, an individual must have a good deal of prior knowledge of air terminals, which is represented in memory by a schema that specifies the relationship between the roles played by various people in the terminal, the objects typically encountered, and the actions that typically ensue. Schema theory assumes that the memory structures for recurrent situations have a major function in the construction of an interpretation of a new situation.

The objects of a schema may be thought of as variables or *slots* into which incoming information can fit. If enough slots of a particular schema are filled, it becomes active. An active schema can then guide the search for information to fill remaining slots. If additional information is not available in the environment, then the schema will fill its slots with information typical of a similiar situation. It may now be easier to think about how problem representations are formed: Essentially, they are determined by the existing schemata and the slots they contain. If a problem is of a very familiar type, it can trigger an appropriate problem schema; if not, some more general schema will be triggered. In any event, the slots in the schema control which features of the problem are incorporated into the representation; features that do not fit into a slot will be ignored.

Once a schema is triggered, if it contains precisely the right procedures it can control the solution. In this case, the solver can proceed easily and rapidly. If it is a general schema, it might only contain a general prescription for how to proceed. In this case, the solver will have to search for procedures that fit the given situation and the general prescription. The solution will then be much more difficult, and may be impossible to reach, if the proper procedures cannot be found. If an inappropriate schema is somehow triggered, the solver will make little progress. Thus, the importance of the knowledge structure, how it is organized into schemata, becomes clear. It is the organization and structure provided by schemata which allow relevant knowledge to be found in memory. Although lack of knowledge may sometimes result in failure to solve a problem, lack of access to that knowledge because of inadequate organization of knowledge may also be the cause.

The problem-solving difficulties of novices can be attributed largely to the nature of their knowledge bases, and much less to the limitations of their processing capabilities, such as their inability to use general problem-solving heuristics or strategies. Novices do show effective use of heuristics; the limitations of their thinking derive from their inability to infer further knowledge from the information in a problem situation. These inferences are necessarily generated in the context of a knowledge structure that experts have acquired. In sum, studies on the solution of problems where a great deal of domain knowledge is involved indicate clearly that a very relevant part of success in problem solving is the access of a large body of well-structured domain knowledge. Hence, one important direction of current research in instruction is to explore how a large body of knowledge is organized and represented, so that it can be easily accessed for successful solving of problems.

MENTAL MODELS

In the course of learning and performing their tasks, individuals develop representations that can be referred to as *mental models,* which drive their performance. These models are not necessarily completely accurate understandings; rather they are useful representations of how a task's component parts or concepts interact. For example people's understanding of devices such as calculators, computers, computer text editors, digital watches, and equipment that they must pilot or maintain varies with their level of skill and the demands of their jobs (Johnson-Laird, 1983). As they learn, and continue to perform a task, individuals develop efficient and flexible models that are determined by their experience and what they need to do. Johnson-Laird (1983) describes this as follows:

> Your model of a television set may contain only the idea of a box that displays moving pictures with accompanying sound. Alternatively, it may embody the notion of a cathode-ray tube firing electrons at a screen, with the beam scanning across the screen in a raster controlled by a varying electro-magnetic field, and so on. You may conceive of an electron as nothing more than a negatively charged particle whose trajectory is influenced by a magnetic field. There may be no need for you to have any deeper understanding, because you can grasp the way the set works without having to reduce everything to its fundamental principles. A person who repairs television sets is likely to have a more comprehensive model of them than someone who can only operate one. A circuit designer is likely to have a still richer model. Yet even the designer may not need to understand the full ramifications of quantum electrodynamics— which is just as well, because nobody completely understands them. (p. 4)

No one of the above models is necessarily increased in usefulness by adding information to it beyond a certain level, but each can be very useful for the particular tasks and functions it serves.

Mental models can be thought of as knowledge structures that are schema-based, but also include perceptions of task demands and task performances. Multiple schemata can be accessed in building a model of a particular problem. A model implies a structure which is constructable and modifiable by the student and instructor. Models can be built, used and altered in the course of learning, and as proficiency is acquired.

The use of models is an important aspect of *inferencing,* which can result in significant learning. There are numerous examples of inference tasks that demonstrate the role of mental models in problem solving and comprehension. Children, or adults who presumably lack proficiency in abstract reasoning abilities, can be made to exhibit more proficient performance by fostering the use of mental models. It also is possible to disrupt inferencing in normally proficient performers by creating situations that make it difficult to construct a mental model. For example, Falmagne (1980) studied children on *modus tollendo tollens* problems (if *p* then *q;* not *q,* therefore, not *p*); problems in which the premises are often misinterpreted (Wason & Johnson-Laird, 1972). Falmagne trained second through fifth graders using relatively concrete premises with which children would be familiar (e.g., If it is Tuesday, Mary has gym; Mary does not have gym, therefore it is not Tuesday). Children were able to answer these more concrete problems accurately. They were able to construct models, because of their familiarity with the information, and to solve the problems. They also eventually gained an understanding of the abstract logical arguments, which enabled them to solve more abstractly presented problems. Similarly, adults, if unable to construct a model of the problem, may not demonstrate what has been called logical competence.

The knowledge one has about a particular domain affects the types of models constructed during comprehension. Voss and his colleagues have examined how people with high and low knowledge of baseball can process and recall text about a baseball game. Information pertinent to the game itself was recalled more often by the high-knowledge people, whereas incidental information was not recalled any better by the high-knowledge individuals. High-knowledge people integrate new information into their existing understanding of a domain. For baseball, this might include the score, teams, number of outs, and so on. Information that is not important in the model of baseball information, such as uniform color, is not processed as well. In addition, high-knowledge individuals' recall is more detailed, well integrated, and more sequentially correct than the recall of low-knowledge individuals. Low-knowledge recall consists of more isolated propositions, which are not recalled in an order typically associated with a baseball game (Voss, Vesonder, & Spilich, 1980).

Problem solving is also affected by the model one constructs in a specific domain. For example, Gentner and Gentner (1983) observed that those individuals who conceived of electricity flow as an analogy to flowing water were apt to solve certain problems more accurately than those who used an analogy of a moving crowd of objects. Conversely, the latter group's model allowed for more efficient solution of other types of problems.

Instruction and Mental Models

In encouraging the exercise of mental models in learning and performance, we can think of a number of tactics useful for instruction. First, there is a need to identify the type of model that an individual brings to an instructional situation. There have been different illustrations of this endeavor. For example, in physics, McCloskey (1983; McCloskey, Caramazza, & Green, 1980) has demonstrated that many individuals, even without training, possess naive theories of physical phenomena. These naive theories lead to incorrect or inefficient problem solving and learning. Discovering the models that people use to understand a situation can assist in effecting a change to conceptual models appropriate for proficient performance.

A second tactic is to track the development of models during the transition from novice to expert performance. In the acquisition of proficiency in solving arithmetic word problems, Riley, Greeno, and Heller (1983) studied the development of subjects' understanding of the semantic structure of different classes of word problems. Improvement in performance occurs when these structures of understanding are elaborated so that mental models are available that can represent distinctions between different problem types. Siegler, in his work, has mapped the development of certain abilities over age. In solving a balance-scale problem, young children's models do not include the same number of features as those of the more proficient performers. Hence, only a subset of the features that need to be processed are attended to, and errors are often made on certain problems. The elaboration of models over development and learning may follow a fixed pattern, so that by understanding the sequence of functional models, an appropriate "next step" for instruction can be devised (Siegler & Klahr, 1982). Longitudinal investigations would obviously facilitate descriptions of and prescriptions for the development of these cognitive models.

A third tactic is to take advantage of the models individuals are currently using to guide their performance, and to build on them. By understanding a student's current state of knowledge, teachers can specify what can be called *pedagogical theories* (Glaser, 1984). These are models that differ from, but are still relatively consistent with, the learner's current model of understanding. They serve to guide interrogation, instantiation, or falsification of the learner's model, helping to organize new knowledge into more proficient models of understanding. An example of this approach has been described by Collins and Stevens (1982). They give a detailed account of recurring strategies that effective teachers used in asking questions that provide the student with counterexamples, possibilities for correct and incorrect generalization, and other ways of applying and testing their models of understanding.

A fourth tactic is to teach explicitly mental models that facilitate performance. An example of this approach was recently reported in two studies by Kieras and Bovair (1983). In Study 1, students were taught how to operate an electrical control device. In one group, the purpose of the device was explained in terms of the system that underlay its operation. This explanation served as a model of the device, and operating procedures were taught in terms of the model. A second group was presented with the device's operating procedures only. The group given the model learned the procedures faster and exhibited better retention. In the second study, one group was given the model and the device, and a second group, only the device. Both groups were asked to infer the operations of the device by testing its performance under certain conditions. The model group was able to make faster and more direct inferences of the system's operating procedures by using the model to guide performance.

In sum, the studies on mental models support current theory that attributes much of the learning process in the acquisition of knowledge and skill to the presence and development of organized knowledge. The more knowledge one has about a certain domain, the more inferences can be drawn and used to construct models, elaborate new information, enhance retrieval, and foster learning. Hence, the acquisition and exercise of well-developed knowledge structures, containing easily accessible knowledge, is a critical goal for instruction. The instructional problem that is raised for investigation is whether to teach general, model-building strategies independent of specific domain knowledge, so that this capability is developed for use generally in learning situations, or whether to concentrate on building up specific knowledge structures which should aid in the construction of domain-specific models, and which may eventually result in a more generalized ability to construct and use mental models.

SELF-REGULATION

A further characteristic of the proficient individual is well-developed self-regulation or *metacognitive awareness*. Proficient people exhibit a greater attentiveness to the demands of the task, the nature of the materials, their own capabilities, and the activities which can be performed to accomplish the task. The good performer is also aware of the interaction of these factors, and controls behavior in a flexible, purposive manner, in accordance with these perceptions. In contrast, the novice demonstrates much less awareness or purposefulness of behavior (Brown et al., 1983).

Self-regulatory skills refer to generalized skills for approaching problems and for monitoring one's performance. These skills are called metacognitive because they are not specific performances or strategies involved in solving a particular problem or carrying out a particular procedure; rather, they refer to the kind of knowledge that enables one to reflect upon and observe one's own performance usefully. As Flavell (1976) has written:

> "Metacognition" refers to one's knowledge concerning one's own cognitive processes and products. . . . For example, I am engaging in metacognition . . . if I notice that I am having more trouble learning A than B; if it strikes me that I should double-check C before accepting it as a fact; if it occurs to me that I had better scrutinize each and every alternative in any multiple-choice type task situation before deciding which is the best one; . . . if I sense that I had better make a note of D because I may forget it . . . Metacognition refers, among other things, to the active monitoring and consequent regulation and orchestration of these processes in . . . the service of some concrete goal or objective. (p. 232)

These metacognitive abilities are present in mature learners and take on the characteristics of an executive control processor—introduced as an overseer in many current models of memory. In the course of learning and problem solving, representative kinds of regulatory performance include: knowing when or what one knows or does not know; predicting the correctness or outcome of one's performance; planning ahead and efficiently apportioning one's cognitive resources and one's time; and checking and monitoring the outcomes of one's solution or attempt to learn. As Brown (1978) writes: "These forms of executive decision making are perhaps the crux of efficient problem solving because the use of an appropriate piece of knowledge or routine to obtain that knowledge at the right time and in the right place is the essence of intelligence." (p. 82)

In studies of intellectual development, there have been numerous demonstrations of the lack of efficient self-regulatory behaviors. Such deficiencies might be attributable, in part, to the immature performer's lack of understanding of those factors that affect cognitive processing. For example, Kreutzer, Leonard, and Flavell (1975) found that young children displayed a failure to distinguish between situations which would detract from or improve their memory performance. Among the many metacognitive differences that have been cited are knowledge of test readiness (Brown & Barclay, 1976), sensitivity to text organization (Danner, 1976), apportionment of study time (Brown & Smiley, 1978), and the ability to detect inconsistencies or inadequacies of oral and written presentations (Flavell et al., 1981; Markman, 1979).

In general, unsuccessful learners are often deficient in the knowledge needed to solve problems, and along with this deficit are apparent regulatory differences which manifest themselves on more difficult problems. These individuals do not adjust to problem difficulty as flexibly as better learners, and do not maintain their processing until the task demands are satisfied. Examining the extent to which these self-regulatory deficits may be amenable to remediation with training is an important issue for research.

Self-Regulatory Skills and Instruction

In fostering self-regulatory, purposive skills, good instruction must inculcate sensitivity and adaptability to task characteristics, such as problem difficulty, the details of one's performance, and progress made toward solution. Sensitivity to task characteristics has been studied and trained by Bransford and colleagues (Franks et al., 1982). Poorly performing fifth graders were initially unable to discriminate the relative ease of learning two passages. The passages differed in that one contained propositions that were elaborated in a way that could facilitate recall. With training, these students were able to distinguish between the two types of presentations, elaborate the information themselves, and increase recall of the input. An effort to train sensitivity to the details of performance was undertaken by Brown, Campione, and Barclay (1979), who trained retarded children to assess their readiness to recall a series of pictures. The training was successful, and generalized to situations in which the materials were simple prose passages.

The teaching of explicit, self-regulatory skills has been a recent, growing endeavor. In addition to the work reported in the theoretical and experimental literature on various metacognitive processes, a number of training programs have been developed. These include such programs and texts as those by Whimbey and Lochhead (1980), Feuerstein et al. (1980), De Bono (1985), Rubinstein (1975), Wickelgren (1974), and Hayes (1981). Although these programs target different skills and different populations, they all emphasize self-regulatory aspects of behavior, and active involvement of the learner in monitoring problem-solving and learning activity.

These programs primarily emphasize the teaching of heuristics and general cognitive strategies and of rules for reasoning, problem solving, and memory elaboration which can facilitate learning. In large part, abstract tasks, puzzle-like problems, and informal life situations are used as content, and avoidance of the complexity of subject matter is typical. It is of interest to note that these programs often focus on process instruction that is, to a large extent, divorced from the development of proficiency in complex knowledge and skill domains. The apparent attractions of these approaches are that they attempt to train general strategies that are intuitively alluring, and that they explicate individual differences in terms of a few general processes. In poor learners, self-regulatory behaviors are obviously deficient, and this leads to the conclusion that their explicit absence is responsible for poor performance. It is also notable that such programs have had some success, although for the most part they need further evaluation.

One exemplary program which includes systematic evaluation was conducted by Brown and Palincsar (1982) to improve reading comprehension and monitoring skills. They encouraged control and activity of the learner by employing what they called a "reciprocal" teaching method, in which the student and teacher would switch roles, so that the student learned to function as the regulator of the interaction. Students were taught to summarize, question their understanding, clarify any misunderstandings, and predict future events, along with other skills involved in self-regulation. The results were successful. The skills taught were maintained over a period of time and carried over into other classrooms. Interestingly, with a brief training procedure, regular classroom teachers were able to use the reciprocal teaching method with the same level of success. Thus, another apparent advantage of teaching general self-regulatory methods is that they can be trained in a relatively short period of time.

Overall, it seems best to emphasize the interaction between structures of knowledge, mental models, and regulatory processes. This forces us to consider instructional theory in terms of *knowledge structure-regulatory process interactions,* rather than in terms of a separation between acquiring specific knowledge, on the one hand, and the acquisition of regulatory processes on this base, on the other. In all probability, however, some combination of specific and general methods needs to be considered. Perhaps a general strategy approach is recommended when there is little evidence of regulation of cognitive activity by an individual across a number of knowledge domains. However, training only general methods will not make the novice an expert. Even when poor performers do learn to regulate their behaviors, although performance improves it seldom reaches the levels of the initially proficient performer (e.g., Stein et al., 1982). We can interpret this as a function of an elaborated knowledge structure and associated well-practiced specific regulatory routines that are more available to the proficient individual.

To become an expert requires a great deal of knowledge and practice in a domain. As we have indicated, this implies facilitating the development of knowledge so that helpful schemata and mental models can be created, which can be efficiently accessed to guide performance. The acquisition of self-regulatory skills may, in fact, occur along with the learning of domain-specific knowledge. With experience in a variety of domains, it is possible that an individual generalizes specific regulatory practices, so that they become general principles of regulation with wider applicability. In actual application, instructional decisions will have to be considered on the basis of knowledge of individual capabilities and the characteristics of the task to be learned. Individuals who display poor self-regulation across domains might benefit from general instruction in self-regulatory skills. Those who fail to regulate their behaviors only in certain domains, might best be taught to acquire specific regulatory skills through practice in manipulating their existing knowledge structures. The relative emphasis of each has to be worked out in the course of analyzing both individual capabilities and the task demands of proficient performance.

REFERENCES

Akin, O. (1980). *Models of architectural knowledge.* London: Pion.

Allen, W. H. (1975). Intellectual abilities and instructional media design. *AV Communication Review, 23,* 139–168.

Anderson, J. R. (1976). *Language, memory, and thought.* Hillsdale, NJ: Lawrence Erlbaum Associates.

Anderson, J. R. (1980). *Cognitive psychology and its implications.* San Francisco: Freeman.

Anderson, J. R., & Bower, G. H. (1973). *Human associative memory.* Washington, DC: Winston.

Anderson, R. C., & Pichert, J. W. (1978). Recall of previously unrecallable information following a shift in perspective. *Journal of Verbal Learning and Verbal Behavior, 17,* 1–12.

Atkinson, R. C., & Shiffrin, R. M. (1968). Human memory: A proposed system and its control processes. In K. W. Spence & J. T. Spence (Eds.), *The psychology of learning and motivation* (Vol. 2). New York: Academic Press.

Attneave, F. (1959). *Applications of information theory to psychology.* New York: Holt, Rinehart and Winston.

Bartlett, F. C. (1932). *Remembering: An experimental and social study.* Cambridge: Cambridge University Press.

Binet, A., & Simon, T. (1916). *The development of intelligence in children.* Baltimore: Williams & Wilkins.

Bower, G. H. (1975). Cognitive psychology: An introduction. In W. K. Estes (Ed.), *Handbook of learning and cognitive processes* (Vol. 1). Hillsdale, NJ: Lawrence Erlbaum Associates.

Bower, G. H., & Hilgard, E. R. (1981). *Theories of learning.* (5th ed.). Englewood Cliffs, NJ: Prentice-Hall.

Bower, G. H., Black, J. B., & Turner, T. J. (1979). Scripts in memory for text. *Cognitive Psychology, 11,* 177–220.

Bransford, J. D., & Franks, J. J. (1971). The abstraction of linguistic ideas. *Cognitive Psychology, 2,* 331–350.

Bransford, J. D., & Johnson, M. K. (1972). Contextual prerequisites for understanding: Some investigations of comprehension and recall. *Journal of Verbal Learning and Verbal Behavior, 11,* 717–726.

Brooks, L. R. (1968). Spatial and verbal components of the act of recall. *Canadian Journal of Psychology, 22,* 349–368.

Brown, A. L. (1978). Knowing when, where, and how to remember: A problem of metacognition. In R. Glaser (Ed.), *Advances in instructional psychology* (Vol. 1). Hillsdale, NJ: Lawrence Erlbaum Associates.

Brown, A. L., & Barclay, C. R. (1976). The effects of training specific mnemonics on the metamnemonic efficiency of retarded children. *Child Development, 47,* 71–80.

Brown, A. L., Bransford, J. D., Ferrara, R. A., & Campione, J. C. (1983). Learning, remembering, and understanding. In J. H. Flavell & E. M. Markman (Eds.), *Carmichael's manual of child psychology* (Vol. 1). New York: Wiley.

Brown, A. L., Campione, J. C., & Barclay, C. R. (1979). Training self-checking routines for estimating test readiness: Generalization from list learning to prose recall. *Child Development, 50,* 501–512.

Brown, A. L., & Palincsar, A. S. (1982). Inducing strategic learning from texts by means of informal, self-control training. *Topics in Learning and Learning Disabilities, 2,* 1–17.

Brown, A. L., & Smiley, S. S. (1978). The development of strategies for studying. *Child Development, 49,* 1076–1088.

Bruner, J. S., Goodnow, J. J., & Austin, G. A. (1956). *A study of thinking.* New York: Wiley.

Chase, W. G., & Simon, H. A. (1973a). Perception in chess. *Cognitive Psychology, 4,* 55–81.

Chase, W. G., & Simon, H. A. (1973b). The mind's eye in chess. In W. G. Chase (Ed.), *Visual information processing.* New York: Academic Press.

Collins, A., & Quillian, M. R. (1969). Retrieval time from semantic memory. *Journal of Verbal Learning and Verbal Behavior, 12,* 1–20.

Collins, A., & Stevens. A. L. (1982). Goals and strategies of inquiry teachers. In R. Glaser (Ed.), *Advances in instructional psychology* (Vol. 2). Hillsdale, NJ: Lawrence Erlbaum Associates.

Conrad, R. (1964). Acoustic confusion in immediate memory. *British Journal of Psychology, 55,* 75–84.

Craik, F. I. M., & Lockhart, R. S. (1972). Levels of processing: A framework for memory research. *Journal of Verbal Learning and Verbal Behavior, 11,* 671–684.

Cronbach, L. J., & Snow R. E. (1977). *Aptitudes and instructional methods: A handbook for research on interactions.* New York: Irvington.

Danner, F. W. (1976). Children's understanding of intersentence organization in the recall of short descriptive passages. *Journal of Educational Psychology, 68,* 174–183.

De Bono, E. (1985). The CORT thinking program. In J. W. Segal, S. F. Chipman, & R. Glaser (Eds.), *Thinking and learning skills: Relating instruction to basic research* (Vol. 1). Hillsdale, NJ: Lawrence Erlbaum Associates.

de Groot, A. (1966). Perception and memory versus thought: Some old ideas and recent findings. In B. Kleinmuntz (Ed.), *Problem solving.* New York: Wiley.

Detterman, D. K., & Sternberg, R. J. (1982). *How and how much can intelligence be increased.* Norwood, NJ: Ablex.

Ebbinghaus, H. (1913). *Memory.* (H. A. Ruger & C. E. Bussenius, Trans.). New York: Teachers College, Columbia University.

Egan, D. E., & Schwartz, B. J. (1979). Chunking in recall of symbolic drawings. *Memory and Cognition, 7,* 149–158.

Elstein, A. S., Shulman, L. S., & Sprafka, S. A. (1978). *Medical problem solving.* Cambridge, MA: Harvard University Press.

Ericsson, K. A., & Chase, W. G. (1982). Exceptional memory. *American Scientist, 70,* 607–615.

Falmagne, R. J. (1980). The development of logical competence: A psycholinguistic perspective. In R. H. Kluwe & H. Spada (Eds.), *Developmental models of thinking.* New York: Academic Press.

Feuerstein, R., Rand, Y., Hoffman, M. B., & Miller, R. (1980). *Instrumental enrichment: An intervention program for cognitive modifiability.* Baltimore: University Park Press.

Fitts, P. M., & Posner, M. I., (1967). *Human performance.* Monterey, CA: Brooks/Cole.

Flavell, J. H. (1976). Metacognitive aspects of problem solving. In L. B. Resnick (Ed.), *The nature of intelligence.* Hillsdale, NJ: Lawrence Erlbaum Associates.

Flavell, J. H., Speer, J. R., Green, F. L., & August, D. L. (1981). The development of comprehension monitoring and knowledge about communication. *Monographs of the Society for Research in Child Development, 46* (5, Serial No. 192).

Franks, J. J., Vye, N. J., Auble, P. M., Mezynski, K. J., Perfetto, G. A., Bransford, J. D., Stein, B. S., & Littlefield, J. (1982). Learning from explicit versus implicit texts. *Journal of Experimental Psychology: General, 111,* 414–422.

Gagné, E. D. (1978). Long-term retention of information following learning from prose. *Review of Educational Research, 48,* 629–665.

Gagné, R. M. (1984). Learning outcomes and their effects. *American Psychologist, 39,* 377–385.

Gagné, R. M. (1985). *The conditions of learning* (4th ed.). New York: Holt, Rinehart and Winston.

Galton, F. (1883). *Inquiries into human faculty and its development.* London: Macmillan.

Gardner, E. T., & Schumacher, G. M. (1977). Effects of contextual organization on prose retention. *Journal of Educational Psychology, 69,* 146–151.

Garner, W. R. (1962). *Uncertainty and structure as psychological concepts.* New York: Wiley.

Gentner, D., & Gentner, D. R. (1983). Flowing waters or teeming crowds: Mental models of electricity. In D. Gentner & A. L. Stevens (Eds.) *Mental models.* Hillsdale, NJ: Lawrence Erlbaum Associates.

Glaser, R. (1984). Education and thinking: The role of knowledge. *American Psychologist, 39,* 93–104.

Glynn, S. M., & DiVesta, F. J. (1977). Outline and hierarchical organization as aids for study and retrieval. *Journal of Educational Psychology, 69,* 89–95.

Glynn, S. M., & DiVesta, F. J. (1979). Control of prose processing via instructional and typographical cues. *Journal of Educational Psychology, 71,* 595–603.

Greeno, J. G. (1978). A study of problem solving. In R. Glaser (Ed.), *Advances in instructional psychology* (Vol. 1). Hillsdale, NJ: Lawrence Erlbaum Associates.

Hayes, J. R. (1981). *The complete problem solver.* Philadelphia: Franklin Institute Press.

James, W. (1890). *Principles of psychology.* New York: Holt, Rinehart and Winston.

Johnson-Laird, P.N. (1983). *Mental models: Towards a cognitive science of language, inference, and consciousness.* Cambridge, MA: Harvard University Press.

Kaplan, R., & Rothkopf, E. Z. (1974). Instructional objectives as directions to learners: Effect of passage length and amount of objective-relevant content. *Journal of Educational Psychology, 66,* 448–456.

Kieras, D. E. (1978). Beyond pictures and words: Alternative information-processing models for imagery effects in verbal memory. *Psychological Bulletin, 85,* 532–554.

Kieras, D. E., & Bovair, S. (1983). *The role of a mental model in learning to operate a device.* (Tech. Rep. No. 13). University of Arizona.

Klatzky, R. L. (1980). *Human memory: Structures and processes* (2nd ed.). San Francisco: Freeman.

Kreutzer, M. A., Leonard, C., & Flavell, J. H. (1975). An interview study of children's knowledge about memory. *Monographs of the Society for Research in Child Development, 40* (1, Serial No. 159).

Lachman, R., Lachman, J. L., & Butterfield, E. C. (1979). *Cognitive psychology and information processing: An introduction.* Hillsdale, NJ: Lawrence Erlbaum Associates.

Larkin, J., McDermott, J., Simon, D. P., & Simon, H. A. (1980). Expert and novice performance in solving physics problems. *Science, 208,* 1335–1342.

Lesgold, A. M., Shimron, J., Levin, J. R., & Guttman, J. (1975). Pictures and young children's learning from oral prose. *Journal of Educational Psychology, 67,* 636–642.

Mandler, J. M., & Ritchey, G. H. (1977). Long-term memory for pictures. *Journal of Experimental Psychology: Human Learning and Memory, 3,* 386–396.

Markman, E. M. (1979). Realizing that you don't understand: Elementary school children's awareness of inconsistencies. Child Development 50, 643–655.

McCloskey, M. (1983). Naive theories of motion. In D. Gentner & A. L. Stevens (Eds.), *Mental models*. Hillsdale, NJ: Lawrence Erlbaum Associates.

McCloskey, M. Caramazza, A., & Green, B. (1980). Curvilinear motion in the absence of external forces: Naive beliefs about the motion of objects. *Science, 210,* 1139–1141.

Miller, G. A. (1956). The magical number seven plus or minus two: Some limits on our capacity for processing information. *Psychological Review, 63,* 81–97.

National Academy of Sciences. (1981). *Outlook for science and technology: The next five years.* Washington, DC: National Academy of Sciences.

Neves, D. M., & Anderson, J. R. (1981). Knowledge compilation: Mechanisms for the automatization of cognitive skills. In J. R. Anderson (Ed.), *Cognitive skills and their acquisition.* Hillsdale, NJ: Lawrence Erlbaum Associates.

Newell, A. (1980). One final word. In D. T. Tuma & F. Reif (Eds.), *Problem solving and education.* Hillsdale, NJ: Lawrence Erlbaum Associates.

Newell, A., & Simon, H. A. (1972). *Human problem solving.* Englewood Cliffs, NJ: Prentice-Hall.

Norman, D. A., & Rumelhart, D. E. (Eds.). (1975). *Explorations in cognition.* San Francisco: Freeman.

Paivio, A. (1971). *Imagery and verbal processes.* New York: Holt, Rinehart and Winston.

Palincsar, A. S., & Brown, A. L. (1984). Reciprocal teaching of comprehension-fostering and comprehension-monitoring activities. *Cognition and Instruction, 1*(2), 117–175.

Pavlov, I. P. (1927). *Conditioned reflexes.* (G. V. Anrep, Trans.). New York: Oxford.

Peterson, L. R., & Peterson, M. J. (1959). Short-term retention of individual verbal items. *Journal of Experimental Psychology, 58,* 193–198.

Posner, M. I., & Keele, S. W. (1970). Retention of abstract ideas. *Journal of Experimental Psychology, 83,* 304–308.

Postman, L. (1961). The present status of interference theory. In C. N. Cofer (Ed.), *Verbal learning and verbal behavior.* New York: McGraw-Hill.

Pressley, M. (1977). Children's use of the keyword method to learn simple Spanish vocabulary words. *Journal of Educational Psychology, 69,* 465–472.

Raugh, M. R., & Atkinson, R. C. (1975). A mnemonic method for the learning of a second-language vocabulary. *Journal of Educational Psychology, 67,* 1–16.

Reder, L. M. (1985). Techniques available to author, teacher, and reader to improve retention of main ideas of a chapter. In S. F. Chipman, J. W. Segal, & R. Glaser (Eds.), *Thinking and learning skills: Research and open questions.* Hillsdale, NJ: Lawrence Erlbaum Associates.

Resnick, L. B. (1981). Syntax and semantics in learning to subtract. In T. P. Carpenter, J. M. Moser, & T. Romberg (Eds.), *Addition and subtraction: Developmental perspective.* Hillsdale, NJ: Lawrence Erlbaum Associates.

Resnick, L. B., & Beck, I. L. (1976). Designing instruction in reading: Interaction of theory and practice. In J. T. Guthrie (Ed.), *Aspects of reading acquisition.* Baltimore: Johns Hopkins University Press.

Richek, M. (1976). Effect of sentence complexity on the reading comprehension of syntactic structures. *Journal of Educational Psychology, 68,* 800–806.

Rigney, J. W. (1978). Learning strategies: A theoretical perspective. In H. F. O'Neil, Jr. (Ed.), *Learning Strategies.* New York: Academic Press.

Riley, M. S., Greeno, J. G., & Heller, J. I. (1983). Development of children's problem-solving ability in arithmetic. In H. P. Ginsburg (Ed.), *The development of mathematical thinking.* New York: Academic Press.

Rips, L. J., Shoben, E. J., & Smith, E. E. (1973). Semantic distance and the verification of semantic relations. *Journal of Verbal Learning and Verbal Behavior, 12,* 1–20.

Rohwer, W. D., Jr. (1975). Elaboration and learning in childhood and adolescence. In H. W. Reese (Ed.), *Advances in child development and behavior.* New York: Academic Press.

Rothkopf, E. Z. (1971). Experiments on mathemagenic behavior and the technology of written instruction. In E. A. Rothkopf & P. E. Johnson (Eds.), *Verbal learning research and the technology of written instruction.* New York: Teachers College Press.

Rubinstein, M. (1975). *Patterns of Problem Solving.* Englewood Cliffs, NJ: Prentice-Hall, 1975.

Rumelhart, D. E. (1975). Notes on a schema for stories. In D. G. Bobrow & A. M. Collins (Eds.), *Representation and understanding.* New York: Academic Press.

Rumelhart, D. E. (1981). *Understanding understanding.* La Jolla, CA: University of California, San Diego, Center for Human Information Processing.

Rumelhart, D. E., & Norman, D. A. (1975). The active structural network. In D. A. Norman & D. E. Rumelhart (Eds.), *Explorations in cognition.* San Francisco: Freeman.

Rumelhart, D. E., & Norman, D. A. (1978). Accretion, tuning, and restructuring: Three modes of learning. In J. W. Cotton & R. L. Klatzky (Eds.), *Semantic factors in cognition.* Hillsdale, NJ: Lawrence Erlbaum Associates.

Salomon, G. (1979). *Interaction of media, cognition, and learning.* San Francisco: Jossey-Bass.

Schank, R., & Abelson, R. (1977). *Scripts, plans, goals, and understanding.* Hillsdale, NJ: Lawrence Erlbaum Associates.

Schank, R., & Colby, K. M. (Eds.). (1973). *Computer models of thought and language.* San Francisco: Freeman.

Shannon, C. E., & Weaver, W. (1949). *The mathematical theory of communication.* Urbana, IL: University of Illinois Press.

Shiffrin, R. M., & Atkinson, R. C. (1969). Storage and retrieval processes in long-term memory. *Psychological Review, 76,* 179–193.

Shiffrin, R. M., & Dumais, S. T. (1981). The development of automatism. In J. R. Anderson (Ed.), *Cognitive skills and their acquisition.* Hillsdale, NJ: Lawrence Erlbaum Associates.

Shiffrin, R. M., & Schneider, W. (1977). Controlled and automatic human information processing: II. Perceptual learning, automatic attending, and a general theory. *Psychological Review, 84,* 127–190.

Shulman, H. G. (1972). Semantic confusion errors in short-term memory. *Journal of Verbal Learning and Verbal Behavior, 11,* 221–227.

Siegler, R. S., & Klahr, D. (1982). When do children learn? The relationship between existing knowledge and the acquisition of new knowledge. In R. Glaser (Ed.), *Advances in instructional psychology* (Vol. 2). Hillsdale, NJ: Lawrence Erlbaum Associates.

Simon, H. A., & Feigenbaum, E. A. (1964). An information-processing theory of some effects of similarity, familiarization, and meaningfulness in verbal learning. *Journal of Verbal Learning and Verbal Behavior, 3,* 385–396.

Skinner, B. F. (1938). *The behavior of organisms.* New York: Appleton.

Skinner, B. F. (1968). *The technology of teaching.* New York: Appleton.

Stein, B. S., Bransford, J. D., Franks, J. J., Owings, R., Vye, N. J., & McGraw, W. (1982). Differences in the precision of self-generated elaborations. *Journal of Experimental Psychology: General, 111,* 399–405.

Sulin, R. A., & Dooling, D. J. (1974). Intrusion of a thematic idea in retention of prose. *Journal of Experimental Psychology, 103,* 255–262.

Tennyson, C. L., Tennyson, R. D., & Rothen, W. (1980). Content structures and instructional control strategies as design variables in concept acquisition. *Journal of Educational Psychology, 72,* 499–505.

Thorndike, E. L. (1913). *Educational psychology: The psychology of learning* (Vol. 2). New York: Teachers College, Columbia University.

Tulving, E. (1972). Episodic and semantic memory. In E. Tulving & W. Donaldson (Eds.), *Organization of memory.* New York: Academic Press.

Tulving, E., & Thomson, D. M. (1973). Encoding specificity and retrieval processes in episodic memory. *Psychological Review, 80,* 352–373.

Underwood, B. J. (1964). The representativeness of rote verbal learning. In A. W. Melton (Ed.), *Categories of human learning.* New York: Academic Press.

Voss, J. F., Vesonder, G.T., & Spilich, G. J. (1980). Generation and recall by high-knowledge and low-knowledge individuals. *Journal of Verbal Learning and Verbal Behavior, 19,* 651–667.

Wason, P. C., & Johnson-Laird, P. N. (1972). *Psychology of reasoning.* Cambridge, MA: Harvard University Press.

Watkins, M. J., & Tulving, E. (1975). Episodic memory: When recognition fails. *Journal of Experimental Psychology: General, 104,* 5–29.

Whimbey, A., & Lochhead, J. (1980). *Problem solving and comprehension: A short course in analytical reasoning.* Philadelphia: Franklin Institute Press.

Wickelgren, W. A. (1974). *How to Solve problems.* San Francisco: Freeman.

Wickens, D. D. (1972). Characteristics of word encoding. In A. W. Melton and E. Martin (Eds.), *Coding processes in human memory.* Washington, DC: Winston.

Wright, P. (1977). Presenting technical information: A survey of research findings. *Instructional Science, 6,* 93–134.

AUTHOR NOTES

Robert M. Gagné is Professor of Educational Research, Florida State University.

Robert Glaser is Director of the Learning Research and Development Center, and University Professor of Psychology and Education, University of Pittsburgh.

4 Instructional Systems Design

Bela H. Banathy
Far West Laboratory & Saybrook Graduate School

In the context of the other chapters of this book, it appeared to be appropriate for this chapter to focus on design and on a systems view of instructional design. I felt comfortable with this focus in view of my long-term involvement with the systems movement; my work and teaching in applying systems theory and systems thinking in educational, organizational, and societal contexts; and in view of my research in systems design.

During the last 30 years, I have directed more than 40 projects that have involved design, many in the area of instruction and curricula. Over this period my perspective on design in general and instructional design in particular has changed markedly, moving toward an increasingly intensive systems orientation—emphasizing an open-systems view. Although some would say the approach to design presented in this chapter is at variance with the conventional instructional design approach, I intend to make a contribution to the field by offering a *complementary* perspective on instructional systems design and proposing a broad, macro-systemic orientation. The chapter presents a set of conceptual systems and related components that explain my conception and understanding of instructional systems design.

THE KNOWLEDGE BASE

The first system presented is a knowledge base of two components. One component is a set of selected concepts of systems inquiry (systems theory, philosophy, and methodology) that seem to be relevant to the topic. The second is a set of characteristics portraying design inquiry. The knowledge base emerges from a synthesis of these two sets (System A).

The knowledge base system is embedded in another system, System B. This system comprises a set of organizing perspectives that I have learned to accept and consider as important in guiding and organizing thinking about instructional systems design. These are the four perspectives:

1. The recognition of a hierarchy of systems in which instructional systems are embedded and a hierarchy of system levels in relation to which instruction is to be designed;

2. A recognition that the learning-experience level is the primary (system) level around which instruction should be organized;

3. A recognition that numerous societal systems are relevant to education and include resources and opportunities, arrangements and situations embedded in those systems that can be employed in designing instructional systems; and

4. Deriving from the knowledge base (System A) and the above three perspectives, a recognition of instructional systems as *open systemic* and design as a process of dynamic "systemic" inquiry, rather than "systematic" engineering.

A synthesis of these four perspectives brings forth an awareness of the multi-level and complex nature of instructional systems and of the significance of a macro-design approach to the formulation of instructional systems.

The outcome of this line of inquiry will lead to the construction of a macro-model of instructional design. In the remaining parts of the chapter, I will develop this topic more fully. Figure 4.1 depicts a summary image—a model—of the entire chapter.

The knowledge base was defined as having two components: one embedded in systems inquiry and the other in design inquiry. The organized knowledge base of these two lines of inquiry is vast. Within the limited space of this chapter, brief references will be made to a few aspects that are relevant to our topic.

A Systems Perspective

A systems perspective is introduced here by presenting a brief rationale for systems inquiry, highlighting its main aspects, and outlining a systems-model approach.

Rationale.   Over the last three decades, we have been faced with increasingly more complex and pressing problems, embedded in interconnected systems that operate in dynamically changing and turbulent environments. In addressing these problems and in working with these systems, we have learned to recognize the limitations of the perspectives, methods, and tools of

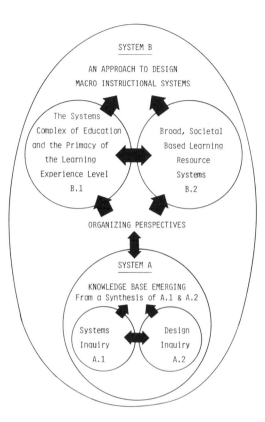

FIGURE 4.1. A systems model
of the contents of this chapter.

analytically oriented traditional disciplines. Thus, of necessity, a new
method of thinking and a new approach to disciplines inquiry has emerged,
namely, *systems inquiry.* Systems inquiry has demonstrated its capability for
effectively attacking highly complex and large-scale problems. It has orchestrated the efforts of various disciplines and introduced systems approaches to
analysis, design, and management.

Systems inquiry incorporates three interrelated streams: systems philosophy, systems theory, and systems methodology. In contrast to the analytical,
reductionist, and linear-causal orientation of classical scientific thinking, *systems philosophy* brings forth a reorientation of thought and world view manifested in an expansionist orientation and a dynamic, nonlinear, synthesis-
oriented, and holistic mode of thinking. The scientific exploration of the iso-
morphism of systems and theories of systems in various disciplines has
brought forth *general theories of systems:* a set of interrelated concepts and
principles. *Systems methodology* provides us with a set of paradigms, strategies, methods, and tools that instrumentalize systems thinking and systems
theory in design, development, and problem solving for complex systems.

The need for this inquiry is nowhere more obvious than in professions involved with studying and working with social systems. The prevailing approach is dependent on discipline-based scholarship that, unfortunately, is limited to gaining merely partial understandings of subsystems, or to description using disparate methods and theoretical frameworks. For example, in education, we study the sociology of the classroom, the economics of educational administration, the psychology of instruction, and so on. This is somewhat reminiscent of the parable of the blind men and the elephant. The combination of compartmentalizing inquiry and using disparate orientations and languages results in unintegrated and incomplete understanding.

For any system of interest, systems inquiry enables us to explore and characterize not only the selected system but the environment(s) in which the system is embedded as well as components or subsystems. We seek to explore, understand, and describe:

1. The characteristics of the hierarchy of systems operating at various interconnected levels, their relationships, and mutual interdependencies;

2. The relationships, interactions, and information-matter energy exchanges between the system of interest and its environment;

3. The purposes and boundaries of the system of interest;

4. The dynamics of interactions among the components of the system and their relationship patterns;

5. The properties and characteristics that emerge at various system levels as the result of systemic integration and synthesis; and

6. The behavior and change of the system, its environment, and its components through time.

Systems philosophy generates insights in ways of knowing, thinking, and reasoning that empower us to pursue this kind of investigation. Systems theory provides us with a large set of concepts and principles, often organized into models, that enable us to express and describe in an internally consistent and externally viable manner our findings. Systems Methodology provides us with strategies, methods, and tools that we can use to operationalize theory.

By observing systems, studying their behavior, and seeking to understand them—through the kind of inquiry described here—we learn to recognize their systemic characteristics and properties, and to express them in terms of systems concepts. When we define a set of systems concepts and discover how relationships among concepts lead to principles, we are in a position to look for relationships between principles and to organize them into conceptual schemes called systems models. A model is a representation of reality, an expression of a mental image, an abstraction. It is useful as a frame of reference within which we can examine and talk about what the model represents.

Findings from the types of systems inquiries introduced herein will produce sets of systems concepts and principles that can be organized into three complementary models:

1. One model examines systems in the context of and in relation to their environments and organizes concepts and principles relevant to this examination. This model is the *systems-environment model* or the *systems-context model*.

2. Another model focuses on what the system is, what it looks like, how it is organized. This is called the *structural model*.

3. The third model examines the behavior of the system over time, and it tells us how the system operates. This model is called the *process model*.

I developed these three models in the context of education (Banathy, 1973), and have found them useful in describing any educational system for which or in which an instructional system is to be designed and developed. A model of the particular educational program enables us to map the instructional system into the larger system and thus make it an organic part.

DESIGN INQUIRY

The second major task of the present chapter is to discuss design inquiry that is compatible with systems thinking and practice in education. A brief summary that follows presents basic characteristics of design. (This section is a partial adaptation of a chapter in Banathy, 1984.)

Design is a creative, disciplined, and decision-oriented inquiry that aims to: (a) formulate and clarify ideas and images of alternative desired states of a system; (b) prepare descriptions, representations or "models" of the system; and (c) devise a plan for the development and implementation of the selected (most promising) model. The design of alternative models enables both conceptual and empirical testing before a system is realized. Design is carried out in iterative cycles. It operates in four arenas or spaces: the *design solution space,* which is embedded in the *knowledge space,* the *contextual space* (which is the environment of design), and the *experience space.* The designer constantly explores these spaces, integrating information and knowledge with emerging images of the design solution. Feedback–feedforward and divergence–convergence are additional attributes of design dynamics. Furthermore, design embraces various system levels and involves various positions and values.

At the most general level, we may define design inquiry as having the following iterative process components:

1. The definition and analysis of the context of design and formulation of the purposes and goals of the system to be designed;

2. The devising of a set of alternative representations of the desired future system;

3. The devising of criteria by which to evaluate the alternatives;

4. The selection of the most promising alternatives by application of the criteria; and

5. The communication of findings in the form of displaying and describing the model of the future system.

The position taken here is that these process components are not completed in a step-by-step, linear fashion, but are carried out through recurring spirals as we explore and re-explore the different arenas (spaces) of design inquiry, and integrate information and knowledge with our emerging images of the future. Even though at any given time only one design process component may be in focus, the designers contemplate the impact of their ongoing work on what they have already done and what they have yet to accomplish.

The predecessors of contemporary design models and methods emerged during and after World War II when we first constructed highly complex man-machine systems. Success in the use of the models, methods, and tools developed during those years often led to their direct transfer to the design of social and educational systems. Thus, we applied "mostly technological models to thinking and design to conceive and build systems in the appreciated world" (Jantsch, 1975, p. 26). Those early design approaches—being characteristic of the fields from which they originated—represented a rather closed systems view, emphasizing steady state and structure, and employing linear thinking. Borrowing heavily from systems engineers, we used their design approach, without having any real understanding of the systems concepts and principles from which their models, methods, and tools were derived. Consequently, these "borrow and use" efforts brought about only meager results at best, and often failed entirely.

As we have learned more about the true nature of societal systems, such as education, we have realized that we need design models, methods, and tools that are specifically applicable to open systems (Checkland, 1981).

As mentioned earlier, design inquiry operates in several conceptual spaces:

1. *The design-solution space* occupies the center of the inquiry and is bounded in the beginning by design purposes and goals and at the end by the model of the system to be created. The design-solution space is surrounded by three other spaces, as follows:

2. *The contextual space,* or the environment of design, is our source for defining, studying, and characterizing design-relevant systems and systems of problems relevant to the design.

3. *The experience space* is created by the designers in order to reality-test design alternatives and the emerging model. This is of great significance in that separating design from reality testing may result in errors in perceiving the real world and in making the design relevant to the real world.

4. *The organized-knowledge space* consists of the knowledge areas that will be explored in order to establish and enrich the knowledge base for the design. (Organized knowledge should embrace both general knowledge that is content- and context-specific to the system to be designed.)

The exploration of the contextual space (often called the "problem space") and the knowledge space is constantly ongoing. In addition to an intensive initial exploration of the contextual and knowledge spaces, as solution alternatives emerge, we continue to draw upon information generated from the ongoing exploration of the contextual (problem) space. As design proceeds, we have increasingly better understanding of what to look for in the contextual space, and information gained there begins to enlighten our design. The same is true with the knowledge base. We draw upon organized knowledge

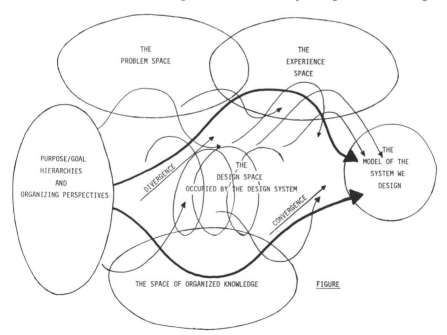

FIGURE 4.2.   A diagram of the interaction dynamics of design inquiry.

increasingly and more effectively as the questions we formulate become ever more clear and better informed by knowledge. Consequently, our exploration of the knowledge base becomes better focused.

The experience space is the remaining arena that surrounds design inquiry and is continuously explored as we proceed with design. In this space, we conceptually test the various design configurations and reality-test the most promising ones. The model (of the future system) evolves as we test and display the most promising solutions. It is shaped thorugh the integration of perceptions, insights, and information coming from the knowledge, the contextual, and the experience spaces. It represents an approximation or image of what may evolve if the system is actually developed.

Figure 4.2 presents an image of interactive dynamics operating in the various spaces of design inquiry.

I shall now outline *design dynamics* and, as an example, draw upon experiences in designing a national model for Experience Based Career Education (EBCE).

Iterative and Spiralic Design

Jones (1963) was among the first who took the position that the phase-by-phase and step-by-step "linear" approach to design is replaced by a process where the designer may pass several times through the various phases of the design cycle. In practice, this means that the designer has to iterate analysis–synthesis–evaluation (Sage, 1977). This notion is compatible with the recurring exploration of the knowledge, problem, and experience spaces, as iterative design brings forth progressively more refined characterizations of the model of the system to be designed.

Feedback and Feedforward

The unfolding spirals of design are interlaced with the dynamics of feedback and feedforward. Thus, designers go back to previous formulations in order to shape emerging design images by asking: How does what we have done earlier affect what is going on now? They may also ask: How does what we do now affect what we did earlier? They realize that the emerging solution changes their perception of the design problem. Feedforward reaches ahead. In an anticipatory mode, we speculate about the impact of current design information and choices on design tasks still ahead of us, as well as the ultimate shape of design.

Divergence-Convergence

In Fig. 4.2, divergence and convergence are shown as intersecting each other in the inquiry space of design. Divergence calls for exploring many alternatives in the beginning, and, as design proceeds, continuing to search for opportunities to make changes as we gradually converge toward the design solution (Jones, 1970). The dynamics of divergence–convergence are manifested as the designer continually goes through alternating sequences of generating variety (divergence) and reducing variety (convergence), while seeking the single most feasible and workable alternative (Rittel, 1972).

Multi-systemic Thrust in Design

Open systems operate at various levels in a hierarchy of interdependence (Miller, 1978). A system existing at a particular level operates in the context of a larger system or systems. Furthermore, the system has its own subsystems, and each of these has its own components. Even though the designer will select a specific system level as the primary level of design, the designer will have to be informed about and concerned with the effect that the system (to be designed) will have on its surrounding environment as well as the environment on the system.

Participative Design

Design brings together various people involved in decision making, including clients/users and others affected by the design. The people involved define positions, gather evidence, and prepare arguments (Ackoff, 1981). Consequently, debate develops, and, when an issue is resolved by scaling and prioritizing concerns, the decision reflects the different positions, The process of arriving at better decisions is not a process of optimization; it is, rather, a process of negotiation among those with different points of view and value systems in order to find a satisfying solution. Dialectics (Churchman, 1982) is the underlying philosophy of this approach, and consensus-building methods provide the technology (Warfield, 1982).

The design dynamics of the preceding paragraphs may be highlighted by an example. In designing and then developing one of the national models of Experience Based Career Education (EBCE) we went through four iterations of design spirals in the eight months of initial design. At the front end the focus was on the analysis of the problem space and the design context in which we elected to conduct the design. As we became informed by our analysis, we created a "rich picture" of all the relevant systems, and soon began to speculate (moving to synthesis) about the image of the shape of the kind of educational system that would be compatible with the specifications given by our sponsor (the U.S. Office of Education) as well as with the findings of our initial explorations.

During our second spiral we focused on the creation of a knowledge base by conducting a number of feasibility studies that our initial exploration had indicated would inform and enlighten our design. This exploration already led us into the experience space as well as helped us to balance analysis and synthesis. We also revisited the problem space and gained a new perspective. Our sponsor defined the system to be designed as *employer-based career education*. During this second spiral of design we realized that the key feature of our system (to be designed) was not that it would be based on employer territories but that it would be experience-based, that is, grounded in the multiple systems of the real world.

The third spiral of design iteration included synthesis, analysis, and evaluation. Its most significant thrust was the creation of a rather large set of alternative design configurations, exemplifying the dynamics of *divergence*. The design of these configurations was informed by both the knowledge base (the synthesis of the feasibility studies) as well as by new information from a revisit of the problem space. During this third cycle we had gained—again—some new insights that led us to propose that the most salient feature of the system to be designed would be a system based on the *learning experience level;* a system of which the learning experience level was the primary level. (This issue will be discussed later in some detail as a primary design perspective.) We tested the alternative design configurations both conceptually and also in real-world settings, by creating small-scale representations of the various design configurations.

The fourth spiral of our design iteration focused on synthesis, which was informed by findings of our conceptual evaluation and real-world testing, as well as the new perspective which emerged during spiral three. Here we began to capture the image of a new type of educational system which drew upon the large sets of potential learning resources, arrangements, and situations available in a great variety of societal systems; a system that would connect the learner with those resources, arrangements, and situations in a purposeful and learning-focused manner.

Our design project also demonstrated the dynamics of embeddedness and multi-systemic thrust. We realized that the system we designed was embedded in several environments and systems, such as the particular school district (in which our system became an alternative program), the many private- and public-employment systems that comprised the learning territory, various community systems, and the state system of education, whose requirements we had to satisfy. In addition, there were a large number of relevant systems that interacted with our system, ranging from transportation systems to labor unions, and several public agencies. The dynamics of participatory design were equally obvious in the design program. We had to involve all "stakeholders"—representatives representatives of the embedding system as well as the relevant systems. We had to build consensus as to the purpose and operations of the system to be designed. Our design work with EBCE was one of several efforts involving the design of large-scale complex systems. In addition we had the opportunity to conduct a two-year comprehensive research project on the design process itself.

In the previous section and in the EBCE example I have highlighted several characteristics of design dynamics in the context of open systems. Viewed comprehensively, these characteristics create an image markedly different from the systematic stage-by-stage linear approaches that many of us, including myself (Banathy, 1968), believed in and attempted to practice as instructional systems design in the 1960s. The emerging design inquiry seems to be dynamic and holistic; interactive and integrative; spiralic and interative; and participatory, dialectical, and consensus seeking.

The type of design inquiry described here is proposed as one which is most compatible with instructional systems design that focuses at the learning experience level.

THE SYSTEMS COMPLEX OF EDUCATION

Earlier in this chapter, I have portrayed System B as the second major conceptual system. System B is composed of a set of organizing perspectives that consititute its four interactive components. In this section, I discuss two of these organizing perspectives: the systems complex of education and the primacy of the learning experience level (Banathy, 1980a). Schooling—the formalized manifestation of education—is viewed as a systems complex operating at several levels. These levels and systems organized at these levels will be characterized first. Next, the rationale for considering a particular level as primary system will be examined. In accordance with the organizing perspectives defined earlier, the systemic consequences of giving primacy to the learning experience level will be explored. This exploration will lead us to a macro-design perspective of instructional-system design.

Education as a System Complex of Various Levels

There is a variety of configurations by which systems concepts and principles can be used to view social systems such as education, and by which such systems can be characterized as *organized complexities*. I have selected a configuration that appears to be particularly relevant to portraying the organization of schooling. This configuration is displayed in the form of a set of inquiries. The set includes the following elements of inquiry:

a. Clarify the levels that constitute the hierarchy of education and identify systems that operate at the various levels;

b. Designate the primary-system level in the hierarchy;

c. Clarify the key-systems entities around which the various systems are built;

d. Specify the purposes of these systems;

e. Specify their input, and

f. Output;

g. Designate control and decision-making authority at the various levels;

h. Display the relationships among the various systems;

i. Define the degree to which the systems are closed or open.

There are two elements in the set of inquiries above which are the normative type and are central to our present topic. These are (a), the issue of the designation of the primary system level, and (b) the degree to which the school system (or other system of education or training) is closed or open. A change in these two elements leads to a change in the very nature of the instructional enterprise. Furthermore, as we shall see, these two elements are interrelated and have a systemic effect on all the other elements. The letters in parentheses permit a comparison with the letters used in the four outlines that follow in which I display various images of the nature of schooling.

I will now comment on the nine elements and their significance. The *systems hierarchy* in education is made up of various *systems levels* (a). At the *institutional level,* the society interfaces and interacts with the administration of schools. The system at the *administrative level* implements decisions made at the institutional level and manages resources that support the instructional level. The systems at the *instructional level* attend to the functions of educating (as well as other functions defined at the institutional and administrative level). Instructional personnel operating at the instructional level deal with the learners. The *learning-experience level* has recently come to the fore with a potential to become a full partner in the systems hierarchy of education.

The designation of the *primary systems level* (b) is probably the least understood aspect of education, even though its designation is probably the most crucial. Depending on which one of the levels is selected as the primary level, several distinctively different models of education emerge. In this chapter I will argue that the learning experience level should be the primary level in the hierarchy of educational systems and that all other systems should be organized around it.

A significant point of inquiry in the systemic characterization of education is to designate clearly the *key system entity* (c), around which each of the systems is built and operates. Often we fail to state explicitly who or what the key entity is, or else we view entities as being interchangeable among the various sytems. Such lack of specificity has led to confusion and has hindered an understanding of problem situations and structuring potential solutions.

The four systems are to be characterized further and understood by the specification of their *purpose* (d), their *input* (e), and their *output* (f). Here systems thinking may help us again to understand the relationship between purpose, input and output. It has become clear to us, for example, that we cannot designate *learning attained* as a direct output at the institutional or instructional levels, but only at the learning-experience level. Systems thinking has also legitimized the purposes and goals of the individual learner as a viable input to the systems of schooling.

The matter of who *controls and who decides* (g) at various system levels must be made clear. The nature of *relationships* (h) among the various systems that comprise the systems complex of schooling is determined by the designation of the primary level and by the nature of intersystems relationships (subordinate, centralized, or egalitarian).

The degree of *openness or closedness* (i) is another critical dimension. Despite the rhetoric to the contrary, the thrust in education has been toward isolating the school from its environment. This tendency has become a major source of discontent, inefficiency, dissatisfaction, and loss of support. It is rather unfortunate that the early systems-approach movement in education borrowed closed-systems models from systems engineering, resulting in a "systematic" approach to education that overlooked the basically open nature of human systems and even failed to view education as an open, human-activity system (Checkland, 1981). We neglected to consider the uniqueness of the various environments in which education is organized and embedded (openness toward the environment) and, most importantly, failed to attend to the uniqueness of learners (openness toward the true client of the system).

The points of inquiry just described will be used next to characterize various configurations in the structure and organizational arrangements of education.

SYSTEM LEVELS AS PRIMARY LEVELS

Depending on which level is selected as the primary one, four distinctively different organizational models of education can be constructed. A display and discussion of these models, their underlying rationale, and their contrasting features will help us see the *learner system* in proper perspective and will help us to recognize the necessity of organizing education around the learning experience level and instituting a macro-design in education. In the following section the characteristics of each model is described in a standard outline form.

The Institutional Level as the Primary System Level

Organizing the educational system around the institutional level (Model A) is usually the organizational construct: (a) in societies where educational authority is centralized (e. g., a national system of education); (b) in cases where education is defined as part of a larger organization, such as a church; and (c) in traditional societies where the only or primary purpose of education is enculturation.

Model A

Institutional Level (School System)
Purpose: To enculturate, indoctrinate children and youth
Key Entity: National, societal (cultural), or organizational goals
Primary Decision-Maker: The educational authority; minister of education; church or societal authority
System Input: Societal definitions, needs, values; financial resources available to education; constraints that limit education
System Output: Educational goals; organizational schemes; established policies, standards, and methods of operation; budgets

Administrative Level (System-wide administration)
Purpose: To establish operational guides to (1) implement input and (2) account for resources
Key Entity: Information received as input and resources allocated to the system
Primary Decision-Maker: Educational managers and administrators
System Input: The output of the institutional level as specifed in previous section
System Output: Guidelines, directives, curriculum specifications, course materials, evaluation programs that regulate behavior at the instructional level

Instructional Level (Instructional programs and departments)
Purpose: To provide instruction in line with the defined institutional purpose
Key Entity: The prescribed curriculum
Primary Decision-maker: Department chairman, principal
System Input: System output from the administrative level
System Output: Specification of instructional experiences, instructional arrangements, textbooks, organization of teachers, staff.

Learning Experience Level (Classes of students)
Purpose: To respond to instruction
Key Entity: Instruction
Primary Decision-maker: Teacher
System Input: The output of the instructional level; instructional materials, aids, lesson plans and tests
System Output: Students passing courses, earning grades, diplomas, certificates

Model A implies a system of education that is rather closed toward the learner in that decisions are being made far removed from the learner. The system complex is regulated by top decision makers who affirm the purpose of the system, namely, enculturating and indoctrinating children and youth in line with societal goals. The model represents the top-down approach of a rigidly controlled, almost mechanistic system, which operationalizes a uniform curriculum and educational experience.

The Administrative Level as the Primary System Level

Organizing the educational systems complex around the administrative level is best evidenced by the way public-education education systems are currently organized in the United States. This way of organizing eduation is displayed in the following outline of Model B.

Model B

> *Institutional Level* (School System)
>> *Purpose:* to enculturate, indoctrinate children and youth
>> *Key Entity:* Societal goals, community expectations
>> *Primary Decision-maker:* Board of Education or similar authority
>> *System Input:* Information on societal needs, values, financial resources available to education, and constraints that limit operations
>> *System Output:* Stated educational goals, policies, organizational schemes, budgets, facilities
>
> *Administrative Level* (System-wide administration)
>> *Purpose:* The management of the operational system of education
>> *Key Entity:* Information received as input and resources allocated to the system
>> *Primary Decision-maker:* Educational managers and administrators
>> *System Input:* The output of the institutional level and information on the needs of the instructional level
>> *System Output:* Specification of educational programs, standards, methods, materials, rules regulations for the use of resources
>
> *Instructional Level* (Instructional programs)
>> *Purpose:* To provide instruction in line with the defined institutional purpose
>> *Key Entity:* The prescribed curriculum
>> *Primary Decision-Maker:* Department chairman, principal
>> *System Input:* The output of the administration level, resources, facilities, and students
>> *System Output:* Specification of instructional experiences: instructional arrangements, scheduling, organization of teachers, staff, students
>
> *Learning Experience Level* (Classes of students)
>> *Purpose:* To respond to instruction

Key Entity: Instruction
Primary Decision-Maker: Teacher
System Input: The output of the instructional level: lesson plans, materials, aids, tests
System Output: Students passing courses, earning grades, diplomas, certificates

Model B indicates a system that is more open than the one described under Model A, that is, open toward the immediate societal system in which the school is embedded. But decision making is quite removed from the learning experience level. In this arrangement, national and societal goals are complemented with perspectives and goals that are formulated in the community in which the school is located (e.g., the Board of Education is typically involved in such formulation). This model allows for sharing in decision making between the two top levels of the hierarchy.

The Instructional Level as the Primary Level

Organizing the educational systems complex around the instructional level as the primary level can be found: (a) in education contexts where instructional systems approaches, aided by instructional technology, have been used during the last 20–25 years; and (b) in departmentalized or discipline-based, higher-education programs. This approach is represented in Model C.

Model C
    Institutional Level (School system)
        Purpose: To provide facilities and resources in support of the operating systems
        Key Entity: Needs, requirements of the environment and the operating systems
        Primary Decision-Maker: Managers, policymakers, boards
        System Input: Societal needs and values, resource requirements of the instructional system, financial resources available
        System Output: General educational goals, allocation of resources in support of operating systems, and policies regulating the use of resources
    Administrative Level (System-wide administration)
        Purpose: Support the instructional level, given a set of policies and resources.
        Key Entity: Formalized information relevant to societal expectations, insitutional policies, and instructional-system needs.
        Primary Decision-Maker: System-wide administrators, school principals
        System Input: The output of the institutional level and requirements of the instructional system level
        System Output: Policies regulating the use of resources and specifying educational requirements

Instructional Level (Instructional systems)
> *Purpose:* To provide instruction to students
> *Key Entity:* Instructional goals and objectives
> *Primary Decision-Maker:* Instructional-systems manager and teacher
> *System Input:* The output of the administration level, instructional aims and design, staff, facilities, students
> *System Output:* Instructional systems, instructional arrangements, instructional delivery-systems, resources.

Learning Experience Level (Classes or groups of students)
> *Purpose:* To optimize instructional arrangements
> *Key Entity:* Instruction
> *Primary Decision-Maker:* Teacher
> *System Input:* The output of the instructional level and implemention plans geared to specific instructional arrangements
> *System Output:* Students who can perform on specified instructional objectives

This model implies a system which is *more open* than those described previously. The system is open to both external and internal influences. Primary educational decisions are made at the middle level of the systems hierarchy, closer to the learner. Consequently, within a specific educational institution, a variety of instructional systems and arrangements of educational experiences may be operationalized. Any given instructional system, however, is relatively closed in that it is designed against predetermined instructional objectives. (The so-called self-pacing, individualized-instruction programs are considered to be a step toward giving more attention to the learning experience level.)

The Learning-Experience Level as the Primary Level

We have had only limited experience with organizing education around the learning-experience level. The ancient tutorial approach of "sitting on the log," and some more recent innovative and alternative educational programs are examples of this approach.

Model D
> *Institutional Level* (Various educational sectors in the community)
> > *Purpose:* To facilitate the availability of resources in support of the instructional/learning system
> > *Key Entity:* Societal expectations; and the requirements of the instructional/learning system(s)
> > *Primary Decision-Maker:* Educational policymakers and representatives of various societal-based resource systems

System Input: Society's educational needs and values, and requirements of the instructional/learning systems. Financial resources and constraints

System Output: General educational goals, allocations of resources available to the instructional/learning system

Administrative Level (System-wide administration)

Purpose: To formalize information about requirements for resources that facilitate learning and negotiate the use of those resources

Key Entity: Instructional/learning resources, educational facilities requirements

Primary Decision-Maker: Managers and administrators for resource acquisition and utilization systems

System Input: The output of the institutional level and the instructional/learner levels

System Output: Policies regulating the use of society's educational resources and establishing overall educational requirements

Instructional Level (Learning resources systems)

Purpose: To provide resources and arrangements that facilitate learning

Key Entity: Learner needs, objectives

Primary Decision-Maker: Managers of the instructional/ learning resources system

System Input: The output of the administrative level; information about learners' procedures, learners' requirements

System Output: Information about the curriculum framework; instructional/learning resources and arrangements; organized, readily available resources

Learning Experience Level (The learners' systems)

Purpose: To master learning tasks; to become educated

Key Entity: Information about desired learning outcomes

Primary Decision-Maker: Learners and resource managers

System Input: The output of the instructional level; learners' needs and objectives; specific plans for making use of instructional/learning resources

System Output: Learning tasks mastered, progress toward becoming a self-sufficient person

Model D projects an educational system that is open toward the learner as well as to sources beyond the boundaries of the school that can support learning. Decisions relevant to the educational experience are made jointly by the instructional-resource system personnel and by the learners. Within an educational setting, there may be as many organized learner systems as learners. Furthermore, the boundaries of the learner systems may be extended into the various societal sectors that can provide opportunities, arrangements, and resources for learning.

Implications of the Models

Whichever model is operationalized in a given societal context depends on several factors, some of which are as follows:

1. *The socio-political configuration of the particular society.* More open and progressive societies will tend to move toward the learning-experience level focused Model D. More closed, autocratic, and traditional societies have schools that are more uniform and prescriptive, like Model A.

2. *The unitary versus pluralistic nature of the society.* A pluralistic society—one that defines itself as such—will not be likely to support a uniform system of schooling like the one represented by Model A.

3. *The prevailing conception of learning and the learner.* If individual differences are recognized and the learner is judged to be capable of making his or her decisions in learning, Model D will be the direction toward which the organization of education will tend to move.

Models A, B, and C are the most familiar to us. The model focused on learning experience, however, is less well known. Even though we currently have several manifestations of Model D, we do not yet have a clear idea of all the implications of such an educational systems complex.

In the next section will we elaborate on learning-experience-level education that is supported by societal-level organization of learning resources and a macro-design approach to instructional-systems design.

LEARNING EXPERIENCE LEVEL ORGANIZATION

In designing and developing educational systems built around the learning-experience level, our thinking has been guided by organizing principles that include the following:

1. The learner is the key entity and occupies the nucleus of the systems space of education.

2. The primary systems function is the facilitation of learning.

3. The primary systems level is the learning-experience level, around which a systems complex is built.

4. There is a large reservoir of learning resources in the society which can be defined, developed, and made available to support learning, and these are not now being used and institutionalized.

5. Left to his or her own devices, the learner cannot attain easy access to these resources.

6. Learning resources need to be identified and developed; their availability communicated to and their use arranged for the learner. This is an essential function of (macro) instructional design.

An elaboration of these principles would provide a rationale for organizing a macro-societal systems complex of education around the learning-experience level (Banathy et al., 1978).

The systems perspective, the organizational models derived from that perspective, and the assumptions (organizing principles) just described lead us to the following propositions:

1. Recognize the learning-experience level as the primary level in the systems complex of education.

2. Identify a new level—the societal level—that should be included in the set of levels at which education is organized.

3. *Define, as a major task, the design of systems that connect the learning-experience level with societal sectors (systems) that have the potential to offer learning resources. This proposition is the central notion of macro-instructional design.*

These ideas were implemented in a series of projects conducted at the Far West Laboratory, leading to the construction of a new formulation of the systems complex of education. This formulation is characterized in the following paragraphs.

In addition to the institutional, administrational, instructional, and learning-experience levels of the educational-systems complex, the societal level is recognized and established as an essential systems level of the complex. At this level we had systems that have the potential to offer resources, opportunities, and arrangements for learning.

The systems that operate at the institutional and administrative levels had to be reconceptualized as systems that have the function of connecting the societal-level systems described previously with systems operating at the instructional and learning experience levels. Systems at the instructional and learning-experience level were integrated and organized for connecting with those systems at the societal level that offer arrangements and resources that facilitate and support learning.

What is emerging from this characterization of systems and their relationship is a new image of education that operates within widely extended boundaries, drawing upon a much larger resource base than the conventional, school-based model of education. The image described here will be elaborated in the section that follows.

In introducing the content of this chapter, I depicted System B (Fig. 4.1) as the second major conceptual system of the chapter and proposed that it is comprised of a set of four organizing perspectives or interacting components. In this section, I explore first the third organizing perspective, namely, the notion of the availability of numerous resources, opportunities, and arrangements relevant to education that can be designed into instructional systems to support learning, and second, the need to use an open systems design in education (Banathy, 1980b).

A Societal View of Education

Education is more than schooling. The development of children and youth and the continuing development of adults intricately mesh with learning opportunities available in all facets of life. Beyond the boundaries of the school, formal and informal learning opportunities are offered in diverse ways: in the home; through the various media; in peer, neighborhood, civic and religious groups; through community, youth, and cultural agencies; in the world of work; and in many everyday-life situations. For too long these learning opportunities have been fragmented and separated from the school and from each other, even though ample evidence suggests that linkage and integration of various purposively focused efforts may generate benefits well beyond that which the total sum of separate efforts might produce.

A powerful potential resides in the notion of an alliance of all societal sectors that are interested in and involved in education. Such an alliance, if formally constituted, could identify, integrate, and energize those forces and components of society that jointly possess a vast reservoir of educational resources and opportunities and can facilitate the full development of the individual. In short, the present proposition is that we could identify and integrate by design all educational opportunities and resources that are available in the society and focus them on supporting learning arrangements and opportunities for all.

In the broadest sense, education is the domain of human activity that comprises all arrangements, resources, and opportunities which facilitate learning and development in children and youth, as well as the continuous learning and development of adults.

In the past, whenever we looked at education in this broader sense, it usually resulted in efforts to extend schools in two possible ways. A more modest way was to relate the subject matter presented in school to real life, thereby allowing students to extend the potential application of their learning beyond the confines of the school. The other way was to bring into the school representatives or representations of the outside world. A more dynamic interaction with the real world has emerged recently through career education. This movement has gone a long way toward opening the outside world as a learning area and involving the private and public sectors in the business of education. However, I attempt in this chapter to envision education even more broadly, via *organizing education at the societal level.* In view of Model D, introduced in the previous section, I propose the establishment of education at a societal (macro-system) level through macro-instructional design. Such a system will have the capacity to integrate *all* means, forces, and entities that can facilitate learning, including those now located in the school. The entity that is at the center of the macro-system is the *individual learner.* Around the learner are systems that have the potential to make contributions to or facilitate the learning and development of the individual. The systems that are closest to the individual are informal in nature. These are the family, peer groups, friends, and other people with whom the individual is in frequent and close contact. We call these systems the *primary social systems;* they have much to contribute to learning in the informal mode.

The *institutions of education*—various schools that are accessible to members of the society—potentially constitute the central coordinating system of societal-based education. Among these systems we include all those societal organizations whose primary function is instruction. Next, social and youth organizations; churches; and various community, civic, and cultural groups, which I call *community educational agencies,* offer a wide range of educational resources.

Another domain that offers sources of information and knowledge includes *communication systems,* such as the news media, TV and radio broadcasting, libraries, the many forms of art groups and exhibits. In a broad sense, all these aim to communicate something that may also constitute viable resources and opportunities for learning. Another area of human experience that has been a rich source of education is the *work system* in both the public and private sectors. These sources offer educational resources by the very nature of their purpose and existence. Beyond these, there is still a large domain which includes life situations, social events, and recreation activities that can offer educational resources in an informal fashion. These could be called *ad hoc learning resource systems.*

The societal level organization of education can be accomplished through formalized interorganizational arrangements for coordinated sharing of resources and functions among the various sectors of society. Such interorganizational cooperation may bring about a manifold increase in the potential of educational resources and instructional systems' potential that may match the continuing demand for quality education and educational excellence.

In developing the macro-system notion of education, I took the position earlier that the learner is the key or central entity of the system. Accordingly, the system should be conceptualized, designed, and organized so that the learner will have ready access to educational resources and functions and to learning opportunities that are potentially available in the various systems that comprise the *macro-societal education system*. The main thrust in designing education at the macro-societal level will be to identify functions and create relationships (or structure) among the various component systems of the potential societal-educational systems complex. These systems can then be designed in a directly cooperative and coordinated relationship to respond to learners' needs in the most effective way. This view is fully compatible with the position taken in the previous section, where the learning experience level was identified as the primary level in education, calling for a more open-systems view of education.

IMPLICATIONS OF SOCIETAL-BASED ORGANIZATION

I shall now explore the implications of what a broad, societal-resources-based organization of education means for design. The first implication is that such a design has the purpose of organizing and integrating the various societal learning-resource systems and connecting them with systems operations at the instructional and learning-experience levels of education. Thus the purposes of this type of design are very different from those of instructional design conducted in the school-based system.

The second implication is that issues and inquiries that are relevant to the design of a societal learning-resources-based organization of education are also markedly different from those of the school-based system. A line of design inquiry would address such questions as:

1. What resources are, or might be, available in the various systems of society that can facilitate learning?

2. What are the specific functions that the various resource systems can perform in offering resources for learning?

3. What arrangements could be made to discover and map resources and delivery systems in which those resources will be made accessible to the learner?

4. How can the application of these resources be optimized for use by the learner?

5. What are the ways by which we can interrelate and integrate the various resource and delivery systems?

6. What are policy issues, interorganizational and structural arrangements that could help to integrate and institutionalize the use of various resource and delivery systems?

7. How can we facilitate, through design, the development of interorganizational coordination relationships among the various systems?

8. What would a system be like that could manage and monitor the integrated use of resources?

9. How could such a system be designed, developed, maintained, supported, and institutionalized?

The type of inquiry introduced above was formulated and pursued in the context of educational-systems design projects that we have conducted at the Far West Laboratory. In addition to the two implications described above, a third major implication emerging from these projects is pertinent to a reconceptualization of the structure and the functions of the systems complex of education. This complex is now seen as having five systems levels. Systems operating at these levels are very different from the school-based model as to their purpose, function, and structure. We labeled this new complex as the macro-societal complex and called its relevant design approach, *macro-design*.

In the school-based arrangement of education, societal systems are outside of the boundaries of schooling. Their functions are to provide financial resources, educational purposes, and directives, and to judge the performance of the school. These functions are managed by a small group of elected or appointed officials, for example, a school or college board or board of regents, who are working with officials of the school system.

In the societal-based arrangement of education, societal systems are within the boundaries of the system complex of education. (The community becomes the classroom.) In the case of this arrangement, in addition to the functions described previously, decision-makers operating at the societal level of the systems complex of education have such functions as: (a) establishing and maintaining arrangements with various societal systems for the offering, development, and use of learning arrangements, opportunities, and resources; (b) formulating political and financial bases needed to support the latter; (c) negotiating and establishing policies and regulations that govern the use of arrangements and financial resources; and (d) monitoring arrangements and the use of societal resources.

In each community or other geopolitically defined area there are several social organizations, such as schools and colleges, the primary purpose of which is education. In the current—conventional—mode of education these organizations are autonomous, directed by an agency of the society (e.g., school board), and are responsible for serving the educational needs of the society. In the school-based mode, officials operating at the administrational level of schooling are managing the use of fiscal resources made available to the school. In the societal-based mode these organizations are *subsystems* of the larger system, rather than autonomous entities. Managers of these subsystems operate the resource management and control systems, (of the systems complex of education) that have such functions as: (a) analyzing and identifying learning resources, arrangements and systems-support requirements, (b) formulating statements of requirements and communicating those to managers operating at the societal level, (c) formulating directives for the use of those resources and arrangements, and (d) allocating resources received and monitoring their use.

In the societal-based system of education, the system level, which in the school-based model is called instructional level, has functions that are also markedly changed. At this level of the societal based system complex, a system is organized that we labeled the learning resources information and arrangement system. This system is charged with the functions in the following list:

1. Assist learners in preparing their curricular program;
2. Develop a plan and instructional arrangements that have the potential to respond to learners;
3. Identify, develop, and maintain learning territories and resources that have the potential to provide learning opportunities;
4. Display information to learners about items 2 and 3.
5. Make arrangements for the learners' use of learning resources and opportunities.
6. Monitor the learners' use of resources, advise them, and provide information on their progress.

In the societal-based system, arrangements and functions at the learning-experience level are also very different from those operating in the school-based mode. In the school-based mode, the interactions of the learner are basically limited to working with instructional level staff. In the societal-based mode, on the other hand, the community becomes the systemic environment of the learner, and thus functions as the learning-resources information and arrangement system. The learner works with a variety of resources, opportunities and people who are available to the learner in a variety of learning resources and arrangement systems of the society.

Previously described are five levels at which the societal-based complex of education is organized. Also identified have been the main functions that are to be carried out by systems operating at those levels, and the highly interactive, integrative, and multiple relationships among the various sytems. Above all, we have seen the need to think about design in the context of the societal-based system that is very different from the conventional instructional design applicable to the school-based model of education. The main tasks of this new type of design are: (a) to map out societal-learning resources and opportunities, (b) to create connecting systems that link societal-based learning resources with the systems complex of societal-based education, and (c) to devise arrangements by which the use of those resources is ensured.

In the remainder of this chapter this new type of macro-design is contrasted to conventional instructional design.

COMPLEMENTARY APPROACHES TO DESIGN

A discussion on the two types of educational systems complexes has helped us to differentiate between those two types as well as to see the need to think about a new approach to instructional design that may very well complement the conventional approach.

The conventional type of instructional design focuses on the instructional-systems level of the systems complex of education. Chapters in this book provide several elaborations and refinements of this type, and represent an instructional-design approach that has developed and matured into a much-respected profession in the course of the last 30 years. The general procedure of this type of design is to: (a) specify and formulate instructional objectives, (b) develop assessment criteria relevant to objectives, and (c) design and develop instructional systems that provide arrangements and materials that enable the learner to perform as specified. This type of design has the following characteristics: (a) a closed system approach to design (that has kinship with system engineering), (b) prescriptive in action and evaluation, (c) operating within clearly defined boundaries, (d) aiming at stability, (e) adjustments made only in order to increase effectiveness, (f) compliance required of the subject (learner), (g) an externally controlled system and (h) implying an extrinsic concept of motivation (Ulrich, 1983). I label this design type *micro-design,* in order to contrast it to the *macro-design* type presented in this chapter.

The macro-design described in this chapter is intended to be *complementary* to the conventional instructional design (micro-design). It is complementary in the sense that it has a different purpose, different systemic characteristics, and uses a different design approach.

The purpose of macro-instructional system design is to provide for societal-based systems of learning resources and arrangements and connect these with the learning-experience level of education. It aims at designing into the educational-system complex various societal systems and resources that can offer opportunities for learning.

The characteristics of macro-design contrast rather sharply with those of micro-design. Macro-design is: (a) purposeful (teleological) in inquiry, action, and evaluation; (b) open to changes in the environment as well as to changes in the systems that comprise the systems complex of education; (c) continuous and dynamic; (d) participative and interactive with all those involved; (e) internally controlled; and (f) intrinsic as to implied concept of motivation (Ulrich, 1983).

A design approach that has the features defined here is fully compatible with the design inquiry described in a previous section (System A).

Closing Thoughts

The post-World War II emergence of the technological society, and the concurrent explosion of information and knowledge, have caused the development of variations in the classroom-based structure of the systems complex of education. New curricula have emerged, coupled with instructional-systems technology and media-oriented methodology, with some attention given to individual differences. Recently, however, these variations of the traditional system appear to experience increasing difficulty as we (a) accept cultural pluralism as a viable societal arrangement, (b) experience diversification of life-styles, and (c) aspire to improve the quality of life and the human condition. Furthermore, increasing emphasis is placed on the full development of individuals' human potential through life-long learning and through the development of cooperative interaction skills and quality-of-life competence, in addition to attaining cognitive and occupational competence. Accordingly, the learning-experience level is becoming the primary level of educational-systems complexes, and learning becomes the key entity around which to build the educational system.

This emerging image of education has led us to recognize the need for the organization of education-systems complexes that include the societal level and for the design and implementation of instructional systems that focus at the learning-experience level. As a consequence of all this, we require a substantially expanded scope and depth of educational resources. Yet simply to adopt and implement provisions that fulfill these requirements—as additives to the present systems—would be to push the cost of education beyond limits. The instructional-design community can confront this predicament by accepting a three-pronged challenge. First, we should restructure our present systems and procedures so that currently available educational resources are used to greater advantage. Second, we should undertake intensive efforts to search out yet uncharted educational resource and arrangement potentials incorporated in various institutions and in the overall societal structure. Thirdly, we should learn to design systems that connect societal-based learning resources with systems at the learning-experience levels.

REFERENCES

Ackoff, R. (1981). *Creating the corporate future.* New York: Wiley.
Banathy, B. H. (1968). *Instructional Systems.* Palo Alto, CA: Fearon.
Banathy, B. H. (1973). *A systems view of education, a systems models approach.* Seaside, CA: Intersystems.

Banathy, B. H. (1980a). Organizing education around the learning experience level. In B. H. Banathy (Ed.), *Systems science and science.* Louisville, KY: Society for General System Research.

Banathy, B. H. (1980b). The school: An autonomous or cooperating social agency. In L. Rubin (Ed.), *Critical issues in educational policy.* Boston: Allyn and Bacon.

Banathy, B. H. (1984). *Systems design in the context of human activity systems.* San Francisco: International Systems Institute.

Banathy, B. H., Haveman, J. E., Wenkers, R., Stigliano, A., Oakley, G., & Jacobs, R. (1978). *The design of a macro-societal model of education and human development.* San Francisco: Far West Laboratory for Educational Research and Development.

Checkland, P. (1981). *Systems thinking, systems practice.* New York: Wiley.

Jantsch, E. (1975). *Design for evolution.* New York: Brazillier.

Jones, J. C. (1963). A method of systematic design. In J. C. Jones and D. G. Thornley (Eds.), *Conference on design methods.* New York: Macmillan.

Jones, J. C. (1970). *Design methods: Seeds of human future.* New York: Wiley.

Miller, J. G. (1978). *Living systems.* New York: McGraw-Hill.

Rittel, M. (1972). Occasional paper. *Design Method Journal,* January 1972.

Sage, A. P. (1977). A case for a standard for systems engineering methodology: *IEEE Transactions on Systems, Man and Cybernectics: 7*(7).

Ulrich, W. (1983). *Critical heuristics of social planning.* Bern, Switzerland: Paul Haupt.

Warfield, T. N. (1982). Organization and systems learning. In *General Systems* (Vol. 27). Louisville, KY: Society for General System Research.

AUTHOR NOTES

Bela H. Banathy is Associate Laboratory Director, Far West Laboratory for Educational Research and Development, and Professor of Systems Science, Saybrook Graduate School.

The material in this chapter is an adaptation of a part of Bela H. Banathy's "The School: An Autonomous or Cooperative Social Agency" from *Critical Issues in Educational Policy: An Administrative Overview* (Louis Rubin, Ed.). Boston, MA: Allyn and Bacon, Inc. 1980.

Design projects of the Far West Laboratory have included: a National Model of Experience Based Career Education, The Design of an Advanced Graduate Program in Educational R & D, The Design of the National Fire Academy, The Design of a Macro-Societal Model for Educational and Human Development.

5 Identifying and Specifying Requirements for Instruction

Roger Kaufman
Florida State University

Sivasailam Thiagarajan
Institute for International Research, Inc.

The tools and techniques of instructional technology often get applied at the wrong time or place. If instructional technology is the solution, then what is the problem? This chapter deals with ways of determining how problems of human performance are presented and how to link them with instructional solutions. For the sake of simplicity, the terms educational technology, instructional-systems technology, and instructional-systems approach are used interchangeably.

CONCEPTS OF INSTRUCTIONAL TECHNOLOGY

In general, instructional technology contributes knowledge to training (and education) that aims to improve the individual's learning, mastery, and competence. Training is understood as having the purposive intention of providing specific skills, knowledges, and abilities required on the job, and education provides the same which are generalizable and applicable to later related performance and life. We will use the single term "training" to encompass both it and education.

Being a successful technologist ordinarily requires that we plan, organize, and communicate subject-matter content in courses (such as English, computer repair, personnel supervision) using the most useful ways and means of delivering learning experiences to achieve learner competence.

The training and education that establishes competence in the individual shows itself in accomplishments that may occur in various social contexts—on the job, in the community, in the home. As instructional technologists, we help people to be successful on the job and in life. The performance of

113

the individual is most typically shown as the individual products of an *organization*. These are building blocks of performance, which extend from individual tasks or jobs through larger accomplishments of one or another organization. These in turn get combined sooner or later, with other products deliverable outside of the organization: a *performance chain* which should properly link from individual to societal consequences. In view of these considerations, it seems reasonable to deal with the learning of individuals by examining its effects on the organization and the organization's effects in society (Kaufman, 1985).

Instructional technology suggests many tools, techniques, and understandings which are useful in designing and delivering results. Together they provide a useful set of means toward accomplishing organizational ends. By putting training into context—a part of a larger whole—one will be able to select and apply the tools, techniques, and approaches which are most useful. It is important to know and be responsive to:

1. *Where* instruction gets delivered,
2. *What* tools and techniques are available to deliver instruction,
3. *When* to use them,
4. *How* to design and deliver successful learning experiences,
5. *Who* gets which content and methods,
6. *Where* is the best place to deliver instruction,
7. *What* do we use to determine if we have met the expectations, and
8. *What* to revise if we have not.

A holistic understanding of instructional technology includes its context: the organization, society, and community. Students do not stop at the front door of the training facility or school . . . they leave our facilities, curriculum, instructors, teachers, and activities, and go out into their jobs and the world. What they do and contribute on the job (and in their lives) determines, in part, how well their organizations do and survive. But how do we assure that we do not waste training time, money, energy, and resources? We should match our resources, learners, and objectives.

A USEFUL FRAME OF REFERENCE

One perspective for instructional and performance technology which relates means and ends, resources and results, tools and objectives, techniques and tasks is called the *Organizational Elements Model* (OEM) (Kaufman, 1982; Kaufman & Stone, 1983). It relates the individual technological how-to with learners and learning, with useful results. Further, the OEM orchestrates these with what organizations use and do, what they accomplish, and how all of these have an effect on the consequences of performance both within and outside organizations. It is applicable no matter what the organization: to link what we use, what we do, and what we accomplish.

The OEM divides (somewhat artificially) the organizational world of efforts, results, and payoffs into three bundles: (1) What organizations use and do; (2) What they accomplish; (3) What impact organizational results have on society.

It should be emphasized that in conventional use and wisdom, instructional technology is concerned with the individual learner, not with the organization. While using the OEM to relate individuals to organizational efforts and results, we still keep a major focus upon the individual learner, and view the organization only as a means to accomplish worthwhile ends.

Another critical consideration which is easy to lose sight of is that this model is not a linear, lock-step process, but rather a dynamic one which requires continual transactions among goals, expectations, objectives, individual differences, environments, the nature of the knowledge to be acquired, methods and techniques of teaching and presentation, evaluation of results, and revision.

Defining and Using the Organizational Elements Model

The OEM places into relationship and perspective people, resources, and results, and allows one to identify and solve performance problems correctly and quickly. It relates means and ends, and further distinguishes between what we use, what we do, and what we accomplish. There are five organizational elements, four of which are internal to an organization, and one which is external to it. Three of these elements are differing (but related) types of results, and two relate to that which organizations use and do. Table 5.1 provides definitions, relations, and brief examples of each.

Organizational Efforts

When we instruct, use resources, and observe the existing policies, laws, rules and regulations, perform formal training, use some of the usual resources available (e.g., buildings, facilities, equipment, staff, training aids) we are operating in the area of *organizational efforts,* as indicated in the final column of Table 5.1.

Together, the existing personnel, facilities, and equipment, along with the rules and regulations, are *inputs* to anything we do. People and equipment are utilized within the confines of existing requirements. Resources (an input) are only useful to the extent to which they are actually put to work.

Processes are the "doing" of things: teaching, learning, speaking, talking, engineering, thinking, training, and working. In fact, any English word which ends in "ing" is a process. When we use a process, we are using resources and inputs. Inputs and processes together make up organizational

TABLE 5.1
Organizational Elements, Examples, and Their
Relation to Organizational and Societal Results

Element	Examples	Efforts/Results
Inputs (raw materials)	ingredients, existing human and physical resources, policies, values, state-of-the-world	Organizational Effort
Processes (how–to–do–its)	means, methods, procedures, techniques, manufacturing, organizational development	Organizational Effort
Products (en route results)	services delivered, reports completed, skills required, production quota met	Organizational Results
Outputs (aggregated products delivered to society)	delivered automobiles, delivered computer systems, patients discharged	Organizational Results
Outcomes (effects in and for society	profit, off welfare rolls, having financial credit, contributing to self and society, customer satisfaction	Societal Impact (the External Element)

efforts. They are the resources and things which we can and do use when training business is carried on. In training (a process), we use inputs such as instructors, learners, existing goals and objectives, buildings, equipment, and facilities. The processes include instructing, studying, reciting, interacting, speaking, writing, and learning.

The following are some examples of inputs and processes which together constitute Organizational Efforts:

Inputs	Processes
instructors	teaching
learners	learning
existing goals and objectives	studying
existing needs	instructing
entry skills, knowledges, and abilities	reciting
motivation	interacting
expectations	planning
buildings	managing
attributions	presenting
equipment	testing
	writing

facilities	computing
laws	lecturing
policies	
administrators	

In training, we use inputs to deliver processes to learners:

INPUTS + PROCESSES = ORGANIZATIONAL EFFORTS.

The success of training depends on how wisely and how well we design and deliver learning opportunities, and this delivery (usually teaching by instructors in classrooms) gets a lot of attention.

In training, we spend most of our time and money on these organizational efforts. Instructional technology is mainly concerned with *inputs* (e.g., characteristics of learners, individual differences, characteristics of instructors) and *processes* (e.g., methods of teaching, learning, instructional design and delivery, evaluating). Most existing instructional-technology models emphasize this arena (e.g., Branson et al., 1975; Dick & Carey, 1985; Gagné and Briggs, 1979; Reigeluth, 1983.) Of course, since each instructional-technology model or process intends to focus on instruction this is not surprising. What is surprising is the extent to which practitioners in the field are willing to assume that excursions into instructional technology are useful further on in the *results chain,* which extends from the individual through the organization to societal consequences. It is by way of this linking that the OEM allows one to relate instruction better to its organizational payoffs.

Organizational Results

The only reason for designing and delivering training is to change learner performance. Instructional technologists seek useful results both in the courses and later in life. Thus, emphasis is placed not upon just any results, but upon several different types of them.

When we use resources (inputs) and deliver instruction or services (processes), we look to see the results obtained. There are two types of results *within* organizations: (a) learner and instructor accomplishments, and (b) total system (or organizational) accomplishments. Let's take a closer look.

Learner and instructor accomplishments. When a learner masters a course, passes a test, or completes an athletic event, there is a measurable result—a *product.* These products are the useful accomplishments of some useful objectives: a Spanish lesson that results in learner mastery and achieved competence, the volleyball team's winning a game. When an instructor successfully teaches troubleshooting of an on-board radar, or accomplishes student mastery in code cyphering, these also are products.

In training establishments, a lot of attention is paid to learner and instructor accomplishments. Products are the building blocks of a training system. Most of what we do in training is focused on these accomplishments. In fact, the bulk of the information in instructional-systems models, techniques, and methods is designed to help identify what products to achieve, and how to achieve them.

Total system accomplishments.   As important as these products are, they are virtually worthless in and of themselves—they are best seen as en-route, building-block accomplishments which must be combined with others to be useful. Let's look at some examples:

1. Passing a course in chemistry is important, but it alone does not allow one to be a successful chemist, or an educated person.

2. Getting certified as an aircraft master mechanic in the area of computer-actuated, servo valves does not make a mechanic who can deal with all aircraft service and repair problems or situations.

Products (learner/instructor accomplishments) are useful when combined with other products to yield an overall organizational accomplishment, such as a graduate or course-completer. The combination of products into an organizational accomplishment is called an *output*.

Below are examples of the two types of Organizational Results—*products* and *outputs*. Notice how each product, by itself, is not useful, but when combined with other products leads to an integrated, useful output:

Products	**Outputs**
(learner/instructor accomplishments)	(organizational accomplishments)
completed physics course	graduation
completed supervision program	certification
completed teller course	hiring into job
completed troubleshooting course	accepted to field service
completed and passed test	
completed instructor training and competence certification	
completed and validated course content and methods	

The accomplishments of learners and instructors contribute to the results an organization can or does deliver outside of itself—to society:

PRODUCTS + OUTPUTS = ORGANIZATIONAL RESULTS

Putting All of the Elements Together

The five organizational elements, when taken together, help us put training, learners, instructors, and success into useful perspective. Linking all of the five Organizational Elements together, we see the following relationship:

INPUTS + PROCESSES + PRODUCTS + OUTPUTS → OUTCOMES

When we take a big-picture, or societal, view of organizational efforts and organizational results we note that four of the elements occur *within* the training organization, and thus are *internal,* and one is located outside of the organization, and thus is *external:*

INPUTS + PROCESSES + PRODUCTS + OUTPUTS → OUTCOMES

INTERNAL ELEMENTS   EXTERNAL ELEMENT

ENDS

What we do and accomplish in our training (using our resources, methods, and techniques) determines what payoff there is for trainees, the organization, and society. The internal activities and results should lead to helping people to be competent, productive, self-sufficient, and self-reliant in today's and tomorrow's worlds. *Means* should lead to useful *ends.*

Most of what we do in training is concerned with *inputs, processes,* and *products.* But that doesn't mean we should forget for a moment that these are all en-route efforts and results which are the building blocks for achieving useful *outputs* and *outcomes.*

Determining Instructional Requirements Based Upon Needs

But from what source do the requirements for training derive? Do we simply ask subject-matter experts about the requirements to do a job, measure gaps in performance and then design instruction (cf. Kilman, 1984), or do we want a more substantial base?

Relating Needs Assessment and Needs Analyses

Needs are gaps in results (Kaufman, 1972, 1982). Using the OEM, there are three types of results, thus three types of needs (those relating to products, outputs, and outcomes). Since there are three types of needs, then there are three types of *needs assessments* (again relating to gaps between "what is" and "what should be" for products, outputs, and outcomes). A needs assessment identifies, justifies, and selects the needs to be closed. After assessing and selecting a need, then a *needs analysis* may be undertaken to identify and document the sources of these needs.

The identification of needs and gaps in processes and inputs (called quasi-needs) is shown in Fig. 5.1 by using the OEM in the two dimensions of "what is" and "what should be." Instruction should be undertaken only when it will: improve human competence and performance, improve job-task performance, and contribute to organizational effectiveness and payoffs.

By using the OEM in this bilevel form, one may identify the *results chain* which leads from useful societal consequences back into organizational and individual payoffs and requirements.

A suggested sequence for determining instructional requirements is the following:

1. Recognize that instruction is a means for closing gaps in performance;

2. Recognize that instruction should be undertaken to close gaps in products (and thus meet product-level needs);

3. Recognize that meeting product-level needs is a first step in meeting output-level needs, and these in turn should be linked to meeting outcome-level needs;

4. Identify gaps in outcomes, and then relate these to gaps in outputs;

5. Based upon output gaps to be closed, identify products gaps to be closed, and then identify those which may be closed most effectively and efficiently using instruction (here is where needs analysis is useful);

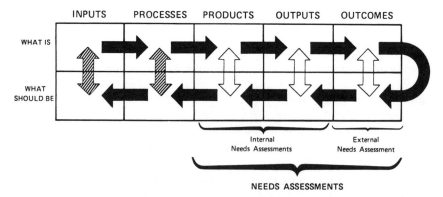

FIGURE 5.1. Relation of *what is* and *what should be* in inputs, processes, products, outputs, and outcomes. Vertical arrows depict gaps that define needs. From Thiagarajan (1984). Reprinted by permission of the copyright owner, National Society for Performance and Instruction.

6. After selecting a performance area which may be properly improved through instruction and the consequent individual competence, which has been documented and justified—based upon the product needs and the resulting performance requirements—perform a job-task analysis to determine the requirements for successfully completing a specific job or task;

7. Based upon the job-task analysis, perform a learning-task analysis to identify those en-route human competencies which must be attained.

8. Select the means and media (processes) to be used (Reiser and Gagné, 1983, provide some guidance on selecting media); remember that all problems are not best solved by instruction (Thiagarajan, 1984);

9. Design and develop the appropriate intervention (possibly instructional); use formative evaluation procedures to assure its preliminary utility, and revise as required;

10. Implement, and collect performance data;

11. Perform summative and goal-free evaluations to determine the extent to which needs have been met; ideally, this evaluation should examine the extent to which needs at all three levels have been met;

12. Revise as required.

SPECIFYING OBJECTIVES

When one has identified a need, then the "what should be" part of that statement is an objective. It meets all of the qualifications as defined by Gagné and Briggs (1979) and by Mager (1975). In addition to the Gagné and Briggs definition, it has specific criteria which will allow the determination of when the objective has been met.

Many practitioners have been concerned with the criteria to be used in writing a measurable objective. Some have claimed that "measurability" results in dehumanization, or capturing the trivial: only unimportant things are easily measurable. While it is true that trival and even destructive events may be written in measurable performance terms, it does not follow that important, useful things cannot.

One way to calibrate the criteria to be employed for a statement of intended results is by noting that some consequences are more suitable for precise, reliable statements of intention than are others, based upon the degree of one's knowledge about the phenomenon. We may state our intended results and select a scale of measurement for these consequences based upon how much we know about the underlying basis for the required result. For example, we may be able to measure precisely the tolerance for setting the focus on a laser-beam generator, but we may not know more about the operator's required personality other than to say that he or she must be "stable." We may appropriately use different scales of criterion measures for different kinds of results.

The determination of criteria to use in a measurable objective may be classified as follows (Kaufman, 1972, 1982):

Type of Results	Scale of Measurement Used
Goal, aim, purpose	Nominal, ordinal
Objective	Interval, ratio

If we only know that an operator must be "stable," then we measure that intention with a nominal (naming) scale. If we were able to state that supervising operators must be taller than their subordinates (so they may see over their shoulders when they are working) then we use an ordinal (greater than, less than, or equal to) scale. Because these are not as precise as other measurement possibilities (another ordinal measure) we label them as "goals," or "aims," or "purposes," simply to indicate their level of precision.

When we know more about the underlying bases for our intentions, then we can be more precise. If we know that our laser focus must be within 5° of the central locus, then we may allow some error, and thus our results are measurable on an interval (an arbitrary zero point, but with equal scale distance between measurement points) scale. If the laser-beam generator has to be certified by the federal inspector as safe and operable on or before June 4, and put out no more than 11.7 units of delta radiation in any 1-hour period, then we have an exact calibration for results measurable on a ratio scale (known zero point with equal scale distances). The more precise we can sensibly be, the greater are our chances to design and evaluate correctly.

This formulation also allows for latitude in indicating expectations. We do not have to "force" our statements of expected results when we do not know enough about them to write an objective. Not all requirements have to be objectives, so when we are not fully aware of the precise result required, we may state it as precisely as our knowledge will allow. However, it does not make sense to define an expected result loosely when we could be quite precise about it: We should not write a goal when we could provide an objective.

When possible, the purposes and expected results of any intervention should be based upon objectives using interval-or ratio-scale measurements. Additionally, when identifying and documenting needs, the gaps between "what is" and "what should be" should also be based upon gaps measured in interval- or ratio-scale terms.

Because there are three types of needs, there may be three levels of objectives associated with each. Those objectives associated with instructional interventions, however, are at the *product* level.

Using needs and then associated derived objectives, the requirements for instruction and the application of instructional technology may be correctly identified and documented. Only by linking, through the results chain, the instructional requirements with organizational payoffs may our technology be truly useful.

The OEM is only useful when put to work. When identifying and resolving problems, the presenting performance symptoms are usually at the process or product level. It is easy for an instructional technologist to simply go in, make a "quick fix," measure a change in performance, and leave. The tools and techniques of *instructional systems* provide ample guidance on what to do. But the professional concern for the usefulness of the intervention is also appropriate.

The following section describes an array of tools, techniques, and approaches which are available. These include needs assessment, needs analysis, instructional design, instructional delivery, evaluation. These all are related to the OEM. Needs assessments relate to products, outputs, and outcomes. Needs analyses are usually restricted to products and outputs. Instructional design relates to stating products (as objective) and then designing and developing the most appropriate processes (methods and means) to achieve them. Instructional delivery is a process. Evaluation compares one's results with their objectives, and thus relates them to products, outputs, and outcomes. The tools of application for specifying requirements and designing instruction may next be examined with the realization of their linking to the OEM.

Specifying instructional requirements amounts to preparing a blueprint for the objectives (or goals), content, materials, methods, and evaluation procedures for the instructional system. These specifications are based on a number of procedures, including needs assessment, needs analysis, systems analysis, performance/task analysis, learner analysis, and media/mode/methods selection. These assessment analysis procedures are applied to three interrelated systems: *instructional design, instructional delivery, and the receiving system.* These terms are defined (and components described) in the following section.

Elements of an Instructional System

The definition of instructional system that takes into account inputs, processes, and products can be formulated in terms of the system's objectives, content, materials and equipment, methods, and evaluation procedures. For example, the objectives for a training workshop for the secretarial staff involve the measurable mastery of a word-processing system. The content for this workshop includes menus, entering text, editing text, copying and moving text, finding and replacing text, and formatting. The materials for the workshop include a workbook, CAI discs, and the word-processing software. The equipment includes a microcomputer. The workshop method involves initial introductory demonstration by a workshop leader, followed by individual practice through a series of graded exercises. This combination of demonstration and practice is repeated with each unit of the content. For evaluation purposes, at the end of each unit, the students are required to apply their skills to edit sample files on a floppy disc. At the end of the workshop, there is a final test which involves the students in typing from a manuscript, proofreading, making corrections, and making revisions according to the changes required in an edited document.

Another example of an instructional system is a printed module on social studies for first grade Liberian children. The objective for this module is for the children to identify correctly and describe several common Liberian foods and their individual contributions to the human diet. The content includes Liberian food, words associated with food—food from animals, food from plants, the demand for food, and important dietary contributions. The material is a programmed teaching module which includes pictures, words, and sentences for the children to see and directions for the teacher to follow. The method involves the teacher's interacting with a group of children. The teacher holds up the booklet and follows the direction in small print on each page. These directions require the teacher to point to some picture, word, or sentence, make a brief explanatory statement, ask a question, give a signal to elicit a choral response from the students, and reinforce or correct the students. The method of evaluation involves asking a series of individual oral questions at the end of the module and comparing the responses with performance standards.

Specifying the instructional requirements relates to all five elements of the instructional system. A complete specification of the instructional requirements will include objectives, content, materials, method, and evaluation. Details of these five elements are listed in Fig. 5.2. Such a specification of instructional requirements provides us with a blueprint for instructional system development and use. When conducting instructional systems activities, check the list to assure you are accounting for all the important dimensions.

Three Systems Related to Instructional Design and Use

Specification of instructional requirements should take into account the concerns of three different groups: the designers, the deliverers, and the receivers. The design system produces the instructional package. The delivery system manages the interaction between the package and the learners. The receiving system utilizes the increased skills, knowledge, and products of the learners.

The design system may include subject-matter experts from the content area. They may determine the objectives and the content for the instructional system if no other objective planning and analysis data are available. The

```
1.  OBJECTIVES/GOALS                                    4.1.3:  Implementation
1.1:  Rationale                                            4.1.3.1:  Introduction/readiness
   1.1.1:  Societal needs                                  4.1.3.2:  Instructional objectives
   1.1.2:  Organizational needs                            4.1.3.3:  Motivation
   1.1.3:  Individual needs                                4.1.3.4:  Information
1.2:  Broader Purposes and Intentions                      4.1.3.5:  Response elicitation
   1.2.1:  Student attitude toward subject-matter area     4.1.3.6:  Feedback
   1.2.2:  Student attitude toward instruction             4.1.3.7:  Branching decision
   1.2.3:  Socialization                                   4.1.3.8:  Practice
   1.2.4:  Independent study skills                        4.1.3.9:  Supporting application
   1.2.5:  Student self-image                           4.1.4:  Follow up
1.3:  Learner objectives                                   4.1.4.1:  Summarizing
   1.3.1:  Cognitive                                       4.1.4.2:  Reviewing/rehearsal
   1.3.2:  Affective                                       4.1.4.3:  Remediation
   1.3.3:  Psychomoter                                     4.1.4.4:  Enrichment
   1.3.4:  Interpersonal                                   4.1.4.5:  Supporting application
1.4:  Specific Objectives                             4.2:  Student role and functions
   1.4.1:  Overall mission objectives                      4.2.1:  Overall role of the learners
   1.4.2:  Enabling objectives                             4.2.2:  Preparation
1.5:  Goals/Objectives from Other Points of View              4.2.2.1:  Acquiring prerequisite skills
   1.5.1:  Trainer-centered                                   4.2.2.2:  Selecting learning modes
   1.5.2:  Administrative                                     4.2.2.3:  Previewing
   1.5.3:  Subject-matter                                  4.2.3:  Participation
   1.5.4:  Client-centered                                    4.2.3.1:  Receiving information
1.6:  Delivery System Objectives                             4.2.3.2:  Responding
   1.6.1:  Cost-effectiveness                                 4.2.3.3:  Receiving feedback
   1.6.2:  Efficiency                                         4.2.3.4:  Practicing
   1.6.3:  Interest level                                  4.2.4:  Follow up
   1.6.4:  Ease of adoption                                   4.2.4.1:  Remedial/revision activities
2.  CONTENT                                                   4.2.4.2:  Enrichment activities
2.1:  Scope                                                   4.2.4.3:  Application activities
2.2:  Sequence                                       5.  STUDENT ASSESSMENTS
2.3:  Topics covered                                 5.1:  Purpose of student assessment
   2.3.1:  Total package                                   5.1.1:  Formative
   2.3.2:  Units                                           5.1.2:  Summative/goal free
   2.3.3:  Lessons                                         5.1.3:  Entry testing
2.4:  Types of content                                      5.1.4:  Criterion testing
   2.4.1:  Core                                            5.1.5:  Diagnostic
   2.4.2:  Optional                                        5.1.6:  Cognitive
   2.4.3:  Enrichment                                      5.1.7:  Affective
2.5:  Range of coverage                                     5.1.8:  Psychomotor
2.6:  Extent of coverage                                    5.1.9:  Interpersonal
2.7:  Relationships to other jobs, products,         5.2:  Types of measuring instruments
        organizational outputs, and societal              5.2.1:  Criterion referenced
        consequences                                       5.2.2:  Norm referenced
3.  MATERIALS                                               5.2.3:  Paper and pencil
3.1:  Components                                            5.2.4:  Performance tests
   3.1.1:  Mainstream                                      5.2.5:  Attitude scales
   3.1.2:  Supplementary                                   5.2.6:  Questionnaires
   3.1.3:  Reference                                       5.2.7:  Transfer tests
3.2:  Support materials                                     5.2.8:  Entry tests
   3.2.1:  Teacher training                                5.2.9:  Pretests
   3.2.2:  Administrative                                  5.2.10:  Posttests
   3.2.3:  Evaluation                                      5.2.11:  Delayed posttests
   3.2.4:  Follow-up                                       5.2.12:  Unit tests
3.3:  Physical requirements                                 5.2.13:  Built-in test items
   3.3.1:  Media                                           5.2.14:  Self-tests
   3.3.2:  Length                                      5.3:  Assessment activities
   3.3.3:  Cost                                            5.3.1:  Teacher/implementer activities
      3.3.3.1:  Installation cost                              5.3.1.1:  Test preparation
      3.3.3.2:  Recurrent cost                                 5.3.1.2:  Student preparation
                Package cost                                   5.3.1.3:  Test administrations
                Annual cost per trainee                        5.3.1.4:  Scoring of tests
   3.3.4:  Print size, typestyle, etc.                        5.3.1.5:  Analysis of results
   3.3.5:  Media production specifications                   5.3.1.6:  Reporting results/making recommendations
4.  METHODS                                                   5.3.1.7:  Using the results
4.1:  Teacher/delivery vehicle role and functions       5.3.2:  Student activities
   4.1.1:  Overall role of the teacher                       5.3.2.1:  Preparation
   4.1.2:  Preparation                                       5.3.2.2:  Test taking
      4.1.2.1:  Lesson preparation                            5.3.2.3:  Utilizing the feedback
      4.1.2.2:  Materials preparation                         5.3.2.4:  Applying mastered skills, knowledges,
      4.1.2.3:  Student preparation                                     and abilities in other contexts
      4.1.2.4:  Facilities, equipment, and materials                   (e.g. work, life)
                preparation
      4.1.2.5:  Time requirements
      4.1.2.6:  Learning environment requirements
```

FIGURE 5.2. Possible elements of the five components of an instructional system.

design system also includes instructional designers with a competency in learning theories and educational psychology. They determine the sequence of presentation, method, and evaluation procedure. The design system also includes methods and media production specialists who convert the objectives and the specification into an actual instructional system.

The delivery system includes the learners, teachers, several members of the support staff (such as librarians and media projection specialists), and administrative personnel (such as principals and supervisors).

The receiving system is the society and the organization or institution which benefits from the increased skills and knowledge of the learners who successfully complete the content of the delivery system. The receiving system consists of clients, consumers, society, the organization, and supervisors.

To return to our examples, the design system for the word-processing workshop includes: specialists in the word-processing system and microcomputers; instructional designers who come up with a blueprint for the workshop package; typists, printers, and computer programmers (who produce the CAI parts of the package). The delivery system consists of the trainees and workshop leaders. They are supported by clerical staff (who assemble and package the materials, arrange the workshop schedule, negotiate with organizations which want to conduct in-house workshops, and check to make sure that there are enough doughnuts and coffee). The receiving system is the organization (nested in a society of consumers) at which the trainees with their improved skills return to work. These could be different organizations if the workshop were open to the general public or a single, specific organization if it were conducted in-house.

In our second example, the design system consists of experts in Liberian food and nutrition, elementary educators, instructional designers, teacher trainers, typists, and illustrators. The delivery system includes children in the first grade of Liberian schools, their teachers, headmasters, supervisors, district education officers, and regional education officers. The receiving system could be the second-grade classrooms, or through a shift in our vantage point, the local community and the Liberian society at large. (In most cases there are multiple levels of receiving systems.)

To return to our word-processing workshop example, and assuming that the workshop is conducted as an in-house training activity of a bank, the receiving system is the bank. The bank, in turn, has a number of receiving systems including local business and industry. All of these clients of the bank have other receiving systems. If we continue tracking this chain, society (the outcome element) becomes the superordinate receiving system. Further on, humanity as a whole is the ultimate receiving system of all instruction (Kanter, 1983; Kaufman, 1982; Pascale & Athos, 1983; Peters & Waterman, 1982).

PROCEDURES FOR SPECIFYING REQUIREMENTS

Instructional requirements are specified through several interrelated procedures. Most of these procedures are undertaken at the beginning of an instructional-system development project. Typically, however, each procedure is repeated frequently to provide refined specifications with more detail. The initial set of requirements may be a tentative starting point. These requirements are modified and fine tuned as instructional designers proceed through stages of development of the system. The number of times the instructional requirements are revised seems to depend on the designer's familiarity with the subject-matter area, the database from which needs and associated performance requirements are derived, types of learners, and the instructional context.

The different procedures for specifying instructional requirements include:

Needs assessment. This is the procedure for identifying (and prioritizing) needs related to societal, organizational, and human performance. Again, needs are gaps in results. The needs are derived from the vantage points of the receiving systems and of the society. There are two types of needs data which may be collected and used: controlled observations of actual performance (called "soft" data because of the perception base). Frequently (and unfortunately) only perceptions of gaps in performance and consequences are used in needs assessments while both types (Fig. 5.3) of data should be used.

Needs analysis. This is the procedure for analyzing the needs identified earlier to determine their underlying causes. During this procedure needs that cannot be efficiently and effectively met through the design of instruction are shifted to alternative interventions.

Systems analysis. This is the procedure for identifying the elements, interrelationships, resources, and restraints of the different subsystems—in OEM terms, inputs, processes, products, and outputs. This analysis reveals critical variables in the receiving system which are likely to facilitate or interfere with the effectiveness of the trained individual.

Systems analysis also identifies the elements, interrelationships, resources, and restraints of the delivery system which manages the training effort. This enables us to produce instructional packages that are compatible with the available resources and restraints in the context in which they are going to be used. Similarly, systems analysis deals with the elements, interrelationships, resources and restraints of the design system which is responsible for the production of the instructional package. It enables us to identify areas where additional information, expertise, and resources are required.

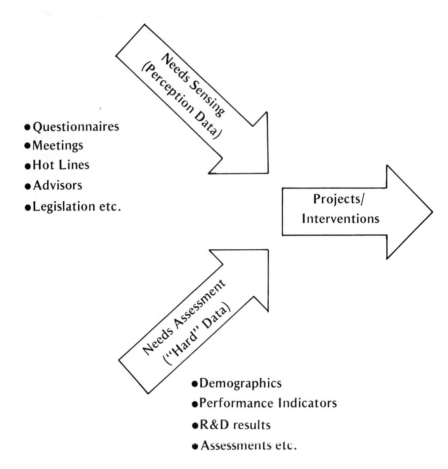

- Questionnaires
- Meetings
- Hot Lines
- Advisors
- Legislation etc.

- Demographics
- Performance Indicators
- R&D results
- Assessments etc.

FIGURE 5.3.   Needs assessment involves objective performance discrepancies as well as perceived gaps (Copyright 1986 by Roger Kaufman).

Performance/task analysis. Needs assessment leads to performance specifications and purposes, and needs analysis helps us identify the objectives for instruction. Performance/task analysis helps us identify specific objectives which will help the trainees achieve the overall purposes. In this procedure various concepts, skills, and informational content to be taught to the learners are identified and analyzed.

Learner analysis.   Learners are an element of the delivery systems, and they are included in the earlier systems analysis. However, they play such an important role in specifying instructional requirements that analysis of the characteristics of the learners deserves a special focus. In this procedure, those characteristics of the learners which are likely to influence their interaction with instruction are identified and analyzed. These factors are, of course, inputs.

Media and mode selection. This is the procedure for selecting appropriate media (e.g., print, videotape, interactive video-disc, or audiotape) and modes (e.g., computer-assisted instruction, programmed instruction, or simulation games) for instruction. (In OEM terms, these are processes.) This procedure uses information from earlier assessment and analyses and selects media and modes on the basis of the instructional goals and objectives, learner characteristics, and resources and restraints in various systems.

Fig. 5.4 summarizes the dimensions and variables. The focus of this section is on needs assessment, needs analysis, and systems analysis. Performance/task analysis is the content of the following chapter. This chapter considers briefly the analysis of learner characteristics. In chapter 8 learner characteristics are treated in greater detail.

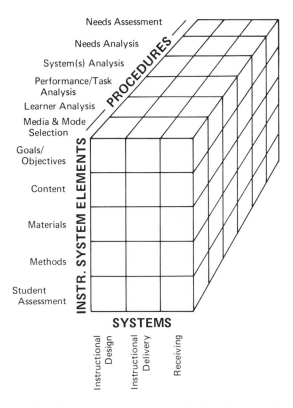

FIGURE 5.4.   Relations among components of instructional requirements.

NEEDS ANALYSIS

This procedure enables us to select from the needs identified during the earlier needs assessment those which can benefit from an instructional intervention. This analysis ensures that we do not apply an instructional solution to an noninstructional problem.

Performance technology (of which instructional technology may be considered a subset) assumes that performance requirements may be generated from a variety of factors. Different types of causes imply different types of intervention. Most performance problems have multiple causes, and performance engineering suggests that we should use appropriate solutions to reduce or eliminate the primary causes.

Gilbert (1978) differentiated between performance problems caused by a lack of skills and knowledge and those caused by a lack of motivation. This insight has been expanded upon by Rummler (1976), Harless (1970), Mager and Pipe (1970), Tosti (1981), Zigon (1983), and Harmon (1984). The following paragraphs describe various possible causes of performance problems.

Superordinate system discrepancies. Performance problems may be created by inappropriate standards, policies, procedures, and actions undertaken by the larger system of which the organization we are studying is a part. As an example of this type of cause for a performance requirement, Harmon (1984) identifies a sales group (the organization being studied) unable to perform effectively because the prices set by the parent company are too high. To give another example, a lack of production among word-processor operators may be traced to the tight corporate budget preventing the purchase of appropriate software packages, or to unreliability of the hardware. Functional policies, not instruction, are required.

Management discrepancies. The management of a specific organization (or a unit) may contribute to some performance requirements. For example, selection and recruitment procedures may be at fault by hiring employees who do not have the requisite skills, competencies, and attitudes. Management procedures may have resulted in unclear or unrealistic standards, policies, and procedures. Management may also use inappropriate work and supervisory procedures. Instruction to workers cannot reduce or remedy performance problems caused by management deficits. Management may have selected the wrong marketable items. What is required are responsive management procedures.

Motivational discrepancies. Often individuals and organizations are capable of appropriate performances but are not motivated to perform. They may lack commitment to the mission, goals, and activities. This lack of commitment could be owing to confusion of what they are supposed to do or to a feeling of meaninglessness and inviability of what they do. Similarly, another motivational deficit could be the lack of feedback on how they are performing, or the lack of incentives for delivering appropriate or excellent performance. It is also possible that in some situations appropriate performance is followed by punishment (e.g., in the classic case of people who complete their chores early being given more chores to do). Similarly, the task could be dull and boring, thus reducing the performance of the individual, or it could be so exciting and dangerous as to immobilize the performer. There could be distractions in the environment, preventing the performer from being able to concentrate on the task. Training cannot eliminate performance problems caused by motivational deficits. What is required is better motivation, incentive, and feedback systems.

Environmental discrepancies. Often the performers are capable of performing the task and are willing to do it. However, they may be prevented from accomplishing the task because of environmental restraints. For example, the temperature, or illumination, or ventilation in the workplace may not be conducive to high rate or quality of performance. The performer may lack the required tools, equipment, and materials. The furniture and facilities may be inappropriately designed, causing fatigue. Training cannot reduce performance problems caused by environmental deficits. What is required is better facilities design in accordance with principles of human factors engineering.

Interpersonal discrepancies. The lack of acceptable performance can be because of interpersonal problems in the organization. For example, members of a unit may lack team spirit and may compete excessively with each other. There could be communications problems in presenting the goals or in providing formative feedback. There could be personality conflicts and political clashes. These interpersonal problems can contribute to slow, low-quality performance. Additional training on job-related skills will not improve the performance in a situation plagued by interpersonal problems. What are required are procedures for successful organizational development, team building, and effective communication.

Health discrepancies. Even under ideal conditions, a performer who is ill cannot deliver peak performance. Job-related training cannot adequately compensate for deficits in physical or emotional health. What is required is individual therapy and preventive medicine.

Skill and knowledge discrepancies. The lack of acceptable performance can sometimes be attributed to an ignorance of basic concepts, or perhaps incompetence on the part of the performers. In this context, finally, the appropriate intervention may be instruction (or it could be selction or assignment).

Different causes of performance problems are listed in Fig. 5.3. The categories in this system are not mutually exclusive. Also, most performance problems are caused by a combination of these deficits.

Several approaches for systematically analyzing performance requirements, to identify the most critical deficits, are available. These include the performance audit (Gilbert, 1978), front-end analysis (Harless, 1970), analyzing performance problems (Mager & Pipe, 1970), and the performance audit (Rummler, 1976).

Needs Assessment and Analysis at Different Levels

Needs assessment and analysis are initially undertaken with a focus on the receiving system. This enables us to identify the societal (outcome) performance problems and to isolate those which lend themselves to instructional solutions.

After we have located skill and knowledge discrepancies, we may then specify the goals for instruction. After we have selected problem areas where instruction is appropriate and derived the goals for instruction, we may repeat the needs assessment and analysis processes with a focus on the delivery and then the design system; we may apply it at each level of the *results chain.* After all, teaching and learning are skilled performances and these performances can be enhanced in a variety of ways.

By applying needs-analysis procedures to the instructional-design and delivery systems, we may identify the standards, policies, plans, and procedures of the receiving organization which interfere with or facilitate effective instruction of its employees. It is possible to identify management characteristics related to the provision and supervision of instruction within the organization. There could also be motivational discrepancies which prevent the trainers from effective teaching and trainees from effective learning. Environmental discrepancies related to physical facilities, materials, tools, and equipment for instruction may also be present. There could be personality conflicts between trainers and trainees and inappropriate interactions among the trainees. Trainees may lack effective skills for learning, and trainers may lack basic skills for instruction. Hence, through the application of needs analysis, any of these factors may be revealed as requirements for instruction.

Systems Analysis

Needs analysis enables us to identify those needs that can be met through instruction. Systems analysis, to be described, enables us to identify the key features of systems that are likely to influence the design and appropriate delivery of instruction.

The effectiveness of an instructional package is a function of both its design and its delivery. It is also a function of the receiving system. If we do not take the characteristics of all three systems into consideration, the instructional package may end up being useless. We must identify the resources and the restraints in the various systems for the optimum design and delivery of the training package. We do this by undertaking a systems analysis of the three different systems, usually parallel to each other.

Information about the design system, the delivery system, and the receiving system are obtained from several key people in these systems. These people may include members of the target population, their supervisors at work, trainers, administrators, and clients. A primary question asked during the systems analysis is: What is the mission of this particular system (or subsystem)? There could be a difference between the stated mission of the system, the perceived mission, and various hidden agendas. Also we should identify different people involved in the system and the ways in which they are grouped together. Groups of people may form subsystems with specific interrelationships. We should find out the inputs provided to various people (or groups), what they are supposed to do with them, and what they actually do. We should also discover the products, outputs, outcomes of each system.

Resources facilitate the required performance and restraints hinder them. The resources available to each system (or subsystem) will include personnel, budget, time, tools, and facilities. The restraints are the other sides of the same coins: restraints in each system (or subsystem) also relate to personnel, budget, time, tools, and facilities.

During systems analyses, we also collect information on the flow of information within and between the systems. The types of information include statements about goals, missions, directives, and feedback.

Learner Analysis

The learners for whom instruction is intended are a critical factor in its design, delivery, and utilization. In the design system, the learners are the target population toward which all instruction is to be aimed. In the delivery system, they are both recipients and potential resources. In the receiving system, their performance is a key variable. Although learners are an important part of all the earlier analyses, a separate learner analysis is usually undertaken by the design system. This analysis begins with a clear definition of the target population—the group of people for whom instruction is intended. Learner analysis ends with an identification of those characteristics of the target population which are likely to influence the design, delivery, and utilization of instruction.

These products of learner analysis affect all aspects of instruction. The objectives for instruction have to be made realistic and compatible with the entry skills of the learners. The content of instruction and the starting point also depend on what the learners already know. Learner characteristics also determine the media and the method of instruction.

Initial definitions of the target population that are too broad (e.g., all TV viewers) or too narrow (e.g., Roger, Thiagarajan) are equally undesirable, but for different reasons. Learner analysis is usually a self-correcting process; we may begin with a broad definition of the target population and in the process of identifying its characteristics we may identify subgroups which require distinct treatments.

Thousands of characteristics of the target population may be analyzed during this procedure. In order to obtain cost-effective information, we should focus on those characteristics which influence the effects of instruction. Some major characteristics to be taken into account are shown in Fig. 5.4. They include factors described in following paragraphs.

Experiences of the learners which are related to the skill, knowledge, and attitudes dealt with in an instructional package form a major component of the learner analysis. Existing knowledge in relevant areas should be carefully gauged. A special aspect of this analysis is identification of misconceptions which the learners bring to the instructional situation and which inhibit their learning. Trainees have to unlearn their previous misconceptions before they can master the new concepts. Among the entry skills, there could be some which interfere with the acquisition of the new skills. For example, in the word-processor training situation, learners' familiarity with the configuration of a previous keyboard may interfere with their mastery of a new one in which the backspace and margin release keys are reversed.

Attitude toward the instructional content is another area for learner analysis. Attitudes might be either positive or negative toward the entire content. It is also possible that the learners have positive attitudes toward some of the elements of the instructional content and negative attitudes toward others.

Most instruction involves language, and we obtain information about learners' language levels. We gather information about their reading level, listening comprehension level, and expressive language skills. If the instruction involves heavy use of nonverbal sources of information, we collect data on the learners' level of visual literacy. In addition to competency levels, we explore learners' language preferences. Among the elements of language preference are style, vocabulary, sentence types, and length of sentence and paragraphs.

Skills related to learning are another part of learner analysis. These include such skills as note taking, scheduling, outlining, memorizing, and test taking. They also include skills related to the specific instructional medium and mode. For example, learning from television requires special strategies, and participating in an instructional simulation game requires collaborative learning and interpersonal skills. In addition to collecting information on learner skills, we should collect information of instructional preferences of the learners. These preferences include media choices (e.g., whether the learners would like to learn through audiotape, print, or videotape), and mode preferences (whether for learner self-instruction, small-group instruction, or teacher-mediated instruction).

Learner analysis focuses on the characteristics of a typical learner. It attempts to average the data collected during this analysis to optimize the instructional requirements. However, our learner analysis may reveal that the target population comes in two or more distinct subgroups with separate clusters of characteristics. It may also reveal that the learners are so diverse and heterogeneous that a flexible branching and individualizing approach is required.

SPECIFICATION OF METHODS, MEDIA, MODES

A critical element in specifying the instructional requirements is the selection of the primary instructional media and modes. The medium is the vehicle through which the instructional message is transmitted. Radio, television, print, and audiotapes are some of the media used in instruction. The mode is the collection of strategies and procedures through which instruction is delivered. For example, programmed instruction, lectures, and simulations and games are some of the instructional modes. Often, different media can be utilized with the same instructional mode. For example, programmed instruction can be presented through print, audiotape, videotape, or computer.

During the media and mode selection activity, we identify the suitable instructional medium (and mode) and specify the requirements for instruction in terms of these two components. Certain media are more cost-effective than others for instruction of certain types of learning and for certain types of learners. Hence specifying the instructional mode enables us to name the most appropriate medium. Similarly, different instructional modes are suited for different types of learning, types of learners, and delivery systems.

The media- and mode-selection activity is undertaken after some tentative needs assessment and analysis, task analysis, systems analysis, and learner analysis. Initial assessment and analysis is then refined on the basis of media and mode selection. For example, we may select audiotapes and lectures as the appropriate media and mode based on preliminary learner preferences. This choice enables us to refine the learner analyses with specific requirements of the medium and the mode. For example, we can now identify learner skills related to the use of audiotapes, preferences toward styles of spoken language, note taking skills, and the ability to use tape recorders.

In general, the procedure for media and mode selection involves matching the needs, resources, and restraints on the one hand and the attributes of different instructional media and modes on the other. The most effective approach to familiarizing oneself with the attributes of different media and modes is actually to experience instructional design in that medium or mode.

Failing this direct, design experience, we should have access to knowledgeable people in relevant areas.

There are three aspects of instruction which have to be taken into consideration in selecting the optimal media and mode: design system, delivery system, and the receiving system. We begin by identifying the attributes required by the instructional goals and objectives. For example, the task of training word-processor operators requires a high degree of realism, and tactile input capabilities. We then identify attributes that are required by the type of learner. For example, in the extreme case of a group of visually impaired learners, auditory capability for the medium is critical. We list the media attributes required (or restraints imposed) by the delivery system. For example, if we are working in a remote village in a developing nation, electricity may not be available. We take this fact into account as a critical restraint. On the other hand, sufficient numbers of competent, literate volunteers may be available in the local community. This resource should also be taken into account. We list the media equipment available in the delivery system as well as equipment which is not available. Production resources and restraints also play a critical role in media and mode selection. For example, if we have a printing press, that is a resource. If there is no one on our staff who is familiar with Computer Assisted Instruction (CAI) authoring languages, that is a restraint. This part of media and mode selection is based on our systems analysis, and takes into account both material and human resources and restraints.

We match the attributes of different media (and modes) with the requirements, resources, and restraints, and identify alternative media which provide all of the critical requirements. If more than one medium (or mode) can provide these requirements, we compare these alternatives, along with logistic and cost considerations, and select the most appropriate combination.

For more detailed discussion of the selection of instructional media, consult the book by Reiser and Gagné (1983). Several instructional modes (labeled as designs) are treated in detail in a series of practical books edited by Langdon (1978, 1980).

SUMMARY

Identifying and specifying requirements for instruction requires us to move through a *results chain*. Needs and associated performance requirements are based upon gaps in societal results, organizational results, and individual contributions. From the identified and documented needs, an analysis of the causes and origin of discrepancies will provide data on interventions which will be successful. When the intervention of choice is instructional, various targeted analyses will provide useful objectives and requirements for instructional design and development.

REFERENCES

Branson, R. K., Rayner, G. T., Cox, J. L., Furman, J. P., King, F. J., & Hannum, W. H. (1975). *Interservice procedures for instructional systems development. Phases I, II, III, IV, V, and executive summary.* (TRADOC Pamphlet 350–30). Fort Monroe, VA: U.S. Army Training and Doctrine Command.

Carter, R. K. (1983). *The accountable agency. Human Service Guide No. 34.* Beverly Hills, CA: Sage.

Dick, W., and Carey, L. (1985). *The systematic design of instruction* (2nd Ed.). Glenview, IL: Scott, Foresman.

Gagné, R. M. (1985). *The conditions of learning* (4th ed.). New York: Holt, Rinehart and Winston.

Gagné, R. M., & Briggs, L. J. (1979). *Principles of instructional design* (2nd ed.). New York: Holt, Rinehart and Winston.

Gilbert, T. F. (1978). *Human competence: Engineering worthy performance.* New York: McGraw-Hill.

Harless, J. (1970). *An ounce of analysis is worth a pound of objectives.* Newnan, GA: Harless Performance Guild.

Harmon, P. (1984). A hierarchy of performance variables. *Performance and Instruction, 23*(10), 27–28.

Kanter, R. M. (1983). *The change masters: Innovation & entrepreneurship in the American corporation.* New York: Simon & Schuster.

Kaufman, R. A. (1972). *Educational system planning.* New York: Prentice-Hall.

Kaufman, R. (1982). *Identifying and solving problems: A system approach* (3rd ed.). San Diego, CA: University Associates.

Kaufman, R. (1985). Linking training to organizational impact. *Journal of Instructional Development, 8,* No. 2.

Kaufman, R. (1983a). A holistic planning model. A system approach for improving organizational effectiveness and impact. *Performance and Instruction Journal, 22*(8), 3–12.

Kaufman, R. (1983b). Planning and organizational improvement terms. *Performance and Instruction Journal, 22*(8) 12–15.

Kaufman, R., and Stone, B. (1983). *Planning for organizational success.* New York: Wiley.

Kilmann, R. H. (1984). *Beyond the quick fix.* San Francisco: Jossey-Bass.

Langdon, D. G. (Ed.). (1978). *Instructional Design Library (Part I)* (20 vol.). Englewood Cliffs, NJ: Educational Technology.

Langdon, D. G. (Ed.). (1980). *Instructional Design Library (Part II)* (20 vol.). Englewood Cliffs, NJ: Educational Technology.

Mager, R. F. (1975). *Preparing instructional objectives* (2nd ed.). Belmont, CA: Pitman.

Mager, R., & Pipe, P. (1970). *Analyzing performance problems.* Belmont, CA: Fearon.

Pascale, R. T. & Athos, A. G. (1981). *The art of Japanese management: Applications for American executives.* New York: Warner Books.

Peters, T. J., & Waterman, R. H., Jr. (1982). *In search of excellence: Lessons from America's best-run companies.* New York: Harper & Row.

Reigeluth C. (Ed.). (1983). *Instructional design theories and models. An overview of their current status.* Hillsdale, NJ: Lawrence Erlbaum Associates.

Reiser, R. A. & Gagné, R. M. (1983). *Selecting media for instruction.* Englewood Cliffs, NJ: Educational Technology.

Rummler, G. (1976). The performance audit. In R. Craig (Ed.), *Training and Development Handbook* (2nd ed.). New York: McGraw-Hill.

Thiagarajan, S. (1984). How to avoid ID. *Performance and Instruction Journal, 23*(4), 6.

Tosti, D. (1981). *Performance based management: Motivating employees.* Boston: Forum Corporation.

Zigon, J. (1983). Performance chain reactions: Performance management the Yellow Freight way. *Performance Management Magazine, 2*(1), 22–25.

AUTHOR NOTES

Roger Kaufman is Professor and Director, Center for Needs Assessment and Planning, Learning Systems Institute, Florida State University.

Sivasailam Thiagarajan is Vice President, Institute for International Research, Inc.

6 Job and Task Analysis

Paul F. Merrill
Brigham Young University

Just as most of us have difficulty in walking a mile in one big step or eating an elephant in one bite, we also find it difficult to learn mathematics or teach someone to read in one step. We must somehow find a way to break down the learning and teaching process into bite-sized chunks. We must also determine which chunks are most important, which should be taught first, and how they are related to one another. The purpose of this chapter is to describe techniques for the analysis of jobs and their associated tasks.

Analysis has proven to be an important process in many fields. The chemist uses qualitative analysis to determine the separate elements in a given compound; the biologist dissects an animal to identify its organs and their relationship to one another; a mechanic breaks down an engine to see how it works; a computer scientist analyzes a procedure in order to write a computer program; and a football coach analyzes the game films of an opposing team to prepare for the next big game. Many problems people face are too large and complex to understand and solve when taken as a whole. Therefore, analytical procedures are used to divide an object, phenomenon, or problem down into its component elements, and to determine how those elements relate to one another and to the whole. Analysis allows us to break down our problems into simpler subproblems which are easier to understand and to address.

Although we could break a watch into components by striking it with a hammer, the resulting pieces would probably not enable us to achieve much of an understanding of how the watch works. The pieces and their relationships would be essentially random. Rather than discovering order, we would find chaos. Obviously, in order for analysis to be productive, we must find and use analysis procedures which identify components with relationships that have some meaning and utility. The analytical procedure used by the chemist would not be very productive for the mechanic. Thus different procedures must be identified and applied to different types of problems. In addition, the same problem may be analyzed from several points of view, using different procedures. Each procedure used could yield a unique set of components and relationships.

Relationships

A relationship is a connection or association between two or more elements. Relationships or connections between elements allow us to place otherwise disparate elements into some predictable sequence or arrangement which organizes elements into units that can be understood. In analyzing jobs and tasks we will find two types of relationships to be very useful: sequential and part–whole.

Sequential relationships. Two or more elements are sequentially related when they are placed in order of succession, one after the other, according to some specified characteristic or scheme. Lines may be ordered sequentially according to their length; musical notes may be sequenced by their pitch; and colors may be sequenced by their wavelengths. Names may be sequenced alphabetically; automobile parts may be sequenced numerically in terms of the order of their assembly; and historical events may be sequenced chronologically. Sequential relationships become very important as we attempt to identify the order in which the steps of a task are to be performed.

Part–whole. Two elements have a part–whole relationship if one is part of the other. A thumb is part of a hand; a page is part of a book; a limb is part of a tree; a battle is part of a war; a minute is part of an hour; and a task is part of a job. The part–whole relationship allows us to break some complex single entity into parts which are less complex. These parts may be further broken down into subparts, which may be further divided into subsubparts, and so on, until simple elements which are easily understood are obtained. This relationship of sub-subparts to subparts and subparts to parts and parts to wholes is hierarchical in nature. The parts are subordinate to the whole, while a part is superordinate to its sub-parts. For example, a ten-speed bicycle may be broken into the frame, the wheels, the brake system, the power train and the steering system. Each of these major systems or parts can be broken into subparts. Thus, bicycle wheels are made up of tires, tubes, rims, spokes, and hubs. A hub subpart can be further disassembled into the subsubparts: axle, bearings, casing, locknuts, and washers.

A part–whole relationship facilitates our understanding of a phenomenon if the individual parts serve some identifiable, independent function. The bicycle described previously could be divided into parts indiscriminately using a hacksaw, but such a division would not be very instructive. Theoretically, if an object has been dissassembled into parts appropriately, it should be possible to reassemble the parts in a straightforward fashion such that the whole will again work properly. This rule of thumb will be examined in greater detail as we discuss analysis techniques.

In order to develop an instructional program which trains individuals to perform effectively on the job, the nature of the job and its component tasks need to be specified clearly. Two different procedures are required to accomplish the needed specification: job analysis and task analysis. Job analysis is a procedure for identifying the component parts or tasks which make up a specific job. The tasks identified through the job-analysis procedure are then further analyzed, using task-analysis procedures. Task analysis identifies the steps of the procedure, which are used to accomplish the task and reveal the relationships between those steps. Job analysis will be examined in the next section, followed by a discussion of task analysis.

JOB ANALYSIS

A job is defined as a set of duties, responsibilities, or tasks assigned to, or performed by a given position or worker. If different individuals perform the same set of tasks, then they are considered to have the same type of job. A job is usually the basic unit for selection, training, and assignment of personnel in the world of work. Examples of jobs include mechanic, schoolteacher, fireman, secretary, car salesperson, nurse, lawyer, scoutmaster, mother.

A job may be analyzed into component tasks according to part–whole relationships. A task is essentially a part of a job. The part–whole hierarchical structure of the components of a job ususally consists of only three levels. In many jobs that involve only a few tasks, there are only two levels. In a three-level structure, the job is first divided into a few major duties. The duties are then further divided into tasks. In a two-level structure, the job is divided directly into a few tasks. In neither case are the tasks further analyzed as part of the job-analysis procedure. That is the purpose of *task analysis,* to be described in a later section.

A job can be analyzed by first identifying the major duties of a task and then breaking the duties into subordinate tasks. However, since the intermediate duty-level is often not necessary, it is generally more efficient to begin at the task level. The recommended procedure for conducting a job analysis consists of the following major steps:

1. Identify the component tasks.
2. Organize the tasks according to relationships between tasks.
3. Produce an appropriate representation of the organized job tasks.

A thorough job analysis requires that several data-collection activities be conducted as part of the first step. Thus, the first step in the job-analysis procedure consists of the following substeps:

1.1 Generate an initial list of job tasks.

1.2 Revise the list based on data from several other sources.

1.3 Validate the list, using data from a sample of jobholders.

The initial list of job tasks can be generated by simply interviewing people who are knowledgeable about the job and asking them to list the tasks that are generally performed by jobholders. This initial list is then revised, based on data obtained from several other sources. Different types of print documents might be available which could serve as alternate sources of information on job tasks. Such a list may not be complete, but it may contain tasks that were omitted from the initial list. A job manual or "how to" book may have been previously published, describing the various tasks involved in performing the job. Trade journals may also provide useful information.

Additional individuals knowledgeable about the job can be interviewed and asked to generate an independent list of job tasks. These new lists can then be compared with the original list. Individuals knowledgeable about the job include jobholders and their supervisors, job trainers, or other job experts.

Two additional ways to obtain information about job tasks include observing an individual actually performing the job or having jobholders maintain a log of their activities on the job. Both of these techniques require considerable time and expense. For many jobs it may be insufficient to use either of these techniques to collect data across only a few days. Many of the tasks that are actually part of the job may not be performed by the jobholder during the period when data are collected. However, these techniques can be useful when combined with the interviews mentioned earlier.

After the initial list has been revised, based on data from several different sources, the list should be validated. The validation procedure requires the preparation of a survey questionnaire which is administered to a representative sample of jobholders. The questionnaire should be constructed to enable job incumbents to rate each of the job tasks identified in the previous step, according to several factors, such as importance, how often the task is performed, the percentage of time spent performing, and difficulty of learning the task. The questionnaire should also allow for the jobholders to add to the list tasks that may have been omitted.

Job-task titles listed on the questionnaire should be stated precisely and concisely. Since a task is part of a job, it is action oriented. Either the performance of the task itself or the results of performing the task should be observable. Therefore, the task titles should include a verb in the present tense and an object of the verb. The list of job tasks should not contain statements of required abilities, knowledge, or training. Such statements would be appropriate in a job description, but are not considered to be job tasks. Examples and nonexamples of appropriate titles for job tasks are shown in the following list:

Examples	Nonexamples
1. Sort Mail	Responsible for sorting mail
2. Type letters	Ability to type
3. Answer phones	Good speaking voice
4. Make change	Be able to add and subtract
5. Purchase food	Know the four basic food groups
6. Interview client	Understand the principles of good interviewing
7. Discipline students	Assure that proper discipline is maintained
8. Contact parents of truant students	Increase student attendance
9. Conduct class discussion	Have a teaching certificate

After the questionnaire has been prepared, it should be administered to a representative sample of jobholders. The responses should then be summarized and tabulated. The mean rating and percentage of responses for each alternative should be calculated for each job task across all scales on the questionnaire. Figure 6.1 shows a section of a report summarizing the data from a job-analysis survey questionnaire. The questionnaire used to collect these data included only two scales: one to measure the perceived importance of the task and another to determine the perceived need for additional training on specific job tasks. The first column of numbers for each scale indicates the percentage of those surveyed who did not respond to a given item. The next five columns indicate the percentage of responses to each alternative of the scale. Thus, for the first task, "prepare and distribute flyers," 2% rated the task as "not important," 35% rated the task as "very important," and 24% rated the task as "extremely important." The last column for each scale gives the mean rating for each task. Thus, the mean rating for task number 6, "contact personal acquaintances," is 4.06 or "very important."

The summarized questionnaire data can be used to generate a final list of job tasks. Tasks which were included on the questionnaire but are hardly ever performed by the respondents should be considered for elimination from

Sales Manager's Questionnaire Data

Instructions	Scale A	Scale B
Please rate the following job tasks by circling the appropriate number under each scale.	How IMPORTANT is the performance of this task to success in your business?	I would like more EDUCATION/TRAINING on this task.
	1. Not important 2. Somewhat important 3. Fairly important 4. Very important 5. Extremely important	1. Strongly Disagree 2. Disagree 3. Neutral 4. Agree 5. Strongly Agree

Sales Manager Tasks	NR	Percentages 1	2	3	4	5	Mean	NR	Percentages 1	2	3	4	5	Mean
1. Prepare and distribute flyers.	9	2	15	15	35	24	3.71	13	0	4	31	28	24	3.83
2. Advertise in newspapers	6	24	20	11	20	19	2.88	15	4	7	33	13	28	3.63
3. Advertise on radio	9	37	20	9	11	13	2.37	17	6	13	33	11	20	3.33
4. Prepare and send direct mail notices.	9	9	15	22	24	20	3.35	19	2	6	30	26	19	3.66
5. Seek and obtain referrals.	7	0	2	11	33	46	4.34	19	0	4	20	15	43	4.18
6. Contact personal acquaintances.	4	2	7	11	39	37	4.06	19	4	2	28	19	30	3.84
7. Discuss products with new people you meet.	6	0	0	6	31	57	4.55	19	0	2	24	17	39	4.14

FIGURE 6.1.   Summary data from job analysis survey questionnaire.

the list.   New tasks added to the questionnaire list by survey respondents may be added to the final list.

Once the final validated list is determined, the next step is to organize the final list according to relationships among the job tasks.   The tasks could be organized according to part–whole relationships or according to sequential relationships.   If there are more than six or eight job tasks then the possibility for superordinate duties should be examined.   Tasks that are part of the same major function may be grouped together as a duty.   When there is a large number of tasks on the initial list of job tasks, it may be advantageous to organize the tasks into a preliminary part–whole hierarchical structure before the list is validated.   This structure could then be represented on the questionnaire in an indented outline listing the subordinate tasks immediately below their corresponding duty titles. After the survey data are summarized, the hierarchical organization could be revised to reflect the final list of tasks.

The job tasks may also be organized according to several different sequential relationships.   The data obtained for each of the survey-form scales could be used to rank-order the tasks.   Thus, the tasks could be sequenced according to their mean ratings of frequency, difficulty, importance, and so forth. It would also be possible to organize the tasks, using both sequential and part–whole relationships by listing tasks subordinate to each duty in sequential order based on their mean ratings.

The final step of the job analysis is to prepare a report which describes the procedure and multiple sources used to generate the initial list of job tasks, outlines the procedure used to validate the list, summarizes the data obtained from the survey questionnaire, shows various representations of the final list of organized job tasks, and presents recommendations for further analysis, instructional development and training based on the job-analysis results. Figure 6.2 shows parts of a job-analysis report where tasks are organized by duty and listed sequentially within each duty according to mean importance and desire for training ratings.

The job-analysis report can be used to help decide which tasks need to be taught in a formal training situation, which can be taught on the job, and

ORDERED RATINGS OF SALES MANAGER JOB TASKS

IMPORTANCE		DESIRE for TRAINING	
Identifying Prospective Customers Duties			
1. Discuss products with new people you meet.	4.55	1. Seek and obtain referrals	4.18
2. Seek and obtain referrals	4.34	2. Discuss products with new people you meet.	4.14
3. Contact personal acquaintances	4.06	3. Contact personal acquaintances	3.84
4. Prepare and distribute flyers	3.71	4. Prepare and distribute flyers	3.83
5. Prepare and send direct mail notices.	3.35	5. Prepare and send direct mail notices.	3.66
6. Advertise in newspapers	2.88	6. Advertise in newspapers	3.63
7. Advertise on radio	2.37	7. Advertise on radio	3.33
Bookkeeping Duties			
1. Process orders and maintain inventory	4.58	1. Submit tax forms and payments	4.05
2. Maintain sales records and distribute bonus checks	4.54	2. Maintain business checking account and record income & expenses.	3.82
3. Maintain business checking account and record income & expenses	4.50	3. Maintain sales records and distribute bonus checks	3.65
4. Submit tax forms and payments	4.33	4. Process orders and maintain inventory	3.56

FIGURE 6.2. Part of job-analysis report showing tasks listed sequentially according to mean ratings within duties.

which can be learned by employees on their own. The report can also provide information for job descriptions and for assigning personnel to specific jobs. Those tasks which will be included in formal training courses will need to undergo further analysis. That is the subject of the next section.

TASK ANALYSIS

Before we can develop materials and courses for training people to perform specific tasks, we must have a thorough understanding of the nature of the task. What are the component elements of the task, and how are they interrelated? In order to accomplish a task, we must learn and perform a series of steps or operations. These may be referred to as a procedure. Thus, for purposes of this discussion, the word *task* is a synonym for the term *procedure*. Task analysis, therefore, entails the identification of the steps of a procedure and the interrelationships between those steps.

Procedures are used in baking a cake, operating a sewing machine, performing long division, determining the correlation between two variables, closing out a cash register, preparing balance sheets, diagnosing diseases, repairing bicycles, and so forth. These few examples demonstrate that procedures are very common and important in our lives. Many procedures involve both cognitive and psychomotor components. Procedures which are essentially cognitive in nature would be classified as *rules* according to Gagné's (1985) categories of learning outcomes. The procedural part of a motor skill has been referred to by Gagné (1985) as an *executive routine*. Landa (1974) has used the term *algorithm* 1to refer to procedures for learning and instruction.

The discrete steps of most procedures may be classified as either operations or decisions. Operation steps usually involve the manipulation of some apparatus or the transformation of some information. In contrast, decision steps involve the evaluation or testing of the results or outcomes of earlier operations in order to determine if certain specific conditions have been satisfied. A decision step serves as the crossroad to alternate paths in the procedure. Decision steps are often referred to as branching points. If the specified condition is satisfied, then one path is followed. If the condition is not satisfied, then an alternate path is taken. Each alternate path contains a different set of steps (Merrill, 1980).

Procedures vary greatly in complexity. Simple procedures involve only a few operations, which are performed in a linear sequence and contain no decision steps. Other procedures consist principally of decision points and contain few operations. The more complex procedures contain many conditional decision steps and many operations. These many decision steps result in a large number of alternate paths.

Hierarchical and Information Processing Task-analysis

Probably the most widely accepted approach to the analysis of tasks was proposed by Gagné (1985) and is referred to as hierarchical task-analysis. This approach entails the identification of a hierarachy of subskills such that lower-ordered skills or behaviors generate positive transfer to skills at a higher level. Thus, the purpose of hierarchical task-analysis is to reveal prerequisite skills, and not to describe the steps of a task or procedure. Such an analysis would be performed by starting with a terminal objective and identifying subordinate skills by asking the question: "What [skills] should the learner already know how to do and be able to recall when faced with the task of learning the new rule, the absence of which would make it impossible for him to learn the new rule?" (Gagné, 1985, p. 272). This question is asked recursively of each subskill identified until the assumed student entry behaviors are reached. The results of this analysis are generally represented in a block diagram showing the hierarchy of skills (see Gagné & Briggs, 1979, p. 109).

Merrill (1971), Scandura (1973), and Resnick (1973) have advocated an alternate approach to task analysis called an *information-processing approach*. This approach includes the following steps (Merrill, 1976):

1. Identify the operation and decision steps of the procedure.
2. Sequence the steps in the order in which they would be performed.
3. Prepare a flow-chart representation of the sequenced steps.
4. Validate the flow-chart, using several different initial inputs.

In a flow-chart, the decision steps are represented by diamond-shaped boxes, while the operations are represented by rectangular boxes (see Merrill, 1978). The sequence of steps is indicated by arrows and the beginning and ending points are shown as ovals.

Although both of these types of analysis are useful, and each provides a different perspective on the nature of a task, it is not readily apparent from the diagrams how the two types of analysis are related to one another. Merrill (1978) attempted to show how a hierarchical analysis and associated diagram could be derived from an information-processing analysis through the use of a procedure advocated by Scandura (1973), called path analysis. With this technique, the various paths through a procedure are identified. These paths partition the domain of problems which can be solved by the procedure into mutually exclusive, equivalence classes. By ordering these equivalence classes according to difficulty, a corresponding hierarchical diagram can be constructed.

Unfortunately, information-processing analysis is fraught with inherent weaknesses. These weaknesses stem from the fact that an information-processing analysis is basically a sequential analysis. The steps of the procedure are identified and organized according to sequential relationships between the steps of the procedure. Sequential relationships are obviously critical in the performance of a procedure. However, recent research and evaluation of computer programs (Yourdan & Constantine, 1979) have shown that complex programs organized according to sequential relationships have several significant deficiencies. These deficiencies manifest themselves in (a) programs which will not work properly, (b) difficulty in finding and correcting errors in programs, (c) difficulty in modifying or expanding programs, and (d) difficulty in reading or understanding programs.

In order to reduce these problems, computer scientists have proposed and validated a new approach to the analysis and design of computer programs. This new approach, called *structured analysis* has significantly reduced each of the problems listed above. Since computer programs are nothing more than procedures which have been defined in terms of operations that can be performed by a computer, might not the structured-analysis approach for the design of computer procedures have application in the analysis of tasks or procedures which must be performed by humans? The answer is yes, and such an approach will be presented in the following section.

Structured Task-analysis

Structured analysis gains its name from the principle or guideline that only a small set of sequential structures of operation and decision steps should be used in the analysis and design of procedures, and that these few structures can be organized according to part–whole hierarchical relationships. Bohm and Jacopini (1966) proved formally that any procedure could be written using only three primitive sequential structures: Linear, Alternate, and Repetitive. A flow-chart representation of these three structures is shown in Fig. 6.3. The linear structure simply consists of a series of operations which are performed one after another. For example, a linear structure can be used to represent the operations involved in opening a locked door: insert key, turn key, grasp knob, rotate knob, pull door forward. In contrast, an alternate structure consists of a decision step with two alternate paths or operations. Some condition must be analyzed or some question answered in order to decide whether to perform one operation or another. For example, before performing the operations involved in getting to work each morning, I must consider the weather conditions. If it is raining, I decide to take the bus; otherwise, I decide to ride a bicycle. The repetitive structure consists of a series of one or more operations which may be repeated several times. The number of repetitions is controlled by a decision step. When adding a column of numbers on a calculator, we repeat the process of entering numbers until we decide that the last one has been entered.

Although any procedure may be written using only the three primitive structures described above, the resulting procedures are not always simple

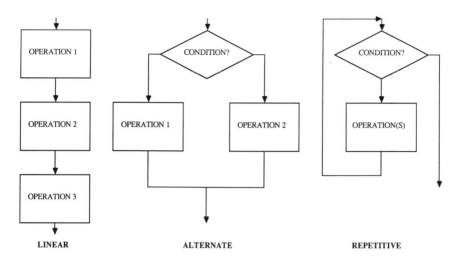

LINEAR   ALTERNATE   REPETITIVE

FIGURE 6.3.   Flow-chart representations of three primitive sequential structures.

and efficient.   The inefficencies resulting from the exclusive use of these three structures may be eliminated by allowing variants to the alternate and repetitive structures.   A variant to the alternate structure is called the *case structure*. This structure allows for several alternate paths at a decision step. For example, our choice of weekend recreational activity may depend on the outside temperature. If the temperature is over 80° then we go swimming; if it is between 60 and 80 we play tennis; between 40 and 60 we play golf; between 20 and 40 we go skiing; and below 20 we stay in and watch television. A flow-chart representation of the case structure is shown in Fig. 6.4.

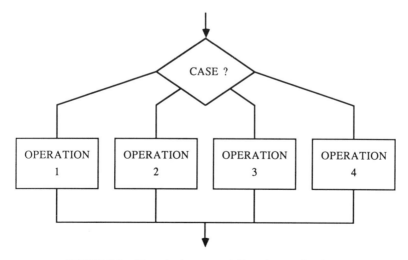

FIGURE 6.4.   Flow-chart representation of case structure.

There are two permissible variants to the *repetitive structure.* In the first variant the decision step may be made by following the operation as shown in Fig. 6.5. The placement of the decision step following the operation implies that the operation will be performed at least once. When the decision step is placed before the operation, as shown in Fig. 6.3, it is possible to exit from the loop without performing the operation at all. By placing the decision step before the operation in the repetitive structure for adding a column of numbers on the calculator, provision is made for the possibility of there being no numbers in the column. On the other hand, by placing the decision step following the operation as in a repetitive structure specifying that a chef should repeat the process of mixing cake batter until smooth, the assumption is made that there would never be an occasion when the batter would be smooth without mixing.

The second variant of the repetitive structure allows for more than one exit path from the loop, as shown in Fig. 6.6. This variant saves considerable time in procedures where a search is being made for a particular item. For example, suppose we want to search through a set of file folders, which are not organized alphabetically, in order to find the folder with the house contract. The first condition would specify that we continue to examine folders until there are no more in the file. However, the second condition would allow an early exit from this loop if the desired folder were found before reaching the end of the file. Without this variant it would be necessary to continue searching, even after the desired folder had been located.

Why restrict the design of analysis of tasks and procedures to these six primitive structures? Certainly many other structures are possible. How

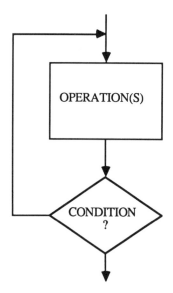

FIGURE 6.5. Flow-chart of variant repetitive structure with decision step following the operation.

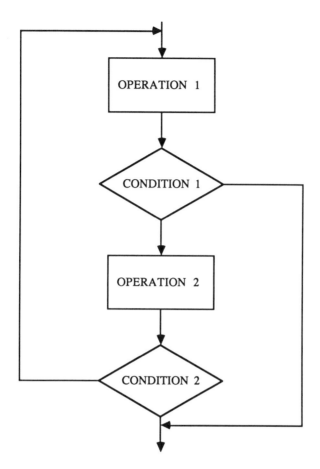

FIGURE 6.6.   Flow-chart of variant repetitive structure with abnormal exit.

does the use of only these structures reduce errors and facilitate understanding? The key lies in the fact that the complexity of a procedure seems to be
proportional to the number of decision steps in the procedure. As the
number of decision steps increases, the number of different paths through the
procedure increases geometrically. Errors are difficult to find because of the
large number of paths which have to be traced. Procedures with many
branching paths are very difficult to follow.

The primitive structures described above significantly reduce the complexity caused by decision steps, since each primitive structure can be treated as
a single entity or whole. By treating each structure as a whole it is possible
to design a part–whole hierarchical organization of a procedure, and then
represent the organized procedure in linear fashion. This reduction in complexity is shown in Fig. 6.7. The complex flow-chart on the left contains

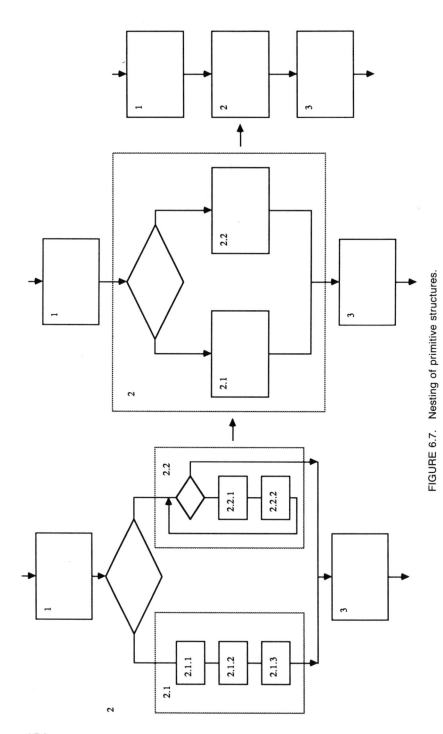

FIGURE 6.7. Nesting of primitive structures.

several decision steps, but it is composed of only primitive sequence structures. In the successive flow-charts to the right, the primitive structures within the dotted lines are reduced to a single, rectangular box, which represents the whole, until a linear sequence is obtained.

The part–whole relationships and underlying linear sequence of a procedure are not readily apparent in a flow-chart representation without the dotted lines around the primitive structures. However, these characteristics of a procedure become very clear if we use a different representation, called structured outlines. A structured-outline representation is an extension of the common, indented outline which is normally used to show the structure and content of a written manuscript. It is also an adaptation of representations referred to as *Structured English* or *Program Design Language* in the computer-science literature (DeMarco, 1979). Structured outlines use a limited vocabulary and syntax of normal English to represent the primitive sequence structures and use indentation to show part–whole hierarchical relationships among the primitive structures. The general format for a structured outline representation of the alternate structure is shown below:

```
IF  <CONDITION>
  THEN
    <OPERATION 1>
  OTHERWISE
    <OPERATION 2>
```

This representation indicates that if the condition is true, then operation 1 is to be performed, otherwise operation 2 is performed. This structured outline representation is directly analogous to the flow chart representation shown in Fig. 6.3. The following is a more specific example:

```
IF Student's GPA  >  3.3
  THEN
    Send letter of admission
    Increment number admitted
  OTHERWISE
    Send letter of rejection
```

The following is the general format for a structured-outline representation of a repetitive structure:

```
REPEAT IF  <CONDITION>
  <OPERATION 1>
  <OPERATION 2>
```

This representation indicates that the indented operations (operation 1 and operation 2) are to be repeated as long as the condition is true. Here is a more specific example:

REPEAT IF MORE PATIENTS
ROLL UP SLEEVE
SWAB ARM WITH ALCOHOL
GIVE INJECTION

This indicates that the operations (roll up sleeve, swab arm, and give injection) should be performed repeatedly as long as there are more patients. There is some flexibility in the exact terms which may be used to indicate how many times the operations should be repeated. For example,

REPEAT IF MORE PATIENTS

could be stated:

REPEAT FOR EACH PATIENT or
REPEAT WHILE MORE PATIENTS

Each of these alternatives indicate that the decision step comes before the operations, and imply that if there are no patients then the operations would not be performed. If the decision step follows the operations then the phrases

REPEAT UNTIL NO MORE PATIENTS or
REPEAT TEN TIMES

would be more appropriate.

The general format and a specific example of structured outline representations of the case variant of the alternate structure are shown below:

SELECT APPROPRIATE CASE	SELECT APPROPRIATE CASE
IF <CONDITION 1>	IF Administrator
<OPERATION 1>	Assign Parking Sticker A
IF <CONDITION 2>	IF Faculty
<OPERATION 2>	Assign Parking Sticker B
IF <CONDITION 3>	IF Staff
<OPERATION 3>	Assign Parking Sticker C
IF <CONDITION 4>	IF Student
<OPERATION 4>	Assign Parking Sticker D
	Charge Fee of $5

These representations indicate that only the operations indented under the appropriate case should be performed. The example on the right specifies that different parking stickers should be assigned, depending on an individual's status within a school community. Thus students are assigned parking sticker D and charged a $5 fee.

The general format and a specific example of structured outlines for the abnormal exit variant of the repetitive structure are shown below:

REPEAT IF <CONDITION 1>   REPEAT IF More file folders
  <OPERATION 1>   Pull Folder
                              Read label on folder
IF <CONDITION 2>   IF label is House Contract
  THEN EXIT REPEAT   THEN EXIT REPEAT
  <OPERATION 2>   Refile folder

These representations indicate that there are two possible conditions under which the repeat loop may be terminated. In the example to the right, the loop is terminated either when there are no more folders or when the folder with the house contract is found.

A complete, structured-outline representation of the procedure for generating the "next numeral in base 3" is shown below:

I. Read the ones digit of numeral

II. REPEAT UNTIL no more digits
  A. IF digit = 2
    1. THEN
      a. Change 2 to 0
      b. Write down 0
    2. OTHERWISE
      a. Increment digit by 1
      b. Write down NEW numeral
      c. EXIT procedure
  B. Read next digit to the left

III. Write "1" in the next position to the left of the last "0" written.

The structured outline is easier to follow than a flow chart, since the outline is simply read from top to bottom as in reading ordinary textual prose; and the parts of the outline (primitive structures) are clearly shown through indentation. (The Roman numerals and letters, etc., are included in this example outline for reference purposes and need not be included in all structured outlines.) The outline consists of four major sections or parts labeled with Roman numerals. Section II is a repetitive structure that is repeated once for each digit until no more digits remain. Nested within the repetitive structure is an alternate structure labeled "A." This structure is used to determine if a given digit is equal to 2. If the digit is equal to 2, the operations labeled a and b under 1 are executed; otherwise, the operations labeled a, b, and c under 2 are executed, not both. Thus, if operations A.1.a and b are executed, the next operation to be executed would be operation B. What operation would be executed after B? Since section II is a repetitive structure, the operations under A would be executed again. In fact, sections A and B would continue to be executed repetitively until no more digits remain. However, note that the operation labeled II.A.2.c is an abnormal exit from the entire procedure. When this operation is executed, the procedure is terminated. If the procedure is not terminated by c, then operation III is executed, only after the repetitive structure under II has been completed (no more digits remain).

Let's use the outline above to find the numerals which follow the number 21 in base three. First we perform operation I and read the ones digit of the numeral (which is digit 1). Since we found a digit we can begin the repeat loop labeled II. We next perform step II.A and check to see if the digit is equal to 2. Since the digit is not equal to 2, we take the otherwise branch and perform steps II.A.2a, b, and c. We increment the digit by 1, write down the new numeral (which is 22) and exit the procedure. Thus the next numeral after 21 in base three is the number 22. Let's continue and find the number following 22 in base three. We start over and read the ones digit (which is now 2). We begin the repeat loop and check to see if the digit is equal to 2. This time the condition is true and we take the "then" branch and perform steps II.A.1a and b (we change the 2 to 0 and write down the 0). We now skip the "otherwise" branch and go directly to step II.B and read the next digit (which is a 2). Since we still found another digit, we continue with the repeat loop and go to step II.A to check if the new digit is equal to 2. The condition is true again, so we change the 2 to a 0 and write down the 0. We go to step II.B and read the next digit to the left. This time there are no more digits and the repeat condition is false. This results in the termination of the repeat loop and we go to step III. We write a 1 in the next position to the left of the last 0 written resulting in the number 100. Thus, the next numeral after 22 in base three is the number 100.

The structured task-analysis approach is analogous to the procedure taught in English classes called outlining. First a thesis is broken down into major topics, which are then divided into subtopics, and so forth. In structured task-analysis, we break the task down into a few major component steps. These major steps are in turn broken down into substeps. Each substep is then divided into sub-substeps and so forth until substeps assumed to be within the repertoire of the target audience are identified. If any steps involve decision points or repetitive loops they should be identified and represented using the structured-outline version of the primitive structures. This task-analysis procedure is similar to the "divide-and-conquer" strategy of problem solving. When the whole is too complex, divide it into its major parts. Each part is then divided into subparts until we reach simple components with which we are able to cope. In computer science a similar process is referred to as *successive refinement*.

Let's walk through the structured-task-analysis procedure described above, using the familiar task of changing a car tire as an example. First, we identify the major steps required to accomplish the task as shown below:

I. Secure car

II. Get tools and spare tire

III. Jack up car

IV. Replace tire

V. Jack down car

VI. Put away tools and flat tire

These steps should be quite general but exhaustive. At least three and not more than ten steps should be identified as major steps. If more than ten steps are identified, then some of the steps should be combined into a more general step.

Second, each of these major steps should be further refined by breaking them into substeps, as indicated by capital letters in the following outline. Step VI is not broken into substeps since it is assumed that it is within the repertoire of the target group of learners.

I. Secure car
   A. Place transmission in park
   B. Block wheels

II. Get tools and spare
   A. Open trunk
   B. Remove spare
   C. Remove jack
   D. Remove lug wrench

III. Jack up car
   A. Set up jack
   B. Operate jack

IV. Replace tire
   A. Remove lug nuts
   B. Remove flat tire
   C. Put on spare tire
   D. Put on lug nuts

V. Jack down car
   A. Set jack lever to down
   B. Operate jack

VI. Put away tools and flat tire

Third, the substeps are examined for accuracy and completeness, and any errors are rectified. If individuals perform all of these steps in the order shown would they be able to accomplish the task? The procedure as outlined above contains a couple of problems. Step I.A would not work if the car had a manual transmission. The step should be stated in more general terms and further analysis should allow for alternate operations, depending on the type of transmission. If we attempt to remove the lug nuts, as indicated in step IV.A, after the car has been jacked up, as indicated in step III, we would find that we are unable to accomplish the step since the wheel is free to turn. This problem can be resolved by adding an additional step to loosen the lug nuts prior to jacking up the car. A similar problem exists with step IV.D, "put on lug nuts." The lug nuts can be put on at this point, but they cannot be tightened while the tire is off the ground. Therefore, another sub-step needs to be added to tighten the lug nuts after the car is jacked down.

Fourth, the substeps are divided into sub-substeps, and decision points and repetitive loops are presented, using appropriate outline structures:

   I. Secure car
      A. Set transmission
         If automatic transmission
            then
               Place transmission in park
            else
               Place transmission in reverse
      B. Block wheels

  II. Get tools and spare
      A. Open trunk
      B. Remove spare
      C. Remove jack
      D. Remove lug wrench

 III. Jack up car
      A. Loosen lug nuts
         Repeat for each lug nut
            Repeat until hand loose
               Turn nut with wrench
      B. Set up jack
         1. Assemble jack
         2. Place jack under car
         3. Set jack lever to up
      C. Operate jack
         Repeat until tire clears ground
            push jack handle

   IV. Replace tire
        A. Remove lug nuts
        B. Remove flat tire
        C. Put on spare tire

D. Put on lug nuts
   Repeat for each nut
      Repeat until hand tight
         turn nut with hand

V. Jack down car
   A. Set jack lever to down
   B. Operate jack
   C. Tighten lug nuts with wrench

VI. Put away tools and flat tire

Fifth, the completed analysis would now be validated by actually having an individual attempt to accomplish the task following the outlined procedure.

All of the steps need not be broken down to the same level of detail. Some of the substeps in the example were probably broken down more than necessary for illustrative purposes. If there is only one step within a repeat loop, it could be described at a more general level with less rigorous language. For example, step III.A could be restated as: III.A. Turn each lug nut with wrench until hand loose. Remember that the task-analysis-structured outline is to serve as a design document to guide the development of instructional materials. The design document is not the final instructional product. Therefore, it is not necessary to continue the analysis to the point that a naive learner would be able to perform the task, given only the outline. However, the outline may serve as a model for a job aid to be included as part of the instruction.

The structured outline serves as an analysis tool and as a final representation of the results of the analysis. It is a very powerful representation, since it shows both the sequential and hierarchical relationships between the steps of the procedure. The sequence in which the steps are to be performed is shown by reading the outline from top to bottom. The hierarchical relationships are revealed by noting the substeps indented to the right. The substeps, A. Loosen lug nuts, B. Set up jack, and C. Operate jack, have a part–whole hierarchical relationship to the major step: III. Jack up Car. Since these substeps are components of the major step, they must be learned before the major step can be learned. Thus the substeps are learning prerequisites to the major step. In the same manner, sub-substeps (1) Assemble jack, (2) Place jack under car, and (3) Set jack lever to up, are learning prerequisites to the substep: B. Set up jack.

It should be fairly clear that the part–whole hierarchy produced by the structured-analysis procedure is analogous to Gagné's learning prerequisite hierarchy. The structured outline shows why one element is prerequisite to another. The structured-outline representation has advantages over the block-hierarchical diagram, and to the flow–chart, since it shows both sequential and hierarchical relationships in a single diagram. It can also be easily constructed and modified, using a typewriter or word processor.

Instructional Sequencing

Task analysis helps us identify the component parts of a task and the relationships between those parts. The identification of the component parts determines what must be taught in order for someone to learn how to do the task. The relationships help determine the sequence in which these parts should be taught. The structured analysis procedure described here reveals two different relationships among the component parts: sequential and hierarchical part–whole. Which of these relationships should be used to determine the instructional sequence? Since the part–whole relationships reveal learning prerequisites, one might naturally assume that the part–whole relationships should be used to determine the instructional sequence. However, this is not always the case. If the task can be taught in one instructional session, it would be better to teach the component parts or steps in the same sequence that the task is normally performed. Such a sequence does not violate the need to teach prerequisite substeps before their superordinate major steps can be taught. A major step and its substeps are essentially taught at the same time. The ideal way to teach such tasks would be to have a subject-matter expert demonstrate how the task is to be performed and then have the learners practice performing the task. Corrective feedback would then be given to correct performance deficiencies. For simple tasks, the steps of the task would be demonstrated and practiced in the sequential order shown in the structured outline of the task.

The part–whole hierarchical relationships are used to determine the instructional sequence for complex tasks which cannot be taught in a single instructional setting. Many mathematical tasks, such as long division, are much too complex to be taught in one session. The subparts such as multiplication and subtraction must have been taught and learned in prior instructional sessions before one can attempt to teach long division. Notice that in such cases the subparts are often independent and functional tasks in their own right. Multiplication is a whole task, independent of its role as a substep within the division procedure.

Procedural Path Analysis

Task complexity is determined by at least three factors: (a) the total number of steps in the task, (b) the number of repetitive-sequence structures, and (c) the number of alternate-sequence structures. The number of steps is the least contributing factor, while the number of alternate structures is the greatest contributing factor. Alternate structures produce multiple paths through the procedure. Repetitive structures with the decision step before the operations also increase the number of paths, while those with the decision step following the operations do not. As the number of alternative structures increases, the number of paths increases geometrically. Even though it contains quite a few steps, the task of changing a tire is relatively simple, because it contains only one alternate structure resulting in just two paths through the procedure: one path for a car with an automatic transmission and another for a car with a manual transmission. In contrast, the task of subtracting whole numbers is much more complex than changing a tire even though it has fewer steps, because it has two alternate structures and a repetitive structure with the decision step before the operations, resulting in nine different paths.

Each path through a procedure is actually a separate task to be learned. Since all of these separate tasks cannot be taught or learned in one setting, further analysis is necessary to determine the relationships between these tasks and the sequence in which they should be taught. This analysis is referred to as *procedural path analysis* and entails the explicit identification of the separate paths through the procedure and the part–whole relationships between those paths.

Scandura (1973) has suggested that each path through a procedure could be represented by a directed graph wherein the decision steps are represented by points and the operations are represented by arrows or arcs. However, such directed graphs are derived from a flow-chart representation of an information-processing analysis. Since we are using structured-outline representations of the procedure, it is more appropriate to represent a given path through the procedure by showing that part of the structured outline actually included within the path.

For example, let's walk through the path analysis of the task for "subtracting whole numbers." Before conducting a procedural path analysis, we would first conduct a structured task analysis as described in the previous section. Such an analysis would yield the following structured outline:

REPEAT FOR each column

   I. Encode top number   3047

  II. IF there is a bottom number   − 285
      A. THEN
         1. IF the top No. is smaller that the bottom No.
           a. THEN
              1. Go to the next column to left
              2. REPEAT WHILE top No. in column = 0
                 (a) Change 0 to 9
                 (b) Go to next column to left
              3. Borrow 1 from top number
              4. Return to original column and place
                 1 in front of top number

> 5. Subtract bottom No. from top No.,
>   using subtraction facts for top
>   No. $\geqslant 10$ and $\leqslant 19$
> b. OTHERWISE
>   Subtract using facts for top No. $\leqslant 9$
> B. OTHERWISE
>   Assume bottom No. is 0
>   Subtract using facts for top No. $\leqslant 9$

By examining this outline we can see that there are two alternate structures and one repetitive structure. The many resulting paths through the procedure indicate that a procedural path analysis would be needed.

In outlining the procedural path analysis, we first examine the structured outline to identify the shortest, most direct path through the procedure. This path is labeled Path 1:

> REPEAT FOR each column
> I. Encode top number
> II. IF there is a bottom number
>   B. OTHERWISE
>   Assume bottom No. is 0
>   Subtract using facts for top No. $\leqslant 9$

Note that this path is simply a small part of the overall procedure and only includes step I and the OTHERWISE part of the alternate structure from step II. This path is only taken when the condition specified in step II (there is a bottom number) is false. Obviously, this path is not a very useful subtask in and of itself, since there are no real subtraction problems which would be solved using this path. However, as we shall see, it does have utility as part of other paths.

We now identify the next most direct path through the procedure, Path 2:

> REPEAT FOR each column
> I. Encode top number   7   4597
> II. IF there is a bottom number $-\ 5$ $-\ 3274$
>   A. THEN   _____   _____
>   1. IF the top No. is smaller than the bottom No.
>   b. OTHERWISE
>   Subtract using facts for top No. $\leqslant 9$

This path is taken when the condition specified in step II is true (when there is a bottom number). However, this path includes a second decision point or alternate structure where the specified condition (the top number is smaller than the bottom number) is false. This path would be used to solve all single-digit subtraction problems where the bottom number is smaller than the top number. However, note that this whole path may be executed several times as specified by the REPEAT FOR repetitive structure. Through repetition we are able to use this path to solve multiple digit subtraction problems in which each bottom digit is smaller than its corresponding top digit. Examples of the types of problems which could be solved by this path or subtask are shown to the right of the structured outline.

Path 3 includes both the THEN and the OTHERWISE parts of step II:

REPEAT FOR each column
I. Encode top number   17   647
II. IF there is a bottom number   − 3   − 25
   A. THEN
      1. IF the top No. is smaller that the bottom No.
         b. OTHERWISE
           Subtract using facts for top No. $\leqslant 9$
   B. OTHERWISE
      Assume bottom No. is 0
      Subtract using facts for top No. $\leqslant 9$

This is only possible because the alternate structure specified in step II is nested within the REPEAT FOR repetitive structure. This path would be used to solve problems where at least the top number has more than one digit and where the bottom number has at least one less digit than the top number (see the examples to the right of the outline). These problems must not require borrowing and the extra digits from the top number must be brought down. Notice that this path incorporates the steps included in both paths 1 and 2.

The next three paths all include the THEN part of the second alternate structure (if the top No. is smaller than the bottom No.) which is executed when the specified condition is true. Thus, each of these paths involves the steps needed for borrowing. Path 4 is used to solve problems which require borrowing but do not require bringing down:

REPEAT FOR each column
 I. Encode top number   647   3647
II. IF there is a bottom number   − 469   − 1829
   A. THEN
      1. IF the top No. is smaller that the bottom No.
        a. THEN
           1. Go to the next column to left
           2. Borrow 1 from top No.

      3. Return to original column and place 1 in
         front of top No.
      4. Subtract bottom No. from top No.,
         using subtraction facts for top
         No. $\geqslant 10$ and $\leqslant 19$
   b. OTHERWISE
     Subtract using facts for top No. $\leqslant 9$

Path 5 is used to solve problems which require borrowing and bringing down:

REPEAT FOR each column
  I. Encode top number   23   364
 II. IF there is a bottom number   − 8   − 85
   A. THEN
     1. IF the top No. is smaller that the bottom No.
       a. THEN
         1. Go to the next column to left
         2. Borrow 1 from top No.
         3. Return to original column and place 1 in
            front of top No.
         4. Subtract bottom No. from top No.,
            using subtraction facts for top
            No. $\geqslant 10$ and $\leqslant 19$
  B. OTHERWISE
     Assume bottom No. is 0
     Subtract using facts for top No. $\leqslant 9$

Path 6 includes all the steps of paths 4 and 5 and is used to solve problems that include at least one column that requires borrowing, one that does not require borrowing, and one that requires bringing down:

REPEAT FOR each column
  I. Encode top number   3647
 II. IF there is a bottom number   − 829
   A. THEN
     1. IF the top No. is smaller that the bottom No.
       a. THEN
         1. Go to the next column to left
         2. Borrow 1 from top No.
         3. Return to original column and place 1 in
            front of top No.

    4. Subtract bottom No. from top No. using
       subtraction facts for top No. $\geqslant 10$ and $\leqslant 19$
  b. OTHERWISE
    Subtract using facts for top No. $\leqslant 9$
B. OTHERWISE
    Assume bottom No. is 0
    Subtract using facts for top No. $\leqslant 9$

The next two paths add the REPEAT WHILE repetitive structure. These paths are necessary for problems which have one or more zeros in the top number. Path 7 requires borrowing across zero with no bringing down:

REPEAT FOR each column

I. Encode top number	607	3602
II. IF there is a bottom number	− 469	− 1235

  1. IF the top No. is smaller than the bottom No.
    a. THEN
      1. Go to the next column to left
      2. REPEAT WHILE top No. in column = 0
        a. Change 0 to 9
        b. Go to next column to left
      3. Borrow 1 from top No.
      4. Return to original column and place 1
        in front of top No.
      5. Subtract bottom No. from top No., using
        subtraction facts for top No. $\geqslant 10$ and $\leqslant 19$
    b. OTHERWISE
      Subtract using facts for top No. $\leqslant 9$

Path 8 requires bringing down in addition to borrowing across zero:

REPEAT FOR each column

I. Encode top number	203	3064
II. IF there is a bottom number	− 8	− 85

  A. THEN
    1. IF the top No. is smaller that the bottom No.
      a. THEN
        1. Go to the next column to left
        2. REPEAT WHILE top No. in column = 0
          a. Change 0 to 9
          b. Go to next column to left
        3. Borrow 1 from top No.

4. Return to original column and place 1 in
   front of top No.
5. Subtract bottom No. from top No.,
   using subtraction facts for top No. ≥ 10 and ≤ 19
   No. ≥ 10 and ≤ 19
B. OTHERWISE
   Assume bottom No. is 0
   Subtract using facts for top No. ≤ 9

Path 9 incorporates the entire procedure, and was shown previously at the beginning of this section. This most complex path is used to solve problems that require every step of the algorithm, such as those with borrowing across zero, columns with normal borrowing, columns with no borrowing, and columns that require bringing down.

As can be seen from these examples, some paths include all the steps of other paths. Such paths have a hierarchical part–whole relationship to one another. These relationships allow us to organize the paths into a hierarchical structure represented by a block diagram as shown in Fig. 6.8.

These hierarchical relationships can be used to specify an instructional or learning prerequisite sequence. Students cannot learn how to accomplish the task specified in Path 6 until they know how to do the subtasks indicated by Paths 3, 4, and 5 since these paths are components of Path 6. However, as mentioned in the previous section, it would be theoretically possible to teach all of the steps involved in paths 3, 4, 5, and 6 in one instructional session. These part–whole relationships indicate that if the complete procedure is to be taught over several instructional sessions, then positive transfer is expected to occur from simpler tasks to more complex tasks when the simpler tasks are included as parts of the more complex tasks (Resnick & Ford, 1976).

Elaboration Theory

The component parts and relationships identified through the use of structured and procedural path analyses described in the previous sections can be used directly to design instructional materials in accordance with the elaboration theory proposed by Reigeluth and colleagues (Reigeluth & Stein, 1983). Elaboration theory prescribes that procedures should be taught in a simple-to-complex or general-to-detailed sequence beginning with the most fundamental ideas that can be directly applied by the student. These fundamental ideas are referred to as the *epitome* of the procedure. The remainder of instruction elaborates on the epitome by adding successive levels of detail or complexity.

Simple tasks which do not involve many paths through the procedure, such as changing a flat tire, can be sequenced in a general-to-specific

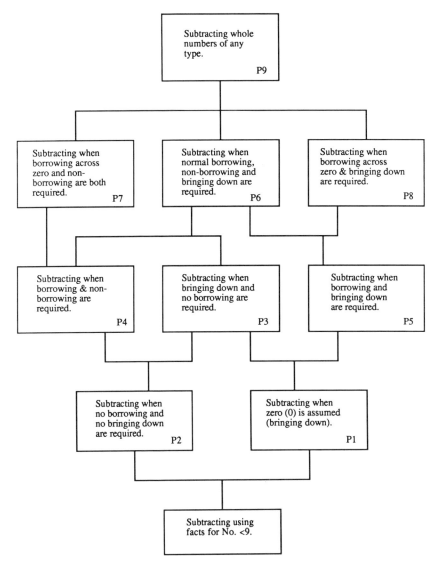

FIGURE 6.8. Block diagram showing hierarchical, part–whole relationships of subtraction task, based on procedural-path analysis.

sequence based on the structured outline of the procedure. Instruction would begin with an epitome or overview consisting of the major steps of the task. Subsequent instruction would elaborate on the major steps by detailing the substeps and then the sub-substeps. For complex procedures containing many alternate paths, instruction would begin with the simplest subtask or path identified through path analysis. Further instruction would elaborate on the simplest path by successively adding more complex paths which include the simpler paths as a components. The resulting sequence for the subtraction task described in the previous section would be that implied in the hierarchical diagram shown in Fig. 6.18. Instruction would begin with the paths shown at the bottom of the diagram and proceed up the hierarchy.

Extended Task Analysis Procedure (ETAP). Reigeluth and M. D. Merrill (1984) have proposed an alternate approach to task analysis, called extended task-analysis, which attempts to combine hierarchical task analysis and information-processing task analysis into a comprehensive procedure. Extended-task analysis is conducted in three phases. The task is first analyzed, using information-processing analysis resulting in a flow-chart representation of the procedure. Second, if necessary, each step of the procedure is further divided into component substeps. This second phase is essentially the same process as described in the previous section on structured-task analysis, where substeps are divided into sub-substeps. The third phase, referred to as *knowledge analysis,* involves the identification of any prerequisite concepts or facts which students must know in order to learn any given substep of the procedure.

The first two phases of extended task-analysis are essentially accounted for in the structured task-analysis procedure described earlier. However, the third phase involves an additional level of analysis not previously described. In many cases, this additional level of analysis would not be necessary since the prerequisite concepts or classification skills would generally be within the entering knowledge or skills of the target audience. However, if this is not the case, the identification of prerequisite concepts would be necessary. These prerequisite concepts are usually identified from the structured outline. They are simply the object of the action verb used to describe each step of the procedure. Thus, in the tire-changing task, one of the steps was identified as "Remove jack." The object of the action verb, *remove,* is the label for the concept *jack.* If this concept or associated classification skill is not within the entry behavior of the target audience, then it would have to be taught either before or at the same time as instruction for this step.

Decision steps indicated by alternate or repetitive structure statements also identify prerequisite classification or discrimination skills. For example, in the structured outline for the subtraction task, step II (IF there is a bottom number), indicates that the ability to identify bottom numbers would be prerequisite to the successful learning and execution of this decision step. Similarly, the ability to discriminate the number zero (0) would be prerequisite to learning the step: "REPEAT WHILE top No. in column = 0." The concepts *top, No.,* and *column* would also be prerequisite.

Extended task-analysis also includes a method for analyzing transfer or soft-skill tasks that are too complex to define completely. For some transfer tasks, the correct procedure for performing the task varies under different situations. Extended task-analysis prescribes a technique for identifying the underlying principles that are followed in performing such tasks. Other transfer tasks require that many different factors be considered in making certain decisions. Extended task-analysis also outlines a method for identifying these factors, so that they may be included in an instructional plan.

SUMMARY

In this chapter we have outlined several procedures which should be followed by instructional developers in the initial stages of designing an instructional program for training individuals on how to perform the essential tasks of a given job. First, the tasks that make up the job must be identified through a process called job analysis. This process involves the generation of an initial list of tasks, the confirmation or revision of the list based on information from several alternate sources, and the validation of the revised list by collection of data such as the importance and performance frequency of the tasks from a sample of jobholder or job supervisors. These data are then summarized, organized, and described in a report.

Each of the validated tasks is then submitted to task analysis. The approach recommended in this chapter involves *structured task-analysis* followed by *procedural path analysis* and *knowledge analysis* when necessary. Structured task-analysis is based on recent research and practice found to be successful by computer scientists in the analysis of procedures to be executed by computers. This approach involves dividing the task or procedure into major parts or steps, then further dividing these major parts into substeps, sub-substeps, and so on, until simple steps assumed to be within the repertoire of the target group of learners have been identified. These substeps are organized according to three basic sequential structures: *linear, alternate,* and *repetitive.* The sequential and part–whole relationships identified through this analysis are represented, using a *structured outline.* This outline indicates what is to be taught and the sequence to be used in instruction.

If the structured outline shows that the procedure has many alternate paths, then a procedural path analysis should be performed to identify explicitly the paths and their part–whole relationships. This analysis is based on the structured outline, and results in a hierarchical diagram that reveals an appropriate learning prerequisite sequence. Knowledge analysis should be used to identify the prerequisite classification and discrimination skills which are not within the entering knowledge of the learners. These prerequisites are identified in the structured outline.

The task-analysis procedures outlined here are congruent with other approaches, such as hierarchical task-analysis, information-processing analysis, and extended task-analysis. However, structured analysis with its structured-outline representation seems to have several advantages. The structured analysis approach reveals the specific steps required to perform the task, the sequence in which those steps must be performed, and the hierarchical relationships between the parts of the task. Thus, the sequence for performing the task and the sequence for learning the task are both identified. Extended task-analysis provides additional methods for the analysis of transfer tasks, when complex knowledge structures are involved.

REFERENCES

Bohm, C., & Jacopini, G. (1966, May). Flow diagrams, Turing machines, and languages with only two formation rules. *Communications of the ACM, 366–371.*

De Marco, T. (1979). *Structured analysis and system specification.* Englewood Cliffs, NJ: Prentice-Hall.

Gagné, R. M. (1985). *The conditions of learning and theory of instruction* (4th ed.). New York: Holt, Rinehart and Winston.

Gagné, R. M., & Briggs, L. J. (1979). *Principles of instructional design* (2nd ed.). New York: Holt, Rinehart and Winston.

Landa, L. N. (1974). *Algorithmization in learning and instruction.* Englewood Cliffs, NJ: Educational Technology.

Merrill, P. F. (1971). *Task Analysis—an information processing approach* (Technical Memo No. 27). Tallahassee, FL: CAI Center, Florida State University.

Merrill, P. F. (1976). Task Analysis—an information processing approach. *NSPI Journal, 15*(2), 7–11.

Merrill, P. F. (1978). Hierarchical and information processing task analysis: A comparison. *Journal of Instructional Development, 1*(2), 35–40.

Merrill, P. F. (1980). Representations for algorithms. *NSPI Journal, 19*(8), 19–24.

Reigeluth, C. M., & Merrill, M. D. (1984). *Extended task analysis procedure (ETAP): User's Manual.* Lanham, MD: University Press of America.

Reigeluth, C. M., & Stein, F. S. (1983). The elaboration theory of instruction. In C. M. Reigeluth (Ed.), *Instructional-design theories and models: An overview of their current status.* Hillsdale, NJ: Lawrence Erlbaum Associates.

Resnick, L. B. (1973). Issues in the study of learning hierarchies. In L. B. Resnick (Ed.), Hierarchies in children's learning: A symposium. *Instructional Science, 2,* 312–323.

Resnick, L. B., & Ford, W. W. (1976). The analysis of tasks for instruction: An information-processing approach. In T. A. Brigham & A. C. Catania (Eds.), *Social and instructional processes: Foundations and applications of a behavioral analysis.* New York: Irvington.

Scandura, J. M. (1973). *Structural learning: I. Theory and research.* New York: Gordon and Breach.

Yourdon, E., & Constantine, L. L. (1979). *Structured design, fundamentals of a discipline of computer program and system design.* Englewood Cliffs, NJ: Prentice-Hall.

AUTHOR NOTES

Portions of this chapter were adapted from Merrill, P. F. (1982). Structured outline representations for procedures or algorithms. In D. Jonassen (Ed.), *The technology of text*. Englewood Cliffs, NJ: Educational Technology Publications. Used by permission of the copyright owner, Educational Technology Publications, Inc.

Paul F. Merrill is Professor, Department of Instructional Science, College of Education, Brigham Young University.

7 Learning Situations and Instructional Models

Charles M. Reigeluth and Ruth V. Curtis
Syracuse University

Let's assume that you have been given the task of developing some instruction. The two most important decisions you will have to make are *what* to teach and *how* to teach it. Everything you do in the instructional-system design (ISD) process is directed toward these two fundamental decisions.

You have already analyzed the requirements for the instruction that you are developing, and have used much of the information from that analysis in performing a task or content analysis, which resulted in a complete determination of *what* to teach. Now it is time to decide *how* to teach it, usually with the help of a subject-matter expert. This activity will result in a "blueprint" of the instruction, much like an architect's blueprint of a building.

When this activity has been completed, you will then usually work with a subject-matter expert to develop the instructional displays and communication in accordance with your design specifications, much as an architect would work with a contractor to build the building in accordance with a blueprint. Finally, you will evaluate and revise the instruction before implementing it. The instruction which you are developing may be for any one of a wide variety of contexts, including such K–12 and higher-education forms of instruction as teacher lesson plans, textbooks, educational software, audiovisual materials, workbooks, handouts, educational films, tutoring programs, laboratory demonstrations, and role-playing activities, and such adult-education forms of instruction as health education, business training, professional updating and recertification, and even recreation- and hobby-related learning resources. As our information society increases its rate of change, the importance of good instruction is likely to increase dramatically (Naisbitt, 1982), as will the variety of contexts within which instructional design expertise will be valuable.

As we proceed with the design of your instruction in this chapter, we will look at a wide variety of situations for which each of those differences is most appropriate. But before we survey the current state of the art, a brief historical perspective may be useful for gaining insights into both the directions in which our knowledge about instruction is developing and the major shortcomings in our current knowledge about instructional design.

Trends in the Field of Instruction

For the first few centuries after the Renaissance, efforts to improve instruction were philosophical in nature. It wasn't until the 1950s that research became the prevalent mode of inquiry. With the quest for the "ideal" instructional model, there evolved a global perspective that attempted to identify *one* instructional method that was superior to all others. As a result, research tended to investigate very general, gross variables and focused on comparison between major methods of instruction. Lecture was compared with discussion. Inductive methods were compared with deductive methods. The discovery method was compared with the expository approach. Mediated instruction was compared with nonmediated instruction.

It soon became apparent that the research results were contradictory—that any one of these methods could be designed and utilized in such a way as to be better than the alternatives. These contradictory results led investigators to realize that there could be more variation within each category of methods than between them, that is, two different discovery methods could differ more than an expository and a discovery method. So the field of instruction entered into an *analysis* phase in which methods of instruction were broken down into elementary components, called instructional strategy components, such as rules and examples (e.g., the ruleg investigations; see Evans, Homme, & Glaser, 1964) and overt responses and reinforcement (e.g., the programmed-instruction investigations; see Crowder, 1960; Skinner, 1969).

Research on individual strategy components has built up a knowledge base of validated principles of instruction—that is, reliable statements about the effects of each component under different situations. The problem with this piecemeal knowledge base is that it is relatively difficult for instructional designers to "mix and match" these components into the best combination for each and every situation. So gradually, various investigators have begun to usher the field of instruction into a *synthesis* phase in which strategy components are combined into *models* of instruction, each of which is supposed to be better than any other known combination for a certain learning situation. Hence, situations provide the basis for prescribing instructional models. Although some promising progress has been made on synthesizing our current knowledge about instructional strategy components, much more work is needed.

Conceptual Framework

It may be helpful to summarize a few points about learning situations and instructional models, in order to provide a conceptual framework that will make it easier to understand the remainder of this chapter. An instructional-strategy component is a part or aspect of a method of instruction. It has an influence on learning outcomes.

1. Knowledge about instruction has two major elements:
    (a) instructional strategy components (what kinds of components exist?) and,
    (b) learning situations (when should we use each strategy component?).

2. Insofar as possible, strategy components should not be prescribed individually; they should be combined into *optimal* models (each of which is better than any other set of components) for different learning situations. (Incidentally, the models and the bases for prescribing them constitute what is referred to as a theory of instruction; see Reigeluth, 1983a.)

3. Since some models differ only in minor ways from others (because their learning situations differ in only minor ways), it is more economical to think in terms of just a few *general models* of instruction plus a series of *variations* which serve to tailor a general model to a precise learning situation (Gropper, 1983).

4. Different models and variations of those models are prescribed for different kinds of learning situations, depending on the nature of the content and the desired outcome. (These will be discussed in further detail in subsequent sections.)

Hence, the remainder of this chapter will describe: (a) the major *general models* of instruction, plus the bases for prescribing each, and, (b) some of the major *variations* on each general model, plus the bases for prescribing each.

Let's return to your task: to develop some instruction. You have already analyzed the requirements for the instruction and have performed a task or content analysis which resulted in a complete determination of *what* to teach. Now you need to decide *how* to teach it. You should start by designing the overall structure and sequence of the instruction, and then proceed to design the instruction on each piece of content within that sequence.

To make your work easier and more effective, you want to select the most appropriate general model for the overall structure and sequence of the course. On the most general level, you must determine whether your goals and objectives are *primarily* motor, affective, or cognitive (Bloom, 1956;

Krathwohl, Bloom, & Masia, 1964) because the nature of the instruction will be very different for each of these three types of goals (i.e., situations on the broadest level of conceptualization).

Motor goals are desired outcomes largely related to performing a physical action, such as typing or swimming. *Affective* goals refer to the development of feelings, attitudes, and values, such as wanting to vote. Goals in the *cognitive* domain deal with learning intellectual knowledge and skills. Although most instruction includes goals in all three domains, one domain is usually dominant and therefore provides the basis for selecting one of the three classes of general models of instruction.

AFFECTIVE DOMAIN

The affective domain (Krathwohl et al., 1964) includes human attitudes and values. Over the years, schools and businesses have assumed an ever-growing role in the development of positive attitudes and values in their learners. If your goals are primarily in this area, then there's not much guidance from instructional design as to what to do. Three models that will be discussed briefly are values clarification (Harmin, Kirschenbaum, & Simon, 1973), cognitive moral development education (Kohlberg, 1976), and social modeling (Bandura & Walters, 1963).

The intention of the values clarification movement of the 1960s and 1970s was to encourage students to identify, select, and act on their currently held values and to motivate students to think about and discuss the moral issues. The values-clarification model requires students to confront a moral issue, state their position on that issue, and reflect on their position and the positions of others (Ryan, 1981).

Moral education is an area within the affective domain which has received growing attention over the last ten years. Perhaps the best known approach to moral education is Kohlberg's (1976) cognitive moral-development education. Kohlberg has identified three levels of moral development. The *preconventional level* is one in which the person approaches a moral question on the basis of his or her own personal interest or perspective. At the *conventional level*, the person approaches a moral question from the perspective of a member of the larger society. The final level is the *principled level*, in which the person makes moral decisions on the basis of his or her own developed set of ethics (Hersh et al., 1980; Ryan, 1981).

Kohlberg (1976) advocates an instructional model "in which the teacher Socratically elicits conflicting student views on a moral issue or dilemma" (p. 20) within an atmosphere of moral reasoning and discussion. The instruction not only corresponds to the student's specific level of moral development, but also attempts to influence and guide that development toward the next higher level. The teacher's first task is to identify the student's present level of moral development. The teacher then carefully chooses and poses a problem or dilemma to the student and provides an atmosphere which encourages the discussion of conflicting moral views, thus helping to raise the student's level of moral reasoning to the next higher level.

Attempts to encourage positive behavior patterns as well as to change negative behavior have also been common. One approach, for example, advocates the acquisition of knowledge through the observation of *human models* (Bandura, 1963, 1969). This observational learning requires: (1) exposure to a model, (2) acquisition of knowledge of the model's behavior, (3) acceptance or rejection of the model's behavior by the individual in future performance (Liebert & Spiegler, 1974). It should be noted that this is a model of learning, not of instruction. Although it should be possible to develop a model of instruction based on Bandura's work, such has not yet been done.

Behavior modification extends the modeling approach through the use of appropriate reinforcements for both desirable and undesirable behaviors. Bandura (1965) found that modeling in which behavior is rewarded is much more likely to be imitated than modeling in which behavior is punished. Therefore, although the behavior may have been learned through observation, performance of that behavior is influenced by the type of reinforcement associated with the behavior. This is clearly an instructional prescription and would be part of the instructional model.

Obviously, our knowledge about effective instructional strategies for affective objectives is inadequate; it does not allow us to provide very useful prescriptions for designing instruction in this domain. More work is needed on what strategy components to use when within each of these three models, but work is especially needed on identifying the situations for which each of these models is better than any alternatives, on identifying situations for which none of these models is very appropriate, and on developing models of instruction for each of those "new" situations.

MOTOR SKILL DOMAIN

Although largely ignored until recently, research into the learning of motor skills has been mainly related to industrial training and sports training contexts (Romiszowski, 1981). Several approaches to instruction have been advocated in this domain: the traditional (or direct) approach and the movement education approach. However, neither can be considered a model of instruction. The traditional approach has focused on selection of content by matching a series of formal motor activities to the stages of child development (Wade & Davis, 1981). The movement education approach uses an organized set of play and dance experiences in order to provide the opportunity for children to discover a variety of fundamental motor behaviors in a problem-solving situation (Wade & Davis, 1981).

Mental practice (Singer, 1972; Singer & Witker, 1970) is an interesting strategy component, which requires the mental or imaginary rehearsal of overt performance of a particular task. Mental practice takes place between practice sessions in order to improve the effect of motor training. It is often intended to reduce anxiety.

In addition, some investigators have advocated the teaching of motor skills for purposes of enhancing cognitive-skill development (Doman et al., 1960), but such work is in the cognitive domain (because it is intended to achieve cognitive outcomes), even though the methods entail motor activities (motor means).

The only work we have found which approaches being an instructional model in the motor-skill domain is that of Gagné (1985; Gagné & Briggs, 1979). This very general model prescribes demonstrations, practice, and informative feedback as the major strategy components, and indicates that sometimes (presumably for more complex motor skills) it is beneficial to divide the motor skill into *part-skills,* each of which is taught in isolation, followed by instruction in putting them all together (Fitts & Posner, 1967; Naylor & Briggs, 1963; Singer, 1972, 1975). Gagné also recommends the use of verbal instructions, checklists, and/or pictures for teaching the learner how to put all the part-skills together.

One can readily see some similarities between this model and models of instruction in the cognitive domain. The relationship between motor-skill and cognitive-skill learning has only recently been recognized. Increasingly, strategy components are being prescribed for both of these domains (see, e.g., Landa, 1983). The roles of goal setting, sequencing, repeated practice, feedback, and motivational considerations are all very similar to their counterparts in the cognitive domain. Strategies such as backward and forward chaining (Gilbert, 1962) and the executive subroutine procedure (Fitts & Posner, 1967) have been used within both domains. In addition, such strategies from the cognitive domain as mastery learning, information processing, cybernetics, and behavior modification are often used in motor-skill instruction.

However, it is clear that much more work is needed in this domain. More detailed prescriptions are needed for each of the general components in Gagné's model, and it seems likely that additional strategy components will be found that are helpful. Furthermore, different types of motor skills are likely to require different treatment. Perhaps gross motor coordination and fine motor coordination each require some specialized strategy components that are not needed for the other. Skills differ with respect to such requirements as speed, accuracy, force, and smoothness (Gagné & Briggs, 1979).

Perhaps differences in such skill characteristics require different strategy components. We hope to see much more research and model building in this domain over the next ten years or so.

COGNITIVE DOMAIN

Here we can provide you with more guidance than for either the affective or psychomotor domain because instructional researchers and theorists have done far more work in this domain. To continue with your task of developing some instruction, let's assume that your goals are primarily cognitive. Most instructional theorists indicate that your first task is to decide how to sequence all of the content (skills and information) that you identified in your task analysis as important to teach (see, e.g., Branson et al., 1975; Gagné & Briggs, 1979). Since this is the broadest level of instructional design, it is referred to as the *macro-level.*

Why is the sequencing of instruction important? Simply stated, if the sequence of a piece of instruction is bad, people won't learn as well. Ausubel (1963) argued that the sequence in which learning occurs influences the stability of cognitive structures and thereby influences long-term retention and transfer.

Gagné and Briggs (1979) recommend a "top-down" approach to designing an instructional sequence, in which you "work from more general goals and objectives down to increasingly specific objectives" (p. 29). First, a needs analysis is conducted to identify the broader "life-long objectives, which imply the continued future use of what is learned after the course is over" (p. 137). Then successive levels of objectives are determined, beginning with end-of-course objectives which state the performance expected immediately after instruction is completed. Once you have identified the general, end-of-course objective, you identify major *course units,* each of which may require several weeks of study. These units "define the performances expected on clusters of objectives having a common purpose in the organization of the total course" (p. 137). These unit objectives may be referred to as *target objectives,* which you then cluster into groups and sequence, thereby forming a general structure of the course.

This process of further analyzing objectives and then sequencing them is repeated for several more levels. You derive *performance objectives,* which are the specific learning outcomes expected, and which are at the appropriate level for task analysis, including information-processing analysis and hierarchical analysis. Then you sequence the performance objectives, each of which will make up a *lesson.* Finally, these performance objectives are broken down into *enabling objectives,* each of which may in turn have several subordinate objectives. The enabling objectives "support the learning of performance objectives either because they are essential prerequisite skills required to learn target objectives or because they facilitate such learning" (p. 137). And, of course, you sequence these enabling objectives within each lesson.

Once the sequence has been designed, you need to design the instruction on each individual skill or piece of information in that sequence. This entails deciding such things as the number and types of examples, practice, visuals, memory aids, attention-focusing devices, and the like. If time and budget permit, a learner analysis should be conducted to provide information on the difficulty level of the content in relation to ability levels of the entry learners. Often, however, constraints on time and budget require reliance on an experienced teacher to provide that information. The result of this process is the listing of strategy components to be used for each skill and piece of information in the sequence, and the order in which those strategy components should be presented.

SEQUENCING STRATEGIES

Many different sequencing strategies have been proposed. Posner and Strike (1976) suggest that five types of organizing principles may be combined to create instructional sequences. The five organizing principles are:

1. World-related sequences—the consistency and relationships among phenomena as they exist in the world;

2. Conceptual-related sequences—the organization of the conceptual world as it relates to the real world;

3. Inquiry-related sequences—"those that derive from the nature of the process of generating, discovering or verifying knowledge" (p. 676);

4. Learning-related sequences—based on knowledge about the psychology of learning; and

5. Utilization-related sequences—either through procedural sequences for problem solving or based on the utilization potential of the content.

Posner and Strike (1976) also identify a variety of sequences within each of these five categories. However, this perplexing plethora of possible sequences can be reduced to a few major types of sequences which researchers, educators, and instructional designers have found to be most helpful to learners. Almost universally, these major types of sequences are some form of simple-to-complex sequence. The following is a brief description of each.

Bruner's Spiral Curriculum

Bruner (1960, 1966) suggests that if an idea is determined to be important for a student to know, it should be introduced as early as possible on an intuitive, experiential *(enactive)* level. The idea is then developed and redeveloped as the learner matures intellectually. This continuous exposure to the idea provides the learner with a deeper and more meaningful understanding of that idea.

Hence, Bruner's spiral sequence prescribes that content be sequenced commensurately with the learner's intellectual development and that the sequence be built around the fundamental ideas in the subject. This approach demands that the same fundamental ideas of a subject be taught at each grade but with increasing levels of sophistication. Therefore, a spiral is produced by this periodical recycling of the same ideas through progressively greater degrees of complexity.

The spiral approach to curriculum sequencing has been used occasionally. Bruner himself was involved in the design of *Man: A Course of Study,* a social-studies text that utilized a spiral approach (Bruner, 1966). However, Bruner did not provide specific guidance as to how to create a spiral curriculum. Hence, it has not been easy for designers to use this sequencing strategy.

Ausubel's Progressive Differentiation

Ausubel (1963) constructed an instructional theory based on his theory of learning, which assumes that learners' cognitive structures are "hierarchically organized in terms of highly inclusive concepts under which are subsumed less inclusive subconcepts and informational data" (1960, p. 267). His instructional theory proposes *advance organizers,* in which general and inclusive ideas are presented first, followed by related ideas of greater specificity and detail. This sequence provides *progressive differentiation* of the initial ideas, such that the learner *subsumes* new, detailed knowledge under previous more general knowledge, resulting in stable cognitive structures that are resistant to forgetting.

In accordance with this theory, Ausubel (Ausubel, Novak, & Hanesian, 1978) advocates a general-to-detailed sequence that begins with more general and inclusive *anchoring ideas,* which in turn serve as organizers for the next level of detail and specificity. The ideas on that next level in turn serve as advance organizers for another level, and so on until the desired level of detail is reached. Unfortunately, Ausubel's instructional theory was primarily intended for the social sciences and other highly conceptual, verbal types of content. For more structured procedural content such as mathematics, his general-to-detailed sequence has not been adequately developed. Also, like Bruner, Ausubel has not provided specific guidance as to how to create this type of simple-to-complex sequence, making its use difficult for instructional design.

Gagné's Hierarchical Sequence

Gagné (1968, 1985) advocates the hierarchical analysis of intellectual skills. A *learning hierarchy* is formed by breaking each intellectual skill into simpler component parts. The component skills are then taught in a parts-to-whole sequence which follows the hierarchy in a "bottom-up" fashion, first teaching the most elemental parts at the bottom of the hierarchy, followed by progressively more complex combinations of the parts. It was found that teaching the prerequisite knowledge first facilitates the learning of the higher-order skills more than teaching the prerequisite knowledge out of sequence (Gagné, 1962; White & Gagné, 1974, 1978). However, there are relatively few unmastered prerequisites for most of the skills taught in most courses. Also, there are other kinds of relationships among skills in a course (besides the prerequisite relationship) that influence the kind of sequence that will most facilitate learning. Therefore, the hierarchical approach is a necessary but not sufficient basis for sequencing instructional content.

Shortest Path Sequence

Procedural content—content which is algorithmic in nature—has long been analyzed by performing an information-processing analysis. P. Merrill (1978) and Scandura (1973, 1983) are among the first who also advocated that a *path analysis* be conducted to identify all possible paths through a flow chart of the procedure (see Chapter 6). The path analysis provides the basis for designing yet another type of simple-to-complex sequence, one in which the operations constituting the shortest path are taught first. The remainder of the sequence consists of a series of paths (expanding sets of operations) which are progressively longer, that is, there are progressively more operations in each path. Therefore, as the instruction proceeds, the procedure or rule, as it is known to the learner, becomes more complex and detailed. This kind of sequence has much intuitive appeal. But what about courses within which procedural content is a relatively insignificant part of the subject matter, such as a social-studies course or an introductory course in economics? Again, this is an important but not sufficient sequencing strategy.

A GENERAL SEQUENCING MODEL

All four of the sequencing strategies described above for the cognitive domain—spiral, progressive differentiation, hierarchical, and shortest path—are variations of the simple-to-complex pattern. The Reigeluth-Merrill Elaboration Theory (Reigeluth & Stein, 1983) proposes an elaboration approach to sequencing which integrates and builds upon all four of these strategies; it uses both an analysis of the structure of knowledge and an understanding of learning theories and cognitive processes to design an instructional sequence.

The elaboration approach has two major features: (1) The earlier ideas *epitomize* rather than summarize the ideas that follow; and (2) The sequence is based on a *single* content orientation (Reigeluth & Stein, 1983). To epitomize is to present a few of the most fundamental and representative ideas at a concrete application (or skill) level (Reigeluth, 1979). Subsequent lessons add complexity or detail to one part or aspect of the overview in layers (called elaborations). The nature of the elaborations will differ, depending on the content orientation: whether the instruction should focus primarily on "what" (concepts), "how" (procedures), or "why" (principles). Careful analysis has shown that virtually every course holds one of these three to be more important than the other two. Hence, the Elaboration Theory proposes that the nature of the simple-to-complex sequence must differ, depending on the kind of content that is considered to be most important to the goals of the instruction.

The Elaboration Theory views an instructional sequence much like studying a picture through the zoom lens of a camera. A person starts with a wide-angle view, allowing the viewing of major parts of the picture and the major relationships among the parts, but without any detail. Once the person zooms in on a part of the picture, more about each of the major subparts can be seen. After studying those subparts and their interrelationships, the person can then zoom back out to the wide-angle view to review the other parts of the whole picture and to review the context of that one part within the whole picture. Continuing in this "zooming in" pattern, the person gradually progresses to the level of detail and breadth desired.

The Elaboration Theory starts the instruction with a special kind of overview containing the simplest and most fundamental ideas, called the *epitome.* Then, subsequent lessons add complexity or detail to one part or aspect of the overview in layers *(elaborations),* while periodically reviewing and identifying relationships between the most recent ideas and those presented earlier. This pattern of elaboration followed by summary and synthesis continues until the desired level of complexity has been reached. The elaboration sequence is highly detailed and precise in terms of its actual operationalization and allows sufficient freedom for the learner to select which part to zoom in on next and how far to zoom in on each one of the major ideas.

In spite of the detail and precision of Elaboration Theory and its firm basis in cognitive-learning theory and the structure of knowledge, many of the prescriptions for this sequencing strategy have not yet been sufficiently tested. Much more research is needed to validate and revise the strategy.

Variations on the Sequencing Model

In reviewing the sequencing strategies of Bruner, P. Merrill, Ausubel, and others, Reigeluth and M. D. Merrill found that each of these strategies used a simple-to-complex sequence (see Reigeluth & Stein, 1983). However, the dimension upon which those sequences were elaborating was different for each of them. That is, Bruner used *principles,* while P. Merrill utilized *procedures,* and *concepts* were the primary target of Ausubel's sequence.

In all the work that has been done on sequencing, the elaboration of concepts, principles, and procedures are the only three we have found, although additional ones may be identified in the future. This finding is consistent with M. D. Merrill's (Merrill, 1983; Merrill & Wood, 1974) identification of three content types for generalizable knowledge. Therefore, the Elaboration Theory proposes three different ways of elaborating, based on those three content types.

Hence, at this point in the development of your instruction, you must decide whether your goals are primarily conceptual (focusing on the "what"), procedural (focusing on the "how"), or theoretical (focusing on the "why"). If your goals are primarily conceptual in nature, as is usually the case in an introductory biology course, then the elaboration sequence should follow the process of meaningful assimilation of *concepts* to memory (Ausubel, 1968; Mayer, 1977). First, according to Elaboration Theory (Reigeluth & Darwazeh, 1982), you analyze and organize the concepts into conceptual structures, which show their superordinate, coordinate, and subordinate relationships. Then you design the instructional sequence by selecting the most important, comprehensive, and fundamental conceptual structure and sequencing its concepts from the top down (i.e., from the most general and inclusive concepts to progressively more detailed and less inclusive concepts). Finally, other concepts and other types of content, including learning prerequisites (Gagné, 1968), must be fleshed onto that skeleton of a sequence at the point where each is most relevant (Reigeluth & Darwazeh, 1982).

Alternatively, your goals might be primarily procedural (addressing the "how"), as in an English composition course. In this case, the elaboration sequence should follow the optimal process of *procedural skill* acquisition. Your first activity is to identify the simplest possible version of the task (usually equivalent to the shortest path through the procedure in P. Merrill's path-analysis methodology) and to identify the *simplifying assumptions* which define that simplest version. Your next task is to design the instructional sequence by gradually relaxing the simplifying assumptions in the order of most important, comprehensive, and fundamental ones first, such that progressively more complex paths are taught. Then the other types of content, including concepts, principles, learning prerequisites, and factual information, are "plugged into" that sequence at the point where each is most relevant (Reigeluth & Rodgers, 1980).

The final possibility is that your goals are primarily theoretical (addressing the "why"), as in an introductory economics course. In this case, the elaboration sequence follows the psychological process of developing an understanding of natural processes (primarily causes and effects), which is usually the same as the order of the historical discovery of such knowledge. After identifying the breadth and depth of principles that should be taught, you design the instructional sequence by asking the question "What principle(s) would you teach if you only had the learners for one hour?" and ". . . one more hour?" and so on until all the principles have been arranged in a sequence that progresses from the most basic and fundamental principles to the most detailed, complex, and restricted principles. During this process, it is often helpful to look at an earlier principle and ask "Why?", "Which way?", "How much?", or "What else?" to identify more complex principles which elaborate on the earlier one. Other types of content are then plugged into that sequence at the point where each is most relevant (Reigeluth, in press; Sari & Reigeluth, 1982).

When you finish designing the sequence, you will have a macro-level blueprint similar to the one shown in Fig. 7.1. It shows all of the organizing content (in this case, principles) allocated to lessons, and it shows the sup-

LEVEL	LESSON	ORGANIZING CONTENT (PRINCIPLES)	SUPPORTING CONTENT CONCEPTS	PRINCIPLES	PROCEDURES	LEARNING PREREQUISITES	FACTS
Epitome	1	*The body gets energy and nutrients from food.		*Different ages and sizes of people require different amounts of energy and nutrients.		*Energy *Nutrients	*4 food groups
1	2	*The body gets energy from food containing protein, carbohydrates, or fat.	*Kinds of food.			*Protein *Carbohydrates *Fat	*List and definition of each other kind of food (remember level)
2	3	*Energy is used through exercise and physical activity. *If too much food is eaten, energy from that food is stored as fat. *Body fat is changed back into energy by reducing the amount of energy readily available.	*Kinds of exercise. *Kinds of physical activity.		*How to figure out amount of energy needed. *How to reduce amount of energy readily available.	*Calorie *Exercise *Physical activity	*One pound of fat is burned by using 3500 calories. *List and definition of each kind of exercise and physical activity (remember level).
2	4	*Protein from food gives you energy and helps develop muscles. *Carbohydrates give you quick energy. *Ingested fat gives you twice as much energy as anything else.				*Muscles *Ingested fat	*Number of calories in common food.
1	5	*Vitamins and minerals provide essential nutrients for proper body growth and function.	*Kinds of vitamins. *Kinds of minerals.	*Vitamin deficiencies cause diseases. *Mineral deficiencies cause diseases.		*Nutrient *Vitamin *Mineral *Body function *Vitamin deficiency	*List of each kind of vitamin. *List of each kind of mineral.
2	6	*Vitamin A makes smooth, healthy skin, develops "night" sight and reduces the chances of catching a cold. *Vitamin B₁ (thiamin) keeps nerves healthy, aids good digestion, and helps your body use other foods for energy. *Vitamin B₂ (riboflavin) keeps mouth and eyes healthy and helps your body use oxygen. *Niacin keeps skin and nerves healthy. *Vitamin C (ascorbic acid) keeps your gums, skin, and muscles healthy, helps keep you from catching a cold. *Vitamin D helps build strong teeth and bones, and makes legs straight and strong.			*How to meet your vitamin needs.	*Definitions of any unknown terms in the principles	*Vitamin content of common foods.
2	7	*Calcium builds strong bones and teeth, and stops bleeding when you cut yourself. *Phosphorus builds bones, teeth and nerves and helps you use other nutrition for energy. *Iron builds healthy red blood. Copper helps build healthy red blood. *Iodine controls how you use energy.			*How to meet your mineral needs.	*Definitions of any unknown terms in the principles.	*Mineral content of common foods.

FIGURE 7.1. A macro-level blueprint for a course on nutrition.

porting concepts and procedures, learning prerequisites, and factual supporting content for each lesson.

Within-lesson sequence.   Next, you need to design a sequence for all content *within* each lesson. The Elaboration Theory offers several guidelines here: (1) Usually put supporting content immediately after the organizing content to which it is most closely related, (2) Put each learning prerequisite immediately before the content for which it is prerequisite, (3) Group coordinate concepts together, and (4) Teach a principle (meaningful understanding of processes) before any related procedure (see Fig. 7.2 for an example of a lesson sequence). Other macro-strategy components are integrated into the lesson sequence, such as summarizers, synthesizers, analogies, cognitive-strategy activators, macro-level motivational-strategy components, and macro-level learner-control options (Reigeluth & Stein, 1983).

Summarizers.   A summarizer is a strategy component used to review systematically what has been learned (Reigeluth & Stein, 1983). It provides (1) a concise statement of each idea or fact that has been taught, (2) a typical,

---

LESSON 3 SEQUENCE

1. Contextual synthesizer.

2. Learning Prerequisites: Exercise, physical activity.

3. Organizing Content: Energy is used through exercise or physical activity.

4. Supporting Concepts: Kinds of exercise. Kinds of physical activity.

5. Organizing Content: If too much food is eaten, energy from that food is stored as fat.

6. Supporting Procedure: How to figure amount of energy needed.

7. Organizing Content: Fat is changed back into energy by reducing the amount of energy readily available.

8. Learning Prerequisite: definition of calorie.

9. Supporting Fact: One pound of fat is "burned" by using an equivalent of 3500 calories of energy.

10. Supporting Procedure: How to reduce the amount of energy readily available.

11. Supporting Fact: List and definition of each kind of exercise and physical activity.

12. Summarizer.

13. Post-synthesizer.

FIGURE 7.2. An example of a within-lesson sequence for one lesson of a course on nutrition.

easy-to-remember example, and (3) some diagnostic, self-test, practice items for each idea. *Internal summarizers* appear at the end of each lesson, while *within-set summarizers* summarize all of the ideas and facts that have been taught so far in an entire set of lessons. A set of lessons is all those lessons that elaborate directly on a single lesson.

Synthesizers. A synthesizer is used to interrelate and integrate ideas. It is intended to (1) provide the learner with a valuable kind of knowledge, (2) facilitate a deeper understanding of the individual ideas, (3) increase the meaningfulness and motivational appeal of the instruction (Ausubel, 1968; Keller, 1983), and (4) increase retention. The Elaboration Theory presently prescribes three types of synthesizers, each of which interrelates ideas of a single content type (Reigeluth & Stein, 1983).

Analogies. An analogy relates new information to a more familiar and hence more meaningful context of organized knowledge that the learner already possesses (Ortony, 1979; Verbrugge & McCarrell, 1977). It reminds the learner of something more concrete within the learner's experience in order to prepare him or her for understanding a more abstract, complex type of idea (Curtis & Reigeluth, 1984; Reigeluth, 1983b).

Cognitive-strategy activators. A cognitive-strategy activator, which activates the learner's use of a generic skill, can be used for any content area. It may be *embedded* into the instruction, as when a mnemonic or analogy is presented, or it may be *detached,* as is the case when the learner is provided only with the directions to use a previously learned cognitive strategy (Rigney, 1978), such as "think up an analogy," or "try to come up with a mnemonic."

Learner control. Learner control may offer the learner options for the selection and sequencing of his or her content and instructional strategies, and thereby control over how he or she will study and learn (M. D. Merrill, 1979, 1983, 1984; Reigeluth & Stein, 1983). Learner control of *content* offers selection of any lesson for which the learner has already acquired the prerequisites, while learner control of *instructional strategies* offers selection of the type, order, and number of such micro-strategy components as examples, practice items, and alternative representations, and type and timing of such macro-strategy components as summarizers, synthesizers, and analogies.

At this point, you have designed the following aspects of your instruction:

1. An elaboration sequence of lessons,
2. A within-lesson sequence for each lesson, including any necessary learning-prerequisite sequences,
3. A summarizer for each lesson,

4. A synthesizer for each lesson,

5. Analogies as needed,

6. Cognitive-strategy activators as needed, and

7. Learner control to the extent appropriate.

MICRO-LEVEL STRATEGIES

Now that you have selected and sequenced all of the skills and information that need to be taught, you need to design the instruction on each individual skill and piece of information (micro-level design). This entails making a number of decisions about a variety of different micro-strategy components, such as examples, practice, feedback, representation forms, memory devices, and attention-focusing devices. The decisions include: (1) which components should be used, (2) how much of each should be used, and (3) what should each component be like.

The macro-level blueprint shown in Figs. 7.1 and 7.2 indicates the sequence for instruction related to nutrition and energy. Micro-design for that course would specify how to teach such ideas as "calories," "the relationship of age and size to nutrition and energy," "how vitamins are used in the body," and others of this general sort.

Much work has been done on each of a wide variety of micro-strategy components. This work has contributed greatly toward the building of a common knowledge base from which much needed optimal models of instruction are beginning to emerge (Reigeluth, 1984b). Evans, Homme, and Glaser (1962) developed prescriptions for the use of rules and examples (ruleg). Skinner's work (1954, 1965) includes prescriptions on the use of overt responses, reinforcement, and shaping. Bruner's work (1960, 1966) includes prescriptions for the use of a variety of representation forms, specifically enactive (the real thing), iconic (representations which bear some resemblance to the real thing), and symbolic (ones which bear no resemblance to the real thing). Rothkopf (1976) has developed prescriptions for the use of *mathemagenic information,* forms of guidance which help the learner to understand new knowledge or to acquire new skills. Kulhavy (1977) has done much work on prescriptions for the optimal form of feedback on practice. Landa's work (1974, 1976, 1983) includes prescriptions for the use of algorithms to aid skill acquisition. Horn (1976) has developed some useful prescriptions for *information mapping* to isolate and label the nature of each component of the instruction.

Most of the work mentioned previously was fairly piecemeal in that it made no attempt to prescribe the full variety of strategy components that should be included in any module of instruction. However, some important efforts have been undertaken to identify optimal combinations of strategy components, which are far more useful to instructional designers than piecemeal prescriptions. Gagné (1968) was a pioneer in attempts to integrate our piecemeal knowledge about instructional strategies on the micro-level. He identified nine *events of instruction* considered to be critical for effective instruction. They include: (1) *gaining attention* through the use of stimulus change; (2) *informing the learner of the objective* to help the learner recognize the importance and relevance of the instruction; (3) *stimulating recall of prerequisite learnings* so that the learner may combine them with new learning; (4) *presenting the stimulus material* in an appropriate manner to the learner; (5) *providing learning guidance* in accordance with the level of complexity and difficulty of the material to be learned and the level of knowledge and ability of the learner; (6) *eliciting the performance* which represents the desired learning; (7) *providing feedback about performance correctness* in order to establish reinforcement of appropriate performance and prevent further inappropriate performance; (8) *assessing performance* in order to evaluate learning; and (9) *enhancing retention and transfer* by providing cues and strategies for retrieval.

Gagné, Wager, and Rojas (1981) assert that all nine events of instruction should be considered, but decisions about which events to include and how to represent and sequence them are dependent on the nature of the learning objective and the intended learners. Gagné and Briggs (1979) provide prescriptions for each event of instruction depending on the type of learning objective—intellectual skill, cognitive strategy, verbal information, attitude, or motor skill—by combining them into a matrix of five distinct models of instruction. An example of their model for teaching *verbal information* includes 1. gaining attention (introducing stimulus change); 2. informing the learner of the objective (specifying the type of verbal question to be answered); 3. stimulating recall of prerequisite learning (recalling a context of organized information); 4. presenting the stimulus material (presenting information in propositional form); 5. providing learning guidance (suggesting verbal links to a larger meaningful context); 6. eliciting the performance (asking the learner to respond through paraphrasing of information); 7. providing feedback (informing about the correctness of a response); 8. assessing performance (requiring the learner to restate the response); and 9. enhancing retention and transfer (providing verbal links to additional complexes of information) (Gagné & Briggs, 1979, p. 166).

Although they have provided some useful examples, Gagné and Briggs have not provided many generalizable prescriptions as to specific instructional strategy components for designers to use to accomplish each instructional event for any given type of objective. Since Gagné and Briggs developed their notion of the nine events of instruction, much work has been done to develop detailed prescriptions about what specific kinds of stimulus change to use when, how to present information in propositional form, what kinds of verbal links to use when, and what type of feedback to employ.

Generalizable prescriptions have been developed for such specific strategy components as mnemonics, visual images, a variety of attention-focusing devices, and other strategies. Although the nine events of instruction do not provide detailed generalizable guidance for instructional designers, this work has made several extremely important contributions to our knowledge base. First, it provides a useful, broad framework that integrates many prescriptions that have been generated about particular instructional-strategy components. Second, it also introduced the notion that different models of instruction were needed for different learning situations, and that the most important type of learning situation for prescribing instructional models is the nature of what is to be learned.

George Gropper (1973, 1974, 1975, 1983) has also done much work to integrate our piecemeal knowledge base about micro-level strategy components into models of instruction. Like Gagné and Briggs (1979) and most other instructional theorists, he prescribes different instructional-strategy components for different types of objectives. Some of those strategy components are always used when teaching most types of objectives. They are called *routine treatments* and include (1) telling students what to do and how to do it, (2) providing a variety of examples, (3) providing rules governing performance, and (4) requiring practice of an intact criterion behavior (Gropper, 1983). But not all of these components are used for every kind of objective. For example, objectives that entail "recalling facts" require only the first and the fourth: "telling students what the facts are" and "requiring students to practice . . . the facts" (Gropper, 1983, p. 149).

In Gropper's instructional theory, other strategy components are included for all types of objectives, but only when the objective is fairly difficult for the learners. They are called *shaping progressions* and include: (1) increasing the strength of cues, (2) reducing the size of the unit of behavior, (3) introducing *recognize* and *edit* as intermediate modes of practice before requiring the learner to *produce,* and (4) introducing easier practice examples before more difficult ones (Gropper, 1983).

Still other strategy components are also used when the objective is fairly difficult for learners, but are idiosyncratic to the specific objective. They are called *specialized treatments.* For example, instruction on objectives that call for defining concepts would use "special cues such as diagrams or information maps that distinguish between instance and noninstance" (Gropper, 1983, p. 151), and instruction on objectives that entail following procedural rules would use "backward chaining for long chains" and "job aids or checklists (cues) to overcome difficulties traceable to the length of a chain" (pp. 153–154). These three types of strategy components are listed here in order of their priority for use, which is based on their relative efficiencies. Each type of component results in progressively longer (less efficient) instruction, and should therefore only be used when the higher-priority components are inadequate. Gropper provides much detailed guidance to the designer as to specific strategy components to use in the micro-level design of instruction.

Concept classification is one of the types of objectives used both by Gagné and Briggs and by Gropper to prescribe an instructional model. Markle and Tiemann (1969), M. D. Merrill and Tennyson (1977), and Klausmeier, Ghatala, and Frayer (1974) have all developed many useful strategies specifically for teaching concepts, including "matched" or "close-in" nonexamples and stages in the development of a learner's knowledge of concepts.

THREE INSTRUCTIONAL MODELS FOR THE MICRO-LEVEL

M. D. Merrill's Component Display Theory (Merrill, 1983; Merrill, Reigeluth, & Faust, 1979; Merrill et al., 1977) builds on the Gagné-Briggs framework and integrates into it much existing knowledge about micro-design considerations. It is comprised of *three models* of instruction, each of which can be used in varying degrees of richness, and a system for using *three categories of objectives* to prescribe those models. The three types of objectives include: (1) Remember a generality or an instance (rote recall or meaningful understanding), (2) Use a generality on new instances (skill application), and (3) Discover a new generality (cognitive-strategy application). These correspond roughly to Gagné's verbal information, intellectual skills, and cognitive strategies, respectively. Component Display Theory (CDT) indicates what combination of instructional-strategy components is most likely to optimize achievement of each of these three desired outcomes.

At this point in the development of your instruction, you must pick one skill or piece of information (concept, principle, procedure, or fact) from one lesson and decide which of the three levels is represented by its objective.

Remember-Level General Model

If the objective for your piece of content calls for it to be learned by rote recall or meaningful understanding with no intention that the learner be able to generalize it to a variety of cases (that would be skill application), then CDT prescribes that the primary components in the instruction be: (1) presentation of the information that is to be remembered and (2) practice in recalling that information. CDT also prescribes a variety of secondary components: mnemonics, attention-focusing devices, and of course immediate feedback on the practice (M. D. Merrill, 1983). These are similar to Gropper's *shaping progressions* and *specialized treatments*.

Variations of the Remember-Level Model

There are several learning situations that call for modifications in this general model. One is that the *richness* of the instruction needs to vary, depending on the difficulty of the content. The easier and more familiar the content, the fewer secondary components are needed. The other modification is that some strategy components will be different, depending on whether the objective calls for remembering *verbatim* (rote recall) or *paraphrased* (meaningful understanding). CDT prescribes that a prototypical example (for remembering a generality) and an alternative representation (e.g., a diagram or paraphrase of the content to be remembered) be included in the instruction only for remembering the paraphrased form.

Reigeluth (1984c) has expanded on this model and its variations. The following strategy components are not necessarily used sequentially:

a. Stimulate and maintain *interest* (if necessary)
   —question   —demonstration   —game
   —novelty   —analogy

b. Create or activate a *meaningful context* (if appropriate)
   —related learner experience (experiential knowledge)
   —subsuming ideas (superordinate knowledge) if any

c. Present the *information*
   —consistent with the postinstructional requirements
   —separated and labeled

d. Provide *enrichment* on the presentation (if appropriate)
   —spaced repetition (for different information)
   —simplified early presentations (for difficult information)
   —bite-sized chunks (for a lot of information)
   —attention-focusing devices (when there is much irrelevant information)
   —alternative representations (for meaningful understanding)
   —reference example (for understanding of a generality)
   —memory devices (for rote recall)

e. Provide *practice* on the information
   —consistent with the post-instructional requirements
   —separated and labeled
   —as soon as possible after presentation of information

f. Provide *enrichment* on the practice (if necessary)
   —spaced repetition (for difficult information) including recognition before recall form of practice
   —bite-sized chunks (for a lot of information)

g. Provide *reinforcement* and feedback
   —immediately after each practice
   —continuous-to-intermittent reinforcement
   —correct answer
   —intrinsic reinforcement

h. Provide *enrichment* on the feedback (if necessary)
   —praise
   —attention-focusing devices (when there is much irrelevant information)
   —alternative representations (for meaningful understanding)
   —repeat the memory devices (for difficult rote information)

Skill-Application General Model

If the objective for your next piece of content calls for learning to apply a skill, the CDT prescribes that the instruction should contain three primary components: a generality, examples, and practice items (M. D. Merrill, 1983). A *generality* is the definition of a concept, description of a procedure, or explanation of a principle, any one of which can be applied to a variety of different cases. For example: "An adjective is a word that is used to describe a noun or a noun equivalent." An *example* is an instance or specific case of that generality, such as "slow is an adjective." A *practice item* offers the learner an opportunity to apply the generality to an instance not previously encountered, such as "Which of the following words is an adjective? *cow . . . pretty . . . jump*" (where none of those words was used in previous instruction on adjectives). Practice items should be followed by some type of *feedback* informing the learner as to whether his or her response was correct, and, if incorrect, it should explain why or should show the process for arriving at the correct response.

When more than one example and/or practice item is required for the instruction, they should be *divergent*—that is, the instances should be as different as possible from each other. In addition, the examples and practice should be presented in a *progression of difficulty* from easy to difficult.

Finally, CDT prescribes the use of several *secondary components:* alternative representations of the generality, examples, and practice; attention-focusing devices on the generality, examples, and practice feedback; analogies; mnemonics; algorithms; and matched example–nonexample pairs for concepts (M. D. Merrill, 1983).

Variations on the Skill-Application Model

There are several learning situations that call for modifications in this general model (M. D. Merrill, 1983). As with the remember-level model, the *richness* of the instruction needs to vary, depending on the difficulty of the content. The easier and more familiar the content, the fewer examples, practice, and secondary components needed.

Another variation relates to *content types.* The nature of the generality, examples, and practice is different for different content types. For example, the generality for a concept should identify the name of the concept, its superordinate concept, its critical (defining) attributes, and the nature of the relationship among the attributes (conjunctive or disjunctive). On the other hand, the generality for a procedure should identify the name of the procedure (if any), its goal, and its steps in sequential order, including any decision steps and branches. And the generality for a principle should identify the changes and the relationship between them, which usually means identifying the cause, the effect, and the fact that the cause caused the effect. The nature of examples, practice, and enrichment components is also different for each type of content. (See M. D. Merrill, 1983, pp. 313–320, for details.)

The *sequence* of the primary components can be varied, depending on whether a deductive or inductive approach is desired. A *deductive approach* requires presentation of the generality before the examples and practice. An *inductive approach* requires presentation of the examples or even just the practice first, so that the learner is required to induce or discover the generality (cf. Collins & Stevens, 1983). The selection of approach depends on the amount of time available for instruction (the inductive approach takes longer), the motivational requirements of the learners regarding the content (the inductive approach is usually more motivational), the age of the learners (younger learners usually benefit from receiving examples first), and whether the ability to discover is a desirable secondary objective (Landa, 1983). One should also keep in mind that the inductive approach tends to facilitate transfer and long-term retention. However, it is less efficient because it takes the learners longer to achieve mastery (Shulman & Keislar, 1966).

Finally, *learner control* (M. D. Merrill, 1984) offers yet another variation. Instruction may be designed so that the learner can easily select which strategy component to study when. If each component is labeled, then the learner can construct his or her own sequence of components. For instance, a learner could skip to the examples first, then go back to the generality, try a few practice items, look at a few more examples, and then go to the more difficult practice. However, research results indicate that learner control is only helpful when the learners have learned how to use it effectively (M. D. Merrill, 1983).

Reigeluth (1984c) has extended CDT's skill-application model of instruction. The following strategy components are not necessarily included sequentially:

a. Stimulate and maintain *interest* (if necessary)
   —question   —demonstration   —game
   —novelty   —analogy
b. Review *prerequisites* (if necessary)
c. Present the *generality*
   —consistent with the postinstructional environment
   —separated and labeled

d. Provide *enrichment* on the generality (if necessary)
   —bite-sized   —alternative representation
   —memory devices   —repetition (spaced)
   —attention-focusing

e. Present some *examples*
   —consistent with the postinstructional environment
   —separated and labeled   —divergent (varied)
   —easy-to-difficult

f. Provide *enrichment* on the examples (if necessary)
   —amount   —alternative representation
   —attention-focusing

g. Provide *practice*
   —consistent with the postinstructional environment
   —separated and labeled   —divergent (varied)
   —easy-to-difficult

h. Provide *enrichment* on the practice (if necessary)
   —amount

i. Provide *reinforcement* and *feedback*
   —immediate   —correct answer
   —-intrinsic   —continuous-to-intermittent
                          reinforcement

j. Provide *enrichment* on the feedback (if necessary)
   —praise   —attention-focusing
   —process   —alternative representation

Cognitive-Strategy-Application General Model

Finally, the objective for your next piece of content may call for learning a cognitive strategy. Cognitive strategies are ways the learner uses to approach novel problems, and if properly applied will facilitate acquisition, retention, and retrieval (Rigney, 1978). They can be thought of as thinking skills and learning skills that can be applied across a variety of different subject areas (Reigeluth, 1983b). There have been many cognitive strategies investigated over the years. Examples are strategies for creating mental imagery, for creating analogies, for discovering, problem solving, note taking, response review, self-programming, and self-monitoring (Dansereau, 1978; Weinstein, 1978).

Although cognitive strategies take longer to learn than intellectual skills, their acquisition may be facilitated through a variety of techniques. As mentioned previously, Gagné and Briggs (1979) have advocated presenting *novel problems* in teaching cognitive strategies. However, it also seems likely that virtually all of the strategy components from the skill-application model can and should be used for teaching cognitive strategies. For example, discovery (a cognitive strategy) can be taught by providing a generality about how to discover new ideas, presenting examples of that generality being used to discover new ideas, and providing practice with feedback on applying the generality to novel problems.

Variations on the Cognitive-Strategy-Application Model

It seems likely at present to assume that all of the variations of the skill-application model would also hold here. However, much more work needs to be done in this area.

MOTIVATIONAL-STRATEGY COMPONENTS

As you design the instruction on each piece of content in your macro-level blueprint, you should also be thinking about the motivational requirements for the instruction, given the nature of the content and the learners. The inclusion of motivational principles in instructional design has only recently begun to receive systematic attention. Keller (1979) has done some integrative and highly innovative work in developing a descriptive theory of motivation as it relates to instruction and performance. Keller's theory is founded upon *environmental theories* concerned with conditioning principles and physiologically based drives (e.g., Hull, 1943; Skinner, 1953); *humanistic theories* attributing free will as the basis for motivation (e.g., Rogers, 1969); and *social-learning theories* which look at the interaction between person and environment (e.g., Bandura, 1969; Rotter, 1954, 1966). In addition, Keller's theory of motivation draws on a broad variety of other ideas, particularly expectancy-value theory (e.g., Porter & Lawler, 1968), which includes the notion that motivation is a multiplicative function of expectancies and values.

Furthermore, Keller has extended his descriptive theory by developing *prescriptions* for the motivational design of instruction (Keller, 1983; Keller & Dodge, 1982). These prescriptions are divided into four types of motivational requirements, represented by ARCS: *Attention* (arouse and sustain), *Relevance* (instruction linked to important needs), *Confidence* (feelings of competence), and *Satisfaction* (reinforcement). A special combination of learner and content analyses identifies the motivational requirements of the instruction, which in turn provide the basis for prescribing specific motivational-strategy components.

These four types of motivational requirements may be related to Gagné's nine events of instruction. Attention corresponds to Gagné's first event: gaining attention. Relevance is provided when the learner is informed of the objective and is stimulated to recall past learning before encountering the stimulus material. Confidence may be achieved through "learning guidance."

Finally, the learner's feelings of satisfaction may be enhanced by providing positive feedback on the learner's performance.

Keller and Dodge have further identified specific strategy components for each of the four dimensions that may be applied to the design of a piece of instruction. Examples for each motivational requirement are:

1. Vary the appearance of the instructional materials (attention);
2. Relate the content to the learner's past experience (relevance);
3. Sequence and present material in gradually increasing levels of difficulty (confidence);
4. Provide positive reinforcement and feedback (satisfaction) (Keller & Dodge, 1982).

The nature of various primary and secondary presentation forms may be greatly influenced by the types of motivational considerations outlined here. For example, in order to sustain attention, lower-ability students often require less print, more illustrations, and more attention-focusing devices on a page of text than higher-ability students. There is much need to integrate this highly innovative work into our expanding knowledge base of instructional models.

APPROACHES TO INSTRUCTION

Once the richness and motivational requirements for the instruction are determined and the appropriate components are prescribed for the instruction, you must then decide on an approach or combination of approaches by which the instruction should occur (Reigeluth, et al., 1982). However, the approach selected for the presentation of instruction is largely based on what the sequencing strategy requirements are for that instruction.

Reigeluth et al. (1982) have organized the types of presentation approaches into a matrix based on the *source* of instruction and the *receiver* of that instruction. The source can be either human or nonhuman. If it is human, it can be a trained professional or an amateur; and similarly, if it is nonhuman, it can be instructionally designed or not designed specifically for instructional purposes. For any one of those kinds of sources of the instruction, the receiver can be an individual learner or a group of learners. The result of this conceptualization is a 4 × 2 matrix defining eight distinct approaches to instruction (see Fig. 7.3). The label most closely associated with each of these eight approaches is shown in the matrix, but in some cases common use of those labels does not perfectly match the category as defined by the matrix.

Source of Instruction

	Human		Nonhuman	
	Professional	Non-Professional	Instructionally Designed Environment	Not Designed for Instruction
Individual	Tutoring	Peer Tutoring	Individualized Resources	Individual Projects
Group	Exposition (Lecture)	Group Discussion	Group Activities	Group Projects

Receiver of Instruction

FIGURE 7.3. Eight instructional approaches as defined by the nature of the source and receiver of the instruction.

Often instructional designers think only of individualized resources when they design instruction. This is not a good practice because other approaches are often more effective or less expensive. The selection of the most appropriate approach or combination of approaches for your instruction should be based on a number of criteria, including practice and feedback requirements, content characteristics, student characteristics, teamwork requirements, and resource considerations. A guide to the selection of these approaches, according to specified conditions, is presented in Fig. 7.4. Also, Reigeluth et al. (1982) provide specific prescriptions for using each approach. These prescriptions identify additional strategy considerations (especially management considerations, as described in the following section) particular to each of the eight approaches, and they integrate those considerations with the Component Display Theory and Elaboration Theory prescriptions.

MANAGEMENT STRATEGIES

Management strategies are methods for deciding when and where to use other instructional strategies. Perhaps the most important model for management-strategy components is mastery learning (Block, 1971; Bloom, 1968, 1971; Carroll, 1971). The major components in this model are: (1) identification of competencies to be mastered by all learners; (2) diagnosis of the learners at the end of the instruction on a competency to determine whether mastery has been reached; and (3) remediation whenever the diagnosis reveals that a learner has not achieved mastery of a competency.

Selection Criteria	Individualized Instruction	Group Activities	Lecture or Demonstration	Teacher or Peer Tutoring	Group Discussions	Individual Projects	Group Projects
1. Practice and Feedback Requirements							
Not required			X				
Rote practice required		X		X			
Immediate, individual feedback neded	X			X			
Perspectives/attitudes of peers important					X		
Responses difficult to evaluate	X			X			
Wide range of responses possible	X			X			
Evaluation/practice conducted in natural environment		X		X		X	X
2. Content Characteristics							
Abstract/complex information	X			X			
Urgent/changing information			X				
Low priority information			X				
Easy to retain			X				
No/low active participation of learner required	X		X				
Problems with no clear answer					X		
Special presentation for special group			X				
Unique task for one/few learners				X			
3. Student Characteristics							
Homogenous	X		X				
Similar verbal/analytical aptitude					X		
Avove-average intelligence			X				
Low achievers	X	X	X	X	X		
Need to alleviate anxiety caused by group work	X			X		X	
Need affiliation with teacher				X			
Need affiliation with peers		X			X		X
Can work independently	X					X	
4. Teamwork Requirements							
Real-life team task		X					X
Interactive skills critical to task		X			X		X
Group consensus needed					X		
Student cooperation/group cohesiveness sought		X			X		X
5. Resource Considerations							
Large number of students	X		X				
Lack of teachers/money/materials			X	X			
Individual records to be managed	X			X		X	

FIGURE 7.4. Guidelines for selecting an instructional approach.

Another important model included in management strategies is learner control. Various components for providing learner control over macro strategies (especially sequencing) and micro-strategies were described earlier. Other management strategies are described in Chapters 14 and 15.

CONCLUSION

The failure of so many instructional programs and materials has often been the result of an emphasis solely on content, with little regard for principles of instructional design to produce effective, efficient, and appealing instruction. A knowledge of instructional models that adapt to a variety of learning situations provides the foundation for optimizing learning outcomes.

This chapter has described the results of some of the most comprehensive efforts to integrate our knowledge about instructional strategy components into theories of instruction, which prescribe different models of instruction for different learning situations. However, the field is just entering its adolescence. We can expect to see the development of a much more cohesive and powerful knowledge base about instruction over the next 10 to 20 years. Readers of this chapter may well become important contributors to that effort.

REFERENCES

Ausubel, D. P. (1960). The use of advance organizers in the learning of meaningful verbal material. *Journal of Educational Psychology, 51,* 267–272.

Ausubel, D. P. (1963). *Psychology of meaningful verbal learning.* New York: Grune & Stratton.

Ausubel, D. P. (1968). *Educational psychology: A cognitive view.* New York: Holt, Rinehart and Winston.

Ausubel, D. P., Novak, J. D., & Hanesian, H. (1978). *Educational psychology: A cognitive view* (2nd Ed.). New York: Holt, Rinehart and Winston.

Bandura, A. (1969). *Principles of behavior modification.* New York: Holt, Rinehart and Winston.

Bandura, A. & Walters, R. H. (1963). *Social learning and personality development.* New York: Holt, Rinehart and Winston.

Block, J. H. (1971). *Mastery learning: Theory and practice.* New York: Holt, Rinehart and Winston.

Bloom, B. S. (Ed.). (1956). *Taxonomy of educational objectives. Handbook I: Cognitive domain.* New York: McKay.

Bloom, B. S. (1968). Learning for mastery. *Evaluation Comment, 1*(2) 1–12.

Bloom, B. S. (1971). Mastery learning. In J. H. Block (Ed.), *Mastery learning: Theory and practice.* New York: Holt, Rinehart and Winston.

Branson, R. K., Rayner, G. I., Cox, J. L., Furman, J. P., King, F. J., & Hannum, W. H. (1975). *Inter-service procedures for instructional system development* (5 vols.). Fort Monroe, VA: US Army Training and Doctrine Command (TRADOC PAM 350–30 and HAVEDTRA 196A).

Bruner, J. S. (1960). *The process of education.* New York: Random House.

Bruner, J. S. (1966). *Toward a theory of instruction.* New York: Norton.

Carroll, J. B. (1971). Problems of measurement related to the concept of learning for mastery. In J. H. Block (Ed.), *Mastery learning: Theory and practice.* New York: Holt, Rinehart and Winston.

Collins, A., & Stevens, A. L. (1983). A cognitive theory of inquiry teaching. In C. M. Reigeluth (Ed.), *Instructional-design theories and models: An overview of their current status.* Hillsdale, NJ: Lawrence Erlbaum Associates.

Crowder, N. A. (1960). Automatic tutoring by intrinsic programming. In A. Lumsdaine & R. Glaser (Eds.), *Teaching machines and programmed learning.* Washington, DC: National Education Association.

Curtis, R. V., & Reigeluth, C. M. (1984). The use of analogies in written text. *Instructional Science, 13,* 99–117.

Dansereau, D. (1978). The development of a learning strategies curriculum. In H. F. O'Neil, Jr. (Ed.), *Learning strategies.* New York: Academic Press.

Doman, R. J., Spitz, E.B., Zucman, E., & Delacato, C. H. (1960). Children with severe brain injuries: Neurological organization in terms of mobility. *Journal of the American Medical Association, 174,* 257–262.

Evans, J. L., Homme, L. E., & Glaser, R. (1962). The Ruleg system for the construction of programmed verbal learning sequences. *Journal of Educational Research, 55,* 513–518.

Fitts, P. M. & Posner, M. I. (1967). *Human performance.* Monterey, CA: Brooks/Cole.

Gagné, R. M. (1962). The acquisition of knowledge. *Psychological Review, 59,* 355–365.

Gagné, R. M. (1968). Learning and communication. In R. V. Wiman and W. C. Meierhenry (Eds.), *Educational media: Theory into practice.* Columbus, OH: Merrill.

Gagné, R. M. (1985). *The conditions of learning* (4th ed.). New York: Holt, Rinehart and Winston.

Gagné, R. M. & Briggs, L. J. (1979). *Principles of instructional design* (2nd ed.). New York: Holt, Rinehart and Winston.

Gagné, R. M., Wager, W., & Rojas, A. (1981, September). Planning and authoring computer-assisted instruction lessons. *Educational Technology,* 17–26.

Gilbert, T. F. (1962). Mathetics: The technology of education. *Journal of Mathetics,* 7–73.

Gropper, G. L. (1973). *A technology for developing instructional materials.* Pittsburgh: American Institutes for Research.

Gropper, G. L. (1974). *Instructional Strategies.* Englewood Cliffs, NJ: Educational Technology Publications.

Gropper, G. L. (1975). *Diagnosis and revision in the development of instructional materials.* Englewood Cliffs, NJ: Educational Technology.

Gropper, G. L. (1983). A behavioral approach to instructional prescription. In C. M. Reigeluth (Ed.), *Instructional-design theories and models: An overview of their current status.* Hillsdale, NJ: Lawrence Erlbaum Associates.

Harmin, M., Kirschenbaum, H. & Simon, S. (1973). *Clarifying values through subject matter.* Minneapolis: Winston Press.

Hersh, R. H., Miller, J. P., & Fielding, G. D. (1980). *Models of moral education: An appraisal.* New York, Longman.

Horn, R. E. (1976). *How to write information mapping.* (Lexington, Mass: Information Resources.

Hull, C. L. (1943). *Principles of behavior.* New York: Appleton-Century-Crofts.

Keller, J. M. (1979). Motivation and instructional design: A theoretical perspective. *Journal of Instructional Development, 2*(4), 26–34.

Keller, J. M. (1983). Motivational design of instruction. In C. M. Reigeluth (Ed.), *Instructional-design theories and models: An overview of their current status.* Hillsdale, NJ: Lawrence Erlbaum Associates.

Keller, J. M. & Dodge, B. (1982, September). *The ARCS model of motivational strategies for course designers and developers.* Fort Monroe, VA: Training Developments Institute.

Klausmeier, H. J., Ghatala, E. S., & Frayer, D. A. (1974). *Conceptual learning and development: A cognitive view.* New York: Academic Press.

Kohlberg, L. (1976). The cognitive-developmental approach to moral education. In D. Purpel & K. Ryan (Eds.), *Moral education . . . it comes with the territory.* Berkeley, CA: McCutchan.

Krathwohl, D. R., Bloom, B. S. & Masia, B. B. (1964). *Taxonomy of educational objectives. Handbook II: Affective domain.* New York: McKay.

Kulhavy, R. W. (1977). Feedback in written instruction. *Review of Educational Research, 47,* 211–232.

Landa, L. N. (1974). *Algorithmization in learning and instruction.* Englewood Cliffs, NJ: Educational Technology.

Landa, L. N. (1976). *Instructional regulation and control: Cybernetics, algorithmization, and heuristics in education.* Englewood Cliffs, NJ: Educational Technology.

Landa, L. N. (1983). Descriptive and prescriptive theories of learning and instruction: An analysis of their relationships and interactions. In C. M. Reigeluth (Ed.), *Instructional-design theories and models: An overview of their current status.* Hillsdale, NJ: Lawrence Erlbaum Associates.

Liebert, R. M., & Spiegler, M. D. (1974). *Personality: Strategies for the study of man.* Homewood, IL: Dorsey.

Markle, S. M. & Tiemann, P. W. (1969). *Really understanding concepts.* Chicago: Tiemann Associates.

Mayer, R. E. (1977). The sequencing of instruction and the concept of assimilation-to-schema. *Instructional Science, 6,* 369-388.

Merrill, M. D. (1979, February). *Learner-controlled instructional strategies: An empirical investigation.* Final report on NSF Grant No. SED 76–01650.

Merrill, M. D. (1983). Component display theory. In C. M. Reigeluth (Ed.), *Instructional-design theories and models: An overview of their current status.* Hillsdale, NJ: Lawrence Erlbaum Associates.

Merrill, M. D. (1984). What is learner control? In R. K. Bass & C. Dills (Eds.), *Instructional development: The state of the art, II.* Dubuque, IA: Kendall-Hunt.

Merrill, M. D., Reigeluth, C. M., & Faust, G. W. (1979). The instructional quality profile: A curriculum evaluation and design tool. In H. F. O'Neil, Jr. (Ed.), *Procedures for instructional systems development.* New York: Academic Press.

Merrill, M. D., Richards, R. E., Schmidt, R. V., & Wood, N. D. (1977). *The instructional strategy diagnostic profile: Training manual.* San Diego: Courseware, Inc.

Merrill, M. D., & Tennyson, R. D. (1977). *Teaching concepts: An instructional design guide.* Englewood Cliffs, NJ: Educational Technology.

Merrill, M. D., & Wood, N. D. (1974). *Instructional strategies: A preliminary taxonomy.* Columbus, OH: Ohio State University (ERIC Document Reproduction Service No. SE 018–771)

Merrill, P. F. (1978). Hierarchical and information processing task analysis: A comparison. *Journal of Instructional Development, 1*(2), 35–40.

Naisbitt, J. (1982). *Megatrends: Ten new directions transforming our lives.* New York: Warner Books.

Naylor, J. C., & Briggs, G. E. (1963). Effects of task complexity and task organization on the relative efficiency of part and whole training methods. *Journal of Experimental Psychology, 65,* 217–224.

Ortony, A. (Ed.). (1979). *Metaphor and thought.* Cambridge: Cambridge University Press.

Porter, L. W., & Lawler, E. E. (1968). *Managerial attitudes and performance.* Homewood, IL: Irwin.

Posner, G. J., & Strike, K. A. (1976). Categorization scheme for principles of sequencing content. *Review of Educational Research, 46,* 665–690.

Reigeluth, C. M. (1979). In search of a better way to organize instruction: The elaboration theory. *Journal of Instructional Development, 2*(3), 8–15.

Reigeluth, C. M. (1983a). Instructional design: What is it and why is it? In C. M. Reigeluth (Ed.), *Instructional-design theories and models: An overview of their current status.* Hillsdale, NJ: Lawrence Erlbaum Associates.

Reigeluth, C. M. (1983b). Meaningfulness and instruction: Relating what is being learned to what a student knows. *Instructional Science, 12(3), [fR197–218.*

Reigeluth, C. M. (1984a, November). Toward a common knowledge base: The evolution of instructional science. *Educational Technology,* 20–26.

Reigeluth, C. M. (1984b, March). *An instructional model of remember-level learning: The integration of instructional design prescriptions.* Paper presented at the annual convention of the American Educational Research Association, New Orleans, LA.

Reigeluth, C. M. (in press). Lesson blueprints based on the elaboration theory of instruction. In C. Reigeluth (Ed.), *Instructional theories in action: Lessons illustrating selected theories and models.* Hillsdale, NJ: Lawrence Erlbaum Associates.

Reigeluth, C. M., & Darwazeh, A. N. (1982). The elaboration theory's procedure for designing instruction: A conceptual approach. *Journal of Instructional Development, 5(3),* 22–32.

Reigeluth, C. M., Doughty, P., Sari, I. F., Powell, C. J., Frey, L., & Sweeney, J. (1982). *Extended development procedure: Users' manual.* Fort Monroe, VA: U. S. Army Training and Doctrine Command.

Reigeluth, C. M., & Rodgers, C. A. (1980). The elaboration theory of instruction: Prescriptions for task analysis and design. *NSPI Journal, 19*(1), 16–26.

Reigeluth, C. M. & Stein, F. S. (1983). The elaboration theory of instruction. In C. M. Reigeluth (Ed.), *Instructional-design theories and models: An overview of their current status.* Hillsdale, NJ: Lawrence Erlbaum Associates.

Rigney, J. W. (1978). Learning strategies: A theoretical perspective. In H. F. O'Neil, Jr. (Ed.) *Learning strategies.* New York: Academic Press.

Rogers, C. R. (1969). *Freedom to learn.* Columbus, OH: Merrill.

Romiszowski, A. J. (1981). *Designing instructional systems: Decision making in course planning and curriculum design.* New York: Nichols.

Rothkopf, E. Z. (1976). Writing to teach and reading to learn: A perspective on the psychology of written instruction. *National Social Studies Education Yearbook, 75*(1), 91–129.

Rotter, J. B. (1954). *Social learning and clinical psychology.* Englewood Cliffs, NJ: Prentice-Hall.

Rotter, J. B. (1966). Generalized expectancies for internal versus external control of reinforcement. *Psychological Monographs, 80.*

Ryan, K. (1981). *Questions and answers on moral education.* Bloomington, IN: Phi Delta Kappa Educational Foundation.

Sari, I. F., & Reigeluth, C. M. (1982). Writing and evaluating textbooks: Contributions from instructional theory. In D. Jonassen (Ed.), *The technology of text: Principles for structuring, designing, and displaying text.* Englewood Cliffs, NJ: Educational Technology.

Scandura, J. M. (1973). *Structural learning I: Theory and research.* New York: Gordon and Breach.

Scandura, J. M. (1983). Instructional strategies based on the structural learning theory. In C. M. Reigeluth (Ed.) *Instructional-design theories and models: An overview of their current status.* Hillsdale, NJ: Lawrence Erlbaum Associates.

Shulman, L. S., & Keislar, E. R. (Eds.). (1966). *Learning by discovery: A critical appraisal.* Chicago: Rand-McNally.

Singer, R. N. (1972). *Psychomotor domain: Movement behavior.* Philadelphia: Lea & Febiger.

Singer, R. N. (1975). *Motor learning and human performance* (2nd ed.). New York: Macmillan.

Singer, R. N., & Witker, J. (1970). Mental rehearsal and point of introduction within the context of overt practice. *Perceptual and Motor Skills, 31,* 169–170.

Skinner, B. F. (1953). *Science and human behavior.* New York: Macmillan.

Skinner, B. F. (1954). The science of learning and the art of teaching. *Harvard Educational Review, 24*(2), 86–97.

Skinner, B. F. (1965). Reflections on a decade of teaching machines, In R. Glaser (Ed.), *Teaching machines and programmed learning, II.* Washington, DC: National Educational Association.

Skinner, B. F. (1969). *Contingencies of reinforcement: A theoretical analysis.* New York: Appleton-Century-Crofts.

Verbrugge, R. R., & McCarrell, N. S. (1977). Metaphoric comprehension: Studies in reminding and resembling. *Cognitive Psychology, 9,* 494–533.

Wade, M. G., & Davis, W. W. (1981). *Motor skill development in young children: Current views on assessment and programming.* Washington, DC: National Institute of Child Health and Human Development. (ED 207 672)

Weinstein, C. E. (1978). Elaboration skills as a learning strategy. In H. F. O'Neil, Jr. (Ed.), *Learning strategies.* New York: Academic Press.

White, R. T., & Gagné, R. M. (1974). Past and future research on learning hierarchies. *Educational Psychologist, 11,* 19–28.

White, R. T., & Gagné, R. M. (1978). Formative evaluation applied to a learning hierarchy. *Contemporary Educational Psychology, 3,* 87–94.

AUTHOR NOTES

Charles M. Reigeluth is Associate Professor of Instructional Design at Syracuse University, and a consultant on educational software programs to Renaissance Learning Systems.

Ruth V. Curtis is an instructional development consultant, a Ph.D. graduate of Instructional Design, Development, and Evaluation, Syracuse University.

8 Learner Characteristics

Sigmund Tobias
City College, City University of New York

The impact of differences in student characteristics on learning in school and training contexts is one of the major themes in the history of research relating psychological knowledge to learning. It is, of course, well known that Binet was originally commissioned to develop a test of student characteristics so that the "uneducable" could be identified and removed from regular schools for specialized placement. Since then, the effects of learning differences among students has been a regular theme in educational research.

Research on the relationship between learner characteristics and instructional outcomes has taken three major forms: correlational studies, main-effect investigations, and interaction research. In correlational studies student learning is related either to one or to a variety of student characteristics. In main-effect research, the learning of students with one set of attributes is compared with that of another group having different characteristics. For example, such studies might compare learning of students high or low in spatial abilities, anxiety, or other characteristics. Finally, in interactive research, differential predictions are made such that students at one end of an individual-difference continuum are expected to perform well with one instructional-method or experimental procedure, whereas those with different characteristics are expected to excel with alternate procedures.

The research reviewed in this chapter will deal with all three types of studies. Since some of the issues in this area are analyzed most clearly in interactive investigations, and since these studies deal with a wide range of learner characteristics, this discussion will begin with an overview of those studies. Research on adaptive instruction will be reviewed next, followed by a discussion of the effects of anxiety. There is an enormous body of literature dealing with student characteristics, greatly surpassing present space constraints. Therefore, an attempt will be made to review the most significant work, and to offer critical evaluations of selected areas, rather than to conduct an exhaustive review.

INTERACTIVE RESEARCH

Cronbach's (1957) call for rapprochement between the fields of correlational and experimental psychology was a milestone for interactive research. Correlational researchers try to identify the nature and dimensions of individual differences, and experimental psychologists study the effects of variations in task parameters, such as instructional methods, on learning. Cronbach proposed a synthesis of these fields, urging researchers to investigate the interactions between individual differences and task parameters. Ultimately, such interactions were expected to identify which instructional methods were optimal for different students.

A book edited by Gagné (1967) summarized the then available knowledge regarding what came to be known as aptitude treatment interaction (ATI) research. Aptitude was generally defined as any individual difference measure related to instructional outcome, and treatment denoted any variation in presenting instructional material to students (Cronbach & Snow, 1969). The underlying logic for this approach was that no one instructional method was expected to be optimal for all students. Instead, some methods were assumed to be ideal for students at one end of the individual difference continuum, whereas others might be most efficient for learners with different characteristics. Cronbach (1967) also suggested adapting the goals of instruction to student characteristics. The Gagné (1967) volume and Cronbach and Snow's (1969) monograph summarized much of the available evidence pertaining to ATI research. Cronbach and Snow (1977) updated their review and this expanded source also offered extensive evaluations of research, theory, and methodology for the conduct of ATI studies.

Perhaps an example of ATI research may clarify this approach. In a widely quoted study, Domino (1971) assigned students to sections of a course taught by a single instructor, one of which was designed to encourage independence and another structured to demand conformity. Student characteristics were determined by two scales assessing students' abilities to achieve either independently, or by conforming to external demands. In general, it was found that students with high scores on achievement via independence performed best in classes encouraging independent functioning, whereas students who were high on achievement via conformity accomplished most in sections demanding conformity.

TYPES OF INTERACTIONS

The most sought-after effect by ATI researchers is a disordinal interaction, such as that depicted in Fig. 8.1. In disordinal interactions the functions for different instructional treatments cross. The crossover shows that at one point of the learner characteristics continuum, represented on the horizontal or *x* axis, one method results in superior achievement, as displayed on the vertical, or *y* axis. After the crossover, another method is superior for students at different points of the continuum.

In ordinal interactions, such as that depicted in Fig. 8.2, there is no crossover; one treatment is superior for all students, irrespective of their standing on the individual-difference continuum. In ordinal interactions, however, the slopes of the functions for the various groups differ, so that the superiority of one group is much larger at one point of the continuum than at others. Ordinal interactions imply disordinality at a point outside of the range of values used in a particular study. That is, if the range of student characteristics displayed on the *x* axis were extended, the differences between the slopes of the two lines in Fig. 8.2 suggest that they will ultimately cross, generating a disordinal interaction. This phenomenon is indicated by the dotted lines in Fig. 8.2.

It may be instructive to compare the types of results sought in ATI research with those found in main-effect studies. The latter typically yield parallel functions, with identical slopes for different instructional methods or experimental treatments. Generally, researchers employing this approach expect the superiority of one treatment or instructional method over another

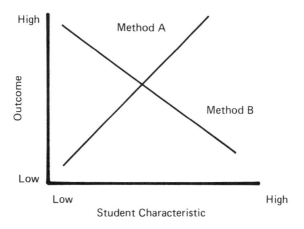

FIGURE 8.1. Example of disordinal interaction.

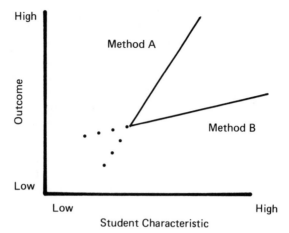

FIGURE 8.2.   Example of ordinal interaction with hypothetical extrapolation shown by dotted line.

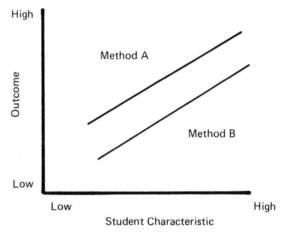

FIGURE 8.3.   Example of main effect without interaction.

to be unaffected by differences in student characteristics. Figure 8.3 displays such results.

Overview of ATI Research Results

From the late 1960s to the late 1970s there was relatively intense ATI research activity. Bracht (1970) reviewed this literature and found few significant disordinal interactions, leading him to question the value of ATI research. Berliner and Cahen's (1973) review indicated that both ordinal and disordinal interactions were of importance for ATI research, for reasons much like those suggested in the previous section. These reviewers expressed "cautious optimism" about the future of ATI research.

Cronbach and Snow (1977) concluded their massive review of the ATI literature by indicating that "no Aptitude X Treatment interactions are so well confirmed that they can be used directly as guides to instruction" (p. 492). They suggested that there was evidence for several patterns of interactions which deserved further investigation. Among these were findings that students high in general ability tended to succeed with unelaborated instructional treatments, whereas those lower in such abilities profited from the addition of augmentations, such as advance organizers, demonstrations, and the like. In the personality domain, Cronbach and Snow found that interactions appeared with some frequency, and concluded that "students with constructive motivation tended to benefit from treatment conditions that provide more freedom and more challenge, i.e., treatments that look to the learner himself to supply a good deal of the structure in the specification of the task" (p.469). The opposite could be expected for those whose motivation was less strongly constructive. Constructive motivation may be defined by high scores on scales measuring a preference to achieve independently and low scores on measures of anxiety, defensiveness, and similar characteristics.

One of the major problems in the ATI field has been the inconsistency of findings. In much of this research the number of significant findings was almost equal to the non-significant ones (Cronbach & Snow, 1977; Tobias, 1981). Even more vexing has been the fact that when significant ATIs were reported they were often difficult to replicate. For example, Peterson (1977) investigated the interaction between instructional methods and a number of personality variables, using a sample of ninth-grade students. The next year, she repeated essentially the same study (Peterson, 1978), using different subject-matter and a new student sample. Surprisingly, the results of the second study were markedly different from the first.

Inconsistent ATI results are troubling to both researchers and practitioners. If minor alterations in the content to be learned, in the instructional methods, or in student characteristics can change interactions substantially, important questions may be raised regarding whether ATI research can ever be expected to develop useful generalizations for instructional designers. Concerns similar to these led Cronbach (1975) to hypothesize that generalizations made from ATI research may well be limited to the particular location in which the research was conducted, rather than being applicable to all populations. Cronbach also suggested that in the social sciences in general, and in ATI work in particular, results may *not* be stable from one decade to another.

Achievement–Treatment Interactions

A good deal of ATI research has used differences in students' prior knowledge of the subject matter, rather than more general aptitudes, as the student characteristic. A general hypothesis (Tobias, 1973, 1976) predicted an inverse relationship between prior knowledge and the amount of instructional support provided by different instructional methods. Prior knowledge is readily identified by students' pretest scores in a particular subject. Instructional support is defined as the assistance given to organize instructional content, maintain attention, provide feedback, and similar forms of assistance. The hypothesis predicted that students with little familiarity with an area might require substantial assistance to learn optimally, whereas knowledgeable students would succeed with minimal support.

In a representative study using the achievement-treatment approach, Pascarella (1978) compared a mastery-based instructional strategy with regular, classroom-based instruction in college calculus. The mastery approach offered instructional support in the form of formative evaluation and remedial loops, both of which were absent in the comparison method. As expected, the mastery strategy was found to be superior for students with limited prior mathematics preparation, compared with the usual classroom approach. Further research on this hypothesis is reviewed elsewhere (Tobias, 1973, 1976, 1982).

The achievement-treatment hypothesis is similar to the formulation subsequently advanced by Cronbach and Snow (1977) and by Snow and Lohman (1984), regarding interactions between ability and instructional augmentation. Snow and Lohman suggested that reducing the complexity of an instructional treatment would be beneficial to students of lower mental ability, whereas complex or incomplete methods ought to be more effective for abler students. They also suggested that the less complex, more directive treatments may actually be harmful to brighter students by providing the types of assistance that abler students provide for themselves more effectively. Such results are sometimes reported in studies using mental ability as the student characteristic, but rarely in studies using the achievement-treatment paradigm.

There are advantages to conceptualizing the ATI problem in terms of prior achievement. When aptitudes are employed as the student characteristics, investigators assume that they are relevant to both the instructional content and method. Such an assumption should, of course, be independently verified in preliminary research, but rarely is. When prior achievement data are used, on the other hand, it can be assumed that they are relevant to the content, since pretests are samples of the instructional content. Furthermore, there is evidence (reviewed in the next section) of variability in relationships between aptitudes and outcomes of instruction as students move from one course segment to another. However, when a pretest is used to predict instructional outcome, the evidence indicates that such predictions are relatively stable.

Aptitude-Outcome Research

Predicting that an instructional method will be optimal assumes relatively stable relationships between aptitudes and tests assessing the outcomes of instruction. Such consistency permits teachers or instructional developers to assign students with different characteristics to methods that will be optimal for them during instruction lasting several days or weeks. Inconsistency in aptitude-outcome relationships, of course, makes it difficult to predict which method will be optimal for students in different segments of instruction. Unfortunately, there has been some evidence of such inconsistency.

Burns (1980) found that there were differences between the correlations of aptitudes and achievement on four units dealing with an imaginary science, indicating that "aptitude-learning relations are not stable over time and that this instability is exhibited in different aptitudes being required at different points during instruction" (p. 793). Federico (1983) gave 24 individual-difference measures to 166 Navy trainees who completed a hierarchically organized, mastery-based, computer-managed instruction course of 11 modules. Correlations between factor scores computed on the 24 tests and student achievement on the modules shifted substantially from module to module.

A re-examination (Tobias & Federico, 1984) of the Federico data assumed that before instruction the best predictors of outcomes are student's pretest scores. Since no pretest data were used in the Federico study, it was reasoned that posttest scores on a preceding module would convey much of the information contained in a pretest, especially in hierarchically organized courses. The re-analysis of the Federico data indicated that "the posttest on the preceding module predicted instructional outcome approximately as well as 24 individual difference measures used by Federico" (p. 111). If posttests of one module are more clearly conceptualized as pretests for the next, they would include, for diagnostic purposes, items dealing with the succeeding content. In that case, correlations between module posttests can be expected to be even more useful for prediction of outcomes.

While there were no instructional-method variations in either the Federico or Burns studies, their results suggested that if aptitude data are used in ATI paradigms, the optimal method for students with different characteristics may well shift from one module to another. The results also indicated that prior achievement may be more stable than aptitudes for the prediction of instructional outcome. These data, and other findings supporting the achievement-treatment formulation (Tobias, 1976, 1981), suggested that this may be a more viable approach to ATI research than the use of more general aptitudes. As with all other ATI research, however, there were also some contradictory findings (Tobias, 1982) regarding this hypothesis, which may be a function of some untested assumptions made in ATI research.

Assumptions of ATI Research

It has been suggested (Tobias, 1982) that whenever different results are expected when the same subject is taught by alternate-instructional methods, one or both of the following are presumed: (1) That the alternate methods invoke different types of cognitive processing of instruction, called macro-processing; or (2) That the methods engage similar macro-processes, but one method requires more frequent or intense processing than the other. If neither of these assumptions is valid, then alternate-instructional methods may appear different superficially, but lead to similar outcomes. These assumptions are implicit in ATI studies and also in research comparing instructional methods without attention to student characteristics.

A second set of assumptions vital only to ATI research is that the student characteristics studied are meaningfully related to the macro-processes engaged by the instructional methods. This assumption should also be verified by research prior to conducting an ATI study, but rarely is. If this and the preceding assumption are valid, ATIs may be expected. That is, if the individual difference measure assesses the type of characteristics which are related to the macro-processes demanded by the instructional methods, then interaction between these two sets of variables may be expected. This analysis suggests that inconsistencies in ATI research results may be attributable to the scarcity of knowledge in two critical areas: (a) the mediating cognitive processes (Doyle, 1978), or macro-processes engaged by instructional methods, and (b) the nature of the individual-difference measures used in ATI studies and their meaningful relationships to these macro-processes. Research on cognitive processes is directed at providing data to answer these questions.

Cognitive Processes Research

Recently, ATI work has fallen somewhat out of vogue, probably because of some of the problems suggested previously. Instructional and individual-difference researchers have embarked on a massive effort to identify the types of cognitive processes engaged by different instructional methods (Resnick, 1981; Wittrock, 1978). An equally active contemporary thrust of importance to ATI research has been the attempt to identify the types of cognitive processes underlying such learner characteristics as intelligence, spatial ability, and other individual differences. (Pellegrino & Glaser, 1980; Snow & Lohman, 1984; Sternberg, 1985). From an ATI perspective, such research may clarify the types of cognitive processes which are readily available to students of different affective or cognitive characteristics. For example, Hunt's (1985) research has shown that students who are high in verbal ability "tend to have larger memory spans for words and digits . . . and to be adept at holding information in working memory while analyzing simple sentences" (p. 47), compared with low verbal ability students. If research indicates that a particular instructional method requires holding information in working memory, such a strategy would obviously be ideal for students high in verbal ability who have such processes readily available to them. Those lower in available to them. Those lower in verbal ability, on the other hand, should be assigned to a different method in order to learn optimally.

Cognitive processes in reading. It may be useful to describe some research intended to clarify the cognitive processes used by different types of readers to illustrate how that approach may eventually help in reformulating the ATI problem. A number of investigators have examined student use of reading strategies such as *lookbacks,* or reviews of previously read material. Garner and Reis (1981) used a task in which lookbacks were necessary to answer some questions on a text passage. Their results showed that only older elementary school students with good comprehension used lookbacks with any frequency; in general, the number of reviews made by students were lower than expected. Alexander, Hare, and Garner (1984) also investigated lookbacks among undergraduate students who were proficient readers. Their results indicated that only 50% of these more knowledgeable subjects used lookbacks at all, and that overall, lookbacks occurred only 30% of the time. It has also been demonstrated (Tobias, 1985) that if readers are required to re-read when there is evidence of comprehension difficulty, achievement will increase compared with those for whom review is optional. Future ATI studies investigating reading may be more fruitful if the methods used vary such characteristics as the support provided to good and poor readers for using lookbacks.

There are studies of reading which examine detection of inconsistencies (Garner, 1980; Garner & Kraus, 1981–1982; Markman, 1977, 1979), the use of strategic behaviors (Baker & Anderson, 1982; Meyer, Brandt, & Bluth, 1980), and other macro-processes (Baker & Brown, 1984; Brown et al., 1983; Kintsch & van Dijk, 1978; Winograd, 1984). These examples of research on cognitive processes in reading suggest that the next generation of ATI studies will have a sounder basis for examining the interaction between instructional methods and student characteristics than was previously the case.

It should be noted, however, that cognitive processes research does not address yet another component of the ATI problem: the psychological processes demanded by different instructional content. Clarification is needed regarding the types of processes required by different subject matters, ranging from algebra to zoology. If variability in the cognitive processes demanded by different domains of content is found, this may be yet another dimension to be considered by ATI research. In that event, not only will it be necessary to investigate interactions between instructional methods and student characteristics, but the interactions of these variables with different types of content will also have to be examined before students can be assigned to methods likely to be optimal for them.

ADAPTIVE INSTRUCTION

Research on adaptive instruction investigates the types of variables which are useful in varying either the method of instruction, its sequence, or aspects of its content (e.g., the number of examples used) to learner characteristics, as students move from one course segment to another. Most ATI research has used relatively short instructional sequences and therefore is not useful in addressing the question of varying instruction as students progress through a course. Field-based, adaptive instructional systems typically are designed to assure that all students reach a predetermined criterion of mastery. In such situations, of course, it is impossible to obtain any variability in relationships between achievement and learner characteristics, since virtually all students attain the same outcome. The time required by different students to attain criterion does vary in such situations, but adaptive programs typically do not report results regarding relationships between time and learner characteristics. Data from such implementations are therefore not useful in clarifying the research base for adaptive instruction. There are some other studies, however, which are relevant to adaptive practices.

Hansen, Ross, and Rakow (1977) taught students a series of mathematical rules. Instructional adaptation consisted of requiring another trial of those students who did not perform well on formative tests, and varying the number of examples for a particular rule. Available test information included a variety of aptitude and personality measures, plus task specific tests, measures of learning styles, and others. Five groups were compared, including an adaptive group, a yoked adaptive group (student path through the material was determined by the sequence assigned to a matched subject in the adaptive group), a mismatched adaptive, plus two fixed groups, one receiving a maximal and the other a minimal number of examples. The adaptive group's initial teaching sequence was based on students' entry-level scores, and data were updated after students progressed through the material.

The results indicated that the adaptive, yoked adaptive, and group receiving maximal number of examples did not differ from one another on the posttest, but did differ from both the minimal fixed and the mismatched group. It was also found that the maximal examples group took the most time and the minimal group the least. There were no time differences between the adaptive, yoked adaptive, and mismatched treatment. In the adaptive group, the best predictor of success on future trials was performance on prior trials.

Ross, Rakow, and Bush (1980) also examined the effect of providing variation in the number of examples given to students while learning a series of statistical rules. Examples varied from one to ten, and adaptation was based on student success on formative tests. The design included an adaptive group, a deliberately mismatched adaptive group, and a group receiving a fixed number of examples. The adaptive method led to the most efficient outcomes (defined as test score divided by instructional time). Interactions with pretest indicated that students with low pretest scores took more time than those with higher scores. Ross and Rakow (1981) extended this group of studies by adding a learner control treatment condition in which students determined the number of examples to be used, compared with a program-controlled prescription. Learner control was found ineffective, regardless of level of prior achievement.

In a series of studies, Tennyson and his associates used a Bayesian statistical model to arrange adaptive instruction based upon general aptitudes, pretest scores, and on-task performance. Instruction was typically presented via computers, and the number of examples provided was varied. Tennyson and Rothen (1977) assigned undergraduate students to a full adaptive strategy, using both pretask and on–task measures, a partial adaptive strategy using only pretask measures, and a fixed strategy. Their results indicated that the full adaptive strategy used 25% less time and had higher posttest scores than the partial adaptive group which, in turn, was 16% more efficient than the fixed strategy. Park and Tennyson (1980) found that an adaptive strategy using on-task information required less time and fewer examples than either a pretask-information strategy alone, or a combination of pretask plus on-task information. A response-sensitive strategy, in which the types of instances presented were based on students' responses, led to superior performance and required less time than a response insensitive strategy.

Tennyson (1981) compared a computer-controlled adaptive condition and two learner-control strategies, one in which students received computer guidance, and another in which they did not. The computer-controlled adaptive condition and the adaptive learner-control condition produced significantly higher posttest scores than the student free-choice condition. Students in the learner-control adaptive condition used 50% more time than those in the learner-control group, but less time than the computer-controlled condition.

ATIs and Adaptive Instruction

The aim of both ATI and adaptive instruction research is to develop a knowledge base that will permit teachers and instructional designers to assign students to instructional methods and materials which are optimal for them. Most present implementations of adaptive instruction contain only very superficial variations of instructional methods, such as changing the number of teachers or size of remedial groups (Wang & Walberg, 1985). The problems of ATI research indicate that it is premature to make generalizations permitting assignment of students with one set of individual characteristics to one instructional method and those with different characteristics to another. In view of this uncertain state of affairs, most recent adaptive-instructional models can be characterized by a heavy emphasis on direct instruction, frequent formative evaluation, and variation in the amount of time students are allowed to spend on different instructional segments (Berliner, 1985; Talmage, 1985).

Research on adaptive instruction has generally indicated that instructional methods which vary the amount of material presented to students according to some criterion are more effective than fixed instruction given to comparable groups. Giving students control of the adaptive strategy has not been found to improve achievement. Finally, measures of prior achievement, in contrast to aptitude information, appear to be most useful for adaptive decisions regarding the content and sequence of instruction. The data also suggest that recent prior achievement information, such as outcomes of preceding trials, are more useful for prediction than pretests or other measures administered before instruction. These results coincide with those obtained in some concept-formation studies (Alvord, 1967; Bunderson, 1967), which also found that the best predictions of success on future trials were made from the outcomes of preceding trials. There is convergence, then, of research results from adaptive instruction, from aptitude-outcome research, and from the ATI area, suggesting that prior achievement may be the most useful measure for adaptive instructional decisions.

ANXIETY

Anxiety is one of the learner characteristics of major importance for instructional concerns. Anxiety has generally been defined as an affective state characterized by unpleasant feelings which are similar to fear or apprehension (Sieber, 1977). Different types of anxiety, such as test anxiety, mathematics anxiety, or speech anxiety are similar in that they describe the unpleasant, fear-like affective state, although they differ with respect to the particular situations which evoke this state. Naturally, there are different tests to measure the various affective states. Of particular importance for instructional concerns is test anxiety, sometimes more generally called evaluative anxiety (Sieber, 1977). Test anxiety refers to students' fear of evaluative situations such as examinations. Research has shown that students high in test anxiety perform more poorly in evaluative situations than their low-anxiety counterparts, even when scholastic ability is held constant (Sarason, 1980; Sieber, O'Neil, & Tobias, 1977).

The lower test performance of anxious students has generally been explained by the presumed interference of anxiety in the retrieval of prior learning when students are being tested. Wine (1971) and Sarason (1972) suggested that the process accounting for such interference might be that highly anxious students divide their attention between task demands and a variety of task-irrelevant concerns composed principally of negative self-preoccupations, feelings of helplessness, and the like. Less-anxious students,

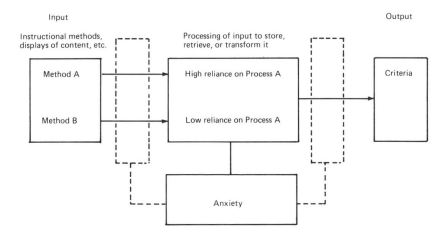

FIGURE 8.4. Model describing the different effects of anxiety on learning from instruction (From Tobias, 1977). Reprinted with permission of the copyright owner, Lawrence Erlbaum Associates, Inc.

on the other hand, have been found to devote a greater proportion of their attention to task demands and less to irrelevant concerns, thus explaining their better test performance.

A model has been proposed (Tobias, 1977, 1979) to integrate the various effects that anxiety can have on learning. The model assumes that since "learning is a process that is essentially cognitively mediated, anxiety can affect learning only indirectly by impacting on the cognitive processes which control learning" (Tobias, 1979, p.575). The model, displayed in Fig. 8.4, separates the instructional process into the three classical information-processing components: input, processing, and output. Input stands for the presentation of instruction to students. Processing denotes the cognitive operations performed by students to encode, organize, and store input. Output represents performance on evaluation after instruction. Figure 8.4 indicates some points at which anxiety can affect learning from instruction most prominently: preprocessing, during processing and after processing, and before output.

Preprocessing Interference

This type of interference represents situations in which instruction is presented but not appropriately encoded by anxious students, perhaps because their attention is diverted to off-task concerns (Sarason, 1972; Wine, 1971). It was hypothesized that any procedure permitting students to reinstitute input will reduce the potential interference of anxiety at this stage. Procedures such as being able to review segments of text, or having the option to rewind audio- or videotapes, were predicted to reduce preprocessing interference and therefore were expected to be differentially beneficial to anxious students.

There is research to support these expectations. Deutsch and Tobias (1980) found that anxious students who studied a set of videotaped modules individually, with the option to review, learned more than similarly anxious students viewing the same tape in groups without the review option. In one part of a study by Tobias and Sacks (1983), students read a text passage, received adjunct questions about the text, and could review the preceding text whenever they wished. The correlations between the number of reviews and test anxiety was .54. Furthermore, the number of correct answers to adjunct questions prior to review had a correlation of −.35 with test anxiety; after review that correlation changed to .50. These findings confirmed the expectations that anxious students would review instruction more frequently than their low-anxious counterparts, and also that reviewing would be differentially beneficial to anxious students.

Processing Interference

At this stage instructional input has been encoded and is processed by the individual. It has been suggested (Tobias, 1984a) that the cognitive representation of anxiety absorbs some portion of cognitive processing capacity, leaving a reduced amount to be devoted to task demands. It is assumed that this reduced capacity is one mechanism by which anxiety interferes in performance. There is substantial evidence (Wine, 1971; Sarason, in press) that during evaluative situations anxious students are more preoccupied with off-task concerns than those lower in anxiety. It is reasoned that such preoccupations must absorb some portion of cognitive capacity.

Paulman and Kennelly (1984) assigned students to work on two tasks (Raven's matrices and backward digit span) sequentially or concurrently. Anxious students had lower scores on the matrices and remembered significantly fewer total digits in the concurrent compared with the consecutive condition. For low anxious students, there were no differences between the presentation modes on digit-span performance. The results supported the cognitive capacity formulation and were interpreted by these investigators to indicate that "test anxiety is associated with an impairment in information-processing capacity. . . . Anxiety by itself seems to signal lower cognitive effectiveness when task demands are high" (p.285). As expected, the processing deficit shows up most clearly when the task calls for substantial cognitive processing since task demands and the cognitive representation of anxiety both make peak demands on limited capacity.

Cubberly and Weinstein (1983) and Walters and Tobias (1985) reasoned that use of a strategy would reduce the cognitive capacity demanded by tasks and therefore be differentially beneficial to anxious students. Cubberly and Weinstein used an imagery strategy, while a word-clustering strategy was employed in the Walters and Tobias investigation. Both studies found that strategies improved the performance of high anxious students compared with their less-anxious counterparts, confirming expectations from the cognitive-processing capacity formulation.

Post-processing Interference

This type of interference is meant to describe situations in which learning is assumed to have occurred, but interference is encountered in retrieving previously learned material during evaluative situations. Such interference is implied when students report that they study carefully but "freeze up" during tests and hence receive lower scores than less anxious students. Postprocessing interference has generally been attributed to disruptions in the retrieval of prior learning by the effects of anxiety (Sarason, in press, 1980; Sieber et al., 1977). Recently, a number of investigators have suggested that the lower scores obtained by anxious students may be caused by less thorough initial learning, because of deficient study or test-taking skills, rather than disruption in retrieving prior learning. The difference between these formulations has become the subject of active research. A review of this research will be undertaken in the following section.

Deficit hypotheses. Relationships between study skills and anxiety have been reported by many investigators. Desiderato and Koskinen (1969), Mitchell and Ng (1972), and Wittmaier (1972) found that anxious students had less effective study skills than students lower in anxiety. Culler and Holahan (1980) found that test-anxious students studied longer than their less anxious counterparts, presumably compensating with more time for poorer study habits. Kirkland and Hollandsworth (1979) reported that study skills and achievement anxiety measures were major predictors of grade point average, excluding scholastic ability, and "raised the question whether anxiety interferes with effective test-taking behavior or whether the lack of effective study skills results in anxiety" (p.435). Benjamin et al., (1981) found that highly test-anxious subjects had poorer scores on different types of tests than those lower in anxiety. Highly test-anxious students also reported more problems during both initial learning and reviewing than those lower in anxiety. Furthermore, the higher the test anxiety the greater the difficulty reported by students while learning, reviewing, and remembering on examinations. In general, these studies document negative relationships between test anxiety and various indices of study skills.

A number of studies suggest that poor student test performance may be attributable to defective test-taking skills, rather than interference in retrieval. Kirkland and Hollandsworth (1980) found that skills-acquisition training resulted in less attentional interference during test taking and in higher performance on an analog test, compared with anxiety-reduction treatment.

Bruch (1981) reported that high and low test-anxiety groups differed in their knowledge of test-taking strategies, determined by questionnaire responses. Being aware of such strategies was significantly related to differences in college grades, even when scholastic achievement was held constant, while anxiety was found to be unrelated to school achievement. Bruch, Juster, and Kaflowitz (1983) reported that test-taking strategies significantly affected performance on simulated essay and multiple-choice tests, but had less effect on a math test. Surprisingly, test performance was *not* related to anxiety, nor to students' self-statements during tests. These findings are at variance with Sarason's (in press) reports of greater cognitive interference from negative self-thoughts during tests among anxious students.

Clear-cut differentiation between the interference or deficit interpretations require data distinguishing between student learning during or immediately after acquisition and again at recall. When mastery at acquisition is established, and students are required to retrieve the learned material during a test administered later, a straightforward test of the deficit or interference interpretations becomes possible by relating both of these indices to student test performance. A number of preliminary studies have addressed this problem.

Studies differentiating between acquisition and retrieval. Wendell and Tobias (1983) studied student's retrieval of learning from six videotaped instructional modules. Prior learning was measured by pretest, acquisition was assessed by posttests administered after each module, and retrieval was determined by a summative posttest, repeating the items from the module posttests, given approximately six weeks later. One retrieval index, comparing test items passed at pretest, passed again on posttest, and failed at recall 6 weeks later had a correlation of .22 (*p.* < .05) with test anxiety. A second index, composed of items failed on pretest, passed on immediate posttest, and failed on delayed posttest, was not significantly related to anxiety. The first index may have been a better measure of retrieval, since attainment of mastery was based on students' passing items on both module pretests and posttests. The second index used items passed only on immediate posttest, suggesting weaker content mastery and, therefore, a more ambiguous assessment of retrieval.

Another study (Tobias, 1984b) used a list learning, free-recall paradigm in which students studied two lists of words. Acquisition was established by requiring perfect recall of the first list. Recall interference was created by a second list, which was studied for only three trials. Mild stress was induced prior to requesting recall of both lists by informing students that performance was related to school achievement. Stepwise regression analyses indicated that worry, a component of test anxiety, was significantly related to List 1 retrieval, while study skills were not. List 2 retrieval was measured by words mastered on acquisition yet failed on recall. This index was significantly affected both by worry and by measures from a group of anxiety scales, whereas study skills had only a marginally significant effect.

Neither anxiety nor study skills affected any of the acquisition indices in the list-learning study. It was reasoned that the absence of acquisition effects might be attributable to the fact that stress was induced only at retrieval. Prior research (Sarason, 1980) had indicated that the debilitating anxiety effects occurred mainly in stressful situations. This interpretation was tested in a succeeding investigation (Tobias & Sacks, 1984) manipulating retrieval and acquisition stress. Unfortunately there was evidence that the stress had little credibility for the students.

These conflicting data, together with the less than definitive results from other experiments, suggest that there is still much to be learned about the relative contributions of test anxiety and skills deficits to students' performance on tests. The attempt to interpret test anxiety effects in terms of cognitive deficits is in accord with the cognitive *Zeitgeist* of contemporary psychology. It remains for future research to establish more definitively the contributions of interference or cognitive deficits to postprocessing interference.

Summary of Research on Anxiety

There are two themes in anxiety research which are similar to those found in the discussion of the ATI area. First, recent research is attempting to identify the cognitive processes impacted by anxiety. It is assumed that such an analytical approach may be fruitful both in clarifying the way anxiety impacts learning, and in improving attempts to ameliorate the effects of anxiety. A second theme implies the importance of interactive research. If anxiety and study skills have complementary effects, it becomes clear that training programs to improve student learning by either reducing test-anxiety or increasing study skills would have to be adapted to differences in student characteristics (Tobias, 1979). That is, test–anxious students with poor study skills would learn optimally from a program addressing both anxiety reduction and study-skills training. On the other hand, test-anxious students with effective study skills would profit optimally from programs emphasizing anxiety reduction without the additional study skills training. A study by Naveh-Benjamin (1985) confirms these expectations and underlines the importance of using an ATI paradigm for research in this area.

The current interest in distinguishing between acquisition and retrieval effects, and between the deficit and interference formulations, may contribute to a better understanding of the effects of test anxiety and study skills. Ultimately, such knowledge will also lead to more effective training programs for students with anxiety and study-skills problems.

STUDY SKILLS, MOTIVATION, AND CONTROL

Study-skills research, already mentioned, and investigations of such learner characteristics as motivation, and students' perception of themselves as having control over the outcomes of their efforts, have important implications for understanding learning from instruction. Recently, there has been considerable theoretical and research activity in these areas. Since space constraints make it impossible to describe this research fully, only a brief overview of this work will be presented.

Study Skills

Research on student study skills or learning strategies, and in the development of study-skills training programs has increased recently. Such skills may be defined as student behaviors during meaningful learning, which are intended to improve the encoding, acquisition, retention, and retrieval of new knowledge (Weinstein & Mayer, 1986). Robinson (1946) proposed a study-skills program four decades ago, demonstrating that there is a history to these concerns.

Weinstein and Mayer (1986) list some of the major components of study-skills programs. These include the following: basic rehearsal strategies, such as repetition; complex rehearsal strategies, such as summarizing and paraphrasing; basic elaboration strategies, such as forming a mental image or a sentence relating items; complex elaboration strategies, such as describing how new information relates to prior knowledge; basic organizational strategies, such as grouping or ordering information to be learned; complex elaboration strategies, such as outlining a passage or creating a hierarchy; comprehension-monitoring strategies, such as checking for failures to understand; and affective strategies, such as focusing attention and reducing evaluation anxiety.

Brooks, Simutis, and O'Neil (in press) suggest that instruction in study skills is unlikely to be the same for all individuals, since students vary in their knowledge of different strategies. In addition, variation in the explicitness of strategy training may be required by students of differing ability. These authors suggest that strategy instruction may also be a function of environmental variables, such as the demands of the task and the nature of incoming information. The combination of these variables will determine the outcomes of study skills instruction on students' performance, their knowledge, and their attitudes.

Motivation and Locus of Control

Both of these constructs are important in determining learning since they relate to the amount of effort that students invest in a task. Locus of control research investigates whether students see the outcomes of their efforts as being attributable to their own behavior, or to factors they cannot control. This research has indicated, for example, that students with an internal orientation work harder (Stipek, 1980), have a more active orientation to learning (Wolfgang & Potvin, 1973), and take more pride in success. Instructional designers would be well advised to keep track of work in this area since it may be of some importance in maximizing learning.

Motivation is another important variable in understanding people's learning from instruction. Anderson et al. (in press) found that motivational factors, such as students' interest in their reading, accounted for an average of 30 times more variance than other variables. Other research (Nicholls, Jagacinski, & Miller, 1986) has shown that curiosity, and intrinsic motivation (valuing an activity for its own sake) lead to more intense task engagement and greater output than extrinsic motivation (valuing an activity for exogenous reasons). Frase, Patrick, and Schumer (1970) found that offering an extrinsic incentive, such as 0, 3, or 10 cents for right answers was more effective than various other conditions. Clearly, motivation is of major importance in facilitating people's learning and should be followed closely by instructional designers.

GENERAL DISCUSSION

The paradigm shift to cognitively oriented instructional psychology is making important inroads on all aspects of the relationship between student characteristics and instructional outcomes. ATI research and studies of adaptive instruction stress the importance of understanding both the cognitive processes available to students and required by tasks. In contemporary anxiety research the importance of clarifying the cognitive processes impacted by anxiety, and the effects of anxiety on acquisition and retention are lively issues. Students' cognitive and metacognitive strategies are major components of affective and conative research and development. Clearly, the detailed analysis and specification of cognitive processes is an important theme underlying most areas in which learner characteristics affect instructional processes.

The rationale underlying ATI research, that no instructional technique could be expected to be equally effective for different types of students, was reviewed at the beginning of this chapter. While research in this field has proven to be much more problematical than initially assumed, variations of the ATI theme appeared in most of the areas discussed here. For example, in the discussion of test-anxiety-reduction programs and skills training, it was suggested that the type of intervention should be adapted to students' status on these variables. In the learning strategies area, it was suggested that the types of strategies to be taught would depend on the individual characteristics

of learners. The idea that training has to vary according to learner characteristics is implicit in research-and-development work on student-control and
motivational strategies. These are, of course, all different illustrations of the
ATI paradigm. While the evidence in support of ATIs is quite variable, the
ATI rationale is invoked in many areas dealing with the effect of student
differences on learning.

The ATI paradigm has some further problems which were alluded to previously. When interactions between student characteristics and instructional
methods are found, these interactions may be specific to the content domain
studied. That is, if an ATI study uses social-studies materials and finds
interactions, such results may be specific to that field. There is no research
demonstrating that interactions generalize from one content domain to
another. In view of the difficulties found by researchers trying to replicate
ATIs, there is reason for skepticism about generalization of interactions
across content domains. While ATIs have been investigated most intensively
in the instructional area, it seems likely that similar problems will arise in
every field in which the ATI paradigm is invoked.

The importance of including the characteristics of the subject matter in
interactive models has been mentioned specifically in the discussion of ATIs
in instructional research. Brooks et al. (in press) also suggest that task
demands and the type of incoming information should be included in study-
skills models. The development of measures to assess anxiety in different
areas, such as mathematics anxiety, speech anxiety, test anxiety, and others,
implies similar concerns about content characteristics. It would probably be
wise to examine whether interactions or main effects are specific to the content domain in which they were found in every area of research on learner
characteristics. Such examinations will determine the limits on generalizations
to be made from the results.

It is possible that the specification of cognitive characteristics may
represent a viable approach to deal with the problem of content specificity.
A number of investigations have examined the cognitive demands of various
subjects such as electronics (Riley, 1984), geometry (Greeno, 1981), and
mathematics (Resnick, 1981). If such analyses determine that different content domains require similar cognitive processes, then presumably interactions established in one domain should generalize to other situations requiring
similar cognitive activities. Of course, it also is to be demonstrated that the
cognitive demands of a subject at the beginning of a task are the same once
students progress into the content, and that similar stability exists in other
domains demanding the same cognitive processes. The research on relationships between outcomes and aptitudes across several modules suggests that
such temporal consistency may be difficult to attain.

It is assumed that detailed process analyses of task demands, instructional
strategies, and learner attributes (cognitive, affective, and conative) will lead

to more precise descriptions of the relationships among these variables. Presumably, these analyses will lead to research hypotheses and instructional prescriptions which will be less general than the preliminary formulations offered by Cronbach and Snow (1977) and by others concerned with these problems. Instead, such process analyses are likely to generate findings describing the recommended mix of specific macro-processes demanded by instruction for students whose cognitive processes match those required by the method, on particular types of subject matter, for specified outcomes.

As many fields of inquiry mature, general theories and sweeping hypotheses are supplanted by more specific and more limited formulations. Apparently research on the impact of student characteristics on learning from instruction follows a similar trend. Presumably, as specific findings continue to accumulate during the next generation of research on individual differences, they will have to be aggregated into more general hypotheses. Such hypotheses may form the basis for a new set of more general theories, leading to more research and application. Whether such a cycle of vague general formulations, succeeded by greater specificity, and then followed again by greater generality, will repeat itself in future generations of research remains to be seen.

REFERENCES

Alexander, P. A., Hare, V. C., & Garner, R. (1984, April). *Effects of time, access, and question type on response accuracy and frequency of lookbacks in older proficient readers.* Paper presented at the annual meeting of the American Educational Research Association, New Orleans, LA.

Alvord, R. W. (1967). *Learning and transfer in a concept-attainment task: A study in individual differences.* Unpublished doctoral dissertation, Stanford University. (University Microfilms No. 68-11, 263)

Anderson, R. C., Shirey, L. L., Wilson, P. T., & Fielding, L. G. (in press). Interestingness of children's reading material. In R. E. Snow & M. J. Farr (Eds.), *Aptitude, learning and instruction: Conative and affective process analyses.* Hillsdale, NJ: Lawrence Erlbaum Associates.

Baker, L., & Anderson, R. I. (1982). Effects of inconsistent information on text processing: Evidence for comprehension monitoring. *Reading Research Quarterly, 17,* 281-293.

Baker, L., & Brown, A. L. (1984). Metacognitive skills and reading. In P. D. Pearson (Ed.), *Handbook of reading research.* New York: Longman.

Benjamin, M., McKeachie, W., Lin, Y., & Hollinger, D. (1981). Test anxiety: Deficits in information processing. *Journal of Educational Psychology, 73,* 816-824.

Berliner, D. C. (1985). How is adaptive education like water in Arizona? In M. C. Wang & H. Walberg (Eds.), *Adapting instruction to individual differences.* Berkeley, CA: McCutchan.

Berliner, D. C., & Cahen, L. S. (1973). Trait-treatment interaction and learning. In F. N. Kerlinger (Ed.), *Review of research in education* (Vol. 1). Itasca, IL: Peacock.

Bracht, G. H. (1970). Experimental factors related to aptitude treatment interactions. *Review of Educational Research, 40,* 627-645.

Brooks, L. W., Simutis, Z. M., & O'Neil, H. F. (in press). Individual differences in learning strategies research. R. Dillon (Ed.), *Individual differences in cognition* (Vol. 2). New York: Academic Press.

Brown, A. L., Bransford, J. D., Ferrara, R. A., & Campione, J. C. (1983). Learning, remembering, and understanding. In J. H. Flavell & E. M. Markman (Eds.), *Carmichael's manual of child psychology* (Vol. 1). New York: Wiley.

Bruch, M. A. (1981). Relationship of test-taking strategies to test anxiety and performance: Toward a task analysis of examination behavior. *Cognitive Therapy and Research, 5,* 41–56.

Bruch, M. A., Juster, H. R., & Kaflowitz, N. G. (1983). Relationships of cognitive components of test anxiety to test performance: Implications for assessment and treatment. *Journal of Counseling Psychology, 30,* 527–536.

Bunderson, C. V. (1967). *Transfer of mental abilities at different stages of practice in the solution of concept problems.* Princeton, NJ: Educational Testing Service. (University Microfilms No. 66–4986).

Burns, R. B. (1980). Relation of aptitude to learning at different points in time during instruction. *Journal of Educational Psychology, 72,* 785–795.

Cronbach, L. J. (1957). The two disciplines of scientific psychology. *American Psychologist, 12,* 671–84.

Cronbach, L. J., (1967). How can instruction be adapted to individual differences? In R. M. Gagné (Ed.), *Learning and individual differences.* Columbus, OH: Merrill.

Cronbach, L. J. (1975). Beyond the two disciplines of scientific psychology. *American Psychologist, 30,* 116–127.

Cronbach, L. J., & Snow, R. E. (1969). *Individual differences and learning ability as a function of instructional variables.* (Contract No. OEC 4–6–061269–1217). Stanford, CA: School of Education, Stanford University.

Cronbach, L. J., & Snow, R. E. (1977). *Aptitudes and instructional methods.* New York: Irvington.

Cubberly, W. E., & Weinstein, C. E. (1983, August). *The interactive effects of cognitive learning strategy training and test anxiety on paired-associate learning.* Paper presented at the American Psychological Association annual meeting, Anaheim, CA.

Culler, R. E., & Holahan, C. (1980). Test taking and academic performance: The effects of study-related behaviors. *Journal of Educational Psychology, 72,* 16–20.

Desiderato, D., & Koskinen, P. (1969). Anxiety, study habits, and academic achievement. *Journal of Counseling Psychology, 16,* 162–165.

Deutsch, T., & Tobias, S. (1980, September). *Prior achievement, anxiety, and instructional method.* Paper presented at the annual meeting of the American Psychological Association, Montreal, Canada.

Domino, G. (1971). Interactive effects of achievement orientation and teaching style on academic achievement. *Journal of Educational Psychology, 62,* 427–431.

Doyle, W. (1978). Paradigms for research on teacher effectivenss. In L. S. Shulman (Ed.), *Review of research in education* (Vol. 5). Itasca, IL: Peacock.

Federico, P. A. (1983). Changes in cognitive components of achievement as students proceed through computer-managed instruction. *Journal of Computer Assisted Instruction, 9,* 156–158.

Frase, L. T., Patrick, E., & Schumer, H. (1970). Effect of question position and frequency upon learning from text under different levels of incentives. *Journal of Educational Psychology, 61,* 52–56.

Gagné, R. M. (Ed.). (1967). *Learning and individual differences.* Columbus, OH: Merrill.

Garner, R. (1980). Monitoring of understanding: An investigation of good and poor readers' awareness of induced miscomprehension of text. *Journal of Reading Behavior, 12,* 55–63.

Garner, R., & Kraus, C. (1981–82). Good and poor comprehender differences in knowing and regulating reading behaviors. *Educational Research Quarterly, 6*(4), 5–12.

Garner, R., & Reis, R. (1981). Monitoring and resolving comprehension obstacles: An investigation of spontaneous text lookbacks among upper grade good and poor comprehenders. *Reading Research Quarterly, 16,* 569–582.

Greeno, J. G. (1981, August). *Problem solving and understanding in mathematics.* Paper presented at the annual meeting of the American Psychological Association, Los Angeles.

Hansen, D. N., Ross, S. M., & Rakow, E. A. (1977). *Adaptive models for computer-based training systems.* Memphis: Memphis State University.

Hunt, E. (1985). Verbal ability. In R. J. Sternberg (Ed.), *Human abilities: An information-processing approach.* New York: Freeman.

Kintsch, W., & van Dijk, T. A. (1978). Toward a model of discourse comprehension and production. *Psychological Review, 85,* 363–394.

Kirkland, K., & Hollandsworth, J. (1979). Test anxiety, study skills, and academic performance. *Journal of College Personnel,* 431–435.

Kirkland, K., & Hollandsworth, J. (1980). Effective test taking: Skills-acquisition versus anxiety-reduction techniques. *Journal of Counseling and Clinical Psychology, 48,* 431–439.

Markman, E. M. (1977). Realizing that you don't understand: A preliminary investigation. *Child Development, 48,* 986–992.

Markman, E. M. (1979). Realizing that you don't understand: Elementary school children's awareness of inconsistencies. *Child Development, 50,* 643–655.

Meyer, B. J. F., Brandt, D. M., & Bluth, G. J. (1980). Use of top level structure in text: Key for reading comprehension of ninth grade students. *Reading Research Quarterly, 16,* 72–101.

Mitchell, K., & Ng, K. (1972). Effects of group counseling and behavior therapy on the academic achievement of test-anxious students. *Journal of Counseling Psychology, 19,* 491–497.

Naveh-Benjamin, M. (1985, August). *A comparison of treatments intended for different types of test-anxious students.* Paper presented at the annual meeting of the American Psychological Association, Los Angeles, CA.

Nicholls, J. G., Jagacinski, C. M., & Miller, A. T. (198). *Conceptions of ability in children and adults.* In R. Schwarzer (Ed.), *Self-related cognitions in anxiety and motivation.* Hillsdale, NJ: Lawrence Erlbaum Associates.

Park, O., & Tennyson, R. D. (1980). Adaptive design strategies for selecting number and presentation order of examples in coordinate concept acquisition. *Journal of Educational Psychology, 72,* 362–370.

Pascarella, E. T. (1978). Interactive effects of prior mathematics preparation and level of instruction support in college calculus. *American Educational Research Journal, 15.* 275–285.

Paulman, R. G., & Kennelly, K. J. (1984). Test anxiety and ineffective test taking: Different names, same construct. *Journal of Educational Psychology, 76,* 279–288.

Pellegrino, J. W., & Glaser, R. (1980). Components of inductive reasoning. In R. E. Snow, P. A. Federico, & W. Montague (Eds.), *Aptitude, learning and instruction: Cognitive processes analysis* (Vol. 1). Hillsdale, NJ: Lawrence Erlbaum Associates.

Peterson, P. L. (1977). Interactive effects of student anxiety, achievement orientation, and teacher behavior on student achievement and attitude. *Journal of Educational Psychology, 68,* 779–792.

Peterson, P. L. (1978). *Aptitude by treatment interaction effects of teacher structuring and student participation in college instruction.* Paper presented at the annual meeting of the American Educational Research Association, Toronto.

Resnick, L. B. (1981). Instructional Psychology. *Annual Review of Psychology, 32,* 659–704.

Riley, M. S. (1984). *The acquisition of problem solving skills in basic electricity and electronics* (Tech. Rep. No 84–50). San Diego, CA: U.S. Navy Personnel Research and Development Center.

Robinson, F. P. (1946). *Effective study*. New York: Harper.

Ross, S. M., & Rakow, E. A. (1981). Learner control versus program control as adaptive strategies for selection of instructional support on math rules. *Journal of Educational Psychology, 73*, 745–753.

Ross, S. M., Rakow, E. A. & Bush, A. J. (1980). Instructional systems for self-managed learning systems. *Journal of Educational Psychology, 72*, 312–320.

Sarason, I. G. (1972). Experimental approaches to test anxiety: Attention and the uses of information. In C. D. Spielberger (Ed.), *Anxiety: Current trends in theory and research* (Vol. 2). New York: Academic Press.

Sarason, I. G. (Ed.), (1980). *Test anxiety: Theory, research, and applications*. Hillsdale, NJ: Lawrence Erlbaum Associates.

Sarason, I. G. (in press). Test anxiety, cognitive interference, and performance. In R. E. Snow & M. J. Farr (Eds.), *Aptitude, learning, and instruction: Conative and affective process analyses*. Hillsdale, NJ: Lawrence Erlbaum Associates.

Sieber, J. E. (1977). How shall anxiety be defined? In J. E. Sieber, H. F. O'Neil, Jr., & Tobias, S. *Anxiety, learning and instruction*. Hillsdale, NJ: Lawrence Erlbaum Associates.

Sieber, J. R., O'Neil, H. F. J., & Tobias, S. (1977). *Anxiety, learning, and instruction*. Hillsdale, NJ: Lawrence Erlbaum Associates.

Snow, R. E., & Lohman, D. F. (1984). Toward a theory of cognitive aptitude for learning from instruction. *Journal of Educational Psychology, 76*, 347–376.

Sternberg, R. J. (Ed.) (1985). *Human abilities: An information-processing approach*. New York: Freeman.

Stipek, D. (1980). A causal analysis of the relationship between locus of control and academic achievement in first grade. *Contemporary Educational Psychology, 5*, 90–99.

Talmage, H. C. (1985). What is adaptive instruction? In M. C. Wang & H. Walberg (Eds.), *Adapting instruction to individual differences*. Berkeley, CA: McCutchan.

Tennyson, R. D. (1981). Use of adaptive information for advisement in learning concepts and rules using computer-assisted instruction. *American Educational Research Journal, 18*, 425–438.

Tennyson, R. D., & Rothen, W. (1977). Pretask and on-task adaptive design strategies for selecting number of instances in concept acquisition. *Journal of Educational Psychology, 69*, 586–592.

Tobias, S. (1973). Review of the response mode issues. *Review of Educational Research, 43*, 193–204.

Tobias, S. (1976). Achievement-treatment interactions. *Review of Educational Research, 46*, 61–74.

Tobias, S. (1977). A model for research on the effect of anxiety on instruction. In J. E. Sieber, H. F. O'Neil, Jr., & S. Tobias. *Anxiety, learning, and instruction*. Hillsdale, NJ: Lawrence Erlbaum Associates.

Tobias, S. (1979). Anxiety research in educational psychology. *Journal of Educational Psychology, 71*, 573–582.

Tobias, S. (1981). Adapting instruction to individual differences among students. *Educational Psychologist, 16*, 111–120.

Tobias, S. (1982). When do instructional methods make a difference? *Educational Researcher, 11*(4), 4–9.

Tobias, S. (1984a, April). *Test anxiety: Cognitive interference or inadequate preparation?* Paper presented at a symposium held at the annual meeting of the American Educational Research Association, New Orleans, LA.

Tobias, S. (1984b). *Test anxiety and postprocessing interference* (Tech. Rep. No. 2). New York: Instructional Research Project, City College of New York.

Tobias, S. (1985, April). *Review, other macroprocesses, and individual differences*. Paper presented at the annual meeting of the American Educational Research Association, Chicago, Illinois.

Tobias, S., & Federico, P. A. (1984). Changing aptitude-achievement relationships in instruction: A comment. *Journal of Computer-Based Instruction, 11,* 111–112.

Tobias, S., & Sacks, J. (1983, October). *Aptitude treatment interaction, adjunct questions, review, and macroprocesses.* Paper presented at a symposium held at the annual meeting of the Northeastern Educational Research Association, Ellenville, NY.

Tobias, S., & Sacks, J. (1984, October). *Test anxiety and post processing interference II.* Paper presented at the annual meeting of the Northeastern Educational Research Association, Ellenville, NY.

Walters, J., & Tobias, S. (1985, April). *The effect of anxiety and strategy training on learning.* Paper presented at the annual meeting of the American Educational Research Association, Chicago, IL.

Wang, M. C., & Walberg, H. (Eds.) (1985). *Adapting instruction to individual differences.* Berkeley, CA: McCutchan.

Weinstein, C. E., & Mayer, R. E. (1986). The teaching of learning strategies. In M. C. Wittrock (Ed.), *Handbook of research on teaching* (3rd ed.). New York: Macmillan.

Wendell, A., & Tobias, S. (1983, October). *Anxiety and the retrieval of information from long term memory.* Paper presented at the annual meeting of the Northeastern Educational Research Asociation, Ellenville, NY.

Wine, J. D. (1971). Test anxiety and direction of attention. *Psychological Bulletin, 76,* 92–104.

Winograd, P. (1984). Strategic difficulties in summarizing texts. *Reading Research Quarterly, 19,* 404–425.

Wittmaier, B. (1972). Test anxiety and study habits. *Journal of Educational Research, 65,* 352–354.

Wittrock, M. C. (1978). The cognitive movement in instruction. *Educational Psychologist, 13,* 15–30.

Wolfgang, A., & Potvin, R. (1973). *Internality as a determinant of degree of classroom participation and academic performance among elementary students.* Paper presented at the annual meeting of the American Psychological Association, Montreal.

AUTHOR NOTES

Sigmund Tobias is a Professor in the School of Education, The City College of the City University of New York.

Completion of this chapter was facilitated by grants from the Basic Research Program of the Army Research Institute and from the Control Data Corporation.

9 Displays and Communication

Malcolm L. Fleming
Indiana University

The design of displays that communicate is not a stand-alone part of the instructional development process, but grows out of prior analyses of learner characteristics, tasks, and learning situations. Consequently, what follows assumes that such preparatory analyses have been done.

This chapter deals with the problem of translating the products of earlier stages of the instructional development process into a specific and detailed design for instruction. This design is typically in the form of a script or story board which includes the words and the pictures that the instructor or the medium will present, though these will be in provisional form—sketches instead of final art or photography. Translating this instructional design into final media forms is a process specific to each medium and is not directly dealt with here.

Paraphrased, the above title might read, "What kinds of displays communicate?" That is the question addressed in this chapter. A more research-oriented statement would be, "What kinds of stimuli tend to lead to what kinds of responses, for example, attention, perception, learning, concept formation?"

The principles presented as guidelines to instructional design are stated in a language and a form that translates readily to practice. These principles are expected to inform the creative processes of the designer, increasing the probability of wise decisions without guaranteeing them. Thus, although the principles are based on large bodies of research, testing of prototype designs is essential, followed by redesign and retesting as needed.

SOME DEFINITIONS

Medium. Several concepts used in the following sections require clarification at this time. To begin with, conceptions of medium range from "the medium is the message" to the medium is only a delivery system. I believe neither view to be satisfactory. Even if we reduce our conception of media to simply that of delivery systems we still must make intelligent choices among them. True, seldom is *one* medium the only appropriate choice (given access to several), but neither is it likely that *all* media will adequately meet a particular instructional requirement.

To avoid some of the conceptual pitfalls associated with use of the word *medium,* I prefer a word that broadens the concept to a position of centrality in the instructional process. The substitute word is *mediator,* which is defined as "an intervening cause or instrument, something that intervenes between parties at variance to reconcile them." There are two advantages. First, mediator defines a role or function, that of arranging effective relations between two key parties to the instructional process: the learner and the subject matter. Learning is a lifelong process between humans and their environment, while instruction (by any mediating person or agency) is a deliberate intervention between learner and subject matter. Hence, effective instruction is seen as mediating optimally between learner and subject matter, taking into account the characteristics of both.

A second advantage of the term mediator is that it is eclectic. Anything in an instructional system that performs the mediational role is a mediator, from live teacher to latest device. Thus, because it denotes a function essential to instruction and because it avoids some undesirable associations with the word media, the concept of mediator serves well within the systems approach, and will be used here to refer to the vehicle which delivers the instructional message. In contrast, *display* will be used to refer to the actual instructional stimulus: the page of a book mediator, the speech of a teacher mediator, the projected image of a film mediator, the images displayed by a computer mediator.

Learner. I use the term learner not simply because one hopes the receiver in the instructional situation does learn, but also because I conceive of that person as a learner wherever he or she is, and at whatever stage in life. Such a person is actively interacting with the environment much of the time, mentally and physically.

The idea of *learner strategy* is pervasive in contemporary research literature. It is presumed that for every kind of subject matter or task there is a corresponding cognitive strategy, which, if applied by the learner, will lead to acquisition of the subject matter or performance of the task accurately and efficiently. According to this conception, the designer of instruction can arrange for a match between a learner's cognitive strategy and a particular task in any of several ways: assume the learner knows and will apply the appropriate strategy, remind the learner to use a known strategy, build the strategy into the instructional method (called embedded strategy, after Rigney, 1978), or teach the strategy as a separate part of the instruction. Full application of the learner-strategy concept to instructional design awaits further study of how to induce or teach the strategies. Some task-specific work has been done, for example, on geometry problems (Greeno, 1978), reading (Cook & Mayer, 1983), language learning (Paivio, 1983). Application of a few general memory strategies is now possible and will be discussed in a following section on learning.

Other chapters in this book focus on learner differences (particularly, Chapter 8). The design principles here are addressed to general learner characteristics. Adapting these principles to different learners is assumed to involve more changes in degree than in kind.

Task. I will use the term *task* here in place of subject matter or content, although knowledge or information are occasionally used to avoid the behavioral aspect of "task." Further, particular kinds of tasks will be referred to by name, for example: skill, concept, problem.

The term *schema* is used here to refer to the way knowledge is represented in memory. A schema is presumed to be an organized cluster of related information in memory. Although the designer may expect the existence of a close relation between the organization of information in a display and the presumed organization of schemata in memory, this relation does not necessarily follow.

Here are a few caveats concerning the communication principles to be described:

1. Principles will be numbered and underlined.

2. Principles have been selected primarily from four areas *(attention, perception, learning, and concept formation)* which are judged to be most pertinent to design decisions.

3. The sources cited in parentheses following each principle are mostly reviews of research. The bibliography in each review may, of course, be consulted for more specific credit to individual studies and investigators.

4. Instructional effects have multiple causes, hence the effects of any one principle may be modified by other factors.

5. The principles are broad, superordinate statements. Qualifications are omitted, hence the limits of appropriate application are not specified.

6. The applications suggested for the principles are intended as illustrative rather than prescriptive.

7. The application of research often involves over-generalization. The risk of misapplication is acceptable, however, if the designer tests and revises each instructional design as necessary.

ATTENTION

Attention, perception, and learning are not discrete processes. They are richly intertwined—both practically and theoretically. Even so, it is frequently advantageous to discuss them separately.

Quite simply, without attention there can be no learning. Designers typically seek both to obtain the learner's attention and to keep it. Influence on attention comes both from the display and from the learner, and the designer has some control of both.

1. *Attention is highly selective* (Treisman, 1974). We can give attention to only a small part of the environment at one time, and of that we see most sharply only the tiny, central portion of the visual field. We cope with the complexities of the environment by continually repositioning the eyes so that bit by bit we construct a functional, perceptual representation. Designers must learn to accommodate to and use this selective process called attention.

2. *Attention is drawn to what is novel or different* (Berlyne, 1970). By manipulating instructional displays the designer can readily introduce novelty. This need not be something that is entirely new to learners; it need only be different from what they have just recently experienced. For example, in speech, change the volume or inflection; in print, change the typeface or color; in film or television, change the pace or introduce a novel element such as a sound effect. In instructional displays, novelty should be used to draw attention to the information to be learned, not to the novel element per se.

Novelty can further be understood as the introduction of change. From that perspective come the following subprinciples:

2a. Changes in brightness and particularly in motion are strong attention-getting factors. Sensitivity to these factors is present even in infants, hence the designer can use them with all ages.

2b. Once attention is gained, continuing changes in the ongoing stream of instruction can help maintain it.

3. *Attention is drawn to moderate complexity* (Forgus, 1966). Obviously, this can be overdone, leading to learner avoidance. On the other hand, a too simplistic display may get very little attention.

4. *Lean displays focus attention.* This has been called attribute isolation (Bovy, 1981). The procedure here is simply to include only the most relevant information. For example, in motion pictures and TV, use closeups; in text, delete nonessentials and use footnotes for less central information; in

pictures delete irrelevant background information and superfluous interior detail in figures.

The above principles do not depend on prior learning, and hence can be used by the designer for all ages.

5. *Learned cues can direct attention* (Bovy, 1981). Examples are arrows, underlinings, circles, or rectangles around items. Such attention-directing cues are effective only with "literate" learners. Another very effective cue is simply to direct the learner verbally to look for or listen to certain features. See Fig. 9.1.

Captions can have a strong effect on the amount and kind of attention given pictures. Pictures without attention-directing prompts may be scanned superficially and processed at a very shallow level (Levie & Lentz, 1982). See Fig. 9.1.

6. *Learner expectations can strongly influence attention* (Eysenck, 1984). The learner's expectations (sometimes called mental set) are a powerful determinant of attention. Designers can have a strong effect on learner set or expectation by means of task instructions. Challenging questions, for example, can strongly influence what a learner attends to in a paragraph or picture, and thus determine what can be remembered.

Expectations can also influence the amount of mental effort that learners are willing to invest in attention to a display. For example, Salomon (1984) has shown that learners may have a set or expectation that television provides entertainment, and hence may not give it the careful attention necessary for systematic learning.

7. *Moderate uncertainty may induce careful attention* (Mouly, 1973). This implies that displays that are too easy or obvious may fail to gain or hold attention. The amount of uncertainty may vary with the task, less for concepts and more for problem solving.

PERCEPTION

Learning is limited by what the learner perceives, and that can be influenced directly by the designer. Subsequent learning is controlled by other less direct factors which will be considered later. Perception is conceived here as an active, ongoing, constructive process. A learner presented with a display may select some part of it, compare it with some schema (organized information) in memory and immediately recognize the displayed object. Or, lacking a match between display and schema, the learner may scan further information in the display or seek another schema for comparison. This interactive, goal-oriented process may continue until an adequate match is found, an existing schema is modified, or a new schema is constructed. While principles of perception operate in all sensory modalities, the following discussion emphasizes the two modalities by which most instruction is received: visual and auditory modalities.

8. *Perception is organized* (Eysenck, 1984). Learners try to construct meaningful wholes from their environment: objects, events, ideas. Unorganized stimulation is difficult to understand and remember. The designer who produces displays that are readily organized reduces the possibility that the learner will organize the material differently and perhaps erroneously. See Fig. 9.1.

8a. Perhaps the most basic organizational step in the perceptual process is the separation of the visual field into figure and ground. For example, key figures (objects, persons) in a picture are selected and given more attention than the background scene. The designer should make the essential information figural and therefore dominant. See Fig. 9.1.

8b. Orderly displays invite systematic perceptual processing (Winn, 1982). Since perception takes time, logically organized displays save instructional time and also increase the probability of correct interpretation. For example, hierarchical orderings can influence comprehension of graphic displays. Other orderings, for example, cause–effect, before–after, can simplify perception.

9. *Perception is relative* (Helson, 1974). Perception is not registered in absolute values; rather, it functions by comparison. The implications are many.

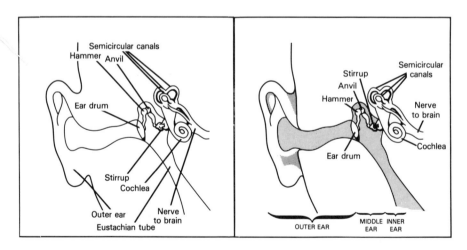

FIGURE 9.1. Effects of display organization. In the improved version (right) important figures stand out more clearly from the background. Labels and arrows are grouped by three major areas, simplifying attention and memory.

9a. Judgments of brightness and loudness are relative. A medium gray may be perceived to be dark gray relative to white and light gray relative to black. The apparent loudness of a musical passage will be influenced by the level of the just preceding passage.

9b. Judgments of size or quantity are relative. The size of an unknown pictured object cannot be determined without reference to some standard, for example, a hand or ruler.

9c. Judgments of depth or distance are relative. For instance, size and depth are inversely related; the smaller a familiar object appears to be the farther away it will be judged to be. Perceived size in a picture or screen is influenced by the frame—large if it's filled and smaller if it's not.

9d. Judgments of time are relative. For example, judgments of time duration are relative to the concurrent activity—short if it's interesting and long if it's not. Moral to designers: keep instruction moving.

9e. Judgments of motion are relative. Perceived motion is relative to some reference point, for example, the frame or background in a picture.

10. *Perception is most influenced by the informative areas of a display.* The informative areas are those which are most effective in reducing uncertainty and providing a match between display structure and learner schema. Examples follow.

10a. Contours are given more attention than uniform areas, probably because there is more information there; contours define figures (Graham, 1965). This may help explain the perceptual effectiveness of outline drawings.

10b. Learners attend to and remember figures better than the details inside the figures (Mandler & Johnson, 1976).

11. *Vision is most sensitive to colors in the middle of the spectrum, yellow and yellow-green, and least sensitive to those at the ends of the spectrum, violet/blue and red. Similarly, audition is most sensitive to pitches in the middle, two to three octaves above middle C, falling off toward both lower and higher pitches* (Murch, 1973; Van Bergeijk, Pierce, & David, 1960). The falling off of sensitivity toward the ends of the range can be partly compensated. For vision, add white pigment or white light (more energy) to the blue or red. For audition, special audio equipment can compensate for losses by boosting the levels of low or high frequencies.

12. *Displays and display elements that appear similar tend to be grouped in perception and associated in memory* (Haber & Hershenson, 1973). Similarity is a pervasive factor whose influence extends to concept formation (grouping and labeling similar things). Similarity can be made apparent in many ways: perceptually (form, size, color) as well as procedurally and conceptually. It follows that the designer has many ways of manipulating similarities; for instance, by accentuating some cues, and by eliminating or rear-

ranging others. When objects, events, ideas are to be related, associated, organized, or conceptualized together, employing similarity factors can be facilitative.

Similarity also influences the amount of transfer of learning from one situation to another. Where extensive transfer is desired, the designer should provide for similar practice in varied contexts.

13. *Displays or elements that appear close together in space or time tend to be grouped in perception and memory* (Murch, 1973). This principle has been called the law of proximity in perception and the law of contiguity in memory. These relationships are critical for the designer to arrange since many instructional processes depend on them.

13a. Proximity is often a determinant of perceived causality, for example, when one event or condition, the apparent cause, is closely followed by another, the apparent effect. Film editors have often used this device to suggest cause–effect or before–after relationships.

13b. Two proximate (side-by-side) displays invite perceptual comparison of similarities and differences. This relationship can be manipulated to emphasize similarities despite differences, and vice versa. See Fig. 9.2 for an example.

13c. Contiguity, either spatial or temporal, is a basic factor in forming associations in memory (Bugelski, 1971). Putting two symbols together in space, for example, a picture of an object together with its label, facilitates associative memory. So, too, does putting two symbols one after the other in time, for instance, words in a spoken sentence.

13d. Classical forms of learning, such as conditioning and reinforcement, depend on contiguity factors.

14. *Displays that are different tend to separate ideas in perception and memory* (Fleming & Levie, 1978). Display differences can be in time of presentation, in spatial location within the display, or in style or format. Such differences are common across mediators: separate paragraphs or chapters in books, fades to black between film or TV sequences, pauses in lectures, verbal cues for change, for example, "before that," "next," "in contrast." Such devices have the effect of signaling the boundaries between ideas.

When two things are quite difficult to distinguish, other methods are required, as follows.

14a. For difficult discriminations a side-by-side (instead of separate) arrangement may be necessary to facilitate perception of the differences.

14b. For discrimination, maximize differences. This can be done by exaggerating critical differences or eliminating similarities.

14c. Begin with examples that are most different (easy to discriminate) and continue with those having finer differences (difficult to discriminate) (Gibson, 1969).

LEARNING

Representing the Information

One might expect this section to begin with the several classical laws of learning (frequency, effect, conditioning). Instead, a generally sequential order of principles is used, depending roughly on when a designer might consider them. Thus, principles dealing with an initial presentation will precede those dealing with repeating it (frequency) and those involving learner responses following it (effect).

Probably the most important objects perceived by learners are the various kinds of symbols used in instruction, for instance, words, numbers, pictures, which refer to important phenomena in the environment. One of the more common and puzzling choices that designers make is among symbol types. Distinctions important to the designer can be made here.

15. *The kinds of mental operations evoked by a display are related to but not limited by the symbol systems used* (Winn, 1982). For example, a displayed picture often arouses mental words as well as mental images. A displayed word may arouse mental images (picture-like) as well as mental words. Displayed numbers can also lead to verbal or imaginal processing. Such dual-processing effects do not necessarily occur, but when they do they may facilitate learning.

16. *The kinds of information that can be presented in a display are dependent on the nature of the symbol systems used.* This is partly a function of the characteristics of the sensory modalities involved. Vision is especially sensitive to changes across space, while audition is especially sensitive to changes across time. Words are perceivable through either modality: through vision as print and through audition as speech. In contrast, pictures are generally perceivable only through vision. These sensory differences affect instruction.

16a. Words are instructionally more flexible than pictures in that they can be perceived through either the visual or auditory modality (Fleming & Levie, 1978). This provides the designer with more mediator choices and the learner with more choices in recording and manipulating the symbols.

16b. Print and pictures are more durable than speech, that is, they are available to processing longer (Fleming & Levie, 1978). This is due to the temporal nature of the auditory channel. Typically, the learner has one moment to perceive a spoken word but can perceive a printed word over more time. (Obviously the mediator involved can limit perception time as well; fixed-pace mediators, such as TV and motion pictures, limit both picture and print duration.)

Thus, print and pictures are more suitable than speech (live or recorded) for presentation of complex tasks which require prolonged attention. Where auditory symbols are desired, very good sound quality and listening conditions are required.

17. *Concreteness in displays facilitates learning* (Gagné & Rohwer, 1969). This principle requires explanation; for, despite its positive effect on memory, concreteness by itself may be undesirable; although it is effective when used to exemplify abstractions. Following are more examples and explanations.

17a. The demonstration or modeling of skills can lead to their acquisition by observers (Berliner & Gage, 1976). Many motor, social, and cognitive skills are learned from models: parents, teachers, peers. The designer can make effective use of live or recorded models; for example, one can use experts in the task being taught.

17b.Pictures are better remembered than words (Gagné & Rohwer, 1969). This has been supported by many controlled studies, but the implications for instruction are not self-evident. For example, a picture may give too much information, and the most essential part for instruction may not be evident. Hence pictures generally need the constraining context of words (Mills, 1980), or selective simplification, as in line drawings (Dwyer, 1972). A common use of pictures is to repeat the information verbally stated in a display. This has been shown repeatedly to increase significantly learning of that information over what is learned from the verbal display alone (Levie & Lentz, 1982).

17c. Concrete words are better remembered than abstract words (Paivio, 1971). One explanation of this well-established finding is that concrete nouns more readily elicit mental images than do abstract nouns. Though designers often cannot avoid use of abstract words, they can define them with concrete words or provide examples or analogies that are concrete.

17d. Concreteness is more effective on the stimulus side of an association than on the response side (Gagné & Rohwer, 1969). This fits well the use of pictures as stimuli and words as responses or descriptions.

17e. Pictures and words can be reciprocally beneficial; words can delimit and interpret pictures and pictures help define, exemplify, and make memorable words (Mills, 1980). Captions and labels can have a determinative effect on how or whether pictures are studied.

17f. Realism per se is not necessarily a virtue in instruction (Winn, 1982). This is probably apparent from the foregoing outline, but needs emphasis because picture-mediator enthusiasts have sometimes overlooked the fact that abstraction is often the intent of instruction.

18. *Meaningful displays facilitate learning* (Eysenck, 1984). An earlier S–R psychology avoided the concept of "meaning," but yielded ample evidence that learners of nonsense syllables resorted to many techniques to make enough sense out of nonsense-syllable stimuli to permit memorization, for example, similarity to words, alphabetical order, phonics, rhymes.

Current cognitive psychologists are more accepting of the concept of meaning but not much more successful in defining it. However, two factors emphasized as strongly influencing it are display organization, for example, advance organizers (Ausubel, 1968), and learners' prior knowledge of display characteristics (Reigeluth, 1983).

To be stressed here is the power of meaningfulness over memory; the more meaningful the display the less drill or repetition necessary to memorize it. Numerous principles in this chapter contribute to meaningfulness: for example, relating instruction to learner's prior knowledge (24), making criterial cues dominant (20), make organization apparent (25), giving corrective feedback (29), and others.

19. *The amount of displayed information that can be processed at one time is quite limited* (Moray, 1967). It follows that the information provided by the designer should be rationed. Following are some important considerations.

19a. Information in a display is divided by the learner into chunks of a size suitable for perception and memory (Miller, 1968). Prechunking by the designer may be facilitative, in effect increasing processing capacity. Displays can be prechunked by spatial grouping, by temporal pacing and pauses, or by semantic grouping of related concepts. For example, a process of 20 steps can be divided into 4 groups of 5 steps. Though more information will be involved, that is, the names of the 4 groups, all of it is likely to be learned more efficiently.

19b. A general limit of seven plus or minus two familiar items can be perceived and reported at one time (Miller, 1968). Perhaps five is a more dependable limit for instruction. Item size, and hence capacity, will depend on prior learning; for instance, a familiar superordinate word can be made to stand for a quantity of subordinate information.

19c. Processing capacity is influenced both by the quantity of information involved and the type or depth of processing required (Eysenck, 1984). For example, explaining the various relationships between objects in a picture would require deeper processing than simply naming the separate objects. Thus, both the size of the display and the complexity of the task need to be controlled to keep within processing capacity limits. (However, deeper or more extensive processing generally leads to more learning.)

19d. Familiar displays or elements require less processing capacity than unfamiliar (Haber & Hershenson, 1973). Thus, including familiar terms or examples, or using analogies to something familiar can increase capacity.

19e. Capacity is partly determined by sensory modality; there can be more when two modalities are used concurrently than when either is used separately (Craik, 1979). For example, using both the visual modality (pictures) and the auditory modality (speech) increases capacity over either one separately. However, this effect occurs when information in the two modalities is related rather than redundant or discrepant. Also, adding more information to both modalities can overload the system so much that the learner must choose to attend to one or the other.

Directly related to the capacity problem, much research has been devoted to finding the optimum size of step in programmed instruction, but without much success. There are apparently too many factors involved to permit simple generalizations. However, Margolius and Sheffield (1961) referred to a useful measure, the *demonstration-assimilation span,* or the amount of information that can be presented before the learner must respond by rehearsing, answering questions, or applying the information. They defined this measure as the amount of information on which 75% of learners tested immediately can score 100%. Similarly, Brophy (1980) reports that effective teachers use small steps but a rapid pace to keep learners involved. The indicator for the teacher is that learners can answer correctly about 70–80% of questions. It thus appears that problems of pace and size-of-step must ultimately be answered through formative evaluation of initial designs.

20. *Displays which make criterial information salient make learning more efficient* (Fleming & Levie, 1978). Two aspects should be noted here. First, criterial information in a complex display is often highly selective (based on a careful task analysis), and hence may not be apparent to a naive learner. Second, salience is required because of the important distinction between the nominal stimulus (what's available in the display and perfectly clear to the designer) and the effective stimulus (what the learner selectively attends to). To minimize the discrepancy between the two, the designer must make the essential part salient, dominant, noticeable. What information is criterial in Fig. 9.2?

The manipulations available to the designer for the above purpose are many: eliminating the nonessential (picture background), adding the essential (definitive examples), selectively emphasizing the essential (making it larger, colored, moving, underlined, repeated). Several emphatic devices have been noted in a previous section.

Special mention should be made here of color. Despite widespread opinion, color has not been shown to have any unique effect on instruction (Lamberski, 1980). True, learners typically prefer it, but they generally learn as well without it. Color seems to be an important characteristic of displays where it is criterial, that is, essential to the subject matter (color which identifies a particular bird), where it is selectively used to direct attention to what is essential (a word printed in red), or where it is used to differentiate or group objects or ideas (color coding of a map).

21. *Contextual information may be necessary to perception, learning, and understanding* (Horton & Mills, 1984). Whereas the previous principle favors a bare-bones display, this one favors adding or retaining some contextual information. The difference is one of degree. Information that is too

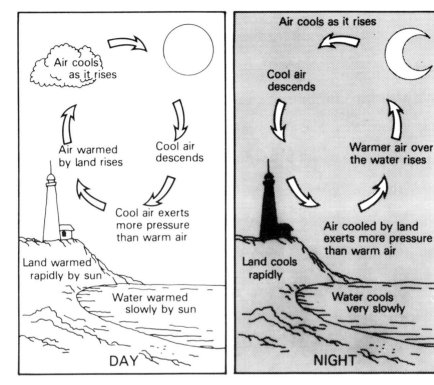

FIGURE 9.2. Side-by-side (proximate) placement invites comparison. Criterial information is contrasted between the two, increasing its saliency. Less important information is held constant.

isolated can be misinterpreted or forgotten. This is because of the basic relational nature of cognition: figures are perceived relative to a ground, memory functions by connecting a and b (assimilating to an existing schema). For example, much recent research on reading demonstrates the dependence of word meanings on a sentence context and sentence meaning on a paragraph context (Horton & Mills, 1984).

22. *Learning can be facilitated where displays in initial learning stages are highly manipulated to influence attention and memory, and where, in subsequent displays, these manipulations are gradually eliminated* (Anderson & Faust, 1973). Maximum assistance is given the learner initially to minimize error. Then the assistance is gradually faded until the learner can respond correctly and without aid to the real situation. This method doesn't avoid maximum manipulation but attempts to remedy its undesirable effects.

23. *Alternately, learning can be facilitated where initial displays are only minimally manipulated. Criterial questions are asked; and additional manipulation, called brightening, is provided only as and if the learner requires it*

to give correct answers (Ellson et al., 1965). This method avoids overmanipulation, but requires a knowledgeable tutor to keep evaluating the learner and providing remedial assistance (more manipulation, more prompts) as needed. However, this procedure can be systematized with a graduated series of questions and prompts so that nonprofessional tutors can be trained to manage it quite effectively.

Also, the degree and kind of manipulations that are desired in instructional displays and processes depend on the characteristics of the learner, a factor dealt with in other chapters of this book. In general, the more skilled and knowledgeable the learner the less the manipulation required.

24. *Learning is highly dependent on the prior knowledge of the learner* (Reigeluth, 1983). The prior knowledge presumably provides a schema which subsumes or modifies the new information. Thus, what is already familiar to the learner can be used to acquire new learning. Many kinds of prior knowledge can be facilitative: knowledge of symbol systems, of related concepts or skills (superordinate, coordinate, subordinate), of preceding steps in a process, of known relationships (alphabetical, hierarchical), of cognitive strategies.

While some newness or unfamiliarity in a display is necessary in order for learning to occur, limiting the new to what is necessarily new—that is, making as much use of the familiar as possible—reduces the processing and memory load, saving capacity for the essential new elements. There is a limit to this principle, for too familiar displays may be given only superficial processing that overlooks essential information. In such cases, some added difficulty in task or unfamiliarity in display may be necessary (Wickelgren, 1981).

Notice that the familiarity principle seems to contradict the novelty principle (2) discussed earlier. The difference is in the designer's intent: to attract attention, use novelty; to facilitate memory, use familiarity. It may be difficult to maintain a proper balance between the two.

Organizing and Sequencing Instruction

Once some of the decisions on the representation of information have been made, the designer faces important alternatives in organization and sequence.

25. *Organized displays facilitate learning* (Winn, 1981). This principle extends an earlier one (8) noting the positive effect of organization on efficient perceptual processing. However, there are several ways to conceptualize and achieve organization. Three representations of organization are: the structure of the knowledge to be taught, the structure of the display, and the structure of the learner's cognitive schemata. The designer's task might be conceptualized as bringing these three representations into congruence. Relating the first two can be fairly straightforward, providing that task

analysis yields a representation of the substantive relationships. For example, a spatial diagram may be employed, probably hierarchical for concepts and sequential for skills. However, dealing with the last factor, cognitive schemata, in any direct and reliable way, is beyond our present capability in most areas of knowledge. However, enough can be inferred from a learner's knowledge about a task and skills for dealing with it to permit the designer to proceed—that is, to train prerequisite skills, or embed them in the design, or assume the learner has the skills (based on pretests or prior instruction successfully completed). The next two principles are intended to influence the learner's selection and development of cognitive processes appropriate to the task at hand.

26. *What occurs in the first display or last display of an instructional unit can have a critical effect on learning* (Gagné, 1978). As a concept in the learning literature the idea of an introduction, whatever it may be called, is widely reported and valued. A sample of the various conceptions follows.

26a. Primacy and recency effects are very common in memory research; what the learner encounters first and last in a stimulus is better remembered than that in between (Berelson & Steiner, 1964).

26b. An introduction that is relatively abstract and provides an organization that subsumes the information which follows can facilitate learning. This kind of introduction, called an advance organizer, is said to provide an assimilative context for what follows. Advance organizers have been widely studied with mixed results, although when the organizers are properly designed and effects are measured by a transfer test, the results are generally positive. This seems especially true when the information is otherwise poorly organized or the learners are poorly informed (Mayer, 1979).

26c. Introductory questions have a determinative effect on learning (Anderson & Biddle, 1975). Information related to the prequestions tends to be better learned than information not related to them. Further, the type of question influences the kind of cognitive processing induced, from recall to analysis, synthesis, and evaluation (Hall, 1983).

26d. Various other kinds of introductory information affect subsequent cognitive processing and facilitate learning: instructions, statements of objectives, and topic sentences (Gagné, 1978); headings and titles (Resnick, 1981). There is evidence that what appears at the top of a display is judged to be superordinate to what follows and thus more inclusive or general, more important, or superior, relative to what follows (DeSoto, London, & Handel, 1968).

26e. Concluding material such as postquestions, summaries, and reviews can also affect what is learned. Postquestions appear to have a broader effect on learning than prequestions in that they facilitate learning of both related and unrelated information (Anderson & Biddle, 1975).

It is apparent from the foregoing that the start and finish positions in an instructional sequence provide the designer with a variety of opportunities to influence the course of cognitive processing.

27. *Repetition increases learning* (Wickelgren, 1981). This is the classical Law of Frequency, and is commonly employed by teachers and learners alike, that is, in drill and practice. It should, however, be used selectively by designers.

27a. Use repetition where meaningfulness is minimal. Use it more for rote memory tasks than for concepts (DeCecco & Crawford, 1974).

27b. Use repetition for skills that need to be maximized in precision (golf swing or basketball free-throw) and in speed (addition, multiplication, reading, writing). Also, repetition may be required to produce automatization of skill (Neves & Anderson, 1981).

27c. The newer the information the more practice and more time per repetition may be necessary (Kumar, 1971).

27d. Spaced or distributed practice generally leads to more learning than massed practice (Wickelgren, 1981). Cramming before a test (massed practice) may appear to be an exception, but does not favor long-term retention.

28. *Repetition with variety is superior to verbatim repetition* (Tulving & Thomson, 1973). This not only makes the repetition less boring but also increases the generality of the learning. Repetition in varied contexts increases transfer of learning.

The designer should keep in mind that repetition and meaningfulness are reciprocal, that is, the more meaningful the display the less need for repetition, and vice versa. Thus, a considerable investment in meaningfulness can be cost effective. See Principle 18.

Feedback to the Learner

At this point, if not earlier, it is important for the designer to consider what learner responses might be to the tentative design resulting from the preceding, and what effect these might have on learning and on next design decisions.

29. *Feedback to learners after they have responded facilitates learning* (Kulhavy, 1977). This is the classical Law of Effect, the basic tenet of reinforcement theorists. What happens after a response is made to a display affects whether that response will be repeated, that is, learned. The association is presumably strengthened where the effect is positive and weakened where negative.

This principle has been very widely studied and applied, and should be known by designers as a central concept behind programmed instruction. However, studies have not found it to be uniformly effective, particularly in studies of programmed instruction in which learners were permitted to peek at the answers before making a response (Anderson et al., 1971). Some limitations and qualifications for its use follow. A common distinction in the literature is between feedback that is intended to reward the learner ("Well done!" "Excellent!") and that is intended to inform the learner ("Correct answer was _____ "). When the learner's response is correct, rewarding feedback may be more reinforcing; while when the response is incorrect, feedback is more informative. With learners of some maturity, Estes (1972) found informative feedback to be more effective than a reward.

29a. Give praise for correct responses and more help for incorrect ones (Levin & Long, 1981). However, feedback after errors is generally more important than confirmation of correct responses (Kulhavy, 1977).

29b. Feedback for incorrect responses should include corrective procedures and further testing and feedback as necessary. This approach was found to be essential in recent research on mastery learning (Bloom, 1984). Corrective procedures can extend to probing learner errors to find why they were made (Levin & Long, 1981). This probing of errors is particularly useful in formative evaluation of an initial design in order to inform the designer of problems to remedy in a redesign.

29c. Immediate feedback is not always essential or even desirable. Delays of 24 hours can sometimes facilitate learning (Kulhavy, 1977). However, immediacy is probably important where the task is difficult or where each step is dependent on correct responding to the previous one.

29d. Feedback should be frequent in initial instruction, then reduced, and finally eliminated (Anderson & Faust, 1973).

All of the above feedback principles assume that a responsive mediator (teacher, computer, or other) is available.

Activity and Strategy of the Learner

The designer can assume the learner is active, overtly or covertly. The problem is that of guiding and sustaining the learner's on-task activity and reducing or eliminating the off-task activity.

30. *Learning is facilitated where the learner reacts to or interacts with the criterial information, and the more activity the more learning, within limits* (Levin & Long, 1981). Although, as noted earlier, repetition can increase learning, the emphasis here is on more varied activity.

30a. Both overt and covert activity can facilitate learning. Thus, mental activity of various kinds is included in the above principle, the designer's problem being how to induce it. This is related to the concept of level of processing, that is, from a rote superficial level to a higher conceptual or problem-solving level. Results from study of processing levels have shown greater learning associated with deeper levels of processing, generally induced through higher cognitive tasks. Though some investigators (e.g.,

Horton & Mills, 1984) have explained this kind of result as mental elaboration or mental effort, the levels-of-processing concept provides the designer a useful heuristic for finding ways to maximize learner cognitive involvement.

30b. Learner involvement varies with type of task, over which the designer has considerable control. For example, as discussed earlier, the insertion of questions in displays can markedly influence the learner's level of activity, both quantitatively and qualitatively. See Fig. 9.3 for an example of the use of questions with an illustration.

As noted in the introduction to this chapter, learners acquire strategies (systematic ways of dealing with information) partly from trial-and-error learning, partly from strategies embedded in instruction, and partly from direct instruction. Two of the best established and most widely useful memory strategies will be discussed here.

31. *A learner strategy that consists of the generation of relational mental images can markedly increase learning* (Eysenck, 1984). A mental image is a representation in the learner's mind that corresponds to some degree to concrete objects and events. Extensive research has established that where two words (concepts) are to be associated, forming a mental image of the object, event, or idea which each word refers to can lead to twice as much learning as subvocal repetition of the word pair, provided the two images interact in some way (Bower, 1972). Several qualities of mental images have been compared. The results suggest that while image vividness and bizarreness may sometimes be helpful, it is essential that there be some interaction between the images to be associated such that a single, composite image be formed.

There is evidence that, for a particular task, provision of a picture of interacting objects may lead to more learning than provision of instructions for the learner to form interacting mental images of the objects (Levin, 1979). However, there is also long range merit in training learners to use mental imagery as a memory strategy that is easy to learn, inexpensive to apply, and widely applicable (Higbee, 1979).

32. *A learner strategy that consists of the generation of a sentence or paragraph context for embedding words to be memorized can increase learning* (Bower, 1973). This is a form of mental elaboration upon the given information, such that meaningful relations are formed between the words to be remembered and the sentence context. This has the effect of raising the level of processing from rote to conceptual. Even the use of simple rhymes can facilitate memory; for example, use "i" before "e," except after "c."

The above two principles raise again the issue as to how far instruction should go in supplanting learner strategies (with pictures or verbal structures) instead of inducing them (mental imagery or mental elaboration). While the designer's decision in any particular case can be argued, there seems to be a consensus that learners can and should be taught a wide range of cognitive

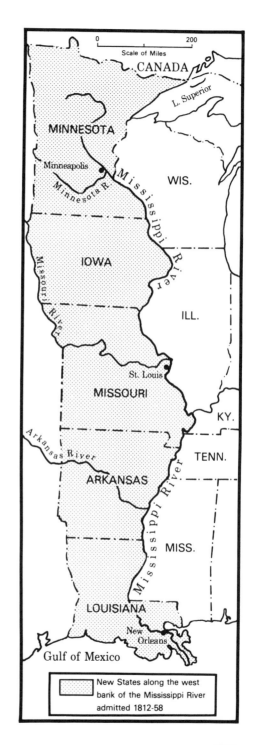

FIGURE 9.3. Use of questions to influence learner involvement. (1) Name the new states created along the west bank of the Mississippi River. (2) Which has an international boundary? (3) What effect might the Mississippi and its tributaries have on settlement to the west?

strategies, such as imagery and elaboration. There is also evidence that repeated performance of a cognitive task can lead to automatization of the strategies involved (Gagné & Dick, 1983). This greatly increases efficiency on that task and may result in strategies that can be transferred to other tasks. There is further evidence that repeated exposure to a certain mediator can induce learning of cognitive strategies characteristic of that mediator. For example, repeated zooming into details of a painting seems to induce a more analytical strategy toward study of subsequent paintings (Salomon, 1979). But such effects may not always be positive. Extensive exposure to broadcast TV may lead to preferences for shallow processing and low investment of mental effort.

CONCEPT FORMATION

Concepts are commonly thought of as names or labels (common nouns) for groups of things. More precisely, concepts are what common nouns refer to, that is, a set of referents (objects, events, or ideas) which have some characteristics or defining attributes in common. Concepts enable us to group a very large number of things into a finite number of categories. Without them, learning to cope with our environment would be very difficult. Concepts are built on the important regularities observed in the environment, and thus are the core of classroom learning.

As implied above, a concept is more than its label. It is also more than its definition. Both label and definition can be memorized, but concept formation ultimately requires a higher cognitive process, a generalization across a varied set of examples. Thus, another group of principles is required to assist the designer in moving learners from memorization processes to conceptualization processes.

Because of recent research, some older concepts about concepts have been modified. The classical view that *all* examples have *common* defining attributes is now seen as largely limited to mathematics and science concepts. For other concepts, the attributes may be only probabalistic and be based on the relative similarity of examples to a prototypical example. Such concepts are common in the social sciences and humanities (Medin, 1984). Thus, despite an effort toward achieving clear-cut classical-type concepts, many remain with fuzzy borders and with examples having a gradient of representativeness.

Just what may be the instructional implications of the above range of concept types is not yet clear. Consequently, the principles which follow will in general assume classical-type concepts, for they have been most extensively studied in learning contexts.

As discussed in the preceding section on learning, what occurs first in concept instruction may have a determinative effect on what follows. For example, prior learning of relevant words (names of attributes, examples, related concepts) and prior familiarization of relevant objects would be facilitative (Brien, 1983).

33. *Concrete concepts are generally easier to learn than abstract concepts* (Clark, 1971). This mainly serves to extend a memory principle encountered earlier (17). It assumes that concrete (more memorable) examples will be used in instruction.

34. *Abstract concepts can be learned from various verbal structures: definitions, descriptions of attributes, descriptions of examples, synonyms* (Klausmeier et al., 1974). While pictures may be more memorable than words, as noted in 17b, abstract concepts are unlikely to have readily picturable examples. Even abstract pictures may include too much without very careful control of noncriterial attributes. Hence, the use of relatively concrete words (more memorable) to describe abstract concepts (less memorable) seems appropriate. Analogies may be very useful as well.

Selection of Examples and Nonexamples

Five kinds of information are useful for concept instruction: name, definition, attributes, and examples and nonexamples; and this is the sequence in which they are often selected and presented by designers. The opposite view is taken here, that is, choose examples first because only from them can the common attributes be reliably determined; and only from those attributes can an accurate definition be derived. However, when the choice has been made to begin with a definition, the designer must be sure to verify it with reference to examples. The definition must reliably and efficiently distinguish between examples and nonexamples.

35. *Use both examples and nonexamples in instruction* (DeCecco & Crawford, 1974). Often instruction includes only examples. However, it is the nonexamples that clarify for the learner just what is distinctive about the concept, that is, what distinguishes examples from nonexamples.

36. *Use a wide variety of examples to represent their full range of divergence* (Tennyson, 1980). These examples would be expected to be alike in criterial attributes but as varied as possible in noncriterial attributes. The effect is to clarify for the learner what defines the concept (doesn't change) and what is irrelevant to it (does change). Figure 9.4 provides an example.

37. *Use non-examples that are close in to (similar to) examples* (Tennyson, 1980). These close-in nonexamples are very important instructionally, for they are the very ones that learners will find confusing and thus require special help with. These nonexamples will be similar to examples in one or more criterial attributes, or noncriterial attributes, or both.

38. *Use sufficient examples to suggest the applicable range of the concept. Use close-in nonexamples to cover the most common and confusing ones and to delimit the concept* (De Cecco & Crawford, 1974). This provides a basis

for controlling the number and kinds of examples and nonexamples needed for instruction.

Presentation of Examples and Definitions

Presentation order has been much debated. The definition (rule) can be presented first and then the examples. This deductive approach has been dubbed "ruleg." Or, the examples can be presented first, followed by the definition (rule). This inductive approach has been called "egrule." A combined approach has much to recommend it. First, present a simple and clear example or two, derive from them a rule (definition or set of criterial attributes), then apply it to a wide range of examples and nonexamples (Engelmann, 1969). The initial example(s) could be eliminated when it is considered that the learner would understand the concept in abstract verbal form, that is, by its definition.

39. *Display of the criterial attributes increases concept learning as opposed to a presentation requiring the learner to discover them* (Anderson & Faust, 1973). This can be done in several ways: present a definition, present a list of attributes, direct attention to the attributes in examples. Where a discovery method is preferred, more examples may be required, and criterial attributes should be as few and as apparent to the learner as possible (Anderson & Faust, 1973).

40. *Initial examples should be representative of the concept, relatively familiar, and with unambiguous criterial attributes* (Anderson & Faust, 1973). *Subsequent presentations should include both examples and nonexamples and be arranged in order of increasing difficulty* (Tennyson, 1980). This is essentially a reiteration of the simple-to-complex order recommended earlier for instruction.

41. *Display examples and nonexamples simultaneously or in close succession while keeping earlier ones in view* (DeCecco & Crawford, 1974). This reduces memory load and permits direct comparisons of similarities among examples (see Fig. 9.4) and differences between examples and nonexamples. This is another application of the proximity–contiguity principle (13).

Some writers (Ali, 1981; Tennyson, 1980) also recommend presentation of matched pairs: an example and then a close-in nonexample, the pair being similar in noncriterial attributes. This would certainly draw learner attention to criterial attributes.

42. *Displaying the concept name in contiguity with examples facilitates associating the two* (DeCecco & Crawford, 1974). Contiguity can mean either close together in space (computer terminal) or in time (voice over picture).

43. *Displaying a definition as an organized list of attributes can increase concept learning over the usual sentence format* (Markle, 1975). This tech-

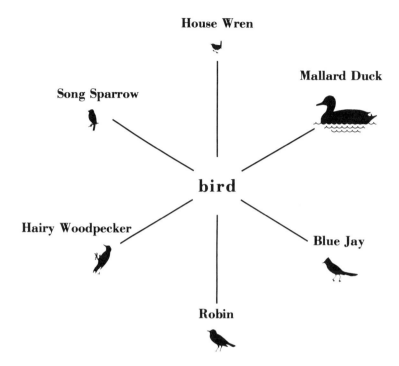

FIGURE 9.4. Concept (bird) related to a range of divergent examples. Common attribute (configuration) is accentuated by similar poses across examples. Irrelevant attribute (size) is eliminated by variation across examples.

nique selectively emphasizes each attribute that might otherwise be lost in a long definition.

44. *When dealing with a concept that is probabilistic (not classical), present the central meaning, then a series of carefully chosen examples, for example, model example, contrary example, related example, borderline example, together with the context of use* (Hall, 1983). As noted in the beginning paragraph of this section, there have not been many studies contrasting instructional methods for this type of concept with those for classical concepts.

Practice with newly learned concepts is important, as would be expected from learning principles such as 27.

45. *Consolidation of new conceptual learning depends on further learner activity, including opportunities to practice identifying additional examples and nonexamples, to describe criterial attributes, and to apply the concept to various situations* (Klausmeier et al., 1974).

OTHER COGNITIVE PROCESSES

Considerable recent research has examined problem solving, primarily with reference to the cognitive processes or strategies employed. Most results appear to be task specific, for example, solving geometry problems, (Greeno, 1978), playing poker (Langley & Simon, 1981), solving spatial-aptitude problems (Cooper, 1980), learning maps (Stasz & Thorndyke, 1980), inductive reasoning (Pellegrino & Glaser, 1980). However, it is generally found that good problem solvers engage in certain kinds of activities, for instance, systematic study of the situation, planning moves, trying alternatives, monitoring the effects, evaluating.

Thus it seems apparent that certain task-specific strategies have been analyzed and can now be taught (Greeno & Simon, in press). Also, general problem solving strategies, if such there be, need further study.

SUMMARY

One way of summarizing this chapter would be through a four-part model of the learner. As here conceived, the learner actively seeks *stimulation* (information) in the environment, is particularly attentive to *order* (regularities) there, requires some *strategy* for dealing with that stimulation and order, and as a general consequence of this ongoing process derives *meaning* from the environment (Fleming, 1980). In general, *any instructional situation should provide for these four learner needs.*

These learner needs can serve as an organizing aid to memory for many of the foregoing principles by forming them into four clusters. Under *stimulation* could be grouped these attention principles: selectivity, and novelty; plus these learning principles: concreteness, prior knowledge, and salient criterial attributes; as well as these concept formation principles: varied examples, and close-in nonexamples. Under *order* could be grouped these perception principles: organization, similarity, and proximity–contiguity; plus these learning principles: limited capacity, similarity, and primacy–recency; as well as this concept-formation principle: simultaneous display of examples. Under *strategy* could be grouped the perception principle: expectancy; and the learning principles: activity, strategy, mental imagery, and elaboration. Under *meaning* could be grouped the attention principle, uncertainty; and the learning principles, meaningfulness and feedback.

REFERENCES

Ali, A. M. (1981). The use of positive and negative examples during instruction. *Journal of Instructional Development, 5*(1), 2–7.

Anderson, R. C. and Biddle, W. B (1975). On asking people questions about what they are reading. In G. H. Bower (Ed.), *The psychology of learning and motivation* (Vol. 9) New York: Academic Press.

Anderson, R. C., and Faust, G. W.(1973). *Educational psychology, The science of instruction and learning.* New York: Dodd, Mead.

Anderson, R. C., Kulhavy, R. W., & Andre, T. (1971). Feedback procedures in programmed instruction. *Journal of Educational Psychology, 62,* 148–156.

Ausubel, D. P. (1968). *Educational psychology: A cognitive view.* New York: Holt, Rinehart, and Winston.

Berelsen, B., and Steiner, G. A. (1964). *Human behavior: An inventory of scientific findings.* New York: Harcourt, Brace & World.

Berliner, D. C. and Gage, N. L. (1976). The psychology of teaching methods. In N. L. Gage (Ed.), *The psychology of teaching methods.* NSSE Yearbook (Vol. 75, Pt. 1). Chicago: University of Chicago Press.

Berlyne, D. E. (1970). Attention as a problem in behavior theory. In D. I. Mostofsky (Ed.), *Attention: Contemporary theory and analysis.* New York: Appleton-Century-Crofts.

Bloom, B. S. (1984). The 2 Sigma problem: The search for methods of group instruction as effective as one-to-one tutoring. *Educational Researcher, 13*(6), 4–16.

Bovy, R. C. (1981). Successful instructional methods: A cognitive information processing approach. *Educational Communication and Technology Journal, 29,* 203–217.

Bower, G. H. (1973). How to . . . ah . . . remember. *Psychology Today, 7*(5), 62–70.

Bower, G. H. (1972). Mental imagery and associative memory. In L.W. Gregg (Ed.), *Cognition in learning & memory.* New York: Wiley.

Brien, R. (1983). Sequencing instruction. A cognitive science perspective. *Programmed Learning and Educational Technology, 20*(2), 102–114.

Brophy, J. (1980). *Recent Research on Teaching.* Paper presented at annual meeting of Northeast Educational Research Association (ERIC No. ED 204280)

Bugelski, B. R. (1971). *The psychology of learning applied to teaching.* Indianapolis: Bobbs-Merrill.

Clark, D. C. (1971). Teaching concepts in the classroom: A set of teaching prescriptions derived from experimental research. *Journal of Educational Psychology, 62.* 253–264.

Cook, L. K., & Mayer, R. E. (1983). Reading strategies training for meaningful learning from prose. In M. Pressley & J R. Levin (Ed.). *Cognitive strategy research, educational applications.* New York: Springer-Verlag.

Cooper, L. (1980). Spatial information processing: Strategies for research. In R. E. Snow, P.A. Federico, & W. E. Montague (Eds.), *Aptitude, learning, and instruction* (Vol. 1). Hillsdale, NJ: Lawrence Erlbaum Associates.

Craik, F. I. M. (1979). Human memory. *Annual Review of Psychology, 30,* 63–102.

DeCecco, J. P., & Crawford, W. R. (1974). *Psychology of learning and instruction: Educational psychology.* Englewood Cliffs, NJ: Prentice-Hall.

DeSoto, C. B., London, M., & Handel, S. (1968). Reasoning and spatial representations. *Journal of Verbal Learning & Verbal Behavior, 7,* 351–357.

Dwyer, F. M. (1972). *A Guide for improving visualized instruction.* State College, PA.: Learning Services.

Ellson, D. G., Barber, L., Engle, T. L., & Kampwerth, L. (1965). Programmed tutoring: A teaching aid and a research tool. *Reading Research Quarterly, 1,* 77–127.

Engelmann, S. (1969). *Conceptual learning.* San Rafael, CA: Dimensions.

Estes, W. K. (1972). Reinforcement in human behavior, *American Scientist, 1972, 60,* 723–729.

Eysenck, M. W. (1984). *A handbook of cognitive psychology.* Hillsdale, NJ: Lawrence Erlbaum Associates.

Fleming, M. (1980). From seeing and hearing to remembering: A conception of the instructional process. *Instructional Science, 9,* 311–326.

Fleming, M., & Levie, W. H. (1978). *Instructional message design: Principles from the behavioral sciences.* Englewood Cliffs, NJ: Educational Technology.

Forgus, R. H. (1966). *Perception: The basic process in cognitive development.* New York: McGraw-Hill.

Gagné, E. D. (1978). Long-term retention of information following learning from prose. *Review of Educational Research, 48,* 629–665.

Gagné, R. M., & Dick, W. (1983). Instructional psychology, *Annual Review of Psychology, 34,* 261–295.

Gagné, R. M., & Rohwer, W. D. (1969). Instructional psychology. *Annual Review of Psychology, 20,* 381–418.

Gibson, E. J. (1969). *Principles of perceptual learning and development.* New York: Meredith.

Graham, C. H. (1965). *Vision and visual perception.* New York: Wiley.

Greeno, J. G. (1978). A study of problem solving. In R. Glaser (Ed.), *Advances in instructional psychology,* (Vol. 1). Hillsdale, NJ: Lawrence Erlbaum Associates.

Greeno, J. G., & Simon, H. A. (in press). Problem solving and reasoning. In R. C. Atkinson, R. Herrnstein, G. Lindzey, & R. D. Luce (Eds.), *Stevens' handbook of experimental psychology.* (Revised ed.). New York: Wiley.

Haber, R. N. & Hershenson, M. (1973). *The psychology of visual perception.* New York: Holt, Rinehart and Winston.

Hall, K. A. (1983). Content structuring and question asking for computer-based education. *Journal of Computer-Based Instruction, 10*(1–2), 1–7.

Helson, H. (1974). Current trends and issues in adaptation- level theory. In P. A. Fried (Ed.), *Readings in perception: Principle and practice.* Lexington, Mass.: Heath.

Higbee, K. L. (1979). Recent research on visual mnemonics: Historical roots and educational fruits. *Review of Educational Research, 49,* 611–629.

Horton, D. L., & Mills, C. B. (1984). Human learning and memory. *Annual Review of Psychology, 35,* 361–394.

Klausmeier, H. J., Ghatala, E. S., & Frayer, D. A. (1974). *Conceptual learning and development: A cognitive view.* New York: Academic Press.

Kulhavy, R. W. (1977). Feedback in written instruction. *Review of Educational Research, 47,* 211–232.

Kumar, V. K. (1971). The structure of human memory and some educational implications. *Review of Educational Research, 41,* 379–417.

Lamberski, R. J. (1980). *A comprehensive and critical review of the methodology and findings in color investigations.* Paper presented at the annual convention of the Association for Educational Communications and Technology, Denver, CO.

Langley, P., & Simon, H. A. (1981). The central role of learning in cognition. In J. R. Anderson (Ed.), *Cognitive skills and their acquisition.* Hillsdale, NJ: Lawrence Erlbaum Associates.

Levie, W. H., & Lentz, R. (1982). Effects of text illustrations: A review of research. *Educational Communication and Technology Journal, 30,* 195–232.

Levin, J. R. (1979). *On functions of pictures in prose.* Wisconsin University, Madison: Research and Development Center for Individualized Schooling. (ERIC No. ED 186847)

Levin, T., & Long, R. (1981). *Effective instruction.* Alexandria, VA: Association for Supervision and Curriculum Development. (ERIC No. 200572)

Mandler, J. M., & Johnson, N. S. (1976). Some of the thousand words a picture is worth. *Journal of Experimental Psychology: Human Learning & Memory. 2,* 529–540.

Margolius, G. J., & Sheffield, F. D. (1961). Optimum methods of combining practice with filmed demonstrations in teaching complex response sequences: Serial learning of a mechanical assembly task. In A. A. Lumsdaine (Ed.), *Student response in programmed instruction.* Washington, DC: National Academy of Sciences, National Research Council.

Markle, S. M. (1975). They teach concepts, don't they? *Educational Researcher, 4*(6), 3–9.

Mayer, R. E. (1979). Twenty years of research on advance organizers: Assimilation theory is still the best predictor of results. *Instructional Science, 8,* 133–167.

Medin, D. L., & Smith, E. E. (1984). Concepts and concept formation. *Annual Review of Psychology, 35,* 113–138.

Miller, G. A. (1968). The magical number seven, plus or minus two: Some limits on our capacity for processing information. In R. N. Haber (Ed.), *Contemporary theory and research in visual perception.* New York: Holt, Rinehart and Winston.

Mills, M. I. (1980). A study of human response to pictorial representations on *Telidon. Telidon Behavioral Research 3.* Quebec: Montreal University.

Moray, N. (1967). Where is capacity limited? A survey and a model. In A. F. Sanders (Ed.), *Attention and performance.* Amsterdam: North-Holland.

Mouly, G. J. (1973). *Psychology for effective teaching.* New York: Holt, Rinehart, and Winston.

Murch, G. M. (1973). *Visual and auditory perception.* Indianapolis: Bobbs-Merrill.

Neves, D. M., & Anderson, J. R. (1981). Knowledge compilation: Mechanisms for the automatization of cognitive skills. In J. R. Anderson (Ed.), *Cognitive skills and their acquisition.* Hillsdale, NJ: Lawrence Erlbaum Associates.

Paivio, A., (1971). *Imagery and verbal processes.* New York: Holt, Rinehart and Winston.

Paivio, A. (1983). Strategies in language learning. In M. Pressley & J. R. Levin (Eds.). *Cognitive strategy research: educational applications.* New York: Springer-Verlag.

Pellegrino, J., & Glaser, R. (1980). Components of inductive reasoning. In R. E. Snow, P. A. Federico, & W. A. Montague (Eds.), *Aptitude, learning, and instruction* (Vol. 1). Hillsdale, NJ: Lawrence Erlbaum Associates.

Reigeluth, C. M. (1983). Meaningfulness and instruction: Relating what is being learned to what a student knows. *Instructional Science, 12,* 197–218.

Resnick, L. B. (1981). Instructional psychology. *Annual Review of Psychology, 32,* 659–704.

Rigney, J. W. (1978). Learning strategies: A theoretical perspective. In H. F. O'Neil (Ed.), *Learning strategies.* New York: Academic Press.

Salomon, G. (1979). Media and symbol systems as related to cognition and learning. *Journal of Educational Psychology, 71,* 131–148.

Salomon, G. (1984). Television is "easy" and print is "tough": The differential investment of mental effort in learning as a function of perceptions and attributions. *Journal of Educational Psychology. 76,* 647–658.

Stasz, C., & Thorndyke, P. (1980). *The influence of visual-spatial ability and study procedures on map learning skill.* (N–1501–ONR). Santa Monica, CA: Rand.

Tennyson, R. D. (1980). The teaching of concepts: A review of instructional design research literature. *Review of Educational Research, 50,* 55–70.

Treisman, A. M. (1974). Selective attention in man. In P. A. Fried (Ed.), *Readings in perception: Principle and practice.* Lexington, MA: Heath.

Tulving, E., & Thomson, D. M. (1973). Encoding specificity and retrieval processes in episodic memory. *Psychological Review, 80,* 352–373.

Van Bergeijk, W. A., Pierce, J. R., & David, E.E. (1960). *Waves and the ear.* Garden City, NY: Anchor Books.

Wickelgren, W. A. (1981). Human learning and memory. *Annual Review of Psychology. 32,* 21–52.

Winn, W. (1982). *Status and trends in visual information processing.* Paper presented at the annual meeting of the Association for Educational Communication and Technology, Dallas, TX.

Winn, W. (1981). The meaningful organization of content: Research and design strategies. *Educational Technology, 21*(8), 7–11.

AUTHOR NOTES

Malcolm L. Fleming is Professor Emeritus, Indiana University Audio-Visual Center and Department of Instructional Systems Technology, School of Education, Indiana University.

Special thanks are expressed to Dr. W. Howard Levie for a thorough critique of the manuscript and numerous thoughtful suggestions for improving it. Appreciated as well are the illustrations by Suzanne Hull, Michael Neff, and Irene Lee, Indiana University Audio Visual Center.

10 Innovations in Telecommunications

Gwen C. Nugent
Nebraska Educational Television

The extension of instructional delivery beyond the confines of the traditional public school and college classroom has led to changing learning environments. Today, instruction is delivered to individuals and groups located in homes, learning centers, military bases, and places of work, as well as in typical classrooms. This diversity of learning environments, with their varying instructional delivery requirements, gives rise to a number of different systems of transmission and media of communication, each with unique characteristics and capabilities. There are transmission systems capable of reaching geographically dispersed audiences and systems more suited for dissemination to groups in close proximity. Delivery systems can also present programming targeted for individual use and for use in small to large groups. New developments have led the way for two-way instruction, promoting dialogue between an instructor and remote learner, and interactivity, which allows individualization by branching students to appropriate instructional points, depending on their sequence of responses.

Current hardware systems can be configured in various ways to meet learning requirements. Telecommunications systems, representing the growing union of television, computer, satellite, and telephone systems, are providing unique instructional possibilities. Broadcast television, for example, is well suited to reaching large numbers of students cheaply. On the other hand, it lacks flexibility and the ability to respond to student feedback. Instructional Television Fixed Service (ITFS) provides a signal capable of covering only a small area, but use of multiple channels permits simultaneous distribution of programming to serve different audiences. Satellite transmission can deliver instruction to large geographical areas and can reach the remotest of locations. Satellite also has the capability for video-conferencing, allowing remote sites to communicate via one- or two-way video and/or audio.

This chapter will focus on developments in telecommunications hardware and its influence on the nature of instructional delivery. The oldest telecommunication system, broadcast television, is discussed first, followed by a description of systems used primarily to deliver linear programming—cable, ITFS, videotape recorders, satellite, and teletext. The chapter concludes with an in-depth look at the newer technologies of videodisc and videotex, which maximize the opportunity for delivery of individualized, interactive instruction.

EDUCATIONAL TELEVISION: BROADCAST

When television first appeared and commercial stations were scrambling to get started, educators were also busy establishing stations for delivery of educational materials. The first ETV station, KUHT-TV, Houston, went on the air in 1953. Instructional television was an integral part of these early operations, prompted in part by a serious teacher shortage and the belief that television could help overcome unequal distribution of educational resources. The theory was that television could multiply students' exposure to master teachers. The development of monolithic, statewide, educational television networks provided an efficient means of beaming instruction into the classrooms. In attempting to obtain legislative funding, administrators could cite low expense; quality instruction could be delivered at a per-child cost equivalent to the cost of a pencil.

As instructional television programming became available, schools scrambled to take advantage of the new marvel. Their efforts were expedited by the availablility of National Defense Education Act funds, which could be used to purchase television-receiving equipment. This funding source, available from the mid-1950s to 1970s, played a major role in equipping schools with television receivers.

The early years were not without problems, however. For one, many stations operated on UHF frequencies, and television sets of that time often could not pick up a UHF signal. If the signal could be received, teachers many times had difficulty tuning the channel, and the reception was often poor.

Another problem related to the inherent nature of broadcast television. Teachers were restricted in their use of televised instruction by the predetermined broadcast schedule. This schedule meant that a teacher had to find when a program was broadcast and arrange the daily routine so that students could view the program at that time. Sometimes the teaching plan had to be adjusted to correlate with the time of year and the order of topics in which the programs were broadcast. This locked-in schedule was a drawback at all levels, but caused particular problems at the high school, where bell schedules seldom coincided with broadcast times.

The late 1960s and early 1970s saw a change in philosophy of instructional television. The teacher crunch was lessening, and stations responded accordingly by reducing the number of long-term, core-curricula offerings and focusing on shorter, supplemental units. To provide greater flexibility in viewing times, more repeats of programs were offered. There were also attempts to use the television medium more creatively, using new production formats. The "talking face," or television teacher on camera, was replaced by dramatization, documentary, or magazine formats.

As the television formats became more complex, production costs rose. It became increasingly difficult for individual stations to justify the expense of local production. One solution was leasing programming from national tape libraries. A pioneering agency in this area was the Great Plains National Television Library, which has placed more than 18,000 separate lesson units in classrooms of levels elementary through college.

Another solution to the high production costs was the development of consortia; individual agencies pooled their resources to fund high quality programming. The consortium effort was pioneered by the Agency for Instructional Television, now the Agency for Instructional Technology, a national clearinghouse located in Bloomington, IN. This organization has coordinated more than 20 consortium television projects to date, used in more than 50 states and provinces.

VIDEOTAPE RECORDERS

The 1960s and 1970s saw an increase in the number of videotape recorders, which gave teachers greater control over classroom television. Today approximately three-fourths of all elementary and secondary schools (Corporation for Public Broadcasting (CPB), 1984) and 90% of colleges (Statistical Research Inc., 1983) have at least one video-recorder, allowing greater flexibility in playback times and the building of local tape libraries.

Colleges are also using video-recorders to provide new ways of reaching students. Stanford University has a program called Tutored Videotape Instruction, which was developed for a company that could not be reached by a broadcast signal. This method utilizes prerecorded videotapes of classroom instruction shown to small groups of students (three to ten). A paraprofessional, skilled in leading discussion, watches the tape with the students and encourages them to stop the playback and ask questions. Students discuss the questions as a group and generally resolve the question themselves. If the tutor or group discussion cannot answer the question, it is referred to the instructor and discussed at the next session. This system combines the positive features of lectures with those of small group discussion. Students are able to remain at their workplace, yet still take advantage of the personal interaction available in on-campus instruction. Studies of this technique at Stanford have isolated several advantages, including the fact that the system is cheaper than either classroom or televised instruction (Gibbons, Kinchelor, & Down, 1977).

INSTRUCTIONAL TELEVISION FIXED SERVICE

Although open-circuit broadcast is the most common means of delivering educational programming, ITFS systems are also prevalent. ITFS is an over-the-air broadcast system that operates on a frequency above that of normal television. Special equipment is required to receive the signal and change the frequency to a normal television signal for viewing on a regular television set. Because ITFS is a low-powered, limited range system, it is less costly than its VHF or UHF system counterparts. Since signals only travel a short distance (approximately 20 miles), ITFS systems are usually found in small areas that are highly populated.

ITFS is intended primarily to provide a means for the transmission of instructional and cultural television materials. It has several advantages:

1. It offers mass distribution with relatively inexpensive operating costs.

2. It provides a degree of confidentiality, since specialized receiving equipment is required to access the signal.

3. Channels are generally awarded by the Federal Communications Commission in groups of four, permitting simultaneous distribution of multiple strands of programming to serve different audiences.

4. It allows on-site, workplace delivery of training that is both efficient and cost-effective.

5. Its capability for two-way communication, including audio feedback and computer interactivity, promotes student-faculty interaction.

ITFS systems have been used by several colleges and universities to distribute continuing education and college-credit programming. The Illinois Institute of Technology, using a transmitter on top of Chicago's Sears Tower, provides specifically designed courses in technical education aimed at employees from area corporations. Companies that subscribe to the service and receive courses at their on-site classrooms include Bell Labs, Western Electric, Honeywell, and Motorola. Students pay regular tuition rates and receive their programming on seven ITFS channels.

This college's system connects participating companies with one-way video, two-way audio transmissions. The course originates in studio class-rooms. The audio feedback allows direct communication between the instructor and remote locations. If a student viewing a class has a question, he or she asks it through a talkback telephone system, and it is heard by both on-campus and off-campus class members. Another interesting feature is the daily courier service, which routes handouts, exams, and homework between student and teacher. This service also serves as a link to the bookstore, registrar's office, and other campus services.

The system has been quite successful. In a study conducted in the fall of 1983, 80% of the television students indicated they would *not* be taking courses if the system were not available (IIT/TV Survey, 1983). The college is capitalizing on telecommunications technology to reach more students and provide a continuing service to the business community.

ITFS can also provide flexibility for delivery of secondary school pro-gramming. South Carolina has undertaken an ambitious ITFS system to pro-vide programming to elementary and secondary schools, as well as to higher education institutions. The system replaces the statewide closed-circuit sys-tem relying on the microwave and cable network leased from Southern Bell. In 1981, the leasing expense of this network had reached $3.8 million, with projections of higher costs. These increasing costs, plus the possibility of expanding coverage, led South Carolina to begin planning a network of ITFS systems. Planners estimate that installing and operating their own ITFS sys-tem could result in savings up to $245 million over the next 20 years. The currently planned system will use 14 local-area ITFS transmitters and 11 wide-area transmitters with six repeaters (Hopkins, 1983). It is an ambitious undertaking, but one which will allow greater flexibility in scheduling and provide a full range of continuing education programming.

There are numerous examples of educational uses of ITFS, but the system's basic philosophy is currently undergoing examination. ITFS is changing from an alternative transmission system reaching hundreds of stu-dents to a medium than can reach viewers in their homes. This change is occurring because in May 1983, the FCC reallocated certain ITFS channels to outright commercial use and ruled that "excess capacity" on the other channels could be leased by educators to commercial users.

In the past, targeting ITFS to home users was impractical because the spe-cial antennas and converters were too expensive. The availablity of new, addressable downconverters (boxes that convert ITFS channels to vacant channels on home television sets) has made home use of ITFS a reality. ITFS is suddenly becoming a high-tech "wireless cable" medium of great interest to commercial operators. It provides an alternative way to deliver entertainment, data, and information services. It is also a relatively inexpen-sive means of reaching densely populated areas where installation of cable lines is becoming increasingly expensive.

CABLE

Cable television was originally established to improve reception, but the advent of satellite technology offered new opportunities and directions. Home Box Office initiated this change in 1975 when it began distributing its programming to cable operators via satellite. Before that time, such distribution would only have been possible through terrestrial microwave, which is prohibitively expensive. The improvements in technology also led to multichannel offerings, with up to 107 channels available on newer systems. Cable has evolved from a way to improve reception in isolated areas to a technology providing many channels and even two-way capability.

In 1984 approximately 39% of homes in the United States were wired for cable (Home Video Market Indication, 1984). Earlier industry projections were for 60% cable penetration by 1990, but the growth of cable is slowing. With fewer new subscribers, the general belief now is that 50% penetration is more realistic (Beville, 1984b). The slowdown is attributed to the large number of disconnects prompted by a lagging economy and the fact that building new cable systems, particularly in urban areas, is becoming increasingly expensive. Operators are eyeing other technologies, such as ITFS, direct broadcast satellite, and fiber optics.

It is clear that cable technology is readily available and reaches or will reach a large number of homes. In the educational arena, Corporation for Public Broadcasting surveys have shown that 39% of public schools (Corporation for Public Broadcasting, 1984) and 28% of colleges and universities (Dirr, Katz, & Pedone, 1981) use programs distributed by cable. Cable's availability to and use by educational institutions clearly varies, however. Early cable franchises were sometimes lax in providing cable access to educational institutions. In cases where free cable drops to schools were stipulated, contracts often did not spell out specific completion dates. The result was that installation was delayed or never occurred.

In 1972 the FCC paved the way for education's involvement with cable by ruling that cable systems in major markets had to offer channels for public access and use by government and education. Unfortunately, the courts later struck down these rules, and the FCC no longer makes such requirements. Any channel allotment for education must now be spelled out in the city franchise agreeement, with resulting disparity as to how educational services are handled.

There are, however, excellent examples of educational uses of cable. The Pennsylvania Learning Network, Pennarama, is a prime illustration. Pennarama is a 24-hour-a-day educational service for cable subscribers. The emphasis is on college-credit courses, supplemented by teleconferences for specific audiences in business, industry, and health professions.

Pennarama represents a unique marriage of the cable industry and higher education. The cable industry in Pennsylvania formed a nonprofit organization to develop a statewide microwave-relay system interconnecting individual cable systems. In September 1983, the networking was capable of serving an estimated 1.5 million cable households. The program schedule is repeated several times a day throughout the week. Pennarama delivers up to 16 full courses, along with live seminars and teleconferences.

SATELLITE

"Live via satellite" is a familiar phrase to today's television viewers, just as the white, dish-shaped earth stations are familiar sights at television stations, hotels, and remote rural locations. Satellite technology has revolutionized television delivery, for it provides transmission of television signals from virtually any part of the world and eliminates the need and expense of terrestrial microwave systems.

The satellite age began in 1957 with the Russians' launching of Sputnik. The United States quickly became involved in satellite technology and added some of its own advances allowing for high–capacity transmission of video, audio, and data communication. The domestic satellite industry began in 1974 when Western Union launched Westar. RCA quickly followed suit with Satcom.

Satellites are orbiting approximately 22,000 miles above earth at speeds coinciding with the rotation of the earth. The result is that they are a fixed target. Each satellite has a number of transponders which receive the television signal and beam it back to earth. The signal is received by dish-shaped earth stations and can then be transmitted via microwave, phone lines, or cable to its destination. The more powerful the transponder, the smaller and less expensive the earth stations need to be, leading to a recent development—direct broadcast satellites. These satellites, approved by the FCC in June 1982, transmit programming directly to a home or school, where umbrella-sized dishes pick up the signal. In 1984, this dish cost $1,000 to $4,000, but projections are that it will come down in price. Although direct-broadcast satellites offer attractive commercial possibilities, the stakes are high. The cost of launching a successful direct-broadcast satellite service has been tagged at $500 million (Beville, 1984a).

Satellite technology has been a major influence in educational telecommunications. Since 1978 the Public Broadcasting Service (PBS) has been distributing programming to its affiliates via satellite. PBS now has a network of approximately 180 earth stations and has eliminated the need for phone lines. Programs are transmitted to more than 300 public televison stations in every state, Puerto Rico, and the Virgin Islands.

Satellite transmission has also facilitated distribution and previewing of instructional programming. Before satellite transmission was possible, the major instructional television distributors had to duplicate videotapes for each program and send them physically to individual stations. Today it is more common to deliver programs by satellite "hard" or "soft" feeds. In both types of feeds the program is "uplinked" to the satellite from a ground station and then "downlinked" to individual user stations. A hard feed retransmits the program to classrooms as it is received from the satellite. A soft feed takes part in recording the program for later transmission.

Direct-broadcast satellites open the door for delivering programming directly to the user. If outfitted with an appropriate user station, a school could receive programming directly from the satellite. Another potential advantage is that computer data can also be delivered via satellites.

TELECONFERENCING

In addition to paving new directions in cable, satellite technology has been the impetus to teleconferencing. Actually the basic technology necessary for teleconferencing has existed for some time, but rising transportation costs and the desire for increased productivity have recently stimulated its growth.

In its most generic sense, teleconferencing is electronic communication between individuals or groups located at different sites. There are various types of teleconferencing systems, which may be used singly or in combination. Audio-conferencing permits several locations to talk with each other using amplified telephone speakers. Freeze-frame or slow-scan teleconferencing transmits still images over phone lines, microwave, or satellite. These images can be photographs or hard copy. Full motion or videoconferencing allows remote sites to interact via one-way or two-way video or audio. This system provides pictorial quality similar to broadcast television. It is, in short, "the next best thing to being there."

Teleconferences move meetings to people, thus reducing the need for travel. In education, they can increase communication between schools and involve more people in the information-sharing and decision-making process. They can provide immediate interaction and minimize misunderstandings because participants can ask questions. Also, presentations can be videotaped, providing a permanent record.

Educational applications of teleconferencing are common. One of the earliest efforts was the Public Service Satellite Consortium (PSSC), established by colleges, hospitals, and other nonprofit institutions to provide information and produce teleconferences for its members. The consortium was so successful that nonprofit agencies began soliciting their help in teleconferencing. As a consequence, in 1981 PSSC formed a for-profit subsidiary, Services by Satellite (Satserv), which handles around 30 video-conferences each year. One of Satserv's principal projects is the development of the Campus College Network, debuting in the fall of 1984, which represents a network of earth stations and viewing sites located on nearly 40 campuses. The network provides teleconferencing and program–distribution services.

Another higher-education example is the National University Teleconference Network, which was created to provide a means of information sharing and exchange. Beginning in 1981, approximately 40 higher-education institutions each provided $1,000 in membership fees to initiate the teleconference services. Today there are more than 100 members representing several categories of higher education (Oberle & Quinn, 1984).

FIBER OPTICS

Broadcast, cable, and satellite are established transmission systems, but a new, high-tech delivery system uses fiber optics. Fiber optics is a transmission technology using an attenuated glass fiber hardly thicker than a human hair, which conducts light from a laser source. A single glass fiber can carry the equivalent of 100 channels of television or 100,000 telephone calls, and even more capacity is possible by encasing many fibers within a cable. Developed by Bell Labs and Corning Glass in the late 1960s, the technology is still relatively new. It does, however, offer several advantages. First, it can carry a tremendous amount of data at high transmission speeds. Second, fiber optics does not experience signal degradation over distance as does coaxial cable. Third, it is a multipurpose system. A bundle of these fibers can bring television, telephone, and radio into the school through a single cable.

While still a new technology, fiber optics has already been successfully demonstrated in some high-visibility applications. AT&T is using a fiber-optics system which can send voice, data, and digital video to large population centers. This system is currently used for phone conversations, but fiber optics has been used to transmit television. A fiber-optics system carries a television signal from the Notre Dame stadium to nearby studios and satellite uplink for telecast of football games (Summerville & Krakora, 1984).

TELETEXT

Teletext is a system which allows for the transmission of information via the vertical blanking interval of a televison signal, the unused lines viewed as the black roll-bar. These lines are currently being used to send closed captions and test data. Digital data are fed into a decoder attached to the television set and stored in a buffer memory. When a user keys in the number of a particular page, the page is transferred to the screen and remains until a new page is requested.

The advantage of teletext is that it gets essentially a "free ride" on the broadcast signal. The disadvantage is the small number of frames or pages that can be stored (generally 100–200 pages). Also, the system is one-way; it does not provide full two-way interactivity. Another problem is that decoders are expensive ($1,000). Predictions are that the service will not become widespread until decoders are built into TV sets, lowering their price.

Teletext demonstration projects have experimented with delivery of a variety of educational materials. KCET (Los Angeles) used teletext to supplement in-school television programs, to provide quizzes complementing the regular school curriculum, and to deliver information facilitating instructional-television use. WGBH (Boston) tested an educational news service for secondary schools, and placed decoders at local museums, public schools, and department stores.

These experiments showed that the teachers believed the materials were highly motivational and offered valuable enrichment to the regular curriculum. Interestingly, results showed a preference for use in small groups, as opposed to class or individual settings. Small groups were able to promote a level of discussion and student interaction not possible in the other two settings (Goldman, 1982; Goldman et al., 1982).

VIDIPLEX

Vidiplex is a digital-electronics system that allows for the transmission of two video signals on a single cable, microwave channel, or satellite transponder. The system essentially doubles the capacity of television transmission and allows for simultaneous feed of independent programs for two audiences. The system requires an encoder at the originating end, which encodes the two video sources on a single channel. Only one field of each signal is recorded so that when the encoded vidiplex signal is viewed on a monitor, it appears like a double exposure, with both pictures visible, but overlapping. At the receiving end, a decoder separates the two signals and electronically "fills in" the missing lines of video. Quality of the reconstituted video signals is excellent, and any difference from a normal video signal would probably go unnoticed by most observers.

A vidiplex system is currently being used in Nebraska to transmit continuing educational programming from the university in Lincoln to western Nebraska. The programming is "piggybacked" on the regular ETV network signal. Since vidiplex does not provide for program audio transmission, audio communication is through standard phone lines. This system, installed for around $235,000, provides a way for students removed from the university to receive university coursework. Its use maximizes utilization of leased interconnection lines.

AUDIO AND VIDEO IMPROVEMENTS

In addition to the developments in broadcast, cable, satellite, and fiber optics distribution, there is also ongoing research to improve video and audio components. For example, considerable work is being done in Japan in the area of high-definition television. In 1981 a group of Japanese companies introduced a high-definition television system that utilizes a 1125-line television screen, as opposed to the current United States National Television Systems Committee (NTSC) standard 525 lines. The picture contains about five times more video information than that of a conventional television set. The result is extraordinary resolution, with rich, saturated colors. The advantages such a system might have for education, particularly in the medical and scientific areas, come immediately to mind. It improves the clarity of text and provides greater detail. Any instructional area that requires sharp, detailed video could benefit from this new technology.

With its inherent advantages, one might question why high-definition TV has not been introduced in the United States. The answer is that despite its attractions, there are certain drawbacks. For one, it requires extraordinary bandwidth. A high-definition television channel must have five times the capacity of a conventional television channel. Another drawback is that the television receivers are estimated to be 30% more expensive than today's most costly sets. Although engineers marvel at the picture quality, there is some question that the general public will view the improvements as worth the increased costs.

Until the television–broadcast system can handle high-definition television's spectrum space requirements or until bandwidth-compression techniques are developed to shrink the space requirements, this technology may find its niche as an alternative to theatrical films. High-definition television combines the visual clarity of film with the lower costs and flexibility of video. It is no wonder that film makers are already experimenting with prototype systems. The system could revolutionize distribution strategies, since movies could be distributed to theaters via satellite.

Another way to improve the video image is to enhance the current NTSC color television signal, and work in this area is proceeding through the use of digital technology. There are digital television sets, priced at more than $1,000, in which an incoming analog signal is converted to digital information, processed, and then converted back to analog for display. This processing procedure improves ghosting and interference problems and provides greater signal stability. Unfortunately, digital processing will not be a panacea for reception problems, although it will improve the picture.

Sets equipped with digital frame store will permit viewers to zoom in on a portion of the picture, freeze a single frame, and watch two or more channels at once through a split-screen function. These features provide obvious instructional advantages. Teachers could use the zoom and freeze-frame functions to emphasize important concepts. The split screen functions could also be used for comparison and contrast strategies.

Spurred by the high quality audio available with videodisc and videocassette, developments are also under way to improve the audio component of broadcast television. The FCC, in March 1984, approved a multichannel-television sound system. Multichannel sound allows stereo, as well as foreign-language translation. Stereo will require additional equipment by the broadcasting entity, as well as adapters or new sets by viewers. Predictions are, however, that this equipment process should be well developed by 1990 (Beville, 1984a).

VIDEODISC

Description and Hardware

Much has been written lauding the features and educational advantages of the laser-optical videodisc, which resembles a grooveless record and is played on a compact player using a low-power laser. Images are displayed through a standard televison set. Each side of the videodisc contains 54,000 individual frames, which can be viewed continuously as motion or individually as single pictures or pages of information. Each frame can be searched out and viewed by the user through the player's remote control. The viewer can also stop the disc at any time, play the information in slow motion forward or reverse, or "step" through the material one still frame at a time.

The many functions of the disc provide tremendous flexibility in presentation of instructional materials. It can present all other media—films, filmstrips, books—and provide multimedia learning experiences in which each medium is used to its best advantage. With such a variety of presentation methods, the videodisc can promote the matching of instructional techniques to individual learning needs of students.

One criticism of technology in the classroom is that it removes instruction from the teacher. The videodisc circumvents this problem because it allows virtual teacher control of all phases of the presentation. Teachers can easily stop the instruction at any point to explain a potentially confusing concept. When they feel that students understand the material, they can continue the presentation by simply pushing a button. Segments can also be accessed and played in any order and as many times as desired. Because the player uses a laser to read encoded information, and nothing comes in contact with the disc itself, stopping and repeating will not harm the disc.

The system also provides for two audio tracks, which can be recorded at two different levels of complexity or in different languages. With the addition of digital compressed audio systems, audio messages can also accompany still frames. With the Sony system, for example, still-frame audio is made possible by converting the analog signal to digital data and encoding the data in frames adjacent to the desired still frames. When the disc is played, the data are read out through an external digital to analog converter. This technique provides for 15.5 audio hours, accompanying 1600 visual frames. There is, however, one stipulation: the maximum audio message is 40 seconds. Thirty-nine video frames are needed to accommodate one still frame and 40 seconds of accompanying audio. In contrast, if real-time audio were used, 1200 frames would be required.

The videodisc can also be used in conjunction with a computer. The digital codes that control disc-frame access and display make a marriage of videodisc and computer a natural, yet revolutionary, development. This combination creates an instructional format in which the motivational, elaborative qualities of visual media are combined with the more pedantic, programmatic characteristics of the computer. The videodisc provides still or motion pictures, and the computer processes responses and initiates appropriate branching.

When the videodisc and a computer are used together, computer images may be superimposed directly over the video image or may be displayed on a separate monitor. Computer information can be used to highlight, reinforce, and update information stored on the videodisc. Also, as the capacity for computer graphics improves, the resulting computer/video image will become even more sophisticated and better able to present complex concepts.

The use of the videodisc with the computer has led to the search for interfaces that facilitate human use. Touch screens are a fairly common input device and are used with the videodisc to simplify user input. The user touches the screen to indicate a response; it is not necessary to respond though a keypad or keyboard. If the videodisc player and computer are enclosed in a carrel or kiosk, users have no sense of the extensive hardware that is processing their responses. The videodisc and computer control are unseen. Although not suited for input of lengthy constructed responses, a touch screen works well with menus or multiple-choice decision points and allows simulation of hands-on training. For example, the videodisc can present a real-life picture of a piece of machinery. The student is then asked to touch particular parts of the machine in response to selected questions.

The videodisc has also been used with bar–code technology, such as seen at supermarket checkout counters. Courseware consists of bar-coded workbooks, a scanning wand, and a videodisc player. The workbook directs the instructional flow. A student reads the material and scans the bar code, which in turn accesses a videodisc segment. Bar codes can also be used at multiple-choice decision points. Users make choices by scanning the bar code next to their choice. This system simplifies the input process and significantly reduces input errors.

A frequently cited drawback to the videodisc is that it is a read-only medium. However, recordable videodisc systems permitting user recordings are available. Their price tags (approximately $30,000 in 1984) make them impractical for educational applications, but such systems have been purchased by a handful of industrial customers. Laboratory projects are also investigating ways to allow recorded information to be changed at will, but none has yet resulted in a commercially viable product.

The videodisc has always been cited as a high density information–storage device, and now the advent of optical memory systems is making this prediction a reality. Systems have been developed to store 20,000 pages of information, the equivalent of four file drawers, on a 12-inch or smaller disc. Entry and retrieval of digital data is possible, allowing users to store huge databases, graphics, documents, and images. The benefits of optical storage technology are high capacity and low cost per bit stored, no media wear, and the ability to mix digital data, still images, motion video, and audio on the same medium. There are drawbacks, however. Presently there are compatibility problems among various systems, high error rates, lack of erasability, and limited shelf life (estimated at 10 years). Although systems are expensive—($15,000 and up)—it is projected that the price range of such hardware will be comparable to that of floppy and hard-disk drives.

Videodisc Applications

The applications of disc technology are far-reaching. Sears placed one of its summer 1981 catalogs on disc, making extensive use of still frames and motion–demonstration sequences. *Dragon's Lair,* an adventure game, popularized the use of videodisc technology in arcades and received positive response to its use of television animation in place of more abstract, computer-generated graphics. Disc technology has been used with computer networking and spatial database-retrieval logic to create an ordering system permitting access to an illustrated catalog of thousands of product parts. There is also the well-known Aspen disc, a movie map or video travelogue, which allows the viewer to take a simulated drive through the streets of Aspen, Colo.

Training is perhaps the predominant use of videodisc technology, and one of the most innovative applications is the disc developed by the American Heart Association to teach cardiopulmonary resuscitation (CPR). The training system consists of a videodisc player, microcomputer, and dummy which the trainee uses to practice techniques. The dummy is equipped with sensors that determine if the person is performing the techniques correctly. If not, signals are sent to the microcomputer, which accesses appropriate videodisc remediation.

Training advantages of videodisc technology are many. For large-scale training applications, a videodisc presentation can provide message consistency not possible with stand-up sessions. Disc-based training also has cost advantages. One company estimated that training a salesperson in a lecture setting costs $475 per day, compared with $130 for disc training (Stokes, 1983). Another study comparing conventional stand-up training and disc-based training found that disc trainees completed the program in 25% less time, scored higher on a final examination, and unanimously preferred the interactive videodisc format (Smith, 1984).

Comparisons between videodisc/computer training systems and self-paced programs relying on media such as linear video and workbooks, also have found no difference in posttraining performance. Students using the disc system completed the work in significantly less time and called the courses more stimulating and motivating than a traditional lecture-laboratory system (May, 1984).

Other studies have compared training on actual equipment with videodisc simulations. Results show no difference in learning between the two groups, but significant cost savings (Young et al., 1981). If equipment is expensive and difficult to schedule for training purposes, a videodisc simulation offers a practical alternative.

There has been considerable videodisc use and research in training, but this technology has also found its way into education. One of the most extensive evaluation efforts was the college-level, science laboratory simulations developed by the University of Nebraska. Comparisons were made between traditional on-campus laboratory instruction and videodisc instruction. Results showed that the videodisc students performed as well as their laboratory counterparts. The videodisc instruction was completed more quickly; however, the result was partly attributable to reduced setup time and the fact that experiments could move more quickly. For example, students did not have to wait for temperature changes but could observe results immediately. The videodisc system also allowed students to examine a wider variety of conditions and more variables. With fewer distractions, videodisc students appeared more task oriented. They also had a lesser sense of failure, since they knew they could stop their experiment at any time or repeat steps if necessary (Davis, 1984).

Other evaluations have also supported the lower study times and equal or better performance for students using disc materials. In a study of college-level biology materials, students using the interactive videodisc had lower study times and higher posttest scores than those reading the text and hearing the lecture (Bunderson, Olsen, & Baillio, cited in DeBloois, Maki, & Hall, 1984).

Videodisc technology has also been used successfully in special education, where its "patience," high visual content, and reinforcement qualities provide definite advantages. Classroom evaluations have shown positive response by hearing-impaired students and their teachers, with teachers citing user control as a major advantage. Users can stop, slow down, and sequence materials, according to learner styles and special needs (Propp, Nugent, & Stone, 1980).

Videodisc technology has been used extensively in military, business, and industrial applications, and to a lesser degree in education. A report by Frost and Sullivan, Inc. showed that in 1982, $49.3 million was spent on laser discs for industrial, government, and military usage, but only $3.9 million for educational and database publishing (Interactive Disc Sales Hit 56 Million in 1982, 1983). Nevertheless, a 1983 report commissioned by Great Plains National, a national distributor of television instruction aids and videodiscs, showed that 15% of public schools and 22% of colleges owned videodisc playback equipment and even more were anticipating purchase of such equipment in the next four years. The study also found that one-fifth of those with players interfaced them with a computer (Science Research Center, 1983).

It is likely that the more limited use of videodiscs in education is not because of their instructional inappropriateness. Indeed, the videodisc coupled with the microcomputer has been promoted as the ideal instructional format. The reason for its slow adoption in education is most likely an economic one. Although the cost of players is fairly reasonable ($1500), discs are expensive to produce. They require a high production level, staff expertise, and considerable time to develop. These factors translate into money. It is not uncommon for videodisc production to cost $2,000 to $5,000 per linear minute, with mastering and replication charges added on. It is no wonder that few educational discs are available. Few individual school districts and colleges are in a position to produce their own discs, and publishers are reluctant to lay out such production costs.

VIDEOTEX

One of the most recent developments in the telecommunications area is the introduction of videotex, which represents a unique hybrid of video and computer technologies, combining television, electronic text, and electronic messaging and data communications. Although the role of videotex is just emerging, the Institute of the Future predicted that almost half of U.S. households will be using videotex services by the end of the century (Tydeman et al., 1982, p. 86). As of 1985 there were three commercial videotex operations—Times Mirror Videotex Service, called *Gateway,* in the Los Angeles area; Knight Ridder's *Viewtron* Service in south Florida, and *Keycom* in Chicago. Another major videotex service, a joint venture of IBM, CBS, and Sears, is scheduled for 1988.

Like teletext, videotex systems require that the viewer have a television set equipped with a special decoder, which translates digital data into a television display. If videotex signals are carried via phone lines, users also need a modem, which interfaces with phone lines. In addition, they may also have to pay long-distance phone charges or a monthly phone usage fee. If videotex signals are carried via two-way cable, users are typically charged a usage fee, which can range from $5 to $75 a month, depending on the type of service offered.

The unique characteristic of videotex is that it allows two-way transmission of information, either through coaxial cable or telephone lines. Two-way transmission means that the user's request is sent upstream to a large computer, where the request is processed and the appropriate response is in turn sent downstream to the user. Videotex can be used for basic services, such as information retrieval, or it can be employed for higher-level applications. On one level, a user can search out restaurants in a particular location by simply working through a series of indices until the desired information is found. At a more advanced level, customers can actually make a restaurant reservation, pay bills, transfer funds, or purchase goods by making selections through their keypad.

Videotex (and teletext) systems can present text and colored graphics. Earlier systems in the United States utilized an alphamosaic approach in which the graphic appears as if it were constructed of individual tiles. The result is a rather crude representation with no curved or diagonal lines. This system is still prevalent in Britain, but the United States and Canada have recently moved toward an alphageometric system, where graphics are assembled from computer-stored patterns, including circles and arcs. The alphageometric system requires a more expensive decoder at the user end, but provides smooth- and high-resolution graphics allowing a representation closer to actual objects.

Although videotex was developed with business interests in mind, it has been used to deliver educational materials, offering an alternative delivery method for computer instruction. Its advantages are that the system can be used at school or in the home. The learner is able to access and interact with a mainframe computer on a 24-hour basis and receive full-color graphics to supplement presentation of textual information. Another advantage is that the system is easily understood by untrained users. It is a system designed for noncomputing or nonelectronic specialists.

Since videotex appears to offer exciting educational possibilities, it would seem natural to look to existing applications and their successes and failures. Experimental videotex projects in this country and Canada have shown that effective instruction can be delivered via videotex, and students do learn from this medium. The educational applications for the medium are broadly based. It can be used for correspondence study (Montgomerie, 1982;

Nugent, 1984); in-class instruction (Trueman, 1982); at-home instruction or classroom instruction supplement (Online Computer Library Center, 1980); informal education (Bamberger, 1984); and as a telecourse supplement (Goodfriend et al., 1982).

Projects have isolated problems, however. For one, a telecourse/videotex combination can reduce the "on-demand" advantage of the videotex medium (Goodfriend et al, 1982). Also, the sophistication of the host system and its computer-programming capabilities influence the quality of interactive instruction that can be delivered (Bamberger, 1980; Montgomerie, 1982). Educational effectiveness is also reduced by problems at the user end, such as lack of dedicated phone lines, cumbersome keyboards, and consistent technical problems (Educational Technology Center, 1983; Nugent, 1984; Online Computer Library Center, 1980).

A review by Carey (1983) concluded that in educational settings, electronic-text services should meet existing needs, fit into existing curricula, enhance or suppplement other materials, not duplicate them, and be easy to use. This basic conclusion was echoed by Dozier, Valente, and Hellweg (1984), who reviewed user reaction to several educational videotex products and concluded that the user's need of the content and the perceived appropriateness of videotex as the delivery medium were critical factors in viewer acceptance.

Videotex is becoming more and more intertwined with the personal computer. Commercially available software allows microcomputers to serve as videotex terminals, eliminating the need for expensive, dedicated decoders. Local disk storage or hard-copy videotex pages has the potential to cut operating costs, particularly phone-line charges. Newer services are utilizing more software at the user end and more offline interaction. Carey (1984) predicts that in 1990 a user will preselect information, access the host database to have the appropriate material downloaded, go through the information offline, and then re-access the host to transmit messages or confirm transactions. As the number of home and school microcomputers increases (and there is every indication that they will continue to proliferate), videotex applications will perhaps become more feasible.

The linkage of videotex with other technologies may also provide a basis for videotex growth and acceptance. For instance, the videodisc, because of its natural computer interface, appears to be ideally suited for a video/ videotex application. Commercial interface hardware and software are already on the market and are being used by business and industry, particularly for point-of-sales and promotional activities.

There are, however, limitations for any educational institution interested in this medium. Commercial videotex operators, with their emphasis on mass-market appeal, have limited interest in educational materials. Given this philosophy, educational institutions are beginning to develop their own videotex systems. Colleges and universities with extensive computing capabilities are in the best position to develop videotex capability for a reasonable cost. In-house, closed-user group videotex systems are currently being implemented by certain businesses and industries. Assuming proper personnel and equipment, higher education would appear to be another candidate.

SUMMARY AND CONCLUSIONS

This chapter has examined both established and futuristic telecommunications systems. In looking at these technologies and projecting their potential for education, several trends seem evident. First, although the numbers of videodiscs and videocassettes are increasing, traditional telecommunications systems are currently serving large numbers of students. In 1983, an estimated 18.5 million public school students received some of their instruction from televison. Television was available in 70% of public-school classrooms, a figure virtually unchanged since 1977. On a positive note, teachers' access to color sets increased from 34% in 1977 to 75% in 1983 (Corporation for Public Broadcasting, 1984).

On the higher–education level, a 1978 survey showed that 71% of colleges and universities used television, with approximately 500,000 students enrolled in television courses. A variety of distribution methods were used, including cable, closed circuit systems, ITFS, and broadcast by both public- and commercial-television stations (Dirr, Katz, & Pedone, 1981).

Another trend is that the technologies are being used together, and unique hybrids are being formed. Satellite and cable have a well-established relationship, with satellite distribution providing a major boon for the cable industry. Video-recorders and videodisc are being linked with computers. And videotex itself is a unique hybrid of television, computer, and data-delivery systems.

The new technologies are providing new types of educational experiences, with more flexibliity and greater interactivity and individualization. The video–recorder eliminates the tyranny of the broadcast schedule. The teacher has more flexibility in time of use and can stop the tape for class discussion or teacher-directed questioning. Also, nonbroadcast programs do not have to be a standard 15, 20, or 30 minutes in length.

The linking of computer and video technologies provides interactive systems that feature immediate feedback, individualization in pacing and presentation, and almost unlimited combinations of text and images. These sophisticated technologies are, however, requiring new ways of simplifiying the hardware–person interface, with resulting experimentation with touch screens, light pens, and bar codes. They are also requiring new instructional design techniques, and designers are experimenting with innovative ways of structuring and individualizing interactive instruction.

New systems are also providing greater access to educational programming. ITFS provides a low-cost alternative to broadcast. Cable allows television delivery to poor reception areas. Satellite can reach even the remotest of locations. ITFS, cable, teletext, and videotex can reach students in their places of work and homes, as well as in schools and college classrooms.

Costs are lowering. Early videodisc systems cost $2500; today's educational/industrial models are in the $1500 range. Satellite dishes are becoming cheaper, paving the way for more use by educational institutions. Prices on videorecorders and computers have dropped. Despite this positive downward trend, however, price remains a critical factor in education. Many of the higher-end technologies are simply beyond the reality of education's economics. This problem is also compounded by the fact that hardware developments always outpace software developments by several years, and many cautious educators are delaying purchase until there is a mass of good generic software.

These new telecommunications systems can have a positive impact, but they can also introduce problems. The high cost of the more sophisticated systems, limiting the number of educational purchasers, could lead to disparity in educational opportunity, with the proverbial "haves" and "have-nots." Those who "have" gain access to tremendous information databases and instructional methods. Those who "have not" are limited to local resources and more traditional ways of delivering instruction.

The use of computer with video systems provides the opportunity for student tracking and grading, but opens the door for multiple access, with resulting loss of confidentiality. To cite an example, a computer/video simulation on courtship, modeling the dating process to illustrate sociological theory, would potentially require students to respond with personal information. Who has access to this information? The teacher? An evaluator? Other students? A videotex system operator? Who has access to students' grades? As control and potential access of collected data shifts from individual or classroom settings to buildings or institutional environments, greater problems of unauthorized access may arise.

The 1970s and 1980s have seen unparalleled developments in telecommunication hardware. Images that appear on television screens now arrive in a variety of ways, with the possibility for multiple presentation modes. New telecommunications sytems are influencing society, with viewers having increased access to a variety of information sources. These systems are also affecting education, providing new methods for delivery of effective and efficient instruction.

REFERENCES

Bamberger, N. J. (1984). The university as an information provider: the San Diego report. In KUON-TV and San Diego State University (Eds.), *Final report: the interactive cable project.* San Diego: San Diego State University, Center for Communications.

Beville, H. M. (1984a). Standard broadcast television is well equipped to survive the onslaught of new technologies. *Televison/Radio Age, 31*(23), 38–94.

Beville, H. M. (1984b). VCR penetration: Will it surpass cable by 1990? *Television/Radio Age, 31*(25), 27–31.

Carey, J. (1983). *Electronic text and higher education.* San Diego: San Diego State University, Center for Communications.

Carey, J. (1984). On the road to _____ . In KUON-TV and San Diego State University (Eds.), *Final report: the interactive cable project.* San Diego: San Diego State University, Center for Communications.

Corporation for Public Broadcasting (1984). *School utilization study 1982–83: Executive summary.* Washington, D.C.: Corporation for Public Broadcasting.

Davis, B. G. (1984, August). *Evaluation of science lab videodiscs.* Paper presented at Fifth Nebraska Videodisc Symposium, Lincoln, NE.

DeBloois, M., Maki, K. C., & Hall, A. F. (1984). *Effectiveness of interactive videodisc training: a comprehensive review.* Falls Church, VA: Future Systems, Inc.

Dirr, P. J., Katz, J. H., & Pedone, R. J. (1981). *Higher education utilization study phase I: final report.* Washington, D.C.: Corporation for Public Broadcasting.

Dozier, D., Valente, T., & Hellweg, S. (1984). Evaluation. In KUON-TV and San Diego State University (Eds.), *Final report: the interactive cable television project.* San Diego: San Diego State University, Center for Communications.

Educational Technology Center. (1983). *A trial in the application of videotex to education.* Adelaide: South Australia Educational Technology Center.

Gibbons, J. F., Kinchelor, W. R., & Down, K. S. (1977). Tutored videotape instruction: a new use of electronics media in education. *Science, 195,* 1139–1146.

Goldman, R. J. (1982). Teletext transforms broadcast television into an interactive medium. *CMLEA Journal, 5,* 12–15.

Goldman, R. J., Gordan, E., Craig, E., & Gingras, R. L. (1982). *Teletext as an educational medium: The Los Angeles school trial.* Los Angeles: KCET.

Goodfriend, K. K., Bamberger, N. J., Dozier, D. M., & Witherspoon, J. P. (1982). *Final report of the KPBS interactive videotext project.* San Diego: KPBS.

Hopkins, G. W. (1983). The new ITFS system in South Carolina. *Educational and Industrial Television, 15,* 50–52.

Home video market indication. (1984). *Video Manager, 7*(5), 10.

IIT/TV Survey. (1983). *The IIT connection.* Chicago: Illinois Institute of Technology, 1983.

Interactive disc sales hit $56 million in 1982. (1984). *Video User, 10*(9), 6.

May, L. S. (1984). Corporate experience in evaluating interactive video information system courses. *Interactive instruction delivery in education, training, and job performance.* Warrenton, VA: SALT.

Montgomerie, T. C. (1982). *Telidon distance education field trial.* Unpublished report commissioned by Alberta Education Department, Edmondton, Alberta.

Nugent, G. C. (1984). *Videotex in higher education: evaluation of videotex correspondence study.* Lincoln, NE: Nebraska ETV.

Oberle, M., & Quinn, H. (1984). The national university teleconference network: born of adventure and experiment. *Educational and Industrial Television, 16*(8), 32–40.

Online Computer Library Center. (1980). *Channel 2000: description and findings of a viewdata test.* Dublin, OH: Online Computer Library Center. (ERIC Document Reproduction Service No. 206–312)

Propp, G., Nugent, G., & Stone, C. (1980). Videodisc update. *American Annals of the Deaf, 125,* 679–684.

Science Research Center. (1983). *Great Plains National Instructional Television Library audio visual director's survey.* Lincoln, NE: University of Nebraska, Science Research Center.

Smith, R. C. (1984). First results from Florida's interactive training program. *Nebraska Videodisc Design/Production News, 6*(2).

Statistical Research, Inc. (1983). *Audio visual market study.* Washington, DC: Public Broadcasting Service Video and Corporation for Public Broadcasting.

Stokes, J. T. (1983). American Bell installs 200-player videodisc network for training. *VideoUser, 6*(3), 1.

Summerville, R., & Krakora, N. (1984). "One for the gipper" via fiber optics. *Educational and Industrial Television, 16*(4), 102–105.

Trueman, M. (1982). Telidon and computer assisted learning—a report of the first experiment using Telidon for CAL. *Proceedings of the 1982 International Videotex Conference, New York City,* 123–131.

Tydeman, J., Lipinski, H., Adler, R., Nyhan, M., & Zwimpfer, L. (1982). *Teletex and videotex in the United States.* New York: McGraw-Hill.

Young, J. J., Tosti, D. T., Hattman, L. L., & Palmisano, S. P. (1981). *Equipment-independent training: Final report.* Fort Monroe, VA: U.S. Army Training and Doctrine Command.

AUTHOR NOTES

Gwen C. Nugent is Assistant Director, Electronic Text, Nebraska Educational Television, University of Nebraska–Lincoln.

11 The Evolution of Computer-Aided Educational Delivery Systems

C. Victor Bunderson
Educational Testing Service

Dillon K. Inouye
Brigham Young University

The use of computer-aided delivery systems is a radical development in the history of education, representing the first qualitative change in delivery-system technology since the printing press. Although other technological innovations, such as the tape recorder, motion-picture projector, and television, have contributed to the refinement of the traditional teacher- and textbook-based delivery system, theirs were contributions of degree and not of kind. The computer offers something qualitatively different, that is, a way of replicating intelligent interactions with the learner, thereby changing not only the kind of delivery but also the meaning and roles of the other parts of the educational system.

DELIVERY SYSTEMS FOR EDUCATION

The potential contribution of current innovations in computer-aided education (CAE) can be more fully appreciated by reviewing the weaknesses inherent in our traditional delivery systems. They may be readily seen by comparing the ideal case with a typical case from the traditional delivery system found in our public schools. The discrepancies between the ideal and the typical illuminate the fundamental problems that modern computer-aided educational delivery systems were designed to address.

In the ideal case, there is one teacher per student. The teacher knows the subject, knows the student, and knows how to teach. The student, on the other hand, is willing and able to learn. He also knows how to learn.

By contrast, the typical classroom diverges widely from the Mark Hopkins-like ideal. Instead of teaching one student, the teacher teaches many. Instead of knowing the subject matter, all too often the teacher may never have had an advanced course in the subject, or may not have had adequate time to prepare. Instead of the students' being known thoroughly, they may be known only superficially. Instead of knowing how to teach, the teacher may have only a rudimentary understanding of pedagogy. These divergences from the ideal on the teacher's part are accompanied by similar divergences on the student's. Instead of being willing and able, the student may be indifferent to learning and may not have developed the study styles and strategies that would optimize his or her performance.

These discrepancies between ideal and reality in our current educational delivery systems may be summarized under the rubric of two general problems: (1) the problem of work, and (2) the problem of knowledge.

We believe that productivity in education will be enhanced to the extent that we are able to ameliorate these two problems. Let us examine them in greater detail. Although we can only offer an elementary analysis at this stage, it will serve as groundwork for the later discussions of this chapter.

The Problem of Work

Education, or the transmission of our total cultural inheritance to succeeding generations, is a labor-intensive enterprise. Every part of the process requires work. The teacher's preparing, presenting, monitoring of student progress, and providing of feedback is the product of intense labor. Likewise the learner's capturing of the teacher's lessons, assimilating them into his own life, doing homework and sharing what he has learned with others also requires dedicated effort. Education runs on work and work is obviously an important factor in determining the productivity of any educational process.

As we define it, the general problem of work is the question of how to make enough work available to accomplish the goals of the educational process, so that the lack of work is not a rate-limiting variable in the attainment of our educational goals. A more specific formulation of the problem which applies to those classroom settings in which there are dramatic insufficiencies of work is the question of how to increase *exponentially* the available work in the classroom. We include the idea of exponential increase in our formulation because we wish to distinguish between those efforts, such as CAE, which attempt both qualitative and quantitative increases in the amount of available work and more traditional efforts, such as the introduction of overhead projectors, which attempt only quantitative increases of degree.

The critical undersupply of work in the traditional classroom has been well documented now by studies that show how students and teachers use their time. These studies have offered more detailed descriptions of the work of the classroom in their attempt to study how students use their learning time. The studies show that the individual student has less than 2 minutes per day of individual interaction time with his teacher (Christensen, 1956; Conant, 1973; Denham & Lieberman, 1980), thus pointing out the dilution in individual attention that usually occurs when there are many students per teacher.

Of course, time for individual interaction with the teacher is only a part of total learning time, but most parents would be troubled to learn how little individual attention and feedback their child receives. The 2 minutes-per-day figure corresponds to our own unpublished studies, which show that in a typical 50-minute period, the elementary teacher may spend 20 minutes on administrative matters, 20 minutes on subject-matter presentations to the students, and only 10 minutes working with selected individual students. The effect of studies like these is to substantiate the acute shortage of the teacher's work, that is, teacher's time available to an individual student in need.

The Problem of Knowledge

If education runs on work, it is guided and informed by knowledge. Knowledge is not only an important end of education, it is also one of its indispensable means. Increasing work is good, but increasing the amount of smart, or knowledgeable, work is better. It is obvious that knowing the subject matter, knowing who is being taught, and knowing how to teach optimally are better than their uninformed alternatives, but how can we realize these desired ends?

The general problem of knowledge is the question of how to make enough knowledge available to accomplish the goals of the educational process, so that knowledge is not a rate-limiting variable in the attainment of our educational goals. As with the problem of work, there is a more specific formulation of the problem which applies to classrooms deficient in the kinds of knowledge discussed above: How can the knowledge available to the learning process be increased *exponentially*? Once again the idea of exponential increase is included to draw upon the capabilities of the new technologies and to distinguish CAE efforts from those that do not aim at qualitative change.

The acute shortage of knowledge in our nation's classroom has been amply documented by a steady flow of articles in popular and professional publications. These articles show that:

1. Educators have low scores on standardized tests of academic achievement;

2. There is a consistent flight of some of our best teachers from education into industry, especially in the areas of math and science;

3. Publishers have by conscious design lowered the difficulty level of their textbooks; and

4. The teacher population is growing less experienced; that is, our most experienced teachers are leaving education to be replaced by younger teachers who have less knowledge of the subject matter and less knowledge about how to teach.

All of these contribute to a "brain drain" in which the amount of knowledge available to guide the educational processes decreases. The trends listed above lower the amount of knowledge available to the learning process and, it is assumed, also lower educational achievement. Although there have been, and continue to be, many admirable attempts to turn the tide of the trends mentioned above, the gap between the knowledge needed and the knowledge available continues to widen. A qualitatively different solution is needed both for students and teachers to address properly the problem of insufficient knowledge.

Solutions Must Be Cost-effective

An assumption undergirding our discussions of the fundamental problems of work and knowledge is that solutions to these problems must be sought within the local constraints of individual educational systems that have finite and limited resources. It necessarily follows that the relative expense of solutions to the problems of knowledge and work is an extremely important factor. We shall point out in our subsequent discussion the dramatic changes that have occurred in the performance/price ratio. As the work and knowledge technologies have evolved, there have been dramatic increases in the amount of performance available per-unit cost.

Present Delivery Systems Are Not the Answer

It is likely that present delivery systems will not solve the two problems of work and knowledge in an economical way. First, there are signs that our present delivery system is nearing or has reached maturity, and that it will be very difficult, within current technical, cultural, and political restraints, to increase academic productivity qualitatively. As evidence that traditional delivery systems have reached maturity, critics point to the fact that although the real dollars spent on delivering education have doubled during the last 25 years, test scores have actually declined (Heuston, 1985). That productivity has decreased despite increased expenditure is a sign that present delivery systems have reached their maturity and that we have passed the point of diminishing returns to scale. According to these critics, we are spending more and more for increasingly less and less.

Second, we have reason to believe that the real deficiencies of the present delivery system cannot be easily changed. Our traditional systems divide rather than multiply the teacher's efforts. Very little paperwork can be automatically processed. These limitations of the system are limitations which arise out of the very nature of the teacher-textbook delivery system, that is, the inability of traditional delivery systems to solve the problems of work and knowledge. Although the educational systems of some countries, such as Japan, which use traditional delivery systems, seem to be more productive than ours, their sociocultural conditions differ in ways which would make such systems difficult to duplicate in our society.

CAE Delivery Systems: Potential Solutions

Computer-aided educational delivery systems are evolving into promising alternatives to traditional delivery methods because they retain many of the advantages of the traditional delivery system while adding the work and knowledge power of new technology. Although much research and development remains to be done and some formidable obstacles remain to be overcome, we believe that modern CAE systems are becoming increasingly capable of addressing the work and knowledge problems of modern education at a reasonable cost.

For the purposes of this chapter, we define computer-aided educational delivery systems as those systems which exploit the use of computers to assist educators in improving learning productivity, where productivity may be defined according to purpose in local settings. This definition is meant to include the use of computers to deliver mainline instruction, the use of computers to deliver supplementary instruction such as drill and practice, and the use of computers to teach people how to use computer tools to enhance personal productivity. By definition, it is the role of CAE to assist teachers in delivering the work and knowledge necessary to sustain the educational processes that lead to these purposes. The definition of CAE is intended to differ from that of Computerized Education in that CAE is not meant to supplant the teacher but rather to provide the teacher and the student with hardware and software tools which enhance their productivity.

From our foregoing discussion, it follows that for CAE, the primary means of increasing productivity is to increase the amount of work and knowledge available to the learning process. Productivity in learning may be measured over time as the rate of growth along one or more dimensions of a master's competence, for example, knowledge, skill, attitude, role perception, commitment. Similarly, the amounts of available work and knowledge may be measured by the extent to which they replicate the work or the knowledge of a master for a given interval of time. One plausible functional relationship between productivity, work, and knowledge may be expressed in the formula:

$$O = aW^b K^c$$

Where O is the teaching power, or product (Output) of an educational delivery system. W is available work, K is available knowledge, a is a constant, and *b* and *c* are exponents whose value is usually less than one, indicating diminishing returns to scale.

There is a need for appropriate units for the measurement of the work and knowledge power of an educational system For lack of a better term, we are provisionally calling the units of replication for work and knowledge *reps,* an abbreviation for the locution "replicated work of a person" in the case of work, and "replicated knowledge of a master, or expert," in the case of knowledge, respectively. These units help us to conceptualize and compare the power of computer-assisted educational delivery systems to replicate the labor and knowledge of an idealized master teacher. An unaided master teacher in a classroom generates one *rep* of teaching power; with the assistance of a properly applied computer-aided delivery system his or her teaching power may be multiplied.

The application of these units in measuring and comparing the relative teaching power of educational delivery systems is simple and straightforward. For example, one CAE delivery system on a drill and practice task may yield 30 reps of work and 1/3 rep of knowledge while another might yield 1 rep of work and 1 rep of knowledge on the same task. Or, alternatively, one CAE system can replicate the work of 30 teacher aides, each of whom has about one third the knowledge of a master teacher, while the other CAE system can replicate the work of one master teacher at the level of knowledge proficiency of the master teacher.

Please remember that we use these units provisionally, until advances in measurement and theoretical conception allow the field to develop a system of interrelated units of measurement like that used in the physical sciences, where a measure of temperature, such as $1°$ Kelvin, is related to a measure of energy, such as $\frac{1}{2} mv^2$, where both *m* and *v* are theoretical constructs that can be operationalized and scaled.

Having introduced a temporary construct for conceptualizing amounts of work and knowledge and a scale of first approximation which will allow us to compare qualitatively our ability to solve the work and knowledge problems at reasonable cost, we are now prepared to talk about evolutionary developments in the field, which have occurred as a function of our ability to:

1. Do more work at less cost, that is, the evolution of our ability to solve the work problem through new work-aiding technologies;

2. Apply CAE to more settings and more important practical problems; and,

3. Do smarter work at less cost, owing to the evolution of our ability to solve the knowledge problem, both through smarter applications and through new technologies for developing *reps* of knowledge.

THE EVOLUTION OF WORK TECHNOLOGIES

The work technologies of computer-aided education are evolving rapidly, enabling us to do more and more work and more kinds of work at the same or lower cost. The key index of merit, the performance/cost ratio, has grown exponentially over the last few decades and is projected to continue to do so through the end of this decade. Although this chapter is not a review of computer hardware—most hardware has a half-life of less than two years—it is important to note the dimensions along which CAE delivery-system hardware is evolving and the implications for education of this evolution.

It is useful to consider four dimensions along which the work technologies have evolved. Each dimension represents a different kind of human work effort. Along each dimension, technology has exponentially increased the amount of work and the kinds of work that an individual, so aided, can do. The four dimensions are: *sensing, remembering, deciding,* and *acting.*

The work of sensing, deciding, remembering, and acting has been automated with varying degrees of success by current technology. When the capacity of a device to simulate one of these forms of work surpasses a given performance/price threshold, then that device may be used in a computer-aided educational delivery system to increase the work reps that the system can deliver. As the technologies meet successively lower thresholds, availability and utilization increase. To the extent that a technology is able to produce work reps, it can free educators to do other things, including work they currently do not have the time and resources to perform.

Before discussing the evolutionary developments of the work technologies along each of these dimensions, let us review the kind of work each dimension represents.

Sensing. Input devices that do the work of sensing pick up information from the learner or the environment, encode it as symbols, and transmit it to the system for interpretation and response. In principle, input information may consist in any of the kinds of information sensed by the five senses, although the ranges of that information may be extended well beyond human capability, as to infrared light or electromagnetic radiation. The information sensed may originate from human beings or from machines (including states of the same machine). It may be decoded as data, communication, or commands.

Remembering. Memory devices that do the work of remembering store information. It is difficult to overstate the importance of the work of remembering. By this the system remembers the step-by-step sequence of operations it is to perform and the instructions and data it is to use. As in humans, memory makes it possible for the machine to recognize signals, decode stored instructions, record data and later adapt to these records of past experience, and organize data into structures so that it can process these higher-order units.

A subcategory of remembering of especial relevance to teaching delivery is the archival storage of files of text, images, and audio used as presentations in teacher-learner interactions. As in humans, timely retrieval is as important as accurate storage.

Deciding.   Central processing devices that do the work of deciding perform the information processing necessary to make decisions. This includes the processing of inputs, the computing, and the making of decisions based upon information in memory. In the system, the work of deciding is done by the processor. It performs the arithmetic and logical operations required to make a decision. It also controls the operation of the machine by turning the computer's other functional units on and off at the appropriate times.

Acting.   Output devices that do the work of acting execute the decisions made by the system. This work may consist in activating output devices that send information, turn on motors, switch lights, display the next unit of instruction, position and activate machine tools, and so forth. The work of acting allows the computer to change the environment or control devices external to the system. It also allows the computer to communicate with people or other machines. The most important subcategory of acting involves controlling display devices for text, images (still or motion), and audio used in teaching presentations.

These four kinds of work may be deployed in educational delivery systems to replicate many kinds of work that educators have hitherto performed. (Some examples where large savings of time and energy have resulted include the scoring of tests, searching large files to retrieve records, computing of statistics, processing of words, and keeping of records.) Depending on the capabilities of the devices that do the work and the relative cost of owning and operating those devices, they can be widely disseminated to increase exponentially the amount of work in the classroom.

The evolutionary changes in performance, price, and categories of capability of computer-aided delivery-system hardware over the last three decades may be illustrated concretely by referring to a few representative examples. A list of these examples is found in Table 11.1.

Although these examples represent only a few points on a path of continuous evolution, they illustrate the following trends in the evolution of work technologies:

1. Elaboration of kinds of devices. The input devices exemplify the trend. They began as crude, general-purpose, binary switches. Now we have key-

TABLE 11.1

The Evolution of Computer-Aided
Educational Delivery System Hardware

Manufacturer (Approximate Year)	Number of Learning Stations	Cost per Learning Station	Description of Capabilities
IBM 1401 (1965)	4	$55,000	IBM selectric typewriter terminals with random-access slides and audio.
IBM 1500 (1967)	up to 32	$10,000	CRT terminals w/primitive graphics and light pen. Random-access slides and audio. 64K RAM and 4 megabytes of mass storage for the whole system.
CDC Plato IV (1975)	hundreds	$12,000	512 X 512 plasma display terminals w/ excellent graphics. Instant random access audio disk with 15 in. floppy disks. Cyber mainframe with hundreds of megabytes of storage for many terminals. Microfiche projection on the back of display terminals.
TICCIT (1975)	up to 128	$ 4,000	Learning keyboard with color TV display. Random-access audio w/ hard disk. Adaptive delta digital audio. 10 videotape players switched between terminals. 175 megabytes of mass storage on 7 25 meg. drives. 2 Nova 800 central processor units with 64K and 32K of RAM, respectively.
WICAT 300 (1984)	30	$ 3,000	Typewriter keyboard with monochrome CRT. 2-3 megabytes (mb.) of RAM for 30 terminals, 1 mb. for digital audio and 1 or 2 mbs. for courseware. 160-474 megabytes of mass storage with streamer tape backup. 1 Motorola 68000 microprocessor and 5 Intel 8088's. Star network. Digitized audio.
Personal computers with local area networks and fileservers (1986)	dozens	$ 3,000	Networked microcomputers each with hard-disk fileserver, color CRT, 512K RAM, and 550 megabytes of CD ROM storage. Icon–driven interface with mouse.
		$ 4,500	May include videodisc player with each learning station.

boards, trackballs, mice, digital pads, joysticks, light pens, voice input devices, touch-screens, and graphics tablets.

2. Improvement in capability stimulated by competition for markets.

3. A decline in price as the economies of mass production and component standardization bring greater efficiency.

4. Increased utilization, from improvements in the performance/price ratio formed by factors listed as 2 and 3.

These trends in the kinds and capabilities per unit-cost of the work technologies are seen in the actual devices used for learning stations in computer-aided delivery systems. As Table 11.1 shows, the following specific trends may be seen along each of the four work dimensions discussed above:

Sensing. Input devices have evolved from limited teletype keyboards and such low-cost and available systems as Macintosh-like interfaces utilizing windows, icons, and a mouse.

Remembering. Memory per work station has increased dramatically. Whereas the earliest systems had only a few kilobytes to share between all of the learning stations, it is not unusual at present to find individual learning stations with from 512 to 1024K of RAM. Even larger amounts of RAM will be used in the future. The early and expensive mass secondary storage devices are being replaced by inexpensive, high-density magnetic and opto-electronic devices. Compact-Disc ROMS and videodiscs will soon allow gigabytes of mass storage per work station.

Deciding. Most CAE delivery systems of the future will utilize microprocessors that handle at least 16 to 32 bits at a time at speeds from 10 to 20 million cycles per second. The evolution is toward larger information-handling capacity at higher speeds. The current state of the art is represented by 32-bit microprocessors which have a full 32-bit architecture, a full 32-bit implementation and a 32-bit data path (bus) to memory. Some (Murphy, 1985) believe that microprocessor performance will eventually exceed that of all but a few of our current mainframes.

Acting. As with the input devices described above, output devices have evolved in performance, price, and variety. Visual displays have improved tremendously since the days of the teletype. Soft-copy displays have become more and more prevalent, most of them in the form of cathode-ray tube (CRT) displays. The CRT is still the soft-copy display of choice for most educational applications, although its competitors, the liquid crystal, the electroluminescent, and the plasma displays, have made impressive gains and are gaining greater currency.

High-resolution graphics have replaced the random-access slide projectors of early times. Color is now a standard item with some displays having resolution of as high as 1800 × 1800 *pixels* (picture elements). The price of an RGB color monitor is still high—in the $600–1000 range, while higher-resolution monochrome transistor-to-transistor logic monitors sell for as little as $150–250. The lower cost and higher resolution of the latter have caused many educators to choose them over color monitors.

Most professional educational delivery systems will now include digitized audio. They also employ daisy wheel, dot matrix, or laser printing-devices for hard-copy output. These devices print at speeds ranging from 12 to 400 characters per second.

The implications of the evolutionary development of the work technologies are far-reaching. Two of these implications seem particularly noteworthy:

1. Improvements in the performance/price ratio lower the cost of available work. When the cost of work falls below certain thresholds, it brings ever larger numbers of consumers into the marketplace. Educational designers can plan and produce curricula for this increasing demand.

2. The capability of hardware has, in general, ceased to be a bottleneck in the development and use of CAE delivery-systems. The current, but soon-to-become obsolete, state of technology represents a quantum leap in capability over even the dreams of the early CAI pioneers, frustrated because of the lack of audio, graphics capability, or memory and processing speed.

The dramatic advances in the evolution of work technologies have been exploited by educators who have harnessed the work technologies in educational applications. It is to this subject that we now turn.

THE EVOLUTION OF CAE APPLICATIONS

One way of looking at the evolution of applications is to consider the work teachers do. How have educators and innovators tried to apply CAE to assist with this work? An outline in the following section provides seven major categories of work performed by classroom teachers or trainers. No one teacher can be a master at all these kinds of work. A glance at the outline makes it easy to see why in a regular classroom only 20 minutes or so of each period is devoted to instruction: there are too many non-instructional tasks to fill the time. As CAE hardware and software has become more accessible in terms of price and capabilities, applications have been introduced in each of the seven categories. There was and is an evolution of applications within each category, not necessarily an orderly and most helpful evolution. For example, in perhaps the most venerable category, teaching delivery, many forms of one-on-one teaching interactions have been developed, ranging in complexity up to very sophisticated computer-video-disc simulations of scientific laboratory work, but CAE aids to group presentations are primitive. Systematic attempts to identify the work that matters most to student growth, to compare it with the work that uses up the most time, and to target CAE applications to ameliorate observed imbalances, are notable in their absence. Instead, there has been a mind-boggling variety of applications targeted at one, or at most a few, line items in the work array listed in the outline. These applications developed because equipment was available and someone saw on application for educational work, or because someone had to get an advanced degree, or someone obtained a research grant, or someone fired with visionary zeal saw release from a disliked form of work, such as grading drill exercises, or saw a way to achieve educational goals now prevented because of limitations in work or knowledge. Always, the scope of CAE projects has not encompassed all of the interlinked aspects of work in the live, classroom situation. Nevertheless the scope of some projects has grown larger and larger.

An Outline of Some of the Work Performed by Classroom Teachers

A. The work of teaching delivery
    1. Information presenter (lecturing, using media)
    2. Coach and tutor (organizing practice and feedback)
    3. Lab instructor (operating and monitoring equipment)
B. Administration of instruction
    1. Course administrator (planning, scheduling)
    2. Committee member (personnel management, textbook selection)
    3. Adviser (advising course selection)
    4. Counselor (counseling on personal problems)
    5. Sponsor (initiating clubs, projects)
C. Developing and collecting materials
    1. Syllabus planner
    2. Group lesson planner
    3. Instructional developer (designing presentations)
    4. Instructional developer (using practice, simulations)
    5. Test developer
    6. Programmer of computer exercises
    7. Assembler of materials
D. Assessing and improving learner productivity
    1. Test administrator
    2. Test and homework grader
    3. Test interpreter
    4. Diagnostician (spotting exceptions, problems)
    5. Prescriber (individual and group educational plans)

      6. Instructor of learning strategies
      7. Work assigner (use of new learning-productivity tools)
      8. Remedial tutor (basic skills instruction)
  E. The work of professional development
      1. Learner of teaching techniques
      2. Representative of teaching profession
  F. Public service instruction
      1. Adult teacher
      2. Teacher of refresher courses
  G. Evaluator and researcher
      1. Designer of evaluation studies
      2. Interpreter of evaluation data
      3. Scholar and writer (pursuing advanced degree)

The following sections are organized around two major trends in application, mainline and computer-centered CAE. Because of space limitations, not all of the seven categories of work can be considered.

An Early Bifurcation of Applications

Two quite different clusters of applications motivated the early CAE researchers, whose pioneering studies began in a few universities and a few industrial laboratories in the late 1950s and early 1960s. One group sought to apply the early, time-shared computers to the delivery of teaching interactions in conventional curricular subjects—to do better what we do now. We will call this approach *mainline CAE.* The other group saw the computer as a new subject matter—a new curriculum in its own right—and computer literacy as having a position of importance equal with the three Rs. We will call this approach *computer-centered CAE.* In terms of the applications in the previous outline, the mainline group sought to use CAE in teaching delivery, and studied drill programs, structured-practice problem sets, tutorial programs, and simple simulations and games. Another branch of this movement built computer-managed (CMI) systems to test for placement in a self-paced curriculum, then to test for progress from module to module of study materials administered using conventional, rather than computerized, materials. The second cluster of applications, computer-centered CAE fits categories C and D of the outline best. The advocates of this emphasis taught students a programming language, and how to use packaged programs. They were encouraged to use these abilities to solve problems, create and execute models, and search databases relevant to any course or topic of interest. Teachers were encouraged to assign computer exercises and integrate them into their classes. New courses and departments were created built around computer uses.

Mainline CAE

The first group has progressed through the applications of the outline in the approximate order: (1) teaching delivery, small learning packages; (2) simple achievement testing and records management (CMI); (3) early authoring software tools to support lesson development; (4) the development of larger curricular libraries to support mainline teaching delivery; (5) teacher training in the use of more complete systems; and (6) advising and counseling; and (7) learner profiling and learner productivity.

Teaching delivery; small learning packages.   Early teletype and selectric typewriter terminals were used for administering drill and practice exercises in arithmetic, then in reading and language arts.   Drill programs embody structured lists of items to be learned, simple forms of feedback, simple record keeping, and branching to the appropriate next drill set.   Neither drill programs nor practice problem sets performed much actual instruction.   It was assumed that this was done in the classroom.   Drill and practice has been a long-lasting application, and continues today.   The noisy, uppercase, text-only teletypes were replaced when cathode-ray tube (CRT) displays, at first character-only, then with graphics, became less costly.

Tutorial programs soon appeared on the early teletype and typewriter terminals.   Their purpose was to present information, teach concepts, and to do so in a didactic presentation–question–feedback–branch mode.   They broadened the instructional purposes for which CAE could be used, but made programming more complex.   They were based on no real instructional model except a mixture of Skinner's admonition to use constructed responses rather that multiple choice (to avoid teaching the student erroneous choices; advice that was commonly ignored), and Crowder's intrinsic-programming concept of branching based on alternative answers.   Much else was borrowed initially from the programmed-instruction (PI) movement, including actual programmed lessons.   The text-based, fill-in-the blank PI style did not lend itself to interesting computer interactions. The main contribution of PI was that its development method and some aspects of its prescriptions for good frames were adopted in some mainline CAI circles (Bunderson & Faust, 1976).

The drill-and-practice programs were more successful than the tutorial because they were highly structured. Thus they were easier to implement in sizable systems of exercises which impacted the school curriculum.   Thus the drill–and–practice vendor Computer Curriculum Corporation, founded by CAE pioneer Patrick Suppes, started early and has survived long (Suppes, Jerman, & Brian, 1968). It influenced far more students with its drill–and–practice curricular adjuncts than other commercial ventures, which tried to get by with insubstantial amounts of more complex tutorial curricula on fancier but more expensive hardware.

Both drill-and-practice and tutorial programs were a reflection of the early software, as well as the early hardware. The *Coursewriter* authoring language developed by IBM lent itself well to tutorials, and was adequate for drills. Standard computer languages, however, became the norm for drill-and-practice programs in large quantity because the repetitive structure of these exercises lent themselves to implementation in standard, full-powered computer languages, rather than limited authoring languages. Computer programs were built which embodied efficient execution algorithms with simple data entry and editing conventions for authors.

Developing adequate libraries of courseware. The problem of materials development in CAE has always been, and remains, one of the most significant of all barriers to its widespread, effective use. It is this problem that the mainline CAE group had to solve, while the computer-centered CAE group largely avoided it. One early response was the use of Computer-managed Instructional Systems (CMI). Another response was the evolution of authoring languages, and later, authoring systems. CMI is a response to the materials-development problem because it allows the use of printed and audiovisual materials, or teacher-led but modular activities, in the framework of an organized sequence of learning modules. The computer enables self-pacing and associated records management. Simple on-line tests or off-line mark sense tests were used, first to place a student into the system of modules at the right starting point, and then on a continuing basis to monitor the performance on each module. After a module test the system was programmed to prescribe alternate activities in the event of a nonpass, or a new module in the event of a pass.

CMI systems made it possible to create large libraries of non-computer-administered curriculum modules and yet to introduce some of the benefits of CAE, without the extensive programming and debugging of tutorial lessons. An evolutionary trend in both CMI and interactive CAE was influenced by Individually Prescribed Instruction (IPI), a system of self-paced learning packages for elementary schools that was popular in the mid-1960s and early 1970s. Developed at the University of Pittsburgh Learning R&D Center and distributed by the Regional Laboratory Research for Better Schools, Inc., this system was influential in shaping the concepts of early CAE pioneers. It influenced both those who favored the CMI approach and those who favored on-line interactions. (Weisgerber, 1971, described both IPI and an early CMI system, Project PLAN).

It is significant that the concept of self-pacing, rather than group pacing, became the dominant concept in mainline CAE. IPI was installed in quite a number of schools in the 1970s, and extensive CMI and CAE systems with a similar individually paced concept have been installed and evaluated, but the schedules and traditions of most schools will not yield easily to such a revolution. Neither computer-aided nor computer-managed systems have achieved lasting acceptance. Even the massive CMI system run by the Memphis Naval Air Station for managing the instruction of thousands in electronics was abandoned in 1984, and the Navy turned the clock back toward group-paced teaching.

Self-pacing as an educational concept has many strengths. Its greatest weakness, limiting lasting acceptance, was the need to transform radically teacher roles and classroom traditions. CAE systems which fit into the conventional schedules have been more successful. The successful drill-and-practice systems, of great value because of their extensive libraries of exercises, fit into the existing school schedules and curricula. They allowed the assignment of groups of students to terminals to finish sets of exercises by a certain time. A number of CAE hardware and software vendors now offer curricula that assume the schedule as a given, and provide scheduling flexibility in the software so schools can pace students through the curriculum as a group, not insisting on mastery of each module. In 1985, when this chapter was completed, total self-pacing in school and college settings was no longer an important movement, yet a residue remained. The concept of individual work at individual terminals was still the norm, rather than the alternative of group presentations with interactive responses by all learners at the same time.

Authoring languages.   The struggle to develop enough curricula to make a difference was taken as a challenge by software experts. Their efforts resulted in a host of early authoring languages, of which *Coursewriter, PLANIT, TUTOR, Pilot,* and *Scholar-Teach* are examples. They dealt directly with the interactions on the teletype printout or CRT screen. Large courseware-development projects involved other media besides the computer display-screen, including computer-controlled audio, film, or video. Computer graphics and videodiscs later added complexity to these languages. An *authoring system* had as its purpose to help in the many aspects of media development and integration. Today, numerous products are called authoring systems, but they are usually software packages that do not deal with design-level work. They emphasize ease in producing displays for the computer screen, and provide for integrating into the CAE program calls to a video-disc player, videotape player, or other analog image or audio source controllable by the computer. The WISE authoring system, developed by Peter Fairweather at WICAT Systems, achieved a milestone in learning and using ease. It was open-ended and facilitated computer-adaptive testing and excellent record-keeping systems, both of which represent a severe challenge to authoring software.

Authoring languages usually have some built-in instructional strategy favored by the groups of authors who influenced the development of the authoring software. In most cases the strategy is quite informal, reflecting the author's tastes. A notable exception is an authoring-software package designed around a coherent instructional strategy—the Authoring Procedure for TICCIT (APT), perfected and marketed by Hazeltine, Inc. As a result of the large, NSF-funded TICCIT project in the early 1970s, the first version of APT was developed at Brigham Young University. It was based on a coherent model of instruction involving the lesson components Rule, Example, Practice, Help, and Advice. (See Bunderson, 1975, for a description of the strategy). It was optimized for concept and rule learning, and was applied to the production of one of the largest early libraries of courseware, in freshman mathematics and English, introduced to that date. Most current authoring systems (really languages) are neutral as to instructional strategy, leaving it up to the author.

Teacher Training and Productivity. When CAE applications were first introduced, little thought was given to teacher training in the productive use of the systems. One of two models was implicitly assumed: (1) The computer was like a resource in the back of the classroom or in a learning center where students could be sent to study, or (2) The computer terminals were the means to implement a self-paced course, and computer-room proctors would be available. The computer-literacy movement opened up a much greater emphasis on teacher training, as more and more teachers gained access to a small number of personal computers for their students. Such stand-alone computers were equipped with programming languages, games, and little else. The emergence of CAE systems with enough material to make a difference in mainline instruction made it painfully obvious that new roles and new skills were required of the teachers. Otherwise the promise of CAE either fell far short or failed miserably. Failures often occurred because the users did not use the system as it was designed. Their expectations and skills did not match those required by the designers of the system. Such failures were no true test of the potential of CAE.

Merely the idea of using computers was itself a frightening challenge to many teachers. The often-hidden but revolutionary assumptions about teaching and learning embedded by the designers into their systems became an even greater obstacle to many. Sweeping changes in society during the last half of the 1970s in the form of the now-ubiquitous calculators, then personal computers, did much to dispel the fear of computers. At the least it made unacceptable the frequent proud refusal to deal with them. Dealing with the new concepts about teaching and learning embodied in these delivery systems was quite another matter. Older innovations in the delivery system, such as better audiovisual media or 1950's teaching machines, could be taken as a matter of course and used or not as an adjunct to a lesson. Mainline CAE systems carried a whole library of curricula, enough to restructure large portions of the day; and worse, they carried accountability in the form of performance tests over the material and reports available to administrators. Good teachers welcome anything that will help them do more for their students, as long as it doesn't require more work. They welcome training programs sophisticated enough to deal with the real issues: the significant role changes that occur when CAE is introduced seriously.

In schools of education and in school districts desiring inservice training, the problem is that no authoritative curriculum exists. No agreed-upon standard exists for what constitutes a master computer teacher. The bifurcation between computer as teacher and computer as the basis for new curricula is part of this confusion. Does a school install clusters of individual stations in classrooms and library for programming, word processing, and other operations of this sort, or does it install a large number of stations networked together to administer a packaged curriculum? The roles and training requirements differ substantially in the two cases.

Learner profiling and learner productivity. This category of applications has the greatest promise for making exponential improvements in solving the problems of work and knowledge. One statement of the problem is this: How can the people in an educational system gain knowledge of the position, direction, and velocity of each student within a curriculum, and of groups of students, then adapt to that knowledge by shifting the resources to aid the growth of the individuals and groups? Such a goal implies both a more visible and quantitative definition of curriculum, and a means to measure and make visible student progress. The self-paced instruction movement introduced some ways to do this. The curriculum was modularized and progress within the defined set of modules was quantified with achievement tests. A student's progress through the set of modules could be charted as the posttests were passed. On failure, extra help could be prescribed. Placement tests were used. In initial studies with self-paced, modular curricula, a number of para-professional clerks had to be hired to take care of all of the required testing and paperwork. In other words, new work had to be introduced in order to gain the knowledge and prescriptive control over position and velocity within the curriculum. Later, CMI systems were introduced to do the work of this army of clerks.

Much was learned from all the testing in self-paced systems. The initial placement tests were disliked. Students always started a new learning session with a failure experience. The fun of showing what they knew was precluded. If given a choice, many students will start with material they can deal with comfortably, and will often spend too much time and avoid venturing into new areas. It was observed that the frequent off-line, paper-and-pencil tests in self-paced and CMI systems were more than a problem in administration and logistics. They were aversive to students long conditioned to paper–and–pencil testing as an unpleasant experience rather than as a help-ful part of learning.

As tests started to migrate onto computers for on-line administration, benefits were gained. The logistical problems of maintaining files of paper test-booklets and sheets were solved. The tests became more interesting and less "test like," as graphics, simulation, and game elements were added. Scoring was immediate and record keeping invisibly and competently done. As CAE module lessons began to be available on-line, the difference between the practice problems and the lesson tests became less visible. Students did not even need to know that they were being tested.

Computerized testing began to become more sophisticated, and its growth in sophistication can be described as an evolution through three generations. The first generation of tests were computer versions of paper-and-pencil tests. A fixed number of items was given to each student. Only scoring and record keeping was performed by the computer, and later graphics. The second generation of tests introduced various forms of computerized adaptive testing, where different items are given, depending on the student's item-by-item performance. In the Wald sequential testing algorithm, a pass-or-fail decision was made as soon as enough items were administered to make a decision, but the items were not selected individually. In the one-, two-, and three-parameter computer-adaptive testing procedures, the items must all be calibrated statistically in advance, using hundreds of student responses. New items were picked after each response—items with a difficulty level about right for the responding student. A new estimate of the student's achievement or ability level was made after each response until the estimate was stable enough to be accepted. Much higher accuracy of measurement was possible, despite using from 20% to 50% fewer items for a given stu-dent (Hulin, Drasgow, and Parsons, 1983; Lord, 1980).

In the third generation of computerized testing, the CAE curriculum exer-cises themselves are calibrated. The authors introduced such a project at the WICAT Education Institute in 1983. The two-parameter model was used, and for calibration, the BILOG program (Mislevy & Bock, 1982). Response vec-tors from student performance on computer-administered exercises in a modular reading curriculum were submitted to the BILOG program to obtain the difficulty and discrimination parameters. The results of this pilot work were very promising, even though item response theory, on which these pro-cedures were based, must be extended to permit its application with lessons instead of items. In this study the item statistics associated with each reading exercise were judged to be more meaningful and accurate than the existing method for assessing reading level using Frye Indices and author judgment to sequence and grade the reading selections. The estimate of student position in the set of exercises could be made very accurately, and the accuracy increased with each exercise worked. Movement up and down grade level could be charted on a daily basis. This third generation of *continuous measurement* promises to go a long way toward solving the knowledge problem of tracking the position, direction, and velocity of students and groups through a calibrated curriculum. It also provides data to grade and sequence the lessons.

The concept of on-line testing in CAE, based on a modular curriculum, which is calibrated to make progress through it visible, is a fertile, new area within educational research and evaluation. Since it takes place within the schools themselves, it represents a new, ecologically valid form of educational research. This field is new and largely unexplored, because there have been so few examples of mainline CAE curricula with enough scope to cover years of the schoolchild's life. Moreover, stable, calibrated measurements have not been available. Some of the most important issues have barely been framed, let alone studied. A case in point is the issue of the mixture of familiar lessons versus new ones, previously mentioned. There are two sides to this issue: Students want the fun and confidence building experiences of doing familiar work; teachers want them to maintain a pace through the new materials that stretches each student optimally.

It is well known that students have different styles and temperaments that affect moving ahead into new material, but information on these differences and what to do about them has not been available in classrooms. CAI makes it possible to define operationally different tactics and strategies through students' response patterns at the CAE terminals. For example, in the calibrated reading exercises at the Waterford School, some students would approach each one with care, would watch their mistakes, and would exit the lesson, rather than risk logging a failure. Other students would brashly and quickly run through the lesson, happy to take a failure just to see what was required, then go right back a second time and pass it. They knew that the failure did not matter, just passing the lesson. These two, and other tactical approaches, are readily visible from computer–generated reports. A subset of such patterns reveals students who are not learning at all, merely putting in time pressing keys.

Learner profiling systems to assess abilities, preferences, and temperaments are needed. Then it will be possible to learn what tactical and strategical patterns go with different learner profiles. The authors initiated and produced an on-line, learner-profile testing system using second generation tests (three-parameter computer–adaptive) at the WICAT Education Institute in 1982–1984 (Inouye et al., 1986). This system is now available on the Plato/ WICAT system 300. A mainline system like this, with powerful record-keeping, is a powerful tool for the extensive research needed to relate learner-profile variables to achievement, whether defined traditionally, or as position and velocity in a calibrated curriculum. This area is one of the first wherein the mainline approach, which set out first to do better what we can do now, has gone beyond into that which was unthought of before.

Computer-centered CAE and Its Outgrowths

The advocates of computer-centered CAE and computer literacy did not see their goal as reducing the work of teachers. They were excited about using the computer as a new intellectual tool for students as well as teachers. Thus, they emphasized *learner productivity* through problem solving and modeling. They encouraged the use of the new computer tools to open up new computer-related course offerings.

They were interested in the entire phenomenon of computing and its impact on thinking and knowledge work, and were interested in trying out the new advances and using them in their own right, rather with the aim of doing better in education what we now do with conventional methods. They began to see that advances in computer software and hardware make possible new approaches to education undreamed of by educators trying to improve conventional methods. In this potential for dramatically different approaches to learning comes the greatest distinction between mainline and computer-centered approaches.

The computer-centered approach saw perhaps its earliest flowering in the work of Kemeny and Kurz and their group of bright undergraduates at Dartmouth on an early time-shared computer. They developed the BASIC language. The title, *Beginner's All-Purpose Symbolic Instruction Code,* had special significance to them, and many million computer beginners have learned BASIC since. Their educational purpose was not teaching delivery, but using computer power as an adjunct to regular learning. For example, classes in math and science would no longer have to restrict student experience to problem sets with easy numbers (e.g., those that came out with perfect squares for easy computation). Real-world problem sets could be provided and solved with the aid of BASIC programs on the computer. A powerful central computer was provided with dozens of terminals for student access across campus. The faculty and students soon raced on to the use of quantitative and procedural modeling in the curriculum, and to the building and accessing of databases in a particular knowledge domain.

With the advent of inexpensive personal computers, all of them equipped with BASIC, this movement has made and continues to make a significant impact on education. Some aspects of this contribution later became implicit in the term "computer literacy," although structured languages, such as PASCAL, are now more often preferred than BASIC. People who share this concept have created a new curriculum about computers and their uses in solving problems, modeling, and manipulating data from the old curricula.

A hybrid between the two movements exists when sets of interactive lessons are written on personal computers in one of their standard languages, usually BASIC or PASCAL. The authors of these packages may have the same purposes as those who have toiled to make mainline CAE effective with time-shared or networked computers. They are limited, however, to applications in teaching delivery, or testing, which do not require shared files in an extensive way. Anyone who has attempted to manage records by capturing them on floppy disks and transferring them to a central archive is well aware that this is not a solution with general applicability.

Computer literacy.   The evolution of the movement we have characterized as *computer-centered CAE* is a part of the evolution of computers in society. Thus landmarks along the way are defined by the development of specific computers and computer languages. Languages grow in usefulness when tied to enhanced hardware capabilities in computers or peripherals. The BASIC language was one of the earliest and most popular, but another early interactive interpretive language, APL, played a significant role in the evolution of CAE. IBM made APL available on the system 360 in the mid 1960s. They also made a subset version of it available on the IBM 1500, one of the first (but unfortunately short-lived) computer systems designed specifically for education. This system was at its peak from 1967 to 1972, and many hundreds of students and teachers learned to use APL on the IBM 360 and 1500 systems for problem solving, modeling, and for developing teaching modules. APL was especially good for drills, simulations, and games, and for problem solving in any of the branches of applied mathematics and statistics. Its notation is unfamiliar and quite mathematical, and it requires a special keyboard. One result of these features was that it did not have the immediate, broad appeal of BASIC. The notation can be viewed as a strength, for when learned, it helps students become familiar with advanced concepts in computing and in applied mathematics. A good computer language always has this property: It gives substance to a set of concepts in the domain it most effectively serves for modeling and problem solving.

Another computer language, LOGO, introduced new concepts from computer science and logic to schoolchildren in a friendly and interesting way (Papert, 1980). LOGO was used to control the motions of a *turtle,* implemented both as a three-dimensional robot that could be programmed to move about on the floor, and as a two-dimensional icon on a computer screen. The turtle could be programmed to draw geometrical patterns, or to trace paths around and through obstacles. A collection of such exercises came to be called "turtle geometry." Students learned much by writing a LOGO program to produce geometrical patterns and to perform sequences of actions. The mathematics curriculum can be greatly enriched by the addition of LOGO and turtle geometry (Abelsen, & di Sessa, 1981). LOGO students are exposed to many new concepts of general utility, not just of demonstrable worth in computer applications. Some of the concepts are iteration, conditional action, recursion, string manipulation, and the modeling of observable phenomena by formally stated procedures.

LOGO's use of computer graphics and icons was one important influence on the development of the SMALLTALK language at the Xerox Palo Alto

Research Center. This language in turn strongly influenced the popular Macintosh man-machine computer interface. The use of windows, iconic communication (of which the turtle icon was an early example), and a mouse as an input device is fast becoming a standard for user-friendly, man-machine communication. As the public is educated in such convenient and easy to learn standard conventions for communicating with machines, developers of both curricular materials and work–productivity tools can adopt these conventions, speeding the processes of design and of user training. Standard and intuitively easy man-machine conventions are opening the world of computers to people who have mistrusted and avoided computers. The first wave of users, most of whom were "techies," liked or at least tolerated the complexity and foolishness of much of computer usage.

Advances in computer science and technology truly create the opportunity for a new curriculum. New concepts and new skills are introduced and are taught to the using public, whether they are students, teachers, or workers in an occupation. Application packages, such as word processors, spreadsheets, business graphics systems, database systems, and communication software, introduce new approaches to doing work–productively and make commonplace some previously unfamiliar concepts. The wide availability of languages such as BASIC, APL, LOGO, PASCAL, and LISP introduces other new terms to express powerful concepts for dealing with information. Now computer graphics and iconic communications are producing a new language for communicating concepts which only a few years ago had to be expressed in words or mathematical symbols, or in abstract computer-program code. The old delivery-system displays, primarily text, are not expressive for many of these concepts. The use of text *and* image processing *and* audio-processing techniques by digital computers makes the concepts easy to express. In addition to all this, a crowning impact on the curriculum of the educated citizen of the twenty-first century may well come about through advances in *knowledge technology,* discussed in another section of this chapter.

Some Emerging and Future Trends in CAE

The fertile imaginations of today's hordes of computer designers and users will thwart any effort at specific prediction, but three major trends seen by these authors to be of considerable significance will be discussed: (1) group interactive teaching, (2) broadcasting superior lessons and data, and (3) publishing interactive knowledge bases.

Group interactive teaching. Even though group teaching has many strengths, the emphasis in the evolution of CAE has been on individual learning at a work station. A few years ago, the authors were involved in an NSF-financed project using an interactive video-disc system which had been programmed with visual, auditory, and simulation materials in developmental biology (Bunderson et al., 1984). Some complex concepts dealing with DNA, RNA, and protein synthesis were taught in a lecture-recitation mode by a biology professor at Brigham Young University for one 50-minute period. He used the rules, examples, and visual sequences from the video-disc archive at his fingertips, and punctuated his lecture with the use of the practice questions on video still-frames. With the practice questions on the screen, the students were encouraged to vocalize their answers. They did so, with active involvement, shouting out the answer. The next video frame showed the correct answer, providing immediate group feedback. The same teacher taught another 50 students (same class of 100, divided in half) using his best overhead transparencies, slides, and film clips. The results on a test given to both groups was that the video-disc group scored one letter-grade higher than the AV-lecture group The validated instructional design, and active involvement in the video-disc group, apparantly improved the learning in this group.

We predict that computer-controlled video-disc systems will increasingly be used by teachers in a group-interactive mode. The disks will contain a substantial archive of validated instructional materials, both visual and textual, and audio where appropriate. Teachers will be able to add their own text, graphics, and audio displays to an associated magnetic disk. The result would be to add a file of the teacher's own "overhead transparencies," some of which were animated. The future system will also include simulations that can be run in a group mode. It will include data that can be retrieved and displayed graphically for all to see.

We further predict the development of individual response units that can be held by each student, probably communicating by infrared so that no wiring to each seat is necessary. This will promote a new kind of group interaction where the consensus of the group, or the teacher's responses to a summary display of the group choices, determines the flow of events. The responses can be recorded and scored to monitor the progress of each student individually, even though the responses were made in a group-paced situation. Quizzes can be given this way.

There are several reasons for this prediction, having to do with economics, teaching traditions, and learning traditions. It is more economical to have one computer-controlled videodisc system per classroom than to have one for each individual student. Even if shared in a resource room, the need is for one per 4–7 students, instead of one per 25–30. It is also more economical in curriculum development. To make lessons stand alone, so that a solitary and possibly subpar learner can have all the explanations needed to proceed alone, is costly in development time and money. In group interactive mode, all of the context and unexpected questions can be handled by the teacher and the knowledgeable students.

Group CAE also fits existing teaching and learning traditions better. As shown previously, when a CAE application jars too many traditions, especially the schedule, it is a candidate for nonsurvival. Why not tap into these traditions and rituals of classroom learning and enhance them with CAE instead of trying to depose them? One-on-one CAE can take the place of individual seat work or study hall, and can evolve from that basis, but group CAE can assume its proper role. It has been several years since Lipson (1976), one of the pioneers in the development of *Individually Prescribed Instruction* (IPI), wrote on its strengths and limits. He emphasized "the hidden strengths of conventional instruction" and cited the schedule common to all, the traditions, and even the ritual significance of some commonplace classroom methods. Teachers and students are socialized into these traditions and rituals, and know them almost instinctively. After a long period of neglect of group methods, CAE will do well to flow with and enhance these strengths.

Broadcasting lessons and data. The second prediction is that satellite broadcasting will be used to download CAE lessons. These lessons will include three forms of data: video pictures, digitized audio, and digital-computer programs. The digital data readable by a computer will include the instructions for all the usual CAE interactions with good graphics display, audio, and response devices.

The school or industrial organization using this method of distribution will have an optical disc-recorder attached to a satellite receiving-dish and will receive a 13- to 15-minute recording. If the 14 minutes were all digitized audio it would translate to more than 9 hours of analog audio. If it were all interactive computer exercises, it could easily translate to dozens of hours of interactive exercises (100 million bytes of digital data). Thus, a 14-minute broadcast made up of some combination of video still-frames, audio, video motion, computer text and graphics, and computer interactions could easily generate a dozen hours of interactive instructions, or of group displays and interactions, or of productivity-improving computer programs. The computer programs could be "locked" so that they could not be used without paying a fee, after receiving over the telephone a unique code number for opening the resource files.

The distribution benefits of this innovation are enormous. The satellite cost to distribute this much data is very low, even though there may be 100 megabytes of computer data, or 23,940 full-color video-frames with 13.3 minutes of accompanying audio or any combination of the above. An hour of satellite time costs $600, so a 15 minute burst would cost $150, but could be delivered to hundreds, and later thousands, of users.

Knowledge-base publishing. New technologies for replicating inexpensively files of information which contain computer-readable digital code, video pictures, and audio will have a major inpact in publishing. The inexpensively replicated files, probably on small, plastic discs, will provide a strong alternative to textbooks as a way of replicating and distributing knowledge. Books have inherent in them all of the representation problems and production problems of the printing technology founded by Gutenburg: how to represent knowledge in words, or at greater costs with the addition of mathematical symbols, line drawings, and perhaps a few photographic images.

By contrast, the knowledge-base discs will offer far more representational and interactive power. To use these discs will require work stations with a powerful CPU, at least a medium-resolution color monitor, a digital-to-analog audio converter, a keyboard, and a mouse. The powerful CPU, equipped with artificially intelligent software, will permit powerful searches, queries requiring deductive reasoning, and editors to add the user's own knowledge to the database.

Products now exist on the market which are the forerunners of such a possibility. One product will transfer a color video image to 65,000 bytes of digital data. Audio can be digitized with good quality at 3,000 bytes per second. Floppy discs are soon consumed by such numbers, but new optical memories can easily handle it. An optical videodisc can store 200 million bytes of digital data, and a small, 5.5 inch CD–ROM *(compact-disc, read-only memory)* will hold 550 million bytes. CDs are available now for digital music, and will be commonplace vehicles for distributing digital data when this chapter is in print. This means that concepts can be represented visually, with full video, accompanied by voice or music, with animation or live motion, or with those dynamic computer graphics presentations that allow us to see the previously unseen. Knowledge can be represented in computer-readable data structures that lend themselves to manipulation by graphics programs, statistical programs with graphing capability, or artificially intelligent programs that reason about the knowledge.

Applied Artificial Intelligence has come into its own in recent years with the development of *expert systems.* An expert system uses a knowledge base of computer-readable symbols representing facts and formal rules about a knowledge domain, and informal rules or heuristics used to reduce search through the knowledge base and to solve problems using informal reasoning. An inference engine uses the data in the knowledge base to answer queries posed by a user that are relevant to the knowledge domain. Search procedures and deduction procedures are used to answer the queries, or to respond with information to help the user sharpen the query. It is called an expert system because the knowledge is obtained by interviewing one or more experts in a domain and getting them to help validate the facts, rules, and heuristics (Hayes-Roth et al., 1983; Waterman, 1986). The completed system performs about as the expert would do in answering an appropriately narrow class of queries put to it.

Experts now toil to write books and articles about their knowledge domains. Soon they will be able to publish the representations they used during the computer-assisted work that led to the development of the knowledge—the word-processor files, the computer graphics, the statistics, the computer programs, and the clean and simple lists of facts, rules, and heuristics.

How will the knowledge bases become clean and simple? It is now possible for a scientist or knowledge worker to formalize facts and rules in the predicate logic, a language first introduced in the sixth grade. Logic is far closer to natural English than is a computer language, and is accessible to knowledge workers of all kinds (Hogger, 1984). After it is entered, knowledge workers can test and refine that growing knowledge base through the power of an inference engine with a theorem prover. Is one assertion a consequence of the existing assertions? The inference engine will find out. Is it inconsistent logically with the other assertions? Some emerging inference engines can tell. All knowledge in any field that can be expressed symbolically can be refined in this manner. (See also Michie, 1983, who describes "The Knowledge Refinery.")

The purchaser of the knowledge base can peruse it, as with a book, but without being limited to representations in the form of words and symbols. More importantly, one can pose questions to the symbolic part of the knowledge base and get answers. One can be given editing tools to add one's own facts and rules to the knowledge base and test and refine the resulting new combination. Not only will computers as tools in the hands of experts enable them to discover and express new concepts, but in the hands of new users will enable the knowledge to be a living thing, quickly growing beyond the conception of the originator. In the hands of an original and skilled user it will evolve far faster than it would with any creation of marginal notes in the books of the old delivery system.

THE EVOLUTION OF KNOWLEDGE TECHNOLOGIES

Knowledge technology includes those methods and mechanisms that mankind has evolved for the *acquisition* of knowledge or expertise from one or more human masters, and the *representation* of that knowledge in appropriately usable form. Once acquired and represented in words, pictures, or interactive algorithms, the knowledge can be *replicated*. A replication of the acquired knowledge is usable in teaching interactions designed to pass that knowledge on to learners. Knowledge technology is involved with materials development. It includes, on the hardware side, the printing press, audio recorders, video-recorders, word processors, text editors, graphics editors, film and videotape editors, and the like. Knowledge technology also has its softer side, including the methodologies for interviewing experts to acquire knowledge; defining tasks and objectives as intermediate representations; determining strategies for re-presenting the knowledge to students; and methods for packaging and disseminating the replicated knowledge and teaching potential. The chapter by Branson on instructional systems development (ISD) in this book emphasizes the softer side of knowledge technology.

CAE has begun to have and will continue to have an important impact on knowledge technology. This impact is usually discussed under such headings as *authoring systems, computer aids to ISD,* and more recently, from the field of artificial intelligence, *knowledge engineering.* In this section it is our goal to trace some significant developments in the evolution of knowledge technologies.

Human Modeling

When we think of a human master teaching one or more students, the ideal case mentioned at the first of this chapter, we think of human modeling (Bandura, 1977). It is one of the earliest and still one of the most powerful methods of transferring knowledge. One person, the master, models a performance, which will generally include both vocalizations and skilled movements. The observers, learners who if they master it will later become formal or informal teachers themselves, attempt to duplicate the performances and receive feedback in the form of corrective advice. They repeat the modeling until they have it right. It is important to mention this at the outset, because human modeling is remarkably strong in teaching, among other things, skilled movements and the subtleties of intonation in vocalizations. These subtleties convey emotions, value, and have an enormous impact on the purposes and motivation of the learner. Delivery technologies, including the printing press and the common types of computer-aided education, are extremely weak in replication of the feedback interactions in correcting movements and vocalizations. This observation and much experience with CAE leads us to the conclusion that teachers are needed in CAE environments for modeling and coaching, especially for movements and vocalizations and the values and motivational affects these convey. Teachers are also needed for many other matters including scheduling and conducting group activities.

The Written Word as a Knowledge Technology

Since human masters can rarely perform as models and coaches for more than a few learners, writing has long been used to replicate a portion of the knowledge of masters. The portion replicated includes their explanations, parables, and sayings, and descriptive or narrative reports by observers. For centuries, replication was limited to the tedious and costly methods of manual copying. The replication worked if you could afford such expensively prepared manuscripts, and if you had the skills to read them. The printing press revolutionized that.

The Replication of Work Models

We use the term *work model* to describe a kind of representation of the performance aspects of a master's knowledge besides, or in addition to, those that can be represented in words. A work model is a small, interactive model of some part of the master's work (Bunderson et al., 1981). It can be presented to the learner, giving the learner an opportunity to perform that work. To be complete, the work model must have provision for corrective feedback. It can be used to demonstrate performances of a task, and then to allow practice with feedback. It is a far more complete description of a class of practice exercises than is a written behavioral objective.

Printing is weak in replicating the opportunities for practice. Unless the master's domain of work tasks happens to be highly symbolic, lexical, or verbal, then practice excercises consisting of paper-and-pencil questions sample poorly from that domain. We would expect little transfer to the real work tasks. Learners need to practice, at first slowly and with errors, the tasks that masters perform with skill and effectiveness. Learners need to have feedback on their performances so that they can correct them as rapidly as possible. For this reason, the existence of an apprentice system persisted during the Middle Ages in the guilds and continues to this day in any number of fields (including graduate education at our universities).

This is where CAE has offered a true discontinuity from the past delivery-system. Even as the printing press permitted the replication of the verbalizations of and about master's performances, CAE allows the replication of work models, organized as a hierarchy of tasks and exercises. This hierarchy extends from simple and partial tasks novices can perform to the complex and totally integrated tasks that masters can perform.

The ability to simulate aspects of a master's work (that is, to execute work models that provide job-like practice for the learner) is a fundamental contribution of CAE. The essence of this seminal contribution is the ability to replicate *interactions*. The learner makes a response to the work-model simulator; the work-model simulator immediately presents feedback as to how the learner's response will affect the system. In addition to natural feedback, which the learner would see from some pictured piece of the work being simulated, the feedback can be evaluative. It can be of the type that a coach would give to correct and guide the learner's responses.

In the remainder of this section, we will discuss the evolution of knowledge technologies for acquiring and representing the two main forms of replicated knowledge, *presentations* and *work models*.

Replicating Presentations

Writing and drawing (or painting) were the first two methods used to replicate the presentations about masters and their mastery. Writing as an early technology involved the forming of the characters, the care of quill pens, ink, and parchments, the selection of different colors, conventions for sub-headings, highlights, indices, and so forth. We are all familiar with the evo-lution of technologies related to writing; the development of movable type, the development of the typewriter, the development of duplication technolo-gies. More recently the evolution includes the development of word proces-sors, text processors, page-layout systems, tele-transmission of text symbols, and other systems. This is a remarkable recent and continuing evolution.

The evolution of technology for replicating pictures has a similar history. It includes the evolution of painting methods and materials, the evolution of woodcuts, copper plates, and other methods of pictorial reproduction, the evolution of photography, and photo-lithograpy. More recently, it includes the development of computer graphics, digitized images, and processing methods for video-camera-scanned pictorial data. This is a revolution now as significant as that in text processing. Today professionals are using powerful computer graphics systems with remarkable software for manipulat-ing digital representations of images, editing them, and enhancing them with software to manipulate texture, shading, and perspective. Where text and pictures are to be intermixed, the software will do it. The output is in a variety of media, ranging from print to film. Even children are using per-sonal computers with bit-mapped graphics to create original graphics. It is easy to integrate them into text presentations and print them out on matrix printers.

Audiovisuals.   An important line of evolution in knowledge presentation runs through the development of photography and radio, the evolutionary steps through silent motion pictures, "talkies," color motion pictures, television, videotape, and now, videodiscs. Video and film allow us to model behavioral sequences or at least to demonstrate skilled movements and subtle vocalizations, with all of the value-laden and emotion-laden affect of back-ground music. The arts of audio recording and editing, video-recording and editing and the technologies of the associated studio equipment are undergo-ing a transformation, due to the power of computer technology. Both video and audio can be digitized and then edited with exponentially more powerful levels of control. Major portions of many motion pictures are now produced by computer graphics. This evolution parallels the developments in text and still-picture processing.

Digitized audio, digitized images and the tremendously enhanced capabili-ties for editing them are transforming production methods. Today's expen-sive video– and audio-studios are introducing large computers and image-processing software. With it they can create more new and special effects, and do old things, such as animation, far faster and more productively. At the other extreme, less elaborate video- and audio-editing and image-processing systems are emerging using much smaller, less expensive video and audio storage systems controlled by inexpensive computers. This is going to put into the hands of many creative people the capability for obtaining new and existing visual and auditory information, digitizing it, editing it, and transforming it in a variety of creative ways, using synthesizing capabilities; and transforming it into final products, which can be replicated on magnetic or optical memories. As predicted in the previous section, these will be distributed on CD-ROMS or vidodiscs, or broadcast to read/write optical discs.

Knowledge Technologies for Work Models

The evolution of knowledge technologies to aid in the design, development, and replication of work models has progressed away from the old print-based delivery system in a series of steps. First, drill programs were developed that modeled workbook exercises but provided scoring. Then tutorials and testing systems were developed to model verbal-knowledge tasks. Recently, more lifelike games and simulations are beginning to predominate. The drills provided practice and feedback with tasks low in the hierarchy of skills in mathematics, reading, and language arts. Computer graphics and audio have enabled drill or practice exercise sets to become work models for a broader class of objectives; that is, tasks that a "master" of school mathematics and language arts can perform.

In order to make practice more interesting and fun, practice exercises are increasingly embedded in game-like situations. Some software publishers have made a good business out of diskettes that package games involving practice on school subjects. These diskettes include limited tutorials, but the game-like interactions make the programs attractive to buyers. At the higher levels of mastery, the games will become true work-model simulations of complex tasks having social value in the world of work. These work models will be used increasingly in job training. Visible examples of this trend exist in computer-controlled videodisc simulations of medical diagnosis and patient management, equipment operation, equipment maintenance, user directions for sophisticated new software packages, and scientific laboratory simulations.

It has been very costly to acquire and represent the knowledge in work-model simulations. It is costly both to figure out what the image and audio material should be, as well as to produce it. It is very costly to write the computer software to make the simulation respond as the real-world system would do to every reasonable action that a person might take. For example, do the authors have to photograph 360 pictures of a sweep radarscope, one picture for every degree the scope might depict? Does the software have to include anticipated branches for every possible permutation of switch settings on a complex instrument panel, with visuals for every possibility? Even if there were only 16 switches or display conditions and they each had only two settings, this would generate the requirement for a software decision table with 2^{16} or 64K separate situations. A videodisc has only 54,000 still frames.

Computer graphics is one solution. A function can calculate the position of the radar sweep and overlay a line on one general-purpose, video image of the blank scope. It can turn a computer-generated "light" on and off on a video image of a control panel. Forcing a limited sequence with only a few branches per choice point is the most common solution to limiting the exponential explosion of possibilites. Unfortunately, this makes the exercise appear "canned" and eliminates many logical sequences a novice might perform on a real-world patient or piece of equipment.

Artificial intelligence and work models. Methods developed in the computer-science field of artificial intelligence (AI) are applicable to the problem of developing better work models more inexpensively. AI methods have dealt with the problem of exponential explosion of possibilities in a variety of ways. These methods can be built into "smart simulators" that are far more than a branching decision table of all the possibilities an author of a simulation wants to consider. For example, a symbolic model of the operation of the radarscope can be written in *predicate logic.* The logical description of the radarscope can be tested to make sure it is correct. It can be linked to computer functions that calculate and display graphics, such as the radar sweep or the lights to be turned on and off. Other functions enable the logic programs to select the video-frame or sequence, or the audio sequence and play it at the right moment.

The logical description of the system to be simulated contains the domain knowledge about the system. Another part of the knowledge base can include intructional prescriptions for generating coaching comments, or changing the sequence or approach, depending on what the student is doing. An inference engine of proper design can both run the simulation and generate the coaching commentary.

Intelligent work-model simulations will be used first in expensive, high-risk training where they are cost-effective compared with three-dimensional simulators of actual equipment, human bodies, or complex environments. Later, as the power of large computers migrates to small chips in personal computers, and the methods are refined, AI methods will become available for developing work models for schools, colleges, regular job training in workplaces, and homes.

AI and the Knowledge Problem

The knowledge problem of education is to do our work with greater smartness. AI methods are perhaps the most promising approach. As expertise grows in any area, the symbolizable parts of it can be acquired from the experts by new educational professionals analogous to AI's knowledge engineers. These people will observe and interview the experts, defining tasks and measurable goals, as in ISD. It is an indictment of ISD that it has not dealt rigorously with domain knowledge. Going beyond ISD, they will represent the expert domain knowledge in some form such as predicate logic. Such representations will form the basis for smart work model simulations to provide the practice and feedback on the specified tasks.

It is not just in a subject matter like medical or equipment diagnosis that they will accomplish these ends, but in the expert work of knowledge acquisition, representation, and transfer itself, for example:

1. The expertise of acquiring knowledge about tasks and goals, representing it in computer-usable forms, editing and evaluating it, can be built into computer tools. An expert system can guide the knowledge analyst in using these tools for front-end analysis.

2. The expertise of producing teaching presentations and work models can be built into expert systems to help instructional developers make wise design decisions.

3. The expertise of writing textual displays for CAE frames can be computerized in an advice-giving expert system for writers.

4. The expertise for using such features as graphics, color, and animation in CAE, can be captured in an advising system for display designers.

5. The expertise of interpreting formative evaluation data and specifying revisions can be made available.

6. The multitude of teaching decisions during on-line instruction using CAE can be made more intelligent. When a student or group is heading for trouble, expert systems can recommend alternative actions having the best hope of success.

The potential of these new knowledge technologies is as significant as that for knowledge-base publishing. Both go together. Knowledge-base publishing has the potential for gradually replacing the old print-based delivery system, as well as the old educational curriculum built within its constraints. The knowledge technologies outlined in this section for acquiring, representing, replicating, and making more intelligent the delivery of the knowledge, are required to expedite the growth of knowledge-base publishing.

SUMMARY

CAE is a rapidly moving field. It is an interdisciplinary adventure; contributions are coming rapidly from many fronts. A chapter like this one can easily become dated. Because of this, we have tried to maintain a balance between what has happened in the past and what is coming in the future. The primary movement is not coming from within the traditional fields of education or training. It is coming from fields of engineering, computer science, artificial intelligence, robotics, and from the applications built by users of new knowledge technologies in information and media fields. The results of the rapid development of knowledge and work technologies are to transform the way jobs are done in all forms of knowledge work, and in much of manufacturing and professional work. Teaching and training work also is subject to the productivity-transforming potential of these new technologies. That cluster of applied information technologies we have called CAE is moving into society at a rapid rate. It is transforming the way information is produced and distributed in the media, and is transforming the nature of many jobs. Education will follow these societal movements, both in using the information technologies to do its own work, and in adjusting its curriculum to the new jobs that are being produced. Such rapid change can be very threatening, but we have attempted to show that the prospects are more hopeful than threatening.

We have argued that the problems of education cannot be solved by the old delivery system, for it has reached its limits and does not inherently have the capability of solving the problems of work and knowledge. The potential for exponentially increasing both work and appropriate knowledge was shown in several ways. First, the technologies themselves were reviewed in a framework of the work that people can do: sensing, remembering, deciding, and acting. Next, we showed how these technologies have been applied, over the past 20 years of the development of CAE, in the two broad trends of mainline CAI and computer-centered CAI. We predicted that three new trends will become important and visible over the next decade: group-interactive CAE, broadcasting of interactive programs involving video, audio, and computer code, and knowledge-base publishing.

These three predictions all depend on, and will follow, developments in what we have called *knowledge technologies*. These technologies are transforming the work of people who produce text, graphics, photos, video, and computer programs. Artificial intelligence is opening up new possibilities for delivering knowledge in forms that will promote new levels of human interaction with that knowledge. In the future, book-like materials will be only one part of the media delivered on a magnetic or optical disk. Simulated work models will allow learners to practice tasks more like those that masters in the field can perform. Advanced users will be able to query the knowledge bases, using machine–aided reasoning, add to the knowledge and discover new relationships within it. An extrapolation of the mainline CAE history promises changes in education and training as we have known it. An extrapolation of the computer-centered CAE and knowledge technology trends suggests that the content as well as the methods of education will be transformed.

REFERENCES

Abelsen, H., & di Sessa, A. (1981). *Turtle geometry: Computation as a medium for exploring mathematics.* Cambridge, MA: MIT Press.

Bandura, A. (1977). *Social learning theory.* Englewood Cliffs, NJ: Prentice-Hall.

Bunderson, C. V. (1975). The TICCIT project: Design strategy for educational innovation. In S. A. Harrison & L. A. Stolurow (Eds.), *Improving instructional productivity in higher education.* Englewood Cliffs, NJ: Educational Technology.

Bunderson, C. V., Baillio, B., Olsen, J. B., Lipson, J. I., & Fisher, K. M. (1984). Instructional effectiveness of an intelligent videodisc in biology. *Machine-Mediated Learning, 1,* 175–215.

Bunderson, C. V., & Faust, G. W. (1976). Programmed and computer-assisted instruction. In N. L. Gage (Ed.), *The psychology of teaching methods.* Seventy-fifth Yearbook of the National Society of Studies in Education. Chicago: University of Chicago Press.

Bunderson, C. V., Gibbons, A. S., Olsen, J. B., & Kearsley, G. P. (1981). Work Models: Beyond instructional objectives. *Instructional Science, 10,* 205–215.

Christensen, P. E. (1956). Work-sampling: A stroboscopic view of teaching. *Educational Administration and Supervision, 42,* 230–243.

Conant, E. H. (1973). *Teacher and paraprofessional work productivity.* Lexington, MA: D. C. Heath.

Denham, C., & Lieberman, A. (Eds). (1980). *Time to learn.* Washington, DC: National Institute of Education, U. S. Department of Education.

Hayes-Roth, F., Waterman, D. A., & Lenat, D. B. (1983). *Building expert systems.* Reading, MA: Addison-Wesley.

Heuston, D. H. (1985). *Some of the critical issues in introducing computer technology into schools.* Unpublished manuscript. WICAT Systems, Orem, UT.

Hogger, C. J. (1984). *Introduction to logic programming.* New York: Academic Press.

Hulin, C. L., Drasgow, F., & Parsons, C. K. (1983). *Item response theory: Application to psychological measurement.* Homewood, IL: Dow Jones-Irwin.

Inouye, D. K., Bunderson, C. V., Olsen, J. B., Hansen, E., & Robertson, J. (1986). *The WICAT learner profile.* Unpublished manuscript. WICAT Education Institute, Provo, UT.

Lipson, J. I. (1976). Hidden strengths of conventional instruction. *Arithmetic Teacher, 23*(1), 11–15.

Lord, F. M. (1980). *Applications of item response theory to pratical testing problems.* Hillsdale, NJ: Lawrence Erlbaum Associates.

Michie, D. (1983). Knowledge refineries. In J. E. Hayes & D. Michie (Eds.), *Intelligent systems: The unprecedented opportunity.* E. Horwood, NY: Halsted Press.

Mislevy, R. J., & Bock, R. D. (1982). *Maximum likelihood item analysis and test scoring with binary logistic models.* Mooresville, ID: Scientific Software Inc.

Papert, S. (1980). *Mindstorms: Children, computers, and powerful ideas.* New York: Basic Books.

Suppes, P., Jerman, M. & Brian, D. (1968). *Computer assisted instruction: Stanford's 1965–1966 arithmetic program.* New York: Academic Press.

Waterman, D. A. (1986). *A Guide to expert systems.* Reading, MA: Addison-Wesley.

Weisgerber, R. A. (1971). *Developmental efforts in individualized learning.* Itasca, IL: Peacock.

AUTHOR NOTES

C. Victor Bunderson is Vice President for Research Management, Educational Testing Service.

Dillon K. Inouye is Associate Professor of Instructional Science, Brigham Young University.

Credit is due to the WICAT Education Institute, with its experimental Waterford School, where Bunderson and Inouye performed research and developed concepts described herein, and to Knowledge Engineering, Inc., source of the AI and knowledge technology concepts.

12 Artificial Intelligence and Computer-Based Learning

Robert D. Tennyson
University of Minnesota

Ok Choon Park
U.S. Army Research Institute

Since the 1960s, the use of computer technology in education has focused on means and methods to enhance the teaching process. For example, computer-managed instruction (CMI) provides teachers with automated record keeping and scheduling of instructional events. Other teaching applications have included simulations and games. In most applications, the purpose of the computer has been to augment teacher-directed instruction.

However, recent research and theory-development in human learning and cognition have narrowed the focus of computer applications to variables and conditions that are directed to the promotion of learning rather than the improvement of teaching (Tennyson & Breuer, 1984). As a result, the distinction between forms of instructional applications (e.g., computer-assisted instruction, computer-managed instruction, simulations) has given way to instructional systems that exhibit direct (and predictable) and theory-based relationships between learning and instructional variables.

Not all the concern has been devoted to the relations of learning theory to instructional theory (Gagné & Dick, 1983); there is also the question of the possible effect of computer technology on the improvement of learning. Therefore, instead of the traditional practice in educational research of testing computer-assisted instruction versus conventional instruction, the research paradigm first defines a learning theory and then identifies possible instructional variables that would facilitate learning. Along with the latter variables, consideration is also given to computer-based variables thought to contribute to improved learning.

The purpose of this chapter is to review the research and development of an important computer-based variable that is making a significant contribution to learning. This variable comes from the computer-science investigations of artificial intelligence (AI). The term intelligence is defined as competency in problem solving; artificial means any humanly formulated method that may accomplish the goal of solving problems. In this context, AI does not imply simulation of human problem solving. It is, rather, any rational means that may be used to enhance the solving of problems.

Within this chapter we will review the initial, and now conventional, applications of AI in computer-based learning (usually referred to as intelligent computer-assisted instruction, or ICAI) followed by a presentation of a specific, AI computer-based learning (CBL) system. A major thesis in our presentation is the growth of theory-based instructional systems during the 1970s. This growth is seen in the movement from model-based to theory-based instructional systems (Park & Tennyson, 1983). Theory-based instructional systems, as contrasted to model-based, represent attempts to make direct and predictable connections between the instructional variables and learning outcomes. Model-based instructional systems, on the other hand, represent attempts to demonstrate a means or method of instruction without the concept of empirical verification. Most ICAI systems are model-based development efforts, aimed at demonstrating the application of AI methods to instruction, that is, efforts to enhance instruction through computer-based variables associated with AI. For example, methods such as natural-language processing, expert tutorials, computer languages developed for instruction, and hardware-software characteristics (e.g., graphics, color, animation) are used extensively. In contrast, the more recent AI developments trace their specific instructional and computer-based design variables directly to definable logic based on learning theory, backed up by empirical verification (Tennyson & Christensen, 1985).

In the next section we will provide a review of the tradition and direction of AI in educational computing. As such, we use the common label usually associated with AI and educational computing. In the third section we further narrow our presentation to a specific AI computer-based learning system: an AI system, that in contrast to the ICAI model-based systems, is a theory-based system. In the present context, the term model-based refers to instructional methods that demonstrate the use of some technique or variable without the direct verification of why it may result in improved learning. For example, visuals are often said to help learners understand information, but the question of why they help is not always understood. The term theory-based implies that the technique of instruction is explained in terms of its effect in aiding learning; the verification of method is not simply assumed.

MODEL-BASED ICAI

For the last decade, AI has generated strong interest and enthusiasm in industry and universities. It has become an important component for research and development in high-technology fields. AI principles and techniques have been applied in education as well; the product is often referred to as intelligent tutoring systems (Sleeman & Brown, 1982) or intelligent computer-assisted instruction (ICAI).

ICAI systems can take many forms, but essentially they arrange various components of an instructional system by using AI principles and techniques in a way which allows both the student and the program flexibility. The learning environment closely resembles what may occur when students and teachers sit down one-on-one and attempt to learn together. Thus, a well developed ICAI system may be able not only to recite specific questions but also to use and process knowledge stored in the system in asking questions and in responding to student questions. Theoretically, the ICAI system does not act on the basis of pre-entered questions, anticipated answers, prespecified branches, and so forth, but on the knowledge accumulated while a student learns (Feigenbaum, 1977). It has general procedural guidelines and criteria that depend on its knowledge structure and also on recent events, such as a student's response history. An important feature of many ICAI systems is that they may be able to carry on natural-language dialogues with the student in generating questions and their corresponding answers. The ability to use a natural-language dialogue allows an interaction between the student and computer in which questions and answers come from both sides.

AI principles and techniques are applied in the representation of the knowledge domain to be taught, the natural-language dialogue, and methods of inference for hypotheses about the student learning-process. In this section, we will review the general structure of ICAI systems, present some examples, and conclude with a discussion of their limitations. The detailed technical procedures involved, including computer programs, are beyond the scope of this chapter.

Three Components of ICAI Systems

As is true of other instructional systems, the operational functions of an ICAI system are determined by three main components: the content (or information) to be learned, the instructional strategy, and a mechanism for understanding the student's current knowledge state. In ICAI systems, these components are referred to as the expertise module, the student-model module, and the tutoring module (Clancey, Barnett, & Cohen, 1982).

Ideally, an expertise module should have its own problem-solving expertise as well as static knowledge of the subject matter; a student-model module should have its own diagnostic capabilities; and the tutoring module should be able to provide intelligent learning guidance with its own explanatory capabilities. Early ICAI systems mainly focused on representation of the domain knowledge. Since the mid-1970s, however, modeling the students' learning behavior and tutorial strategies for presenting the materials have been some of the main issues in the development of ICAI systems (Sleeman & Brown, 1982).

The ultimate goal of an ICAI system is to have a program which has powerful models in each of these three components, and to have these components working together to produce the most effective learning environment possible. Each of the three components is elaborated below.

Expertise modules.   An expertise module consists of the domain knowledge that the system presents to the student. The instructional information includes both the content to be taught and the application of that knowledge to solve related problems. The former of these is referred to as declarative knowledge and the latter as procedural knowledge. The procedural knowledge represents the methods used by experts in solving problems of the specific type.

Because the expertise module is charged with the task of generating questions and assessing the correctness of a student's problem solution, information must be organized in the structure of a computer program for the intelligent manipulation of the data in the teaching and learning process. That is, ICAI developers determine how to encode the information in the system's data structure and procedures. The domain knowledge of a subject matter may be organized in a data structure by using one or more of the following methods:

1. Semantic nets in a large, static database which incorporates all the facts necessary to teach the knowledge. A net consists of codes representing objects, concepts, events, and links between the nodes, representing their interrelations.

2. Procedural representation that corresponds to subskills in well-specified situations that a student must learn in order to acquire the complete skill being taught. In a procedural representation, knowledge consists of small subskills preceding specific tasks in well-specified situations.

3. Production rules that are used to construct modular representations of skills and problem-solving methods. The basic idea of production rules is that the knowledge database consists of rules, called productions, in the form of condition–action pairs: "If this condition occurs, then do this action."

4. Frames that are data structures, including declarative and procedural information in predefined internal relations. A frame for a generic knowledge domain has specific knowledge slots for facts that are typically known about the generic knowledge and attached procedures for determining the specific nature of the facts.

5. Logic that is a kind of calculus of the process for making inferences from facts. From the representation of knowledge in a formal logic database, there is a set of rules, called the rules of inference in logic, by which facts that are known to be true can be used to derive other facts that must also be true.

Although all of the above methods of knowledge representation are interchangeable, for most cases one method may be better than others depending on the characteristics of the knowledge to be represented. Also, multiple representations of the same information with different methods may be used simultaneously for different purposes. Knowledge structured in an expertise module may be used for acquiring more knowledge with its self-learning capabilities, for retrieving facts from the knowledge base relevant to the given problem, and for reasoning about these facts in search of a solution.

Student-model module. The student-model module deals with the method of representing the student's learning progress of the material to be learned. This module is used to make hypotheses about the student's misconceptions and suboptimal performance strategies so that the tutoring model can point them out, indicate why they are wrong, and suggest corrections.

Because in ICAI a student's knowledge state is basically represented as a subset of an expert's knowledge base, the model is constructed by comparing the student's performance with the computer-based expert's behavior on the same problem (*overlay model,* Goldstein, 1982). Another approach is to use a student's misconceptions, which are not primarily subsets of the expert's knowledge, as variants of the expert's knowledge (*buggy model,* Brown & Burton, 1978). A buggy model represents domain knowledge as rules and potential misconceptions as variants of the rules (*mal-rules;* Sleeman, 1982).

Modeling the student knowledge uses: (a) simple AI pattern-recognition techniques to evaluate the student's knowledge acquisition process from the response history and (b) flags in the subject-matter semantic net (or the rule base), representing components on which the student has demonstrated mastery. Major information sources for maintaining the student model are: (a) student problem-solving behavior observed by the system, (b) direct questions asked of the student, (c) assumptions based on the student's learning experience, and (d) assumptions based on some measure of the difficulty of the subject-matter materials (Clancey et al., 1982).

Information collected by the foregoing methods should be useful for making inferences about which subskills (or skills) the student does not have when there is a failure on a task and for explaining the student's behavior as a collection of knowledge components. Also, the information can be used for handling disorganized data arising because a student's mistakes come not only from mislearned information but also for other reasons (e.g., fatigue, distraction, cognitive overload).

Tutoring module.   A tutoring module is a set of instructional specifications of how the system should present materials to the student. The module integrates knowledge components structured in the expertise module, pedagogical methods, and AI techniques for employing natural-language dialogues.

This module interacts with the student in selecting problems to be solved, monitoring, and critiquing the student's performance, providing assistance upon request, and selecting remedial materials. Teaching methods are basically determined on the basis of diagnostic information obtained in the student modeling process. The program debugs the student's understanding by posing tasks and evaluating responses. The program's feedback specifically indicates which knowledge components the student has used incorrectly or less optimally, and may provide the knowledge components that the student should learn.

Representative methods used in ICAI systems are:

1. The Socratic method, which provides questioning in a way that encourages the student to think in terms of debugging his or her own knowledge. In the debugging process, the student is assumed to reason about what he or she knows and does not know and thereby to modify his or her conceptions (Stevens & Collins, 1977).

2. A coaching method in which the student is engaged in some activity like a computer game to provide an environment for the learning of related skills and general problem-solving ability. The goal of the program is to have the student enjoy and learn as a consequence of fun. In developing a tutoring model of this sort, various types of instructional strategies can be applied to determine desirable interactive formats and processes between the student and the program.

In consequence of the size and complexity of the AI domain, not all three of the components just described are fully developed in every system. Most systems focus on the development of a single part of what would constitute a fully usable system. The contribution of these three components to the development of ICAI is not limited to the single module. (See Clancey et al., 1982, for a comprehensive description of the three components.)

Development of ICAI

Carbonell's (1970) SCHOLAR system for teaching South American geography served as an impetus for the development of ICAI systems. SCHOLAR uses a complex but well-defined structure in the form of a network of facts, concepts, and procedures as a database. The elements of this network are units of information, defining words, and events in the form of multilevel tree lists. In SCHOLAR, the Socratic style is used. The system first attempts to diagnose the student's misconceptions and then presents materials that will help the student to recognize his or her own error (Collins, Wornock, & Passafiume, 1975). SCHOLAR's inference strategies for answering student questions and evaluating student answers are independent of the content of the semantic net and applicable in different domains.

SCHOLAR is extended by the WHY program (Stevens & Collins, 1977). WHY tutors students in the causes of rainfall, a complex geophysical process that is a function of many unrelated factors. WHY implements Socratic heuristics which describe the global strategies used by human tutors to guide the dialogue.

O'Shea developed a system referred to as the self-improving quadratic tutor (O'Shea, 1978). This system has two principal components: one is an adaptive-teaching program, which is expressed in a production rule; and the other is the self-improving component, which makes experimental changes in the production rules of the teaching program. The system is designed to conduct experiments on the teaching strategy by altering the production rules. Data are kept on the effectiveness of the changes, and those modifications which result in improved student performance are incorporated into the set of production rules. This work is particularly interesting in its adaptive nature, but has not been investigated.

Brown, Burton, and Bell (1975) developed the SOPHIE system, which is an attempt to create a reactive learning environment in which the student acquires problem-solving skills by trying out his or her own ideas rather than by receiving direct instruction from the system. SOPHIE incorporates a model of knowledge domain along with heuristic strategies for answering a student's questions. It provides critiques of the student's current learning paths, and generates alternative paths (Brown & Burton, 1978). SOPHIE allows the student to have a one-to-one relationship with a computer-based expert, who helps with the generation of the student's own ideas, experimenting with these ideas, and, when necessary, with debugging them. The principles of SOPHIE have been applied to constructing a diagnostic model (BUGGY) in learning basic, mathematical problem-solving skills and for developing a computer-coaching model in a discovery-learning environment (Burton & Brown, 1979). The BUGGY program provides a mechanism for explaining why a student is making a mistake, as opposed to simply identifying the mistake. BUGGY allows teachers to diagnose the underlying causes of students' errors by prescribing examples of systematic, incorrect behavior.

The coaching model is developed to identify diagnostic strategies required to infer a student's misunderstandings from observed behaviors and to identify various explicit tutoring strategies for directing the tutor to say the right thing at the right time. WEST is a coaching program designed to teach the appropriate manipulation of arithmetic expressions in a computer-gaming environment (Burton & Brown, 1979).

Clancey's (1979) GUIDON, another program for teaching diagnostic (medical) problem-solving, is different from other ICAI programs in terms of its mixed-initiative dialogue. GUIDON uses the prolonged and structured teaching interactions that go beyond responding to the student's last move (as in WEST) and beyond repetitive questioning and answering (as in SCHOLAR and WHY).

In GUIDON, the tutoring rules are organized into discourse procedures. The subject materials (medical diagnostic rules) are hierarchically grouped into a separate system, called MYCIN. This is a computer-based consultation system for diagnosis and therapy of infectious diseases. GUIDON's failure as a teaching system demonstrated that domain knowledge of expert systems cannot be effectively used as a knowledge base for ICAI systems without supplementation of other levels of domain knowledge during the teaching process, to help explain and organize the knowledge.

Suppes and his associates also applied AI techniques to the development of a proof checker (EXCHECK) capable of understanding the validity of a student's proof (Suppes, 1982). EXCHECK has no student-model module, but its inference procedures in the expertise module allow it to make assumptions about a student's reasoning and track the student's solutions. Thus it provides a reactive environment similar to that of SOPHIE.

Limitations of ICAI

ICAI systems seem to represent the state of the art in what "could be" in applying computer attributes to instruction. They appear to have the potential of offering fertile research opportunities in exploring how students learn and how we might be more effective in teaching them. However, the overall performance of ICAI systems is not satisfactory. Sleeman and Brown (1982, p. 3) have described the shortcomings of ICAI systems as follows:

1. The instructional material produced in response to a student's query or mistake is often at the wrong level of detail; the system assumes too much or too little student knowledge.

2. None of these ICAI systems can discover, and work within, the student's own (idiosyncratic) conceptualization to diagnose his or her "mind bugs."

3. The tutoring and critiquing strategies used by these systems are excessively ad hoc, reflecting unprincipled intuitions about how to control student behavior.

4. User interaction is still too restricted.

The overall performance of ICAI systems could be significantly improved by integrating learning theories and instructional design principles proposed by psychologists and instructional researchers. However, to overcome these shortcomings entirely seems to be difficult because of the following limitations for the development of ICAI systems:

First, the lack of a natural means for communication between the student and the computer is a major stumbling block for the development of ICAI systems. At this point, the natural-language dialogue is only possible within structured corrections of the information elements in the knowledge base (i.e., the system cannot generate or understand dialogues for newly encountered learning situations).

Second, the ability to capture a student's learning processes from the knowledge representation in the expertise module being used by the system is limited because it requires the ability to understand the different reasoning processes of individual students.

Third, the amount of work and technical skills required to specify the knowledge domain and the tutorial strategies in a system is a significant problem. Although some versions of AI programming languages are available on a personal computer, most ICAI systems still require processing machines that employ very powerful AI language (e.g., LISP, PROLOG).

Fourth, the AI techniques are less clearly applicable in the less structured subject-matter areas such as the humanities. Most existing ICAI systems are developed in well-structure taxonomic subject domains, such as mathematics and games.

A final issue which limits the theoretical and practical value of ICAI systems is that most systems have focused on the development of man-machine interaction capabilities (e.g., natural-language dialogue on very limited topics, rather than on issues of learning and instruction). Most problems and issues treated in ICAI systems are trivial and task-specific, with little generalizability. Considering these limitations, favorable future development of effective CAI systems should be based on instructional theories, rather than on intuition about and technical manipulation of man-machine interactive capability.

THEORY-BASED AI CBL

In the previous section we described computer-based instructional models that in various forms demonstrate the use of artificial-intelligent methods. Because the developers of these models were interested in advancing the art of instructional computing beyond the then-current design practices implied by the stimulus–response paradigm, there was little direct instructional theory development.   In this concluding section, we will present a specific computer-based learning (CBL) system that reflects our concern for a theory-based approach to AI CBL.

From an educational perspective, an instructional theory should deal with the processes of learning, memory, and cognition. The theory should define instructional variables and conditions that predictably improves: first, the acquisition of information; second, the storage and retrieval of knowledge; and third, the productive thinking process. A theory accounting for these three concepts might at first thought seem beyond the capabilities of conventional teaching forms. However, the potential of the computer in terms of its power and speed for variable manipulations and calculations makes possible the construction of a CBL system of considerable complexity. Such a system is capable of effecting the application of a theory which accounts for learning, memory, and cognition.

In two other articles (Park & Tennyson, 1983; Tennyson & Park, 1984) we review several CBL systems that exhibit various degrees of sophistication in applying AI methods as well as in attempting to be consistent with modern learning theory. Here, we will restrict the scope of this chapter to an in-depth description of one of these systems, the Minnesota Adaptive Instructional System (MAIS) (Tennyson, 1984).

The two main components of MAIS are built around the three concepts of learning, memory, and cognition. See Fig. 12.1. These two components are termed *macro,* referring to curriculum, and *micro,* referring to instruction. Within the macro-level, we define variables that relate directly to the concepts of memory and cognition, while the micro-level variables relate to events associated with learning. The variables within the macro-component establish the conditions of instruction, while the micro-component adjusts the instruction to meet moment-to-moment individual student learning needs. Both components interact in an iterative fashion; the initial conditions of instruction established in the macro-components adjust according to learner progress and needs in learning while in the micro-component. To discuss MAIS, we will first briefly review the computer-based AI methods of the management system. (Details of the actual program statements are available in Tennyson, Christensen, & Park, 1984.) Subsequent sections contain descriptions of each component.

AI Methods

As stated in the introduction to this chapter, AI methods have been applied in a wide range of applications. Many of the methods developed are in fact derived from specific needs, with little or no generalizability. In the area of behavorial sciences, most recent research work in AI methods has focused on

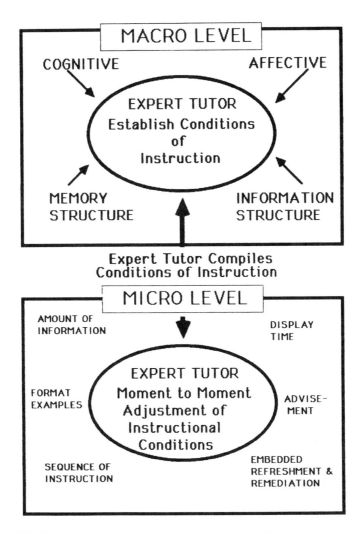

FIGURE 12.1 Minnesota Adaptive Instructional Systems (adapted from Tennyson & Christensen, 1985).

expert systems, using various algorithmic methods or tree structures for management of the learning. The purpose of these expert systems is to facilitate the retrieval of information in problem-solving applications; but not in problem formation. Conventional AI programming techniques closely resemble tree structures that string together possible data points that can then be interpreted to solve problems. Thus, the expert system approach to AI is a programming methodology to help experts solve problems (Amarel, 1983). Obviously, these expert systems are model-based, relying on the unique characteristics of the given expert from whom the structure is derived. This particular approach does not appear to be appropriate for design of learning management systems (Tennyson, 1984).

In contrast to the formal heuristic or tree-structure expert systems, are those employing informal heuristic methods. The use of informal heuristic methods in learning systems is built around a direct connection to cognitive-psychology theories of learning. An informal heuristic can be defined as a rule-of-thumb search strategy composed of variables that can be manipulated to provide increasingly better decisions as more knowledge is acquired. Frequently, program designers refer to informal heuristics as *fuzzy logic* statements because, unlike the production-rule statements used in formal heuristics, informal heuristics can be written as abstract, flexible statements which acquire assumptions with experience. Therefore, an informal heuristic can start to understand a situation and "think" about possible outcomes that do not exhibit correct or incorrect solutions. Also, informal heuristic methods differ dramatically from the formal heuristics methodology of AI programming in that they are usually written as conditional probability statements. In educational terms, an informal heuristic may be thought of as a higher-order rule statement rather than a depository of domain-specific information (Dörner, 1983).

We selected the informal heuristic approach for the MAIS management system because the flexibility offered by such programming techniques allows us to integrate various theory-based learning variables, and thus to avoid being forced to adjust the variables to a given programming method (e.g., few learning variables fit a tree-structure format). Additionally, informal heuristic systems conserve time by controlling the number of operations the system must perform to make a decision. Here is an important instructional-systems concept that is usually not a concern of formal heuristic-based ICAI systems, since they seldom directly address efficiency of decision making.

Macro-component

The primary purpose of the macro-component is to establish the initial conditions of instruction by considering the interaction of individual-difference variables with the content domain of a given curriculum. The term dynamic is used to describe the relationship between the macro- and micro-components of MAIS. At the micro-level, the conditions of instruction are adaptively adjusted to improve learning at any given moment. As the learner progresses through the instruction, appropriate information is sent continuously back to the macro-level to improve decision making constantly with regard to the conditions of instruction.

Figure 12.1 shows five main variables of the macro-component. The cognitive, affective, and memory structure variables represent areas of individual differences. Each of these three variables has differing effects on learning, and requires constant adjustment based on the information-structure variable. The fourth variable represents the unique features of the information domain to be learned in the curriculum. The fifth variable, expert tutor, establishes the conditions of instruction. The conditions of instruction represent specific instructional strategies based on the learning needs associated with Gagné's (1985) three types of cognitive behavior: verbal information, intellectual skills, and cognitive strategies. Within this chapter, we will discuss only the instructional variables and strategy associated with intellectual skills. The purpose is to limit our presentation to that part of the system which contrasts most to conventional ICAI systems. In dealing with verbal information, MAIS uses drill-and-practice variables that adapt to individual learning needs on both repetition placement and time. For cognitive-strategy learning, MAIS uses simulation techniques for student practice in using knowledge for productive and creative thinking (Breuer, 1985; Tennyson & Breuer, 1984). The macro-level conditions of instruction initially set the parameters of the micro-level instructional variables, which then adjust adaptively to the individual learning needs of each student.

Cognitive variable. Earlier we described how the three concepts of learning, memory, and cognition form the basic theoretical structure of MAIS. It is our view that theories of memory and cognition are appropriately applied at the curricular level of educational design. Although each has implications at the instructional level, delineation of persisting student characteristics (traits) makes them fit the parameters of the curricular decision-making level rather than those of the instructional level. For the variables of cognition, a number of basic factors seem to offer valuable weights in establishing the conditions of instruction. Our current MAIS program incorporates cognitive measures of intelligence, aptitude, ability, and cognitive style. We define intelligence as skill in problem solving, and view it in reference to intellectual competence. Intelligence, along with aptitude and ability, seem to be indices that remain fairly stable over extended periods of time; however, MAIS is capable of adjusting to individual learner differences in these areas, especially in developmentally oriented curricula. For example, there is evidence that mathematics ability may be subject to more dynamic improvement if conditions of instruction provide quality learning environments.

Cognitive style is a controversial area in education because of attempts by researchers to use it as a direct instructional variable without considering its interaction with other variables. However, research findings are of sufficient strength to recommend inclusion of cognitive style at the macro-level of decision making. At the present time, we have not included *learning style* as a component of this variable because of the apparent overlapping with cognitive style and the current absence of evidence regarding powerful interactions of learning style with instructional variables (Park, 1984).

Memory variable.   Our intent with respect to this variable is to account for knowledge currently in a learner's memory.   Recent experimental evidence appears to support strongly the importance of the learner's knowledge structure in learning (Tennyson, 1982).   The memory variable includes achievement measures on four types of necessary knowledge: background, associate, prerequisite, and prior knowledge. Briefly, we define each type of necessary knowledge as follows: Background refers to knowledge that is general and is only indirectly connected to the information to be learned.   Associate refers to knowledge that can be directly connected with the to-be-learned information.   For example, in learning educational statistics, background knowledge would be an understanding of the context in which specific examples are used, while associative knowledge would be an understanding of the various mathematical rules being used in a given statistical operation. Prerequisite refers to supportive knowledge that the student should already have in memory. And prior knowledge refers to that part of the information to be learned that the student already knows. Achievement in backgound knowledge is a major predictor of success in learning new information. However, given the range of possible scores in background knowledge, the interaction with the other three variables certainly establishes a different learner macro-profile than one which would include only a single variable of necessary knowledge.

The other three achievement measures of prerequisite, associate, and prior knowledge influence the conditions of instruction in terms of remediation and amount of instruction for the to-be-learned information.   Each measure becomes increasingly important the longer the curricular program—that is, they progressively assume more influence over the conditions of instruction. These factors are readily affected by the heuristic approach used in MAIS.

Affective variable.   This variable, long recognized as important but long neglected by instructional designers, lends itself well to the informal heuristic AI methods employed in MAIS. For example, research findings on motivation make it one of the most powerful variables in learning. But the answer to how it can be accounted for in instruction has been elusive (Tennyson & Breuer, 1984). Within MAIS, we can profile a learner's initial *motivation* and then progressively adjust its interactive influence as the learner progresses through the curriculum. Rather than considering motivation as a constant, it can be treated as a fluid factor adjusting with and to the other instructional variables. Similarly, *self-esteem* can be a major influence on the conditions of instruction, and can be adjusted within the curriculum while simultaneously affecting other variables.

Information structure.   The macro-level variables provide direct assessment information on each learner. This fourth variable brings into the decision-making process the structural conditions of the information to be learned. Cognitive learning theory recognizes the idea that the structure of information will influence learning (E. Gagné, 1985). Unfortunately, research findings call into question contemporary principles of *context analysis* without offering a replacement conception. Current content-analysis procedures dictate a taxonomic approach, using attributes of the content as the structure (Mandler, 1979). Recent research shows that information analyses which follow schematic structures may be the more suitable means for use in learning improvement (our own work in Tennyson et al., 1985, is an example). At the present time, MAIS uses as guidelines in content analysis, an information analysis that employs a schematic (or thematic) approach (Siaw, 1984). Unlike some of the other macro-variables, the information-structure variable influences directly a number of parameters in helping to establish the conditions of instruction.

Basically, we consider the relational structure of information in terms of its conceptual network. This helps to establish the schematic structure of information, which in turn influences the sequencing of the presentation. Additionally, the characteristics of the information's concepts are considered in terms of their dimensions and degree of variability (Tennyson & Cocchiarella, 1986). At this point there is an interaction with the memory-structure profile, making it possible to specify for the individual learner a unique information structure for information to be learned.

Expert tutor variables. The informal heuristics, the decision-making processes of Mais, are embedded within an expert tutorial which compiles the information from the four variables of the macro-component to establish the conditions of instruction. These conditions of instruction include type of learning outcome (i.e., verbal information, intellectual skill, and cognitive strategy), information structure, instructional strategies, forms of remediation, and mode of presentation.

To summarize, the macro-level component includes variables that interact with instruction according to individual differences, content structure, and instructional conditions. The variables, although trait-like in nature, undergo adjustments as additional data are acquired on each individual learner. With this progressive updating of the variables, the system becomes increasingly better at making decisions about conditions of instruction. These conditions make initial settings of the instructional variables of the micro-level component of MAIS.

Micro-component

The purpose of the micro-level component of MAIS is to individualize the instruction to learner differences, rather than merely making it self-instructional. In an article by Tennyson and Rothen (1977), the basic structure of MAIS was developed around Bayes's conditional probability method. At the present time, the micro-component at the intellectual-skills level is composed of six instructional-design variables that focus on the improvement of concept and rule learning. It does not directly deal with specific display characteristics, such as the use of color, graphics, and display layout. These variables are important elements of instructional development, and we follow them in the design of CBL, but the research literature does not offer sufficient evidence for them to be included as management variables at the present time. The current six design variables of MAIS at the micro-level are as follows: (1) amount of information, (2) sequence of information, (3) format of examples, (4) learning time, (5) refreshment and remediation of the necessary knowledge, and (6) advice on learning progress. Although these variables are listed here in a given order, there is no intent to indicate their value; they all interact within the expert tutor to enhance the instruction.

Amount of information. With expository instruction, a major concern is the amount of information necessary for the learning of a given concept or rule. Most often the information is presented in a definitional or declarative format with minimal development of either conceptual or procedural knowledge. The purpose of this instructional variable is to adjust the amount of both expository (statement) and interrogatory (question) information based on a learner's progress in learning. The parameters, using Bayesian methods, are determined from the heuristics of the expert tutor in the macro-component. The level of instructional need in learning concepts and rules varies according to how well a learner acquires the use of new information in solving problems. Therefore, the purpose of this variable is to decide how much information a learner needs at any given moment. Too little information can result in insufficient learning while too much information can cause boredom, fatigue, and loss of interest.

The amount-of-information variable constantly monitors the learner's progress and adjusts the amount accordingly; and does so until the point of desired learning is reached or the system recognizes a need for special help. In either case, the macro-component sets the statistical parameters for each learner and then the micro-component monitors continuously the moment-to-moment learning progress. Additionally, factors included in this variable control prompting and feedback, and monitor learner effort (Tyler et al., 1979).

Sequencing of information. Computer-based learning systems have typically used branching routines to sequence learners through the instruction. However, the work of Atkinson (1972) showed that a response-sensitive approach to sequencing based on error patterns would be more beneficial to learning. Park (1984) extended this response-sensitive strategy to the learning of concepts. The sequencing strategy used at the micro-level determines the selection of concepts (within the information structure established at the macro-level), according to responses to interrogatory examples. For example, a correct solution indicates progress in learning, and therefore sequencing can be random; an incorrect solution in early instruction shows a conceptual knowledge problem, and thus the need to have additional information from that given concept. In later instruction, incorrect solutions indicate a procedural knowledge problem, and imply the need to have additional information from the concept for which the solution was taken. This is an example of a simple but very powerful informal heuristic. It is theory-based, and it also allows for fuzzy logic in deciding when "later" instruction has actually arrived.

Format of examples. Closely associated with the sequencing variable is the means for determining the format of examples. In complex problem situations, learners may not have sufficient knowledge to make a correct solution and must, therefore, either not attempt a solution or make an incorrect attempt (Mawer & Sweller, 1982). In such situations, learning can be improved by showing learners worked-out (expository) examples. With expository examples the learners have the opportunity to encode complete information rather than being forced into the generation of possible misconceptions. Park and Tennyson (1986) propose that the strategy format presented after an incorrect solution to an interrogatory problem be an expository example. Again, this is a simple informal heuristic in terms of management, but powerful in the improvement of learning.

Learning time. The learning of new information is a difficult process, and one in which monitoring of the learner is especially crucial in the early stages. A particularly important variable that has only recently received research attention is the monitoring of the instructional-display time interval. Given the nature of expository information, it appears that pacing should involve control over how slowly a learner proceeds. However, with interrogatory examples, monitoring of time must be more carefully observed. With respect to the learning-time variable, our research has shown that learners need to receive, early in their learning, information designed to improve conceptual knowledge. For example, when the macro-component establishes the conditions of instruction, the values for the time variable assume a conservative position on conceptual knowledge, thereby allowing only minimal time on interrogatory examples for problem solution. When the focus is on conceptual knowledge formation, if a learner does not answer a given problem within the time interval provided, the interrogatory example changes to an expository example. This results in presentation of more information at the initial stage of the instruction, when encoding of information is necessary.

Later on, more time can be allowed when the learning focus shifts away from encoding and toward the development of procedural knowledge.

By monitoring learning time, the learner's attention is constantly on task in an efficient manner. Unlike the circumstances obtaining in a discovery format, the learner has a reduced chance of encoding incorrect information or forming misconceptions (Schoenfeld & Herrmann, 1982). Once the learner has sufficient conceptual knowledge and can start solving problems, more and more time can be allocated. The heuristic for this variable is complex because of the number of conditions necessary to determine the display time. But because the heuristic is a separate entity within MAIS, complexity does not interfere with the other variables described earlier.

Embedded refreshment and remediation. An important advancement in instructional design brought about by cognitive-learning theory is the connection in memory between the information to be learned and knowledge already stored in memory. Cognitive theory implies that acquisition of information begins in the working memory, where the learner decodes appropriate necessary knowledge from long-term memory to help in understanding and encoding of the new information. Instruction can enhance this process by providing support (and structure as discussed in the macro-level variable) to the learner in selecting appropriate knowledge from memory and in making appropriate connections between the new information and previously acquired knowledge.

Earlier attempts in this area to support the learner in initial learning were made exclusively in pre–task activities. For example, review of prerequisite knowledge was employed as an attempt to accomplish retrieval of necessary prerequisite information; or advance organizers were used to help establish an initial schema. Both forms of refreshment were found ineffective because of the limited storage available in working memory. Review information and advance organizers in complex learning situations are usually too extensive for a learner to keep in working memory simultaneously with the acquisition of new information. The more complex the information they contain, the less useful are these forms of instructional help. What seems to be necessary as help is to provide at the moment of learning direct information as to the specific prerequisite knowledge. The assumption is that the prerequisite knowledge is in memory, and that what the learner needs is help in decoding that knowledge to working memory. Thus, two objectives are involved: first, the decoding and retrieval to working memory of only the specifically necessary prerequisite knowledge, and second, facilitating the connection between the to-be-learned information and the previously stored knowledge.

The heuristic for sensing this need is embedded within the presentation of interrogatory examples. If a learner either fails to respond in the display-time interval or provides an incorrect solution, the embedded refreshment variable immediately provides the specific prerequisite information. This contrasts to the usual teaching practice of providing feedback on the correct solution. The focus of learning then shifts from acquiring the new information to refreshment of specific prerequisite knowledge. The improvement in learning occurs because the learner is provided linkage to specific knowledge in memory at the moment of need. Review schemes and advance organizers do not provide such discriminations. This research is reported in Tennyson, Christensen, Hajovy, and Chan-Tam (1985).

Associated with refreshment of prerequisite knowledge is the problem posed by the learner who has either forgotten or has never learned the prerequisite information. Needed then is some form of remediation. The purpose of this heuristic is twofold: (a) determine a lack of prerequisite knowledge, and (b) redirect the instruction to the prerequisite information.

Unlike typical CAI remedial branching routines, embedded remediation is instruction on the specific domain of the prerequisite information: assessing complete understanding of the prerequisite domain before returning to the instruction of the information to be learned. The two variables of embedded refreshment and embedded remediation are instructional heuristics based on interpretations derived from cognitive learning theory. Their purpose is to sense learner need at any given moment and redirect the instructional focus for the specific need.

Advisement. The sixth variable of the micro-level component of MAIS involves a means by which the learner can understand how the instruction, and the learner's own effort, are contributing to the acquisition of the to-be-learned information. In ICAI systems, as well as in most other instructional situations, learners are usually not sure of their learning progress (Hannafin, 1984). For example, in our research (Tennyson, 1981) we have found that learners become more confident of their problem-solving skills during instruction in a given domain of information even if they are not actually learning. At the beginning of learning something new, learners have low confidence in their ability to solve problems, but after any form of instruction they become more confident, regardless of their actual ability to make correct solutions. One purpose of the advisement variable is to help learners in understanding their problem-solving skills while they are learning them.

The advisement variable keeps the learners informed of their individual learning progress throughout the instruction. Not only does this keep them informed of their skill development, but for instructional programs that include forms of learner participation, the learner has the continuing progress reports as help in making informed instructional decisions. In our most sophisticated form of MAIS, transfer from program control to learner control is done 'as the learner demonstrates increased skill in understanding instructional decision-making. This occurs over time, as information continues to be returned to the macro-level following performance at the micro-level.

SUMMARY

MAIS is viewed as the next generation of intelligent computer-based learning systems because of its foundation as a theory-based system. Each of the two main components of the system includes variables derived from learning theory and verified by empirical research. At both the macro- and micro-levels, the included variables interact in a very great variety of instructional conditions and events. Of special note is the ability of the entire system to adjust parameters in accord with both group experience and individual learner experiences. Informal heuristics are formed with currently available information and data. As experience is gained from both sources, the heuristics adjust accordingly. Currently, the heuristics adjust to both internal and external influences. Internally, certain heuristics have "fuzzy" logic statements that adjust as newly obtained data indicate. All heuristics can be adjusted by the instructional designer as need is determined. Because the heuristics are independent of both hardware and software conditions, they can be easily transferred and generalized to other systems, and can accommodate new developments in both hardware and software.

For an example, using a school mathematics curriculum, the conditions of instruction would differ for each student, according to the interaction of such variables as intelligence, motivation, prerequisite knowledge, cognitive style, and the specific mathematics information to be learned. If a given student had high intelligence, poor achievement in background knowledge, and low motivation and self-esteem, the prescribed conditions of instruction would differ dramatically from those intended for a student with equally high intelligence, but with high background knowledge achievement and high motivation. In each of these two cases, the macro-level conditions of instruction would initially set the parameters of the micro-level instructional variables (or events), which would then adjust according to the individual learning needs of each student. At the micro-level, for the first of these students, the need for immediate embedded remediation of backgound knowledge and form of advice would be very different than for the second described student.

FUTURE DIRECTIONS OF AI CBL

MAIS is basically an instructional research system rather than an operational system. Therefore, two future directions of the MAIS effort are in the continuation of the research program of the past decade, and in extending the system to additional applications. Within the research program, the direction of effort includes refinement of the interactions within and between the two main components, and the movement toward domain-specific variations and individual difference variables. Refinements will occur because of the nature of the informal heuristics; the need here is for longitudinal studies to increase the efficiency of the heuristics, which will also lead to advancements in knowledge about the interactive effects of the component variables.

Because much of the future directions of learning and instructional research will be with domain-specific variables, the basic research on MAIS will likewise move in that direction. Indeed, information useful for learning is increasingly being viewed by educators as knowledge rather than as subject matter. We expect interest to be directed to two types of instructional variables: those defined as generic, having across–content application; and those defined as domain-specific, having only within-content applications. Because of the focus on knowledge acquisition, research on information to be learned will see increased collaboration between learning psychologists and subject-matter experts. The initial work in expert systems is an example of this cooperation. Instead of conducting learning research in laboratories with artificial tasks, the experimentation will take place in "real-world" learning environments.

Another area of future research will be that on individual differences. This research will be directed not toward how to define differing learning outcomes because of differences, but on how to enhance instruction to benefit all individuals, with equal access to knowledge. Individuals differ on a wide range of variables, but understanding and using information cannot be compromised by these differences. Intelligent CBL systems can offer assistance in providing management systems that accommodate individual differences so that learners can successfully acquire the knowledge necessary to reach their potential.

In terms of hardware and software, the future seems to lie in the increasing use of internal operations to lessen the noncreative aspects of working with computers. For example, in the hardware area, computers will have input devices more directly related to specific types of applications. Use of symbolic and iconic inputs for quantitative and spatial information is becoming standard. Voice-recognition inputs and outputs allow for simultaneous processing of information. Computer memory developments are likely to alter the way we write program codes, so that AI methods will be more readily applicable. Instead of hardware controlling computer design, the science of cognition will increasingly influence hardware development.

The future of software developments will include reduction in the need for programming languages in favor of authoring systems in which the software writes the programming code. Current authoring systems, such as the initial ICAI systems, are models demonstrating a given technique (in this case, having the software write code) but controlling also much of the design process. The next few years will see the development of authoring systems that effectively write code, but leave the design and management decisions up to the instructional designer (who will, it is hoped, use theory-based principles of design).

Finally, in terms of the application of computer technology in education, the future growth will most likely be in adult learning environments. There are going to be increased numbers of computers in conventional school settings (K–12), but the more innovative applications will be in the business and governmental sectors. Learning for adults in the future will be increasingly through electronic media and less through classroom-like teaching. To conclude, we are inclined to restate the proposition that the direction of AI CBL is toward application of research and theory of the sort that deals with improvement in learning rather than in teaching. Finding means for enhancing instruction to improve learning is the goal of AI CBL.

REFERENCES

Amarel, S. (1983). Problems of representation in heuristic problem solving. Related issues in the development of expert systems. In R. Groner, M. Groner, & W. F. Bischof (Eds.), *Methods of heuristics*. Hillsdale, NJ: Lawrence Erlbaum Associates.

Atkinson, R. C. (1972). Ingredients for a theory of instruction. *American Psychologist, 27*, 921–931.

Breuer, K. (1984). Zur Lehr-lerntheoretischen Grundlegung der Computerunterstuetzten Unterricht. *Log In, 2*(2), 11–14.

Breuer, K. (1985). Computer simulations and cognitive development. In K. A. Duncan & D. Harris (Eds.), *Proceedings of the World Conference on Computers in Education*. Amsterdam: North Holland.

Brown, J. S., & Burton, R. R. (1978). A paradiagramatic example of an artificial intelligent instructional system. *International Journal of Man-Machine Studies, 10*, 323–339.

Brown, J. S., & Burton, R. R., & Bell, A. G. (1975). SOPHIE: A step toward creating a reactive learning environment. *International Journal of Man-Machine Studies, 7*, 675–696.

Burton, R. R., & Brown, J. S. (1979). An investigation of computer coaching for informal learning activities. *International Journal of Man-Machine Studies, 11*, 5–24.

Carbonell, J. (1970). AI in CAI: An artificial intelligence approach to computer-assisted instruction. *IEEE Transactions on Man-Machine Systems, 11*, 180–202.

Clancey, W. J. (1979). Tutorial rules for guiding a case method dialogue. *International Journal of Man-Machine Studies, 11*, 25–50.

Clancey, W. J., Barnett, J. J., & Cohen, P. R. (1982). Applications-oriented AI research: Education. In A. Barr & E. Feigenbaum (Eds.), *The handbook of artificial intelligence:* (Vol. II). Los Altos, CA: Kaufmann.

Collins, A., Warnock, E. H., & Passafiume, J. J. (1975). Analysis and synthesis of tutorial dialogues. *Psychology of Learning and Motivation, 9*, 48–87.

Dörner, D. (1983). Heuristics and cognition in complex systems. In R. Groner, M. Groner, & W. F. Bischof (Eds.), *Methods of heuristics*. Hillsdale, NJ: Lawrence Erlbaum Associates.

Feigenbaum, E. A. (1977). The art of artificial intelligence. *Proceedings of the 5th International Joint Conference on Artificial Intelligence*. Cambridge, MA: Massachusetts Institute of Technology Press.

Gagné, E. (1985). *The cognitive psychology of school learning.* Boston: Little, Brown.

Gagné, R. M. (1985). *The conditions of learning* (4th ed.). New York: Holt, Rinehart, and Winston.

Gagné, R. M., & Dick, W. (1983). Instructional psychology. *Annual Review of Psychology, 34,* 261–295.

Goldstein, I. P. (1982). The genetic graph: A representation for the evolution of procedural knowledge. In D. Sleeman & J. S. Brown (Eds.), *Intelligent tutoring systems.* New York: Academic Press.

Hannafin, M. J. (1984). Guidelines for using locus of instructional control in the design of computer-assisted instruction. *Journal of Instructional Development, 7*(3), 6–10.

Mandler, J. M. (1979). Categorical and schematic organization in memory. In C. R. Puff (Ed.), *Memory organization and structure.* New York: Academic Press.

Mawer, R., & Sweller, J. (1982). The effects of subgoal density and location on learning during problem solving. *Journal of Experimental Psychology: Learning, Memory, and Cognition, 8,* 252–259.

O'Shea, T. (1978). A self-improving quadratic tutor. *International Journal of Man-Machine Studies, 11,* 97–124.

Park, O. (1984). Example comparison strategy versus attribute identification strategy in concept learning. *American Educational Research Journal, 21,* 145–162.

Park, O., & Tennyson, R. D. (1983). Computer-based instructional systems for adaptive education: A review. *Contemporary Education Review, 2,* 121–135.

Park, O., & Tennyson, R. D. (1986). Response-sensitive design strategies for sequence order of concepts and presentation form of examples using computer-base instruction. *Journal of Educational Psychology, 78,* 153–158.

Schoenfeld, A., & Herrmann, D. (1982). Problem perception and knowledge structures in expert and novice mathematical problem solvers. *Experimental Psychology: Learning, Memory, and Cognition, 8,* 484–494.

Siaw, S. N. (1984). Developmental and population comparisons of taxonomic and thematic organization in free recall. *Journal of Educational Psychology, 76,* 755–765.

Sleeman, D. H. (1982). Assessing aspects of components in basic algebra. In D. H. Sleeman, & J. S. Brown (Eds.), *Intelligent tutoring systems.* New York: Academic Press.

Sleeman, D. H., & Brown, J. S. (Eds.). (1982). *Intelligent tutoring systems.* New York: Academic Press.

Stevens, A. L., & Collins, A. (1977). *The goal structure of a Socratic tutor.* Paper presented at the annual conference of the Association for Computing Machinery, Seattle, WA.

Suppes, P. (1979). Observations about the applications of artificial intelligence research in education. *Advances in Computers, 18,* 173–229.

Tennyson, R.D. (1981). Use of adaptive information for advisement in learning concepts and rules using computer-assisted instruction. *American Educational Research Journal, 18,* 425–438.

Tennyson, R. D. (1982). Interactive effect of cognitive learning theory with computer attributes in the design of computer-assisted instruction. *Journal of Educational Technology Systems, 10,* 175–186.

Tennyson, R. D. (1984). Artificial intelligence methods in computer-based instructional design: The Minnesota Adaptive Instructional System. *Journal of Instructional Development, 7*(3), 17–22.

Tennyson, R. D., & Breuer, K. (1984). Cognitive-based design guidelines for using video and computer technology in course development. In O. Zuber-Skerritt (Ed.), *Video in higher education.* London: Kogan.

Tennyson, R. D., & Christensen, D. L. (1985, April). *Intelligent curricular management system.* Paper presented at the American Educational Research Association, Chicago.

Tennyson, R. D., & Christensen, D. L. (In press). MAIS: An intelligent learning system. In D. H. Jonassen (Ed.), *Instructional designs for microcomputer courseware.* Hillsdale, NJ: Lawrence Erlbaum Associates.

Tennyson, R. D., Christensen, D. L., Hajovy, H., & Chan-Tam, P. W. (1985). Interactive effect of content structure with prerequisite knowledge in rule learning using computer-based instruction. *Journal of Educational Psychology, 33,* 213–223.

Tennyson, R. D., & Christensen, D. L., & Park, S. (1984). The Minnesota Adaptive Instructional System: An intelligent CBI system. *Journal of Computer-Based Instruction, 11,* 2–13.

Tennyson, R. D., & Cocchiarella, M. J. (1986). An empirically based instructional design theory for teaching concepts. *Review of Educational Research, 36,* 40–71.

Tennyson, R. D., & Park, S. I. (1984). Process learning time as an adaptive design variable in concept learning using computer-based instruction. *Journal of Educational Psychology, 76,* 452–465.

Tennyson, R. D., & Rothen, W. (1977). Pretask and on-task adaptive design strategies for selecting number of instances in concept acquisition. *Journal of Educational Psychology, 69,* 586–592.

Tennyson, R. D., Welsh, J., Christensen, D. L., & Hajovy, H. (1985). Interactive effects of content structure, sequence, and process learning time on rule-using in computer-based instruction. *Educational Communications and Technology Journal, 33,* 213–233.

Tyler, G. H., Hertel, P. F., McCallum T. J., & Ellis, B. G. (1979). Cognitive effort and memory. *Journal of Experimental Psychology: Human Learning and Memory, 5,* 607–617.

AUTHOR NOTES

Robert D. Tennyson is a Professor in the Department of Educational Psychology, University of Minnesota.

Ok Choon Park is a Research Scientist in the U. S. Army Research Institute.

13 Assessing Instructional Outcomes

Eva L. Baker
Center for Study of Evaluation, University of California, Los Angeles

Harold F. O'Neil, Jr.
University of Southern California

This chapter is addressed to the topic of assessing instructional outcomes. It occupies, conceptually, an interesting point in the consideration of instructional technology. On the one hand, the hallmark of technology is its repeatable utility based upon its use of verified knowledge produced from research. Assessment is clearly a requirement to determine if one has a technology that works. On the other hand, in practice, the serious consideration of assessing educational outcomes is often overlooked in the excitement of exploring innovation or in the day-to-day tedium of producing sufficient amounts of courseware or other instructional products on schedule and within budgetary constraints. Because of the lack of attention to the issue of educational-outcome assessment, measuring outcomes in the recent history of instructional design has been treated routinely, more as a historical obligation than as a tool integrally related to the improvement of instructional effectiveness. For this reason, it is important to see that the measurement of instructional outcomes has two critical functions: (1) It is both a means to assess how well the product, courseware, or other technology performs, and (2) It is a mechanism to intervene in and to improve the process of instructional design and development itself.

Basic to the understanding of the assessment of instructional outcomes is the role of *tests*. Unfortunately, this conjures up some of the least useful forms of assessment and restricts the instructional designer's view of the full range of information useful for making important inferences about the effects of learning. While basic understanding of testing is important, and will be treated in this chapter as well, it is not sufficient. It is more important to think broadly first about information needed to make instructional decisions,

343

and secondly, about the inferences one can draw from such information to make decisions about the equality of instructional efforts.

At the heart of both the information base and the inferencing process is the notion of validity, and it should be the overriding concern in the process of assessment. The formats of assessment, where they take on the coloration of typical tests or even look very different from the tests we have seen and taken in school, are at best secondary concerns. Our intent is to raise the salience of assesement in the entire design and development process by identifying the critical attributes of valid information and inferences. Then we will move to discussion of the various sorts of testing and other assessment options and consider their strengths and limitations against a framework of validity.

MEASUREMENT: THE BASICS

Without deeply investigating psychometric theory, an instructional designer can still treat the assessment issue seriously. A few straightforward points need to be reviewed. First, all measurement is imprecise. Everything we infer is exactly that: inferencing about learning that has occurred (or is potential) in the learner. As measurement begins to use some of the newer techniques in the biotechnical area, readings of magnetic fields, heat, and other electrical brain activity, then we may appear to be closer to the direct measurement of learning. But since we are dealing with the mind, we will still remain in the land of inference and inevitably be left to piece together what has actually been experienced by the learner.

Second, a good deal of what is measured is inaccurate because we have chosen the wrong thing to measure. We may have chosen an approach inappropriate to the subject matter, chosen to measure performance in a particular way because of its practicality and convenience rather than for reasons related to accuracy. So even if we were to improve our precision, we would err by selecting, some of the time, the wrong matter.

Third, we must remember we are dealing with people, not plastics. People are dynamic; they all change from second to second. The meanings they ascribe to events become successively refined and restructured with experience. They are blurry targets for precise metrics. As we all know, people not only change continuously but they differ from one another enormously. They have color preferences, various language facilities, and predispositions to certain subject matter, for instance. They also have very different perceptions of themselves as learners, of their abilities to succeed, and of the reasons they succeed and fail (see Weiner, e.g., 1979). Some are desperately anxious when they are given tests (O'Neil & Richardson, 1980), some worry about only one sort of test, such as essays or multiple choice, and some are relatively accepting of whatever tests come their way.

People also think in different ways. Their approaches differ not only as a function of the level of ignorance or expertise they have about a single subject, but their general background or world knowledge. They also approach problems very differently. One style is methodical and analytical; learners of this sort see the world in terms of components that get built up or decomposed into smaller parts. Others see the world in broad patterns, seek integration, use metaphors, and focus on the whole rather than its parts. And many people use both approaches described, switching within the same problem sometimes to understand through one or another means. These approaches were described simply and archetypally to make a point. But, it should be remembered that, regarding style of learning, much comes automatically to the learner. Only infrequently is learning style a volitional matter, although there have been moderately successful attempts to affect the use of various learning strategies. (Dansereau et al., 1986; Moore et al., 1985; O'Neil, 1979).

Our primitive measurement tools will miss a good deal of this complexity. So even if we had precise methods, and were confident that we were assessing the correct type of learning, we would still be sure to miss a good deal of the truths of what our effects have been.

For all these reasons, we cannot claim to have proved that our instruction is effective, just as we cannot prove that a scientific theory is right. We have to repeat our measurements, find multiple approaches to assess the outcomes we are intending, and still couch our conclusions tentatively. In the educational marketplace, of course, tentativeness goes by the board. Instructional designers compete with claims about materials proven effective, quality assurance, and other slogans designed to loosen resources from program managers either in business or in government. But, in the secret recess of one's own mind, it is important to know what we don't know, even if our roles or organizations require different public proclamations.

Purposes of Assessment

Central to the problem of assessing instructional outcomes is the issue of purpose: For what purpose are we to assess outcome? One common-enough response is to assess the quality of our intervention in meeting its particular goals. If a program or system is devoted to teaching reading comprehension, then it is appropriate to assess the extent to which comprehension is affected by exposure to the intervention. A second purpose of assessment in instructional contexts is related to the improvement of the program itself. We wish to assess instructional outcomes, again—reading comprehension in the example just given—for the purpose of revising instructional processes in the desired direction. These two purposes of assessment interact, often sharing the same sets of data collection processes and measures.

With both these outcome-assessment purposes, the principal focus has been on the achievement produced by the intervention, the what and how well students learn. Recently, the focus of outcome assessment has been broadened in a number of ways: (1) to assess both cognitive and affective outcomes other than those intended by the intervention; (2) to include measures of attitudinal development and satisfaction; (3) to assess how students go about learning, emphasizing processes rather than products. An additional but largely unsatisfied quest is to determine for which students—based on student individual differences such as cognitive preference, experience, and ability—various instructional interventions are most effective (Clark, 1983; Cronbach & Snow, 1977).

But a critical focus is on the assessment of learning outcomes. The means to accomplish such assessment has been *criterion-referenced measurement* (CRM), and that is the major focus of this chapter.

Criterion-Referenced Measurement

Criterion-referenced measurement has had many definitions. The merits of each and implications of different wording will later be discussed at some length. At the outset, we offer the reader a small sample of definitions which capture the range in the field.

> A criterion-referenced test is one that is deliberately constructed so as to yield measurements that are directly interpretable in terms of specified performance standards (Glaser & Nitko, 1971, p. 65).

> A criterion-referenced test is used to ascertain an individual's status (referred to as a domain score) with respect to a well-defined behavior domain (Popham, 1975, p. 130).

> A pure criterion-referenced test is one consisting of a sample of production tasks drawn from a well-defined population of performances, a sample that may be used to estimate the proportion of performances in that population at which the student can succeed (Harris & Stewart, 1971, p. 2).

The history of achievement testing has been described in part by a range of scholars, each operating from a differing frame of reference (Buros, 1977; Cronbach & Suppes, 1969; Levine, 1976; Nifenecker, 1918; Spearman, 1937). The particular path of development of criterion-referenced testing is less well documented, although partial attempts at description have been produced by Millman (1974), Brennan (1974), Popham (1978), Hambleton (1978), and Baker (1980). A point of contention, for example, is when CRM began. It seems to have two major sources: curriculum development inquiry and instructional psychology. Its early roots can undoubtedly be traced to Rice's assessments (1897), continuing with Thorndike's experiments, and Washburne's applications to school objectives (1922). The impact of Ralph Tyler's contribution cannot be underestimated, with his widely disseminated writing on curriculum development and evaluation (Smith & Tyler, 1942; Tyler, 1943, 1950, 1951). There is similar evidence, from the work of instructional psychologists, of the early development of CRM techniques for the assessment of instruction, for instance, films produced for training in World War II (Hovland, Lumsdaine, & Sheffield, 1949). In these early examples, content was sampled from the instructional universe of films, as is recommended currently by CRM specialists. The psychological bases of CRM were later exhibited in the experimental analysis of human and animal behavior (Skinner, 1958).

When reviewing the psychological roots of CRM, the source of nomenclature associated with CRM can be identified. For example, *criterion* itself simply means a *terminal* or ending frame in a sequence of programmed instruction, where the response opportunity for the learner was unprompted (or without cues supporting the correct answer). Only later were such criterion trials aggregated into a *criterion test* of the sort Glaser described. Programmed instruction absorbed the attention of many psychologists concerned with changing student performance, providing us with concepts such as task analysis (Gagné, 1965, 1977), performance level (Mager, 1962), and individualized instruction (Holland & Skinner, 1961; Lindvall & Cox, 1969).

CRM was first conceived to be a dependent measure for instructional sequences which were concrete and carefully designed. Thus the purpose of CRM was twofold: (1) to provide an operational definition for the skills developed by a given sequence, (2) to be used as a mechanism for formative evaluation (Scriven, 1967) to improve instruction. The use of test information to revise instruction was a tenet of programmed instruction, and was also called developmental testing (Markle, 1967) or field trials (Lumsdaine & May, 1965). Of great importance, however, was that the test and instructional sequence were intimately connected, which made elaborate description of what the test measured unnecessary.

Early Applications

The movement in American education relating to behavioral objectives was nurtured by both the programmed-instruction movement and the broader curriculum-development and evaluation concerns of Tyler (1950) and Bloom et al., (1956). Advocates of such objectives (Mager, 1962; Popham & Baker, 1968) argued that specification of goals allowed teachers greater efficiency in their instructional tasks as well as concrete means for assessing the success of their instruction. Although the movement often resulted in enthusiastic overspecification, with hundreds of tasks identified for a single course, the progressive refinement of the idea resulted in fewer objectives (to aggregate discrete objectives into clusters that made more sense for learning and instruction). The emergence of more generalizable classes of behavioral goals and the recognition that the evaluation of these goals (testing) needed to derive from the clear statements led to the development of specification-oriented testing, or CRM.

From the Tyler tradition, and elaborated by the work of Carroll (1963), Bloom (1968), and Keller (1968), teacher-oriented notions of *mastery learning* developed. These models shared an important philosophical view, adopted, it appears, from the work of the programmed-instruction designers: that student success was the shared responsibility of the teacher and the learner. Teacher-training models were concomitantly developed, based on this point of view (Michigan State University, 1968; Popham & Baker, 1970, 1973). In addition, the curriculum development renewal, spurred by federal support of regional educational laboratories and research and development centers, integrated Tylerian and programmed-instruction traditions (see, e.g., products developed by the Southwest Regional Laboratory in California, or the Learning Research and Development Center, University of Pittsburgh). These instructional systems, whether purely programmed-instruction, teacher-mediated, or comprehensive systems, depended for their evaluation on quality criterion measures. Thus, the initial utility of CRM was almost always as a part of an instructional system. The tasks assessed by CRM were circumscribed by the goals of the instructional system.

CRM AS A FIELD OF STUDY

As shown earlier, critical definitions of CRM include the notion that performance is assessed relative to a particular task domain and that the representative samples of tasks that form this domain are organized to make a test (Glaser & Nitko, 1971). Glaser's work spurred that analysis of CRM as a measurement model rather than only as a part of an instructional system.

Early discussions of CRM, after Glaser christened the fledgling approach, struggled to contrast CRM to traditional testing theory. In their well known and referent article, Popham and Husek (1969) contrasted *CRM* and *norm-referenced tests* (NRT) on the basis of test development procedures, test-improvement procedures, analysis, and interpretation routines. NRTs were so named because their reporting procedures required that individual scores be transferred to a common scale and characterized as ranks in a distribution of scores. Thus, a score had meaning only in comparison with other scores in a particular distribution. Data were reported in terms of percentile, stanine, or quartile. It became gradually clearer to researchers that the norming process not only depended on the selection of appropriate comparison groups of students, but also that it significantly influenced the development procedures of the test items themselves. The development procedure was bound by the requirement of performance variance to permit normal curve interpretation. Thus, early distinctions between norm- and criterion-referenced tests were drawn in terms of what was expected to happen to this variance after instruction. Because norm-referenced tests were developed to provide discriminations among individuals and relatively stable estimates of individual performance, instruction was expected to affect students about equally. The shape of a norm-referenced distribution of scores would not change as a function of instruction. Everyone was simply expected to move up a few notches (as the phrase *grade-equivalent* suggests). The relative rank of a student's score in a distribution was not expected to change. In contrast, criterion-referenced distributions should alter dramatically after the treatment of related instruction. Before teaching, the retest distribution might be homogeneously clustered and low on the scale for peculiarly obscure tasks or, for more general areas, randomly distributed; following instruction, it was conceivable for the great proportion of students to be achieving very high levels of performance, with relatively small variance. Before too long, researchers recognized the effect of reduced score variability on the utility of extant statistical procedures for examining test adequacy.

The Problem of Identity

Just as a young child probes the limits of his or her own identity and seeks to separate and distinguish oneself from his or her parents, so did the writers in the area of CRM continue to seek to differentiate CRM from norm-referenced testing. Streams of articles attempted to describe what CRM was, including Popham and Husek (1969), Simon (1969), Lindquist (1970), Ivens (1970), Block (1971), Ebel (1971), Harris & Stewart (1971), Glaser & Nitko (1971), Emrick (1971), Cronbach, et al (1972), Kriewall (1972), and Livingston (1972). Much of these discussions focused on the model underlying CRM. There were two basic points of contention. First, the question was raised whether the term *criterion* meant a criterion set of behaviors, or essentially a task domain, whether it meant rather a standard or performance level, such as 70% of the items correct, or whether it was to be used as an external criterion, such as in *criterion validity* (Brennan, 1974). A second point of contention was how well specified were the domains from which the items were drawn. Some suggested that a CRM needed careful specification of both content and behavioral domains. The recognition of different degrees of specification led to analyses that not only contrasted norm and criterion-referenced tests, but also attempted to distinguish subsets of CRM, such as *objective-based, domain-referenced,* and *ordered sets.* (See, e.g., Berk, 1980a,b; Denham, 1975; Glaser & Nitko, 1971; Hambleton et al., 1978; Harris, Alkin, & Popham, 1973; Millman, 1974; Popham, 1978; Sanders & Murray, 1976; Skager, 1975). The recency of some of the entries suggests clarity is not rampant in the field and, in fact, which concepts are subsumed by which appears to be a matter of personal preference.

Conflict

A good many of these articles and books attempted to distinguish between CRM and NRM by casting doubts on the worth of one or the other (see, e.g., Ebel, 1972; Haney, 1980; Perrone, 1975). Such doubts were easy to support on either side, for assessments of the quality of available commercial achievement tests, both norm-referenced, (Haney and Madaus, 1978; Hoepfner, 1971–1976) and criterion-referenced (CSE Criterion-referenced Test Handbook, 1979) were generally negative.

From the literature alone, it is difficult to gauge the intellectual environment in which these discussions occurred, but in fact, a good deal of rancor was generated by contending advocates for norm- and criterion-referenced testing. Within active memory were rather vitriolic exchanges between purveyors of the "upstart" form of assessment, the CRM devotees, and those firmly grounded in traditional psychometric theory. Debates were held at research associations. National professional groups published resolutions in favor of one or another sort of testing, and then sometimes switched sides. A joint committee of the American Psychological Association, the American Education Research Association, and the National Council for Measurement in Education (1977) made an attempt to mediate differences (American Psychological Association, 1974). CRM advocates saw themselves as student- and teacher-oriented, interested in testing in the name of formative evaluation and the improvement of education. Norm-referenced test authorities held fast to the long and scholarly psychometric traditions upon which NRT was based. They could point to well-developed concepts of individual differences, robust parametric analyses to assess the quality of their measures, and a thriving industry of users.

The sum of the criticisms of CRM by this group was that it was largely atheoretical nonsense. Should one review some of the early examples of CRM, such criticism is clearly appropriate. As will be detailed later, test construction in the name of CRM proceeded at a superficial level. Items were generated and reviewed under less than rigorous conditions (justified, of course, because the empirical analyses available to improve norm-referenced tests could not be directly applied and interpreted for CRM).

Social Context and the NRT-CRM Debate

One of the great ironies of this period of CRM development, the late 1960s and early 1970s, occurred as a function of the social reaction in American education. Precisely at the time CRM was emerging and differentiating itself under the banner of more educationally and instructionally relevant assessment, a strong reaction to technology of any sort took place. Both NRT and CRM advocates were tarred by the same brush by representatives of the counterculture, activists who rebelled against institutionalized testing and its attendant philosophy of logical positivism. Thus, CRM and NRT were thrown together as "the enemy," and distinctions between models of assessment were overshadowed by the general rejection of "irrelevant" and competitive educational activity. These reactions, scholars avow, were in part caused by social disruption, the limited success of the Great Society (Aaron, 1980), and evidence of the perversion of political power.

At the same time, and causing additional conflict in the practical world of education, was the increasing public attention and support of testing (Atkin, 1980). The evaluation requirements attached to federal categorical-aid programs spread the amount of testing throughout the nation. The interpretation by the courts of test data, such as reported in the Coleman study (1966), the trends toward statewide achievement programs, and the development of school-leaving examinations as a criterion for high-school graduation (Pipho, 1978) raised the testing stakes. What had started as an academic squabble among educational psychologists grew to an issue of considerable proportion in public policy. As the testing issue became more visible, and involved life choices of individuals, so did the need to identify problems in the testing field become more urgent. Consumer-advocate groups (such as Nader's) attacked testing institutions; questions regarding test security were raised concomitantly (Haney, 1978); teacher organizations presented forceful points of view (National Education Association, 1977; Ward, 1980); contention was fed by court cases, and legal analyses of tests were issued (McClung, 1978). Another broad irony is that most of these analyses of test properties were based on work of psychometricians, a professional group with relatively little school experience and almost no involvement with instructional programs.

Especially noteworthy in reviewing the development of CRM is that only rarely were the core philosophical distinctions between NRT and CRM clearly articulated. Bloom (1968), in his classic article on mastery learning, pointed out the difference in expectation such a model could make for children and outlined some of the benefits of allowing learning time rather than student competency level to vary. One clear consequence was the sharing of instructional responsibility by teacher and student. Not yet solved, however, are the practical difficulties of implementing such an idea in the face of continued social and financial pressures on schools. These difficulties include problems associated with reallocation of resources to students who require more time, the nature of shared responsibility in the face of high student absentee rates, and the tendency for *mastery* to be set at lower rather than higher levels (Baker, 1978).

TEST DESIGN FOR CRITERION-REFERENCED MEASUREMENT

When one imagines what ought to be in a section called test design, a prominent contender is how to make a test, that is, the nuts and bolts of actual item writing and test assembly. While such activity has rarely been regarded as at the higher end of the intellectual continuum, nonetheless rules, procedures, and routines for test construction have been developed, for use by either the professional test builder or by teachers. In this section, some contrasts will be presented between test construction activities and test-design efforts, the former characteristics of typical achievement-test development and the latter examples of test development in CRM.

Norm-Referenced Test Development

Certain steps in achievement-test construction were developed in traditional practice. It should be emphasized that the routines were created: (1) to assure a broad representation of item and content types; (2) to avoid gross technical error. The major burden of test development for the norm-referenced achievement test (NRT) fell on empirical analyses.

Typically, in NRT, a general content-behavior matrix was first developed, so that test items could be generated to tap the full range of topics and eligible response modes. Then items were reviewed to assure that they did not inadvertently cue the learner to the correct answer, that the length and syntax of response options were comparable, and that the correct answer was keyed accurately. These items were also inspected for content quality and screened for obvious technical errors. Most important in test development processes, however, was the use of empirical procedures to determine test quality. Techniques such as item analysis, reliability estimates, and quantitative indicators of validity were created to help the test item selection process. These techniques were based upon parametric statistics used by researchers in analyzing experimental data. Such techniques depended, as did certain experimental research models, on classical notions of science: predictability and control.

Underlying empirical test-refinement practices was a relatively simple idea. A norm-referenced achievement test was to measure a general ability, pertinent to an area of knowledge or skill. The underlying "explanatory concepts . . . accounting for test performance" were called constructs (Cronbach, 1971). An individual's performance included chance exposure to relevant experience, broadly aggregated, as well as to in-school or other purposive instructional experience. Constructs, definitionally, required more than one measure. Performance on any single test measuring a general construct (such as reading ability) was thought to provide a relatively stable estimate of an individual's performance when compared with other similar individuals. The role of change (as in learning due to instructional exposure) was noticeably unclear. As such achievement measures were to assess important dimensions formulated as constructs, the argument ran, then they should not be reactive to relatively small variations in the learner's total experience, for instance, whether or not a child received a particular one-month reading comprehension program. Such a model was almost universally accepted and maintains strong and eloquent supporters (see, e.g., Ebel & Anastasi, in Schrader, 1980). They describe a view of achievement as a *developed ability,* with the other end of a continuum anchored by *aptitude* (the capacity or predisposition, without the relevant experiences). This notion of achievement was supported by statistical analysts who conceived of testing in terms of prediction. Changes in test score from occasion to occasion were formulated as *unreliability* or *error* (see, e.g., Harris, 1962) by such methodologists.

Certainly no one worries much about models underlying test construction or any other human endeavor when certain conditions hold: (1) performance looks good; (2) significant decisions do not hinge on the model's products; and (3) a body of prestigious support is available for the practice. Such was the comfortable status of norm-referenced achievement testing for many years. Measures now show a less than rosy view of student achievement, and explanations for declines have not been satisfactory (Harnischfeger & Wiley, 1975; Wirtz, 1977). Decisions about admission to professional schools, coveted undergraduate institutions, and even the award of the high-school diploma, increasingly depend on test performance. Obviously important is the lack of scholarly consensus on the quality and utility of achievement measures. Because these issues focus attention on the effectiveness of schools, a different philosophy about education has developed vocal, if not always coherent, support. That view is also simple: that schools exist to produce change, in other words, specific learning. In this view, change is not regarded as score unreliability, but is itself the most desired product of education. One should note the level on which discussion of this issue has occurred. Joseph Califano, then Secretary of Health, Education, and Welfare, made a public statement in which he avowed that the federal government wished to *reduce* the predictability of performance based on socioeconomic or race classifications (1978). Since relationships in status on these demographic variables and standardized test performance run very high (between .60 and .80), depending on the reliability of the test, and student performance on similar tests correlate, over time, at .80 or higher (Bloom, 1980), one may infer that this statement challenges the test development community to build measures able to detect effects of educational practices within the school's control. In contrast to earlier formulations, change is to be valued over predictabilty. This perspective shift has great implications for test construction. Procedures used to develop measures of traits thought to be essentially stable over time are not the same ones that should be used to create change-responsive outcome measures (O'Neil & Richardson, 1977).

Specifying Educational Outcomes

CRM developed, it was earlier noted, out of two traditions, each actively promoting change: instructional psychology and curriculum development.

Both of these sources, although from different governing frameworks, hit upon the practice of specifying objectives or goals for change. The practices in CRM development grow from the answers to various questions related to this specification or description: What is specified? At what level of detail? Where do the specifications come from?

In the earliest days, specification of tasks for assessment were thought to flow very nicely from a clear statement of an instructional objective (Mager, 1962). Although these objectives could be developed to cover course-level material, they were usually created for shorter units of instruction. The belief was evident that, once figuring out how to state an objective clearly, test development would be a cinch. In rules designed to help in the assessment of educational programs, Popham (1975) suggested that the critical measurement issue was the classification of forms of stimuli and responses. As an early advocate of diverse forms of measurement, Popham classified assessment tasks into four cells: (a) Student behavior could be either process (throwing a ball) or product (test paper); (b) Elicitation conditions could be either formal (school) or natural (out-of-school or surreptitious). Additional writing around this time focuses on how specific the specification needed to be for the assessment ("to take a test" was a negative example, considered much too vague). Also of interest were conditions under which the test was to be taken (time limits, extra materials) and ways of establishing desired performance standards (such as 75% correct). While Tyler and others since had noted that an objective consisted of both behavior and content, a good deal of early attention in objectives-referenced measurement was devoted to specifying behavioral requirements and very little in developing the content parameters. Good items were thought to match the behavioral statement in the objective.

The Problem of Content

In the absence of routines for specifying the *what* (content) of testing in favor of the *how* (test behavior), two rather different modes of practice developed. Test items were selected or rejected on the match between the objective statement and nuances of the test-taker's behavior (was the student directed to cross out a letter when the objective called for a machine-scored, blacked-in response?) In one mode, content was left to vary freely without any specification ("important mathematics concepts" or "American novels"). In the other, each particular content unit was specified ("In the play *Othello,* identify . . ."). The tradeoffs appeared clear: in the first case, the task was cast in a generalizable form, for almost any particular content would be eligible for inclusion in the test. In the second, particularization of content allowed for highly targeted instruction and congruent testing, but forsook generalizability. Discussions of the merits of these tradeoffs, generalizability versus specific content, were held in workshops and training sessions of the

American Education Research Association during the years 1967 to 1973. However, real confrontation with the content of tests, that is, the subject-matter areas to be assessed, was generally limited. Although there were analyses of new curricula, new math, the process-oriented new sciences, the new linguistics, these were not specifically analyzed for their utility in developing performance-oriented instruments. Content people were generally too "soft" for the hard-edged requirements of behaviorism, and remarkably few content specialists were interested in testing specifically. During the mid-1960s, an impetus for a new view of content in objectives-based testing was needed.

DOMAIN-REFERENCED ACHIEVEMENT TESTING

The work of Osburn (1968), Hively et al. (1968), and Hively (1974) provided that impetus. Using a model developed from set theory, Hively described the identification of a universe of content and behavior, a *domain*. Hively demonstrated that broad classes of performance could be assessed by using algorithmic rules to generate items. This domain could then be theoretically sampled to yield representative instances of test items. Performance on the sample would allow the estimation of performance for the larger content/behavior domain. Hively, in refinements with colleagues (1973, 1974) demonstrated how a technology for *domain-referenced* test (DRT) generation could be developed. He suggested the use of an item form, or shell, that included basic behavioral requirements. Into this shell could be inserted replacement content instances, substituted from the "universe." A simple example of an item form is the addition problem: $x + y =$ ____, where x is any two-digit number and y is any one-digit number. While the item shell might be changed to:

$$\begin{array}{r} x \\ + \ y \\ \hline ? \end{array}$$

the content parameters would be identical. Two digit and single digit numbers were to be added. Any members of that set in the specified combination might actually show up as a test item.

Hively's suggestions had great impact for a number of reasons. First, as described earlier, there was dissatisfaction with current test-development processes in the field. While there was recognition that available empirical procedures were inappropriate to apply to new outcome measures, no alternative procedure had been agreed upon to produce quality test items. Hively's work probably also indirectly capitalized on the widespread knowledge of Bloom, Krathwohl, and colleagues' (1956) efforts at taxonomic organizations of educational objectives. The term *domain* used in these works was understandable to all. An additional explanation for the success of Hively's ideas was his development and demonstration of domain-referenced achievement testing in concrete form. He provided a real example to researchers in the field, an example couched in a theoretical context, but with practical implications. He had actually created test items using such procedures.

Forms of Item Forms

Hively's rules for the creation of items included the specification of the format of the item, the rules for generating the stem, the response alternatives, and the directions. When fully explicated, his item-form directions appeared detailed and formidable. Such detail was clearly required in order to develop unambiguous item domains. Yet his procedures, because of their sophistication, seemed designed principally for use by a team of item writers. Baker's adaptation, reported in Hively's book (1974), focused on specifications as they might be modified for teachers and others familiar with behavioral objectives. The elements of a domain specification included a statement of the objective, the content limits, the wrong-answer population (for multiple choice tests) or response criteria (for production tasks), for item format, the directions, and a sample item. Popham (1975) further modified domain specifications to what he termed an *amplified objective.* In his scheme, stimulus attributes and response attributes were to be specified; however, distinctions between the behavioral and content requirements of the item were not made. The Popham and the Baker adaptations represent less rigor than the Hively approach, but were justified in terms of likely comprehensibility among teachers and instructional designers. At the outset, these approaches were applied to single domains, and the problem of creating tests across a number of related domains was not addressed.

Hively's work (1973; 1974) was particularly important because of its connection with instruction. Unlike the curriculum-development people, who saw specification of objectives and measures as one of the first steps in the process, Hively had directly referenced his efforts to existing instruction. He used content generated by lesson writers as the primary source for the creation of his item domains. Similar to the way in which programmed instruction linked its criterion-frames to instruction, so Hively's item forms were linked to the concepts in actual lessons. Although his work was extended by Popham, Baker, and others, to the objective–instruction–assessment sequence, his ideas remained firmly grounded in instruction. Domain-referenced testing (DRT) immediately formed a new category of criterion-referenced measurement, and writers described applications in teacher training, program evaluation, and accountability.

DRT generated fodder for intellectual rumination lasting until most recently. Questions were raised, and almost endlessly discussed, by Popham

(1978), Millman (1974), Hambleton (1978), Baker (1978), Brennan (1974), Harris (1980), Haladyna and Roid (1977; 1978), Nitko (1974), and Anderson (1972). Numerous problems in DRT were identified and lists of unresolved problems published in 1974 appear to continue in that status.

Problems of Domain-Referenced Testing

Among some of the early problems associated with DRT was the attempt to deal with content parameters outside the field of mathematics and science. Although it was very clear how one might go about generating a set of parameters of generation rules for computational questions, doing so in the liberal arts appeared to be a messy process. Hively's procedure was based upon an algorithmic approach to content selection. Thus it was especially applicable to content areas that had well-defined structural relationships, such as an early example of DRT in a linguistically oriented reading program (Baker, 1968). In that example, a specific set of rules governing content, such as syntactic and spelling rules, allowed for the explication of a universe of content and the compilation of tests that sampled the defined universe.

The attempt to apply DRT to other subject-matter areas were many, and included social studies, writing, English literature, the health sciences, and reading comprehension. A major fact soon became evident: Few subject-matter areas had sufficiently well-defined structures to permit the use of algorithmic approaches to content generation (Landa, 1974). In the absence of sufficient clarity in subject-matter fields, would-be users of DRT fell back on an alternative process. Their choice was to define the parameters of content operationally themselves, without reference to any subject-matter analyses. They would decide, for example, that four causes of economic decline existed, list and define such causes, and develop examples of each. A DRT could then be created by selecting an appropriate range of examples. This method was clearly vulnerable to charges of both arbitrariness and curriculum control. Defenders of this strategy pointed to the void in current practice and suggested that this technique was preferable. As a coincidence, Gagné (1977), in an audiotape developed for the American Educational Research Association, discussed two forms of concept learning. The first type, *concrete,* were those derived from perception. The second category of concepts were those he called *defined* concepts, where the instructional designer (or test writer) would explicate the dimensions of a concept and the learner would discriminate examples or generate instances based on these defined or agreed-upon limits. The use of such defined concepts supported the DRT-content specifications. A large and unresolved issue remained: Who was to decide on the arbitrary features of a defined concept. No satisfactory and practical answers have been suggested, beyond the usual discussion of constituencies and judgment by reasonable persons. The advances in cognitive science, however, presage improvement in specifications. Both cognitive skills and precise content representation may contribute to resolving this issue (Baker, 1985; Baker and Herman, 1983; Curtis & Glaser, 1983).

A second major problem was what to do in cases in which the subject matter itself defied algorithmic definition, even an arbitrary one, in a case such as literature. While one can conceivably specify arbitrary rules for generating examples of lyric poetry, the exercise seems relatively futile because of the variation of examples within that literary genre. Taking a cue from Hively, some DRT writers identified domains not by *generation* rules (for all possible instances) but by *enumeration* of a limited set (for instance, poems 1–9 found in Smith's anthology). Such a tactic reduced the power of DRT to claim estimation of a total domain (such as poetry), reduced the likelihood of generalization (that perhaps performance levels would be similar from poem to poem), but preserved the "fairness" with which items might be sampled by circumscribing the set of content to that contained in the particular anthology. Thus, at least, students, teachers, and test writer would know what content was fair game for testing.

Another fall-back tactic for content specification was to define by illustration and axiom a set of content. Hively provided the example of the front page of the *New York Times* as a content set for assessing reading comprehension. Clearly the explication of generating rules or algorithms for content such as the *Times* is beyond both the funds and attention spans of researchers. In another example, the operational definition of a *clear sentence,* including forms of reference, semantics, and so on, similarly overcomplicates a domain more intellectually accessible by example. As provided in any number of style handbooks, clear sentences can be clearly contrasted to unclear writing. The *rules* are more efficiently perceived in the examples themselves, rather than exhaustively written. Again, this form of specification, while short of the purity of item-generation rules, clearly communicates to teacher and learner what is to be tested and what should be learned.

The problem of the completeness of content-domain specification can be recast as a problem in automation. How fully automated should DRTs be? The extent to which test-item writing can be fully automated is presently unknown, but approximations using domain specifications of syntactic rules have been attempted. Bormuth (1970) provided essentially linguistic transformations to permit the generation of test items. In a series of studies to assess the automaticity of item writing, Roid and Haladyna (1978) were surprised that item-writing "subjectivity" was not removed by the provision of rules to two item-writers. In another study using prose passages, Roid, Haladyna, and Shaughnessy (1979) found some algorithmic practices controlled item-writing production. The study supported the importance of linguistic analyses of items, in addition to other specification-matching routines. This study was also limited, however, by the use of only a few (four) item-writers. Undaunted, they continued (Roid, Haladyna, & Shaughnessy, 1980) with six item writers directed to use linguistic-versus-subjective (match with an objective) strategies. Although lengthy analyses are provided, the item-writer interaction suggests that item-writer behaviors were not sufficiently affected. The authors posit the need for further trials with more empirical tryouts. However, tryouts under conditions of good, medium, or rotten instruction would likely affect the resulting data set. Baker and Aschbacher (1977) achieved considerable success in controlling item production through the use of rules. The automation problem has not been discussed in most research in this area. The use of the computer to automate item writng routines has been less well developed to date than one might hope, with only relatively simple content substitutions used. Millman and Outlaw (1977) conducted a project in this area and Finn (1978) reported on multiple-choice item generation. Hsu and Carlson (1973) earlier used the PDP-10 system, and other automated experiments involved efforts by Olympia (1975) and Fremer and Anastasio (1969). This work needs to be linked and made more relevant to the content parameters of domains. Perhaps availability of better natural language processing options would improve computer utilization in this important area (cf. Frase, 1980).

New Approaches to Content Specification

While computer technology has long been employed to score and to administer tests (Dunn, Lushene, & O'Neil, 1972; Hedl, O'Neil, & Hansen, 1973), its exploration may have some utility in the content specification problem of domain-referenced achievement testing. Specifically, the development of expert systems provides an opportunity for specific knowledge domains to be identified, structured, and incorporated into computer software. Basically, these approaches focus on the problem of representing expert knowledge and its relationships in algorithms that the computer can use (Buchanan, 1981). Modeling knowledge via expert systems has, by and large, focused on relatively narrow knowledge domains, such as subtraction (Brown & Burton, 1984), but efforts have been made to attack more complex areas, such as computer programming (Johnson & Soloway, 1983), infectious diseases (Clancey, 1982), story generation (Dehn, 1981) and understanding narrative (Dyer and Lehner, 1982; Frederiksen & Warren, 1985). Research is also under way to develop procedures for less well-defined areas, so-called fuzzy content (Spiro, 1984), where content does not fall into mutually exclusive categories.

The techniques used to represent knowledge developed for AI expert systems could be used in the vexing problem of assuring full content representation on tests (Freedle, 1985).

Quality Control

Another nagging question about DRT is how one knows an item is a good instance of the set. Most writers suggest some judgment scheme, usually matching the item realistically against characteristics explicated in the specifications. Research on this problem has demonstrated that raters may make their discriminations on superficial item-features; for example, Does the number of response alternatives in the item match the specifications?, rather than on the more difficult issues of cognitive complexity or content appropriateness. Some research has been conducted relating to the need to provide guidelines for such judgments (Polin & Baker, 1979).

Using defined concepts and operating from an instructional perspective, rules and routines for matching instances with classes have been developed by Markle and Tiemann (1974), Tiemann, Kroeker, and Markle (1977) and Tiemann and Markle (1978a). Merrill and Tennyson (1977) have also provided excellent analyses and examples of processes needed to match examples of concepts to specifications or concept definitions. Because this work takes place in the context of instructional rather than test design, these authors have received less than their due recognition for contribution in the testing field.

Of the research conducted on providing guidelines for judgment in a test-design context, Hambleton (1980), Haladyna and Roid (1977), Baker and Quellmalz (1977), Doctorow (1978), and Polin and Baker (1979) have made contributions. Set theory, or more particularly the concept of *fuzzy sets,* has been applied in this research to estimate the degree of congruity between an item and its specification. This research demonstrates the futility of using obvious and superficial indicators (such as the number of foils in the specifications); and factors such as level of cognitive complexity and related linguistic features were highlighted as needing more study. A number of writers have reported training efforts undertaken to teach specification-item matching (Hambleton & Simon, 1980; Merrill & Tennyson, 1979; Tiemann & Markle, 1978). Baker, et al. (1980) have developed training materials designed to teach the rudiments of DRT judgment to teachers and to graduate students. Such training seems to be required before individuals can match test items with their specifications. Baker et al. (1980) make the argument that students must be able to match relevant items with their generation specifications (i.e., to label concepts, to demonstrate that the items cohere). This rather demanding requirement might be acceptable if students were first trained specifically in identifying the critical attributes in DR items. In the absence of such training on relevant dimensions, students might group items under true, covarying, but instructionally irrelevant features (such as sentences starting with the letter T). In the development of the review process described earlier investigated by Polin and Baker (1979), the critical issue was training item classifiers on instructionally relevant item features.

Empirical Studies

The foregoing problems that deal with the match by inspection of specifications and items represent what Bormuth (1970) calls problems of item-writing theory. His second category deals with item-response theory, or more accurately empirical indices used to substantiate the existence of a domain. Millman (1974) also attempted to distinguish between problems of item selection which were judgmental and those for which empirical data were necessary. Popham (1978) also distinguished between descriptive validity (that is, does the item fit its specifications and are those specifications clear?) and functional validity (does performance classify the student as anticipated?). Early interpretations of the DRT process included high expectations of item homogeneity, as discussed by Nitko (1974). The idea was that item difficulties and variances for items produced by DRT procedures should be similar. Items were expected to cluster together (Baker, 1979; Macready & Merwin, 1973; Stenner & Webster, 1971). Baker et al, (1971) discussed procedures by which individual item-writers would be able to produce items which resulted in similar empirical characteristics. Although this demand for homogeneity has diminished in the light of actual data sets, one may still be troubled by the idea that item performance, particularly one developed by DRT procedures, was assessed in the absence of clear documentation of the instructional conditions preceding its use. A similar issue may be looming for the advocates of new empirical procedures thought to obviate the requirement for meticulous matching of specifications with items. The Rasch model (Wright, 1967) has been put forth and scooped up by users of CRM as an empirical solution to the issue of item quality. What is still unclear, however, is the extent to which this model, and in fact other *latent-trait* models are robust in the face of highly targeted instructional interventions (Bock, Mislevy, & Woodson, 1982). Research by Roid, Haladyna, and Shaughnessy, 1980), albeit exploratory, does not lead one to expect good news. Somehow empirical analyses, combined with judgment of specification to item matches, conducted under known instructional interventions, will be necessary before we can uncritically adopt solutions such as the Rasch model proposes.

Matching items to specifications or the generation of item sets according to specifications is based on a pigeon-hole view of the relationship of given items to a domain. Each item would be sorted as it fits according to the exhibition or absence of N features explicated in the domain specification (Choppin, 1980). It is altogether possible that limitations of item writers, subject-matter structure, and technology will conspire to promote alternative, perhaps supplementary models to DRT. One such area of analysis involves the linguistic features of test items, beyond the readability indices presently computed. A similar technique area once again ripe for exploration is the area of facet analysis and concept mapping (see Engle & Martuza, 1976; Guttman, 1969; Harris, 1976). Key words and the improved natural-language processing capacity of computers may also enrich our DRT technology. One principal incentive for such work may be the need for procedures for the development of access and retrieval routines for computerized item banks. Such techniques could easily influence item development and review processes and result in significant improvement.

The foregoing discussion pertains principally to the technology of comparing sets of generated items with their parent specifications. Only oblique discussion has hinted that the content and behavioral requirements themselves might require review. Along what dimensions might specifications be judged? In much the same mode that goals and objectives were to be judged by relevant constituencies, so too might domain specifications be reviewed for relevance and importance in school learning. Some critical questions still need research before we could even begin to open the review process to less technical participants.

For example, how big is a domain? The answer was at first thought to depend on empirical data (to wit, a domain has items that cohere), but as strict expectations for item homogeneity faded, so have guidelines for the restrictiveness of domains. How much complexity in a domain? Any homogeneous response modes required? Does a domain include the task to be tested as well as relevant subtasks in an identified skill-hierarchy? Do such subtasks need enumeration or do they also require verification empirically? How are domains organized with respect to one another? In parallel? By content area? In more than one way? How are task requirements best determined? As pointed out, for the most part specifications have grown from the analysis of content areas and rather gross, behavioral requirements. In some cases, instruction itself has generated the parameters. What should be the relationship of instructional analyses to domain design?

Integration of Testing and Instruction

The relationship of domain specification to instruction is an area which might profitably be addressed. Certain models start with instruction or content (see Hively et al., 1973) and reference the domain to that set. Others start with the test specifications, and then develop instructionally relevant learning opportunities (see Rankin, 1979). Thus from given domains are generated test specifications, item pools, and instructional practice exercises. This system does not completely specify all instruction but it is designed to integrate some aspects of domain design with testing and instructional functions. In mastery learning (Block, 1971; Bloom, 1969), a natural oscillation between instruction and testing occurs.

Researchers are presently at work attempting to find ways to connect instruction and testing at deeper levels than in the past. Rather than developing tests to reference extant instruction (see Baker, 1968) or to map extant tests on instructional texts (Floden et al., 1980), ways to unify the design of test and instruction should be explored. Initial development of this sort has taken place with the creation of Project Torque (Schwartz & Garet, 1982), a math program where exercises serve almost indistinguishable functions of teaching and testing. The cognitive specifications for such a set of activities probably needs additional refinement. Frase (1980) has worked on the integration of testing and instructional domains using computerized language projects, and the research in writing assessment (Baker, Quellmalz, & Enright, 1982; Purves, 1980; Quellmalz, 1980) has potential for a similar sort of unification. Such a merger of instruction and testing will not come about easily. For one thing, it violates our traditional patterns of thought. Brennan (1974) expresses little patience with those who continually blur the distinctions between testing and instruction and impede, he believes, serious progress in either. On the other hand, a scholar as prestigious and traditionally grounded as Harris (1980) has seen the need to integrate testing and instruction complexes.

Most writers on instruction and testing have, in recent years, seen tests leading instruction, as in "teaching to the test." Mastery learning made a great contribution toward the integration of instruction and testing in two ways. First, the intervals between instruction and tests were reduced and made more frequent. Second, they were individually tailored for individuals (Rudner, 1978) or groups. Adaptive testing, using the computer to administer tailored items is a current example of this approach. Thus, the pattern was changed from formal and extended periods for testing and instruction (courses with only one mid-term examination and one final examination) to more flexible and naturally occurring events. But in the hearts and minds of many, instruction is still the *treatment* or intervention and testing is still the *dependent measure.*

By way of analogy, recall some of the early processes in the attempt to teach young children to read. An important and persistently difficult skill was the blending of initial consonants and phonograms, so that when a child was presented with the elements T and AN, he or she could pronounce TAN. For some reason, instruction focused on reducing the interval between the pronunciation of elements. By shaping the child's behavior so that the time between the pronunciation of T and AN was very short, the child would come, it was thought, to understand the process of blending. In fact, no such insight typically occurred. Children showed remarkable resiliency and ability to keep the two elements separate, even when the time between them was essentially eliminated.

Children did learn to blend easily, however, when the focus was not on reducing the time interval, but on changing the framework in which the blending instruction took place. In early experiments (Baker, 1968), children were taught first to understand the unified outcome that was desired, that the units had meaning, and blending was a process similar to saying SAND-

BOX. When presented with T + AN, no hesitations occurred and blending skill became well developed. Similarly, a new dimension must be found to underlie both testing and instruction so that these functions lose their uniqueness. Of great promise is the work in cognitive psychology, which, if united with theories of content structure and language, could allow the generation of experiences useful to develop and assess, in a piece, the desired outcomes of schooling. An excellent analysis of the future has been described by Curtis and Glaser (1983).

Narrow Definition of Testing

As previously stated, most individuals writing in the field assume a test is a paper-and-pencil vehicle, usually in multiple-choice format. They also seem to assume: (1) that the test has one correct answer and that other alternatives are no more than "foils" to the right answer; (2) that the test is kept separate from instructional activities; and (3) that the present practice is probably most efficient.

There is only occasional mention of "performance testing," and a few writers grope to find words to distinguish other than multiple-choice testing. They use words like appraisal, evaluation, assessment, their Roget's litany, to avoid the constrained "test" connotation. In reflecting on this review, the reader would be wise, we believe, to make the effort to break out of a confined view of testing. The research in this area should be judged as it could or might be expanded to generalize to formats of the sort listed in Table 13.1.

EVALUATING INSTRUCTIONAL TECHNOLOGY

One of the most useful options in considering outcomes of computer-based instructional interventions is to use the technology of delivery as a means of collecting information related to student outcomes. Not only can the computer deliver tests that are embedded in instruction but it can also tabulate

TABLE 13.1
Test Format Options

Format	Examples
1. Oral language	Formal speeches, conversational facility
2. Written composition	Essay examinations, expository analyses, description
3. Physical activity	diving, tennis stroke
4. Creative production	art, carpentry
5. Technical exhibition	piano recital

indicators of other instructional outcomes. For example, in the evaluation of a set of computer-based instruction, the latencies of student responses, the numbers of options they select and the frequency with which they select harder problems can be incorporated as an additional outcome measure of program effectiveness. In some sense, these indicators involve using processes as outcomes. The student is encouraged not only to improve his level of attainment but his fluency and exploratory behavior as well. Other automatically recorded information can provide indices of student attitudes— for instance, persistence and attention.

It is true that scholars working in the measurement area are moving toward a fuller concern with the understanding of student learning processes leading to particular levels of attainment. For example, Linn (1985) describes a measurement approach that tracks metacognitive processes that learners employ as they encounter new reading requirements. Furthermore, Shavelson and Salomon (1985) undertake a study of the relationship of the symbol system in which the test is conveyed and the conative processes that students use to develop their responses.

The availability of new computer technology for assisting in assessment problems has both positive and negative sides. On the one hand, it can encourage the integration of assessment into the instruction context, so that it is more representative, less ceremonial, and less artificial than tests of the past. On the other hand, our analysis of what has been happening to testing as implemented in new technology is relatively negative. Short-answer and multiple-choice formats abound, and as a result, the performance tested is at the lowest common denominator. Tests, however, only mirror the approach taken toward instruction. When tests are molecular and discrete, rather than integrated and comprehensible, one can make inferences about the quality of thought behind the instructional development effort even before seeing the data. We expect to see, in future assessment, expansion and integration: where a common database can be explored to make inferences about performance, levels of attainment, relationships to individual differences, cognitive processes, and attitude development. Such an integrated database approach is possible now. However, as long as assessment continues to be regarded as the stepchild of instruction, a necessary evil for reporting requirements, rather than an integral instrument in the design of instruction and the teaching of students, few developers take the risk.

Assessment in the Evaluation of New Technology

While the foregoing sections have focused on assessment and the underlying measurement ideas, it is important to place concern for outcome measurement in context. What else needs to be included in the assessment of *instructional technology* that is especially relevant to the technological character of the innovation? In other words, what else needs to be addressed beyond measures useful for the assessment of instruction that is not technology-based? Let us turn, for the conclusion of this chapter, to the issues related specifically to evaluating technology. Our assumption is that the best ideas posited for the measurement of instructional outcomes will be necessary but not sufficient for this evaluation task.

Assessment, and the evaluation processes which support it, is represented to be a productive mechanism for the improvement of educational systems and products. And there is hard evidence of the utility of evaluation in actually improving technology-based products and efforts in instructional development (Baker, 1972; Rosen, 1968). Assessment is known as well to contain a strong negative potential. Evaluation can identify weaknesses in such a way as to inhibit exploratory behavior and risk taking on the part of researchers and developers. Playing it safe may be seen to be the winning strategy. Evidence of evaluation utilization studies suggests that when the focus of the assessment is classification or accountability (good vs. bad; useful vs. wasteful), the openness of R&D project personnel to evaluation processes in inhibited. Formative evaluation, on the other hand, is evaluation whose specific function is to identify strengths and weaknesses for the purpose of improving the product or system under development (Baker, 1974; Baker & Alkin, 1973; Baker & Saloutos, 1974; S. M. Markle, 1967). The trick, of course, is in determining what should be studied, in what context the evaluation should take place, when evaluation processes are most useful, and in skilled hypothesis generation about what improvement options logically and feasibly may be implemented. In addition, the identification of weaknesses (no matter how benign the intentions of the evaluation may be) creates a documentary trail that might be misused by project managers or funding agency monitors.

These issues take on special dimensions when the evaluation addresses the effectiveness of new technology. All technology development of necessity focuses on the initial problem of system operation: Can the envisioned delivery system work at all, as opposed to the refinement of what the system's merits may be or what effects might be planned or imagined? Outcome assessment is a goal often deferred. When dealing with emerging technology, the boundaries between technology development and science become especially blurred. The creation of technology may be a pleasant side-effect for the creator, whose perception of the main task may be knowledge production, rather than instructional effectiveness. Intellectual exploration is a premium for new technology development, and assessment processes can be seen to inhibit or be irrelevant to invention.

Recent writing in the field of evaluation planning has emphasized a stakeholder perspective in evaluation implementation. Simply put, this means that interested parties must have an opportunity to understand and to shape the nature of the evaluation questions and methods so that they will be more invested in the process and more apt to use any results generated (Bryk, 1983).

With this discussion as context, a special model of evaluation can be designed to be adapted especially to the problem of new technologies. Briefly, we will detail the features of this model, as applied to new technology, a particularly difficult area characterized by weak boundary conditions between research and application goals.

A Model to Assess Technology

The model underlying the formative evaluation of technology is composed of a minimum set of pieces. They include the goals and specifications, the intervention, the context of use, the information base, and the feedback loops. Figure 13.1 displays this model linearly, but in fact it could be arrayed in a circle or in three dimensions. Points of entry to the model could vary, depending on the designer's commitment to prespecification of outcomes. The extensiveness of alternatives could differ, with some designers interested in contrasting alternative instructional treatments and others interested in a broad array of outcomes, including attitudinal and social goals beyond those detailed in the system specifications.

The following is a list of four desired attributes for a model to assess new technology. These characteristics respond to particular attributes of technology development. In brief, these include: weak boundary conditions between research and applications goals of the developers; levels of risk in technology development; and the constant pressure to develop and sustain management support and necessary resources to complete the tasks of interest.

1. *The information must provide an enhanced documentary base for the processes of new technology development.* A characteristic of new technology is lack of documentation describing the process leading to the development of

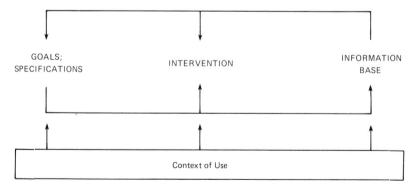

FIGURE 13.1.   Information features and functions for a model to assess new technologies.

the system or product. The purpose of a strong documentary base is to provide the trace of developmental processes so that the field can improve overall. Aggregating across a series of case histories of projects can allow the inference about productive strategies to be made. In addition, a good documentary base can inform about dead ends in substance as well as in developmental processes. Since most R&D reporting is based upon positive findings, it is difficult to avoid useless but unreported paths.

This lack of documentation exists for a variety of reasons. First, the process of early design of technology is complex, iterative, and nonlinear. All of us are familiar with documents of development which retrospectively rationalize and make "neat" processes that are chaotic, or at best, hard to track. Furthermore, the metacognitive awareness required of designers to document their own processes, while at the same time working on problems of interest, presents an almost insurmountable attention burden, even if there were predisposition on the part of the research and development personnel to do so. Solving the problems at hand appears to be more important. Contributing to an abstraction such as *R&D processes* attracts less compelling energy, despite the intellectual apprehension that the field overall can be improved by a "lessons learned" perspective. Another inhibition is the precedence of proprietary knowledge, well known in the private sector, but of potentially increasing import in a public R&D environment characterized by competitive procurement policies.

In an attempt to meet this overall goal in instructional technology, some case histories were prepared 20 years ago (see D. Markle, 1967) and a historian was even on the payroll of another large R&D facility. But these persons can be as pestering and diverting as media reporters, trying to get the idea of what's going on without true understanding of the processes involved. In new technology development, the problem is obviously exacerbated.

Fully participating formative evaluators provide another model, however, if they are linked early on in the development process, and if the R&D management and staff understand the intent is to assist as well as to document process.

2. *The information must use state-of-the-art evaluation methodology, including both quantitative and qualitative approaches to measurement.* One of the reasons evaluation processes have been received with healthy skepticism is that they appear to be so content-free, on the one hand, and methodology-driven, on the other. The history of assessment and of evaluation, as in any new mode of inquiry, is replete with "new" models that propound a particular methodological view of the world. A good deal of the discredit done to evaluation has occurred with the support and consent of its most famous practitioners, who advocated one or another highly quantitative design and analysis method as the preferred mode for solving all evaluation problems (see Baker, 1983, for a list).

Obviously, an analytical approach to evaluation design should be driven by what information is required by whom by when, by the credibility needed by the information analysts to do their job, and most importantly by the nature of the project or activity under review (Cronbach, 1980). Such precepts would suggest an electic approach, mixing journalistic, documentary, and effectiveness information as appropriate.

3. *The information must provide policy feedback to the supporting agencies.* This feature assumes that the funding source is either a contracting agency or an in-house manager. What kinds of policy feedback are appropriate? That depends in part on the nature of the formative-evaluation team selected. Clearly, issues of project management might be a necessary concern. However, it is more likely that the substance to which the technology is directed—instruction—is a more useful area for feedback. At minimum, the formative evaluators should attend to the fidelity of the process by the project to the project's stated goals and procedures and to the kinds of contractual, monitoring, and other oversight arrangements that might be useful in the future. Furthermore, the evaluation report can consider specifically the features or tasks that might be included in the specification of future activities of the sort evaluated.

The tension of providing such information in a way that does not undo either the project activities under study or the receptivity of future projects to evaluation cannot be ignored. A fine line needs to be walked, keeping track of both the professional ethics applicable to contracting agency relationships (i.e., telling the truth) and to maintaining positive connections to the target R&D communities.

4. *The information must provide timely and useful alternatives for the formative evaluation of the project(s) under study.* This platitude takes serious effort to implement. It depends in no small measure on being informed accurately and intimately with the state of development of the project; and in the evaluation staff's sensitivity to the form as well as the substance of findings that might be useful to the project staff. This requirement also depends strongly on the level or stage of development of the technology activity. Early on, certain suggestions can be made and have potentially large effects. However, the evidentiary base of such recommendations is likely to be weak. Later on, good evidence of project benefits and weaknesses can be more fully drawn; however, modification of the technology may be considerably less likely and may cost more.

Thus, the model addresses macro or executive features of the development process rather than micro (or instructional) characteristics. Effectivness data, based on careful assessment of an appropriate range of outcomes, constitute the critical feature of this model; for good management and good documentation have little importance when the question of "does it work?" is not well treated. We look toward a future in which such models will be routinely used and rational design and evaluation activities will actually drive instructional development. It remains for the field to decide if it wishes to implement them, and how seriously.

SUMMARY

We have tried to present in this chapter a discussion of outcome assessment that puts into context how measurement has evolved to its present state. We have attempted to detail the background of alternative viewpoints so that the reader can make informed professional decisions. We have also attempted to keep our eye on the ball of instruction, and we urge those interested in outcome assessment not to get diverted by the intriguing, but occasionally irrelevant, technical debates that suffuse the field of psychometrics. Good assessment depends more on hard thinking and good analysis than on empirical solutions. It is for this reason that we advocate the use of criterion-referenced measurement for the assessment of instructional technology outcomes, with the caveat that such measurement is difficult and must proceed beyond the often mindless way in which it is implemented at present.

We believe that evaluation of technology outcomes of technology-based instruction is different from that of instructional assessment, and that special attention to attributes of the assessment are required.

REFERENCES

Aaron, H. (1977, October). Remarks before the Evaluation Research Society National Conference, Washington, DC.

American Psychological Association. (1974). *Standards for educational and psychological tests.* Washington, DC: American Psychological Association.

Anderson, R. C. (1972). How to construct achievement tests to assess comprehension. *Review of Educational Research, 42,* 140–170.

Atkin, M. J. (1980). The government in the classroom. *Daedalus, 109*(3), 85–97.

Baker, E. L. (1968). *Developing a researched based kindergarten reading program.* Inglewood, CA: Southwest Regional Laboratory for Educational Research and Development.

Baker, E. L. (1971). The effects of manipulated item writing constraints on the homogeneity of test items. *Journal of Educational Measurement, 8*(4), 305–309.

Baker, E. L. (1972). *Using measurement to improve instruction.* Paper presented at a symposium of the annual meeting of the American Psychological Association, Honolulu.

Baker, E. L. (1974). Formative evaluation of instruction. In J. Popham (Ed.), *Evaluation in education.* Berkeley, CA: McCutchan.

Baker, E. L. (1978, January). *Is something better than nothing? Metaphysical test design.* Paper presented at the CSE Measurement and Methodology Conference, Los Angeles.

Baker, E. L. (1980). Achievement tests in urban schools: New numbers. *CEMREL Monograph on Urban Education, 4,* 9–15.

Baker, E. L. (1983, October). *Evaluating educational quality: A rational design.* Paper presented to a seminar on educational policy and management, University of Oregon, Eugene, OR.

Baker, E. L. (1985, August). The impact of advances in artificial intelligence on test development. In *Institutional grant proposal for an NIE center on testing, evaluation, and standards: Assessing and improving educational quality.* Los Angeles, CA: UCLA Center for the Study of Evaluation.

Baker, E. L., & Alkin, M. C. (1973). Formative evaluation in instructional development. *AV Communication Review, 2*(4).

Baker, E. L., & Aschbacher, P. (1977). *Test design project.* Los Angeles: UCLA Center for the Study of Evaluation.

Baker, E. L., & Herman, J. L. (1983). Task structure design: Beyond linkage. *Journal of Educational Measurement, 20,* 149–164.

Baker, E. L., Polin, L. G., Burry, J., & Walker, C. (1980, August). *Making, choosing and using tests: A practicum on domain-referenced testing.* Report to the National Institute of Education, Washington, DC, (Grant No. OB–NIE–G–78–0213). Los Angeles: UCLA Center for the Study of Evaluation.

Baker, E. L., & Quellmalz, E. A. (1977). *Conceptual and design problems in competency based measurement. Long range plan, 1978–1982.* Los Angeles: UCLA Center for the Study of Evaluation.

Baker, E. L., Quellmalz, E., & Enright, G. (1982). *A consideration of topic modality.* Paper presented at the annual meeting of the American Educational Research Association, New York.

Baker, E. L., & Saloutos, W. A. (1974). *Formative evaluation of instruction.* Los Angeles: UCLA Center for the Study of Evaluation.

Berk, R. A. (1980a). *A consumer's guide to criterion-referenced test "reliability."* Paper presented at the annual meeting of the National Council on Measurement in Education, Boston.

Berk, R. A. (1980b). *Domain-referenced versus mastery conceptualization of criterion-referenced measurement: A clarification.* Paper presented at the annual meeting of the American Educational Research Asssociation, Boston.

Block, J. H. (1971). Criterion-referenced measurements: Potential. *School Review, 69,* 289–298.

Bloom, B. S. (1968). Learning for mastery. *Evaluation Comment, 1*(2).

Bloom, B. S. (1969). Some theoretical issues relating to educatiohnal evaluation. In R. Tyler (Ed.), *Educational evaluation: New roles, new means.* Sixty-eighth Yearbook of the National Society for the Study of Education (Pt. 2). Chicago: Unviersity of Chicago Press.

Bloom, B. S. (1980, November). Presentation made at UCLA campus. University of California, Los Angeles.

Bloom, B. S., Englehart, M. D., Furst, E. J., Hill, W. H., & Krathwohl, D. R. (Eds.). (1956). *Taxonomy of educational objectives: the classification of educational goals. Handbook I: Cognitive domain.* New York: David McKay.

Bock, R. D., Mislevy, R. J. & Woodson, C. (1982). *Educational Researcher, 11*(3), 4–11, 16.

Bormuth, J. R. (1970). *On a theory of achievement test items.* Chicago, IL: University of Chicago Press.

Brennan, R. L. (1974). *Psychometric methods for criterion-referenced tests.* Albany, NY: University Awards Committee, State University of New York.

Brown, J. S., & Burton, R. R. (1984). Diagnostic models for procedural bugs in mathematics. *Cognitive Science, 2,* 155–192.

Bryk, A. (Ed.). (1983). *Stakeholder-based evaluation. New Directions for Program Evaluation* (Vol. 17). San Francisco: Jossey-Bass.

Buchanan, B. C. (1981). *Research on expert systems.* Report No. CS–81–837, Computer Science Department, Stanford University, Stanford, CA.

Buros, O. K. (1977). Fifty years in testing: Some reminiscences, criticisms, and suggestions. *Educational Researcher, 6,* 9–15.

Califano, J. (1978). U.S. needs in testing. Speech presented at the Department of Education National Conference on Testing, Washington, DC.

Carroll, J. B. (1963). A model of school learning. *Teachers College Record, 64,* 723–733.

Choppin, B. C. (1980, August). *The IEA item banking project.* Paper presented at the International Education Association Conference, Jyvaskyla, Finland.

Clancey, W. J. (1982). Tutoring rules for guiding a case method dialogue. In D. Sleeman & J. S. Brown (Eds.), *Intelligent tutoring systems.* New York: Academic Press.

Clark, R. E, (1983). Reconsidering research on learning from media. *Review of Educational Research, 53,* 445–459.

Coleman, J. S., Campbell, E. Q., Hobson, C. J., McPartland, J., Mood, A.M., Weinfeld, F. D., & York, R. L. (1966). *Equality of educational opportunity.* Washington, DC: U.S. Government Printing Office.

Cronbach, L. J. (1980). *Toward reform of program evaluation.* San Francisco: Jossey Bass.

Cronbach, L. J., Gleser, G. C., Nanda, R., & Rajaratnam, N. (1972). *The dependability of behavioral measurements: Theory of generalizability for scores and profiles.* New York: Wiley.

Cronbach, L. J., & Snow, R. E. (1977). *Aptitudes and instructional methods.* New York: Irvington.

Cronbach, L. J., & Suppes, P. (Eds.). (1969). *Research for tomorrow's schools—disciplined inquiry for education.* Report of the Committee on Educational Research of the National Academy of Education. New York: Macmillan.

CSE Criterion-referenced Test Handbook. (1979). Los Angeles: UCLA Center for the Study of Evaluation.

Curtis, M. E., & Glaser, R. (1983). Reading theory and the assessment of reading achievment. *Journal of Educational Measurement, 20,* 133–147.

Dansereau, D. F., Rocklin, T. R., O'Donnell, A. M., Hythecker, V. I., Larson, C. O., Lambiotte, J. C., Young, M. D., & Flowers, L. F. (in press). *Development and evaluation of computer-based learning strategy training modules.* (Tech. Rept.). Alexandria, VA: U.S. Army Research Institute for the Behavioral and Social Sciences.

Dehn, N. (1981). Story generation after tale-spin. *Proceedings of the 7th International Joint Conference on Artificial Intelligence,* Vancouver, British Columbia, pp. 16–18.

Denham, C. (1975). Criterion-referenced, domain-referenced, and norm-referenced measurement: A parallax view. *Educational Technology, 15,* 9–13.

Doctorow, O. (1978). *Some theoretical suggestions for a commutative test item operation.* Unpublished manuscript.

Dunn, T. G., Lushene, R., & O'Neil, H. F., Jr. (1972). The complete automation of the Minnesota Multiphasic Personality Inventory. *Journal of Consulting and Clinical Psychology, 39,* 381–387.

Dyer, M. G., & Lehner, W. (1982). Questioning answering for narrative memory. In J. F. Levy & W. Kingston (Eds.), *Language and comprehension.* New York: North Holland.

Ebel, R. L. (1971). *Some limitations of criterion-referenced measurement.* Paper presented at the annual meeting of the American Educational Research Association, Minneapolis.

Ebel, R. L. (1972). *Essentials of educational measurement.* Englewood Cliffs, NJ: Prentice-Hall.

Ebel, R. L., & Anastasi, A. (1980). Abilities and the measurement of achievement. In W. Schrader (Ed.), *New directions for testing and measurement, measuring achievement: Progress over a decade.* San Francisco: Jossey-Bass.

Emrick, J. A. (1971). An evaluation model for mastery testing. *Journal of Educational Measurement, 8,* 321–326.

Engle, J. D., & Martuza, V. R. (1976, September). *A systematic approach to the construction of domain-referenced multiple-choice test items.* Paper presented at the annual meeting of the American Psychological Association, Washington, DC.

Finn, P. J. (1978, March). *Generating domain-referenced, multiple choice test items from prose passages.* Paper presented at the annual meeting of the American Educational Research Association, Toronto.

Floden, R. E., Porter, A. C., Schmidt, W. H., & Freeman, D. J. (1980). Don't they all measure the same thing? Consequences of standardized test selection. In E. Baker & E. Quellmalz (Eds.), *Educational testing and evaluation, design, analysis, and policy.* Beverly Hills, CA: Sage.

Frase, L. T. (1980). The demise of generality in measurement and research methodology. In E. L. Baker & E. S. Quellmalz (Eds.), *Educational testing and evaluation: Design, analysis, and policy.* Beverly Hills, CA: Sage.

Frederiksen, J. R., & Warren, B. M. (1985). *A cognitive framework for developing expertise in reading.* Cambridge, MA: Bolt, Beranek & Newman.

Freedle, R. (1985). *Implications of language programs in artificial intelligence for testing issues.* Final Report, Project 599–63. Princeton, NJ: Educational Testing Service.

Fremer, J., & Anastasio, E. J. (1969). Computer-assisted item writing—I. Spelling items. *Journal of Educational Measurement, 6*(2), 69–74.

Gagné, R. M. (1977). Analysis of objectives. In L. J. Briggs (Ed.), *Instructional design: Principles and applications.* Englewood Cliffs, NJ: Educational Technology.

Glaser, R. (1963). Instructional technology and the measurement of learning outcomes: Some questions. *American Psychologist, 18,* 519–21.

Glaser, R., & Nitko, A. J. (1971). Measurement in learning and instruction. In R. L. Thorndike (Ed.), *Educational Measurement* (2nd ed.). Washington, DC: American Council on Education.

Guttman, L. (1969). Integration of test design and analysis. In *Proceedings of the 1969 Invitational Conference on Testing Problems.* Princeton, NJ: Educational Testing Service.

Haladyna, T., & Roid, G. (1977). *An empirical comparison of three approaches to achievement testing.* Paper presented at the annual meeting of the American Psychological Association, San Francisco.

Haladyna, T., & Roid, G. (1978). *The role of instructional sensitivity in the empirical review of criterion-referenced tests.* Monmouth, OR: Teaching Research.

Hambleton, R. K. (1978). On the use of cut-off scores with criterion-referenced tests in instructional settings. *Journal of Educational Measurement, 15*(4), 277–290.

Hambleton, R. K. (1980). Test score validity and cut-off scores. In R. Berk (Ed.), *Criterion-Referenced testing: State of the art.* Baltimore: Johns Hopkins University Press.

Hambleton, R. K. & Simon, R. (1980). *Steps for constructing criterion-referenced tests.* Paper presented at the annual meeting of the American Educational Research Association, Boston.

Hambleton, R. K., Swaminathan, H., Algina, J., & Coulson, D. B. (1978). Criterion-referenced testing and measurement: A review of technical issues and developments. *Review of Educational Research, 48,* 1–47.

Haney, W. (1980). Trouble over testing. *Educational Leadership, 37*(8), 640–650.

Haney, W., & Madaus, G. (1978). Making sense of the competency testing movement. *Harvard Educational Review, 48*(4), 462–484.

Harnischfeger, H., & Wiley, D. (1975). *Achievement test score decline: Do we need to worry?* Chicago: Cemrel.

Harris, C. W. (1962). *Measurement of change.* Milwaukee: University of Wisconsin Press.

Harris, C. W. (1972). An interpretation of Livingston's reliability coefficient for criterion-referenced tests. *Journal of Educational Measurement, 9,* 27–29.

Harris, C. W. (1974). Problems of objectives-based measurement. In C. W. Harris, M. C. Alkin, & W. J. Popham (Eds.), *Problems in cirterion-referenced measurement.* Los Angeles: UCLA Center for the Study of Evaluation.

Harris, C. W. (1980, July). *Final report to National Institute of Education* (Grant No. NIE-G–78–0085, Project No. 8–0244). Los Angeles, CA: UCLA Center for the Study of Evaluation.

Harris, M. L., & Stewart, D. M. (1971). *Application of classical strategies to criterion-referenced test construction: An example.* Paper presented at the annual meeting of the American Educational Research Association, New York.

Harris, N. D. C. (1976). A course mapping technique. *Instructional Science, 5,* 153–180.

Hedl, J. J. Jr., O'Neil, H. F., Jr., & Hansen, D. N. (1973). The affective reactions towards computer-based intelligence testing. *Journal of Consulting and Clinical Psychology. 40,* 217–222.

Hively, W. (1973). Introduction to domain-referenced testing. *Educational Technology, 14,* 5–10.

Hively, W. (1974). *Domain referenced testing.* Englewood Cliffs, NJ: Educational Technology.

Hively, W., Maxwell, G., Rabehl, G., Sension, D., & Lundin, S. (1973). Domain-referenced curriculum evaluation: Technical handbook and a case study from the MINNEMAST Project. *CSE Monograph Series in Evaluation,* (No. 1). Los Angeles: UCLA Center for the Study of Evaluation.

Hively, W., Patterson, J., & Page, S. (1968). A "universe defined" system of arithmetic achievement testing. *Journal of Educational Measurement, 5*(4), 275–290.

Hoepfner, R., Stern, C., Nummedal, S. G., et al. (1971). *CSE-ERIC preschool/kindergarten test evaluations.* Los Angeles: UCLA Center for the Study of Evaluation.

Holland, J. G., & Skinner, B. F. (1961). *The analysis of behavior: A program for self-instruction.* New York: McGraw-Hill.

Hovland, C. I., Lumsdaine, A. A., & Sheffield, F. D. (1949). *Experiments on mass communication.* Princeton, NJ: Princeton University Press.

Hsu, T., & Carlson, M. (1973). Test construction aspects of the computer–assisted testing model. *Educational Technology, 13*(3), 26–27.

Ivens, S. H. (1970). *An investigation of item analysis, reliability and validity in relation to criterion-referenced tests.* Unpublished doctoral dissertation, Florida State University.

Johnson, W. L., & Soloway, E. (1983). *Proust: Knowledge-based program understanding (Tech. Rept. YaleU/CSD/RR#285).* New Haven, CT: Computer Science Department, Yale University.

Keller, F. S. (1968). Goodbye, teacher . . . *Journal of Applied Behavior Analysis, 1,* 78–89.

Kriewall, T. (1972). Aspects and applications of criterion-referenced tests. *Illinois School Research, 9*(2), 5–21.

Landa, L. N., Kopstein, F. F., & Bennett, V. (1974). *Algorithmization in learning and instruction.* Englewood Cliffs, NJ: Educational Technology.

Levine, M. (1976). The academic achievement test—its historical context and social functions. *American Psychologist, 31*(3), 228–238.

Lindquist, E. F. (1970). The Iowa testing program: A retrospective view. *Education, 81,* 7–23.

Lindvall, C. M., & Cox, R. C. (1969). The role of evaluation in programs of individualized instruction. In R. W. Tyler (Ed.), *Educational evaluation: New roles, new means.* Sixty-eighth Yearbook of the National Society for the Study of Education, Part II. Chicago: University of Chicago Press.

Linn, R. (1985, August). Instructional testing. In the *Institutional Grant Proposal for NIE Center on Testing, Evaluation, and Standards: Assessing and Improving Educational Quality.* Los Angeles, CA: UCLA Center for the Study of Evaluation, 38–48.

Livingston, S. A. (1972). Criterion-referenced applications of classical test theory. *Journal of Educational Measurement, 9*(1), 13–26.

Lumsdaine, A. A., & May, M. A. (1965). Mass communication and educational media. *Annual Review of Psychology, 16,* 475–534.

Macready, G. B., & Merwin, J. (1973). Homogeneity within item forms in domain-referenced testing. *Educational and Psychological Measurement, 33*(2), 352–360.

Mager, R. F. (1962). *Preparing instructional objectives.* Palo Alto, CA: Fearon.

Markle, D. G. (1967). *An exercise in the application of empirical methods to instructional systems design. Final report: The development of the Bell system first aid and personal safety course.* Palo Alto, CA: American Institutes for Research.

Markle, S. M. (1967). Empirical testing of programs. In P. C. Lange (Ed.), *Programmed instruction.* Sixty-sixth Yearbook of the National Society for the Study of Education, Part II. Chicago: University of Chicago Press.

Markle, S. M. & Tiemann, P. W. (1970). Conceptual learning and instructional design. *Journal of Educational Technology, 1*(1), 1–11.

McClung, M. S. (1978). Are competency testing programs fair? Legal? *Phi Delta Kappan, 59*(6), 397–400.

Merrill, M. D., & Tennyson, R. D. (1977). *Teaching concepts: An instructional design guide.* Englewood Cliffs, NJ: Educational Technology.

Michigan State University. (1968). *B-Step: A teacher education curriculum.* Unpublished manuscript, Michigan State University, East Lansing, MI.

Millman, J. (1974a). Criterion-referenced measurement. In W. J. Popham (Ed.), *Evaluation in Education.* Berkeley, CA: McCutchan.

Millman, J. (1974b). Sampling plan for domain-referenced tests. *Educational Technology, 14*(6), 17–21.

Millman, J., & Outlaw, W. S. (1977). *Testing by computer.* Ithaca, NY: Cornell University Extension Publications.

Moore, N. K., Shaffer, M T., & Seifert, R. F. (1985). Basic skill requirements for selected Army occupational training courses. *Contemporary Educational Psychology, 10,* 83–92.

National Education Association. (1977). *Guidelines and cautions for consdering criterion-referenced tests.* Washington, DC: National Education Association.

Nifenecker, E. A. (1918). Bureaus of research in city school systems. In G. Whipple (Ed.), *The measurement of educational products.* Seventeenth Yearbook of the National Society for the Study of Education, Part II. Bloomington, IL: Public School.

Nitko, A. (1974). *Problems in the development of criterion-referenced tests: The IPI Pittsburgh experience. In C. W. Harris, M. C. Alkin, & W. J. Popham (Eds.), Problems in criterion-referenced measurement.* Los Angeles, CA: UCLA Center for the Study of Evaluation.

O'Neil, H. F., Jr. (Ed.) (1979). *Learning strategies.* New York: Academic Press.

O'Neil, H. F., Jr. & Richardson, F. C. (1977). Anxiety and learning in computer-based learning environments: An overview. In J. E. Sieber, H. F. O'Neil, Jr., & S. Tobias (Eds.), *Anxiety, learning, and instruction.* Hillsdale, NJ: Lawrence Erlbaum Associates.

Olympia, P. L., Jr. (1975). Computer generation of truly repeatable examinations. *Educational Technology, 15*(6), 53–55.

Osburn, H. G. (1968). Item sampling for achievement testing. *National Elementary Principal, 54*(6), 96–101.

Perrone, V. (1975). Alternative to standardized testing. *National Elementary Principal, 28,* 95–104.

Pipho, C. (1978). Minimum competency testing in 1978: A look at state standards. *Phi Delta Kappan, 59*(9), 585–588.

Polin, L. G., & Baker, E. L. (1979). *Qualitative analysis of test item attributes for domain-referenced content validity judgments.* Paper presented at the annual meeting of the American Educational Research Association, San Francisco.

Popham, W. J. (1975). *Educational Evaluation.* Englewood Cliffs, NJ: Prentice-Hall.

Popham, W. J. (1978). Practical criterion-referenced measures for intrastate evaluation. *Educational Technology, 18*(5), 19–23.

Popham, W. J., & Baker, E. L. (1968). *Rules for the development of instructional products.* Inglewood, CA: Southwest Regional Laboratory for Educational Research and Development.

Popham, W. J., & Baker, E. L. (1970). *Systematic instruction.* Englewood Cliffs, NJ: Prentice-Hall.

Popham, W. J., & Baker, E. L. (1973). *Teacher competency development system.* Englewood Cliffs, NJ: Prentice-Hall.

Popham, W. J., & Husek, T. R. (1969). Implications of criterion-referenced measurement. *Journal of Educational Measurement, 6*(1), 1–9.

Purves, A. C. (1980, August). *International study of achievement in written composition.* Paper presented at the International Education Association Conference, Jyvaskyla, Finland.

Quellmalz, E. A. (1980, June). *Test design: Aligning specifications for assessment and instruction.* Paper presented at a conference on evaluation in the 80's: Perspectives for the national research agenda. Los Angeles, CA: UCLA Center for the Study of Evaluation.

Rankin, S. (1980). *Detroit Public Schools' use of a test-triggered improvement strategy.* Paper presented at the annual meeting of the American Educational Research Association, Boston.

Rice, J. M. (1897). The futility of the spelling grind I & II. *Forum, 23,* 163–172, 409–419.

Roid, G. H., & Haladyna, T. M. (1978). A comparison of objective-based and modified Bormuth item writing techniques. *Educational and Psychological Measurement, 38,* 19–28.

Roid, G. H., Haladyna, T., & Shaughnessy, J. (1979). *Item writing for domain-based tests of prose learning.* Paper presented at the annual meeting of the American Educational Research Association, San Francisco.

Roid, G. H., Haladyna, T., & Shaughnessy, J. (1980). *A comparison of item-writing methods for criterion-referenced tests.* Paper presented at the annual meeting of the National Council on Measurement in Education, Boston.

Rosen, M. J. (1968). *An experimental design for comparing the effects of instructional media programming procedures: Subjective vs. objective revision procedures. Final Report.* Palo Alto, CA: American Institute for Behavioral Sciences.

Rudner, L. M. (1978). *A short and simple introduction to tailored testing.* Paper presented at the annual meeting of the Eastern Educational Association, Williamsburg, VA.

Sanders, J. R., & Murray, S. (1976). Alternatives for achievement testing. *Educational Technology, 16*(6), 17–23.

Schwartz, J. L., & Garet, M. S. (eds.). (1982). *Assessment in the service of instruction.* Report to the Ford Foundation and the National Institute of Technology.

Scriven, M. (1967). The methodology of evaluation. In R. W. Tyler, R. M. Gagné, & M. Scriven (Eds.), *Perspectives of curriculum evaluation. AERA Monograph Series on Curriculum Evaluation, No. 1.* Chicago: Rand McNally.

Shavelson, R. J. & Salomon, G. (1985). Information technology: tool and teacher of the mind. *Educational Researcher, 14,* 4.

Simon, G. B. (1969). Comments on "Implications of criterion- referenced tests." *Journal of Educational Measurement, 6,* 259–260.

Skager, R. (1975). *EPT material. Abstract of: Critical characteristics for differentiating among tests of educational achievement.* Paper presented at the annual meeting of the American Educational Research Association, Washington, DC.

Skinner, B. F. (1958). Teaching machines. *Science, 128,* 969–977.

Smith, E. R., & Tyler, R. W. (1942). *Appraising and the recording of student progress.* New York: Harper.

Spearman, C. (1937). *Psychology down the ages* (Vol. 1). London: Macmillan.

Stenner, A. J., & Webster, W. J. (1971). *Educational program audit handbook.* Arlington, VA: Institute for the Development of Educational Auditing.

Tiemann, P., Kroeker, L. P., & Markle, S. M. (1977). *Teaching verbally-mediated coordinate concepts in an on-going college course.* Paper presented at the annual meeting of the American Educational Research Association, New York.

Tiemann, P., & Markle, S. M. (1978). *Analyzing instructional content: A guide to instruction and evaluation.* Champaign, IL: Stipes.

Tyler, R. W. (1943). *Constructing achievement tests.* Columbus, OH: Ohio State University.

Tyler, R. W. (1950). *Basic principles of curriculum and instruction.* Chicago: University of Chicago Press.

Tyler, R. W. (1951). The functions of measurement in improving instruction. In E. F. Linquist (Ed.), *Educational measurement.* Washington, DC: American Council on Education.

Ward, J. G. (1980). Issues in testing: The perspective of organized teachers and professors. In R. Bossone (Ed.), *Proceedings: The Third National Conference of Testing: Uniting testing and teaching.* New York: Center for Advanced Study in Education.

Washburne, C. (1922). *School and Society, 29,* 37–50.

Weiner, B. (1979). A theory of motivation for some classroom experiences. *Journal of Educational Psychology, 71,* 3–25.

Wirtz, W., et al. (1977). On further examination: report of the Advisory Panel on the Scholastic Aptitude Test Score Decline. New York: College Entrance Examination Board.

Wirtz, W. (1978). *Report of the advisory panel on the SAT scores decline.* New York: College Entrance Examination Board.

Wright, B. D. (1967). *Sample free test calibration and person measurement.* Invitational Conference on Testing Problems. Princeton, NJ: Educational Testing Service.

AUTHOR NOTES

The project reported here was partially supported by grant #NIE-G-83-0001 from the National Institute of Education, Department of Education. However, the opinions expressed herein do not necessarily reflect the position or policy of the National Institute of Education, and no official endorsement by the National Institute of Education should be inferred.

Eva L. Baker is Professor in the Graduate School of Education and Director of the Center for the Study of Evaluation, University of California, Los Angeles.

Harold F. O'Neil, Jr. is Professor in the Department of Educational Psychology and Technology, School of Education, University of Southern California.

14 Planning for Instructional Systems

Robert M. Morgan
Florida State University

In preceding chapters the application of systems-analytical approaches to the design of instruction has been described. These applications have been made, in some instances, to individual courses or training programs and in others, to more comprehensive blocks of instruction. The development and implementation of individualized instruction, which was pioneered by schools in the Philadelphia, Duluth, and Bloomfield Hills, Mich., school districts, are examples of the use of Instructional Systems Design (ISD) on a fairly broad scale (Esbensen, 1968; Glaser, 1964; Morgan, 1969). The systems approach, as a tool for planning, got its start in education as teaching innovations such as programmed instruction and individualized learning were being introduced into classrooms (Flanagan,1967). The focus of these events was on the direct instructional processes and often ignored other conditions in the school, many of which directly or indirectly affected the success of the innovation which was being introduced (Corrigan & Kaufman, 1965). Such variables as class scheduling, teacher roles, facilities design, fund availability, administrative functions, and many others, were often fixed, or at least difficult to alter. When treated as "givens" in the school environment some of these variables could significantly constrain teaching innovations and limit their potential for improved learning quality (Morgan & Bushnell, 1967).

As researchers encountered these barriers to educational change they became aware of the need to broaden their perspectives and to plan more carefully the introduction of innovational activities, taking into account those conditions and aspects of the educational system that would impinge upon the innovation (Morgan, 1969). Formal education, a publicly controlled process, is enormously complex and the variables having potential for effect on educational change are seemingly almost limitless (Griffiths, 1959). Not apparent to many educational developers is the circumstance that education is essentially a political and economic phenomenon. Failure to take into account the financial and economic constraints under which most schools presently operate has doomed the operational implementation of many new instructional practices that had shown great promise in their pilot or experimental stages (Vaizey & Chesswas, 1967). Some of the better programmed instruction (PI) of the mid-1960s for example, was demonstrably superior to conventional instruction. That PI often cost more for one course of instruction than a school had budgeted for instructional materials for all subjects for the year made PI's qualitative improvement irrelevant. The PI material was simply not affordable. Less obvious, but equally potent, are the social-political processes that characterize educational decision making (Churchman, 1965). Every citizen is a stockholder of the corporate school system and every level of government—local, state, and federal—influences or controls certain features of public education. Sometimes the influence or control overlaps across these levels, and this compounds the confusion (Banathy, 1969).

The introduction of a program such as Instructional-systems Design (ISD) or any other innovation is, to a greater or lesser degree, both disruptive of and constrained by the environment into which it is introduced (Lane & Kyle, 1968). Careful comprehensive planning must be undertaken well in advance of implementation if the disruptive and restrictive effects are to be diminished to acceptable levels (Heinich, 1968; Johnson & Miller, 1969).

PLANNING FOR SYSTEM MAINTENANCE

The professional who undertakes educational planning should be aware that there are different types of planning for different purposes. Most organized planning is intended for efficient operation and maintenance of the existing system (Banghart, 1969; Banghart & Trull, 1973). Individual schools, local districts and state departments of education all have people who are involved in the planning processes. At the local school-level, the planner may be the principal, who communicates to the district office any changes anticipated in course offerings, enrollments, or personnel assignments. This type of information is aggregated at the central district level and results in a district budget and an allocation of instructional-support resources to each school (Novick, 1965). Typically, the latitude a school has in determining the nature and allocation of these resources is limited. Limits are imposed by resource availability, local-board policy, state and federal regulation, and the district's history of practices. This approach to planning is essentially enrollment-driven, where the numbers of expected students at their various levels determine almost automatically how many and what kind of resources will be given to each school (Quade, 1966).

In the United States this planning and budgeting function is predominantly controlled by the states and local communities. The federal government has traditionally limited its intervention to the funding of special programs deemed by Congress to be in the national interest. Some of these special programs have been in place for many years and are by now more routine than special. Agriculture education and the hot-lunch programs are examples of long-standing federal commitments to public education. While the federal contribution to the operational costs of schools has grown appreciably in recent years, local communities and the states still bear the largest share of this burden. The implications of this for the educational planner are that, independently of the level at which the planner is working—state, local or federal—the planners and administrators at the other levels must be taken into account as plans are developed (Kraft, 1969).

This delegation of responsibility and authority for public schooling is not typical of other nations. In most other countries the national government, usually by means of a ministry of education, exercises far more control. (Coombs, 1968). This usually results in a single, uniform national curriculum, at least through the elementary and secondary levels. Course content, instructional materials, and organizational and adminstrative processes are the same for all schools. In some countries this control extends to the point of requiring approval from the ministry of education for the hiring or removal of clasroom teachers, or for any deviation from the national educational plan. While it can be argued that such control tends to stifle local improvement initiatives, it does nevertheless ensure a measure of uniformity in the quality of instructional processes. Moreover, when a decision is taken centrally to initiate a change or reform measure, implementation at the school level occurs much faster than is possible in a highly decentralized system. By assigning to a single organization the responsibility for budgeting and program definition, some aspects of planning are greatly facilitated. Decisions to divert resources from one level of education to another may be justifiable from a national perspective, while not an apparent priority to the local educator. On the other hand, planners who spend most of their time working in the national capital may not be aware of conditions in remote schools.

PLANNING FOR SYSTEMS CHANGE

Educational programs that cannot be changed cannot be improved. Yet there are few nations possessing organizations that have as their primary missions the change and improvement of education (Witherell & Morgan, 1981). To rely for major educational improvements on institutions such as universities or government agencies, whose primary purpose is not educational improvement, has not been very successful because research linked to innovation is simply an "add-on" to their traditional functions. And their success or survival depends much more on accomplishing their usual goals rather than those associated with educational change (Morgan, 1979). Despite this absence of dedicated organizational support, many individual educators continue to work for educational improvement. This is particularly true of instructional-systems designers and educational technologists. If the assertion that most educational planners are presently focusing their efforts on maintenance of existing educational systems is true, then it is essential that professionals concerned with the change and improvement of education become creative and proficient planners.

Planning for change is very different than planning for continued, routine operation of an educational system. Many more system variables need to be taken into account (Bennis, Benne, & Chin, 1961). Undertaking planning for change within the context of the systems approach implies that instructional events will be organized and delivered to accomplish predetermined outcomes, and that the accomplishment of these outcomes will be the criteria by which the efficiency of the instructional system will be measured (Morgan & Chadwick, 1971).

During the past three decades a great many instructional innovations have been shown to contribute to improving the efficiency of one aspect or another of education. That these innovations are not today in widespread use in schools is, in many cases, due to the failure to plan at the outset for their success (Bennis, 1966). Indeed, many educational developers could have saved a great deal of effort if they had realistically forecast the barriers to widespread implementation of the new process or product they were developing (Ryans, 1963). In some instances a little thought at the beginning of a development project would have revealed that the innovation was not a realistic alternative to the existing practice. Conversely, this kind of advance analysis and planning might have highlighted features of the innovation which, without seriously jeopardizing the project's purposes, could have been changed at the beginning to make the innovation more realistically implementable in ordinary, nonexperimental schools (Morgan, 1973). When any educational reform effort is being anticipated, whether large or small, a comprehensive analysis of the variables in the system environment is essential.

ANALYSIS OF MACRO-EDUCATIONAL SYSTEMS

Rarely will the instructional systems design specialist be engaged in simple maintenance of an educational system. ISD professionals are trained to engineer change and improvement in educational programs. For this reason, it is essential that they be competent in organizing the analysis of variables in the education or training system targeted for change, and be capable of systematically describing the relevant conditions of the system. The operational phrase here is "organizing the analysis," because few ISD specialists would possess the range of expertise to deal with all the relevant elements of a macro-educational system. These include fiscal and cost issues, personnel and staffing, management, administative and logistical considerations, legal and policy issues, and all the dimensions related to the teaching/learning process (Windham, 1975). It is only in this latter domain that most ISD professionals are comfortable. Clearly, for the kind of comprehensive analysis required for planning for educational change, an interdisciplinary team of analysts is necessary (Windham, 1980). The range of interdisciplinary competencies required will be determined by the level and breadth of the system in which it is anticipated that the change will be introduced. Generally, the broader the system in question the greater the variety of needed specialists.

An additional argument for an interdisciplinary team approach to macro-systems analysis is that as planning is undertaken following the analysis, innovations, or teaching/learning approaches which are unknown to the planners will not be considered for inclusion in the newly designed system (Chadwick & Morgan, 1979). A number of specialists from diversified backgrounds, as opposed to one or only a few, are likely to be more knowledgeable about new approaches which should be considered for inclusion in the new system.

MACRO-SYSTEM VARIABLES

Most often the ISD specialist is working with a limited block of instruction—a course or sequence of courses. In approaching education more comprehensively, a larger number of elements take on relevance to the instructional design process. Following are brief descriptions of some of these important variables.

Fiscal Capacity

Fiscal capacity refers to the ability of the responsible government entity to support financially the recurrent and development costs for its educational system. Insufficient funding is the reason most often given for the problems besetting public education and more funding the most frequently offered solution (Kraft, 1969). Fiscal capacity issues include the general economic and budget issues, the projections of enrollments, and the derived projections of facilities, materials, and staff requirements. Since nearly all schools operate under severe financial restrictions, this variable is a major inhibitor of educational innovation (Miller, 1967). It is ironic that improving the cost efficiency of existing educational systems is virtually precluded if the funding of improvement measures must be taken from operational budgets (Coombs, 1970). While school systems in the United States vary considerably in their per-student annual budget allocations, nearly all systems consume nearly all of their annual funding for routine operations, with little or nothing left over for system renewal or change. The implication of this for the educational planner is that funding of development research nearly always must be sought from sources other than a local school district. The federal government and the national foundations have traditionally been the best sources with only a few states having funded research–and–development programs.

How the development of an innovational program is to be funded is a secondary question. What effect the innovation will have on the cost efficiency of school operation if it is adopted for widespread use, is a far more important question (Morgan, 1973). Is the cost of the innovation additive or substitutive? If it is additive, is there a measurable improvement in some desired educational outcome sufficient to justify the increased cost (Peters, 1969)? If the cost is substitutive, then at the expense of what?

The planner also needs to forecast changes in the educational budget. Will the availability of funding increase or decrease relative to the operational demands of the system? For most school districts in the United States there seems to be little reason to be optimistic about funding increases for education in the foreseeable future and, in fact, funding for many schools for the past several years has failed to keep pace with inflationary increases. The sources of school revenues should also be examined by the educational planner, with particular reference to whether these sources might change with changing economic conditions, or be amenable to purposeful change through government or public decision (Harbison, 1964). Finally, the fiscal analyst needs to examine carefully how the funds are allocated for programmatic use and how readily alterable are the allocation patterns.

The fiscal area of planning is one in which the ISD specialist, and for that matter, most educators, are ill equipped to work. The issues related to fiscal capacity can best be dealt with by an educational economist, and this speciality should probably always be represented on a team for macro-systems analysis.

Management and Administration

In any short- or long-range plan in which significant change in educational practice is anticipated, the management and administrative capabilities of the system must be taken into account in the planning process. In relation to school-system management and administration there are a number of analyses which will be important. Descriptions of the organizational structures within the system will reveal the formal and informal lines of communication and authority. It is essential to know the directional flow of information that affects decision making within the system. Which individual managers, or which positions, have responsibilty for which operational decisions? At what levels are system policies determined? What latitude of decision making, within the policy framework, is permitted at which working levels? What is the relationship between school policy and the operational practices of the school (Churchman, 1964)?

Another aspect of management and administration which should be examined during the analysis is the capability within the system in these areas. Are the individuals charged with managing the system trained and capable in the relevant skill areas? At the individual school level such routine support requirements which depend on effective management include teacher assignments, facilities maintenance, timely distribution of instructional-support resources, and record keeping (Flynn & Chadwick, 1970). At the higher administrative levels, such items as budget planning and allocation, community relations, school construction, hiring standards, curriculum definition, graduation and certification requirements, are determined. Inefficiencies due to management and administrative practices may be a result of poor organizational structure, a failure to delineate responsibility adequately, or inadequate communication flow among the administrative levels. Managerial effectiveness of even highly qualified persons will be inhibited if one or more of these conditions prevails. Even if the management-support conditions are ideal, poorly trained or incompetent managers in key positions will lead to system inefficiencies.

The planner needs to know these things for two reasons. First, if there are system inefficiencies attributable to the management processes, then this area becomes a target for improvement interventions. Second, even if school management is not a major problem, the people who occupy these positions at the several levels will represent major "gatekeepers" for any anticipated change in the system. For this reason they should be involved early in the analysis and planning activity (Morgan & Bushnell, 1967).

Staffing

Staffing patterns and the qualifications of teachers is a crucial variable in all school systems. In most instances, quality improvement of schools has focused on upgrading the skills of the teachers. Given the critical role in the instructional process of the teacher in the traditional classroom, it is not surprising that the teacher becomes a principal object for improvement. In the analysis of system characteristics, the properties of the teacher population should be carefully assessed, in terms of formal qualifications, experience, stability of the teaching force, and teacher availability. In the United States there has generally been a sufficient supply of trained and formally qualified teachers, except, from time to time, in such subject areas as mathematics, science, and foreign languages. In many other nations, particularly third world countries, this has not been true, and even minimally qualified teachers have been in short supply (Chadwick & Morgan, 1979; Coombs, 1969).

Education is a highly labor-intensive endeavor, and a very large share of the educational budget is allocated to personnel costs. If a desired result in improving the efficiency of education is reduced cost the only reasonable cost category for consideration is personnel (Morgan & Chadwick, 1971). In planning for increased efficiency the planner must decide how much of the development budget can be reasonably invested in upgrading personnel and how much should go to other improvement strategies. Arguments can be made that investments in upgrading teacher qualifications are not good long-term investments, for a variety of reasons. First, the relationship between additional training for the classroom teacher and student learning is tenuous. Second, with the normal attrition rate of teachers in many nations, any benefits from training investments must be realized in rather short time-periods. Third, investments in curriculum materials and processes which are designed to add to and support the teaching process appear to have more tangible and enduring benefits (Witherell & Morgan, 1981). In any case, the planner must take the teacher into account as a major variable. The conventional system places heavy reliance on the individual classroom teacher and any change intended to improve student learning must either strengthen the teacher's impact on learning or provide for additional or alternative means.

In addition to an analysis of the teacher force as a major variable in the educational system, the analyst should examine the institutional means by which new teachers are trained. How, and by whom, is the curriculum of the teacher-training institutions determined? The planner may wish to call for an instructional innovation that will require teacher roles or behavior that depart from those traditionally taught. Can these programs be changed to incorporate the modified role? How feasible are effective in-service teacher-training programs? This phase of the analysis will be facilitated by including a specialist in teacher training on the analysis team (Morgan & Bushnell, 1967).

Legal and Policy Issues

All school systems operate in the context of a sizable body of law, regulation, and policy. These are often determined at the local, state, and national level and provide the guidelines for school operation. In some cases, they are general enough to allow a fairly high degree of programmatic flexibility, but in others they are tightly prescriptive of educational practice (Bennis, Benne, & Chin, 1961). In addition, standard operating-procedures sometimes determine educational events. Laws and regulations are written, but policies and procedures may be either written or merely a matter of conventional practice. The planner must be familiar with these, for they define the boundaries within which an instructional innovation may be introduced. If major changes in existing practices are contemplated it will probably be necessary to get exemption from some of the rules and regulations. Such waivers may be obtainable at the local or district level; others may require changes in legislative authority. A few states have laws that allow, with appropriate approvals, innovational development within schools, even when the innovation is in conflict with existing regulation and policy. This is rare, however, and the educational planner will more often have to seek special approval for such new programs. It is usually not too difficult to obtain authorization for pilot or experimental projects, especially if these appear to be logical improvement measures and if they are not too disruptive of ongoing practices. Approval for the operational implementation of an innovative practice, the worth of which has been demonstrated in pilot testing, will generally require more deliberation and review at the different levels of educational jursidiction. Since this is a slow process, the planner should anticipate early what the approval requirements will be and initiate appropriate steps of information and persuasion before resources are dedicated to the project (Shin, Chang, & Park, 1984). There should be a reasonable probability that the innovational practice will be put into routine use if it meets some agreed-upon performance standard.

External Efficiency

External efficiency refers to the extent that educational systems provide an educational experience that is relevant for the activities of its students after they graduate (Cash, 1965). In this case the evaluation of the system would be in terms of external referents, that is, how well the school has prepared students for continuing in the educational sequence, for productive employment, and for their multifaceted adult roles (Corrigan & Kaufman, 1965). Fairly good data are available on the progression of students within the elementary and secondary levels. Some high schools also maintain records on which and how many of their students enter college following graduation. Much less information is available on school-leavers who do not continue in the formal education stream. Few longitudinal tracer studies have been done to assess the characteristics of those who have left formal education in favor of employment, military service, or other activities (Kraft, 1968).

Historically, external efficiency of schools has not been an important factor in school planning nor in curriculum decision making (Peters, 1969). However, with growing public sensitivity to quality of school programs and increasing inclination to hold schools accountable for their productivity, it is likely that more attention will be given to the outcomes indicative of external efficiency. Thus far, the focus on school accountability has been on in-school outcomes, such as achievement levels in the basic-skill areas. It is not unreasonable to anticipate increased public concern with school effectiveness in preparing students for postschool roles. Whether or not this occurs, the planner should attempt to relate what happens in schools to the intended preparation of students for adult living (Tuckman, 1979).

Internal Efficiency

Internal efficiency of schools refers to the extent to which available resources are utilized to achieve the maximum desired educational outcomes (Cieutat, 1983). Quantitative as well as qualitative inefficiencies are characteristics of many education programs. Improvements in quantitative efficiency can be made by focusing on the variables related to student flow and taking steps to reduce repetitions and dropouts. The educational planner will need to gather data on the numbers of students who are required to repeat grades and those who drop out. That there are grade repeaters and dropouts doesn't necessarily indicate a need for changes in the instructional program. Such a condition may point out the need for improved guidance and placement of students in the educational sequence. On the other hand, if the numbers of these is judged excessive by the system managers, an examination of the conditions of instruction that contribute to grade failure and dropout should be undertaken (Harrison & Morgan, 1982).

Probably of greater interest to most educators are the qualitative indicators of internal efficiency. Achievement levels of students by subject and level are the most widely recognized measures of school effectiveness. Baseline data on the achievement variables should be gathered in the analysis phase to indicate the instructional areas with the most urgent need for improvement, and to serve as the base of comparison in the event new approaches are implemented (Tuckman, 1979).

Measuring student achievement is not a simple process, since there are many different dimensions to student learning. Some schools rely on student performance assessments made in courses, and these can be normative or criterion-referenced assessments. Normative measures refer to assessing a student's achievement in relationship to what other students in his group have achieved. Criterion-referenced assessment is done in terms of some performance standard. This is sometimes called competency-based assessment, where the concern is with what each student knows or is able to do with respect to expected standards. Other indicators of the quality of learning are the degree to which the learning is retained through time, and the generalizability of the learning to new situations. Because the standards across schools are potentially so variable, some educators prefer to rely on standardized national examinations with norms based on the performance of large numbers of students (Morgan & Jeon, 1979). Such exams have the advantage of discounting the evaluation idiosyncrasies of individual schools, and the disadvantage to the planner of not pinpointing with much precision the particular weaknesses of instructional programs. In introducing a large-scale innovation, the planner is probably safer to gather student achievement data through both locally developed and standardized measures.

Access and Equity

Access refers to the proportion of a target population participating in a program, and equity refers to the degree to which program participation is nonrestrictive to factors beyond an individual's control (Cieutat, 1983). Governments usually define the populations they intend their various educational levels to serve, consistent with the resources the nation can dedicate to education. Many factors enter into the decisions that determine which citizens will be eligible for public education (Mayo & Hornik, 1983). National revenues, economic and manpower requirements, and sociopolitical purposes are some of these factors. Nearly all nations aspire to universal enrollments through at least the primary level of education, though many fall short of this goal (Coombs 1970). Expanding educational opportunity is an aim of virtually all societies, even the industrialized nations, which already provide relatively open access to education. The principal constraint on expanding educational opportunity is the availability of funding to pay for more schools and teachers. The planner needs to examine the degree of access and the fairness with which access occurs, and attempt to identify the conditions in the community and in the schools which inhibit access and equity. There is a large range of conditions that may affect access and equity. Only some of these are potentially amenable to control by the schools. Special-education programs for handicapped learners are far more available than they were 20 years ago. Transportation is provided for students in rural areas. And more attention is being given to adapting instruction to accommodate the increasing variation among learners. As enrollments grew, and a larger proportion of age cohorts entered public education, it became apparent that the instructional programs which had evolved with students of relatively homogeneous characteristics were not optimum for student groups which were far more heterogeneous in learning aptitude. While public policy and a prospering economy have permitted increased educational opportunity, public education has been slow in adapting educational processes to realize this aim fully (Morgan, 1969).

If the planner is working with an educational system in which improving access and equity are ambitions of the system, then he will need to be concerned with the cost of instruction—how much is spent per student and what are the constituent parts of this cost (Harbison & Myers, 1964). If means can be found to reduce unit costs, then larger numbers of students can be enrolled without increasing the total budgets for education. Instituting larger student/teacher ratios is one way to reduce unit costs, as is simply paying teachers lower salaries. The former has been less acceptable to the public than the latter. A worthy challenge for the planner is to reduce per-pupil costs and simultaneously raise the measurable quality of the instruction. Instructional technologies, such as individualized and mastery learning, and communications media, such as radio, television, and computers, are promising means of increasing educational cost efficiencies (Morgan, 1973). An alternative to reducing per-pupil costs, when improved access and equity is desired, is to raise the overall level of funding for education within the state or nation. This has not been a realistic alternative for the last three decades, however. Many societal sectors—health, transportation, defense, welfare—compete vigorously for public funds, and in most nations educational budgets have barely kept pace with inflation.

Instructional Support Capacity

Finally, the planner must examine the other elements which are critical to instructional efficiency. These include the facilities, curriculum content, instructional materials, student performance-assessment practices, and the instructional-development capacity of the educational system. For example, an analysis should be made of how the goals and purposes of the educational program reflect national needs. Are the goals and purposes stated with sufficient operational definition to have any practical meaning for educational planning? If not, can processes be initiated to examine the educational goals to ensure that they are relevant to contemporary needs and to derive goal statements of sufficient concreteness to be useful to educational planners and administrators? Is there continuity from the broad goals to curriculum aims and instructional practices? At the course level, an assessment should be made of the tangibility of instructional objectives. Are these stated in operational terms, so that desired learning outcomes can be observed under specified conditions and evaluated against established standards? Are the learning objectives complete and appropriately sequenced within and across the related courses? In reality, in most school systems these definitions of educational purposes and objectives will not be adequately developed and must be inferred from the curriculum and instructional materials being used (Harrison & Morgan, 1982).

The planner should examine the instructional materials and the means used to evaluate student learning, to determine if the materials are effective teaching instruments, and if there is congruence between what is taught and what is tested. The linkage between goals, purposes, course objectives, instruction, and student learning is often tenuous, and careful analysis may reveal the need to strengthen these links. If the quality of learning and student achievement is lower than desired, these instructional variables are good targets for improvement efforts (Miller,1967).

Any initiatives to change and improve educational efficiency will require that the system have available to it, either from within or from outside sources, the means to undertake the change (Morgan, 1979). Improvement measures might involve changes of any one or more of the system variables, and range from something that can be done quickly and without great expense, to development programs encompassing several variables, and requiring considerable funding and time to complete (Morgan, 1973). Education has, historically, been highly successful at resisting change, and improvement efforts intended to have significant impact on educational efficiency will generally need to be comprehensive and large-scale (Morgan, 1969). A precondition of undertaking large-scale educational-reform efforts is a capability in the state or nation for such development work. If this capability does not exist, and is otherwise unavailable, then it must be developed at the outset.

EVALUATION AND RESEARCH REQUIREMENTS

As the systems analysis is progressing, and as it reaches completion, it will often be evident that certain key information is not readily available. For example, a school system wishing to maximize its external efficiency may need to undertake longitudinal tracer studies to determine what has happened to its school leavers. Or a system might be concerned with student achievement in process behaviors such as creativity, analytical thinking, or problem solving. In order to determine if a problem exists in these areas it may be necessary to undertake research studies to provide this missing information (Tuckman, 1979). One of the values of the systems-analytical approach is the identification of data gaps where more research and evaluation information is required for informed decision making (Corrigan & Kaufman, 1965). As plans are formulated for system improvement it will often be desirable to undertake pilot tryouts of instructional elements, either by themselves or in combination with other elements. If new types of instructional materials, such as programmed instruction, are to be used, it would be prudent to test the use of these with ordinary teachers and students. This will permit an assessment of their effectiveness and highlight any problems which should be dealt with before widespread implementation. As the innovation becomes more complex and when many instructional elements are simultaneously changed, the need for thorough pretesting becomes even more important. In such instances, an iterative series of tryouts with between-tryout revisions may be required. Data from such research and evaluation efforts will result in improved and more realistic planning (Shin, Chang, & Park, 1984).

THE PLANNING PROCESS

When the macro-system analysis is completed the planner is ready to begin the design for change. The analysis should reveal any major deficiencies in the efficiency of the system, and provide enough related information to permit the planner and the system managers to prioritize, and to select from among these problems those which should be addressed first. The part of the system targeted for improvement may be large, such as all of elementary education, or it may be narrower, such as improving the science instruction in the secondary schools. Whatever the target is, the boundaries for improvement need to be well defined, and the criteria for success need to be established. These criteria can be highly varied, including such aims as reducing per-pupil costs, increasing student achievement, reducing learning time, reducing grade repetition and dropouts, increasing school access, or combinations of these. Once the criteria have been set, then agreement needs to be reached on how these are to be measured. The planners and system managers need to concur on what evidence will be accepted as indicators of success.

Most improvement efforts will require the mounting of an organized development project, and one of the planners' responsibilities is to coordinate the design of the project. The planning group will need to determine what is to be done, how long it will take, what kinds and numbers of specialists will be required, for how long and at what time intervals, and how the project will be managed, evaluated, and controlled. All of these project needs can be translated into funding requirements. Ordinarily, summary preliminary estimates on these needs and the predicted project outcomes will be required by the system managers before authorization to proceed with the development is given. In addition to estimates of development costs, the planners should also estimate two other kinds of costs. The first of these is the cost for system-wide implementation, that is, how much it will cost to install the new program in all the target schools. Second, what the recurring operational cost of the new program will be. Of the three types of cost—development, implementation, and operation—the latter is of far greater importance. The first two types of cost are essentially one-time investments, while the latter goes on for as long as the program is used, and generally must be multiplied by the number of students (Morgan & Chadwick, 1971).

In addition to costs, there are a number of other considerations which the planner should attend to as an improvement project is being considered. One important question is: Who will be affected by the project and what constituency does this involve? A corollary question is what orientation and information should be given to these constituents to forestall their misunderstanding and resistance to the project. Such concerned groups will typically include parents, teachers and their professional associations, government officials, and others. Informing and involving these groups early can greatly ease project implementation. Another consideration is the possibility of conflicts between the improvement project and existing regulations and policy. As was mentioned earlier, it is easier to get approval for experimentation than for operational use of a new approach to instruction. If a problem exists here it should be confronted before the project is undertaken. One reason that so many successful experiments have failed to result in changed operational practice is that the eventuality of success was not given sufficient thought at the outset (Morgan, 1973).

The plan should identify any staff training that will be needed, and include provisions for the development of the training materials. If new instructional materials for student use are anticipated, consideration needs to be given to the problems of publication and distribution. Some innovations may require changes in administrative practices, logistical support, or physical facilities. Account needs to be taken of all elements in the system that will affect or be affected by the new program, and the plan should spell out how these interrelationships will occur. In order for a plan to be a plan it must be written, and in sufficient detail to explain fully the specific project purposes, the scope of work anticipated, all of the human and material resources required, and how the project is to be formatively and summatively evaluated. Large-scale projects should utilize program evaluation and review techniques (PERT) or other appropriate management and control measures. The plan should be a detailed blueprint for action.

APPLICATIONS OF ANALYSIS AND PLANNING

Perhaps the first large-scale system analysis and planning effort, where major educational improvement was the initial intent, was undertaken in the Republic of Korea in 1970 (Morgan & Chadwick, 1971). Korea, confronted with a rapidly expanding and diversifying economy, and a supply of trained manpower insufficient to sustain the expansion, needed to modernize and expand its educational program. The country was already devoting 20% of its national budget to education and, with the military-defense posture it needed to maintain, could not increase the overall funding for public education. An interdisciplinary team of specialists from Florida State University was invited to conduct a comprehensive analysis of Korea's total education program, to see if means could be found to increase the efficiency of the educational system enough so that enrollments could be expanded without increasing expenditure. Analysis and planning professionals involved in this effort included specialists in instructional-systems design, teacher training, educational administration, economics, manpower planning, and educational technology. The analysis and planning effort took 7 months—3 months gathering the types of information described earlier, and 4 months analyzing these data and developing recommendations and a plan of action for the Korean government. The elementary and middle schools were recommended as the targets for major improvement and enrollment expansion. A new instructional-delivery system was described, which was predicted by the team to be qualitatively equal to the existing program and capable of reducing unit costs by enough to permit the enrollment of all the children in the elementary and middle-school age cohorts. This would result in an enrollment increase of nearly a million children, at the middle–school level. Korea had already attained nearly universal enrollment at the elementary level.

Included in the team's report was a plan for a development project for the design and tryout of the new curriculum. The plan estimated the costs for developing and demonstrating the new program, and the costs of implementing and operating it, if it were to be successfully demonstrated. Also specified were the time and resource requirements for the project, and specification for a national educational-development institute, which would have responsibility for developing and testing the proposed instructional-delivery system. The government created the Korean Educational Development Institute in 1971 and work began on the project as the Institute was being developed (Morgan, 1979). As parts of the new program were developed, they were tested in schools and then revised, based on feedback from the learners. Through time these parts were aggregated into larger blocks of instruction, and teacher training programs were developed. By 1978 the entire elementary curriculum had been developed and was ready for a full test. It was implemented for a complete academic year in a number of schools throughout the nation, including nearly a quarter-of-a-million children. The results were highly favorable, with the children in the experimental curriculum significantly excelling in achievement, compared with children in the control schools, in every subject and grade (Shin, Chang, & Park, 1984). The overall difference between the mean achievement of two groups was nearly 25% in favor of children taught with the new curriculum. During the life of the project, the focus was deliberately shifted by the Korean developers away from reduced unit cost to an emphasis on qualitative improvement.

The U. S. Agency for International Development, the World Bank, and other international agencies are now employing a refinement of the approach used in Korea called an Education and Human Resources Sector Assessment. Sector assessments have been completed in such countries as Liberia, Haiti, Botswana, Somalia, and Yemen. In several instances, these analysis-and-planning efforts have led to major educational-reform efforts with foreign donor assistance (Cieutat, 1983).

One of the important lessons learned from these experiences is the need of close coordination of the analysis, research, evaluation, planning, and policy-formation processes (Hoban, 1965). When these functions are not linked, with one leading to another, the resulting fragmentation leads to ill-informed decision making, and educational systems that are not as efficient as they could be.

REFERENCES

Banathy, B. (1969). *Instructional systems*. Palo Alto, CA: Fearon Publishers.

Banghart, F. (1969). *Educational systems analysis*. London: Macmillan.

Banghart, F., & Trull, A. (1973). *Educational planning*. New York: Macmillan.

Bennis, W., Benne, K. D., Chin, R. (1961). *The planning of change*. New York: Holt, Rinehart and Winston.

Bennis, W. (1966). *Changing organization*. New York: McGraw-Hill.

Cash, W. C. (1965). A critique of manpower planning and educational change in Africa. *Economic Development and Cultural Change, 14*, 33–47.

Chadwick, C. B., & Morgan, R. M. (1979). Educational technology assistance for developing countries. *Educational Technology, 9*, 24–30.

Churchman, C. W. (1964). An approach to general systems theory: In Mihajlo Mesarovic (Ed.), *Views on general systems theory*. New York: Wiley.

Churchman, C. W. (1965). On the design of educational systems. *Audiovisual Instruction, 5*, 361–365.

Cieutat, V. J. (1983). *Planning and managing an education sector assessment*. Washington, DC: U. S. Agency for International Development.

Coombs, P. H. (1968). *The world educational crisis: a systems analysis*. New York: Oxford University Press.

Coombs, P. H. (1969). Time for a change of strategy: In C. E. Beeby (Ed.), *Qualitative aspects of educational planning*. Paris: UNESCO.

Coombs, P. H. (1970). The need for a new strategy of educational development. *Comparative Educational Review, 14*, 75–89.

Corrigan, R. E., & Kaufman, R. A. (1965). *Why systems engineering?* Palo Alto: Fearon.

Esbensen, T. (1968). *Working with individualized instruction: the Duluth experience*. Palo Alto, CA: Fearon Publishers.

Flanagan, J. C. (1967). Functional education for the seventies. *Phi Delta Kappan, 39*, 27–32.

Flynn, J., & Chadwick, C. B. (1970). A study of teacher role behaviors in an innovative school. *Educational Technology, 2*, 49–55.

Glaser, R. (1964). Components of the instructional process: In J. F. DeCecco (Ed.), *Educational Technology*. New York: Holt, Rinehart and Winston.

Griffiths, D. E. (1959). *Administrative theory*. New York: Appleton-Century-Crofts.

Harbison, F. (1964). Human resources and development. *Economic and social aspects of educational planning*. Paris: Unesco.

Harbison, F., & Myers, C. A. (1964). *Education, manpower and economic growth*. New York: McGraw-Hill.

Harrison, G. V., & Morgan, R. M. (1982). *An evaluation of Improved Efficiency of Learning project: the Republic of Liberia*. Monrovia, Liberia: U. S. Agency for International Development.

Heinich, R. (1968). *Technology and the management of the institution*. Washington, DC: Association for Educational Communications and Technology.

Hoban, C. F. (1965). From theory to policy decisions. *AV Communication Review, 13*, 121–139.

Johnson, D. W., & Miller, D. R. (1969). A system approach to planning for the utilization of technology in education: In E. Morphet & D. Jesson (Eds.), *Designing education for the future.* New York: Citation Press.

Kraft, R. H. P. (1968). *Education and economic growth.* Tallahassee: Florida State University.

Kraft, R. H. P. (1969a). *Strategies of educational planning.* Tallahassee: Florida State University.

Kraft, R. H. P. (1969a). *Cost-effectiveness of vocational-technical training and technological change.* Tallahasee: Florida State University.

Lane, R. E., & Kyle, D. W. (1968). The application of systems analysis to educational planning. *Comparative Educational Review, 12,* 35–36.

Mayo, J. K., & Hornik, R. C. (1983). Evaluation's role in the planning, devlopment, and support of nonformal education: In J. C. Bock & G. J. Pappagianis (Eds.), *Nonformal education and national development.* New York: Praeger.

Miller, R. I. (1967). *Perspectives on educational change.* New York: Appleton-Century-Crofts.

Morgan, R. M. (1969). ES '70—A systematic approach to educational change. *Educational Technology, 7,* 49–54.

Morgan, R. M. (1973). An educational reform project in the Republic of Korea: In S. Winkler (Ed.), *Applications of learning technology.* Washington, DC: Corporate Press.

Morgan, R. M. (1979). *The Korean Educational Development Institute—its organization and function.* Paris: Unesco.

Morgan, R. M., & Bushnell, D. S. (1967). Designing an organic curriculum. *National Business Education Quarterly, 2,* 34–52.

Morgan, R. M., & Chadwick, C. B. (1971). *Systems analysis for educational change: the Republic of Korea.* Tallahassee: Florida State University.

Morgan, R. M., & Jeon, U. H. (1979). *Field evaluation processes in formal and nonformal education.* Tallahassee: Florida State University.

Novick, D. (1965). *Program Budgeting.* Cambridge, MA: Harvard University Press.

Peters, J. (1969). The meaning of quality in education: In C. E. Beeby (Ed.), *Qualitative aspects of educational planning.* Paris: Unesco.

Quade, E.S. (1966). *Systems analysis techniques for planning–programming–budgeting.* Santa Monica, CA: Rand Corp.

Ryans, D. G. (1963). *An information systems approach to education.* Santa Monica, CA: Systems Development Corp.

Shin, S. H., Chang, S. W., & Park, K. S. (1984). *Study of impact of E–M project on Korean education.* Seoul: Korean Educational Development Institute.

Tuckman, B. W. (1979). *Evaluating instructional programs.* Boston: Allyn and Bacon.

Vaizey, T., & Chesswas, T. D. (1967). *The costing of educational plans.* Paris: Unesco.

Windham, D. M. (1975). The macro-planning of education—why it fails, why it survives, and the alternatives. *Comparative Education Review, 2,* 187–201.

Windham, D. M. (1980). Micro-educational decisions as the basis for macro-educational planning: In H. N. Weiler (Ed.), *Educational planning and social change.* Paris: Institut Internationale de Planification d'Education.

Witherell, R. A., & Morgan, R. M. (1981). *Korean elementary—middle school project: a national impact evaluation.* Washington, DC: U. S. Agency for International Development.

AUTHOR NOTES

Robert M. Morgan is Professor and Director of the Learning Systems Institute, Florida State University.

15 Instructional Systems Development

Robert K. Branson and Gerald Grow
Florida State University

Instructional Systems Development (ISD) spans a broad range of activities. It has one foot planted in an abstract realm—a place where professors conduct measurements in the laboratory, theoreticians debate fine points of cognitive style, and engineers design microchips. The other foot of ISD, however, is planted in the field, where applications take place—among soldiers in tanks, autoworkers at the plant, students in classrooms, clerks in retail stores, and Nicaraguan villagers learning mathematics by radio. The beauty of ISD is that it connects the rarefied world of research, learning theory, and experimental psychology with the ordinary world, where people need skills to work and live. The connection is a fruitful one. Laboratory research provides better methods for teaching people what they need to know; from experience trying to train numerous people in a variety of skills, ISD professionals have been led to conduct new kinds of research on people whose needs are not met by traditional schooling. In ISD, theory guides practice and practice grounds theory, while enriching it.

The application of ISD in the world, however, has proved to be challenging and complex. This chapter will briefly review the place of ISD in the history of the transfer of knowledge, discuss one of the comprehensive systems models of ISD, then concentrate on what happens to ISD in application, when the model meets the world.

ISD AND THE DISTRIBUTION OF KNOWLEDGE

The creation of new knowledge is a fundamental quest of humankind. Equally fundamental is the distribution of knowledge; for each new generation must be trained in the arts of being human. In the brief survey that follows, we will trace the history of knowledge distribution and show that, although ISD grows out of that history, it revolutionizes knowledge-distribution practices.

The oral tradition served the human race well for millions of years. At the climax of the oral tradition in ancient Greece, scholars met to conduct complex discussions on the nature of life, thought, and knowledge. But the oral tradition is an inefficient way to distribute knowledge widely. Also, as we still see today, an oral public forum provides an easy target for governments, kings, and religions that seek to control the development and distribution of ideas. After they organized schools, scholars could stop wandering and spend considerably more time transmitting the knowledge of the generations to those who had come to study with them. A scholar in residence speaking directly to a student, though, still represents a way of distributing knowledge that is cumbersome. Nevertheless, some scholars achieved enough influence over their pupils to become threats to those institutions seeking to teach the "approved" version of things.

The lecture ranks high among early innovations in educational technology. Using the lecture method, a scholar could distribute ideas to everyone within voice range, limited only by acoustics and the inverse–square law. Through the technology of the organized lecture, the amount of information exchange increased dramatically from what was possible with the one-to-one method.

After Gutenberg invented printing, knowledge could be distributed far beyond the range of the scholars' voices. Then a new profession intervened between the scholars (who created knowledge) and the students (who learned it). These were the publishers, whose job was not only to print books but to edit or transform scholarly writings so that readers could understand them. In translating, popularizing, and distributing the knowledge of others, publishers became the first instructional developers.

As book publishers slowly evolved product lines suitable for use by students of all ages, these books became the cornerstone of school curricula. Schools with the greatest libraries had the greatest stores of information to offer to aspiring scholars. Later, when educational institutions began catering to the general public in addition to the economic elite, vastly increasing the number of enrollments, it soon became apparent that the existing product lines were not suitable for the mass-education market, and special-purpose *instructional materials* were developed and sold. Hornbooks, spellers, readers, and catechisms were widely used in the American colonies (Reynolds, 1976). These textbooks were not meant to document knowledge; they were meant to distribute it.

The social impact of this early instructional development was profound, because, for the first time, *teachers* became part of the process. As book-selection procedures evolved, governments relied on the technical expertise of teachers to choose which books to buy. Teachers and school administrators became the most important members of the *commercial* feedback loop in textbook publishing. The publishers of *McGuffey's Fifth Eclectic Reader* (rev. ed., 1879) recognized the contribution of teachers who commented on the previous edition.

Although now more elaborate, the same general book-selection procedure has been in use for a hundred years. Then, as now, if teachers chose controversial books, those selections could be overridden by community leaders or power groups. Indeed, litigation by power groups has become much more common, and, in the end, some instructional materials are finally selected by the courts.

Most students today use teacher-chosen textbooks; these selections are not always the best. Trying to improve textbook selection, Florida and California have passed laws requiring booksellers to show that their materials have been verified and revised, based on student use. Unfortunately, enforcement of the spirit of learner verification laws has yet to be done effectively and enforcing the letter of the law has a negligible impact. Legislation alone does not increase the sophistication of the teachers who decide which texts to buy, and the marketplace continues to decide the quality (or lack of quality) in the textbooks adopted.

This, then, is how knowledge reached students before the advent of instructional systems development. Knowledge generated by scholars and experts gradually moved into appropriate distribution channels through tomes, technical books, monographs, and journals. These materials were then simplified, translated, and modified for instructional purposes by textbook authors, published commercially, adopted by school boards, and used in classrooms. Knowledge reached adult learners outside the classroom through a roughly parallel route. Instead of going through teachers, the knowledge reached adults through books, magazine writers, popular authors, or through apprenticeship methods of one-to-one contact, such as on-the-job training.

Practitioners of ISD bring something new to history by adding a new direction to the traditional flow of knowledge. Instead of beginning (as publishers do) with the *scholar's knowledge* and trying to sell it to teachers, ISD professionals start with *organizational needs,* then design a system to deliver knowledge in a form that fills those needs. Unlike pure scholarship, ISD is not concerned with the dissemination of knowledge for its own sake; it fills identified needs by delivering the required knowledge to the designated students. Figure 15.1 shows graphically our conceptualization of this history.

The focus of ISD is not on what experts know, but on how students perform. ISD is supremely pragmatic. Yet, for all of its practicality, any given application of ISD is rooted in the abstract realms of research and systems

1. The scholarly book:

2. The published book used as text:

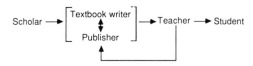

3. The Commercially - Produced textbook:

4. The ISD approach centers on organized needs:

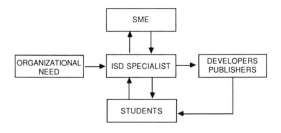

Before ISD, the flow of knowledge originated from the scholars. In ISD, the flow of knowledge originates from a defined need and a specied outcome.

FIGURE 15.1   Historical origins and changes in the flow of knowledge and feedback.

analysis, and guided by an idealized approach called The Model. We refer to the products and processes resulting from using The Model as *educational technology.*

ISD Models: The Ideal

ISD is a method for teaching students how to do specifically defined things—applying research-based methods through a systems approach to the problem. The students may be anyone—children, army recruits, executives, autoworkers, or others. The learning can theoretically be anything, as long as you can precisely define what it is and measure when someone has achieved it. The approach of ISD uses research-based methods of instruction, expanding the art of teaching with the results of experiments. The overall approach taken by ISD—which we will look at first—takes place in the context of a *systems approach to training* (SAT) model.

Henri Fayol (1917; see 1949 translation), the French industrialist and mining engineer, is responsible in part for the principles and intellectual constructs upon which all systematic management models and subsequent SAT models are based. However, it is unlikely that a generic SAT model will perform well for any instructional purpose, unless it is properly modified and integrated into the using organization. It is important that for any established need, an ISD or SAT model be adopted or adapted; but the universal, all-purpose model does not exist (see Butler, 1972; Zemke & Kramlinger, 1982). Robert B. Miller (1953, 1954) is normally credited with conceptualizing the first SAT model presented in Fig. 15.2. O'Neil (1979) has recently documented the currently critical issues and practices of ISD; also, see Gagné (1962).

The necessity to codify an organizational approach to training development has been criticized, both by Montemerlo and Tennyson (1976) and Thi-

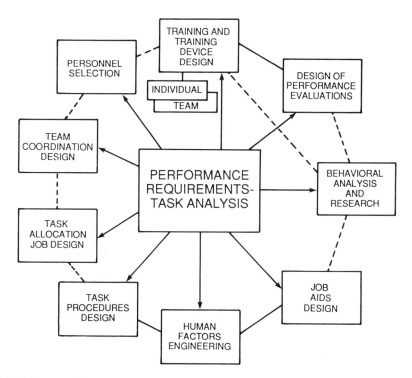

FIGURE 15.2 The early conceptualization of the systems approach to human resources development and training (adapted from Miller, 1953).

agarajan (1976), on the basis that there are already too many SAT models in the literature. These objections are based on the false premise that there exists a generic SAT model that will apply to all organizations. By now, hundreds of SAT models have been developed and used to satisfy specific organizational requirements; they remain instances of the generic model from which they were adapted and will probably not be readily transferred to other organizations.

Andrews and Goodson (1980) reviewed some 40 SAT models, one of which, the Interservice Procedures for Instructional Systems Development (IPISD) model (Branson et al., 1976; Branson, 1981) is used here as an example (see Fig. 15.3). The IPISD was chosen because it is a completely modular input-output model.

The purpose of all ISD models is to provide a conceptual framework into which compatible procedures can be integrated to produce effective and efficient instruction. The IPISD represents these conceptual functions in the five phases shown in Fig. 15.3.

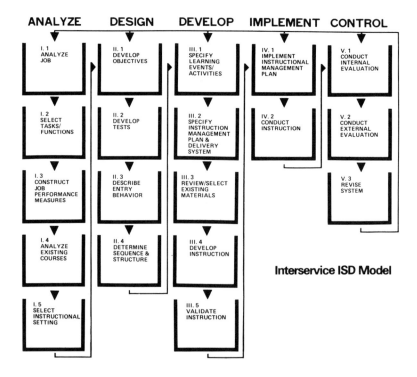

FIGURE 15.3 The model of Interservice Procedures for Instructional Systems Development (IPISD). (Branson et al., 1976).

Within each phase or function, there are alternative procedures that ISD professionals have at their command with which to construct an approach to those performance problems addressed in the procedures. Specifically, IPISD was organized to address training *primarily in single and multiple procedural tasks.* That model does not take into account analyzing jobs and designing instruction for what Reigeluth and Merrill (1979) refer to as *transfer tasks.* The learning of single and multiple procedural tasks involves practicing the tasks themselves, whereas transfer tasks occur under such a variety of circumstances that only attributes of tasks are learned (principles, rules, concepts) rather than specific tasks.

In the *analyze* phase, the ISD professional studies documentation, observes performance, and may conduct interviews about tasks to be learned. These steps may require considerable intellectual work, research, and application of sophisticated computer software. During this stage, project participants come to an agreement on job content and how they will test job performance. Consideration of alternatives to instruction (e.g., job performance aids) must take place here.

In the *design* phase, instructional specifications and training tests are developed. Entry skills are specified to identify those qualified for the instruction. While the first two steps in ISD are dominated by abstract concerns, the last two steps, *implement* and *control,* typically require more practical, managerial, even political, skills. Implementation takes place in the real world, with intractable objects and equally intractable people. This is the arena in which fuses blow, mail is lost, funds run out, and the river rises. It is there that real instruction takes place, under conditions you can never fully control, with people you can never fully know. This is where experience counts, and adaptability is the law of survival.

The *control* phase provides the specific basis on which to compare the operating results with the specifications so that any discrepancies may be identified. These discrepancies are then evaluated by managers to see what corrective action must be initiated. The model also requires quality-control and quality-assurance components. According to Juran et al. (1974), quality control is the process of ensuring that the product or service developed conforms to the specifications set forth at the outset of the project.

The most significant process of quality control is that of inspection, in which ISD products and processes are compared with the explicit or implicit intention of what each ought to be. While inspection in the quality-control function is the process of deciding whether what occurred resembled what was planned, *evaluation* in quality assurance is the process of deciding whether the developed product is fit for the intended use. While it is possible to have a product that conforms to specifications, yet falls far short of its planned accomplishments, it is not possible to have a product that rates high on the quality assurance dimension if it does not conform to specifications.

The first law of quality states: *Quality cannot be inspected into a product; it must be built in.*

In the middle, poised between the more abstract stages of *analyze* and *design* and the more applied stages of *implement* and *control,* sits the *development* phase. Development results in production of materials (products and descriptions of processes) with which to bridge the gap between requirements and results.

ISD approaches any instructional problem with an extensive repertoire of analytical tools, research findings, and understanding of how different people learn different things. That alone makes it powerful and would often be enough to make it good. But ISD's most significant attribute is in the use of feedback (Deterline & Branson, 1972).

Feedback

Based on a control-theory model, a feedback mechanism is built into each ISD subsystem. The provision for feedback across all major subsystems contains the assumption that ISD professionals cannot know everything in advance. Planning in advance to use feedback assumes that conditions may change, and programs may have to change to meet them. Plans to incorporate the results of feedback assume that there will be discrepancies between what occurred and what was planned—but that they can be set back on course. Through feedback, the results of a system are used to correct it, steer it closer to the ideal course.

ISD practitioners differ from traditional educators in this crucial sense. No matter how good an ISD plan is, no matter how right it looks, or how well it worked "the last time," ISD practitioners bow to a profound professional humility that leads them to try it out, see how close they came, and use those findings to improve the program.

Developers use feedback to correct materials and processes so they come closer to the target, but they must first have a target. The existence of a target—a clearly defined, operationalized set of learner outcomes, along with ways of measuring those outcomes—also distinguishes ISD from tradition. Unless it is set to 70°, a thermostat cannot use its built-in feedback mechanism to correct room temperature so that it hovers around 70°. Unless ISD professionals can clearly define just what learners are supposed to do after being instructed—and have the client in full agreement—feedback can't help much. Indeed, in the absence of definable goals, ISD itself will not work, and probably should not be attempted at all. Nothing is gained by using an elaborate system for getting good at something if you don't have a clear idea of what that something is. Under those conditions, you may as well improvise.

ISD requires not only that trainees be evaluated (as they have always been), but also that the training program be evaluated. In the IPISD Control

Phase, procedures are described to collect data for two distinct purposes: for *revision* of the products and processes of the program, and for *feedback* to the students and instructional staff. When the instructional products and processes fail to meet design specifications, the instruction may be revised. When students fail to meet the required standards, actions to improve the performance of individual students or classes can also be initiated.

When revisions in the *instructional materials* are required, based on operating results, the activity resembles product manufacturing. When instructional procedures for individual students are revised as a result of feedback, the activity resembles a continuous-process activity, such as that of a refinery or chemical plant (Friend, Searle, & Suppes, 1980). Evaluation will be more intense during the early phases of implementation. After the instructional system has operated long enough to collect adequate data on it, it may be necessary to make revisions in the program—or to continue development on the program until it reaches the current design objectives. Because revision is one form of instructional development, revision continues as long as there is a requirement for the instruction.

ISD is distinguished, in part, from other forms of instruction by these features:

1. Valid need for instruction has been established;
2. Trainees must reach minimum acceptable performance; and
3. Alternatives to instruction have been proposed and rejected.

Instructional systems *design* refers to those activities used to convert requirements into instructional specifications. Instructional systems *development* is the process of producing those materials, products, and processes that will be used by the target audience. In larger projects, development can include computer programming, print materials, video or film or audio forms of instruction, and conducting extensive instructor and manager training (Tracey, 1971).

The Model that governs any given ISD project is a way of organizing all the development steps so that the purpose is always clear, the goals identified, all necessary steps spelled out, all cross-checking done, and the outcome compared with the goals to fine-tune the project. ISD follows results-oriented procedures that, under ideal circumstances, lead to the particular learning required.

But models don't rule the world, and, in practice, ISD is messier, more varied, and far more creative than any model of it. In the sections that follow, we will look at some of the dragons met and the maidens rescued by people who search for the grail of systematically developed instruction.

THE MODEL MEETS THE WORLD: APPLICATIONS

Alternative Ways to Organize ISD

It is not the purpose of ISD to sell solutions. Among its most distinctive characteristics are the procedures used to generate alternatives for consideration: alternatives to instruction, alternative forms of instruction, alternative media, and alternatives to instructional management. In this section we will examine some of the many ways the guiding ideals of ISD have taken form in the world, how ISD wraps itself differently around different kinds of projects, and how organizations have institutionalized ISD.

One of the classic problems in the manufacture of any product is the deliberate decision to *buy* its component parts or *make* them. Business-school professors have long used the buy-or-make problem to challenge their students in systematic analysis and decision making. Users of instructional products face the same decision, and Fig. 15.4 presents an example of the buy-or-make issue applied to instruction.

Since the late 1950s, a sizable ISD industry has been growing to serve government and corporate markets. These contractors range from single professionals, through small enterprises with no more than 50 employees, to major corporations having the capability to manufacture training devices, simulators, and other sophisticated products.

Many organizations, however, make more instruction than they buy. Some have internal ISD groups dedicated to developing in-house instructional

	SOME	ALL
BUY	When requirements are greater than internal capacity to produce. For peak loads. For specialized products.	When requirements are unpredictable or sporadic. When internal cost control is a critical issue.
MAKE	When security problems, trade secrets, or limited internal capacity requires supplemental development assistance.	When the expertise and commitment are internal. When the need for control is extreme. When there are no available qualified contractors.

FIGURE 15.4   Some considerations in deciding whether to buy or to make instruction.

products. Others do some work internally, and buy the rest from contractors. If an organization seldom needs ISD programs, it probably makes more sense to hire a contractor each time. If an organization will require numerous ISD products over time, it may pay to have a dedicated internal ISD service group. The entire defense industry of the United States is based on a prime-contractor–subcontractor model that permits contractors to capture the expertise of outside experts.

While any organization could use a decision-theoretical approach to arrive at an optimum choice, it is far more likely that executives will decide the buy-or-make issue based on their personal experiences—and government procurement regulations. The advantage of in-house ISD is its availability to work on priorities established by management. Later, as the development group learns more about its employer's business, it becomes considerably more capable of developing quality products.

The disadvantage of captive ISD groups is that they represent a constant item of overhead and might often be assigned low-priority work—work that might not be done at all if they were not available. An advantage of contracting for development is that, when the work effort is completed, the contractor is no longer on the payroll. Contractors also often provide new ideas, and the buyer has the freedom to consider alternative offers from various contractors and pick the best.

Within organizations, ISD groups can function in a variety of ways (see Clymer, 1984). Some groups are assigned to a specific division, department, or cost center, where they work exclusively on internal problems (Fig. 15.5). In other organizations, the ISD group is located at headquarters or corporate staff levels, where its developers serve numerous clients throughout the different branches of the organization. These ISD services may be provided

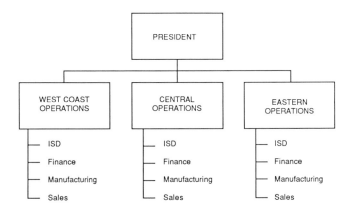

FIGURE 15.5 Centralized ISD groups dedicated to a separate profit center within an organization.

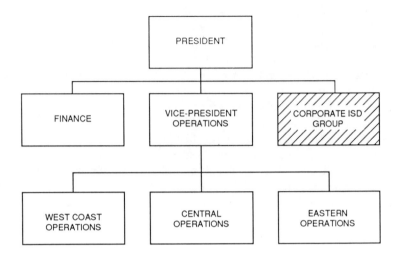

FIGURE 15.6 Placement of a centralized ISD group in an organization where configuration management and uniformity of instruction are critical.

as a part of the normal overhead of doing business; but more commonly, centralized ISD services are charged to each division. Under the centralized model, an ISD staff in San Francisco may provide service to divisions throughout the world. Fig. 15.6 presents the centralized model. Fig. 15.7 presents a model showing the ISD group as one of many profit centers.

Which organizational approach is best? As with so many questions in life, the answer depends on numerous organizational policies and preferences, the nature of the business, and its size. Regulated industries are probably best advised to consider first the centralized model. Firms with highly decentralized organization and multiple product lines may be better off with the ISD group dedicated to each division or profit center. To make the best individual choice, an external audit of the company should be made by

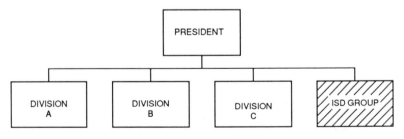

FIGURE 15.7 Organizational model showing an ISD group positioned so that it can be commissioned by any division to produce training. Here, the ISD group may be a profit center.

experienced ISD professionals, who can provide a clear rationale for a management decision.

Alternative Approaches to ISD Projects

Whether ISD is done in-house or by contractors, there are numerous approaches developers can take, depending on the size of the project. Many small ISD programs have been conducted by subject-matter experts (SMEs) who have been trained to do ISD work. Normally, either the in-house staff or contractor will train these experts—such as engineers, noncommissioned officers, industrial trainers, or technical workers—to use ISD to solve organizational problems. With appropriate coordination and supervision, these SMEs develop the required instruction themselves.

In other cases, it is more efficient to assign one ISD specialist to work with one SME to develop the training program. This arrangement has the advantage that the ISD professional is available to translate SME expertise into an effective training program. The first generation of microcomputer manuals were largely written by SMEs (programmers and engineers), and many of those manuals were notoriously difficult to use. Recently, the computer industry has begun to hire instructional designers to extract knowledge from the SMEs and convey that expertise through easily usable manuals.

This method can be quite efficient; a two-person group can get work done in a short time. The disadvantage is that unless the results are verified by others, content validity is in question. To improve content validity, organizations often assign a group of two or more SMEs to work with the ISD practitioner—who then must develop some way of achieving consensus among them (see the subsequent section on consensus).

On large projects, ISD specialists are often assigned entirely to a subspecialty within the organization. For example, ISD professionals can be assigned to the analysis function, a second group to the design function, a third group to the development function, a fourth to implementation, a fifth to control (see Fig. 15.8). In developing materials under this arrangement, there are clear-cut interfaces where the work of one group stops and the other starts. To keep the lines of communication clear, these interfaces must be explicit. In the IPISD, the input–output specifications describe the form of the product as it leaves one phase and enters the next. That feature permits users to organize their management systems according to the various phases of the model. After the IPISD appeared, the U.S. Army reorganized the schools in the Training and Doctrine Command to conform to the IPISD phases. The subsequent specialization of functions permitted the Army to develop considerable expertise (Department of the Army, 1976).

The shape of any ISD project depends not only on the nature of the organization sponsoring it, but also on the complexity of the project. Some projects can be completely carried out by a single person acting alone. Such

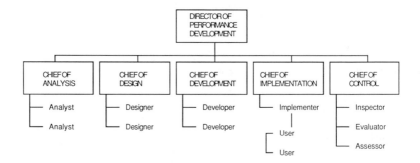

FIGURE 15.8 The departmentalized approach to ISD where numerous projects move through each of the separate specialized functions.

projects can often be found in university instructional development centers that provide a variety of services to faculty. The ISD specialist in a university may seek out faculty members, perhaps in large undergraduate courses, and work with them until the course is completely redesigned according to ISD procedures. In such cases, the ISD specialist may perform virtually all of the design and development work, with the possible exception of producing the media, and may monitor the course once it is installed. Alternatively, a single faculty member trained in ISD may carry out the entire development alone, from design through implementation.

In more complex projects, the ISD specialist is unlikely to be expert in all areas and will probably consult with other experts to produce the quality of course that the client requires. For example, many courses require more complex tests than an ISD generalist has been trained to prepare. In those cases, it would be wise to select a test-development specialist to assist in the unique aspects of a course. While measurement may be the most obvious form of expertise the ISD specialist needs, it would also be prudent to consult with other professionals in needs analysis, media development, job analysis, and task analysis.

In projects that are both large and complex, the project manager should have leeway in organizing the work. If a project requires an extensive development effort, for example, the project manager may divide the project among different development *teams.* Each team would be assigned to develop specific courses or lessons and would be totally responsible for establishing requirements and developing the instruction (Fig. 15.9).

Alternatively, the project manager could *departmentalize* the project, making one group responsible for analysis, a second for design, and so on. The advantage of the team approach is that project responsibility and management-by-objectives are easier to implement. The disadvantage is that it is more difficult to maintain consistent quality across all of the design teams.

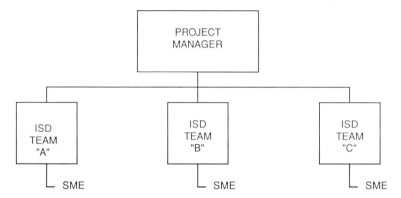

FIGURE 15.9 ISD organizational concept in which teams are each assigned similar tasks.

As the U. S. Army discovered, the departmental approach has the advantage that people become much more adept at performing the specialized function than in performing the generalized function. A second advantage is that it is easier to maintain a constant level of quality across the entire range of lessons. The principal disadvantage of the departmental approach, however, is that the product can be no better than the work of the front-end analysis group. To accomplish more effective front-end analysis, the Army's Training Developments Institute has regularly conducted training programs for the personnel in charge of analysis.

That is a serious problem. *No instructional program can be better than the quality of the analysis that precedes it.* If the front-end analysis is not done well, no amount of attention to instructional design and developmental detail will make the instructional program good. Conversely, if the front-end analysis is done well, wide variations in development and implementation quality are tolerable.

Specialties Required for Larger ISD Projects

To be successful, an ISD project must be preceded by a competent needs analysis that defines the problem for which ISD is the solution of choice. All of the specialties that follow are based on the assumption that there is a documentable need for the project. The *problem analyst,* consultant, or needs assessor is a key member of the ISD team.

Typically, the ISD professional will function as the *project manager.* That role has been debated for years with subject matter experts, but more and more funded projects are directed by ISD professionals. Often the logic for choosing ISD professionals is that they presumably have no vested interest in the content being studied. Since there are often conflicts among SMEs about who really knows the truth, process skills become an important part of the

ISD professional repertoire. One or more competent SMEs must guide the content of the materials. Using SMEs is a process skill that has often been described in the technical literature (Bratton, 1979–80; Walter & Earl, 1982). The role of SMEs is discussed further in a later section.

Job analysts are used to describe the critical attributes of the jobs in question. While job analysis is a learnable skill, it is not always obvious to beginning practitioners how really important a competent job analysis is.

Working in conjunction with the job analyst is the *measurement specialist* who will prepare the job performance measures. A job performance measure defines operationally how the using organization measures the results of the job. That measure is used to design training programs, serve as a criterion variable for selection test development, and provide a basis for the performance-appraisal system.

From a practical point of view, each of these specialists is considered to be a journeyman in the profession—a fully trained, independent practitioner who can solve all but the most difficult problems that must be assigned to the professional master.

Instructional designers use the output of the job analysis and the job-performance measures to design the instruction. Based on the analysis, the designer writes objectives and training tests, lays out the course structure, and develops the entry-skills specifications and tests. The instructional designer's output provides the specifications used by the developers. To be effective, instructional designers must have good analytical, documentation, and writing skills.

The *editing* function is critical to project success. In an earlier section, we argued that book editors were the first instructional designers, since they bridged the gap between scholars and students. That ISD function is normally performed by experienced editors, familiar with instructional materials, who are then given necessary training in instructional design.

Professional *production staff members* translate the instructional specifications into the products and processes. These may include systems analysts and programmers in CBI projects, television and videodisc specialists, print-media producers, and the necessary supporting staffs, including artists, tape editors, and others.

Production coordinators, expediters, and *schedulers* are often required to maintain project control. These people must know the status of each element of the program, be able to locate materials, run and rerun the PERT, CPM, or other scheduling programs to ensure that the necessary events are occurring, and produce management reports.

Administrative officers must be adept at circumventing Murphy's Law. They must see to it that all equipment, people, and other resources are available when required. Creative administrative officers are the only effective defense against a well-organized bureaucracy. They must develop and track the budget constantly, and report any deviations from plans to the project director.

Customer representatives, including program managers, reviewers, implementers, SMEs, and trainees must all be taken into account. Most ISD projects are not initiated by people in the field; they are ordinarily started by someone in management who is aware of a performance discrepancy and wants to find a way to fix it. Consequently, the manager of an ISD project must be aware that the ISD fix for a problem in the field will virtually never be welcomed by those who are to receive it.

It should be clear that we believe that no ISD project of any size can be successfully completed by amateurs. Montemerlo and Tennyson (1976) presented this assertion best when they argued cogently that procedures manuals could not be properly used by unqualified and untrained staff.

ISD In Business and Industry

Business and industry probably include the largest users of ISD products. When national or international firms bring the same product or service to market throughout the world, they need valid, standardized, and effective training for both employees and customers. To manage instructional configuration and take advantages of the payoffs from technology, many corporations (such as IBM) use videodiscs, computer-based instruction, and other media that provide consistent implementation in a wide range of environments. For example, General Motors provides new product and servicing information to its dealers through a videodisc system that is updated each model year. They ensure that all users get the same information and that all maintenance and repair personnel are given the latest technical orders and repair instructions. Sales personnel use the system to identify models and features that customers want to know more about. It takes much less time for a customer to use the videodisc to learn about the available features than it would take to read a stack of brochures (Perecman, 1980).

Simulators and training devices have been developed for operator training in numerous occupations, from keypunch operators to credit managers, from oil-well servicing personnel to bank tellers. Some employees are seeking the efficient acquisition of skills, while those in occupations requiring more complex judgments are provided numerous situational alternatives to consider in decision making.

In addition to General Motors, many other organizations are finding effective applications for interactive videodisc and videotape technology, along with videodiscs combined with microcomputers, to provide an impressive array of instructional hardware. Instructional development activities for interactive videodiscs rely on the expertise of a variety of specialists, including television producers, instructional designers, computer specialists, and others. The 3M company has developed a videodisc-based training package to train its customers how to make interactive videodiscs. The message is truly in the medium (*Producing interactive videodiscs*, 1982).

ISD in Government and Military Agencies

According to Roberts, Lawson, and Neal (1975), in the early 1970s the U. S. Army undertook what was probably the largest single procurement of ISD materials. The Training Extension Course (TEC) program originated in the Army's elite Combat Arms Training Board at Fort Benning, with the intention of overcoming training deficiencies that had been identified by an internal review board. Out of that action came the development and distribution of literally thousands of TEC lessons to Army operating units in the United States and abroad. These lessons were developed either in paper-and-pencil, audio, or audiovisual format, depending on the content requirements. Most lessons were audiovisual and could be used on the Besseler Cue-See projector.

To carry out the TEC project, the Army developed a specific instructional–design model to be used in procurement so that TEC contractors would understand precisely what the Army wanted to buy. When the bids came in, the reviewers considered the ability of each of the bidders, all small specialty firms, to perform according to specifications, based in part on each firm's personnel qualifications. The initial TEC buy was a significant departure from the way instructional materials were previously purchased by the Army in that it required a tryout and revision cycle prior to delivery. The term "empirically designed instruction" was used by the Army to describe TEC.

To produce the TEC lessons, each contractor assigned work to various internal ISD specialists, who were responsible for developing lessons according to the specifications. In the early days of the TEC program, as many as 100 lessons were under development at any given moment, each produced by a contractor.

We consider the award of the first TEC contract to Florida State University in 1973 as the watershed for ISD professionals. Before that, contracts were awarded mostly on the basis of subject-matter expertise to contractors who had manufactured the equipment. Since that time, it has become commonplace for buyers to insist that projects be staffed with ISD professionals.

The next step the Army took in ISD was profound. It developed a Military Specification, *Integrated Technical Documentation and Training* (Shriver & Hart, 1976), and required in procurements that the IPISD Model be used in the development of new training programs delivered with equipment systems. Prior to that time, technical manuals and training courses were developed by engineers and were often unfit for soldier populations.

In the Navy, instruction is often developed at one location and delivered in another. The technicians who develop the instruction may not be those who deliver it. Though controversial, this independence of development and delivery can be the greatest advantage of the ISD process in large organizations (Scanland, 1978). By contrast, consider how apprehensive most traditional schoolteachers would feel if they were required to design effective and valid courses that would then be taught by another person in another location.

Because the intellectual capabilities of recruits in the all-volunteer force vary greatly from year to year, the Army decided to implement a functional basic skills program to correct any entry-skills deficiencies that would interfere with efficient training. Since equipment and jobs are getting increasingly more complicated, the problem of training is also more difficult. At the same time, the Army did not want to spend unnecessary time correcting basic skills problems.

After commissioning a job analysis of 85% of the jobs that soldiers perform, the Army contracted for the required instruction to be delivered principally by computer. The computer-based Job Skills Education Program (JSEP) is intended to be implemented on all Army posts in the United States beginning in mid-1988, using the PLATO® and MicroTICCIT® computer-based instruction systems. Each of these systems has features that make it more suitable for some locations than others; and being able to buy the systems from different vendors preserves business competition. The JSEP program diagnoses individual deficiencies and provides instruction on only those specific skills soldiers need before they can learn their jobs.

ISD in Education

Although ISD is widely used in industry and government, applications in education on any wide scale have been limited (Terrell & Shrock, 1984). The Open University in Great Britain and some international radio and television projects are notable exceptions. Most good resident educational applications have been on a small scale, involving only one or two courses. A significant exception, Oakland Community College in Michigan, was in 1965 the first public institution of higher learning that planned and implemented ISD on an institution-wide basis (Canfield, 1968).

Prophets in their own countries, the leading ISD faculty have not been able to persuade their universities to adopt ISD to any significant degree, although individual faculty members have developed courses using this model. In higher education, two paths of action are typical: (1) A professor in an academic department adopts a generic model, such as the Keller Plan (Keller, 1968) or Postlethwait's (1969) Audiotutorial System, then develops a course based on these systems; or, (2) Individual professors are approached by campus instructional development service groups, who convince them to develop systematic instruction for their courses. Accounts of such courses have appeared in various journals, notably the *Journal of Instructional*

Development and the *Journal of Educational Technology Systems.* Campus instructional-development groups proliferated during the late 1960s and early 1970s, but their numbers have recently fallen (Gustafson & Bratton, 1984). The offices of research in medical education—counterparts to university ISD service groups—have also declined in numbers in recent years (Grover, Smith, & Schimpfhauser, 1985).

Local efforts at implementing ISD courses have had little impact on higher education, but many writers believe that courses developed through these methods have been successful (Kulik, Kulik, & Cohen, 1979; Lasco, 1971). The decision to retain these locally developed courses is vested with individual professors. If the professors move to other courses, the investment made in the developed course is often lost. Administrators are reluctant to undertake costly development efforts only to see the results lost because professors pursued other interests and their successors had no interest in teaching someone else's course.

Perhaps because of the enthusiasm for ISD among the dedicated faithful, or because there were no alternatives available to them, proponents of systematic instruction have wasted millions of hours and even more dollars on in-service training for schoolteachers, often with the naive hope that those teachers would then improve results through better instruction.

It is mind-boggling to consider how many different algebra and science teachers have each written their own unique behavioral objectives and test items for courses in these subjects. Once the objectives are written, teachers use them to develop courses. After that fruitless exercise is over, virtually no checks are ever made on either the quality or content validity of the instruction. Nevertheless, in-service training marches on, and half-implemented projects continue to give ISD a bad name.

Commercial Off-the-Shelf (COTS) Courseware

One of the more fascinating studies of ISD occurs when one reviews the development history of commercial off-the-shelf (COTS) courseware. The attempt to develop COTS courseware was based on the publisher's distribution models, either for the public schools, industry, or individual buyers.

Starting in about 1960, the most significant source of COTS ISD courseware for individual use came through the development and sale of printed, programmed-instruction materials. At that time, the most significant compliment paid to the ISD community occurred when major encyclopedia companies used programmed instructional materials, developed according to the best-known learning principles, as premiums to sell their encyclopedias.

Encyclopedia Britannica, The Grolier Society, and other national marketing organizations, including supermarkets, sold programmed textbooks and teaching machines to individuals and to the schools. Major developers of programmed texts and teaching machines sold by the encyclopedia companies were Teaching Machines, Inc. (founded by Homme and Evans in 1959) and General Programmed Teaching Corporation (founded by Morgan, Branson, and Ellis in 1961). Other corporations, including Basic Systems, Inc., (now Xerox Learning Systems), and Learning, Inc. were entrepreneurial ventures started by Skinnerian psychologists. Although other textbook publishers offered programmed instructional materials later, the encyclopedia companies were the first serious sellers.

When visiting large supermarkets, drugstores, and discount houses, notice the great care paid by the retailer to point-of-purchase sales messages, product displays, and packaging. These selling methods work well to cause buyers to choose their products. When you open the box of deodorant or other personal or cosmetic product, you can see that the box occupies considerably more space on the shelf than the dimensions of the product require. This packaging feature creates the impression that the package inside contains more than the label says. The same general marketing concepts apply to COTS courseware. Product appearance is typically the most important consideration, followed by how quickly the product actively engages the user, and the degree to which the user perceives it as fun to use. These factors, and perhaps referrals or recommendations from others, are all taken into account in the decision to buy.

Personal computers. The intricacies of the marketplace and the nuances of design that attract buyers have distinctly important messages for ISD products. Since more and more personal computer households are capable of using COTS courseware, marketers will need more than ever to be in close contact with their customers. This admonition has been enthusiastically endorsed by Peters and Waterman in the best-selling *In Search of Excellence* (1982).

Relatively few people have been exposed to ISD. And even with such exposure, most users of ISD products do not get to choose them. Choices are made for them by teachers, training managers, professors, clubs and professional societies, and parents. For the first time, educational software presents this choice to millions of potential customers. But marketing products to professionals who will scrutinize them critically is considerably different than offering speculative products to the general public through trade outlets. Consumers buying individual instructional products are rarely influenced by statistical evidence that the materials were faithfully developed using the most significant attributes of the ISD process. Instead, individuals will buy instructional products because they need them, want them, know people who use them, or because they have fallen for the advertising-induced phobia that their children may already be permanently damaged by being deprived of the latest educational game.

THE MODEL MEETS THE WORLD: ADVICE TO DEVELOPERS

Customer Acceptance—User Characteristics

An ISD project has to take the customer into consideration—or rather, the customers. A developer has to work with a number of different people—not only those who receive the instruction, but also those who paid for it and those who administer it. We will look first at how certain characteristics of the user have an important impact on any ISD project. It is rare to have a program adopted solely because it has been demonstrated to be technically superior to the status quo.

There are five significant attributes of an audience that have a direct impact on instructional development activities. These are:

1. Whether or not the users are captive (e.g., in the military services);
2. Whether there is a free market (as in commercial computer courseware);
3. Whether there is a direct relationship between the instruction and some economic benefit (such as may be found in corporate training programs);
4. Whether the users are paid or unpaid; and
5. Whether the trainees must meet a defined, minimum-performance standard.

If the trainees are captive and if there are built-in incentives for completion, then the design and development strategies for the instruction can be quite different. It isn't terribly important whether a captive audience likes the instruction. Neither the public schools nor the military services spend much time trying to make instruction more attractive to the users. Attempting to achieve performance improvements through making instruction more attractive to students is probably not a defensible expenditure, and reports in the literature have rarely claimed statistically significant differences.

However, if one is attempting to market commercial computer courseware, the primary considerations will be how effectively the product is sold and how well the customer likes it. Product competition in a true evaluation is not likely to be a factor in the decision to buy. The customer often does not know the results of tryouts and comparisons made by professional evaluators.

The Problem of Consensus

Instructional systems projects can arise from several sources: from development teams within an organization, from outside organizations under contract to produce the materials, or from people who develop instructional materials on a speculative basis to sell to a variety of clients (Dalgaard, Simpson, & Carrier, 1982). In organizations, ISD projects usually begin in one of two distinct ways: The developer is asked either to develop a specified product, or to solve a problem.

When developers are given a problem to solve, they can use the full power of the ISD approach. In those cases, a systematic front-end analysis must be done to arrive at the specifications for the project, after considering a variety of alternative solutions. Developers, however, do not always have the luxury of practicing all of their art. When the clients have already decided what they want produced—when they have specified, say, a series of computer-based courses in a given subject—this hastens the development, but it also introduces a real danger.

Even when developers do their own front-end analysis, they may have difficulty achieving consensus among the experts. Several points should be made about the question of achieving consensus. First, if a group of experts cannot agree on the essential facts, principles, or elements of a situation, it may be that valid knowledge in the field does not exist. If such knowledge does not exist, developing good instruction will be extremely unlikely; ISD will not help.

Second, there is no easy method for achieving consensus among experts. Unless groups of SMEs are carefully orchestrated, they can deliberate trivial questions endlessly. Several years ago, when we were developing the IPISD at Florida State University, the interservice review panel convened and, with the assistance of two external consultants, managed to spend a complete business day deciding whether the proper term was *behavioral objectives, performance specifications, terminal performance specifications,* or any of several other equally appropriate terms. Even though there was consensus on the proper configuration of objectives, different groups championed their own terminology.

Accordingly, procedures should be established to extract the content information and consensus from SMEs effectively (see Riner, 1982). It is important not to overlook a certain tension inherent in the nature of the relationship between ISD professionals and SMEs—a tension which is almost always present, regardless of how well individuals are able to perform their roles (Osterman, 1979). Remember that the ISD professional is often replacing the SME as the prime contractor or project director and that a shift of power will have occurred. Rarely do professionals relinquish turf voluntarily.

Design and Performance Specifications

It is important for the ISD professional to distinguish between design specifications and performance specifications. *Design specifications* refer to the prepared descriptions of attributes that the instructional products and processes will have. These include quality of paper, appropriateness of content, quality of audio or video production, depth of presentation, and so on. These design features are then built into the product by the developer and, when satisfied, should constitute good performance on contracts.

Performance specifications more explicitly refer to the expected outcomes from appropriately used instruction, rather than an enumeration of its design features. Sophisticated buyers will write performance specifications, if at all possible, while relatively inexperienced buyers will be heavily influenced by design specifications. Generally, since performance specifications are more difficult and more costly to meet than design specifications, they should be used only when a clear performance requirement has been established (see Corrigan & Kaufman, 1965).

The value of instructional materials to a sophisticated buyer cannot be assessed until after the target population has used the material in the intended context. That is, the outcome of use must be satisfactory. On the other hand, COTS courseware will rarely if ever be subjected to careful professional scrutiny. While it may be reviewed in some professional literature, it is by no means certain that buyers will read these reviews.

Perhaps the most difficult discriminations that astute buyers must make are those concerned with the normal professional activities used to establish the worth of instructional materials. These include evaluation reports, statistical data, and reactive or impressionistic data provided by the users. While in COTS courseware the key issue is whether the buyer likes the material, in performance products the most critical feature is whether the buyer is convinced that the intended behavior occurred as a result of use.

It takes a much better informed user to respond to the latter as opposed to the former. Accordingly, ISD professionals should pay absolute attention to the requirements from their clients in order to avoid urging performance specifications on design buyers, thus increasing the costs, and ignoring the performance and design expectations from the more aware buyers.

Packaging Counts

In the United States, as well as other mass-communications-intensive societies, the merchandising organizations and commercial media, including magazines and television, have raised our expectations about the attributes of a product by advertising and the design of its package. Those who buy and use ISD products are in touch with the larger society. As a result of the constant hype, buyers frequently insist on seeing expensive and nonfunctional attributes of instructional programs included in the package. Those ISD professionals who choose to compete in the marketplace should take packaging considerations quite seriously and not save all of the quality artwork and jazzy features of the instructional materials for the final product. Provide your project officer with nice samples to display early.

The issues of appearance and packaging have been a serious consideration in book marketing for many years. Darnton (1984) quotes this 200-year-old complaint about a book: "The fourth (edition) from which I include a sample sheet has been execrably produced both in printing, which is full of mistakes, and in the paper which is detestable. I wouldn't give thirty sous for it. If the (book) you are offering is like the fourth edition, you needn't bother to send it" (p.223).

Approach and Solution

Instructional Systems Development is a special case of the generic systems engineering model. The major feature that distinguishes the systems approach from traditional management methods is the creation of alternative solution strategies. The basic issue is whether one is urging a solution—self-paced instruction, lock-step instruction, computer-based instruction—rather than creating a list of alternatives whose features can be traded off against requirements until an acceptable approach is found. Creators and researchers are typically solution bound—they have a particular vested interest to pursue. For example, virtually no one who is indifferent to computer-based instruction does research in the area; consequently, active researchers become proponents. Such vested interests are similar to those which sell only one product line. If the office copier that your firm sells does not reduce, do multiple copies, and blow up images, the sales message you must exploit is that of dramatizing the most important feature—printing on cheap paper, totally portable, perfect copies every time, or instant service. It is not your job to do an evaluation of significant features for others. But remember that solution selling, no matter how well motivated the seller, is not systematic analysis.

Interplay of Ideal and Real

As an approach, ISD is elegant and systematic. In practice, however, ISD can be messy. To be successful, a practitioner of ISD must be at home not only in the pure universe of systems planning, but also in the ego battle of boardrooms. ISD is more than an idea of how things ought to be done; it is a body of hard-nosed, pragmatic professional experience in how things actually do get done a little bit better than last time. Things do not get done in models, or by model-makers. Things get done by practitioners and managers, working with the problems of institutions: funding, hidden agenda, resistance, professional jealousy, careers, outright hostility, devastating indifference, and the permanent assistance of Murphy's Law. Instructional systems *design* is the guiding light that keeps developers on the straight and narrow track toward worthwhile objectives. Instructional systems *development* is the jousting arena where graying knights in dented armor, guided by the infinite light of the perfect model, try to make some small improvement in the real world.

We believe, though, that both design and development can occur in essential vacuums, according to reasonable principles and with some attributes of the laboratory. The distinction comes with implementation. Three phases of utilization distinguish the truly successful practitioner from the novice: first implementation, then institutionalization, and finally routinization. Based conceptually on Lewin's fundamental change model, ISD implementation requires a singleness of purpose and willingness to participate for the duration. No description of this requirement to persist is better said than to quote the soldier's law from World War II: *illegitimi non carborundum.*

THE WORLD MEETS THE MODEL: PROSPECTS FOR ISD

While ISD practitioners have been diligently learning the skills necessary to make their theories function more effectively in the world, the world has been changing in ways that may make it more receptive to ISD.

There is now a new urgency for more effective instruction. Recent publications have re-sounded the national alarm for educational reform (National Commission on Excellence in Education, 1983). Furthermore, demographers predict a serious teacher shortage by the early 1990s (Gubser, 1985). With fewer teachers and a greater urgency for good instruction, ISD now sounds better to more people. It is an idea whose time has come. The considerable strength of the teachers' unions, however, will urge only the solution of paying teachers higher salaries. No student of systematic analysis has ever witnessed an improvement in performance caused by paying the incumbents more money, but this is the universal solution offered by vested interests.

We do not believe that teachers' unions are the cause of the original school problem—that is, declining student academic performance. The operational model used in the schools is obsolete; the single teacher, independent-classroom model reached asymptotic performance long before research-and-development activities in the early 1950s established new approaches. The results from using the traditional church model in schools will never be better than they were in the early 1950s.

The reason is straightforward: any operating model that has reached maturity through 200 years of practice has no significant opportunity for improvement. All obvious gains were made long ago. Without a fundamental change in operating concept, no additional improvement is likely. Trying to increase the quality of the educational system by somehow improving the quality of teachers without, at the same time, implementing an improved model of operations is an approach doomed to failure, no matter how often it is attempted or by whom it is endorsed.

A practical example from another field may serve to illustrate the point more clearly. During the early years of flight, aircraft designers added and subtracted wings, increased payloads, and attached more engines to achieve the mission performance required. They traded off three major variables to accomplish these ends: speed, range, and payload. It is not possible to maximize all three. During the 1940s, the jet engine was introduced for operational aircraft. That change was fundamental in that it provided a totally different concept of power and vastly increased all three major flight variables. All jet-powered aircraft now can go farther, faster, and carry more payload than propeller aircraft.

What is required to improve school performance is a fundamental technological advancement similar to the introduction of the jet engine. To be effective, it must be well understood and used by both designers and practitioners. Most important of all, it must be well managed to ensure that the intended results are accomplished. We believe that some specially designed and adapted ISD model would serve that purpose in education, much as the jet engine revolutionized aircraft capabilities.

Various technological developments have also made ISD feasible in more applications than ever before. Microcomputer-controlled videodisc learning carrels that provide perhaps the most advanced educational hardware in history are now available (Branson & Foster, 1978; Society for Applied Learning Technology, 1984). Computer-based instruction that used to require a few million dollars worth of mainframe computers is now beginning to run on microcomputers costing a few thousand. The proliferation of personal computers is providing the consumer with one of the most extraordinary devices ever conceived for delivering interesting instruction cheaply at home.

While the availability of the technology is a fundamental and necessary condition for change, it is not sufficient. How the technology is applied to solve widespread student performance problems and managed to that end is, by far, the most important question. These applications are considerably easier in performance environments, but even there, they are by no means simple. There is now a better mousetrap—the job remaining is to use it.

Because of the time, expertise, hardware, and other expense involved, the lessons created for computer-based instruction often require considerably more planning and development than ordinary classroom instruction. As a result of this expense, ISD is becoming a highly attractive method for major software houses to use in developing instruction and manuals of operating procedures.

Implied Merchantability

According to the basic concept of quality assurance, an ISD process should yield a product that is fit for the intended use. Such a product is the result when appropriate design and development procedures have been followed. Quality assurance refers to the process by which one makes products that serve their intended purpose (Lessinger, 1976). For example, if one sells a shovel one ought to expect it to dig gardens or holes when properly used, not collapse on the first use, and not to be so designed that it would be impossible to dig with it. The American legal system has recognized implied merchantability and implied warranty of manufacture in the Uniform Commercial Code, which lists some responsibilities of sellers.

If one develops instruction entitled *Algebra I,* it is only reasonable that a consumer would expect the subject matter to be appropriate. Only recently have sellers offered the additional feature that the ISD product would be fit for its intended use. Accordingly, an ISD course *Algebra I* not only should be appropriate in subject-matter content, but should also establish specified behaviors when correctly used. The significance of this last statement cannot be overemphasized. Numerous lawsuits have been filed and won, due to faulty training programs offered to police officers, public servants, and others.

Your Money Back

Many instructional developers strive to achieve the offer made by major mass merchandisers—satisfaction, or your money back—by developing instruction that works. There is virtually no resemblance between a textbook in *Algebra I* and ISD products that provide the specified skills in that subject matter. And, while mass merchandising has not yet enabled the ISD community to offer "complete satisfaction or your money back," it should remain an ideal for professional practice.

The Future of ISD

In creating a modularized set of ISD procedures and conceptual model, one aim of the IPISD effort was to ensure that future developments could be incorporated without sacrificing the general integrity of the model. Some evidence for this modularity was gained in the early 1980s by Reiser et al. (1981), when they published a substitute media-selection model for Blocks III.1 and III.2 of the IPISD. Their procedures could be substituted for the existing approach while the inputs and outputs remained consistent with the model.

Before that, The Human Resources Research Organization (HumRRO) (Schulz & Farrell, 1980) had worked out a set of job-performance aids to assist Army instructional designers and developers to apply the concepts and procedures of the IPISD. While the model remained virtually intact, the approach for instruction had been vastly improved by these job-performance aids.

There has been intense interest in the past few years in developing approaches to expert systems, artificial intelligence, and other highly-automated approaches to systematic instruction (Brown, Collins, & Harris, 1981). David Merrill (1984) has reported on progress made on an Apple-based system to apply systematic design automatically. Whether Merrill's efforts are transportable to other computer operating systems remains to be seen. However, the implications for research appear to be rich. Chapters 11 and 12 in this volume treat these issues in considerably more detail.

Several researchers have approached the problems of computer-aided authoring and computer-aided design of instructional systems and products. The Naval Training Equipment Center has seen attempts at automation of ISD and training programs (Brecke & Blaiwes, 1982; Braby & Kincaid, 1982). There is every reason to believe that these efforts to assist and automate the ISD process will continue and will become increasingly successful.

Within the professional field, there is continued growth of both the supply of journeyman ISD practitioners and the demand for their services. Compensation packages offered new graduates at the Master's level are comparable with those for the MBA. Compensation for those with a Ph.D is even better, and this degree offers considerably more occupational choices.

SUMMARY AND CONCLUSIONS

The ISD process has brought to the school and to education and training environments two important innovations: outcome-based instruction and instruction based on clearly defined needs. Outcome-based instruction is achieved through the design-development process which has become more widely used during the past 20 years. Instruction based on individual need, however, is a historic achievement which differs in a fundamental sense from traditional knowledge-distribution methods.

It takes careful systems-engineering efforts to define situations in which ISD efforts can be successful and to identify those in which ISD will probably not succeed. In addition to the normal forms of resistance found with any change or innovation, introducing ISD into an organization requires particular finesse. Often, the new users oppose, on an intellectual as well as an attitudinal basis, any attempts to employ research-based development. These facts must be taken into account when disseminating ISD-based courses.

Finally, the field of ISD has grown rapidly during the past 25 years and appears to be gaining in influence through time. Graduates of ISD programs as well as self-taught individuals can find many more employment opportunities than ever before.

REFERENCES

Andrews, D. H., & Goodson, L. A. (1980). A comparative analysis of models of instructional design. *Journal of Instructional Development, 3*(4), 2–16.

Braby, R., & Kincaid, J. P. (1982). Computer-aided authoring and editing. *Journal of Educational Technology Systems, 10*(2), 109–124.

Branson, R. K. (1981). Applications research in instructional systems development. *Journal of Instructional Development, 4*(4), 14–16, 27–31.

Branson, R. K. (1982). On teaching well what shouldn't be taught at all. *Journal of Instructional Development, 5*(3), 38–9.

Branson, R. K., & Foster, R. W. (1978). Educational applications research and videodisc technology. *Educational Technology Systems, 8*(3), 241–262.

Branson, R. K., Rayner, G. T., Cox, J. L., Furman, J. P., King, FJ, & Hannum, W. H. (1976). *Interservice procedures for instructional systems development* (5 vols.) (TRADOC Pam 350-30 and NAVEDTRA 106A). Fort Monroe, VA: U. S. Army Training and Doctrine Command. (NTIS No. ADA-019 486 through ADA-019 490)

Bratton, B. (1979–80). The instructional development specialist as consultant. *Journal of Instructional Development, 3*(2), 2–8.

Brecke, F., & Blaiwes, A. (1982). CASDAT: An innovative approach to more efficient ISD. *Journal of Educational Technology Systems, 10*(3), 1981–82.

Brown, J. S., Collins, A., & Harris, G. (1981). Artificial intelligence and learning strategies. In H. F. O'Neil (Ed.), *Computer-based instruction: A state-of-the-art assessment.* New York: Academic Press.

Butler, F. C. (1972). *Instructional systems development for vocational and technical training.* Englewood Cliffs, NJ: Educational Technology.

Canfield, A. A. (1968). A rationale for performance objectives. *Audiovisual Instruction, 13,* 127–129.

Clymer, E. W. (1984). The project-oriented matrix and instructional development project management. *Journal of Instructional Development, 7*(1), 14–18.

Corrigan, R. E., & Kaufman, R. A. (1965). *Why system engineering?* Palo Alto, CA: Fearon.

Dalgaard, K. A., Simpson, D. E., & Carrier, C. A. (1982). Coordinate status consultation: A strategy for instructional improvement. *Journal of Instructional Development, 5*(4), 7–14.

Darnton, R. (1984). *The great cat massacre and other episodes in French cultural history.* New York: Basic Books.

Department of the Army. (1976). *Staffing guide for U. S. Army service schools* (final draft, revised) (DA Pam 570-558). Washington, DC: Headquarters, Department of the Army.

Deterline, W. A., & Branson, R. K. (1972). *An empirical development model.* Palo Alto, CA: Sound Education.

Fayol, H. (1949). *General and industrial management.* New York and London: Pitman.

Friend, J., Searle, B., & Suppes, P. (Eds.). (1980). *Radio mathematics in Nicaragua.* Stanford, CA: Stanford University Institute for Mathematical Studies in the Social Sciences.

Gagné, R. M. (Ed.). (1962). *Psychological principles in system development.* New York: Holt, Rinehart and Winston.

Grover, P. L., Smith, D. U., & Schimpfhauser, F. (1985). Patterns of change in offices of research in medical education: 1979–1984. *Journal of Instructional Development, 8*(1), 33–37.

Gubser, L. (1985). Is new technology education's last hope? *TechTrends,* February–March, 12–16.

Gustafson, K., & Bratton, B. (1984). Instructional improvement centers in higher education. *Journal of Instructional Development, 7*(2), 2–7.

Juran, J. M., Gryna, F. M., & Bingham, R. S., Jr. (Eds.). (1974). *Quality control handbook* (3rd ed.). New York: McGraw-Hill.

Keller, F. S. (1968). Good-bye teacher. . . . *Journal of Applied Behavior Analysis, 1,* 79–88.

Kulik, J. A., Kulik, C. L. C., & Cohen, P. A. (1979). A meta-analysis of outcome studies of Keller's Personalized System of Instruction. *American Psychologist, 34*(4), 307–318.

Lasco, R. A. (1971). The effect of pacing of instruction on the effectiveness and efficiency of a course serving college-level geology. Unpublished doctoral dissertation, Florida State University, Tallahassee.

Lessinger, L. (1976). Quality control and quality assurance in education. *Journal of Educational Finance, 1,* 503–515.

Logan, R. S. (1982). *Instructional systems development.* New York: Academic Press.

McGuffey's fifth eclectic reader (rev. ed.). (1879). Cincinnati, OH: Van Antwerp Bragg.

Merrill, M. D. (1984). Computer-guided instructional design. *Journal of Computer-based Instruction, 2*(2), 60–63.

Miller, R. B. (1953). *Handbook on training and training equipment design* (Tech. Rept. 53-136). Wright-Patterson Air Force Base, OH: Wright Air Development Center.

Miller, R. B. (1954). *Some working concepts of systems analysis.* Pittsburgh: American Institutes for Research.

Montemerlo, M. D., & Tennyson, M. E. (1976). *Instructional systems development: Conceptual analysis and comprehensive bibliography* (NAVTRAEQUIPCEN-257). Orlando, FL: Naval Training Equipment Center. (ADA 024 526)

National Commission on Excellence in Education. (1983). *A nation at risk.* Washington, DC: U.S. Government Printing Office.

O'Neil, H. (Ed.). (1979). *Issues in instructional systems development.* New York: Academic Press.

Osterman, D. N., (1979). Transmitting instructional development to university faculty: Two approaches. *Journal of Instructional Development, 2*(4), 12–16.

Peters, T. J., & Waterman, R. H., Jr. (1982). *In search of excellence.* New York: Harper.

Postlethwait, S. (1969). *The audiotutorial system* (2nd ed.). Minneapolis, MN: Burgess.

Producing interactive videodiscs: An interactive instructional unit [Videodisc]. (1982). St. Paul, MN: Optical Recording Project/3M.

Reigeluth, C. M., & Merrill, M. D. (1979). Classes of instructional variables. *Educational Technology, 19*(3), 5–24.

Reiser, R. A., Gagné, R. M., Wager, W. W., Larsen, J. Y., Hewlett, B. A., Noel, K. L., Winner, J., & Fagan, C. (1981). *A learning-based model for media selection: Media selection flowchart and user's guide* (Research Product 81-25c). Alexandria, VA: U. S. Army Research Institute.

Reynolds, J. C. (1976). American textbooks: The first 200 years. *Educational Leadership, 33*(4), 274–276.

Riner, R. W. (1982). *The ranking of job incumbents using CODAP overlap values to compare task inventories developed by a modified Delphi technique and a more traditional method.* Unpublished doctoral dissertation, Florida State University, Tallahassee.

Roberts, W. K., Lawson, W. G., & Neal, W. D. (1975). TEC: A Manhattan Project in educational technology. In *Proceedings of the 17th annual conference of the Military Testing Association.* Washington, DC: U. S. Government Printing Office. (ADA 024 735)

Scanland, F. W. (1978) Centralized course development in the Navy. *Educational Technology, 18*(3), 24–27.

Schulz, R. E., & Farrell, J. R. (1980). *Job aid manuals for the Instructional Systems Development Model* (Tech. Rept. 80-18). Alexandria, VA: U. S. Army Research Institute. (ADA 088 920 through 24)

Shriver, E. L. & Hart, F. L. (1976). *Study and proposal for the improvement of military technical information transfer methods.* U. S. Army Human Engineering Laboratory Technical Report, TM 29-75.

Society for Applied Learning Technology. (1984). *Proceedings from sixth annual conference on interactive videodisc in education and training.* Warrenton, VA: Author.

Terrell, W. R., & Shrock, S. A. (1984). ID in higher education: A paradox. In R. K. Bass & C. R. Dills (Eds.), *Instructional Development: The State of the Art, II. Dubuque, IA: Kendall/Hunt.*

Thiagarajan, S. (1976). Help, I am trapped inside an ID model! Alternatives to the systems approach. *NSPI Journal, 15*(9), 16–17.

Tracey, W. R. (1971). *Designing training and development systems.* New York: American Management Association.

Walter, S., & Earl, R. S. (1982). Contracting for instructional development: A follow-up. *Journal of Instructional Development, 5*(2), 26–30.

Zemke, R., & Kramlinger, T. (1982). *Figuring things out: A trainer's guide to needs and task analysis.* Reading, MA: Addison-Wesley.

AUTHOR NOTES

Robert K. Branson is a Professor in the Department of Educational Research, Development, and Foundations, and the Director of the Center for Educational Technology at Florida State University.

Gerald Grow is a Research Associate in the Center for Educational Technology at Florida State University and an Associate Professor of journalism at Florida A & M University.

16

Factors Affecting Utilization

Ernest Burkman
Florida State University

Do you want to see an instructional designer wince? Just ask to be shown a situation in which one of his or her design products is working as planned within an organization. Such a request almost always results in a blank stare or an evasive response. Standard evasive responses include giving a list of the constraints that prevented superior efforts from being implemented, gnashing of teeth over the incompetence of the people on the firing line that sabotaged some really noble project, or passing along a dusty example of a 10-year-old product along with a tale about how well it worked before being abandoned.

It is widely believed that the most critical problem facing instructional designers is to find ways to get their products off the drawing board and into use (Butler, 1982). Many designers have become very good indeed at spelling out models for designing instruction (Andrews & Goodson, 1980), and some have been able to produce instructional programs that work well under specified conditions. But, as has been recently documented by Back and McCombs (1984) and others, the instructional design (ID) process often breaks down when designers try to get their products properly used by others who must operate under real-world conditions and who may not share the designer's point of view.

The failure of practitioners to implement ID's products has not been confined to any particular setting. The problem is probably most severe for designers who try to influence instruction in primary and secondary schools (Berman & McLaughlin, 1974, 1977, 1978) but it is also well known in colleges and universities (Centra, 1976; Dressel, 1982). Even in military and industrial training settings, where it might be expected that the command structure would permit the use of ID products to be mandated, many utilization problems have developed (Branson, 1981; Miles 1983). All in all, the implementation record for ID has not been good.

Why has it been so difficult for designers to get their products into practice? What can they do to improve their success? This chapter deals with these two questions. Its thesis is that utilization can be improved if designers will systematically design their products to be user friendly and will see to it that instructors and other users receive the follow-up support that they require. To develop this thesis, we will draw heavily upon experience from fields outside of ID. Most especially, we will use generic concepts and models proposed by Rogers (1983) regarding the communication and dissemination of innovations and specific suggestions by Urban and Hauser (1980) regarding the development of new commercial products for the market.

The chapter has four major sections. The first section will sharpen the utilization problem and introduce some key concepts and terms. The second section will describe the standard approach to getting instructional designers' products into use. Then we will describe an alternative approach—user-oriented instructional development (UOID). The final section will briefly discuss some of the issues related to implementing UOID.

THE ID UTILIZATION PROBLEM

Introduction

Instructional designers' problems in getting their products used are by no means unique. They are shared by just about anyone who uses the research–development–diffusion (RDD) paradigm for solving social problems. This approach involves having experts identify problems and then systematically designing products, which are then turned over to others to be used to solve the problem at hand (Havelock, 1973). However, whether the problem involves introducing new medical and agricultural practices into underdeveloped countries, or getting sophisticated business executives to use personal computers, people who have tried to introduce predeveloped innovations have almost invariably encountered resistance from potential users.

It has been suggested that the only way to avoid the problems with getting innovations like ID into practice is to replace the RDD paradigm with a more user-oriented approach (Guba & Clark, 1974). One proposed alternative is a sort of problem-solving paradigm in which problem identification is left to people on the firing line, who then develop their own solutions (Lippett, Watson, & Westley, 1958). The problem-solving paradigm assumes that the feeling of ownership fostered by local generation of solutions will ensure their adoption. R&D products fit into the problem-solving model only if they happen to be chosen by firing-line people as solutions to problems that they have identified. A primary criticism of this model is that firing-line people are often not technically equipped to come up with quality solutions and often do not have the time or inclination to do so (Havelock, 1973).

Almost by definition most instructional designers are engaged in work that is encompassed by the RDD paradigm. With this in mind, we will deal with their utilization problems within that framework. As will be evident, the power of ownership in stimulating adoption is impressive. However, we will try to posit a way to achieve a feeling of ownership among potential users without sacrificing the advantages gained by having ID products systematically designed by experts.

The Innovation-Decision Process

For purposes of this chapter, individuals or other decision making units that might logically use an innovative instructional program will be referred to as *potential adopters*. And it will be assumed that most potential adopters go through the five-step process proposed by Rogers (1983) as they pass from first knowledge of such a program to full use of it. This model has been widely adopted and is fairly typical of the way diffusion scholars presently view the innovation-decision process. Briefly described, the steps in the Rogers model are as follows:

1. At the *knowledge* step the potential adopter becomes aware of the program and gets a rough idea of how it works or what it does.

2. At the *persuasion* step the potential adopter seeks more detailed information and forms a favorable or unfavorable attitude toward the program.

3. *Decision* occurs when the potential adopter carries out activities that lead to a choice to adopt or reject the program. *Adopt* means to decide to make full use of the program. *Reject* means to decide not to adopt or not to consider adoption.

4. At the *implementation* stage the adopter puts the program into use. This is also referred to as *implementing the program.*

5. *Confirmation* occurs when the adopter collects information to confirm the adoption decision. Positive information leads to continuance of the program. Negative information leads to discontinuance or reinvention (modification) of it.

It will be assumed that the big problem that an instructional designer faces in trying to get products into practice is finding ways to optimize the chances that the outcome of each of the five steps is favorable. And it will be posited that this result depends primarily on two actions. First, designers' products must be designed to include attributes that are perceived favorably by the potential adopter; and second, the right kind of information and support must reach the potential adopter at the right time.

Instructional Designers and the ID Process

Part of the reason for the apparent failure of instructional designers to get their products adopted and implemented properly is semantic. Not everyone means the same thing when using terms like "instructional designer" and "ID product" or when stating that ID products are not being used properly. In fact it sometimes appears that every designer has a unique model for designing instruction (Andrews & Goodson, 1980).

To avoid parochialism we will define an instructional designer in fairly broad terms as anyone who meets the three following criteria:

1. An instructional designer's principal objective is to induce targeted learners to perform in prespecified ways. Normally the first steps in the ID process are to prepare specific learning objectives and to establish criteria for measuring their accomplishment.

2. Instructional designers achieve results by developing and implementing documented and replicable procedures for organizing the conditions for learning. Normally the procedures are incorporated into instructional programs that include instructional materials for use by learners and directions for use of the materials.

3. Instructional designers define and measure their accomplishments in terms of learner performance. Normally performance measures of the learning objectives are prepared and testing results are used to guide the ID process and to document the effectiveness of the final product.

This definition for instructional designers implies a comparable fairly broad way of conceptualizing the instructional design process. We will consider ID to be any procedure for improving instruction that includes: (a) prespecification of learning outcomes in performance terms, (b) development and dissemination of documented and replicable procedures for organizing the conditions of learning, and (c) evaluation in terms of learner performance criteria.

The definition for an instructional designer also helps to detail the nature of the products that designers generate and try to get into use. The principal product for most designers is instructional materials that incorporate learning objectives, procedures for organizing the conditions of learning, and measuring devices for evaluating student performance. Designers who produce such a product will be referred to as *materials developers* and their products will be called *materials*. Materials developers tend to think of valid implementation of their products as a two-step process. First, their validated materials must be used in the way that was intended, and second, the targeted learners must learn to perform as specified.

Some designers are one step removed from materials development. Their product is a model that spells out how to generate learning objectives, measuring devices and instructional procedures. This type of designer will be referred to as a *model builder*. For most model builders good utilization is a three-step process. First, someone other than the designer must use the model as intended to generate explicit objectives, validated tests, and instructional materials. Next, the materials must be used as intended with learners. Third, and finally, the targeted learners must learn to perform as specified.

We will tend to focus on the adoption and implementation problems of materials developers and will pay less attention to those of model builders. There are two reasons for this. First, the distinction between the two is somewhat artificial because model builders often participate in the subsequent development and dissemination of materials. And second, experience suggests that most potential adopters react much more favorably to concrete products than they do to abstract models (Brickell, 1971). Furthermore, there is evidence that the dissemination of models almost invariably fails because of wide variations in the way users interpret and use them (Farrar, DeSanctis, & Cohen, 1980). This suggests that model builders who are interested in seeing ID implemented with reasonable fidelity might consider taking the next step and developing appropriate materials for dissemination.

Variations in ID Tasks

Within the broad definitions given previously, instructional designers can be sorted into two categories in terms of the situations in which they operate and the utilization problem they face. Those that will be called *micro-instructional designers* operate on a fairly small scale and aim to affect individual learners. On the other hand, *macro-instructional designers* aim to introduce their products into complex organizations that instruct large numbers of students. As we shall see, these two sorts of designers face quite different utilization problems.

The Micro-instructional Designer

Micro-instructional designers aim to influence directly the behavior of individual learners. Normally they are materials developers rather than model builders. Sometimes, as in the case of a person learning a new trade at home via microcomputer-based instruction, it is expected that the target learners will work in isolation. In this case, the micro-designer usually produces self-paced materials that are delivered or sold directly to the learner, who then proceeds to use them independently. This situation is often referred to as "distance education" (Feasley, 1982), and it places a heavy demand on the designer's ability to communicate with the learner. However, since most learners in distance education situations are strongly motivated to complete their work, there is no utilization problem at the student level. The absence of an instructor eliminates the problem at that level as well. Getting institutions to adopt distance education can be a problem presenting many difficulties, but their discussion is beyond the scope of this chapter.

Micro-designers often deal with learners who are clustered together into a class that meets at a specified time and that is led by an instructor who has control over what takes place. In this situation the instructor represents an intermediate user who must be convinced and trained by the designer before the target learners will receive the intended instruction. Frequently, as is often the case in a military or industrial training unit, the instructor is under orders from superiors to use the micro-designer's materials. But this circumstance does not lessen his or her power to sabotage the designer's intentions once the classroom door closes (Branson, 1981). And to date, micro-designers have not been very successful in getting instructors to perform as intended. This is one of the two types of utilization problems that will be of primary interest here.

The Macro-instructional Designer

As indicated earlier, macro-designers operate in a more complex setting than micro-designers. They can be model builders or materials developers and they aim to change the instructional practices of complex organizations such as schools, school systems, government departments of education, or military and industrial training units. In the final analysis the macro-designer's utilization problem is the same as that of the micro-designer—to convince and train instructors to use materials properly. However, the numbers of instructors to be influenced is large and this compounds the difficulty. And before they can turn their attention to the instructor, macro-designers must influence the decision-makers in the target organization to adopt their product and to make it available to instructors.

The major complicating factor for macro-designers is that the power to determine instructional policy and to select instructional materials is often shared by numerous individuals within organizations, and that outsiders sometimes exert an influence as well. Typically the making of these decisions involves instructors, their superiors, policy boards, and often many others. Usually this sharing of power means that someone has to sell the virtues of ID to many individuals with widely divergent perspectives before the macro-designer's product can be adopted and distributed to instructors for implementation. Even if the organization decides to adopt the materials, their effects on the targeted learners can be severely distorted by the subsequent actions of instructors and others who provide support for instruction.

The macro-designer faces the ultimate ID utilization problem—the one that most people think of when they observe that instructional designers have not been successful in getting their products into use.

The Effect of Setting

For both the micro- and macro-designer the task of getting ID products adopted and implemented is different in different settings having different missions, types of personnel, and authority structures. In general, settings can be sorted into two categories with respect to these matters. Military and industrial training units fall into one category. They tend to be rather receptive to adopting ID products, but good implementation does not necessarily follow (Back & McCombs, 1984). The second category is schools and colleges. These units tend to be less prone to adopt ID products and tend not to implement them as intended (Berman & McLaughlin, 1977).

Table 16.1 compares the military-industrial setting with the school-college setting on six variables that probably affect ID adoption and implementation decision. As can be seen, military and industrial units, with their emphasis on efficiency, have considerably greater incentives to adopt and implement ID products. And school and college instructors are much more likely to resist explicit suggestions from outsiders as to what or how to teach than are military or industrial instructors. This suggests that designers who aim to impact schools or colleges can usually expect more resistance than their military-industrial counterparts.

Summary of the ID Utilization Problem

For the purpose of this chapter, then, we will consider an instructional designer to be anyone who tries to improve instruction through a process that includes prespecified learning outcomes, evaluation in terms of learner performance, and the development of replicable and documented procedures for adjusting the conditions of learning. For designers to be referred to as *model builders,* the product to be disseminated is a model to be used by others for developing learning objectives, performance measures and instructional procedures. But the focus here will be upon the dissemination problems of *materials developers*—designers who product is instructional materials.

It will be assumed that potential adopters of ID products go through five stages as they pass from first knowledge of the product to full use of it. The stages are knowledge, persuasion, decision, implementation, and confirmation. Adoption is defined as deciding to make full use of a program, and implementation is defined as putting the program into use.

The focus will be on two varieties of the ID utilization problem: (a) the micro-designer's problem of convincing individual instructors to adopt and properly implement validated instructional materials, and (b) the macro-designers' problem of first convincing organizations to adopt ID products and

TABLE 16.1

Comparison of Six Variables of Instruction in Industry and the Military Services, and in Public Education

Variable	Industry/Military	Public Education
Structure	Centralized: information flow rapid vertically and horizontally. Instructors part of chain of command	Decentralized: information flow slow but better horizontally than vertically. Individual schools and teachers fairly autonomous
Mission of Training and Education	Accommodate turnover and growth in personnel; accommodate changes in knowledge and skills required by organization and personnel; improve skills and performance of job incumbents	Transmit accumulated knowledge of society to future participants in society. Some recent emphasis on projected employment skills.
Focus of performance of skills and knowledge learned	Immediate application of skill and knowledge to new or existing job; transferability (relevancy) of learning	Actual performance delayed; little emphasis on learning transfer
Economic basis	Training must provide minimum competency at minimum cost for maximum number of people; training is nonproductive (i.e., it costs money)	No requirement to rush education; teachers not concerned (for the most part) with cost-effectiveness of instructional methods
Degree of academic freedom	Fairly low—limited by demand for efficiency	High; what to teach broadly described by curriculum scope & sequence— method is teacher's decision almost exclusively
Role of instructor	Temporary subject-matter expert; not well versed in methods; anxious to get back to the field; not hired as an instructor	Perceived as subject matter and methods expert. Career is teaching and was hired as a teacher

subsequently getting instructors to use them properly. For both macro-designers and micro-designers, it makes a difference whether the target is a military-industrial setting or a school-college setting. In general, military-industrial settings tend to be more hospitable to designers, at least in terms of product adoption.

Finally, it should be noted that the learner, who is the ultimate target of both the macro-designer and the micro-designer, rarely participates directly in deciding either to adopt or to implement the designer's products. As we shall see, this has profound implications for designers who aim to get their products into proper use.

QUALITY AS A STIMULUS FOR ADOPTION

Now that the utilization problem has been clarified, we will turn to a discussion of possible ways of dealing with it. A simple and widely practiced remedy is simply for designers to improve upon what they are doing now—developing effective and efficient instruction. But as will be seen, there are problems with this approach.

Many designers cannot understand why ID has not been adopted more widely and better implemented. They point to the fact that ID achieves the primary goal of everyone involved in education and training—more effective and efficient learning. This premise leads to the assumption which undergirds most current approaches for getting ID into use—that a good product will automatically be attractive to potential adopters and will be demanded by them.

If a strong user demand for ID products is assumed, then dissemination can be thought of as a postdevelopment task that consists of two parts: (a) bringing well-designed products to the attention of the potential adopters, and (b) after adoption more or less automatically occurs, providing training and other support for proper use of the materials. This is the way that many prominent ID models depict the implementation process (Andrews & Goodson, 1980). And this way of thinking about the problem implies that the best way to improve ID utilization would be to: (a) find ways to make products instructionally more effective and efficient, (b) find better ways to communicate with users, and (c) provide better instructor training and other support for implementation. In general, this is the way that most designers have proceeded.

This is a comfortable way for designers to think about the utilization problem because it suggests that everything will come out all right if they continue doing what they like to do, only do it better. But, as we have seen, potential users at both the organization level and the instructor level have been rejecting ID products and many of those that do adopt have not used them as designed (Goldman, 1982).

Much evidence suggests that at least part of the reason for the present problem in getting ID into proper use traces back to designers' implied assumption that materials that are instructionally effective and efficient will automatically be attentive to potential adopters' needs (McCombs, Back, & West, 1984). The fallacy of this assumption is well illustrated by a case history of a failed innovation project that was described in detail by Parkinson (1972).

The Case of the Inefficient Typewriter

In 1873, companies that were planning to market the newly invented typewriter had a dilemma. The placement of the type bars on early typewriters led to jamming when the keys were hit too rapidly by a fast typist. To compensate for this it was decided to arrange the keyboard to make it difficult for anyone to type fast enough to get into trouble with jamming. After much thought and field testing, Christopher Sholes came up with a masterpiece of inefficiency. In the Sholes keyboard designer the letters QWERTY were placed along the left side of the home row of keys. This arrangement assured that a typist would have long reaches for keys at inopportune times, thus severely limiting the typing speed that could be reached. Jamming was virtually eliminated and soon the QWERTY keyboard became the standard for all typewriters.

Later, after typewriters had been redesigned to eliminate jamming, efforts were launched to get around the inefficiency of the QWERTY keyboard. One of these was to try to design a new keyboard, this time with efficiency in mind rather than inefficiency. The result came in 1932 and was the Dvorak arrangement (named after its inventor, August Dvorak). In this design, the letters were placed on the keyboard to minimize reaching and awkward moves by the typist. This arrangement was found to be easy to learn and to lead to many fewer errors and much greater typing speed than the QWERTY one.

When the designers of the Dvorak keyboard tried to get it into general use, they were totally rebuffed. A few pioneering efforts were made to introduce the new design, but these failed badly. And to this day, the QWERTY keyboard, which was designed to be inefficient, is found on almost all typewriters, and few people have ever even heard of the highly efficient Dvorak keyboard.

Why did the Dvorak keyboard, with its built-in efficiency, fail to replace the obviously inferior QWERTY arrangement? This is a complex question with many facets, but the nub of the answer is fairly simple. Clearly, taken as a group, those who would have been affected by introducing the new keyboard (the potential adopters) did not collectively perceive it to be more personally advantageous than the old one. And so the collective decision was to leave the old keyboard in place. It is important to note that the potential adopters included typewriter manufacturers, sellers, repairers, and those who taught typing, as well as typists. Clearly such matters as changeover costs, short-range discomforts, and job disruptions weighed as heavily as did typing efficiency on potential adopters' thinking. Also communication was probably such that some potential adopters may have gotten a distorted view of the potential effects of the new keyboard or perhaps heard very little about it. But after all was said and done, the apparently superior product was rejected. Although it may seem strange, this result has been observed again and again with products of all kinds (Rogers, 1983).

Implications for Instructional Designers

The typewriter keyboard story contains many lessons for instructional designers who aim to get their products into use. Three of the key ones are: (a) the way potential adopters perceive that a product will affect them personally tends to determine whether it will be adopted (and to some extent how it will be implemented), (b) demonstrated effectiveness and efficiency in performance are not the only attributes that potential adopters consider in judging new products (often these do not even have the strongest influence), and (c) changing the attitudes that underlie potential adopters' reactions to new products is not easy even if logic is on the side of the new product.

The lack of a direct correlation between a product's effectiveness and efficiency and its likelihood of being adopted and implemented as designed has been well documented (Marquis, 1969). The absence of this relation has been noted again and again in virtually all endeavors that involve trying to get people to adopt new ways of doing things. Whether the objective is selling a new brand of soap, introducing new agricultural products to underdeveloped countries, or writing a novel that will make the best-seller list, it has become quite clear that innovators who are interested in generating wide acceptance for their products will have little success unless their products reflect what users want and are willing to accept (Meadows, 1968).

USER-ORIENTED DEVELOPMENT

The evidence suggests that instructional designers who aim to get their products into use cannot assume that better quality will automatically lead to better acceptance. Instead, it suggests that they should take steps to ensure that the products meet the perceived needs of instructors and other potential users. One way to try to do this would be to mount an advertising campaign aimed at convincing skeptical potential users of the value of the existing products. But the QWERTY keyboard experience and many others like it suggest that the attitudes of potential adopters will not be easily changed. And the fact that ID products have not been highly attractive to date suggests that some adjustment in them may be a prerequisite to generating favorable perceptions.

How then can ID products be designed to be more favorably perceived by instructors and other potential adopters? The generic equivalent of this question has been asked again and again by designers of all kinds and has been of special interest to people who design new commercial products. Efforts to find answers have led to generic models for systematically designing products that have a high probability of being adopted (bought?) (Urban & Hauser, 1980). Some of the elements of these market-oriented models are relevant to the ID usage problem.

The five-step model outlined below describes one way of conceptualizing a user-oriented instructional development process (UOID). The model assumes that the potential adopters of ID products go through an innovation-decision process somewhat like the one proposed by Rogers, as described in the first section of this chapter.

Step 1: Identify the potential adopter.   In this step the designer determines who would be affected if the planned product were to be adopted and especially those who would be involved in the decision to adopt. For most micro-designers the potential adopters are the instructors who would use the product. But macro-designers normally must identify other decision-makers or support personnel within the target organization as well.

Step 2: Measure relevant potential adopter perceptions.   Next the designer determines (a) how the potential adopters perceive that instruction should be done and, (b) the attributes of instructional products that they perceive to be important. Macro-designers normally discover that these perceptions vary between the different types of potential adopters that they must deal with.

Step 3: Design and develop a user-friendly product.   Once the perceptions of potential adopters are known, the design-and-development process begins. Normal ID procedures are used but with two modifications. First, the designer aims to incorporate into the product as many as possible of the attributes that are valued by the potential adopter and tries to make the presence of the attributes as apparent as possible. Second, the criteria used by the designer to evaluate the product formatively and summatively are expanded to include the degree to which the potential adopter: (a) perceives the product favorably, and (b) tends to adopt it and implement it properly.

Step 4: Inform the potential adopter.   At this point a good user-friendly product has been developed that has attributes that the potential adopters value. The next step is to inform the potential developer about the product, stressing its user-valued attributes. The channels of communication that are selected should optimize the chances for stimulating favorable user perceptions. Macro-designers must often use different messages and communication channels for different types of potential adopters.

Step 5: Provide postadoption support. Once adoption has occurred, the instructor (and to some extent others in the adopting organization) must be given the tools needed to implement the product. All hardware must be delivered on time and any required adjustments in the instructional environment made. The adopter must be given appropriate training and encouragement as needed.

There are three major differences between standard ID practices and the UOID model just outlined. First, designers do not normally measure potential adopters' perceptions of their products or try to use them in establishing product attributes. Second, it is not usual for designers to formulate messages about their products or to select communication channels with the objective of creating favorable potential adopter perceptions. And third, designers do not often use adoption and implementation success rates as criteria for evaluating their products. We shall look at these matters more closely; but first we need to acknowledge a potential problem with user-oriented development.

Designers and User-Oriented Development

Designers who work in academic settings often wince when confronted with a user-oriented approach to ID such as the one outlined above. There are two reasons for this. First, as has been nicely pointed out by Kilman (1965), academics feel uncomfortable with attempts to manipulate systematically their product designs and their communications with potential users intending to optimize the chances for favorable impact. Academics might concede that market-oriented design processes work with respect to selling products like soap and political candidates, but they may not agree that such processes are appropriate for improving education. This is clearly a matter for individual judgment. However, the discussion of this subject by Kilman (1965) is recommended reading.

The second reason for caution by designers in accepting UOID procedures relates to their fundamental objectives. Many designers might concede that ID products designed in this way might be more appealing to users, but they are unlikely to see a way of attending to the perceived needs of potential adopters without compromising their own principal interest—instructional quality. Whether this concern is valid depends on the skill of the designer in resolving the feedback obtained from potential adopters. Clearly, dealing with user requirements such as low implementation cost makes it more difficult to design effective ID products. But skillful designers have done it.

And the evidence suggests that if it were to be done the impact of ID would be increased.

Key Attributes of Innovative ID Products

It is almost axiomatic that the way potential adopters perceive a product or a new way of doing things will bear heavily on whether they will adopt it. Research findings support the general principle that innovations perceived favorably by potential users will be more quickly and widely adopted than those that are perceived unfavorably (Myers & Marquis, 1969). Thus it would be to the advantage of impact-oriented designers to include in their products attributes that will favorably influence the perceptions of potential adopters.

Clearly the best way to determine the perceptions of potential adopters relating to a particular instructional product is to measure them directly. Excellent survey research techniques have been perfected for collecting such measures (Calder, 1977; Lehmann, 1979). However, several researchers have compiled generic lists of perceived characteristics of innovations that have been demonstrated to be more or less well related to adoption or rejection (Brickell, 1971; Kester, 1976; Zaltman, Duncan & Holbek, 1973).

Perhaps the best known among the lists of innovation attributes considered to be favorable to adoption is the one by Rogers and Shoemaker (1971). After reviewing more than 3,000 papers dealing with fields from agriculture to marketing, Rogers and Shoemaker concluded that five variables were relevant. These were the relative advantage and compatibility of the innovation with respect to the potential adopter's existing needs and values; and the complexity, observability, and trialability of the innovation. Perceived relative advantage, compatibility, trialability, and observability were considered to be positively correlated with adoption. Perceived complexity was considered to be negatively correlated with adoption. Descriptions of each of these attributes and of the way they might relate to ID products follow.

Relative Advantage and Adoption of ID Products

Relative advantage is defined by Rogers and Shoemaker as "the degree to which an innovation is perceived by the potential adopter as being better than the idea or thing it supersedes" (p. 138). They also describe relative advantage as the "strength of the reward or punishment for adopting the innovation." Many authorities consider relative advantage to be the attribute that most powerfully influences decisions to adopt or reject innovations and it is one of those for which there is probably the greatest research support (Tornatzky & Klein, 1982).

What attributes do potential adopters consider when they decide whether an ID product has a relative advantage over something else? It is not possible to construct a single, comprehensive list of attributes that would apply to all potential adopters in all situations. However, experience suggests that the breakdown given in the next section includes many of the key factors that have operated in most settings.

Relative Advantage from the Instructor's Point of View

For most experienced instructors, judging whether a new ID product is relatively advantageous has boiled down to comparing the personal consequences of its use with what these instructors had been doing in terms of two variables: (a) the amount of work required to implement and use the product; and (b) the effect of use upon their relationships with learners. Some of the key elements of such a comparison are as follows:

The nature of instructor-learner interactions.   Most experienced instructors have preferred to have relatively constant personal interaction with learners and have preferred to deal with learners as a group rather than one at a time. Consequently they have tended to reject or modify products that imply either reduced instructor-learner interaction or self-instruction by learners (Bennis, Benne, & Chin, 1969).

Degree of the management requirement.   Many experienced instructors do not like to manage things, do not feel they have time for much classroom management, and are not especially good managers. Consequently they have tended to reject or modify products that involve considerable formal record keeping, scheduling, or keeping track of materials (Turnbull, Thorn, & Hutchins, 1974).

Potential for motivating learners.   Many experienced instructors believe that instruction that focuses upon learners interacting with materials tends to be unmotivating. Thus they have tended to reject materials-based teaching methods (Bennis, Benne, & Chin, 1969).

Experienced instructors of unmotivated learners have tended to assume that any materials used must be of interest to their students. Accordingly they have tended to demand that materials be well formatted, contain language that the instructor perceives to be at the level of the learner, and include a prominent high-quality visual component. Unillustrated or sparsely illustrated text has tended to be rejected by such instructors.

Quality of student learning.   Instructors obviously want their students to learn. Therefore they have favored products that they believe will improve learning. However, they have had to be convinced that any content that is taught is important and they have often depended upon their intuitive judgment in evaluating either the quality of objectives or the effectiveness of materials (Kester, 1976).

Relative Advantage From the Organization's Perspective

Decision-makers in organizations that deliver instruction have tended to use criteria different from those used by instructors in evaluating the relative advantage of adopting a new ID product rather than staying with their present practices. Here are some of the attributes that have often been considered.

Cost. Most mature instruction-oriented organizations must operate within tight annual budgets that vary little from year to year. Consequently the perceived cost of implementing and maintaining ID products has often been *the* key factor in decisions as to whether to adopt. Products that are perceived to require large initial outlays or heavy continuing expenses for maintenance have tended to be rejected or modified so as to lower costs. In addition to money, expenditures of time, personnel, space, equipment, books and other resources have often been considered to be part of cost (Bickell, 1971). It should be pointed out that there is presently no consensus on how actually to measure cost of instruction (Back & McCombs, 1984).

Disruptiveness. Decision-makers in mature instruction-oriented organizations tend to abhor disruptions. Consequently, they have tended to favor ID products that they think will have wide acceptance among members of the organization and, where appropriate, among the organization's benefactors and clients. They have also favored products assumed to require few adjustments in the organization's policies and operating procedures (Turnbull et al., 1984; Wolf, 1973).

Quality of student learning. Like instructors, mature instruction-oriented organizations want learners to learn. Furthermore, many such organizations are under pressure to instruct as efficiently as possible. And so they have tended to favor ID products assumed to lead to effective and efficient instruction. However, this attribute has often been given lower priority than low cost or low disruptiveness.

Other Variables

The remaining four variables on the Rogers and Shoemaker list of key attributes of innovations are probably less important than *relative advantage* in influencing the judgments of potential adopters of ID products. Consequently, they will here be dealt with less comprehensively. The descriptions of the attributes are listed in the probable order of their influence.

Complexity is probably second to relative advantage as an influence on potential adopters' attitudes toward ID products. Complexity refers to the degree to which an innovation is perceived to be difficult to understand and use. Both instructors and decision-makers in organizations have tended to reject or modify new ID products that they perceive to be complicated (Turnbull et al., 1974). And to them complicated has often tended to mean that the success of the innovation absolutely depends on a large number of things being done right by people in the organization, by the instructor, or by the learners. As the list of essentials for successful use of an innovation has grown longer, and as the requirements for precision have become greater, the tendency to reject or modify it has grown. The presence of large numbers of essential components and the need for complicated implementation instructions for administrators, instructors, or students are clues that a product may be too complex for wide adoption to occur.

Compatibility refers to the degree that an innovation is perceived to be consistent with existing values, past experiences and the felt needs of potential adopters. All mature instruction-oriented organizations and instructors acquire a belief as to the way instruction should be carried out. This perspective arises out of what the instructor or the organization values and wants and what their experience suggests is right. Often, these perceived values become operationally defined as formal rules, laws, and operating procedures. Examples are company policies, classroom discipline rules, and state textbook adoption codes. Clearly, both instructors and organizations have tended to reject or modify ID products that have not fit their perceived norms for carrying out instruction (Brickell, 1971). The chances for adoption have been especially dim if the product is incompatible with formal established rules, laws, or policies (Rosencranz, 1975).

Trialability and *observability* are probably the least important of the Rogers and Shoemaker attributes to instructional designers. They refer to the ease with which an innovation can be tried out on a small scale by potential adopters and the degree to which the positive results of an innovation are visible to others. Independent, instruction-oriented organizations have often insisted upon a low-cost, short-duration trial of a product before considering its adoption. Products with a format that facilitates low-cost, small-scale testing have tended to be favored by such organizations as well as by some instructors. Nonsequential modules of instruction are an example of a trialable format. A hardbound textbook with sequential chapters is not an example. Also, both instructors and organizations have tended to be attracted to ID products that have observability—those that produce easily detected results (especially if they are achieved quickly). In part, this is probably due to the fact that such products attract potential adopters' attention. But another attraction is that they are easy for decision-makers to use to satisfy demands for results by political constituencies (Nelson & Sieber, 1976). An example of the effect of observability is the fact that computers and other hardware tend to be adopted more quickly and easily than software innovations.

Designing ID Products to be User-Friendly

The implication of the last few pages is obvious. Assuming that potential adopters continue to react as they have in the past, designers who want to get their ID products better and more widely adopted should be sure that they are perceived by instructors to be simple to use rather than complex, compatible with existing ground rules, easy and cheap to experiment with, and likely to produce quick and dramatic results. Also, the instructor should perceive the product to foster, or at least permit, instructor-learner interactions, to require minimum instructor management effort, to motivate the target learners, and to communicate easily with the learners. Of course, ID products also need to be effective and efficient in stimulating learning and should be perceived that way by instructors. Finally, products of macro-designers who aim to influence organizations should also be perceived by the appropriate decision-makers to be inexpensive and nondisruptive of the organization.

Product Attributes and Implementation

Notice the emphasis on perceptions in the discussion of attributes. The decision to adopt a product appears to depend strongly on the potential user's subjective perceptions of it. And these may or may not correspond to reality (Urban & Hauser, 1980). Instructors have been known to reject summarily as impractical instructional programs that had not been examined because they had been described as "programmed instruction." On the other hand, administrators have become enthusiastic about programmed instruction when it was described as "cost-effective" or "highly efficient."

Once an innovation has been adopted, and the process of implementation begins, perception tend to be displaced by reality. Adopters begin to compare their actual experiences with the product against what they had expected from it when they chose to adopt. For a product to remain credible the perceived relative advantages that led to its adoption must turn out to be real advantages during use. And the program that was perceived to be inexpensive must not turn out to have large hidden costs or to force the instructor to invest an inordinate amount of time and effort in planning. If the gap between preadoption beliefs and postadoption realities is negative but small, adopters tend to adapt the product to fit their needs. But if there is a large negative gap, the adoption is often reversed and the adopter is left with a negative attitude toward the product.

Accordingly, the designer employing UOID must think about user-favored attributes in two ways as they are designed into ID products. First, they must be displayed so that the potential adopter perceives the product favorably enough to adopt. Second, the attributes must be real enough to retain the adopters' enthusiasm during and after implementation. Otherwise the result may be rejection or potentially damaging modification.

Procedures for Informing the Potential User

Once a designer has developed a user-friendly product the next step in the UOID process is to inform the potential users of the product's existence and to supply the information that is required for them to decide to adopt. If the designer aims to optimize the chances for adoption to occur, the message that is communicated to the potential adopter should emphasize the attributes of the product that earlier surveys have indicated will be perceived favorably. An especially effective technique for designing messages is to "position" the product—to emphasize those attributes that are not only perceived favorably by potential users, but that also tend to distinguish the product favorably from its competition (Urban & Hauser, 1980).

Experience suggests that the choice of communication channel helps to determine the influence of a message about a new product. Mass media such as newsletters, group meetings, or radio and television can reach large numbers of people quickly and easily (Sikorski et al., 1976). But does the message really get through? Experience suggests that it does if the potential adopter is in the early stages of deciding about a product and is seeking only general information (Rogers, 1983). But later, when a decision is imminent, there tends to be need for face-to-face contact with an advocate who is trusted by the potential adopter (Copp et al., 1958). The adjective "homophilous" is often used to describe a person who is similar to a potential adopter (and therefore trusted by him or her) (Lazarsfeld & Merton, 1964).

Many prominent models for the innovation-diffusion process suggest that potential adopters' decisions are influenced by the person who delivers a message about a new product as well as by the nature of the message and the communication channel. Research has shown that potential users adopt new products at different times after they have heard about them. For purpose of analysis, potential adopters have been classified as innovators, early adopters, early majority, late majority, and laggards in terms of their propensity to adopt (Midgley, 1977). It is generally posited that some of the innovators and particularly some of the early adopters (referred to as "opinion leaders") can exert a word-of-mouth influence on the others to adopt (Robertson, 1971).

The innovation-diffusion models suggest a strategy for instructional designers to use to communicate effectively with potential adopters of their product. Simply stated, designers who want to encourage adoption should identify the opinion leaders within the potential adopter group(s) and concentrate the initial communication effort on trying to get these people to adopt, or at least to express their approval of the product publicly. Experience from noneducational settings suggests that, if this can be done, a sort of bandwagon effect will be set in motion in which adopters will influence other potential adopters to adopt (Coleman et al., 1966; Whyte, 1954). Conversely, the models suggest that it would not be very productive to concentrate early efforts upon the innovators (they will probably adopt anyway) or those in the late majority or laggard categories (they will be very slow to adopt).

Obviously this strategy depends on the ability of a designer to classify potential adopters according to their propensity to adopt, and especially to identify the opinion leaders. Measuring opinion leadership involves picking out the individuals within a group of potential adopters who command the most peer respect. Rogers (1983) suggests four methods for doing this: (a) direct questioning of group members, (b) collecting ratings from selected informants, (c) obtaining self-ratings from group members, and (d) direct observation of social-contact frequencies. All of these techniques have been used with success, but all have definite limitations (Rogers, 1983).

Two points should be kept in mind in trying to use opinion leaders as vehicles for influencing potential adopters. First, opinion leaders within organizations tend to reflect the norms of the organization (Rogers & Rogers-Agarwala, 1976). Thus, when a social system's norms favor change, opinion leaders tend to be innovative, but when a system's norms do not favor change, opinion leaders are not especially innovative. With this in mind, designers can expect resistance from opinion leaders when they try to introduce their products into an organization with a conservative value structure. A second important point is that opinion leadership can be product-area specific (Silk, 1966). And so it should not be assumed that a person who is an opinion leader with respect to military strategy will necessarily command high respect when it comes to selecting training packages.

Supporting Implementation

As we have seen, the decision to adopt often depends on the subjective judgments of decision-makers as to how well an innovation will solve some problem. But once the adoption decision has been made, someone has to implement the innovation (make it work) and doing this often depends on practical matters, such as money, facilities, equipment, and training. Much evidence suggests that the failure to supply adequate support along these lines accounts for many of the problems in getting ID properly implemented (Fullan & Pomfret, 1977).

Before turning to the specifics of providing support for implementing ID, we need to briefly consider the way users tend to approach implementation. Situations in which an instructor implements a new instructional program just as the developer specified appear to be the exception rather than the rule (Yin, 1978). What appears to happen more often is what Rogers (1983) has called "reinvention," or adapting of a product to fit local conditions. This process was studied in detail by Hall and Loucks (1978), who concluded that users typically move from nonuse through mechanical use, to what they consider to be higher levels of use that involve making fairly substantial departures from the way the product is used initially. This tendency of users to adapt rather than blindly to adopt new products has led some authors to propose that developers should deliberately build flexibility of use into their products to make them more acceptable and usable (Bezuszka, 1975).

Need for Preimplementation Planning

Sometimes inadequate support for implementing a new product can be traced back to an uninformed adoption decision. Such decisions occur most often in macro-systems in which the decision-makers lack contact with the firing line and are under time or political pressure to make changes in the system (Pincus, 1974). Under these circumstances, it is not unusual for those who must actually implement a newly adopted product to discover that they must do so under impossible time or resource constraints. These circumstances often lead to poor implementation, bad results, and finally discontinuance or damaging reinvention. Good ID examples of this situation are most common in public education, when legislators or public officials decide in haste to introduce a new technology (Task Force on Educational Assessment Programs, 1979).

Perhaps the most important step that an organization can take in providing the necessary support for implementation is to avoid hasty decisions of the sort just described. Probably the best way to do that is to be sure that those who must implement a new product participate in the decision to adopt, especially in being sure that the potential adopter organization has the resources required to put the new product to good use (Zaltman et al., 1973). As a check on the validity of initial judgments of support requirements, organizations often run small-scale tests of a product prior to making final decisions (Benne, 1972).

There appear to be at least three things that an instructional designer can do to reduce the likelihood of hasty decisions to adopt. First, they can make their products as explicit as possible, especially with respect to the resources that are required for implementation. (This requirement is a major reason for the earlier caution about trying to implement models for the ID process.) Also, designers can facilitate small-scale testing by designing their products to be trialable (see the earlier discussion of *trialability*). Finally, designers can arrange for direct (i.e., face-to-face) or indirect (i.e., mediated) preadoption counseling of potential adopters with respect to the resources required for proper use of their products.

Space limitations prevent treatment in detail of all of the specific types of support that may be needed by persons who implement ID products. However, it is possible to classify these four categories: moral support, tactical support, training support, and material support. The following brief descriptions indicate the nature of each category.

Moral support refers to pats on the back and other forms of encouragement to use the innovation that are provided to the person who is trying to implement it. In the case of ID products, the recipient of moral support is normally an instructor and the giver is a superior, a colleague, or an agent of the ID. Moral support can take the form of kind words or formal rewards such as salary differentials, adjustments in work loads or citations. Experience is almost uniformly positive about the implementer's needs for moral support, especially if a major change in behavior is involved (Berman & McLaughlin, 1975; Zaltman et al., 1973).

Tactical support refers to removing or changing organizational practices and procedures that impede implementation. Again the recipient of tactical support in an ID implementation setting is normally the instructor. But the giver must be someone from within the adopting organization who has the authority to change policy. Some examples of tactical support for ID product implementation are (a) replacing norm-referenced grading practices with pass-fail grading, (b) changing the criteria used to evaluate instructors' performance, and (c) changing the criteria for selecting instructional materials (e.g., state textbook-adoption codes). Normally, the instructional designer's role in providing tactical support is limited to recommending actions. It should be noted that the degree of tactical support required to implement a new product tends to be inversely related to its adoption and implementation (see the earlier discussion of compatibility). Back and McCombs (1984) have described examples of the need for tactical support in an important ID setting—the U.S. Air Force.

Training support refers to the need to ensure that all who will be affected by the introduction of an innovation are prepared to do whatever will be required of them. In most ID implementation efforts the principal recipient of training is the instructor, but often others such as school principals and purchasing agents must be dealt with as well. Research generally supports the proposition that training support facilitates implementation of new instructional programs, but there is disagreement about the nature of optimal instructor-training programs (Fullan & Pomfret, 1977).

Materiel support refers to providing any supplies and materials that are needed for implementation on time and in sufficient quantity. Once again the instructor is the primary recipient of material support for implementing ID products. ID material support includes providing for such things as books, classroom space, computer software, overhead projectors and objects to be used by students, along with appropriate storage space and inventory procedures. Start-up material support is required to get product implementation under way and maintenance support is required to keep quantities of essential elements available and to ensure that items are in good repair (Back & McCombs, 1984). Designers can play a major role in material support by ensuring that developed products and their components are easily available.

IMPLEMENTING USER-CENTERED DEVELOPMENT

A major theme of this chapter is that adoption and implementation rates for ID products are strongly influenced by the degree to which the products are perceived by potential adopters as meeting their felt needs, and ultimately by how well those needs are actually met. A second prominent theme is that potential adopters of ID products base their judgments on many factors in addition to the product's effectiveness and efficiency in promoting learning. These points have led to the suggestion that designers who aim to get their product adopted and used well should consider adopting a user-oriented approach to ID, such as the five-step approach outlined as follows:

Step 1. Identify the persons who would be affected if the planned new instructional product were to be put into use (the potential adopters).

Step 2. Measure the perceived needs of the potential adopters with respect to instructional procedures and instructional products.

Step 3. Design and develop the ID product to meet the potential adopters' perceived needs (as well as the requirement of being effective and efficient in promoting learning).

Step 4. Inform the potential adopter about the finished ID product, emphasizing those attributes that relate favorably to perceived needs.

Step 5. Facilitate the implementation of the finished ID product by arranging for four types of support for the instructor or other implementer: moral support, tactical support, training support, and materiel support.

There is nothing especially novel in user-oriented development. This approach has been used with success for years by businesses that bring new products to the market. And it is not surprising that the keys to applying UOID successfully are: (a) to become very knowledgeable about the potential user's problems and preferences, (b) to establish good rapport and lines of communication with the potential user, and, (c) to attend to many details. Unfortunately, getting these things done often calls for knowledge and skills that many designers do not have.

It is not unusual for instructional designers to find that they lack some aspect of the knowledge and skills that are required to do their job. In fact, it has become more or less standard practice for designers to team up with experts in the subject matter (SMEs) and with editors, graphics designers, computer programmers, and other specialists in mediating instructional products (Misselt & Call-Nimwick, 1978; Roblyer, 1981). More recently some designers have been adding instructors and other types of potential adopters to their design-and-development teams (Burkman, 1974). Including users on design teams is based on the assumption that they will inject useful ideas into the design process about teaching procedures, learners' capabilities and classroom conditions, and that they will be able to help to communicate with the potential users about the product and to help with adopter training. User involvement, of course, applies directly to instituting user-oriented development.

What should be the role of instructors and other potential adopters on a team that is implementing UOID? There are three logical roles. First, they can be instrumental in identifying constraints to product adoption and implementation and user perceptions about instruction and the instructional process. In this regard, potential adopters on the development team can contribute their personal ideas and can help to collect and interpret data from others. The second role is to aid in determining when the product reflects the attributes that users will require. And finally the potential adopter-team member can be used to communicate with colleagues, or at least to pass judgment on the effectiveness of communications.

It will be noted that the suggested role of the potential user on an ID design and development team is not cosmetic. It clearly improves the credibility of a product with potential adopters to say that one or more of their colleagues has been involved in its development, but this is not the most important advantage of user involvement. By listening attentively to perceptive potential adopters and acting on their suggestions, designers can shape their products to better fit users' perceived needs. Also, the evidence is quite clear that potential adopters are more likely to be influenced by contacts with persons like themselves than by those who are perceived to be different (Rogers & Shoemaker, 1971).

User involvement on ID development teams can be a negative influence if task assignment is not well done. Instructors and other potential adopters are not likely to have well-honed skills in instructional design, evaluation, written communication, or media production. And they are not necessarily experts in the content of subjects they teach. The proper way to involve potential users in UOID is to be sure that they have strong input *in their areas of expertise.* Normally those areas are knowledge of the learner, of the operating constraints, and of the potential user. As is the case with any development team member, it is unwise to assign potential adopters to tasks for which they are not qualified.

A Last Word

Clearly, user-oriented instructional development is a much more complex process than straightforward instructional design. It requires that extra time and effort be spent in measuring and accounting for user perceptions and requirements and in informing and supporting users. This extra effort, in turn, means that costs will be higher. The fact is that dissemination costs money. And, if the development and dissemination are linked, as is proposed in UOID, projects will be bigger and longer and development costs will be higher. Nevertheless, ID in use is a far different product from ID on the shelf. And, as the saying goes, "there ain't no free lunch."

REFERENCES

Andrews, D. H., & Goodson, L. A. (1980). A comparative analysis of models of instructional design. *Journal of Instructional Development, 3(4),* 2–16.

Back, S. M., & McCombs, B. L. (1984). *Factors critical to the implementation of self-paced instruction: A background review* (TP-84-24). Lowry Air Force Base, CO: AFHRL/ Training-Systems Division.

Bennis, W. G., Benne, K. D., & Chin, R. (Eds.) (1969). *The planning of change: Readings in the applied behaviorial sciences.* New York: Holt, Rinehart and Winston.

Berman, P., & McLaughlin, M. W. (1974). *A model of educational change. Vol. 1 of federal programs supporting educational change (R-1589/1-HEW).* Santa Monica, CA: Rand. (ERIC Document Reproduction Service No. ED 099 957)

Berman, P., & McLaughlin, M. W. (1975). *Federal programs supporting educational change, Vol. IV: The findings in review.* Santa Monica, CA: Rand.

Berman, P., & McLaughlin, M. W. (1976). Implementation of educational innovation. *Educational Forum,* pp. 347–470.

Berman, P., & McLaughlin, M. W. (1977). *Factors affecting implementation and continuation. Vol. 7 of federal programs supporting educational change (R-1589/7 HEW).* Santa Monica, CA: Rand. (ERIC Document Re production Service No. ED 140 432)

Berman, P., & McLaughlin, M. W. (1978). *Implementing and sustaining innovations. Vol. 8 of federal programs supporting educational change (R-1589/8-HEW).* Santa Monica, CA: Rand Corporation. (ERIC Document Reproduction Service No. ED 159 289)

Bezuszka, S. J. (1975). *Future Shock in Mathematics.* Paper presented to the Northwest Mathematics Council, Eugene, OR.

Branson, R. K. (1981). Applications research in instructional systems development. *Journal of Instructional Development, 4(4),* 14–16.

Brickell, H. M. (1971, August). *Alternative diffusion strategies.* Paper prepared for the Center for Vocational and Technical Education, Columbus, OH: Ohio State University, Institute for Educational Development.

Burkman, E. (1974). An approach to instructional design for massive classroom impact. *Journal of Research in Science Teaching, 11(1),* 53–59.

Butler, D. (1982). 22 Obstacles to educational innovation—and how to overcome them. *Instructional Innovator, 27(6),* 18–20.

Calder, B. J. (1977). Focus groups and the nature of qualitative marketing research. *Journal of Marketing Research, 14(8),* 353–364.

Centra, J. (1976). *Faculty development practices in U. S. colleges and universities.* Princeton, NJ: Educational Testing Service.

Coleman, J. S., Katz, E., & Menzel, H. (1966). *Medical innovation: A diffusion study.* New York: Bobbs-Merrill.

Copp, J. H., et al. (1958). The function of information sources of the farm practice adoption process. *Rural Sociology, 23,* 146–157.

Dressel, P. L. (1982). Curriculum and instruction in higher education. *Encyclopedia of Educational Research,* pp. 400–405. New York: Free Press.

Farrar, E., De Sanctis, J. E., & Cohen, D. K. (1980). The lawn party: The evolution of federal programs in local settings. *Phi Delta Kappan, 62(3),* 167–171.

Feasley, C. E. (Ed.) (1982). Distance education. *Encyclopedia of Educational Research,* pp. 450–460. New York: Free Press.

Fullan, M., & Pomfret, A. (1977). Research on curriculum and instruction implementation. *Review of Educational Research, 47,* 335–397.

Goldman, H. D. (1982). *Comments on self-paced instruction in ATC.* Unpublished manuscript. Randolph AFB, TX: Headquarters, Air Training Command.

Guba, E. G., & Clark, D. L. (1975). The configurational perspective: A new view of educational knowledge production and utilization. *Educational Researcher, 4*(4), 6.

Hall, G. E., & Loucks, S. F. (1978). *Innovation configurations: Analyzing the adoptions of innovation.* Austin, TX: University of Texas, Research and Development Center for Teacher Education.

Havelock, R. G. (1973). *The change agent's guide to innovation in education.* Englewood Cliffs, NJ: Educational Technology.

Kester, R. J. (1976, April). *Evaluating the process of educational change: A method.* Paper presented at the meeting of the American Educational Research Association, San Francisco.

Kilman, H. C. (1965). Manipulation of human behavior: An ethical dilemma for the social scientist. *Journal of Social Issues, 21*(2), 31–46.

Lazarsfeld, P. F., & Merton, R. K. (1964). Friendship as social process: A substantive and methodological analysis. In M. Berger et al. (Eds.), *Freedom and Control in Modern Society.* New York: Octagon.

Lehmann, D. R. (1979). *Market research and analysis.* Homewood, IL: Irwin.

Lippett, R., Watson, J., & Westley, B. (1958). *The dynamics of planned change.* New York: Harcourt Brace.

Marquis, D. G. (1969). The anatomy of successful innovation. *Innovation, 1*(7), 28–37.

McCombs, B. L., Back, S. M., & West, A. S. (1984). Factors critical to the implementation of self-paced instruction in Air Force technology (TP–84–23). Brooks Air Force Base, TX: AF Human Resources Laboratory.

Meadows, D. L. (1968). Estimate accuracy and project selection models in industrial research. *Industrial Management Review, 9*(3), 105–19.

Midgley, D. F. (1971). *Innovation and new products marketing.* London: Croom Helm.

Miles, M. B. (1983). Evaluating four years of ID experience. *Journal of Instructional Development, 6*(2), 9–14.

Misselt, A. L., & Call-Himwick, E. (1978). *Analysis of Sheppard AFB computer-based education project* (MTC Rep. No. 21). Urbana, IL: Computer-Based Education Research Laboratory.

Myers, S., & Marquis, D. G. (1969). *Successful industrial innovation: A study of factors underlying innovation in selected firms* (SF 69–17). Washington, DC: National Science Foundation.

Nelson, M., & Sieber, S. D. (1976). Innovations in urban secondary schools. *School Review, 84,* 213–231.

Parkinson, R. (1972). The Dvorak simplified keyboard: Forty years of frustration. *Computers and Automation, 21,* 1–8.

Pincus, J. (1974). Incentives for innovation in public schools. *Review of Educational Research, 44,* 113–144.

Robertson, T. S. (1971). *Innovative behavior and communication.* New York: Holt, Rinehart and Winston.

Roblyer, M. D. (1981, May). *Instructional design vs authoring of courseware: Some crucial differences.* Paper presented at the meeting of the Association for Educational Data Systems, Minneapolis.

Rogers, E. M. (1983). *Diffusion of innovations* (3rd ed.). New York: Free Press.

Rogers, E. M., & Rogers-Agarwala, R. (1976). *Communication in organizations.* New York: Free Press.

Rogers, E. M., & Shoemaker, F. F. (1971). *Communication of innovations: A cross-cultural approach* (2nd ed.). New York: Free Press.

Rosencranz, A. D. (1975, December). Who decides what pupils read? *Compact,* 11–13.

Sikorski, L. A., Webb, P., Lynch, K., & McWilliams, F. (1976). *Targeting information to market segments: An action oriented study of attitudes toward vocational education among target populations.* San Francisco: Far West Laboratory for Educational Research and Development.

Silk, A. J. (1966). Overlap among self-designated opinion leaders: A study of selected dental products and services. *Journal of Marketing Records, 3*(3), 255–59.

Task Force on Educational Assessment Programs. (1979). *Competency Testing in Florida. Report to the Florida Cabinet, Part I.* Tallahassee, FL: Author.

Tornatzky, L. G., & Klein, K. J. (1982). Innovation characteristics and innovations adoption—implementation: A meta-analysis of findings. *IEEE Transactions on Engineering Management, 29*(1), 28–45.

Turnbull, B., Thorn, L., & Hutchins, C. L. (1984). *Promoting change in schools: A diffusion casebook.* San Francisco, CA: Far West Laboratory for Educational Research and Development.

Urban, G. L., & Hauser, J. R. (1980). *Design and marketing of new products.* Englewood Cliffs, NJ: Prentice-Hall.

Whyte, W. H. (1954). The web of word-of-mouth. *Fortune, 50*(5), 140–43.

Wolf, W. C., Jr. (1973). *Some perspectives on educational change.* Amherst, MA: University of Massachusetts and Temple University.

Yin, R. F. (1978). *Changing urban bureaucracies: How new practices become routinized: Executive Summary* (NSF Grant No. PRA 76–15207). Santa Monica, CA: Rand.

Zaltman, G., Duncan, R., & Holbek, J. (1973). *Innovations and organizations.* Toronto: Wiley.

AUTHOR NOTES

Ernest Burkman is a Professor in the Department of Educational Research, Development, and Foundations, Florida State University.

Author Index

457

Subject Index

A

Adaptive instruction, 216–218
Adoption of ID products, 437–439
  quality, 437
Anxiety
  interference with learning, 219–222
  post-processing interference, 221–222
Aptitude-treatment interaction (ATI), 208–213
  achievement-treatment, 211–212
  adaptive instruction, 217–218
  assumptions, 213–214
  post-processing interference, 221–222
  preprocessing interference, 219–220
  processing interference, 220–221
  research results, 210–211
  types, 209–210
Assessment
  basics of measurement, 344–345
  criterion-referenced, 346–348 (*See also* criterion-referenced measurement)
  evaluation of technology, 365–370
  purposes, 345–346
Artificial intelligence (AI)
  computer-based learning, 319–320 (*See also* Ch. 12)
  intelligent computer-assisted instruction (ICAI), 321
Attention, in communication, 236–237
Audiovisual devices, 12–20
  birth of movement, 13–15
  early forerunners, 12–13
  instructional television, 17–18
  modern views, 18–20

National Defense Education Act, Title VII, 16
period of World War II, 15
Audiovisual systems, knowledge presentation, 312–313

B

Behavioral objectives, contribution to instructional technology, 23–24

C

Cognitive strategies, 66–68
  learning, 66–67
  problem solving, 67–68
  remembering, 67
Communication
  activity of the learner, 249–252
  attention, 236–237
  concepts, definitions, 233–235
  feedback to learner, 248–249
  learning, 241–246
  organizing instruction, 246–248
  perception, 237–240
  pictures, side-by-side, 245
  principles, 235
  representing the information, 241–246
Computer-aided education (CAE)
  broadcast lessons, 307
  computer-centered, 303–305
  computer literacy, 304–305
  delivery systems, 293–295